Handbook of Personality Development

Handbook of Personality Development

Edited by

Daniel K. Mroczek
Todd D. Little

2006
LAWRENCE ERLBAUM ASSOCIATES, PUBLISHERS
Mahwah, New Jersey   London

KH

Lawrence Erlbaum Associates, Inc., Publishers
10 Industrial Avenue
Mahwah, New Jersey 07430
www.erlbaum.com

Cover design by Tomai Maridou

Library of Congress Cataloging-in-Publication Data

Handbook of personality development / edited by Daniel K. Mroczek
 and Todd D. Little.
     p. cm.
 Includes bibliographical references and index.
 ISBN 0-8058-4716-2 (cloth : alk. paper)
 ISBN 0-8058-5936-5 (pbk. : alk. paper)
 1. Personality development. 2. Developmental psychology. I. Mroczek, Daniel K.
  II. Little, Todd D.
 BF698.H3343 2006
 155.2'5—dc22   2005055203
                                                                    CIP

Printed in the United States of America
10 9 8 7 6 5 4 3 2 1

8/6/07

Contents

III   Personality Development in Childhood and Adolescence

IV   Personality Development in Middle and Older Adulthood

V Capstone

Preface

The idea for the *Handbook of Personality Development* stemmed out of a chance meeting at a conference that we had with Debra Riegert from Lawrence Erlbaum Associates. At the time, Todd Little was still at Yale and Dan Mroczek was at Fordham. The closeness of New Haven to the Bronx, as well as the proximity of both to Lawrence Erlbaum Associates' offices in Mahwah, New Jersey, facilitated a number of meetings that resulted in the solidification of the plan.

We thought then, as now, that the time was right for such a volume. The study of personality development had entered a period of rich activity in the 1990s, a period that continues to the present. Just as important, the area was no longer confined to the study of personality in childhood. It was true that it had long been breaking out of its origins in early and middle childhood, as exemplified by the groundbreaking work of Jack Block, Paul Costa & Jeff McCrae, and others in the 1970s and 1980s. These investigators had included adolescents, adults, or both in their longitudinal studies of personality development. Yet the 1990s saw a widespread surge in research on personality development, almost equaled distributed across the various segments of the human life span. Strides were made in understanding temperament and personality from infancy to old age, in areas as diverse as traits to life narrative. It was the energy and spirit of this work that led us to conclude that putting together this handbook would be a useful and fruitful endeavor.

We hoped to produce a volume that was not only life span in scope, but also relatively broad in the topics it covered. Our overall goal was to provide a broad view on the area of personality development, in both domain as well as developmental era. We wanted coverage of the key domains and topics within the area, but also strove for perspectives on personality developments across the entire life span, from infancy to old age. Readers will decide how successful we were in achieving this goal, but we think there is no question that this book exceeds any prior volume in both breadth of topic and in coverage of the full life span.

We believe it will prove an invaluable resource for students, researchers and teachers of personality development. Students, researchers and teachers in personality, developmental, social and clinical psychology will find this volume useful, but we also believe that those outside of psychology will find it interesting and relevant to their own research. Students, researchers and teachers of human development, family studies, sociology, education, social work, nursing, and certain other health- or human-service professions will also find many of the chapters germane to the topics they study.

This book is organized around both topic areas as well as developmental era. Early in the volume, the book is largely topic-focused, with several chapters on theoretical and methodological perspectives on personality development. The later sections deal with personality development within particular segments of the life span, such as childhood, adolescence, midlife, and older adulthood. Yet sections of the life span and content domains are not the only themes around which this book is organized. Over the past decade or so, we believe five major types of advances have characterized the burst of activity in the study of personality development, and all of these are represented in this Handbook as well.

These are: a) new theoretical perspectives, b) more and higher-quality empirical studies, c) the application of novel and more sophisticated designs and analyses, d) attention to development across the life span, and e) the growing prominence of interdisciplinary approaches to personality development. Every chapter in this volume represents at least one of these five advances.

If this volume accomplishes nothing else, we hope that the child development researchers who acquire this book read the chapters that focus on adult development and vice versa. Todd Little is primarily known as a child and adolescent development researcher, although he has made some contributions to the literature on aging. Dan Mroczek has mostly stayed within the study of adult development and aging, although he has made some forays into the study of personality in adolescence. Although we represent the separation present in the field, with childhood and adulthood researchers staying with their own kind, we have enlightened each other with insights from our respective areas. We hope that readers of this volume will be similarly enlightened. If each reader simply read one chapter out of his or her domain and one chapter outside the developmental segment that he or she focuses on, we believe that the field would benefit from the cross-fertilization and integration that would result.

We wish to thank Nava Silton and Kamala Ramadoss, who were Dan Mroczek's research assistants at Fordham and Purdue, respectively, for the tireless hours they put in during the preparation of this book. We also thank Debra Riegert of Lawrence Erlbaum Associates for her unflagging support as we encountered problems, issues and delays. Without her enthusiasm for the project, the *Handbook of Personality Development* would not be.

—Daniel K. Mroczek
West Lafayette, Indiana

—Todd D. Little
Lawrence, Kansas

I
Introduction

1

Theory and Research in Personality Development at the Beginning of the 21st Century

Daniel K. Mroczek
Purdue University

Todd D. Little
University of Kansas

The scholarly study of personality development began with Sigmund Freud's writings on psychosexual development. Freud was the first to theorize on how personality developed over time, and during the early decades of the 20th century his view was the only game in town. However, other perspectives on personality development emerged after Freud's death in 1939. Harry Stack Sullivan, Erik Erikson, Henry Murray, Karen Horney, and others offered theories, some of which became enormously influential within personality, developmental, social, and clinical psychology. By midcentury, there was a plethora of personality development theories.

This abundance of theories, however, was a problem for the field. Most work on personality development in the first half of the 20th century was theoretical. Empirical research was almost unheard of. Empirical studies are required to verify theories, and although there was plenty of the latter there was not much of the former, placing limits on how much scholars could understand about personality development. Harry Harlow was perhaps the first to conduct empirical work in personality development, and the data-based literature on the topic steadily increased through the 1960s, 1970s, and 1980s with the work of Jack Block, Glen Elder, Jerome Kagan, Ravenna Helson, Paul Costa, Jeff McCrae, and others.

In the 1990s, the study of personality development enjoyed a burst of scholarly activity that continues to this day. The area is vibrant and flourishing, but more importantly, theoretical and empirical work is more balanced than it was 50 years ago. It is within this milieu that the *Handbook of Personality Development* is presented.

3

The advances characterizing this burst of activity in the study of personality development are represented herein and include new theoretical perspectives, more and higher quality empirical studies, the application of novel and more sophisticated designs and analyses, attention to development across the life span, and the growing prominence of interdisciplinary approaches to personality development. Each chapter represents at least one of these five advances. Moreover, the roster of authors includes many who, in their prior work, have pushed the field forward in one or more of these five ways.

THEORETICAL PERSPECTIVES

The era of grand theories of personality (e.g., those of Freud, Allport, or Murray) is largely over. So too has passed the broad theory of personality development. In one sense, this passing is sad because there is something appealing and idealistic about the broad, general theory. However, the empirical literature has taught us that many people do not conform to the pattern of personality development put forth in the broad theory. One of the key tenets of personality psychology is that people display individual differences on an array of characteristics. The same is true of personality development. Many individuals will not develop or behave in the way the broad theory predicts. This marked variability among individuals was a contributing factor in the decline of the grand theories of personality and personality development.

However, the more recent round of theorizing in personality development is more appreciative of individual differences in development, and has stayed close to the empirical literature. Because it is more focused and more data based, recent theorizing has given rise to more accurate predictions than many of the broader, midcentury theories. Several chapters in this volume are excellent examples of this focused theorizing (e.g., Roberts & Wood, chap. 2; Fleeson & Jolley, chap. 3; Little, Snyder, & Wehmeyer, chap. 4). These theoretical chapters are followed by others on original theory (Hawley, chap. 8; Walls & Kollatt, chap. 12; Harter, chap. 16; Helson, Soto, & Cate, chap. 17; Freund & Riediger, chap. 18; Diehl, chap. 19; Wrosch, Heckhausen, & Lachman, chap. 20). These and other chapters contain theory that is well-grounded in data and evidence. This is a positive direction for the field, and it meshes well with the next point.

EMPIRICAL ADVANCES

The empirical work in personality development has grown tremendously in the past 15 to 20 years. The extant literature has expanded to include studies on personality development during every portion of the life span and on the development of almost every type of personality variable. The most extensive empirical literature is perhaps the one on traits and the temperamental precursors of traits (Roberts & Wood. chap. 2; Krueger, Johnson, & Kling, chap. 5; Saucier & Simonds, chap. 6; McCrae & Costa, chap. 7; Mroczek, Almeida, Spiro, & Pafford, chap. 9; Shiner, chap. 11 Helson, Soto, & Cate, chap. 17). However, empirical work on the development of nontrait personality characteristics has burgeoned in the last decade, especially with respect to self-representations, goals, coping styles, and various aspects of self-regulation. The literature on the development of these elements of personality may soon match the voluminous literature on the development of temperament and trait dimensions (Little, Snyder, & Wehmeyer, chap. 4; Hawley, chap. 8; Saarni, chap. 13; Tobin & Graziano, chap. 14; Donnellan, Trzniewski, & Robins, chap. 15; Harter, chap. 16; Freund & Riediger, chap. 18; Diehl, chap. 19; Wrosch, Heckhausen, & Lachman, chap. 20; Levenson & Aldwin, chap. 21).

Although the empirical studies described, compared, and integrated in the pages of this volume are highly varied and range across many different areas and types of variables, it is nonetheless possible to extract a few common themes. First, it is clear that throughout the development of personality, the person is an active agent. The person does not simply unfold in the classic sense of Rosseau or Freud, nor is the individual a puppet that is subject to external circumstances and reinforcers in the sense of Skinner. Children, and later adolescents and adults, play a major role in shaping their own development. Organismic theorizing is well-established in developmental psychology (Lerner & Busch-Rossnagel, 1981), yet not many personality psychologists are familiar with this notion. It is a powerful idea that is congruent with what personality psychologists have been arguing for decades—that what a person brings to the situation (traits, beliefs, emotions, and strivings) shapes and changes the situation itself. The empirical literature described within this volume largely upholds this viewpoint.

Second, the *Handbook* authors document that personality development continues throughout the life span. The midcentury theories, with Erik Erikson's as the main exception, did not give consideration to what aspects of personality change and what stays the same as people move through adulthood and into older age. There is more on this later, but the empirical advances described in this *Handbook* are not limited to a single segment of the life span.

Third, the empirical literature demonstrates that people show wide individual differences in personality development. Not everyone develops in the same way or has the same trajectory. This inherent variability does not mean that personality development is random or completely idiosyncratic. Indeed, patterns of development are observable, and normative trajectories for many personality traits and processes have been established. However, around these general patterns and normative trends lies individual variation. This idea is not new—it was proposed quite some time ago (Baltes, 1987; Baltes, Reese, & Nesselroade, 1977; Nesselroade, 1991). The recent empirical literature on personality development indicates that for a variety of personality characteristics, people differ from one another in the way they develop. One of the fundamental phenomena that personality psychology has concerned itself with over its history is individual differences. Typically, this focus has meant the study of individual differences in personality variables as static entities. Yet, it is clear from many chapters herein that there are individual differences in the way personality develops as well.

USE OF NEW DESIGNS, METHODS, AND STATISTICS

Many of the empirical advances that the *Handbook* authors have described so well (and often executed in the context of their respective research programs) are a direct result of improved research designs and analyses that investigators of personality development have fruitfully employed. Experience sampling methods, daily diary designs, facial expression coding, and other techniques have all been utilized in personality development research. In several chapters, some of these methods are described because they are essential to understanding the substantive questions. For example, chapter 5 (Krueger,

Johnson, & Kling) describes new models and designs in behavior genetics research, as they have been placed in the service of understanding genetic influences on personality development. Similarly, chapter 3 (Fleeson & Jolley) explains and delineates experience sampling designs and statistical models for analyzing them, and chapter 6 (Saucier & Simonds) addresses lexical factor analytic techniques.

The aforementioned chapters are primarily substantive, and the techniques they describe necessarily occupy a secondary position within the contributions. Two chapters, however, focus primarily on technical and methodological issues, and both deal with a central concern in the study of psychological development; namely, the assessment and analysis of change. Chapters 9 (Mroczek, Almeida, Spiro, & Pafford) and 10 (Little, Bovaird, & Slegers) describe various aspects of modeling change and how such models have informed, and can continue to inform, the understanding of personality development.

AN EMPHASIS ON PERSONALITY DEVELOPMENT ACROSS THE LIFE COURSE

The way to best assess change over time, especially over long periods of time, brings us to an emphasis on personality development across the life course. For a long time, the empirical study of personality development was largely the purview of child development research. The study of temperament, attachment, emotion regulation, and interpersonal maturation dominated the area. The study of personality development in adults did not begin to pick up steam until the 1970s, and today it flourishes and enjoys extensive interest.

Personality development is, at this point, where the area of cognitive development was perhaps from 15 to 20 years ago. The study of cognitive development extends across the entire life span, with some researchers studying infant cognition, others studying cognition in centenarians, and many others studying it at every age in between. Research in aging and cognition is as lively and active an area as research on child cognition. The area of personality development is headed in a similar, positive direction, and it is reflected in the contributions of the *Handbook*.

Section III (chaps. 11–16) is devoted to personality development in the infant, child, and adolescent years. Section IV (chaps. 17–22) is dedicated to personality development in early, middle, and older adulthood. However, within each section are chapters addressing issues that cut across the full life span. Although the chapters are segregated, this is one of a few volumes on personality development that is not restricted to a particular segment of the life span. Although the readers may be tempted to skip the sections covering a portion of the life span in which they are less interested, they are encouraged to peruse all of the chapters. As in other areas of developmental study, theory or research that arises from scholars focusing primarily on one part of the life course may prove informative and valuable to those working on another part.

THE GROWTH OF INTERDISCIPLINARY APPROACHES TO PERSONALITY DEVELOPMENT

There is clear evidence that the development of personality is influenced by a range of factors, including those that are biological, cultural, social, or familial in nature (e.g., Caspi et al., 2002, 2003). A growing body of interdisciplinary research has elucidated these influences, and these studies are very exciting. However, such interdisciplinary studies are still a small proportion of the total number of studies done in the area of personality development. The area would certainly benefit greatly from greater exposure to relevant work in other disciplines as well as more collaboration with scholars from different fields. The work by Caspi and colleagues (Caspi et al., 2002, 2003) is an excellent example of such collaboration, with geneticists, psychiatrists, sociologists, and psychologists working together to produce findings that greatly advance the area. Such work is hard to do, but the potential yield is large.

Several chapters have a primary focus that is interdisciplinary, including chapter 5 on behavior genetics (Krueger, Johnson, & Kling), chapter 7 on cross-cultural issues (McCrae & Costa), chapter 8 on evolutionary perspectives (Hawley), chapter 21 on health (Levenson & Aldwin), and chapter 22 on social relationships (Lang, Reschke, & Neyer). Of course, other chapters draw on other disciplines as well, reflecting the growing emphasis on looking outside psychology for useful insights into personality development.

The authors have done a superlative job of covering the interdisciplinary developments in the area. However, this is one advance where we hope this volume will soon become outdated! We say this in a sense of hope and optimism. If the area of personality development continues to build strong ties to other disciplines, and continues to be informed by multiple disciplines and advances in measurement and methodology, then it will find itself in an enviable position. To support this contention, we note that some of the most successful and interesting intellectual and scientific enterprises of recent years have been interdisciplinary. Watson and Crick were, respectively, a chemist and physicist by training, whose work shaped two different disciplines: biology and medicine. Today, mathematicians are contributing to biology via the area of bioinformatics; economists are collaborating with cognitive scientists on financial decision making; and physicists, neuroscientists, and physicians are working together to improve medical imaging.

The more the area of personality development can cast itself broadly, attracting scholars from many different fields, the greater the rewards will be. Our understanding of personality development will be deeper and our findings more exciting. We see the seeds of such interdisciplinary work in the pages of this volume.

CONCLUSION

We were motivated to assemble this volume because we were impressed with the growing breadth and depth of research on personality development emerging from numerous camps. This breadth and depth includes the constructs under investigation, the methodology employed, and the theoretical perspectives used. This *Handbook* reflects a relatively representative and comprehensive assembling of this growing breadth and depth in the area of personality development. True to our focus on development, each contributor was encouraged to go beyond the traditional summary of where the field has been, and to provide readers with a clear roadmap of where the field is headed in the next 5 to 10 years. Moreover, we were also keen on providing an integrative, big picture assessment of the field of personality development. To this end, we are delighted to have Dan McAdams and Jon Adler providing an integrative capstone chapter. All told, we hope readers will find knowledge and inspiration from the contributions that we have assembled and focus their future research in a way that continues to broaden and deepen our understanding of personality development across the life span.

REFERENCES

Baltes, P. B. (1987). Theoretical propositions of life-span developmental psychology: On the dynamics between growth and decline. *Developmental Psychology, 23,* 611–626.

Baltes, P. B., Reese, H. W., & Nesselroade, J. R. (1977). *Lifespan developmental psychology: Introduction to research methods.* Monterey, CA: Brooks/Cole.

Caspi, A., McClay, J., Moffitt, T., E., Mill, J., Martin, J., Craig, I. W., Taylor, A., & Poulton, R. (2002). Role of genotype in the cycle of violence in maltreated children. *Science, 297,* 851–853.

Caspi, A., Sugden, K., Moffitt, T., Taylor, A, Craig, A. S., Harrington, H., McClay, J., Mill, J., Martin, J., Braithwaite, A., & Poulton, R. (2003). Influence of life stress on depression: Moderation by a polymorphism in the 5-HTT gene. *Science, 301,* 386–389.

Lerner, R. M., & Busch-Rossnagel, N. (1981). *Individuals as producers of their development: A life-span perspective.* New York: Academic Press.

Nesselroade, J. R. (1991). Interindividual differences in intraindividual change. In L. M. Collins & J. L. Horn (Eds.), *Best methods for the analysis of change* (pp. 92–105). Washington, DC: American Psychological Association.

II

Theoretical and Methodological
Perspectives on Personality Development

2

Personality Development in the Context of the Neo-Socioanalytic Model of Personality

Brent W. Roberts
Dustin Wood
University of Illinois at Urbana-Champaign

Over the last several decades, a coherent picture has emerged from numerous longitudinal studies concerning the nature of personality development in adulthood. Personality traits are quite consistent across long periods of time and increase in consistency with age (Conley, 1984; Roberts & DelVecchio, 2000; Schuerger, Zarrella, & Hotz, 1989). In addition, personality traits also show meaningful and statistically significant mean-level change in young adulthood, middle age, and even old age (Helson & Kwan, 2000; Roberts, Walton, & Viechtbauer, 2006; Srivastava, John, Gosling, & Potter, 2003). People increase on traits related to social dominance (a facet of extraversion), agreeableness, conscientiousness, and emotional stability, in some cases well into old age. Finally, these changes are related to life experiences in young adulthood (Pals, 1999), midlife (Roberts, 1997; Roberts & Chapman, 2000), and old age (Mroczek & Spiro, 2003). The picture drawn from the empirical data seems eminently reasonable: Personality traits increase in consistency as people age, reaching levels that are quite high, but not so high as to rule out the possibility or reality of meaningful shifts in traits over time. Development in normative and individual terms continues well into middle age and sometimes later, typically in a less dramatic fashion than would be expected if personality was ruled solely by the environment. Unfortunately, existing theories of adult and personality development fail to capture or account for this temperate perspective on personality trait development.

Traditional theories of adult development have focused on the social structures of life, such as careers, marriages, families, and their changing meaning as people age (Erikson, 1968; Levinson, 1978). New theories of adult development have focused on cognitive factors and the motivational strategies used to cope with the inevitable decline in functioning that comes with age (Baltes, 1997; Heckhausen, 1997). Personality theories, like the Five Factor model, have set aside personality traits from the remaining aspects of personality as specialized units that do not develop through experience, but only through genetically determined means (McCrae & Costa, 1999). Thus, no theories capture the empirical reality represented by longitudinal research.

The present chapter offers an alternative theory that reconciles the empirical data with the existing ideas concerning human nature. It represents an ongoing attempt to develop a theory of personality development (Roberts & Caspi, 2001, 2003; Roberts, Robins, Caspi, & Trzewsneski, 2003). Previous writings have focused mostly on personality trait development, but this chapter briefly outlines a more general theory of personality, borrowing heavily from socioanalytic theory (Hogan, 1982; Hogan & Roberts, 2000). This more general theory is linked to principles of personality development that have been derived from ongoing longitudinal research and synthesis of longitudinal findings.

The first part of this chapter introduces a brief overview of the neo-socioanalytic theory of personality. The second part shows how the theory can be used to address general questions and principles of development distilled from empirical research to date. The third section outlines areas of future research that derive from the theory.

A NEO-SOCIOANALYTIC THEORY OF PERSONALITY

This is referred to as a "neo" theory, in part, because it pays homage to many of the primary components of socioanalytic theory (Hogan, 1982; Hogan & Roberts, 2000). It also is new because it moves beyond previous conceptualizations of socioanalytic theory, mostly in specifying in greater detail the organization of personality units within the individual. One of the primary reasons for relying on socioanalytic theory is that it is one of the few personality theories that incorporates traits and social situations in an informed and integrative fashion. Of the two dominant theoretical perspectives in personality psychology today, the social cognitive school (Bandura, 1999; Mischel & Shoda, 1995) tends to emphasize patterns of behaviors in situations and ignores personality traits, whereas the Five Factor model (McCrae & Costa, 1999) tends to diminish the significance of social situations, especially their potential effect on traits. Neither position is tenable in light of the developmental research noted earlier. A comprehensive and constructive theory of personality must successfully integrate person variables, like traits, with situation variables, like social roles (Funder, 2000). One of the few theories to do so is socioanalytic theory.

Figure 2.1 depicts the primary units of focus in the neo-socioanalytic theory. It is a topographical model because it identifies the major units of personality—the hills and valleys of personality—and approximately how they are related to one another. Like a topographical map, this map of personality points researchers in directions they have been and where they need to go, but it does not necessarily identify the underlying processes and mechanisms of the personality landscape—much like the division between geography and geology.

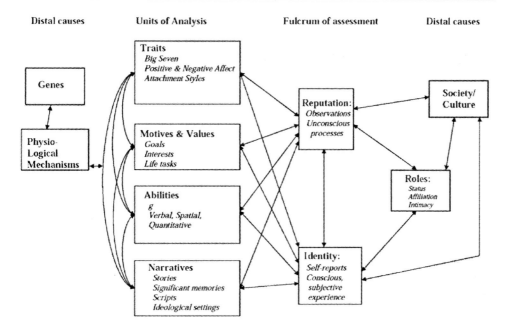

FIG. 2.1.   A neo-socioanalytic topographic model of personality psychology.

Units of Analysis in Personality Psychology

The first thing to note about Fig. 2.1 is that there are four "units of analysis," or domains, that make up the core of personality: traits, values/motives, abilities, and narratives. These four domains are intended to subsume most, if not all, of the broad categories of individual differences. There are very few studies that have examined multiple domains simultaneously. Those studies that have done so tend to support the contention that the domains are separate but related (Ackerman & Heggestad, 1997; Roberts & Robins, 2000; Winter, John, Stewart, Klohnen, & Duncan, 1998). Conceptualizing these domains as separate but related components of personality has important implications for both personality psychology and the conceptualization of personality development detailed later. It also contrasts sharply with existing theories that tend not to include cognitive ability or life narratives, and often consider traits to be superordinate causes of goals, motives, and interests.

Personality Traits.   The first domain, *traits*, subsumes the enduring patterns of thoughts, feelings, and behaviors. Or, more euphemistically speaking, traits refer to what people typically think, feel, or do. In this regard, traits are viewed from a neo-Allportian perspective (Funder, 1991). From this perspective, traits are real, not fictions of people's semantic memory. They are causal, not just summaries of behavior. Moreover, they are learned. Even with identical genetically determined temperaments, two individuals may manifest different traits because of their unique life experiences.

Much attention has been dedicated to finding a working taxonomy of traits, and many accept the Big Five as a minimal number of domains (Goldberg, 1993). But the

Big Seven (Benet-Martinez & Waller, 1997), which adds global positive and negative evaluation to the Big Five, is a better representation of the trait domain, in large part because people do use extreme evaluations to describe themselves and others and these evaluations serve an important social function. Moreover, other constructs, such as defense mechanisms and attachment patterns, need to be added to this domain, as they are often traitlike and serve many of the same functions as traits (Cramer, 1998; Fraley, Waller, & Brennen, 2000).

The domain of traits, and the remaining domains, are viewed in hierarchical terms (see Hooker, 2002; Hooker & McAdams, 2003; Roberts & Pomerantz, 2004). For example, within the trait domain at the broadest level are the personality traits found in standard omnibus personality inventories; these are often the traits that make up the now ubiquitous measures of the Big Five. The midlevel of the continuum can be conceptualized by a number of different constructs such as affective experience (e.g., Diener, 2000); "narrow" traits, such as the subfacets of the Big Five (Roberts, Bogg, Walton, Chernyshenko, & Stark, 2004); attachment patterns (e.g., Fraley et al., 2000); or role identities (e.g., Roberts & Donahue, 1994). These constructs are broader than discrete behaviors but less broad than traits because they are often constrained to specific roles and interpersonal contexts (e.g., relationships, work, and friendships). Presumably, these midlevel constructs are more stable than discrete behaviors and less stable than broad traits (e.g., Conley, 1984). At the most narrow level are the constituent elements of traits: thoughts, feelings, and behaviors. Clearly, thoughts, feelings, and behaviors should be less consistent than the higher order, minimally contextualized trait.

Moving to a hierarchical model means that to some extent all lower order constructs can be subsumed by higher order constructs but the lower order constructs may be the mechanisms by which the higher order constructs exert their influence (see Fleeson, 2001; Graziano, Hair, & Finch, 1997; Graziano, Jensen-Campbell, & Finch, 1997; Hooker & McAdams, 2003). Moreover, a key understanding into the nature of the relations among the levels of the hierarchy may be achieved by acknowledging that each level indicates a certain level of aggregation (Epstein, 1983). That is to say that one moves up a level of breadth, in part by aggregating lower order constructs. This aggregation results in the common variance among lower order constructs being captured by the level of breadth above it. It also leaves the specific variance, sometimes referred to as "unique" variance, at the lower level of breadth. Thus, traits capture only the common variance in thoughts, feelings, and behaviors and leave the unique variance below. To the extent that important unique variance is not captured in the aggregation, the study of lower order constructs is not only quite interesting but also critical. For example, Neuroticism may capture the common variance in a measure of avoidant attachment and work distress. But, these lower order constructs should still predict relationship and work-related outcomes above and beyond a broad measure of Neuroticism.

Values/Motives. The second domain of personality, *values* or *motives*, subsumes all of the things that people feel are desirable—that is, what people want to do or would like. Thus, this category includes the classic notion of motives and needs (e.g., Murray, 1938), in addition to values, interests, preferences, and goals. Like the trait domain, this category is explicitly hierarchical, and the structure of goals and motives has been discussed by numerous researchers (Austin & Vancouver, 1996; Emmons, 1986). The broadest level in this domain is occupied by values (e.g., independence, freedom), which subsume goals such as personal strivings or life tasks (e.g., "I want to become financially independent from my parents."), which in turn subsume current concerns or proximal goals (e.g., the goal to search for a job, get a new suit for an interview, etc.).

Socioanalytic theory posits that this domain can be organized around two primary motivations: the need for status and the need for belonging (Hogan, 1982). Status motives subsume the desires for social status, money, fame, and social regard for people's success. Belongingness motives subsume desires to have a family, close friendships, and some form of identification with a social group or groups (Baumeister & Leary, 1995). Although clearly insufficient to capture the entire domain of values/motivation, it is also clear that these two motives show up across implicit motives (e.g., nPower, nAffiliation), explicit goals (Roberts & Robins, 2000), and values (Schwartz, 1992).

Abilities. The third domain reflects abilities and the hierarchical models identified in achievement literatures—that is, what people can do (Lubinski, 2000). Although still somewhat controversial, the hierarchical model of g, which subsumes verbal, quantitative, and spatial intelligence, is a widely accepted model encompassing the majority of the domains of existing intelligence measures. Alternative theories of intelligence exist (cf. Gardner, 1983), but as of yet, no satisfactory measurement systems have been devised to assess these more comprehensive models. Setting aside the debates within this domain, the most radical feature of the system is that individual differences in ability should be a primary focus of personality researchers. How people differ on abilities from one another is clearly important from both pragmatic and theoretical perspectives and any description of an individual life would be inadequate if it were not included.

Narratives. The final domain, narratives, focuses on the devices people employ to tell the stories they use to understand themselves and their environments (McAdams, 1993). A critical point to consider in any model of personality is that whereas individuals can be classified in terms of traits, abilities, and goals, they often (if not generally) communicate information about themselves quite differently than a simple nomothetic classification on these characteristics, and one common strategy is the use of illustrative stories (McAdams, 1993) or scripts (de St. Aubin, 1999). People find it very easy to tell stories about themselves, others, and their environments. These narratives, in turn, help people create meaning and purpose in their lives and predictability in the events they observe and experience, and provide explanations of how people have come to be in their present circumstances.

The importance of narratives is only beginning to be explored among personality psychologists. Being specific to a person and a given historical period, narratives are more grounded in specific contexts than the other domains of personality. However, tools or stylistic elements that individuals use to construct their narratives, such as narrative tone, coherence, recurrent themes, and complexity, can be abstracted from stories and compared across individuals (McAdams, 1993). The current evidence suggests that these tools vary across people in ways usually only reflected weakly in the other domains (McAdams et al., 2003). Nonetheless, understanding the ways individuals tell stories is important to understanding a number of outcomes. Individuals who typically incorporate "redemptive" themes into their stories are adept at finding happy endings to stories that involve negative events, whereas the tellers of "contamination" stories chronically see good situations turning bad over time, and these story-writing tendencies have been found to have strong relations with dispositional positive and negative affect (McAdams, Reynolds, Lewis, Patten, & Bowman, 2001). Moreover, narratives are organized hierarchically just as the other domains of personality (Hooker, 1992; Hooker & McAdams, 2003). For example, the act of telling stories is often constrained to specific episodes and is also tailored to the audience (Fiese, Hooker, Kotary, Schwagler, & Rimmer, 1995).

As can be seen in the left-hand portion of Fig. 2.1, it is assumed that all of the domains of individual difference are influenced by genetic factors. With the exception of the narrative domain, numerous twin studies have demonstrated that each of these domains is in part the result of genetic factors (Plomin & Caspi, 1999). Clearly, genetic factors act through specific physiological mechanisms. These brain structures, neurotransmitters, and hormone factors are now becoming the focus of research. For example, Caspi et al. (2002) showed that the expression of the gene that affects synthesis of monoamine oxidase (MAO) neurotransmitters can serve as a protective factor for children exposed to abuse. The expression of the gene itself had no direct effect on delinquent behavior. Rather, the gene's expression in delinquency was dependent on the type of abuse the child experienced. Typically, children who are abused grow up to commit greater levels of delinquent acts than their peers. The presence of the MAO gene and its expression buffered the effect of abuse, such that boys with the gene looked surprisingly like boys who experienced no abuse on a battery of psychological and behavioral indicators of delinquency. Conversely, boys without the gene who were abused showed the highest levels of delinquent behavior in adolescence and adulthood.

The identification of these four domains is cursory and deserves greater attention. Nonetheless, this is a good start to organizing the units of analysis found within personality psychology and more clearly than other systems identifies what should be studied.

The Methodological and Conceptual Fulcrum: Identity and Reputation

According to socioanalytic theory, the components of personality are both manifest and organized around two psychological and methodological media: the *identity*, or self-reports, and the *reputation*, or observer reports. The methodological medium reflects the fact that there are primarily two privileged, yet flawed, ways to access information about people: what they say about themselves and what others say about them. Classically, "objective" personality inventories would represent prototypical self-report methods. This category also includes basic trait ratings, self-concept measures, such as self-esteem, as well as measures of goals and values. Observer methods encompass observer ratings of behavior, projective tests, implicit measures, and even physiological factors Typically, self-reports are derogated for being biased by response sets, such as social desirability responding. Observer methods are afforded greater respect within personality psychology, but in industrial organizational

(I/O) psychology where they are used more often, it is widely known that they suffer from biases such as halo error.

These two flawed methods of assessment in personality psychology correspond to two global psychological constructs, identity and reputation that have meaning above and beyond the methods themselves. *Identity* reflects the sum total of opinions that are cognitively available to a person across the four units of analysis described earlier. The term *identity* was chosen for several reasons. The most important is the fact that identity pertains to both the content of self-perceptions and the metacognitive perception of those same self-perceptions. Specifically, people can simultaneously see themselves as "outgoing" and a "carpenter" and feel more or less confident about those self-perceptions. These latter metacognitive aspects of identity, reflected in constructs such as identity achievement, identity clarity, and importance, play a significant role in personality development (Roberts & Caspi, 2003).

Reputation is the perspective on the part of others about a person's traits, motives, abilities, and narratives. Some have argued that the only true way to understand personality is through the lens of the observer (Hofstee, 1994). Regardless, the collective perception of a person not only exists, but could be the focus of more research in personality (Funder, 2000). Reputations clearly guide significant decisions, such as whether to hire a person, admit them to graduate school, marry them, or simply to interact with them. Nonetheless, the concept is summarily ignored in most personality theorizing and research.

Rather than proposing that there is one ideal way of assessing personality, accepting the fact that there are two flawed and distinct ways to understand a person confronts and solves one dilemma that has plagued personality psychology for decades—self-presentation or social desirability responding. For example, it automatically incorporates the fact that people can and do attempt to manage their identity in order to shape their reputation. People do not always tell the whole truth about themselves to employers, friends, family, and strangers. Self-presentation is a fact in human nature and must be successfully incorporated into any theory of personality and cannot be incorporated without an objective division between identity and reputation (Goffman, 1959).

These two perspectives differ in part because they afford different types of information (see Meyer et al., 2001). Clearly, identity-related assessments permit greater access to internal states and experiences that do not happen or are not visible in the company of others. Reputations, on the other hand, may be less tarnished with self-enhancement tendencies and provide a more objective profile of the information that is publicly available to people or experts (Hofstee, 1994). Reputational information may not be ideal because its validity is undermined by the fact that observers do not have complete access to a person's thoughts, feelings, and behaviors (Spain, Eaton, & Funder, 2000), whereas individuals may be unaware of some of their own behavioral tendencies that impact their reputations. Using both and understanding their relation is paramount for any theory and science of personality.

Social Roles: The Conduit for Environmental Influences

One of the most promising aspects of neo-socioanalytic theory is that it explicitly incorporates the social environment, primarily through social roles (Hogan & Rob-

erts, 2000). Social roles tend to fall in two broad domains that correspond closely to
the two primary motives already highlighted: status and belongingness roles. *Status
roles* encompass work and social position roles. *Belongingness roles* encompass friendship, family, and community roles. Moreover, people have to confront the two domains of roles in their universal tasks of living (Helson, Kwan, John, & Jones, 2002).
Across all cultures, individuals tend to gravitate toward finding a mate and establishing a family. In order to thrive, people have to get along with their family, friends,
and members of the community. Individuals also must to establish themselves in
some social position in their community that communicates their social value or
power to their social group.

Many of these roles are age-graded. For example, the importance placed on
creating a family or establishing status positions in society through occupations
reach a peak in young adulthood (Modell, 1989). The age-graded nature of roles
dictates, in part, the progression of personality development across the life course.
When people make serious decisions concerning their position in society and the
constitution of their families and communities, they are forced to confront the
demands of social roles. Accommodation, or change in terms of personality, will
occur in concert with these role expectations. This leads to the first hypothesis:
Personality development will occur primarily in relation to age-graded adult social
roles. One of the most important factors determining personality development will
be when and how these roles are confronted as well as committed to.

As can be seen in the right-hand portion of Fig. 2.1, culture shapes the types and
qualities of roles afforded to individuals. For example, the roles afforded women in
Western cultures are far more diverse than those afforded women in other countries.
Inevitably, the limited role opportunities may limit expression of individual
differences in some samples. In addition, cultures may directly affect individual
differences in dispositions, motives, abilities, and stories through cultural
mechanisms such as religion, mass communication practices, and formal social and
political policies. These cultural effects play out through expectations, demands,
and ideals found in specific roles afforded to people in those cultures.

In closing this brief overview of the neo-socioanalytic model of personality, a few
aspects of the model in Fig. 2.1 deserve comment. First, the model is meant to be a
conceptual, rather than mathematical, model. In its present form, it would not make
for a parsimonious latent variable model. Moreover, it is underspecified, in that we
have not objectively included the product of each box, which is typically thoughts,
feelings, or behaviors (see Hogan & Roberts, 2000, for an example). Clearly,
outcomes, such as health behaviors or episodic emotions, are overdetermined in the
neo-socioanalytic framework. Any given behavior will be the result of multiple
causes, including individuals' traits, goals, abilities, in addition to their social
environment and role enactments. Another feature unique to this model is that all
the paths have double-headed arrows, indicating that no feature of personality is
ultimately causally prior to any other. Moreover, not only are individual differences
being caused by environments and cultures, environments and cultures are being
caused by individuals. Finally, another implication of the bidirectional arrows is that
development can arise not only because of experiences in social roles, but also
because other aspects of personality change. For example, traits may change because
of changes in someone's abilities or goals.

PERSONALITY TRAIT DEVELOPMENT IN THE CONTEXT OF THE NEO-SOCIOANALYTIC MODEL OF PERSONALITY

This uses the tenets of the neo-socioanalytical model of personality to organize and synthesize the patterns and mechanisms of continuity and change in personality traits across the life course. This focus is on personality traits, in large part because that is where our expertise lies, and a review of development in the remaining domains of personality is beyond the scope of the present chapter. First, consider our basic assumptions that lead naturally to a set of questions concerning how and why personality traits develop in adulthood. In the process of addressing the question of personality development, we outline general principles that we have distilled from our review of the literature and from our own research. These principles are defined in Table 2.1.

The first and overarching assumption is that personality traits remain changeable throughout adulthood. This is described as the *Plasticity Principle* (see Roberts, 1997). Built into this principle is the assumption that personality, and personality traits in particular, remain open systems that can be influenced by the environment at any age (Baltes, 1997). This does not mean they are necessarily influenced by the environment or they must change, but that they have the capacity for change at any age. Although this position is seemingly radical in contrast to current perspectives on personality traits (McAdams, 1994; McCrae & Costa, 1999), it actually harkens back to positions espoused by the forefathers of personality psychology who proposed that traits were not only changeable but responded to environmental contingencies (Allport, 1961; Cattell, 1979). It is only recently that traits have been defined as "invariant" or essentially "fixed," and thus not developmental phenomena (McCrae & Costa, 1994). These more recent, and truly radical positions, are the unfortunate

TABLE 2.1
Principles of Personality Development

Principle	*Description*
Plasticity:	Personality traits are open systems that can be influenced by the environment at any age.
Cumulative Continuity:	Personality traits increase in rank-order consistency throughout the life span.
Maturity:	People become more socially dominant, agreeable, conscientious, and emotionally stable with age.
Corresponsive:	The effect of life experience on personality development is to deepen the characteristics that lead people to those experiences in the first place.
Identity Development:	With age, the process of developing, committing to, and maintaining an identity leads to greater personality consistency.
Role Continuity:	Consistent roles rather than consistent environments are the cause of continuity in personality over time.
Social Investment:	Investing in social institutions, such as age-graded social roles, outside of the self is one of the driving mechanisms of personality development in general and greater maturity in particular.

legacy of the person–situation debate that resulted in extreme definitions of traits, either to criticize them or to justify their scientific utility (see Roberts & Caspi, 2001).

When we initially proposed the idea of plasticity, this was more of an assertion than an empirical fact. Given the results of dozens of recent studies, it is more fact than assertion. For example, we find less than perfect rank-order stability even in old age (Roberts & DelVecchio, 2000). Mean-level changes in personality traits have been demonstrated in young adulthood (Helson & Moane, 1987), midlife (Dudek & Hall, 1991), and old age (Field & Millsap, 1991). Numerous studies have demonstrated that individual differences in personality trait change exist and are related to environmental experiences in young adulthood (Helson, Mitchell, & Moane, 1984), midlife (Helson & Wink, 1992; Roberts, 1997; Roberts, Helson, & Klohnen, 2002), and old age (Mroczek & Spiro, 2003; Small, Hertzog, Hultsch, & Dixon, 2003). The latter finding that individual differences in personality trait change exists in old age is by far the most significant. It directly refutes the argument that either personality traits do not change or the changes that are demonstrated are governed entirely by genetic mechanisms (McCrae et al., 2000). It is very difficult to arrive at a parsimonious genetic explanation of individual, unique patterns of personality development, especially when these individual patterns of change contradict general patterns of change, and are linked to experiences in social environments (Robins et al., 2001). It seems much more reasonable to assume that both genetic and environmental factors contribute to patterns of development, in light of the correlations between environmental experiences and individual differences in personality trait change (e.g., Roberts, Caspi, & Moffitt, 2003).

Another implication of the Plasticity Principle is that we are now forced to ask questions about personality trait development that have not as yet been given sufficient attention (cf. Helson & Kwan, 2000; Helson & Moane, 1997; Helson & Stewart, 1994). These questions form the basis of the remainder of this chapter and the inspiration for the remaining principles of development outlined on Table 2.1. Specifically, the fact that personality traits continue to change in adulthood drives four related questions. First, what are the patterns of trait development? Second, why do people maintain or increase consistency with age? Third, why do people change? And fourth, why don't people change more than they do? People face numerous changes in their environment across the life course and especially in young adulthood (see Roberts et al., 2001), yet they do not go through commensurate, dramatic shifts in personality traits. This invites the question of why environmental change does not have a one-to-one correspondence to personality change.

How Do Personality Traits Develop in Adulthood?

The question of how people develop in terms of personality traits can be further broken down into three more specific questions. The first question concerns the general patterns of continuity demonstrated across the life course, such as whether traits demonstrate uniformly high levels of continuity, increasing continuity, or some more complex pattern, such as that shown by self-esteem (Trzesniewski, Donnellan, & Robins, 2003). The second question pertains to the patterns of mean-level changes over the life course. The third pertains to the individual patterns of change.

For each of these, we have distilled principles of development that we believe apply to most people.

Patterns of continuity in personality traits demonstrate a clear pattern across the life course. As mentioned before, there is a tendency for the relative consistency of personality traits to increase throughout the life span, peaking, perhaps at age 60, and even then not being quite fixed (Roberts & DelVecchio, 2000). This is termed the *Cumulative Continuity Principle*.

People become more consistent with age across all personality traits. For example, the differences across the Big Five domains are minimal for average levels of rank-order stability. Moreover, men and women do not differ in their levels of consistency across the life course. It is argued that people exhibit this pattern of increasing in the continuity of traits throughout the life course because of several factors identified in the neo-socioanalytic model of personality, including genetic factors and the processes surrounding identity development (discussed later).

The existence of rank-order stability does not preclude other types of change (see Block, 1971). Specifically, people demonstrate clear patterns of mean-level change in personality traits across the life course. Most people become more socially dominant, agreeable, conscientious, and emotionally stable (Roberts, Robins, Caspi, & Trzesniewski, 2003). This pattern is born out in large-scale cross-sectional studies (McCrae et al., 1999; Srivistava et al., 2003) and in compilations of longitudinal studies (Roberts, Walton, & Viechtbauer, 2006). For example, Roberts, Walton, and Viechtbauer (2006) examined patterns of change across 92 different longitudinal studies covering the life course from age 10 to age 101. The findings show that people become more socially dominant, especially in young adulthood. They become more conscientious and emotionally stable through midlife. Finally, individuals demonstrated gains in openness to experience and social vitality in adolescence, and then equivalent declines late in life.

This pattern of change is described as the *Maturity Principle* because it corresponds quite closely to definitions of maturity that are functional in nature. Hogan and Roberts (2004) argued that maturity is characterized by those qualities that serve to facilitate functioning in society—mature people are more liked, respected, and admired in their communities, social groups, and interpersonal relationships (Hogan & Roberts, 2004). This definition is quite similar to Allport's (1961) characterization of the mature person as happy, showing fewer traces of neurotic and abnormal tendencies, and having the capacity for warm and compassionate relationships. From this perspective, maturity is marked, at a minimum, by higher levels of emotional stability, conscientiousness, and agreeableness. According to the empirical patterns of trait change, it appears that people do become more functionally mature with age. People become warmer, more considerate, self-controlled, responsible, and emotionally stable, especially between age of 20 and age 40.

The interpretation of this definition as functional is bolstered by research demonstrating that people who score higher on these traits tend to be more effective in the tasks of social development. For example, they tend to achieve more success in their careers (Judge, Higgins, Thoresen, & Barrick, 1999), perform better on the job according to their supervisors and peers (Tett, Jackson, & Rothstein, 1991), do more for their organizations than their peers (Hogan, Rybicki, Motowidlo, & Borman, 1998), have more stable marriages (D. Cramer, 1993; Kelly & Conley, 1987), take fewer health risks (Caspi et al., 1997), and live longer (Friedman, Tucker, Tomlinson-Keasey, Schwartz, Wingard, & Criqui, 1993).

The third way that people change concerns individual differences in change. Specifically, we have argued that the most common effect of life experiences on personality development is to deepen the characteristics that lead people to those experiences in the first place (Roberts & Caspi, 2003; Roberts, Caspi, & Moffitt, 2003; Roberts & Robins, 2004). This is the *Correspansive Principle*. Specifically, life experiences that are corresponsive (i.e., that elicit behaviors consistent with their dispositions) will be viewed as validating and thus rewarding to a person, resulting in an elaboration of the dispositions being rewarded by experience. In contrast, people who enter social spheres that have demands that are extremely different from their personality (e.g., a shy person called on to work in an "extraverted" occupation, such as sales or telemarketing) will be disaffected or alienated and will work to avoid or escape prolonged exposure to the experience.

The corresponsive principle is an elaboration on the idea of reciprocity, which holds that certain individual differences will predict experiences in social contexts, and those experiences will in turn affect changes in the predicting disposition. Corresponsiveness goes beyond reciprocity to propose that the pattern holds across dispositions. It also goes to explaining one of the key features of personality trait development in adulthood: its modest nature. Typically, individuals do not go through dramatic transformation in terms of personality traits. Change seems to occur at a modest rate over long periods of time (e.g., 10 years), and often in the direction of the traits that led individuals to those social contexts in the first place.

Support for the corresponsive principle comes from several areas. First, there has been a long history of studies in sociology pointing to the reciprocal relation between work experiences and psychological development. Specifically, people who are more intellectual tend to acquire jobs that have more intellectual stimulation, and in turn this intellectual stimulation is associated with increases in intellectualism (Kohn & Schooler, 1978; Schooler, Mulatu, & Oates, 1999). Data from two recent longitudinal investigations provides more definitive support for applicability of the corresponsive principle to personality trait development. In the first, Roberts et al. (2003) tested whether the personality traits that were predictive of specific work experiences would be the traits that changed in relation to those same work experiences in a sample of young adults making the transition from school to work. They found that across 98 predictive effects, 83% of the change effects were similarly patterned. Moreover, the range of predictive effects correlated .87 with the change effects. For example, people who were more socially dominant were drawn to jobs with more power and, in turn, power was associated with increases in social dominance. In a second longitudinal study of college students, Roberts and Robins (2004) found that adolescents who were less agreeable and more emotionally stable fit better in the highly competitive environment of a large university. In turn, coming to fit better in this environment was associated with decreases in agreeableness and increases in emotional stability—the students responded to the press of the environment and shifted toward the value system of the university over time.

As alluded to at the beginning of this chapter, the picture of development captured by these three principles is eminently reasonable. In terms of personality traits, people become more consistent with age, and according to the mean-level changes, people arguably improve with age too. Consistent with the correspondence principle, idiosyncratic patterns of development can and do occur, but these are in part the result of our preexisting proclivities. Therefore, personality trait development is mostly positive in nature and much less dramatic than that proposed by radical contextualists (e.g., Lewis, 1999).

Why Do Personality Traits Become More Consistent With Age?

One of the most elegant features of the neo-socioanalytic conceptualization of personality is its ability to incorporate many of the mechanisms thought to promote continuity and change in personality (see Caspi & Roberts, 1999; Roberts & Caspi, 2003). For example, genetic and environmental factors have been implicated in maintaining personality continuity over time. In addition, person–environment transactions, such as selection, evocation, and reactance are embedded in the relations between identity, reputation, and role experiences. The next section outlines the primary mechanisms believed to facilitate increasing consistency in personality across the life course.

Clearly, the genetic component of personality is a key component of the neo-socioanalytic model, and apparently it is linked to personality trait consistency. The best evidence for the role of genes in maintaining consistency has been provided by longitudinal studies that track monozygotic and dizygotic twins over time. For example, McGue, Bacon, and Lykken (1993) administered personality tests to monozygotic and dizygotic twins over a 10-year period. Their estimates of overall consistency were similar to other studies (ranging from .4 to .7), showing that there was a balance of consistency and change. Most interestingly, the authors estimated that 80% of the personality consistency demonstrated by their sample of twins was attributable to genetic influences. More recently, Eley, Lichtenstein, and Moffitt (2003) found similar estimates of the effect of genes on levels of consistency in delinquent behaviors in a sample of adolescent twins.

A second factor that contributes to increasing consistency in individual differences are personality traits themselves. That is, certain personality traits tend to facilitate consistency across the life course. For example, Asendorpf and Van Aken (1991) found that ego resiliency, which is partly related to emotional adjustment (Klohnen, 1996), predicted personality consistency over time in a longitudinal sample of children. More specifically, children who were more resilient tended to be more consistent over time. Similarly, Schuerger et al. (1989) found that clinical samples, which it can be assumed are less emotionally stable, were less consistent than nonclinical samples. In an 8-year longitudinal study, men and women who were more controlled, less neurotic, and more prosocially oriented demonstrated less change in personality traits and greater profile consistency across personality traits (Roberts, Caspi, & Moffitt, 2001). Also consistent with the maturity hypothesis is the proposal by Clausen (1993) that the trait of planful competence predicts higher levels of personality consistency in adulthood. People who are planfully competent tend to be more self-confident, dependable, and intellectually invested. Interestingly, planful competence also includes intelligence as a key component predicting consistency, which supports the inclusion of cognitive ability in the scope of personality detailed earlier.

The third factor that facilitates increasing personality consistency derives directly from the neo-socioanalytic model. With age, the process of developing, committing to, and maintaining an identity leads to greater personality consistency (Roberts & Caspi, 2003). This is the *Identity Development Principle*. Although an individual's identity is made up of the constituent elements previously described, people are not entirely clear about their own personality attributes, interests, abilities, and life story when they are young. Thus, an individual's confidence in their metacognitive perspective on their identity is tied to personality consistency. For example, intrinsic to the identity development process is people's search for an identity that fits with their values, abilities, and predispositions (Erikson, 1968). Thus, one of the overriding concerns of adolescence and young adulthood is selecting and building an identity that fits with their characteristics. We see in this process the manifestation of the selection process identified by P. B. Baltes and M. M. Baltes (1990) and others (Buss, 1987; Caspi & Roberts, 1999; Ickes, Snyder, & Garcia, 1997; Snyder & Ickes, 1985), which presumably contributes to personality consistency. The assumption is that if a person chooses an identity that fits well, then there will be less press for change. For example, Roberts and Robins (2004) showed that students that fit better with the value system of their college or university demonstrated less personality change over time.

Aspects of identity achievement, certainty, and consolidation also are related to dispositional factors linked to personality consistency. For example, having an achieved identity was found to be related to higher levels of psychological well-being (Helson, Stewart, & Ostrove, 1995). Vandewater, Ostrove, and Stewart (1997) showed that having an achieved identity was directly related to higher family and work role quality and indirectly to life satisfaction and psychological well-being. Roenkae and Pulkkinen (1995) found that having a clear career line, akin to the notion of an achieved identity, was related to fewer problems in social functioning in adulthood. Identity achievement also has been shown to be related to higher levels of self-esteem, autonomy, and moral reasoning, and lower levels of anxiety (see Marcia, 1980). Likewise, self-certainty is related to an increased sense of control over future situations (Trope & Ben-Yair, 1982); clarity of the self-concept is associated with higher levels of self-esteem (Campbell, 1990); and identity consolidation is related to less marital tension, positive feelings about mothering, work satisfaction, and personality variables such as self-confidence, positive well-being, competence, affiliation, and independence (Pals, 1999). Therefore, identity, and aspects of identity such as achievement, certainty, clarity, and consolidation, are linked to higher levels of psychological well-being and adjustment, which in turn are related to higher levels of personality trait consistency (Roberts, Caspi, & Moffitt, 2001).

Having a well-developed identity may promote other personality-consistency mechanisms. For example, to the extent that a person's identity becomes known to others in the form of a reputation (Hogan & Roberts, 2000), other people may react to individuals in a way that is consistent with their personality (evocative person–environment transaction). For example, if a person has a reputation of being outgoing, others may invite this individual to social engagements more often. Or, if a person has a reputation for being domineering, others may avoid or act submissive in that person's presence, which in turn engenders more domineering behavior.

Of course, the final mechanism typically invoked to explain consistency is the environment itself. Personality consistency is thought to derive from being in a consistent, unchanging environment. Unfortunately, there is no empirical evidence to support this idea. No one has ever done the appropriate longitudinal study in which some measure of environmental stability is linked to personality stability. Moreover, there is a tremendous amount of evidence to the contrary. For example, the level of rank-order stability in a study of college students going through little or no serious environmental transitions (Robins et al., 2001) was identical to the rank-order stability found in a heterogeneous sample of New Zealanders, most of whom made major shifts from their family of origin to independent living (Roberts et al., 2001).

This problem may be solved by using a more psychologically meaningful operationalization of the environment. In particular, a more appropriate "environmental" variable that could help to explain consistency is the role concept embedded in the neo-socioanalytic framework. Rather than a consistent objective environment facilitating consistency, it may be the consistent subjective environment in the form of roles that people enact across transitions that promote consistency. This is the *Role Continuity Principle*. For example, adolescents who play specific roles in high school, such as being a jock or a brain, tend to adopt similar roles in later life stages such as in college or in their chosen occupation or leisure interests (Barber, Eccles, & Stone, 2001). This coherence of social roles transcends the physical environment that facilitates personality consistency over time.

In sum, it is clear that numerous factors intrinsic to the neo-socioanalytic model of personality play a role in facilitating increasing continuity over the life course. Genetic factors, patterns of personality trait development, and identity development are all implicated in the inevitable stabilization of personality traits that comes with age. Clearly, other potential factors remain (e.g., the stability of roles) that also come with age, but these factors remain to be investigated.

Why Do Personality Traits Change With Age?

Most of the previously identified mechanisms of personality change (Caspi & Roberts, 1999) can be located within the neo-socioanalytic framework. Most of these mechanisms of change reside in the path from roles to identity. First, people might simply change in response to contingencies in the environments found in social roles. For example, the child role is one in which many parental demands and expectations are placed on a person, which presumably result in some form of behavioral change. The second and third change mechanisms are watching ourselves and watching others, especially in new contexts. Caspi and Roberts (1999) argued that changes occur through watching ourselves do things differently, often in the context of a new role or in response to new role demands. Moreover, the ability to model (watching others) also is embedded in roles such as those found at work.

The final change mechanism, listening to others, is unique as it resides in the path from reputation to identity. This can be seen in the formal mechanism of performance feedback. Employees may be under the impression that they are performing well (identity perception), until their supervisor provides less than flattering performance feedback (reputation). Similar feedback mechanisms may affect change in traits and interests as people acquire information about their social reputation from others in the environment.

Most of these mechanisms of change are enacted when individuals make changes in their identity that force them to confront new role demands and expectations, acquire role models, and receive feedback from new endeavors and activities. This process is the *Social Investment Principle*. The social investment principle states that investing in social institutions, such as age-graded social roles, outside of the individual's current identity is one of the driving mechanisms of personality development in general and greater maturity in particular. This principle is a natural corollary of the Cumulative Continuity Principle and it also highlights one of the unique components of the neo-socioanalytic model of personality—age-graded social roles. This principle builds on the fundamental feature of identity development that to create an identity entails making commitments to social institutions in the form of social roles, such as work, marriage, family, and community. Moreover, most people make commitments to normative social roles, such as being married and having a career versus not being married and not having a career. The dominant pattern of role investments seen in quasi-universal tasks of social living, such as developing a career and career identity (Helson et al, 2002), helps explain the normative patterns of personality change that result from role investments (see Maturity Principle).

What are the mechanisms through which investments in social roles impart change in personality traits? The crux of the process lies in people committing themselves to social institutions outside of their existing identity structure. This act exposes a person to the contingencies contained in the social role. These contingencies come in the form of role expectations for appropriate behavior (Sarbin, 1964). These role expectations come from the self and from the collective other. For example, people will come to their first job with a set of expectations for how they should act that are derived from their experiences watching significant others in the same types of roles, such as parents, mentors, friends, and other influential people (Caspi & Roberts, 1999). In addition, individuals in a person's social circle will hold a set of expectations for how the person should act and will reward or punish the person according to whether or not they act consistently with those expectations.

These role expectations can affect change through either punishing inappropriate behavior or rewarding appropriate behavior. So, for example, some researchers argue that role expectations exert social control over behavior, such that if a person violates the expectations they will be punished. Sampson and Laub (1990) argued that one reason why delinquent boys relinquished their life of crime upon getting married was that their wives kept them in line through threats and admonishments. Similarly, Hirschi and Stark (1969) indicated that commitments to conventional institutions and the relationships therein, such as religion, exerts a form of social control because behavior is directly supervised and monitored by friends and family members who also participate in the typically conventional organization. Implicit in this idea is the fact that people perceive violations of social control resulting in some form of punishment, typically through loss of social regard or acceptance.

In addition, role expectations can facilitate personality change by serving as guides for what behavior should be rewarded. The rewarding aspect of role expectations may be mediated by the perception the person has of the people in their social roles. For example, Kochanska and Murray (2000) identified the *mutually reinforcing orientation* (MRO) between a young child and their parent as a major factor contributing to the acquisition of a conscience. The mutually reinforcing orientation is the positive relation between parent and child in which the child comes to admire the parent. Children who have mutually reinforcing relationships with their parents are more likely to internalize parental values for moral behavior. According to Kochanska, children with MRO relationships with their parents do this because they like and admire their parents and experience positive emotions when they act in ways consistent with parental expectations and ideals.

In the context of MRO relationships, we see the development of enduring characteristics stemming from a desire to establish positive relationships with people that are liked and admired. These general processes also occur for adults. Specifically, if a person likes and admires the individuals in their social settings who are communicating role expectations, and they enjoy and are satisfied with their relationships and their experiences, they will be more likely to acquire and enact the expected role behaviors. It is especially important to note that the direction of personality change in adulthood will not necessarily be in a direction of improvement because sometimes others do not communicate entirely positive role expectations. So, for example, one reason why executives might acquire unethical behavior patterns is that they like and admire their mentors. These same mentors may have many positive and desirable qualities, yet may unfortunately participate in unethical activities. Through their identification with their mentor, subordinates may inadvertently acquire undesirable behaviors as part of the total identification package. Ironically, it may often be the positive views toward an individual's work that lead to negative behavioral patterns such as corruption, harassment, and exploitation.

Empirical support for the social investment principle is just beginning to accumulate. For example, there is now consistent evidence that social investments in work, marriage, and community facilitate increases in traits related to conscientiousness. Roberts (1997) tracked the reciprocal relation between levels of participation and success in the paid labor force and changes in personality traits in a longitudinal study of women. In the transition from young adulthood to midlife, women who achieved higher levels of occupational attainment tended to increase on achievement, responsibility, and self-control; demonstrating that more continuous investment in work was related to increases in traits from the domain of conscientiousness. In an ongoing longitudinal study of both men and women, Roberts, Caspi, and Moffitt (2003) found that psychological commitment to work was associated with increases in facets of conscientiousness from age 18 to 26. In addition, Robins, Moffitt, and Caspi (2002) found that remaining in a close intimate relationship in young adulthood was related to increases in constraint, a facet of conscientiousness related to impulse control. These longitudinal studies show that investment in social roles may explain, in part, the increases in conscientiousness found in young and middle adulthood.

In sum, people change by responding to contingencies, modeling others, and through receiving persistent feedback that contradicts closely held views of the self. Moreover, the most likely source of these forces of change arises through investing in conventional social institutions, such as marriage, work, and community. These institutions, embodied in social roles that are intrinsic to the makeup of identity, bring with them expectations and demands for prosocial behaviors, responsibility, and emotional stability. Of course, sometimes people select new identities in order to change (Snyder & Ickes, 1985). But this is the least likely pathway through which personality traits change. Rather, change is most likely the result of the long-term press of social environments chosen for reasons other than personality trait development (e.g., interests, abilities, or goals).

Why Don't Personality Traits Change More?

One of the most striking features of the longitudinal studies tracking the relation between life experiences and personality change is the relatively small effect that environmental contingencies have on personality change (see, e.g., Roberts, 1997; Roberts, Caspi, & Moffitt, 2003; Roberts & Chapman, 2000; Roberts, Helson, & Klohnen, 2002). Despite robust shifts in environments, people do not demonstrate dramatic shifts in terms of personality traits in response. This invites the last question of personality development: Why don't we find more evidence for personality trait change?

The answer to this question arrives at a set of three mechanisms that also could be thought of as factors that facilitate consistency in personality. Nonetheless, these mechanisms are a specialized set of tools that people use mostly in response to environmental contingencies that demand change, but they tend not to result in change because of what people do to the information gleaned from the experience in the environment. The first set concerns actively avoiding new environments or avoiding making the social and emotional investment that would result in change. The second set involves a set of individual difference characteristics that seem to buffer or enhance susceptibility to environmental contingencies. The third set encompasses strategies of information processing designed to inoculate or diminish the significance, relevance, or meaningfulness of environmental press to change.

In most socialization theories, the typical assumption is that the path from environments to person is unidirectional and direct. This perspective is described as the "exposure" model of personality development in which it is often assumed that mere exposure to the social structure, role, or context will facilitate change in personality (Roberts et al., 2003). Exposure models underestimate the complexity of the relation between personality and social structure. For example, it is clear that several factors moderate the relation of the path from social roles to identity in Fig. 2.1. First, if the expectations are too different from a person's set of characteristics that they bring to the role, then the person might choose to leave the context rather than change (Schneider, Smith, Taylor, & Fleenor, 1998). Second, experiences early in the process of acquiring the role may not be internalized because of the inevitable identity negotiations that take place. People do not simply respond to role contingencies, they may try to shape the role to fit themselves better and it may take time before these strategies are exhausted and the person has to come to terms with a set of expectations that contradict their strongly held self-perceptions. In both situations, although the investment has occurred demographically, it has not occurred psychologically because the individual has not made the complete emotional and cognitive commitment to the role.

An additional set of moderators is a person's personality characteristics. Certain people are less inclined to respond to environmental contingencies more than others. For example, in a study of Asian students living in Canada, Ryder, Alden, and Paulhus (2000) found that the degree of endorsement of either Western or Eastern ethnic identities was associated with high conscientiousness, emotional stability, and agreeableness. Specifically, people who are less disorganized, anxious, and disagreeable tend not to accept ethnic identities regardless of their content. In work settings, Chatman and Barsade (1955) purported that people who were less cooperative were less likely to adopt a competitive stance when the organizational culture demanded it. Similarly, Roberts and Helson (1997) found that unconventional, less adjusted women were less likely to change in ways consistent with the changing cultural climate of the 1960s, 1970s, and 1980s. In addition, it could be hypothesized that certain defense mechanisms, such as denial and projection, would hinder individuals' ability to successfully integrate new information about themselves (Roberts & Caspi, 2003). Accordingly, it would be assumed that people suffering from certain personality disorders, such as narcissistic personality disorder, would not have the necessary psychological skills to respond to role contingencies and would thus change less in response to role expectations or feedback than others; unless, of course, the role expectations call for the person to become more narcissistic (see Robins & John, 1997; Robins & Paulhus, 2001).

A final set of identity-related factors that would moderate the effect of environmental demands for change are a person's existing cognitive and emotional schemas designed to protect the identity when it is threatened. These factors are strategic information-processing mechanisms. These factors subsume a wide range of conscious and unconscious information-processing factors. These mechanisms share one thing in common: They all act to reconfigure the meaning of experience, not experience itself.

The first mechanism drawn from life-span developmental theory is termed "accommodative" strategies (Brandtstadter & Greve, 1994), and refers to the adjustments one makes in goals or self-evaluative standards in order to maintain consistent self-views. Brandtstadter (1992) showed that people increase the use of flexible goal adjustment with age and simultaneously diminish their tenacious goal pursuit. Thus, with age, people recalibrate their goals rather than persist in attempting to achieve specific outcomes (e.g., earning enough for retirement rather than earning enough to become rich). By recalibrating goals, people can maintain consistent self-views (e.g., I am successful). One of the most effective means with which people can maintain consistent views of themselves is to re-norm their self-evaluative standards. For example, with age, individuals inevitably face decreasing physical and cognitive abilities, especially in comparison with young people. Rather than comparing themselves against young people or people in general, older individuals can maintain the perception that they are active and sharp by re-norming their evaluative standards exclusively against other older people.

Similarly, the optimization and compensation strategies from the Selection, Optimization, and Compensation model (SOC; P. B. Baltes and M. M. Baltes, 1990) can be seen as continuity-promoting mechanisms. *Optimization* refers to emphasizing goals and activities that reflect a person's strengths rather than emphasizing something new or untested (e.g., selection). *Compensation* reflects the inevitable tailoring of goals and activities to make up for the natural degradation of abilities in old age. So, for example, individuals can both emphasize and come to depend on crystallized knowledge more than fluid intelligence because of the diminishing information-processing speed that accompanies old age. Both of these mechanisms entail emphasizing, if not fostering, existing characteristics or skills. Applied to the sphere of personality traits, it is easy to see that the successful utilization of optimization and compensation strategies would facilitate the maintenance of personality traits. For example, despite decreasing expenditure of energy at work (e.g., a propensity to work hard), people's impression that they are conscientious may be maintained if they can emphasize other facets of conscientiousness, such as their organization skills or ability to be efficient. With age and decreasing energy, a person may be forced to fall back on organizational skills to compensate for a lack of energy and efficiency.

Brandtstadter and Greve (1994) described a fourth information-processing factor, *immunization,* which is defined as processes that protect the self from self-discrepant evidence. These mechanisms include deemphasizing the personal relevance of an experience, searching for and finding an alternative interpretation, and questioning the credibility of the source of information. In relation to personality consistency, imagine individuals receiving reputational feedback from a friend or acquaintance that they are neurotic. If these individuals feel that they are not neurotic, then immunizing mechanisms may be employed to discount the friend's opinion. In order to maintain a consistent self-perception, these people may attempt to trivialize the importance of the relationship, or attribute the feedback to the friend's own issues (alternative interpretation), or question the friend's ability to make such interpretations (question credibility). All of these strategies would serve to maintain their self-perception that they are not neurotic or at least not as neurotic as the friend claims.

Accommodation, optimization, selection, and immunization mechanisms are assumed to be cognitive schemas that can be accessed in conscious awareness. *Defense mechanisms,* a fifth information-processing factor, are assumed to perform similar functions to the conscious information-processing mechanisms identified earlier, but do so unconsciously (Norem, 1998). Contemporary perspectives define defense mechanisms as unconscious mental operations that function to protect the individual from experiencing excessive anxiety (Cramer, 1998). Defense mechanisms are seen not only in the classical psychoanalytic sense as acting to filter individuals' unacceptable internal thoughts, impulses, or wishes, but also in the contemporary sense as filtering out experiences and information that threaten their self-esteem or self-integration (Cramer, 1998).

If we assume that, in part, personality change results from experiencing events that contradict closely held views of the self or from receiving feedback from others that individuals are different than originally expected, then defense mechanisms should buffer the effect of this type of experience. What can be more anxiety provoking for people than being told that they are wrong about themselves, or to do something like fail at an important task that is critical to their identity? Indeed, people tend to become anxious when presented with information that contradicts their self-perceptions, even if that new information is more positive than their closely held self-concept (Swann, Pelham, & Krull, 1989). The anxiety, whether or not conscious, that is invoked should by its very nature call up the use of defense mechanisms. Take, for example, the incident described earlier where people receive feedback that they are neurotic. Rather than consciously reshaping the nature of the information, an alternative would be to unconsciously project back the information on the person delivering the feedback. The person providing feedback is now considered neurotic and needs the attention, if not sympathy, of the person originally deemed to be neurotic. Alternatively, people could conveniently forget (repress) that they were described as neurotic, or "isolate" the event from other cognitions and emotions (Baumeister, Dale, & Sommer, 1998), so that it is quickly forgotten or deemed to be of little importance. Needless to say, personality continuity should be maintained to the extent that defense mechanisms can transform or inoculate disconfirming experience or feedback.

Accommodation, optimization, compensation, immunization, and defense mechanisms are "strategic" information processing because each serves the agenda of maintaining continuity in self-perceptions and continuity in self-integrity in response to environmental contingencies that normally would result in change. Combined with identity negotiations, and individual differences in personality traits themselves, people are potentially well defended against environmental presses to change their character. Thus, change is typically modest in relation to putatively dramatic environmental contingencies. Unfortunately, the buffering of these mechanisms has not been tested in longitudinal studies of personality development.

CONCLUSIONS, CAVEATS, AND FUTURE DIRECTIONS

This relatively brief introduction to the neo-socioanalytic theory of personality and personality development has inevitably oversimplified complex ideas and ignored important issues. For example, it has not accounted for the specifics of age-graded development like that found in Levensonian and Eriksonian theories of adult development. Moreover, it has overlooked the conundrum of how to assess both continuity and change. The understanding of, and perspective on, personality development shifts as different indices of change, such as rank-order consistency, mean-level change, and individual differences in change are examined (Mroczek & Spiro, 2003). The latter, individual differences in change, is likely one of the most underappreciated and important phenomena in personality development. The existence of unique patterns of development that contradict general trends renders obsolete theoretical perspectives that pose no influence of the environment on personality trait development or general genetic proclivities being the only force behind personality development. Conversely, ignoring the tremendous continuity in personality over time renders insufficient, simplistic environmental models of personality development that posit individuals as nothing more than fodder for environmental canons.

Apologies aside, there is a tremendous amount of potential and opportunity for research in the theory proposed. First, many of the principles and mechanisms described earlier are supported by provisional evidence at best. It would be especially important to initiate studies testing the mechanisms of continuity and change in a truly longitudinal context.

In addition to these types of investigations, many research questions wait to be addressed. For example, compared to the trait and cognitive ability domain, very little longitudinal research has been carried out on the narrative and motive/interest domains. Nobody knows how consistent life narratives are over time. Moreover, very few studies have tracked multiple levels of different phenomena over time. For example, because of existing ideological differences within the field, it is impossible to find longitudinal studies that track traits simultaneously with social cognitive units of analysis, such as self-efficacy.

An additional overlooked possibility is to track multiple personality domains simultaneously over time, such as goals and traits or goals and abilities. For example, both the motive and ability domains may prove to be necessary for understanding trait development. One reason why emotional stability may increase with age may be the accumulated knowledge, or wisdom, concerning how to better deal with social and emotional situations. With time and experience, people may learn to avoid certain situations (e.g., not sending the first draft of a memo), thus diminishing the likelihood of experiencing elevated distress. This accumulated knowledge is best thought of as part of the ability domain and this knowledge accumulation may be critical for successful development. As another example, Astin (1993) reported that SAT Verbal scores taken at the beginning of college prospectively predicted change in political liberalism over the next 4 years in U.S. undergraduates. This may be caused by highly intelligent students becoming more embedded in and subsequently conforming to a liberal college environment, suggesting an interplay of many processes discussed in this chapter. It is clear that by inclusion of multiple domains, relationships are found in individual development that would otherwise be empirically unobservable and untestable. Certainly, countless relationships of this sort are waiting to be found once materials from multiple domains are administered in a repeated fashion longitudinally.

Another distinct oversight in most longitudinal studies of personality development is the inclusion of meaningful assessments of situations, contexts, or roles (cf. Helson & Moane, 1987; Helson & Picano, 1990; Helson & Wink, 1992). Typically, longitudinal researchers rely too heavily on simplistic, often dichotomous demographic variables to represent important social context or role variables. In contrast, much richer conceptualizations of role variables, such as role expectations, demands, and experiences are available, but simply not included in most studies.

Surprisingly, another aspect of the neo-socioanalytic model of personality has been seldom seen in a longitudinal context. Few studies have bothered to gather identity and reputational information simultaneously on individuals and tracked both over time. We know very little about how reputations are built and maintained over time and what it takes to change a reputation. For example, people may see significant change in themselves that is not seen by others for many years after the change has occurred. Moreover, reputations may themselves be indirect mechanisms of consistency by acting to effectively force a person to behave as they are expected to act.

Two broad issues deserve much greater attention. First, given the provocative role of genetics in determining the expression of phenotypic traits, interests, and abilities, it is incumbent on developmental psychologists to combine forces with behavior geneticists and track monozygotic, dyzygotic, and adoptive siblings over time. This design, especially in combination with rich context information, can provide definitive conclusions to the latent nature–nurture debate, which despite calls for its demise, still informs many perspectives in personality and developmental psychology. The second, ultimately ignored domain is studying personality development cross-culturally. There are little or no known longitudinal studies examining personality development outside of the United States and Western Europe. Given the relevance of longitudinal data to issues critical to cultural psychology, this oversight needs to be addressed.

Finally, a set of ideas germane to both the "analytic" and identity development aspects of the neo-socioanalytic framework should be made an explicit focus of future research: *fit* and its converse, *conflict*. Of course, conflict is intrinsic to analytic models of personality. In this context, it does not have to carry the psychodynamic connotations of the past (e.g., between the id and superego). Rather, there is the potential for much conflict among the units of personality identified in Fig. 2.1. A person may have a conflict between their new role (as a teacher), and their motivation for money and status. Moreover, a person may have conflict between their aspirations (to be a CEO) and their abilities (no leadership skills). As others have shown, conflict can arise within domains, such as the conflict between goals (Emmons & King, 1988). Conversely, the overarching goal of identity development is for people to find an identity that fits with their attributes and thus diminish conflict. This idea is manifest in the organizational ideas of person–environment fit and could be applied to the process of identity and personality development. Clearly, one of the implicit and explicit goals of development is to find one's niche. The processes that people go through to establish their niche deserves greater attention in studies of personality development.

In conclusion, this chapter has outlined a general theory of personality and tied this theory to personality development in adulthood. Three unique aspects of this theory should be highlighted. First, traits are only one of four domains of personality and all four domains should be considered when attempting to understand a person or our field. Second, identity and reputation are separate entities that should be considered in unison. Implicit in this structure is the assumption that neither perspective should be dominant in defining personality. Finally, the third unique aspect of the neo-socioanalytic theory is the inclusion of social roles as the primary conduit through which environments affect personality.

The final useful feature of the neo-socioanalytic framework is that it anticipates many of the factors that affect personality development and provides numerous testable hypotheses concerning other potential mechanisms. So, for example, we know that genes and culture affect personality development and this is the first theory to successfully integrate these two factors. Moreover, identity development and role experiences are clearly identified as critical factors that facilitate both personality continuity and change. The hope in proposing this new theory is that it can account for the patterns of continuity and change that already are known to exist, and to provide fertile ground for generating testable hypotheses for future studies of personality development.

REFERENCES

Ackerman, P. L., & Heggestad, E. D. (1997). Intelligence, personality, and interests: Evidence for overlapping traits. *Psychological Bulletin, 121,* 219–245.

Allport, G. W. (1961). *Pattern and growth in personality.* New York: Holt, Rinehart & Winston.

Asendorpf, J. B., & Van Aken, M. A. (1991). Correlates of the temporal consistency of personality patterns in childhood. *Journal of Personality, 59*, 689–703.

Astin, A. W. (1993). *What matters in college? Four critical years revisited.* San Francisco: Jossey-Bass.

Austin, J. T., & Vancouver, J. B. (1996). Goal constructs in psychology: Structure, process and content. *Psychological Bulletin, 120*, 338–375.

Baltes, P. B. (1997). On the incomplete architecture of human ontogeny. *American Psychologist, 52*, 366–380.

Baltes, P. B., & Baltes, M. M. (1990). Psychological perspectives on successful aging: The model fo selective optimisation with compensation. In P. B. Baltes & M. M. Baltes (Eds.), *Successful aging: Perspectives from the behavioural sciences* (pp. 1–34). New York: Cambridge University Press.

Bandura, A. (1999). Social cognitive theory of personality. In L. A. Pervin & O. P. John (Eds.), *Handbook of personality: Theory and research* (2nd ed., pp. 154–196). New York: Guilford.

Barber, B. L., Eccles, J. S., & Stone, M. R. (2001). Whatever happened to the jock, the brain, and the princess? Young adult pathways linked to adolescent activity involvement and social identity. *Journal of Adolescent Research, 16*, 429–455.

Baumeister, R. F., Dale, K., & Sommer, K. L. (1998). Freudian defense mechanisms and empirical findings in modern social psychology: Reaction formation, projection, displacement, undoing, isolation, sublimation, and denial. *Journal of Personality, 66*, 1081–1124.

Baumeister, R. F., & Leary, M. R. (1995). The need to belong: Desire for interpersonal attachments as a fundamental human motivation. *Psychological Bulletin, 117*, 497–529.

Benet-Martinez, V., & Waller, N. G. (1997). Further evidence for the cross-cultural generality of the Big Seven Factor model: Indigenous and imported Spanish personality constructs. *Journal of Personality, 65*, 567–598.

Block, J. (1971). *Lives through time.* Berkeley, CA: Bancroft.

Brandtstadter, J. (1992). Person control over development: Some developmental implications of self-efficacy. In R. Schwarzer (Ed.), *Self-efficacy: Thought control of action* (pp. 127–145). Washington, DC: Hemisphere.

Brandtstadter, J., & Greve, W. (1994). The aging self: Stabilizing and protective processes. *Developmental Review, 14*, 52–80.

Buss, D. M. (1987). Selection, evocation, and manipulation. *Journal of Personality and Social Psychology, 53*, 1214–1221.

Campbell, J. D. (1990). Self-esteem and clarity of the self-concept. *Journal of Personality and Social Psychology, 59*, 538–549.

Caspi, A., Begg, D., Dickson, N., Harrington, H., Langley, J., Moffitt, T. E., & Silva, P. A. (1997). Personality differences predict health-risk behaviors in young adulthood: Evidence from a longitudinal study. *Journal of Personality and Social Psychology, 73*, 1052–1063.

Caspi, A., McClay, J., Moffitt, T., Mill, J., Martin, J., Craig, I. W., Taylor, A., & Poulton, R. (2002). Role of genotype in the cycle of violence in maltreated children. *Science, 297*, 851–854.

Caspi, A., & Roberts, B. W. (1999). Personality continuity and change across the life course. In L. A. Pervin & O. P. John (Eds.), *Handbook of personality: theory and research* (2nd ed., pp. 154–196). New York, NY: Guilford.

Cattell, R. B. (1979). *Personality and learning theory.* New York: Springer Publishing.

Chatman, J. A., & Barsade, S. G. (1995). Personality, organizational culture, and cooperation: Evidence from a business simulation. *Administrative Science Quarterly, 40*, 423–443.

Clausen, J. A. (1993). *American lives: Looking back at the children of the Great Depression.* New York: The Free Press.

Conley, J. J. (1984). The hierarchy of consistency: A review and model of longitudinal findings on adult individual differences in intelligence, personality, and self-opinion. *Personality and Individual Differences, 5*, 11–26.

Cramer, D. (1993). *Personality and marital dissolution. Personality and Individual Differences, 14*, 605–607.

Cramer, P. (1998). Defensiveness and defense mechanisms. *Journal of Personality, 66*, 879–894.

de St. Aubin, E. (1999). Personal ideology: The intersection of personality and religious beliefs. *Journal of Personality, 67,* 1105–1139.

Diener, E. (2000). Subjective well-being: The science of happiness and a proposal for a national index. *American Psychologist, 55,* 34–43.

Dudek, S. Z., & Hall, W. B. (1991). Personality consistency: Eminent architects 25 years later. *Creativity Research Journal, 4,* 213–231.

Eley, T. C., Lichtenstein, P., & Moffitt, T. E. (2003). A longitudinal analysis of the etiology of aggressive and non-aggressive antisocial behaviour. *Development and Psychopathology, 15,* 383–402.

Emmons, R. A. (1986). Personal strivings: An approach to personality and subjective well-being. *Journal of Personality and Social Psychology, 51,* 1058–1068.

Emmons, R. A., & King, L. A. (1988). Conflict among personal strivings: Immediate and long-term implications for psychological and physical well-being. *Journal of Personality and Social Psychology, 54,* 1040–1048.

Epstein, S. (1983). Aggregation and beyond: Some basic issues on the prediction of behavior. *Journal of Personality, 51,* 360–392.

Erikson, E. H. (1968). *Identity: Youth and crisis.* New York: W. W. Horton.

Field, D., & Millsap, R. E. (1991). Personality in advanced old age: Continuity or change? *Journal of Gerontology, 46,* 299–308.

Fiese, B. H., Hooker, K. A., Kotary, L., Schwagler, J., & Rimmer, M. (1995). Family stories in the early stages of parenthood. *Journal of Marriage and the Family, 57,* 763–770.

Fleeson, W. (2001). Toward a structure- and process-integrated view of personality: Traits as density distributions of states. *Journal of Personality and Social Psychology, 80,* 1011–1027.

Fraley, R. C., Waller, N. G., & Brennan, K. A. (2000). An item response theory analysis of self-report measures of adult attachment. *Journal of Personality and Social Psychology, 78,* 350–365.

Friedman, H. S., Tucker, J. S., Tomlinson-Keasey, C., Schwartz, J. E., Wingard, D. L., & Criqui, M. H. (1993). Does childhood personality predict longevity. *Journal of Personality and Social Psychology, 65,* 176–185.

Funder, D. C. (1991). Global traits: A neo-Allportian approach to personality. *Psychological Science, 2,* 31–39.

Funder, D. C. (2000). Personality. *Annual Review of Psychology, 52,* 197–221.

Gardner, H. (1983). *Frames of mind: The theory of multiple intelligences.* New York: Basic Books.

Goffman, E. (1959). *The presentation of self in everyday life.* New York: Doubleday.

Goldberg, L. R. (1993). The structure of phenotypic personality traits. *American Psychologist, 48,* 26–34.

Graziano, W. G., Jensen-Campbell, L. A., & Finch, J. F. (1997). The self as a mediator between personality and adjustment. *Journal of Personality and Social Psychology, 73,* 392–404.

Heckhausen, J. (1997). Developmental regulation across adulthood: Primary and secondary control of age-related challenges. *Developmental Psychology, 33,* 176–187.

Helson, R., & Kwan, V. S. Y. (2000). Personality development in adulthood: The broad picture and processes in one longitudinal sample. In S. E. Hampson (Ed), *Advances in personality psychology* (pp. 77–106). Philadelphia: Taylor & Francis.

Helson R., Kwan, V. S. Y., John, O. P., & Jones, C. (2002). The growing evidence for personality change in adulthood: Findings from research with personality inventories. *Journal of Research in Personality, 36,* 287–306.

Helson, R., Mitchell, V., & Moane, G. (1984). Personality and patterns of adherence and nonadherence to the social clock. *Journal of Personality and Social Psychology, 46,* 1079–1096.

Helson, R., & Moane, G. (1987). Personality change in women from college to midlife. *Journal of Personality and Social Psychology, 53,* 176–186.

Helson, R., & Picano, J. (1990). Is the traditional role bad for women? *Journal of Personality and Social Psychology, 59,* 311–320.

Helson, R., & Stewart, A. (1994). Personality change in adulthood. *Can personality change?* (pp. 201–225). Washington, DC: American Psychological Association.

Helson, R., Stewart, A. J., & Ostrove, J. (1995). Identity in three cohorts of midlife women. *Journal of Personality and Social Psychology, 69,* 544–557.

Helson, R., & Wink, P. (1992). Personality change in women from the early 40s to the early 50s. *Psychology and Aging, 7,* 46–55.

Hirschi, T., & Stark, R. (1969). Hellfire and delinquency. *Social Problems, 17,* 202–213.

Hofstee, W. K. B. (1994). Who should own the definition of personality? *European Journal of Personality, 8,* 149–162.

Hogan, R. T. (1982). A socioanalytic theory of personality. In *Nebraska Symposium on Motivation* (pp. 55–89). University of Nebraska Press.

Hogan, R. T., & Roberts, B. W. (2000). A Socioanalytic perspective on person–environment interaction. In W. B. Walsh, K. H. Craik, & R. H. Price (Eds.), *New directions in person–environment psychology* (pp. 1–24) Mahwah, NJ: Lawrence Erlbaum Associates.

Hogan, R., & Roberts, B. W. (2004). A socioanalytic model of maturity. *Journal of Career Assessment, 12*(2), 207–217.

Hogan, J., Rybicki, S. L., Motowidlo, S. J., & Borman, W. C. (1998). Relations between contextual performance, personality, and occupational advancement. *Human Performance, 11,* 189–207.

Hooker, K. (2002). New directions for research in personality and aging: A comprehensive model for linking level, structures, and processes. *Journal of Research in Personality, 36,* 318–334.

Hooker, K., & McAdams, D. P. (2003). New directions in aging research: Personality reconsidered. *Journal of Gerontology: Psychological Sciences, 58,* 296–304.

Ickes, W., Snyder, M., & Garcia, S. (1997). Personality influences on the choice of situations. In R. Hogan, J. A. Johnson, & S. Briggs (Eds.), *Handbook of personality psychology* (pp. 617–647). San Diego: Academic Press.

Judge, T. A., Higgins, C. A., Thoresen, C. J., & Barrick, M. R. (1999). The Big Five personality traits, general mental ability, and career success across the life span. *Personnel Psychology, 52,* 621–652.

Kelly, E., & Conley, J. (1987). Personality and compatibility: A prospective analysis of marital stability and marital satisfaction. *Journal of Personality and Social Psychology, 52,* 27–40.

Klohnen, E. C. (1996). Conceptual analysis and measurement of the construct of ego-resiliency. *Journal of Personality and Social Psychology, 70,* 1067–1079.

Kochanska, G., & Murray, K. T. (2000). Mother–child mutually responsive orientation and conscience development: From toddler to early school age. *Developmental Psychology, 71,* 417–431.

Kohn, M. L., & Schooler, C. (1978). The reciprocal effects of the substantive complexity of work and intellectual flexibility: A longitudinal assessment. *American Journal of Sociology, 84,* 24–52.

Laub, J. H., & Sampson, R. J. (1998). The long-term reach of adolescent competence: Socioeconomic achievement in the lives of disadvantaged men. In A. Colby, J. B. James, and D. Hart (Eds.), *Competence and character through life* (pp. 89–112). Chicago: University of Chicago Press.

Levinson, D. J. (1978). *The seasons of a man's life.* New York: Ballantine.

Lewis, M. (1999). On the development of personality. In L. A. Pervin & O. P. John (Eds.), *Handbook of personality: Theory and research* (2nd ed., pp. 327–346). New York: Guilford.

Lubinski, D. (2000). Scientific and social significance of assessing individual differences: Sinking shafts at a few critical points. *Annual Review of Psychology, 51,* 405–444.

Marcia, J. E. (1980). Identity in adolescence. In J. Adelson (Ed.), *Handbook of adolescent psychology* (pp. 159–187). New York: Wiley.

McAdams, D. P. (1994a). A psychology of the stranger. *Psychological Inquiry, 5,* 145–148.

McAdams, D. P. (1994b). Can personality change? Levels of stability and growth in the personality across the life span. In T. F. Heatherton & J. L. Weinberger (Eds.), *Can Personality Change?* (pp. 299–313). Washington, DC: American Psychological Association.

McAdams, D. P. (1993). *The stories we live by: Personal myths and the making of the self.* New York: Morrow.

McAdams, D. P., Anyidoho, N. A., Brown, C., Huang, Y. T., Kaplan, B., & Machado, M. A. (2003). *Traits and stories: Links between dispositional and narrative features of personality.* Unpublished manuscript, Northwestern University.

McAdams, D. P., & Bowman, P. J. (2001). Narrating life's turning points: Redemption and contamination. In D. P. McAdams, R. Josselson, & A. Lieblich (Eds.), *Turns in the road: Narrative studies of lives in transition* (pp. 3–34). Washington, DC: American Psychological Association.

McAdams, D. P., Reynolds, J., Lewis, M., Patten, A. H., & Bowman, P. J. (2001). When bad things turn good and good things turn bad: Sequences of redemption and contamination in life narrative and their relation to psychosocial adaptation in midlife adults and in students. *Personality and Social Psychology Bulletin, 27*(4), 474–485.

McCrae, R. R., & Costa, P. T., Jr. (1999). A five-factor theory of personality. In L. A. Pervin & O. P. John (Eds.), *Handbook of personality: Theory and research* (2nd ed., pp. 139–153). New York: Guilford.

McCrae, R. R., Costa, P. T., Jr., Ostendorf, F., Angleitner, A., Hrebickova, M., Avia, M. D., Sanz, J., Sanchez-Bernardos, M. L., Kusdil, M. E., Woodfield, R., Saunders, P. R., & Smith, P. B. (2000). Nature over nurture: Temperament, personality, and life span development. *Journal of Personality & Social Psychology, 78,* 173–186.

McCrae, R. R., Costa, P. T., Jr., Pedroso de Lima, M., Simões, A., Ostendorf, F., & Angleitner, A., et al. (1999). Age differences in personality across the adult life span: Parallels in five cultures. *Developmental Psychology, 35,* 466–477.

McCrae, R. R., & John, O. P. (1992). An introduction to the five-factor model and its applications. *Journal of Personality, 60,* 175–215.

McGue, M., Bacon, S., & Lykken, D. T. (1993). Personality stability and change in early adulthood: A behavioral genetic analysis. *Developmental Psychology, 29,* 96–109.

Meyer, G. J., Finn, S. E., Eyde, L. D., Kay, G. G., Moreland, K. L., Dies, R. R., et al. (2001). Psychological testing and psychological assessment. *American Psychologist, 56,* 128–165.

Mischel, W., & Shoda, Y. (1995). A cognitive-affective system theory of personality: Reconceptualizing situations, dispositions, dynamics, and invariance in personality structure. *Psychological Review, 102,* 246–268.

Modell, J. (1989). *Into one's own: From youth to adulthood in the United States 1920–1975.* Berkeley, CA: University of California Press.

Mroczek, D. K., & Spiro, A. (2003). Modeling intraindividual change in personality traits: Findings from the Normative Aging Study. *Journal of Gerontology: Psychological Sciences, 58,* 153–165.

Murray, H. A. (1938). *Explorations in personality.* New York: Oxford University Press.

Norem, J. K. (1998). Why should we lower our defenses about defense mechanisms? *Journal of Personality, 66,* 895–917.

Pals, J. L. (1999). Identity consolidation in early adulthood: Relations with ego-resiliency, the context of marriage, and personality change. *Journal of Personality, 67,* 295–329.

Plomin, R., & Caspi, A. (1999). Behavioral genetics and personality. In L. A. Pervin & O. P. John (Eds.), *Handbook of personality: Theory and research* (2nd ed., pp. 251–276). New York: Guilford.

Roberts, B. W. (1997). Plaster or plasticity: Are adult work experiences associated with personality change in women? *Journal of Personality, 65,* 205–231.

Roberts, B. W., Bogg, T., Walton, K. E., Chernyshenko. O. S., & Stark, S. E. (2004). A lexical investigation of the lower-order structure of conscientiousness. *Journal of Research in Personality, 38*(2), 164–178.

Roberts, B. W., & Caspi, A. (2001). Personality development and the person-situation debate: It's déjà vu all over again. *Psychological Inquiry, 12,* 104–109.

Roberts, B. W., & Caspi, A. (2003). The cumulative continuity model of personality development: Striking a balance between continuity and change in personality traits across the life course. In R. M. Staudinger & U. Lindenberger (Eds.), *Understanding human development: Lifespan psychology in exchange with other disciplines* (pp. 183–214). Dordrecht, NL: Kluwer Academic.

Roberts, B. W., Caspi, A, & Moffitt, T. (2001). The kids are alright: Growth and stability in personality development from adolescence to adulthood. *Journal of Personality and Social Psychology, 81,* 670–683.

Roberts, B. W., Caspi, A., & Moffitt, T. E. (2003). Work experiences and personality development in young adulthood. *Journal of Personality and Social Psychology, 84,* 582–593.

Roberts, B. W., & Chapman, C. N. (2000). Change in dispositional well-being and its relation to role quality: A 30-year longitudinal study. *Journal of Research in Personality, 34,* 26–41.

Roberts, B. W., & DelVecchio, W. F. (2000). The rank-order consistency of personality traits from childhood to old age: A quantitative review of longitudinal studies. *Psychological Bulletin, 126,* 3–25.

Roberts, B. W., & Donahue, E. M. (1994). One personality, multiple selves: Integrating personality and social roles. *Journal of Personality, 62,* 199–218.

Roberts, B. W., & Helson, R. (1997). Changes in culture, changes in personality: The influence of individualism in a longitudinal study of women. *Journal of Personality and Social Psychology, 72,* 641–651.

Roberts, B. W., Helson, R., & Klohnen, E. C. (2002). Personality development and growth in women across 30 years: Three perspectives. *Journal of Personality, 70,* 79–102.

Roberts, B. W., & Pomerantz, E. M. (2004). On traits, situations, and their integration: A developmental perspective. *Personality and Social Psychology Review, 8,* 402–416.

Roberts, B. W., & Robins, R. W. (2000). Broad dispositions, broad aspirations: The intersection of personality traits and major life goals. *Personality and Social Psychology Bulletin, 26,* 1284–1296.

Roberts, B. W., & Robins, R. W. (2004). A longitudinal study of person-environment fit and personality development. *Journal of Personality, 72,* 89–110.

Roberts, B. W., Robins, R. W., Caspi, A., & Trzesniewski. K. (2003). Personality trait development in adulthood. In J. Mortimer & M. Shanahan (Eds.), *Handbook of the life course* (pp. 579–598). New York: Kluwer Academic.

Roberts, B. W., Walton, K., & Viechtbauer, W. (2006). Patterns of mean-level change in personality traits across the life course: A meta-analysis of longitudinal studies. *Psychological Bulletin, 132,* 1–25.

Robins, R. W., & John, O. P. (1997). Effects of visual perspective and narcissism on self-perception: Is seeing believing? *Psychological Science, 8,* 37–42.

Robins, R. W., Moffitt, T. E., & Caspi, A. (2002). It's not just who you're with, it's who you are: Personality and relationship experiences across multiple relationships. *Journal of Personality, 70,* 925–964.

Robins, R. W., & Paulhus, D. L. (2001). The character of self-enhancers: Implications for organizations. In B. W. Roberts & R. T. Hogan (Eds.), *Personality psychology in the workplace. Decade of behavior* (pp. 193–219). Washington, DC: American Psychological Association.

Robins, R. W., Trzesniewski, K. H., Fraley, R. C., & Roberts, B. W. (2001). A longitudinal study of personality change in young adulthood. *Journal of Personality, 69,* 616–640.

Roenkae, A., & Pulkkinen, L. (1995). Accumulation of problems in social functioning in young adulthood: A developmental approach. *Journal of Personality and Social Psychology, 69,* 381–391.

Ryder, A. G., Alden, L. E., & Paulhus, D. L. (2000). Is acculturation unidimensional or bidimensional? A head-to-head comparison in the prediction of personality, self-identity, and adjustment. *Journal of Personality and Social Psychology, 79,* 49–65.

Sampson, R. J., & Laub, J. H. (1990). Crime and deviance over the life course: The salience of adult social bonds. *American Sociological Review, 55,* 609–627.

Sarbin, T. R. (1964). Role theoretical interpretation of psychological change. In P. Worchel & D. Byrne (Eds.), *Personality change* (pp. 176–219). New York: Wiley.

Schneider, B., Smith, D. B., Taylor, S., & Fleenor, J. (1998). Personality and organizations: A test of the homogeneity of personality hypothesis. *Journal of Applied Psychology, 83,* 462–470.

Schooler, C., Mulatu, M. S., & Oates, G. (1999). The continuing effects of substantively complex work on the intellectual functioning of older workers. *Psychology and Aging, 14,* 483–506.

Schuerger, J. M., Zarrella, K. L., & Hotz, A. S. (1989). Factors that influence the temporal stability of personality by questionnaire. *Journal of Personality and Social Psychology, 56,* 777–783.

Schwartz, S. H. (1992). Universals in the content and structure of values: Theoretical advances and empirical tests in 20 countries. *Advances in Experimental Social Psychology, 25,* 1–65.

Small, B. J., Hertzog, C., Hultsch, D. F., & Dixon, R. A. (2003). Stability and change in adult personality over 6 years: Findings from the Victoria Longitudinal Study. *Journal of Gerontology: Psychological Sciences, 58,* 166–176.

Snyder, M., & Ickes, W. (1985). Personality and Social behaviour. In E. Aronson & G. Lindzey (Eds.), *Handbook of social psychology* (pp. 248–305). New York: Random House.

Spain, J. S., Eaton, L. G., & Funder, D. C. (2000). Perspectives on personality: The relative accuracy of self versus others for the prediction of emotion and behavior. *Journal of Personality, 68,* 837–867.

Srivastava, S., John, O. P., Gosling, S. D., & Potter, J. (2003). Development of personality in early and middle adulthood: Set like plaster or persistent change? *Journal of Personality and Social Psychology, 84,* 1041–1053.

Swann, W. B., Pelham, B. W., & Krull, D. S. (1989). Agreeable fancy or disagreeable truth? Reconciling self-enhancement and self-verification. *Journal of Personality and Social Psychology, 57,* 782–791.

Tett, R. P., Jackson, D. N., & Rothstein, M. (1991). Personality measures as predictors of job performance: A meta-analytic review. *Personnel Psychology, 44,* 703–742.

Trope, Y., & Ben-Yair, E. (1982). Task construction and persistence as means for self-assessment of abilities. *Journal of Personality and Social Psychology, 42,* 637–645.

Trzesniewski, K. H., Donnellan, M. B., & Robins, R. W. (2003). Stability of self-esteem across the life span. *Journal of Personality and Social Psychology, 84,* 205–220.

Vandewater, E. A., Ostrove, J. M., & Stewart, A. J. (1997). Predicting women's well-being in midlife: The importance of personality development and social role involvements. *Journal of Personality and Social Psychology, 72,* 1147–1160.

Winter, D. G., John, O. P., Stewart, A. J., Klohnen, E. C., & Duncan, L. E. (1998). Traits and motives: Toward and integration of two traditions in personality research. *Psychological Review, 105,* 230–250.

3

A Proposed Theory of the Adult Development of Intraindividual Variability in Trait-Manifesting Behavior

William Fleeson
Wake Forest University

Stephanie Jolley
University of Maryland

The same person acts differently on different occasions and in different situations (Fleeson, 2004a; Mischel & Shoda, 1995; Nesselroade, 1991). This simple truth has been one of the greatest challenges for personality psychologists to explain, because the more that the typical individual acts differently from occasion to occasion, the less useful it is to label him or her as acting a particular way, that is, to describe his or her personality. This chapter describes a new theory of personality that organizes and interprets the implications of intraindividual variability for personality and for personality development. In particular, it describes how intraindividual variability, slowly but finally, has been transformed from a challenge into an opportunity for new research directions and discoveries in both personality (Brown & Moskowitz, 1998; Epstein, 1982; Fleeson, 2001; Larsen, 1989; Mischel & Shoda, 1995) and adult personality development (Larson, Moneta, Richards, & Wilson, 2002; Nesselroade, 1991).

The chapter first reviews recent findings determining the extent to which individuals act differently or similarly across occasions (Epstein, 1979; Fleeson, 2001; Mischel, 1968), describes a new approach to incorporate intraindividual variability into the model of personality (Fleeson, 2001), and discusses three important implications of these findings. First, these findings have engendered a new view of personality as a flexible resource that supports adaptation to the moment but resiliently returns to its general contours. Second, they help bring an end to the person–situation debate, allowing personality psychology to move forward (Epstein, 1994;

Fleeson, 2004a; Funder, 2001; Mischel & Shoda, 1995). Finally, these findings open up new questions in personality about the causes of, consequences of, and individual differences in intraindividual variability.

Next, the chapter assesses the implications of intraindividual variability for adult personality development. There are at least three reasons intraindividual variability is particularly important in adult personality development. First, this is an approach to personality that is inherently developmental from the start, because the amount of, nature of, and reasons for intraindividual variability are all likely to vary across the life span (Nesselroade, 2001). Also, such an approach adds two new classes of personality variables to examine for personality development—amounts of and contingencies of variability—that expand the traditional exclusive focus on development of individuals' trait levels only (Berry & Jobe, 2002; Hooker, 2002; Nesselroade, 1991). Third, this approach discovers what is happening at the very interface of person and context—everyday behavior in situations—where many developmental theories locate the processes of adult development (Caspi & B. W. Roberts, 2001).

THE CHALLENGE AND THE OPPORTUNITY OF INTRAINDIVIDUAL VARIABILITY

A leading definition of traits is as "dimensions of individual differences in tendencies to show consistent patterns of thoughts, feelings, and actions" (McCrae & Costa, 1990, p. 23). This definition captures the powerful intuition that different individuals have different characteristic ways of acting, feeling, and thinking. This definition also highlights the fact that some type of consistency in behavior is required for most concepts of personality. If the typical individual acts similarly across occasions, then he or she has a characteristic way of acting which can be described as his or her personality. In contrast, if the typical individual acts very differently across occasions, then he or she does not have a characteristic way of acting that can be usefully described with traits. Thus, the possibility that the same individual may act in different ways on different occasions (i.e., intraindividual variability) represents a challenge: the more intraindividual variability, the less regularity, the less personality, and the less personality development. Indeed, initial studies found surprisingly low degrees of consistency in select behaviors (reviewed in Mischel, 1968).

Density Distributions

The density distributions approach to personality was developed to obtain and interpret the first direct evidence of just how much intraindividual behavioral variability there is (Fleeson, 2001). Such evidence requires observing many behaviors of the same individual (Larsen, 1989), measuring those behaviors on a dimension that allows comparing them to each other, and then quantifying the amount of variability or similarity on that dimension.

The density distributions approach to personality (Fleeson, 2001) was developed also as a new way to describe personality that is rooted in the accumulation of the everyday behavior of an individual. *Behavior* is emphasized because it is the manifestation of personality; when describing personality, one of the things that should be described is behavior. *Accumulation* is emphasized because the assumption is that although some singular acts can define an entire personality, it is more often the patterns and frequencies of behaviors that reveal the individual. *Everyday* is emphasized because it is the life as lived and in context that the theory describes (Allport, 1937; Buss & Craik, 1983).

The central assumption is that, just as people have personality traits, they also have personality states (Nesselroade, 1991). A personality state is the person's personality at a given moment, described in the same terms as are personality traits. For example, how extraverted individuals are acting at the moment are their extraverted states. States are assessed just like traits, with rating scales, except that the respondents are instructed to describe how they are at the moment rather than what they are like in general. For example, a score of 5 on a 7-point extraversion dimension means that the individual is acting moderately extraverted at the moment.

The accumulation of many personality states over a period of time creates a density distribution recording the frequency with which the individual was in each state. The proposal is that the way to characterize an individual on a trait is not by a certain level on that trait (e.g., highly extraverted), but rather by the distribution of corresponding states in its entirety. A narrow distribution means that the individual is frequently in similar states, that is, acts very similarly across occasions. A wider distribution means the individual regularly and routinely is in all states, that is, acts very differently from occasion to occasion.

To obtain distributions for several individuals, experience-sampling methodology (ESM) was employed (Larson & Csikszentmihalyi, 1983). College students carried Palm Pilots for a couple of weeks and every few hours they described their current behavior using about 25 trait adjectives. The resulting data provided a quantified distribution of an extensive sample of each individual's behavior, directly translated into trait terms. This was the first opportunity for personality psychologists to observe and quantify how similar one individual's behaviors are to each other across multiple occasions.

Variability as a Threat

To quantify amount of variability, Fleeson (2001) calculated the standard deviations of each person's distribution for each trait. Although standard deviations differed by trait, the typical individual had a standard deviation on each trait of about 1.0. On a 7-point dimension, a standard deviation of 1.0 is about as large as a distribution can be and still be normal, meaning that individuals were quite variable in their behavior. Comparing this standard deviation to other comparison standard deviations buttressed this conclusion. The amount that one typical individual varied in his or her behavior across 2 weeks (a) was almost as much as the total amount that behavior varied in the entire sample both between and within individuals, meaning that knowing who is acting adds little information about how the person is acting; (b) about the same as the amount of within-person variation in affect, something that is commonly known to vary so much that affect is thought of first as a temporary state and only occasionally as a stable trait; and (c) more than the amount of variability between individuals, meaning that individuals differ from themselves more than they differ from others. This high degree of intraindividual variability makes it clear that there is very little regularity in behavior and the same person changes his or her behavior quite rapidly and quite frequently, presumably in response to changing situations.

Thus, when it comes to the Big Five and to single behaviors, person-focused regularity is not a prominent feature of behavior. Rather, the typical individual's states make up a relatively wide distribution, routinely and regularly covering the whole range of possible behaviors.

Looking Elsewhere for Consistency

It is possible to acknowledge this variability in single behaviors but to nonetheless find substantial consistency in personality-relevant behavior. Following Nesselroade (1991), Epstein (1979), and others, Fleeson (2001) looked for consistency not in individual behaviors but rather in the parameters of the distributions of behaviors. That is, the notion of the entire distribution draws attention away from single behaviors and focuses it on parameters such as the distribution's central point, its width, and its shape.

The first parameter of a distribution is its central point, representing the individual's mean personality state averaged across several moments from a large time period (e.g., from a week). Stability of the mean would be indicated when successive center points from successive long time periods are similar to each other. Fleeson (2001) split the data in half and calculated two central points for each individual, one for each half, and then correlated them to learn how similar they were to each other. The remarkably high resulting correlations (around .90 for each trait) meant that successive center points were nearly identical to each other and that differences between individuals in their average tendencies were highly stable and highly predictable. This finding has also been demonstrated several times and is no longer a matter of dispute (Epstein, 1979; Mischel & Shoda, 1995). Thus, individuals do act very similarly to themselves from one longer time period to the next, showing consistency.

A second parameter is the distribution's width—variability itself may be a consistent aspect of personality (Bem & Allen, 1974; Fiske, 1961). A similar analysis showed that each individual's standard deviations were also found to be similar across successive time points, although the stability correlations were smaller than for the central point (around .50). Thus, individual differences in variability exist and are consistent aspects of personality as well. Shape parameters, represented by skew and kurtosis, even showed some week to week stability.

IMPLICATIONS OF INTRAINDIVIDUAL VARIABILITY FOR PERSONALITY

There are at least three important implications of the fact that sizable intraindividual variability and sizable stability coexist comfortably. The first implication is that behavior is both inconsistent and consistent (Epstein, 1994; Fleeson, 2004a; Funder, 2001; Mischel & Shoda, 1995). A person's momentary behaviors are indeed very different from each other, so not very consistent from moment to moment. A person's averages from larger occasions are nonetheless very similar to each other, so very consistent from week to week. Personality can move forward studying both approaches.

The second implication is the possibility of a new view of traits. Rather than only the level being used to characterize an individual's standing on a trait, the entire distribution can be seen as a useful way to characterize the individual's trait. Most individuals demonstrate a wide range of extraversion states routinely and flexibly, presumably representing adaptive responses to shifting contexts. Even highly introverted individuals regularly acted extraverted and even highly extraverted individuals regularly acted introverted. However, each individual's range is centered at a different location on the dimension, so it is possible to describe what a person is like in general. The way to do so is in terms of the distribution as a whole.

The third implication is that variability can itself be an exciting topic of study for personality psychologists. Why does the same person act so differently on different occasions, rather than acting more in character? Why do people differ in how variable they are? For that matter, what enables maintaining a unique central point across successive time periods? Finally, individuals may differ not only in their amount of variability but also in the contingencies of their variability (Mischel & Shoda, 1995). That is, individuals may differ in when and under what conditions they change their behavior and in how strongly they do so. Such contingent personality variables are a potentially rich source of individual differences (Hooker, 2002), may provide insight into individuals' adaptivity and functioning, and have potential for elucidating adult personality development (Larsen, 1989).

EXPLAINING INTRAINDIVIDUAL VARIABILITY

Rather than take a traditional top-down approach to answering these questions, by using broad and abstract personality characteristics as explanatory variables, this chapter proposes using a bottom-up approach. A bottom-up approach tries to identify processes explaining the level of a personality state at the moment, and then builds up explanations of broader characteristics from these basic processes (Allport, 1937; Mischel & Shoda, 1995). The following paragraphs outline a theory of adult development of within-person variability in personality states. Six propositions form the theory's framework, as shown in Table 3.1. It begins with explaining an individual's current state by identifying causes of that state. It ends with a prediction of declining but high within-person variability across the life span. Indeed, a basic element of the theory is the characterization of individuals as actively trying to make the best of their shifting circumstances to improve the quality of their lives.

Proposition 1 identifies six potential influences on an individual's current personality state. The Cognitive-Affect Personality System (CAPS) approach (Mischel & Shoda, 1995) argues for the hypothesis that behavior is a result of cognitive-affective units (e.g., encodings, expectancies) triggered by situations and by individual differences in those cognitive-affective units. Applying this to the states that manifest traits suggests *interpretations of situations* as one influence, that is, variability in trait-manifesting states partially represents flexible and discriminative changes in behavior due to interpretations of changing situations.

Second, *purposes* include goals, motives, desired identities, and other teleological variables (Cantor & Fleeson, 1994). Although purposes involve cognitive-affective processing, they appear as a separate influence, because they may play a special role in influencing behavior. Specifically, all courses of action may ultimately be evaluated in terms of their impact on purposes. *Temporal trends* refers to the fact that states may continue over time, and processes such as inertia or cycles may result in individuals acting a given way

TABLE 3.1
Outline of a Theory Regarding Adult Development of Intraindividual Variability
in Personality States

Proposition 1:   Six potential influences on an individual's current personality state include:

Psychologically active elements of situations

Purposes

Temporal trends

Stabilizing forces

Resource availability

Error

Proposition 2:   Individual differences in amount of variability on a trait arise from individual differences in the strength or variability of one of the influences on states (as described in Prop. 1).

Proposition 3:   Five mechanisms underlie adult personality development:

Genetics

Environment

Learning

Identity

Developmental regulation

Proposition 4:   Age differences in amount of variability on a trait arise from age differences in the strength or variability of one of the influences on states (as described in Prop. 1).

Proposition 5:   Developmental mechanisms (Prop. 3) affect variability by affecting the strength or variability of one of the influences on states (as described in Prop. 1).

Proposition 6:   Amount of variability in all five traits will decline slightly over adulthood (declining due to environment, identity, and learning, but staying high due to self-improvement, environment, and genetics), as individuals engage in a lifelong effort to actively adapt to changing circumstances in the pursuit of important personal goals.

because they were acting that way in the recent past (Brown & Moskowitz, 1998; Hemenover, 2003; Larsen, 1989). *Stabilizing forces* refers to possible internal physiological or cognitive structures that serve to return states toward a certain more-or-less fixed level, perhaps through homeostatic processes (Caspi & B. W. Roberts, 2001; Gallagher, 2005). *Resource availability* refers to skills, emotions, or psychopharmacology that may temporarily or permanently prevent certain behaviors (Paulhus & Martin, 1987). Finally, *error* refers to the fact that some states are unpredictable to some extent (Epstein, 1979), reflecting true mistakes or capriciousness. Identifying the steps and mechanisms through which each of these influence trait-manifesting states is the first theoretical task to be undertaken. Demonstrating that states do indeed covary with these influences is the first empirical task to be undertaken.

Identifying the Psychologically Active Elements of Situations

Because of the situation's history as a foil to traits, it was intriguing to begin by testing situations as an explanation for trait-manifesting states. The first task was to determine whether trait-manifesting states indeed covary with situations. This in turn required identifying the elements of situations that are psychologically active for each trait (Mischel & Shoda, 1995; Shoda & LeeTiernan, 2002). Focusing on the elements of a situation that are active is in contrast to the more usual focus on the "nominal" or "categorical" characterization of situations. Normally, situations are classified by their type, category, or physical surround (e.g., as "social," "academic," "family," "classroom," or "house"). The goal behind the density distributions approach is to identify what is psychologically meaningful about, for example, a classroom, that triggers particular behavior on the part of the individual (Shoda & LeeTiernan, 2002).

CAPS provides an important and useful meta-theoretical guide to developing social-cognitive theories of personality (Mischel & Shoda, 1995), so its features were incorporated in this endeavor. Identifying the elements that trigger a given state may be facilitated by an analysis of the state: the kind of behavior, the consequences of acting that way on the self, the effects acting that way has on the situation (including other people), the vulnerabilities created by acting that way, and the resources expended and needed to act that way. Unfortunately, very little is known about this for most traits; this kind of analysis therefore likely will also expand understanding of the basic nature of and processes underlying traits. The state of extraversion, for example is active, loud, and impactful; it increases positive affect, raises status, and accomplishes more goals; it grabs others attention; it opens one up to ridicule or even retaliation; and it requires energy. Situation elements that reward or encourage this type of behavior, provide resources for it, and minimize the vulnerabilities are likely to trigger those behaviors. For extraversion, such situations are those in which happiness is relevant, there is an opportunity to accomplish relevant goals, energy is conveyed to the individual, and there is a low chance of ridicule or retaliation. The situation elements of others' friendliness, interestingness, others status, and the number of people may characterize such situations.

In one experience sampling study, participants rated the degree to which several situation elements were present at the moment and also their current state on each of the Big Five, as they navigated through many situations in a few weeks of their daily lives. Multilevel linear model (MLM) analyses were then conducted separately for each potential trait-element contingency: For each subject, a regression predicted the current state from the degree to which the situational element was present (Fleeson, in press). The resulting betas indicated how much each subject varied that state with the occurrence of that situation element. For example, MLM indicates for each individual how much and in which direction his or her level of extraversion state is contingent on the friendliness of others in the situation. MLM provides a significance test on the average of these betas; a significant and positive beta indicates that the typical individual increases his or her level of the given trait when the element is present in the situation.

MLM revealed a large beta for friendliness of others, $\beta = .43$, meaning that the typical individual's extraversion is strongly related to the friendliness of others. The beta for interestingness of the situation was .32, meaning that individuals indeed became more extraverted as the situation became more interesting. Importantly, this is a within-person function, describing the ongoing psychological functioning of individuals. Specifically, the comparison is within one person at a time; the typical individual was more extraverted on those occasions in which the situation was interesting than on those occasions in which the situation was not so interesting. The beta for number of others was also .32, meaning the number of others is a psychologically active element of situations for the trait of extraversion. Finally, the status of others had a nonsignificant beta of .10, meaning being with high status others, contrary to predictions, is not related to reduced levels of extraversion. These results show successful identification of some situation elements that are active for extraversion, specifically, friendliness of others, number of others, and the interestingness of the situation.

MLM also provides significance tests on the individual differences in contingencies, and all four of these contingencies differed significantly between individuals in their strength or direction. These individual differences are a new method for testing interactionism and if–then contingencies (Mischel & Shoda, 1995). For example, the individual differences in the potency of others' friendliness for extraversion means that for some individuals, extraversion is not contingent on others' friendliness or even may be negatively contingent. An advantage to this approach is that it may help rejuvenate interactionism (Endler & Parker, 1992). Although nearly all developmental, social, and personality psychologists claim to be interactionists, very few actually carry it out in practice (Endler & Parker, 1992). Partly this is due to identified problems with the methods people have applied to date; the current approach provides a new method that may not suffer from these problems (Fleeson, in press).

Individual Differences in Amount of Variability

The second proposition concerns how understanding the influences on the current state in turn can be used to explain individual differences in variability. This begins the move up from the bottom level of in-the-moment states to explaining higher level personality characteristics. Individual differences in variability turn out to be stable and to vary across traits within an individual. This class of personality variables has just begun to be studied and may be very relevant to life outcomes, mental health disorders, and adaptivity (Ghisletta, Nesselroade, Featherman, & Rowe, 2002). Furthermore, flexibility may develop in adulthood in theoretically meaningful ways. Specifically, Proposition 2 states that individual differences in amount of variability arise in individual differences in the strength or variability of one or more of the six influences on the current state. The stronger an influence, the more impact it will have on variability when it varies. For example, individuals who have stronger contingencies among situational elements and states will have more state variation in reaction to situation variation. Similarly, individuals with stronger stabilizing forces are likely to have less intraindividual variability. Similarly, the more variable an influence, the more variable the triggered behaviors. For example, an individual who experienced more variability in extraversion-relevant situation elements would thereby exhibit more variability in extraversion. Similarly, individuals who pursued more variable goals would likely exhibit more variable states.

The previous study tested whether individual differences in variability on a trait were in fact associated with individual differences in strengths of contingencies for that trait. The correlations were very strong, meaning that one strong predictor of who is more flexible on a trait is how much the individual's behavior on that trait is contingent on variability in the relevant situation elements. However, tests of this proposition are in only the initial stages.

In sum, density distributions theory provides the elusive defacto integration of person/structure and situation/process, by showing that the structural variables (traits) are manifest (made real) by the operation of cognitive processes, of reaction to situations and of physiological resources. Thus, this theory organizes many diverse approaches to personality psychology into one framework. It also demonstrates and then explains the variability and adaptiveness of human beings in their everyday behavior. And it does so in a way that may be intriguing to adult developmental theory.

PERSONALITY DEVELOPMENT ACROSS THE LIFE SPAN

As this volume attests, the last two decades have witnessed considerable interest in whether personality changes or is stable across the adult life span (Berry & Jobe, 2002; Caspi & B. W. Roberts, 2001). This section considers the implications of intraindividual variability for adult personality development, and in particular how it stands as an opportunity rather than a challenge in this domain as well. Much of our thinking in these matters develops from the work of the pioneers in intraindividual variability in adulthood and adolescence, John Nesselroade and Reed Larson and their colleagues.

Intraindividual variability in trait-relevant behavior may be particularly interesting to adult developmentalists as they move into second generation questions (Berry & Jobe, 2002) for at least four reasons: Variability and the contingencies of variability are two new classes of variables essential to personality so a full account of adult personality development will include reference to variability; intuitions about personality differences across adult ages may refer to amounts of variability as much as to levels of any particular traits; intraindividual variability inherently conceives of the person in context, an important concern of developmentalists; and behavior in reaction to situation is the crucible for many theorized mechanisms of development. That is, just as the nature of personality is crucial to determining how the person develops, development is crucial to determining the nature of personality (B. W. Roberts & Pomerantz, 2004). Next is a very brief review of accumulated findings and underlying developmental mechanisms as used to characterize adult development of trait levels. Those mechanisms are then applied to make predictions about the adult development of variability in traits. These predictions show the potential for research on the development of variability.

Personality Development—Trait Levels

There is evidence of universal mean level changes in the Big Five traits from young to older adulthood—including decreases in neuroticism, extraversion, and openess, along with increases in agreeableness and conscientiousness—although most authors consider the magnitude of change small (Field & Millsap, 1991; McCrae et al., 1999). From comparisons of individual trait items, the changes found are due to more active thrill-seeking in young adulthood and more modesty and self-discipline in older adulthood. Block (1971) noticed increases in ego control, the delay of gratification, and ego resiliency, the ability to adapt personal level of ego control, during this same period of adulthood. Positive affect, negative affect, and life satisfaction also show improvements at least through the 60s (Fleeson, 2004b; Mroczek & Kolarz, 1998; Mroczek & Spiro, 2003). With age, people become more agreeable and conscientious and better at adapting their behavior in context.

In their meta-analysis, B. W. Roberts and DelVecchio (2000) provided a comprehensive account of rank-order changes in personality. Findings from over 152 longitudinal studies led the authors to conclude that 7-year stability correlations increase from childhood into old age, where they reach a plateau around the ages of from 50 to 70 at about .74. The authors' second conclusion was that the peak level of rank-order consistency is below what would be expected of complete personality stability, so traits remain susceptible to change throughout adulthood. Thus, both continuity and change describe adult development (Helson, 1993). Furthermore, individuals differ in the extent to which they change (Jones & Meredith, 2000; Mroczek & Spiro, 2003).

Developmental Mechanisms Underlying Stability and Change

Research has shown the potential for continuity and change in personality development, so the second question psychologists must answer concerns why these patterns occur. Although there has been much less emphasis on explaining than on documenting patterns of stability and change, we have identified in the literature five mechanisms that have been proposed to account for adult personality development and that may be particularly relevant for development of variability: genetics, environment, learning, identity, and developmental regulation (Bertrand & Lachman, 2003; Caspi & B. W. Roberts, 2001).

First, there is evidence that personality is heritable (Shiner, 1998; Turkheimer, 1998). To the extent that gene effects remain constant throughout life, this is a strong force contributing to stability rather than change. However, two *genetic* forces may lead to increased rather than dampened change. Maturation, the unveiling of the complete organism over time, may mean that some genetic effects on personality are not evident until adulthood. Similarly, evidence from twin studies reveals that the amount of change in personality is heritable (Dworkin, Burke, Maher, & Gottesman, 1976), meaning genes can prescribe a person's susceptibility to change.

A second mechanism driving development is the *environment*, a broad category that includes immediate situations, other individuals, roles, major life events, norms, community, and the culture as a whole (Caspi & B. W. Roberts, 2001; Helson, Jones, & Kwan, 2002). Each aspect of the environment likely exerts some influence over personality; in fact, one of the main wellsprings of interest in adult personality development is the question of how and how much such environmental events shape personality (B. W. Roberts, 1997; B. W. Roberts & Helson, 1997). Environment can be a source of stability in personality when environments and their effects do not change over adulthood. For example, adults typically stay in the same job and marriage for extended periods. But when environments change, personality may change as well, as when work experiences are associated with increased agency (B. W. Roberts, 1997) or childrearing is associated with increased self-confidence in women (Wink & Helson, 1993). When there are major life events in a person's environment, such as marriage, parenthood, or death, then that person may respond with changes in personality (Helson et al., 2002). It is also the case that environmental effects are not unidirectional, from environment to the individual, but transactional, such that individuals select and evoke situations as well as react to them (Buss, 1987; Caspi & B. W. Roberts, 2001), and the results are likely to influence development. The pathways by which environment influences personality are just beginning to be assessed and will be a high interest topic for new adult personality research (Berry & Jobe, 2002).

The third mechanism underlying adult personality development is one of the larger topics in the history of psychology. *Learning* refers to learning stimulus–response contingencies through direct experience but also to social learning and reflected or symbolic learning (Caspi & B. W. Roberts, 2001). As individuals grow older, they accumulate larger and larger stores of knowledge, both factual declarative knowledge and procedural knowledge. Such learning is primarily associated with change: As individuals learn something new, their behavior and thus perhaps their personality may change. However, learning also can be a powerful force for stability. Once learned, a habit may be maintained for decades, and the longer individuals have lived, the greater weight of the prior learning to overcome by anything new.

Identity processes make up an important fourth mechanism underlying development (Erikson, 1963; Marcia, 2002; Pals, 2001; Whitbourne, Sneed, & Skultey, 2002). Typically, identity is described as an exploratory process during individuals' adolescence and early adulthood, followed by commitments to established ways of being and beliefs about themselves. Thus, these processes would predict more change in early adulthood followed by more stability in later adulthood, echoing the conclusion concerning mean levels (B. W. Roberts & DelVecchio, 2000).

Finally, development can be directed, as individuals not only are the products, but are also the producers of their own development; a fifth mechanism underlying adult development is *developmental regulation*, or the intentional effort at self-improvement (Fleeson & Baltes, 1998; Freund & Baltes, 2002; Heckhausen, 2002). In childhood, such efforts are universal and formal, such as education. As individuals age, these efforts often become more individualized and less formal, such as getting promotions, soliciting therapy or other treatment, improving relationships, timing childrearing, developing hobbies, self-improvement such as getting more organized, and lifestyle changes involving health, work style, or eating habits. Self-improvement can also be a powerful force for stability when individuals make deliberate efforts to maintain already desirable aspects of their lives, such as trying to maintain positive relationships, hold the line on their weight, or maintain physical competencies as they age.

ADULT DEVELOPMENT OF INTRAINDIVIDUAL VARIABILITY IN TRAIT BEHAVIOR

The preponderance of research on adult personality development has focused on the development of individuals' trait levels, that is, on whether individuals' levels of a trait change as the individuals develop. This chapter proposes that the amount an individual varies on a trait is also an important part of personality, which may develop across the life span in interesting ways. In fact, such differences may be behind some of the intuitions about what changes in personality in adulthood. For example, intuitions about stormy adolescence or stable midlife may refer to the amount of within-person variability in behavior at the different ages, rather than referring to the mean levels of any particular traits. Furthermore, considering adult personality development from a variability standpoint is particularly appealing because variability is inherently contextual. That is, such an approach directly addresses the person developing in context (Berry & Jobe, 2002; Endler & Parker, 1992). Because variability is defined as state changes across occasions, characteristics of the occasions (e.g., the situations) are directly implicated in the concept of within-person variability. Thus, this approach provides a naturalistic laboratory for investigating the processes presumed to underlie development.

Nesselroade, Featherman, and their colleagues have pushed such research into development of within-person variability, and have demonstrated systematic individual differences among older adults in amount of variability of health and activity (Ghisletta et al., 2002), social relationships and self-efficacy (Lang, Nesselroade, & Featherman, 1997), worldviews (Kim, Nesselroade, & Featherman, 1996), depression (Nesselroade & Featherman, 1991), and self-definition (Freund & Smith, 1999). Furthermore, amount of within-person variability has been shown to predict mortality rates and mental abilities (Eizenman, Nesselroade, Featherman, & Rowe, 1997; Li, Aggen, Nesselroade, & Baltes, 2001). The density distribution approach builds on this work by examining within-person variability in the traits of the central model of traits (i.e., the Big Five) and by developing a model of how developmental mechanisms may influence amount of intraindividual variability across the life span.

Investigating development of amount of variability on a trait is analogous to investigating development of level on a trait, except variability rather than level is the outcome. For example, just as researchers have investigated whether level of responsibility increases during early adulthood, research can investigate whether amount of variability in responsibility increases, decreases, or stays the same during early adulthood. A decrease in variability would mean that a typical young adult swings between the extremes of low and high responsibility over the course of a few days whereas a typical older adult would swing less extremely and stay closer to whatever his or her usual level of responsibility is.

Amount of intraindividual variability can change in the same ways as level and is assessed with the same basic methodological and statistical tools as is trait level. First, as amount of variability is a class of variables rather than a single variable, multidirectionality of development is as likely for amount of variability as is the case for levels (Baltes, 1987). That is, some traits may show developmental increases in amount of variability, whereas others show decreases or no change. Second, amounts of variability can be investigated both for mean-level, or group-normative, change and correlation, or rank-order, change. Normative change would be evident when a cross-sectional or longitudinal study revealed that the average person's amount of variability differed across ages; rank-order change would be evident when a longitudinal study revealed low correlations of amount of variability across ages. This chapter focuses predictions on mean-level, or normative, changes across adulthood in the amount of variability as we are at an early stage in investigation of variability phenomena.

It is worth noting that there is another class of variables that may develop across adulthood, specifically, the situation element-trait contingencies that determine momentary states. For example, the contingency of rudeness on other individuals' rudeness may weaken as individuals age and learn to personalize less. Predictions would need to be made for each contingency individually, a task that will wait until there is more information about intraindividual variability across the life span. However, the rich possibilities of such theories points out the potential created by taking as a starting point that individuals vary their behavior considerably from hour to hour.

Propositions 4 and 5 guide the predictions. Proposition 4 is that age differences in amount of intraindividual variability on a trait are due to age differences in the variability or strength of the influences on states. For example, age differences in the strength or variability of everyday situations would result in age differences in variability in states. Proposition 4 is the age-relevant corollary of Proposition 2: For variability to change, the states must change, and the way for states to change is via one of the influences on states. Proposition 5 is that the mechanisms of development affect intraindividual variability by affecting the variability and strength of the influences on states. Because the route to affect variability is via the five influences on states, developmental mechanisms will work their effects through that route. The theory accordingly develops our predictions by considering how developmental mechanisms may impact one or more of the six determinants of personality states. For example, genetics may maintain the strength of the stabilizing force throughout adulthood and thereby serve to maintain the amount of intraindividual variability at a constant level throughout adulthood.

A difficulty to keep in mind is that the mechanism must work by affecting the amount that different states from one or two days differ from each other. For example, a decrease in the intraindividual variability of agreeableness has to be brought about by decreasing the amount that states in the course of a couple of days differ from each other in their agreeableness (e.g., by reducing the amount that the individual's agreeableness is contingent on changing situational elements).

Applying the Five Developmental Mechanisms to the Five Determinants of States

In this regard, genetics is primarily a force for stability. Individual differences in intraindividual variability are most likely heritable (Turkheimer, 1998), meaning that individuals are likely to stay near their personal amounts of variability as they age. Furthermore, genetics may represent the stabilizing forces influence on current personality state (Fraley & Roberts, 2005). That is, genetics may represent the influence that acts as a counterweight to situational or other influences and that pulls the individual towards his or her average state. As long as the strength of this force does not vary across the life span, genetics will lead to stability in the amount of intraindividual variability across the life span. There are not yet expectations that genetics will alter the strength or variability of any of the other influences on current personality states.

The environment is where many effects on the adult development of intraindividual variability are expected. In particular, situations, roles, and life events are all expected to decline in variability after young adulthood or adolescence. The immediate situation likely varies more during the course of an adolescent's than an adult's day (Almeida & McDonald, 1998; Csikszentmihalyi, Larson, & Prescott, 1977). Compare the student athlete, who has to balance school work, practice, employment, and relationships, with a retired person who does not work, participate in sports, or attend school, or a middle-aged adult for whom workplace and home make up the bulk of the situational contexts. As a result, retired and midlife individuals may vary less than adolescents in their behavior from day to day and from hour to hour (Brown & Moskowitz, 1998). Thus, environment should serve to reduce intraindividual variability across adulthood by reducing the variability in the situations that affect personality states. However, situations should remain at least moderately variable, so personality states should remain correspondingly at least moderately variable (Almeida & McDonald, 1998).

Another way in which the environment may affect the adult development of intraindividual variability is by the concentration of major life events. There may be a sharp increase in intraindividual variability during young adulthood (at least in Western culture) when there is the highest rate of major life events (Glenn, 1980). During young adulthood, many individuals choose a career/job, partner, home, family, and so on. These major life events create a disruption in the prior life course and potentially in the daily schedule. While trying to adjust, people will probably vary in their reactions. That is, such events are likely to increase the daily variability of situations, of personal goals, and of error (erratic responding).

Learning likely has at least three effects on the development of variability. As individuals age, they may develop stronger connections among situations and states. This would increase variability in behavior by increasing the strength of situations. From this perspective, intraindividual variability is adaptive because it allows individuals to respond appropriately to a variety of situations, and the ability to adapt may be enhanced with experience. Conversely, age may lead to decreased error in responding to situation elements as individuals become more effective at matching their behavior to situational elements, thereby reducing the amount of variability (Caspi & B. W. Roberts, 2001; M. L. Roberts & Nesselroade, 1986). A third way in which learning may affect variability is by reducing extreme responding. Novices may respond more extremely to slight variations but temper this propensity with training. The same pattern may be true of responding to situation elements with behavior. For example, mood varies more rapidly and to further extremes in adolescence than adulthood (Buchanan, Eccles, & Becker, 1992; Larson et al., 2002). The net effect of these processes, because error reduction may be the most powerful, may be a slight reduction in overall intraindividual variability across the life span.

Identity, the fourth developmental mechanism, is the only mechanism that is commonly elucidated in terms of variability. To learn who one is, a major task of adolescence, a person will try several different roles, activities, and goals, each corresponding to particular personality behaviors (Erikson, 1963; Marcia, 2002; Pals, 2001; Whitbourne et al., 2002). Another way individuals may experiment is by reacting to a greater variety of situations, thus increasing variability (Whitbourne et al., 2002). Experimentation is likely to also mean less consistent and more arbitrary responding to the same situation element at different times (Whitbourne et al., 2002). Such increased error variance in behavior adds to the total intraindividual variation. Experimentation is also likely to be manifest in shifting personal goals. Although most of those shifts will occur over longer periods than described by intraindividual variability (e.g., weeks or months), some will occur more rapidly over a matter of days, in which case personality state variability would again be increased in adolescence. And to the extent that beliefs about oneself contribute to the stabilizing force and are less firm in adolescence, the stabilizing force will be weaker in early adulthood and thus allow greater variability (Neugarten & Associates, 1964). In sum, identity processes suggest that intraindividual personality state variability will be higher in adolescence and early adulthood, due to a wider variety of powerful situations, more varying purposes, weaker stabilizing forces, and more error in responding. As the individual commits to an identity, intraindividual variability should ease somewhat, but not completely (Freund & Smith, 1999).

Self-improvement is the final mechanism underlying adult personality development. Although self-improvement efforts become less formal and universal as individuals age, and more so for some than for others, individuals nearly always have multiple developmental goals at once (Fleeson & Baltes, 1998; Freund & Baltes, 2002; Heckhausen, 2002). The more goals individuals have, the more they will switch between them in the course of a few days and thus the more their relevant states will vary. Fewer developmental goals with age may reduce variability to some extent. On the other hand, individuals may get more efficient at switching their behavior to more effectively accomplish their goals (Caspi & Roberts, 2001); such increased strength of goals in influencing states may counteract any drop in variability due to having fewer goals.

FUTURE RESEARCH DIRECTIONS

Intraindividual variability has long been considered a challenge to the existence of personality: Individuals cannot have a personality if their personality changes substantially every moment. However, as argued by Nesselroade (1991), Cattell (1973), Larsen (1989), Mischel and Shoda (1995), and others, intraindividual variability can now be seen as an opportunity for personality: An individual's personality is not contrary to the personality changes but in fact consists of the personality changes. That is, personality may be the accumulation of personality states combined into a unique distribution (Fleeson, 2001). This new view of within-person variability can help put an end to the person–situation debate and point to some next topics in personality psychology. The person–situation debate can end because psychologists recognize that, due to human flexibility, traits do not predict momentary behaviors very well but that traits predict trends in behavior exceedingly well. The next topics to address include explaining variability, individual differences in variability, and individual differences in the contingencies of variability; each is a rich road to understanding how individuals try their best to adapt to situations in ways that makes progress toward or sometimes undermine their meaningful personal goals.

Intraindividual variability is also an opportunity for adult personality development, as pushed by Nesselroade (1991). This is especially true given the timing; now that consensus is being reached about how levels of traits develop, adult developmentalists are moving to second generation questions (Berry & Jobe, 2002), such as identifying the mechanisms of development (Caspi & B. W. Roberts, 2001; Hooker, 2002), and addressing the development of other parameters of trait distributions. Intraindividual variability may prove useful for both of these endeavors in that amount of intraindividual variability has been shown to be an individual differences characteristic that is likely to develop in interesting ways across the life span, and intraindividual variability is in the crucible of development. That is, much of development is likely to start with behavioral changes, typically in response to situations or in pursuit of goals.

A particularly exciting design for studying these issues may be the "measurement burst" design (Nesselroade & Boker, 1994) in which individuals' density distributions and contingencies are assessed more than once. This would allow useful longitudinal analysis of questions about variability and its contingencies.

A new theory was outlined leading to the proposition that developmental mechanisms affect amount of intraindividual variability by affecting the strength or variability of the influences on personality states. The overall expectation is that there will be high levels of intraindividual variability throughout life, because genetic, environmental, learning, and self-improvement mechanisms will continue to operate throughout life, but some reduction in variability is expected as adults age, due to establishing an identity, reduced environmental variation, accumulated learning of contingencies, and progressively less effort into self-improvement. That is, adults throughout the life span will remain active, flexible creators who change their behavior appropriately and effectively in the pursuit of personally meaningful goals, although they may become more efficient and less erratic in that variability.

ACKNOWLEDGMENT

Preparation of this chapter was supported by Natioanl Institute of Mental Health Grant R01MH70571.

REFERENCES

Allport, G. W. (1937). *Personality: A psychological interpretation.* New York: Holt.
Almeida, D. M., & McDonald, D. (1998). Weekly rhythms of parents' work stress, home stress, and parent–adolescent tension. In A. C. Crouter & R. Larson (Eds.), *Temporal rhythms in adolescence: Clocks, calendars, and the coordination of daily life. New directions for child and adolescent development* (No. 82). San Francisco: Jossey-Bass/Pfeiffer.
Baltes, P. B. (1987). Theoretical propositions of life-span developmental psychology: On the dynamics between growth and decline. *Developmental Psychology, 23,* 611–626.
Bem, D., & Allen, A. (1974). On predicting some of the people some of the time: The search for cross-situational consistencies in behavior. *Psychological Review, 81,* 506–520.
Bertrand, R. M., & Lachman, M. E. (2003). Personality development in adulthood and old age. In I. B. Weiner (Series Ed.), R. M. Lerner, M. A. Easterbrooks, & J. Mistry (Eds), *Handbook of psychology: Developmental psychology* (Vol. 6, pp. 463–485). New York: Wiley.
Berry, J. M., & Jobe, J. B. (2002). At the intersection of personality and adult development. *Journal of Research in Personality, 36,* 283–286.
Block, J. (1971). *Lives through time.* Berkeley, CA: Bancroft.
Brown, K. W., & Moskowitz, D. S. (1998). Dynamic stability of behavior: The rhythms of our interpersonal lives. *Journal of Personality, 66,* 105–134.

Buchanan, C. M., Eccles, J. S., & Becker, J. B. (1992). Are adolescents the victims of raging hormones? Evidence for activational effects of hormones on moods and behavior at adolescence. *Psychological Bulletin, 111*, 62–107.

Buss, D. M. (1987). Selection, evocation, & manipulation. *Journal of Personality and Social Psychology, 53*(6), 1221.

Buss, D. M., & Craik, K. H. (1983). The act frequency approach to personality. *Psychological Review, 90*, 105–126.

Cantor, N., & Fleeson, W. (1994). Social intelligence and intelligent goal pursuit: A cognitive slice of motivation. In R. Dienstbier (Series Ed.) & W. D. Spaulding (Volume Ed.), *Nebraska symposium on motivation: Vol. 41. Integrative views of motivation, cognition, and emotion* (pp. 125–179). Lincoln: University of Nebraska Press.

Caspi, A., & Roberts, B. W. (2001). Personality development across the life course: The argument for change and continuity. *Psychological Inquiry, 12*, 49–66.

Cattell, R. B. (1973). *Personality and mood by questionnaire.* San Francisco: Jossey-Bass.

Csikszentmihalyi, M., Larson, R., & Prescott, S. (1977). The ecology of adolescent activity and experience. *Journal of Youth and Adolescence, 6*, 281–294.

Dworkin, R. H., Burke, B. W., Maher, B. A., & Gottesman, I. I. (1976). A longitudinal study of the genetics of personality. *Journal of Personality and Social Psychology, 34*, 510–518.

Eizenman, D. R., Nesselroade, J. R., Featherman, D. L., & Rowe, J. W. (1997). Intraindividual variability in perceived control in an older sample: The MacArthur successful aging studies. *Psychology and Aging, 12*, 489–502.

Endler, N. S., & Parker, J. D. (1992). Interactionism revisited: Reflections on the continuing crisis in the personality area. *European Journal of Personality, 6*, 177–198.

Epstein, S. (1979). The stability of behavior: On predicting most of the people much of the time. *Journal of Personality and Social Psychology, 37*, 1097–1126.

Epstein, S. (1982). A research paradigm for the study of personality and emotions. *Nebraska Symposium on Motivation*, 91–154.

Epstein, S. (1994). Trait theory as personality theory: Can a part be as great as the whole? *Psychological Inquiry, 5*, 120–122.

Erikson, E. (1963). *Childhood and society.* New York: Norton.

Field, D., & Millsap, R. E. (1991). Personality in advanced old age: Continuity or change? *Journal of Gerontology: Psychological Sciences, 46B*, P299–P308.

Fiske, D. W. (1961). The inherent variability of behavior. In D. W. Fiske & S. R. Maddi (Eds.), *Functions of varied experience* (pp. 326–354). Homewood, IL: Dorsey.

Fleeson, W. (2001). Toward a structure- and process- integrated view of personality: Traits as density distributions of states. *Journal of Personality and Social Psychology, 80*, 1011–1027.

Fleeson, W. (2004a). Moving personality beyond the person-situation debate: The challenge and the opportunity of within-person variability. *Current Directions, 13*, 83–87.

Fleeson, W. (2004b). The quality of American life at the end of the century. In O. G. Brim, C. D. Ryff, & R. C. Kessler (Eds.), *How healthy are we?: A national study of well-being at midlife* (pp. 252–272). Chicago: University of Chicago Press.

Fleeson, W. (in press). Using experience-sampling and multilevel linear modeling to study person–situation interactionist approaches to positive psychology. In A. D. Ong & M. van Dulmen (Eds.), *Handbook of methods in positive psychology.*

Fleeson, W., & Baltes, P. B. (1998). Beyond present-day personality assessment: An encouraging exploration of the measurement properties and predictive power of subjective lifetime personality. *Journal of Research in Personality, 32*, 411–430.

Fraley, R. C., & Roberts, B. W. (2005). Patterns of continuity: A dynamic model for conceptualizing the stability of individual differences in psychological constructs across the life course. *Psychological Review, 112*, 60–74.

Freund, A. M., & Baltes, P. B. (2002). The adaptiveness of selection, optimization, and compensation as strategies of life management: Evidence from a preference study on proverbs. *Journal of Gerontology: Psychological Sciences, 57B*, P426–P434.

Freund, A. M., & Smith, J. (1999). Methodological comment: Temporal stability of older person's spontaneous self-definition. *Experimental Aging Research, 25,* 95–107.

Funder, D. C. (2001). Personality. *Annual Review of Psychology, 52,* 197–221.

Gallagher, M. P. (2005). *Investigating stability in trait behavior: The contra-trait energy hypothesis.* Unpublished maser's thesis, Wake Forest University, Winston-Salem, NC.

Ghisletta, P., Nesselroade, J. R., Featherman, D. L., Rowe, J. W. (2002). Structure and predictive power of intraindividual variability in health and activity measures. *Swiss Journal of Psychology, 61,* 73–83.

Glenn, N. D. (1980). Values, attitudes, and beliefs. In O. J. Brim, Jr. & J. Kagan (Eds.), *Constancy and change in human development* (pp. 596–640). Cambridge, MA: Harvard University Press.

Heckhausen, J. (2002). Developmental regulation of life-course transitions: A control theory approach. In L. Pulkkinen & A. Caspi (Eds.), *Paths to successful development: Personality in the life course* (pp. 257–280). New York: Cambridge University Press.

Helson, R. (1993). Comparing longitudinal studies of adult development: Toward a paradigm of tension between stability and change. In D. C. Funder, R. D., Parke, C. Tomlinson-Keasey, & K. Widaman (Eds.), *Studying lives through time: Personality and development* (pp. 93–119). Washington, DC: APA.

Helson, R., Jones, C., & Kwan, V. S. (2002). Personality change over 40 years of adulthood: Hierarchical linear modeling analyses of two longitudinal samples. *Journal of Personality and Social Psychology, 83,* 752–766.

Hemenover, S. H. (2003). Individual differences in rate of affect change: Studies in affective chronometry. *Journal of Personality and Social Psychology, 85,* 121–131.

Hooker, K. (2002). New directions for research in personality and aging: A comprehensive model for linking level, structures, and processes. *Journal of Research in Personality, 36,* 318–334.

Jones, C. J., & Meredith, W. (2000). Developmental paths of psychological health from early adolescence to later adulthood. *Psychology and Aging, 15,* 351–360.

Kim, J. E., Nesselroade, J. R., & Featherman, D. L. (1996). The state component in self-reported worldviews and religious beliefs of older adults: The MacArthur successful aging studies. *Psychology and Aging, 11,* 396–407.

Lang, F. R., Nesselroade, J. R., & Featherman, D. L. (1997). Social self-efficacy and short-term variability in social relationships: The MacArthur successful aging studies. *Psychology and Aging, 12,* 657–666.

Larsen, R. J. (1989). A process approach to personality psychology: Utilizing time as a faced of data. In D. M. Buss & N. Candor (Eds.), *Personality psychology: Recent trends and emerging directions* (pp. 177–193). New York: Springer-Verlag.

Larson, R. W., & Csikszentmihalyi, M. (1983). The experience sampling method. *New Directions for Methodology of Social and Behavioral Science* (15), 41–56.

Larson, R. W., Moneta, G., Richards, M. H., & Wilson, S. (2002). Continuity, stability, and change in daily emotional experience across adolescence. *Child Development, 73,* 1151–1165.

Li, S. C., Aggen, S. H., Nesselroade, J. R., & Baltes, P. B. (2001). Short-term fluctuations in elderly people's sensorimotor functioning predict text and spatial memory performance: The MacArthur successful aging studies. *Gerontology, 47,* 100–116.

Marcia, J. E. (2002). Identity and psychosocial development in adulthood. *Identity, 2,* 7–27.

McCrae, R. R. & Costa Jr., P. T. (1990). *Personality in Adulthood.* New York: Guilford.

McCrae, R. R., Costa, P. T., Jr., de-Lima, M., Simoes, A., Ostendorf, F., Angleitner, A., Marusic, I., Bratko, D., Caprara, G., Barbaranelli, C., Chae, J., & Piedmont, R. L. (1999). Age differences in personality across the adult life span: Parallels in five cultures. *Developmental-Psychology, 35,* 466–477.

Mischel, W. (1968). Personality and assessment. New York: Wiley.

Mischel, W., & Shoda, Y. (1995). A cognitive-affective system theory of personality: Reconceptualizing situations, dispositions, dynamics, and invariance in personality structure. *Psychological Review, 102,* 246–268.

Mroczek, D. K., & Kolarz, C. M. (1998). The effect of age on positive and negative affect: A developmental perspective on happiness. *Journal of Personality and Social Psychology, 75,* 1333–1349.

Mroczek, D. K., & Spiro, A., III. (2003). Modeling intraindividual change in personality traits: Findings from the normative aging study. *Journal of Gerontology: Psychological Sciences, 58B,* P153–P165.

Nesselroade, J. R. (1991). Interindividual differences in intraindividual change. In L. M. Collins & J. L. Horn (Eds.), *Best methods for the analysis of change: Recent advances, unanswered questions, future directions* (pp. 92–105). Washington, DC: APA.

Nesselroade, J. R. (2001). Intraindividual variability in development within and between individuals. *European Psychologist, 6*(3), 187–193.

Nesselroade, J. R., & Boker, S. M. (1994). Assessing constancy and change. In T. F. Heatherton & J. L. Weinberger (Eds.), *Can personality change?* (pp. 121–147). Washington, DC: APA.

Nesselroade, J. R., & Featherman, D. L. (1991). Intraindividual variability in older adults' depression scores: Some implications for developmental theory and longitudinal research. In D. Magnusson, L. R. Bergman, G. Rudinger, & B. Toerstad (Eds.), *Problems and methods in longitudinal research: Stability and change* (pp. 47–66). Cambridge, MA: Cambridge University Press.

Neugarten, B. L., & Associates (1964). *Personality in middle and late life: Empirical studies.* Oxford, England: Atherton.

Paulhus, D. L., & Martin, C. L. (1987). The structure of personality capabilities. *Journal of Personality and Social Psychology, 52,* 354–365.

Pals, J. L. (2001). Identity: A contextualized mechanism of personality continuity and change. *Psychological Inquiry, 12*(2), 88–91.

Roberts, B. W. (1997). Plaster or plasticity: Are work experiences associated with personality change in women? *Journal of Personality, 65,* 205–232.

Roberts, B. W., & Helson, R. (1997). Changes in culture, changes in personality: The influence of individualism in a longitudinal study of women. *Journal of Personality and Social Psychology, 72*(3), 641–651.

Roberts, B. W., & DelVecchio, W. F. (2000). The rank-order consistency of personality traits from childhood to old age: A quantitative review of longitudinal studies. *Psychological Bulletin, 126,* 3–25.

Roberts, B. W., & Pomerantz, E. M. (2004). On traits, situations, and their integration: A developmental perspective. *Personality and Social Psychology Review, 8,* 402–416.

Roberts, M. L., & Nesselroade, J. R. (1986). Intraindividual variability in perceived locus of control in adults: P-technique factor analyses of short-term change. *Journal of Research in Personality, 20,* 529–545.

Shiner, R. L. (1998). How shall we speak of children's personalities in middle childhood? A preliminary taxonomy. *Psychological Bulletin, 124,* 308–332.

Shoda, Y., & LeeTiernan, S. (2002). What remains invariant?: Finding order within a person's thoughts, feelings, and behaviors across situations. In D. Cervone & W. Mischel (Eds.), *Advances in personality science* (pp. 241–270). New York: Guilford.

Turkheimer, E. (1998). Heritability and biological explanation. *Psychological Review, 105,* 782–791.

Whitbourne, S. K., Sneed, J. R., & Skultety, K. M. (2002). Identity processes in adulthood: Theoretical and methodological challenges. *Identity, 2*(1), 29–45.

Wink, P., & Helson, R. (1993). Personality change in women and their partners. *Journal of Personality and Social Psychology, 65*(3), 597–606.

4

The Agentic Self: On the Nature and Origins of Personal Agency Across the Life Span

Todd D. Little
C. R. Snyder*
Michael Wehmeyer
University of Kansas

This chapter examines personality development using the human agency concept as an overarching theme. It first articulates fundamental assumptions about agency, with a quick sketch of its organismic metatheoretical roots. Second, it explores the philosophical and historical underpinnings of agency as a central concept in both past and present psychological theories. It then examines the various layers of agency and discusses their development antecedents and consequences. Finally, building on the rich historical literature and recent theorizing, it concludes with some comments and suggestions on future directions.

FUNDAMENTAL ASSUMPTIONS OF AGENCY

Both current and past theories of agency share the metatheoretical view that organismic aspirations drive human behaviors. This organismic perspective presumes that humans are the "authors" and active contributors to their behavior and development. Most human behavior is seen as volitional and described in terms of self-regulated, goal-directed *actions*, where actions are defined as self-initiated and purposive activities (Boesch, 1991; Brandtstädter, 1998; Chapman, 1984; Ryan, 1993). Because of this inherent propensity toward activity and self-regulation, the individual is described in terms of personal agency or as an agentic self.

The concept of personal agency does not reinvent constructs such as self-esteem, self-efficacy, self-concept, and so on. Rather, it helps to organize such concepts into

*This chapter is dedicated to the fond memory of our friend and colleague C. R. "Rick" Snyder (12-26-1944/1-17-2006).

the multilayered model of the self that is premised on volitional goal-directed actions (see Fig. 4.1). Key characteristics of actions include the following:

1. Actions are motivated by both biological and psychological needs (Hawley, 1999; Hawley & Little, 2002; Little, Hawley, Henrich, & Marsland, 2002; Ryan & Deci, 2002).
2. Actions are directed toward self-regulated goals that service the biological and psychological needs, both short term and long term.
3. Actions are propelled by specific understandings about the links among agents, means, and ends (Chapman, 1984; Little, 1998; Skinner, 1995, 1996), and they are guided by general action-control behaviors that entail self-chosen forms and functions (Little, Lopez, & Wanner, 2002; Skinner & Edge, 2002; Vanlede, Little, & Card, in press).
4. Actions give rise to self-determined governance of behavior and development that can be characterized as hope-related individual differences.
5. Actions are triggered, executed, and evaluated in contexts that provide supports and opportunities, as well as hindrances and impediments to goal pursuit.

Being active in their development, individuals are integrated in their organismic functioning. Various processes are called on to establish and maintain a balanced sense of self throughout development. In this process, individuals must negotiate the boundaries and opportunities of the surrounding contexts. Accordingly, each person progresses steadily along a predominantly self-guided developmental path. Actions are given form and meaning along the way and they continually define, refine, and update a person's sense of self. Every action represents a choice made by the individual. From an organismic perspective, individuals plot and navigate their own courses through the challenges of the surrounding environments, which vary in their degree of uncertainty. Similar to trade winds and currents, environments sometimes may bolster, hinder, or alter the course of a developmental route (Little et al., 2002).

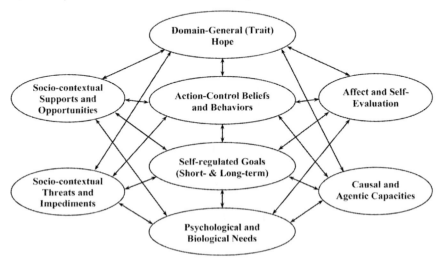

FIG. 4.1.   The various layers of human agency and the construction of the self.

Through self-evaluative feedback processes, persons continuously interpret and evaluate actions and their consequences. In an organismic model of personality development, humans continually discover and refine who they are and the activities of which they are capable in varying situational and developmental contexts. People learn under what conditions their actions can or cannot have desired effects. Under optimal circumstances, this continually evolving and actively monitored self-system gives rise to a strong, stable, and effective sense of personal agency and hope. Different individuals with differing experiences and differing predispositions, however, will yield varying profiles of hope because the sense of agency is a multifaceted and striated system of needs, motives, goals, beliefs, and behaviors (Fig. 4.1; Hawley & Little, 2002; Little et al., 2002; Little & Wanner, 1997).

As individuals begin to discover who they are and of what they are capable, the evolving competence system contributes to an integrated sense of personal agency—an agentic self. The resulting systems of action-control motives, goals, beliefs, and behaviors provide a foundation that is used to negotiate various subsequent developmental tasks and life course challenges. In facing these challenges, agentic individuals are the primary origin of their actions, have high aspirations, persevere in the face of obstacles, see more and varied options, learn from failures, have a strong sense of well-being, and so on. A nonagentic individual, on the other hand, is primarily the pawn of unknown extra-personal influences, has low aspirations, is hindered with problem-solving blinders, and often feels both helpless and hopeless (Little, 1998; Little et al., 2002; Ryan, Sheldon, Kasser, & Deci, 1996; Skinner, 1995; Weisz, 1990). These latter undesirable characteristics can stimulate additional negative feedback, such as teasing and victimization from others (Graham & Juvonen, 1998). In short, agentic persons are on a positive carousel wherein benefits often continually incur, whereas nonagentic persons often spiral into one negative outcome after another.

In addition to the metatheoretical underpinnings of the agency concept as a core feature of personality development, numerous historical precedents point to the importance of agency as an organizing feature of developmental theories about the self. This chapter selectively samples three of the historical giants—Heider, Lewin, and Piaget. Although the ideas of these three pioneers typically have not been examined with an eye toward the agency concept and its basis in developmental theorizing, they provide crucial insights for understanding the role of agency in personality development (see Harter, 1999, for additional histories).

HISTORICAL PRECEDENTS

Human Agency According to Fritz Heider

Heider, who is credited with being the father of theory and research on attributions (see also Kelley, 1983), was fascinated with the human propensity to explain why events—especially interpersonal ones—occur (Heider, 1958). Heider also was captivated by the importance of the human agency concept (Heider, 1944, 1983). His career focused on that part of the action sequence related to the formation of attributions. His underlying interest in agency, however, is intimated in his description of this process as "causal" attributions. Human agency, in Heider's view, was an imperative cause—the motivational force underpinning most human actions across the life span (this propensity to ascribe agency to people rather than to the surrounding environment also led to the fundamental attribution error concept).

According to Heider, agency motivation reflects the individual's perceptions of having "effective personal force" in the course of unfolding events (also see White, 1959). In this regard, Heider (1958, p. 83) believed that such a force is underpinned by a combination of power or personal ability, the intentions to try, and any relevant environmental factors (with the latter often going unrecognized or underemphasized by many). At its earliest onset (at least as early as toddlerhood), the effective and ineffective use of personal force begins the synergistic dance between governing one's actions and adapting to their outcomes. Clearly, Heider's theorizing revolved around the central role that human agency plays in psychology in particular, and human development more generally.

The Role of Agency in Kurt Lewin's Theorization

Although Lewin did not emphasize cognitive processes per se, he did focus on the relation of thoughts to actions. Furthermore, Lewin believed that behavior was best understood by exploring the underlying paths to people's goals (Weiner, 1972). Although Lewin did not use the term *agency* in describing how people use these paths to goals, he did use the concept of "tension"—or the inherent arousal that attends teleological thought (Lewin, 1926, 1938, 1951)—as an analog for agency.

Historically, Lewin's attention to agencylike processes began with his attempts to refine Ach's measurement of "strength of will" (Lewin, 1917). In the early 1900s, psychology was in the throes of Gestalt emphases on perception and mental associations. Noteworthy within this Gestalt camp was Ach (1910), who argued that mental couplings created by association provide the "force of will" (sometimes also called the associative principle of cause). Although Lewin borrowed many Gestalt ideas (see Lewin, 1935), he broke away from Ach's emphasis by suggesting that mere association alone did not provide a sufficient impetus for action; in this debate, Lewin highlighted motivation (the Lewin–Ach Controversy; see Weiner, 1972).

In responding to Ach's views about association, Lewin distinguished between two types of associations or habits. First, there was tension, which was seen as the need that necessitates satisfaction. This tension or need was conceptualized as the source of energy that leads to action. Second, there was an execution habit (e.g., pulling a lever up or down) that is not a source of action in itself. These execution habits were posited to rely on the tension need in order to lead to action. In Lewin's (1951, pp. 5–6) words:

> Dynamically, an "association" is something like a link in a chain, i.e., a pattern of restraining forces without intrinsic tendency to create a change. On the other hand, the tendency to bring about action is basic to a need. This property of a need or quasi-need can be represented by coordinating it to a "system in tension." By taking this construct seriously and using certain operational definitions, particularly by correlating the "release of tension" …, a great number of testable conclusions [are] made possible.

Within Lewin's subsequent field theory and level of aspiration work, he highlighted the role of goals as the objects that produce motivational tensions in humans.

Lewin (1938, 1951) posited that goals, by their very nature, set up tensions or intentions that involve a state of disequilibrium. When a goal is realized, according to Lewin, then the level of tension within the system is reduced and a psychological equilibrium is reinstated. For Lewin, such goal attainment did not necessarily translate to "consumption" of the desired goal object. Rather, memory or thinking about a goal could lessen the goal tension. Lewin used the famous experiments on the recall and resumption of unfinished tasks—what has come to be called the Zeigarnik effect (see Zeigarnik, 1927; see also Ovsiankina, 1928)—in order to test and support his assumptions about the important role of tension reduction in goal pursuit activities. In other words, Lewin viewed such tensions as the fuel for the expression of agency across the life span.

Self-Regulated Actions and Piaget's Theorizing

Although Piaget focused on cognitive developmental acquisitions, the basic tenets of his ideas are readily applicable to both intra- and interpersonal understandings (Carpendale, 1987; Chapman, 1984). At a time when behaviorism dominated much of the North American scholarly zeitgeist (e.g., Watson, 1913), Piaget was building his constructivist view of human beings as active agents. Being an active agent in their own development implies that individuals function as integrated organisms. In this regard, the same assimilative and accommodative processes that are invoked to maintain equilibrium in cognition also are invoked to sustain balance in both social cognition and a person's sense of self (Carpendale, 1987). Likewise, these inherent processes that provide cognitive templates for understanding the physical and material world give rise to stable schemata about the self and the social world.

From a Piagetian view, subjective perceptions of causality and temporal dynamics, which are established through mental simulations and active experimentation, create the conduits to overt actions (see also Boesch, 1991, on symbolic action theory). Using self-generated schema, individual actors produce explanations and predictions of behavior. This process makes action control and meaningful adaptation to change feasible both cognitively and behaviorally (see also Laukkanen, 1990).

THE AGENTIC SELF: EXAMINING THE LAYERS

Numerous contemporary theories have incorporated the concept of agency and action plans either implicitly (e.g., Bandura, 1997) or explicitly (e.g., Chapman, 1984). As exemplified in Fig. 4.1, however, the ways in which agency has been incorporated into contemporary theories is multilayered. The following paragraphs examine some of the ways in which the agency concept appears at the different layers that comprise the fully functioning individual.

Biological and Psychological Needs

A starting point for understanding the development of the agentic self is the assumption that all organisms require resources for physical growth and development (Darwin, 1859; Hawley, 1999; Little et al., 2002; Ricklefs, 1979). Resources are the appetite for biological needs (see Fig. 4.1). There exists, however, an evolutionarily inevitable duality in the pursuit of resources. To meet basic needs that are difficult or impossible to obtain individually, a person can participate in a social group where the presence of others facilitates acquisition of resources. This social group, however, can become a source of competition for the very resources that it facilitates. This duality creates competition for resources within the social group. Thus, as group members, individuals experience wins and losses. These interpersonal patterns of wins and losses lead to what ethologists describe as a dominance hierarchy. Hawley (e.g., 1999) defined such hierarchies as the emergent ordering of individuals based on their relative competitive abilities. By definition, therefore, highly agentic individuals achieve the lion's share of wins, whereas social subordinates experience a disproportionate quantity of losses (Hawley, 1999, chap. 8 in this volume; Little et al., 2002).

As Little et al. (2002) argued, the history of both early and lifelong win–loss experiences influence the development of personal agency, and these early experiences can be viewed as the seeds of agency. Agentic competitors learn that their goals can be met, their efforts pay off, they can control their environment, and their future efforts are likely to be successful. Persistence is both an antecedent and consequence of winning efforts in the pursuit of fulfilling needs (Hawley & Little, 2002). Agency and persistence both are causes and effects of present and future attempts at attaining resource control. On the other hand, children who experience losses early on are at risk. Persistent losses lead to a self view that one cannot achieve desired goals, personal efforts will not pay off, the environment cannot be controlled in the presence of others, and future efforts are likely to be futile. These agentic and nonagentic profiles characterize the extremes of a dominance hierarchy (Hawley & Little, 2002; Little et al., 2002).

One important feature in the development of an agentic self is that different behavioral strategies can be used in these evolutionarily predicated skirmishes. Hawley (1999; Hawley & Little, 1999, 2003; chap. 8 in this volume) outlined two classes of strategy that individuals may use. First, there are coercive strategies such as aggression, manipulation, deception, and so on. Second, there are prosocial strategies such as helping, appeasement, alliance formation, and so on. Individuals develop consistent patterns in the use of strategies to pursue their goals. These consistently used strategies and the ratio of wins to losses represent building blocks to the developing self-system. However, consistency of use and the success ratio depend on specific social and physical contexts.

In addition to the biological needs that drive behavior and precipitate the development of agency, at least three fundamental psychological needs are at play: competence, relatedness, and autonomy (Ryan & Deci, 2002). Competence is the basic need to successfully engage, manipulate, and negotiate the environment (see White, 1959). Relatedness reflects the necessity for close emotional bonds and feelings of connectedness to others in the social world (see Sroufe, 1990). Autonomy reflects the degree to which an individual's actions are predicated on the self or, when nonautonomous, by causes external to the self (Ryan & Deci; Wehmeyer, 2001).

Little et al. (2002) argued that goal pursuit in the service of these needs is yet another driving force in the development of personal agency. Here, the need for autonomy is perhaps the most critical. For actions to be optimally agentic (i.e., to possess a strong sense of personal empowerment), they must be autonomous. In this regard, autonomy is the quality of owning actions and making action choices that are integrated with the self and serve one's needs. As Deci (1996) reasoned, "Without choice, there would be no agency, and no self-regulation" (p. 222). Therefore, autonomy is crucial for the self-determination that underpins the agentic self. Self-determined actions can be directed toward various goals, but the paramount goals are those that service the needs of resource control, autonomy, relatedness, and competence.

Self-Determination, Self-Regulation, and Goal Pursuit

Self-determination is a function of self-regulated agentic action. Wehmeyer (1996, 1998, 1999, 2001) defined self-determined behavior as "acting as the primary causal agent in one's life and making choices and decisions regarding one's quality of life free from undue external influence or interference" (1996, p. 24). Self-determined individuals act (i.e., self-regulate) in such a way that their actions and behaviors are "self" caused (autonomous determinism; cf. intrinsic motivation, Ryan & Deci, 2002), as opposed to "other caused" (heteronymous determination; cf. extrinsic motivation, Ryan & Deci, 2002). From this perspective, self-determined people are *agents* "with the authority" to initiate actions.

Although actions are purposeful (i.e., performed to achieve an end), behaviors are governed by many interacting influences. In this sense, people are "contributors to, rather than the sole determiners of, what happens to them" and therefore "agency refers to acts done intentionally" (Bandura, 1997, p. 3). Agentic behavior can be in response to circumstances that are not planned, but such circumstances nevertheless can be acted on purposefully. The "end" toward which an action is directed varies in terms of specific outcomes, but it ultimately supports self- (vs. other-) determination (Ryan & Deci, 2002; Skinner & Edge, 2002). Thus, all actions function as the means whereby people achieve valued goals, exert control, and, ultimately, maintain (or enhance) their sense of personal agency.

A number of factors are involved in the self-regulation of goal pursuit. These factors include the capability to perform actions, which can be subdivided into causal capacity and agentic capacity, and the challenges to one's self-determination that serve as a catalyst to action, which can be seen as either opportunities or threats (see Fig. 4.2).

Capability refers to having the requisite ability to execute chosen actions to accomplish a particular task. Agentic individuals possess various capacities that enable them to respond to challenges. Two types of capabilities are important to the agentic self: *causal capability* and *agentic capability*. These capabilities differentiate between two aspects of actions: initiating goal pursuit (causal capability) and directing actions toward a preferred end (agentic capability).

Causal capability includes the knowledge, behavioral skills, self-perceptions, and beliefs about one's environment (see causality beliefs; pathways thinking later) that are necessary to express agentic behavior. Examples of causal capacities include goal setting, pre-action problem solving, and decision-making skills. Having the capacity to engage in goal pursuit provides the needed impetus to prioritize and choose among various goal options.

Agentic capability involves possessing the requisite skill, knowledge, and beliefs that one is capable (see agency beliefs; agency, later). In addition, it involves the be-

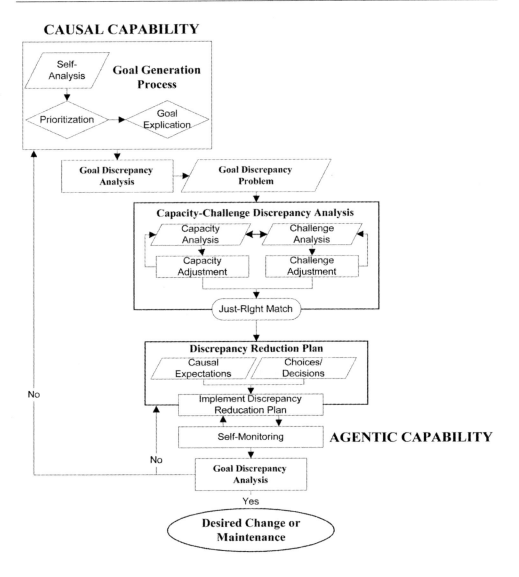

FIG. 4.2.   Overview of action schema.

lief that if individuals act, they can reasonably expect positive outcomes (see control-expectancy beliefs later). Agentic capacity largely involves self-regulatory and self-management skills that enable persons to compare their current states with goal states and to self-monitor, self-evaluate, and self-regulate progress.

Contextual Influences on Self-Regulation

An organismic approach to understanding the developing person explicitly focuses on the interface between the self and surrounding environmental context (Lerner,

1995, 1996; Little et al., 2002; Ryan et al., 1996). Contexts reflect multiple influences, spanning the molar and microlevels that both constrain and promote behaviors (Bronfrenbrenner, 1995; Gottlieb, 1997). Taken as a whole, these contexts create what can be called a psychological "carrying capacity" within which the individual operates (i.e, the maximal level of functioning given an individual's personal resources and the limits and/or supports of the surrounding contexts).

Contexts provide challenges that are the catalysts for actions. A challenge is any circumstance that engages a person's abilities or resources to resolve a problem or threat as well as to achieve a goal. Human actions reflect responses to sociocontextual challenges. Challenging circumstances elicit volitional actions aimed at maintaining or enhancing a person's sense of personal agency.

Two classes of challenges exist: opportunities or threats. First, opportunity refers to situations that engage actions to achieve a planned and desired outcome. Opportunity implies that the situation allows the individuals to make something happen based on their causal capability. An opportunity is bound to the person's causal capability. If the person has no capability, then the situation is not an opportunity. If a person has the capability to act, the situation or circumstance can be construed as an opportunity. If the person is unable to act because of limitations, however, this may be termed a *missed opportunity*. Opportunities can be *found* (unanticipated, happened on through no effort of one's own) or *created* (the person acts to create a favorable circumstance). Second, there are the challenge conditions involving situations that threaten, hinder, or impede goal-directed actions. Such conditions provoke individuals to engage their agentic capabilities to maintain a preferred outcome or create change that is consistent with their preferences and goals.

Affect and Self-Regulation

Another operant in self-regulation is *affect*. Causal affect refers to the emotions, feelings, and other affective components that influence human behavior. For example, emotions (a response involving physiological changes as a preparation for action) often are evoked in response to challenges, be they opportunities (joy, excitement) or threats (anger, anxiety) that heighten or limit the organism's capacity to respond. Similarly, feelings are cognitively mediated emotions with long-lasting impacts on both causal and agentic capability, thereby influencing the ways that the person will respond to future challenges.

Features of an Action-Control Sequence

Agentic individuals respond to challenges by using the capabilities that allow them to direct their actions to achieve either a desired change or maintain a preferred status. Both causal and agentic capability work together in complex ways to achieve or maintain a desired goal (i.e., a schema for self-determined action; see Fig. 4.2).

In response to challenges, the agentic self begins with a *goal generation process*, consisting of self-analysis and exploration concerning an individual's strengths, limitations, preferences, values, and wants with regard to the challenge circumstance. This process identifies needed actions, which are prioritized based on salience to the challenge. Once actions have been prioritized, the person frames the most urgent or important action in terms of a goal state. With a goal state in mind, the agentic person engages in a *goal discrepancy analysis* wherein the current status and the goal status are reconciled. The agentic individual frames the outcomes from this discrepancy analysis in terms of a *goal discrepancy problem* to be solved. This process is followed by a *capacity challenge discrepancy* analysis. Individuals evaluate their capacity to solve the problem and examine the degree to which the challenge will support goal attainment. In this process, the agentic self maximizes adjustment in capacity (e.g., acquires new or refines existing action skills) or adjusts the challenge presented to create a "just-right match" between capacity and challenge so as to optimize the individuals' probability of solving the goal discrepancy problem (Mithaug, 1996; Wehmeyer & Mithaug, in press).

Once people have optimized capacity and challenge, they create a *discrepancy reduction plan* that is regulated by their action-control beliefs. Such beliefs influence the setting of expectations (what can I expect to achieve?), making choices about strategies to reduce the discrepancy, and finalizing and implementing a discrepancy reduction plan. One component of such a plan is the self-monitoring that enables the individual to collect information about progress toward the goal state. During the action sequence, the person will engage in goal discrepancy reanalyses, as needed, using information gathered through self-monitoring, to self-evaluate progress toward reducing the discrepancy between current status and goal status. If the person determines that the discrepancy reduction plan has solved the goal discrepancy problem, then the desired change or maintenance is achieved. If progress is satisfactory, then the person will continue implementing the discrepancy reduction plan. If progress is not satisfactory, then the person either reconsiders the discrepancy reduction plan and modifies that component, or returns to the goal generation process to reexamine the overall goal, its priority, and, possibly, cycling through the process with a revised or new goal.

Action-Control Beliefs During Goal Pursuit

During the life course, individuals develop key understandings about what it takes to achieve a given goal (causal capacity) and about whether they possess what it takes (agentic capacity). People develop these action-control beliefs about themselves and the environmental contingencies in pursuing volitional activity. At this level, personal agency is examined as the possible beliefs a person may have about the relations among the primary constituents of intentional action (Chapman, 1984; Little, 1998; Skinner, 1995; Stetsenko, Little, Gordeeva, Grasshof, & Oetingen, 2000).

The three constituents of an action sequence are the actor, the goal, and the various means by which the goal (or end) can be obtained. Agentic action reflects an agent's general awareness of goals and the means to the goals, taking personal responsibility in pursuing a chosen goal, and the ability to select and utilize potential means (Chapman & Skinner, 1985). Given the three constituents of volitional activity, a number of belief types about the relations among these constituents are possible.

Figure 4.3 displays six of these belief types (see also Skinner, 1996). *Control expectancy* beliefs reflects general expectations about the link between the self and the

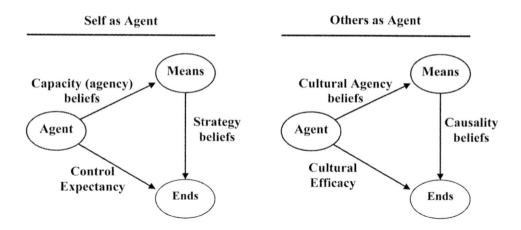

FIG. 4.3.   Relations among the three constituents of human action, both when the self is the agent and when others are the agent. [*Note.* Means can vary from personal attributes such as effort and ability to external aids such as friends and teachers. From Little, 2002].

goal (e.g., "when I want to do ____, I can."). *Cultural efficacy*, on the other hand, reflects the belief link between the person's focal cultural group and the goal. *Agency beliefs* reflect the links between the self and the various means that are relevant for attaining a chosen ends ("I'm able to put forth enough effort to do this," "I possess the necessary skills to do this"). The counterpart linkage, when others are viewed as the agent of behavior, can be termed *cultural agency beliefs*. Similarly, the link between the various means and ends can have two levels of meaning. When the self is the agent, the resulting system of beliefs would reflect *strategy beliefs* (i.e., what means work for me). *Means-ends* (or *causality beliefs*), on the other hand, reflect general views of the utility or usefulness of a given means such effort, luck, or ability for attaining a particular goal (Chapman et al., 1990; Little et al., 1995; Oettingen et al., 1994; Skinner et al., 1988).

Ample research has supported these distinctions (see Little, 1998; Skinner, 1996, for overviews). A defining feature of the action-control view that separates it from other similar models of control perceptions is the explicit means-ends analysis of actions. For example, because ability is considered separately from other means such as effort and access to powerful others, Stetsenko et al. (2000) were able to identify a means-specific gender bias in the action-control beliefs of school-age children. Girls, whose actual school performance was on par with boys, reported lower beliefs in their own ability to get good grades than did boys. All other beliefs about their personal agency, such as effort, luck, and access to teachers, were on an equal footing, as would be expected from equally performing groups of children. Only the girls' beliefs in their access to ability revealed the bias. By focusing on the unique means that are utilized to achieve a goal, Stetsenko et al. identified a specific source of bias in girls' personal agency profile that may hinder them developmentally. Similarly, Baker, Brownell, and Little (2003) were able to integrate the action-control view of perceived control in the Theory of Planned Behavior and found significant differences in the predictive utility of different means. In sum, in order to adequately assess agency across the life span, it is advantageous to focus on differentiating among the available means and evaluate each as a unique dimension and source of an action-control profile of the agentic self.

Hope and the Agentic Self

At the highest level of integration for the agentic self is hope (see Fig. 4.1). Snyder (1994) derived an organismic-agentic concept of hope based on intensive interviews in which people talked about having a sense of agency to pursue their goals, along with the abilities to produce routes to those goals. At this level, personal agency can be thought of in terms of both agency and pathways goal-related thinking, which comprise the definitional components of hope. As such, Snyder, Irving, and Anderson (1991, p. 287) defined hope as a, "positive motivational state that is based on an interactively derived sense of successful (a) agency (goal-directed energy), and (b) pathways (planning to meet goals)."

Goals provide the cognitive anchor of hope (Snyder, 1994), and they can vary in terms of their time frames, with some being short term and others long term. Goals must be of sufficient value that people will continue to think about them consciously. Generally, hope should operate within perceived intermediate degrees of goal attainment difficulty (called "stretch" goals; Snyder, 2002; see capacity challenge discrepancy analysis, earlier, and Fig. 4.2).

The higher the individuals' hope, the more confident they will be about finding effective routes. High-hope, as compared to low-hope, people are more likely to ascribe positive and affirming internal pathways messages to themselves (e.g., "I'll find a way to get this done!"; Snyder, LaPointe, Crowson Jr., & Early, 1998). Such thought typically necessitates imagining a credible route and plausible alternate routes for anticipated goal blockages. High- versus low-hope persons actually are very good at producing alternative routes when faced with blockages (Snyder, Sympson, et al., 1996).

Agency thought taps the perceived capacity to initiate (causal capacity) and sustain (agentic capacity and action-control beliefs) movement toward desired goals. High-hope people embrace agency self-talk phrases such as "I can do this" and "I am not going to be stopped" (Snyder et al., 1998). Agency thinking is important in all goal-directed thought, but it takes on special significance when people encounter impediments. During these blockages, agency thought helps people channel the requisite motivation to the best alternate pathways (Snyder, 1994). Positive emotions result when people perceive themselves as being successful in goal pursuits. Negative emotions, on the other hand, result when people perceive themselves as being unsuccessful in a specified goal pursuit (Diener, 1984; Snyder, Sympson et al., 1996).

The elaborated model of Hope theory is shown in Fig. 4.4. The model depicts the proposed events that occur as the goal-directed thought sequence proceeds temporally. The etiologies of the pathways and agency thoughts can be seen in the far left of Fig. 4.4 above the "Learning History" phase (for more in-depth descriptions of these developmental antecedents, see Snyder, 1994, pp. 75–114). Beyond the "hope self beliefs," people also approach goal-related activities with varying "emotional sets" with high-hope persons being filled with positive approach-like emotions and low-hope persons being filled with negative avoidance-like emotions (see also Elliot & Covington, 2001).

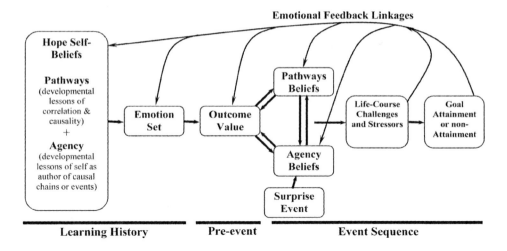

FIG. 4.4.   The development of hope as a feature of the agentic self.

The model implies that high-hope, as compared to low-hope, people should generate more goals. The advantage of having several goals appears when a primary goal
is unreachable, and the person thereby has another readily available goal. The model
also implies that people consider the outcome values of various goals before selecting
a specific one (i.e., the "Pre-Event" phase; Fig. 4.4). If a goal is based on a person's
own standards, this should have greater value than goals that reflect the desires of
other people (see also Ryan & Deci, 2002). Research related to this issue indeed
shows that high- more than low-hope people will select stretch goals based on their
outcomes in previous similar tasks (Snyder et al., 1991).

If a goal is of sufficiently high value to individuals, then they will pay attention,
and move to the next analysis in the "Event Sequence" phase. Throughout the itera-
tive pathways and agency thinking of this "Event Sequence" phase, however, the
person should engage in an outcome value check-back so as to ascertain whether the
potential outcome appears to be important enough to warrant the maintenance of
goal-directed activities.

In the initial "getting started" portion of the "Event Sequence" phase, as long as
things appear to be going well, then feedback should involve positive emotions that
reinforce the goal pursuit. Individual differences in dispositional hope, however,
should influence the content of such emotional feedback. Because persons who are
high in trait hope generally enjoy goal pursuit activities, their self-talk should be of an
engaged, positive, challenge-like nature. Such self-talk should sustain attention and
motivation to the goal. Low-hope persons, however, often are apprehensive about
goal pursuits in general, and chances are high that their attentions will be diverted
from task-relevant cues. This low-hope person also may begin to worry about "how
things are going," and experience a rush of seemingly uncontrolled negative emotions. These negative feelings then produce yet more self-critical ruminations, and it
becomes more likely that the pathways-agency cognitions will become "off-task" in
foci (Snyder et al., 1991; Snyder, Sympson, et al., 1996).

Although cognitions drive emotions, those emotions in turn should inform the thoughts of the person—even during a given goal pursuit sequence. Accordingly, there is a functional role for emotions in that they "establish our position vis-à-vis our environment, pulling us toward certain people, objects, actions, and ideas, and pushing us away from others" (Levenson, 1994, p. 123).

As shown in the middle of the "Event Sequence" phase of Fig. 4.4, goal pursuit sometimes may be impeded by life course challenges and everyday stressors. A stressor represents any impeding circumstance that is sufficiently large so as to place hopeful thought at risk. Should the person perceive that a desired goal is not going to be attained, then disruptive negative emotions should cycle back so as to impact the person's trait and situational hopeful thinking (see also Wrosh et al., chap. 20 in this volume). Some individuals, such as those who are dispositionally high in hope, should experience stressors as challenges rather than threats. Accordingly, an effective strategy when encountering a stressor, or goal blockage, is to develop an alternate pathway, and rechannel personal agency to that new pathway.

In circumstances where there is no stressor, or when the stressor has been surpassed, pathways and agency thoughts continue to iterate (see the bidirectional arrows) and aggregate through the remaining portion of the goal pursuit sequence; in turn, the resulting thoughts should impact the person's later endeavors in pursuit of that same goal. The individual should have perceptions about the success (or lack thereof) and the associated approach-based (or avoidance-based) emotions will cycle back at all points in the goal pursuit sequence (see also Elliot & Covington, 2001).

Once a specific goal pursuit sequence has been completed, the person's attainment (or nonattainment) thoughts and the associated positive (or negative) emotions should cycle back so as to affect the later outcome value attached to that activity, and perceived pathways and agency capabilities in that particular situation and other situations in general (i.e., the narrow-lined, right-to-left arrows in Fig. 4.4 illustrate this latter feedback process). The emotional feedback thereby shapes subsequent goal-directed thinking. Some people should be effective in using such feedback (i.e., high hopers) to do better when facing similar future goal pursuit circumstances, whereas others (i.e., low hopers) should be ineffective.

As can be seen in the lower center of Fig. 4.4, a surprise event may occur. When such an unexpected event is personally relevant to individuals, they experience a rapid rise in arousal. In other words, there is an increase in agency that has yet to be "attached" to any goal. Rapidly, the agentic energy is transferred to a goal and related pathway that fit the circumstances (Snyder, 2002). For example, consider a father who watches his 6-year-old daughter fall off the tree branch she was climbing. Filled with agency-like arousal at the sight of his screaming offspring, the father immediately becomes motivated (agency) to take his daughter to the physician (note pathways and goal here). Although the surprise event occurs outside of the hope model, the way people cope with the vicissitudes of events is explicable in terms of that model.

SUMMARY AND FUTURE DIRECTIONS

Understanding the complexities of organismic activity clearly requires an understanding of how aspects of individuals such as their motives, beliefs, and behaviors coordinate together in the pursuit of life course goals. The linkages among the layered aspects of the agentic self are best examined when the operational nature of each layer stems from a common metatheoretical perspective: in this case, the organismic perspective. A number of commonalities emanate from the overarching organismic metatheoretical perspective that unites the different layers of agentic action. For example, because actions are coordinated in specific domains of goal-directed activity, the motives, goals, beliefs, and behaviors of agentic activity will have considerable domain specificity. In addition, because a specific action is chosen from among a number of possible actions, agentic activity can be examined in terms of its means specificity. Last, because of the domain-specific and means-specific nature of actions in service of self-chosen goals, agentic actions can be classified and categorized in terms of a means–ends, form–function analytic framework.

Issues of personal agency and agentic action are increasingly important in numerous applied settings. A primary emphasis in these settings involves teaching people the skills they will need to exert greater control over their lives, including problem-solving, goal-setting, and decision-making skills. Such instruction is particularly critical for disadvantaged individuals, such as those with disabilities, those from economically impoverished areas, and those of traditionally underrepresented populations.

In terms of future directions, there are at least three avenues that would benefit from further theorizing and empirical scrutiny. A first direction for future research is to focus on integrating the layers of personal agency into a coherent structuring of the agentic self. The various layers presented in Fig. 4.1 are rarely examined in a synergistic fashion. Understanding the direct and indirect linkages between needs, motives, goals, beliefs, behaviors, and hope is the challenge that will reveal the likely mechanisms of development and self formation. Identifying the various linkages would begin to answer the question of how people progress from needs to hope and give rise to an agentic self.

A second direction of future research is to develop more precise theoretical models of contextual opportunities and hindrances, as well as bring the required methodological tools to bear on the analysis of contextual impacts on self-development. Clearly, the linkages from needs to hope and their reciprocal feedback will be significantly influenced and altered by the supports and impediments of the biological, social, and cultural contexts. Current theoretical models that outline the levels of contextual influence (e.g., Bronfrenbrenner, 1995) have slid to the periphery of mainstream inquiry, even though few would consider contextual impacts to be unimportant. In regard to these latter lacunae, the most likely explanation is that the methodological and statistical analyses required to model the contextual influences on development are rather daunting in their complexity. The dauntingness stems from the lack of adequate methodological pedagogy that specifically addresses how to incorporate contextual factors into the study design, and to appropriately model the complex patterns and paths of influence.

A third direction of future inquiry would be to adopt a person-centered viewpoint with a particular eye to identifying the profiles that characterize different types of individuals. As Magnusen, Bergman, and others argued (Bergman, Magnusson, & El-Khouri, 2003), the nomothetic assumption that a model of interrelations among key constructs is the appropriate model for all individuals is less tenable as the complexity of the models increases. The constellations of needs, motives, beliefs, and behaviors that characterize agentic individuals would reveal profiles that are to a degree individuated by the self-direct governance of the individual. Numerous profiles can yield adaptive, effective, and agentic activity. One important implication of this perspective is the need to examine the nature of these profiles over time in order to determine their stability as well as the antecedents and consequents of a given profile. Such an examination requires a network approach to examine the linkages among the profile dimensions in terms of proximal and distal influences, direct and indirect pathways, as well as unidirectional and bidirectional causal influences (Kelley, 1983).

In closing, human action not only is at the epicenter of psychological theory and research across the life span, but it also is an imperative force that drives the quality of human lives. Positive growth and development hinges on both personal and collective efforts of our agentic selves. As such, the agentic self deserves to be a priority in the agendas of scientists and practitioners alike.

REFERENCES

Ach, N. (1910). *Über den willensakt und das temperament* [On deliberate action and temperament]. Leipzig: Quelle und Meyer.

Baker, C. W., Little, T. D., & Brownell, L. D. (2003). Predicting adolescent eating and activity behaviors: The role of social norms and personal agency. *Health Psychology, 22,* 189–198.

Bandura, A. (1977). Self-efficacy: Toward a unified theory of behavioral change. *Psychological Review, 84,* 191–215.

Bergman, L. R., Magnusson, D., & El-Khouri, B. (2003). *Studying individual development in an interindividual context: A person-oriented approach* (Paths Through Life monograph series, Vol. 4). Mahwah, NJ: Lawrence Erlbaum Associates.

Boesch, E.E. (1991). *Symbolic action theory and cultural psychology.* New York: Springer-Verlag.

Brandtstädter, J. (1998). Action perspectives on human development. In W. Damon (Seires Ed.) & R. M. Lerner (Vol. Ed.), *Theoretical models of human development: Vol. 1. Handbook of child psychology* (5th ed., pp. 807–863). New York: Wiley.

Bronfenbrenner, U. (1995). Developmental ecology through space and time: A future perspective. In P. Moen & G. H. Elder, Jr. (Eds.), *Examining lives in context: Perspectives on the ecology of human development* (pp. 619–647). Washington, DC: American Psychological Association.

Carpendale, J. (1997). An explication of Piaget's constructivism: Implications for social cognitive development. In S. Hala (Eds.), *The development of social cognition* (pp. 35–64). East Sussex, England: Psychology Press.

Chapman, M. (1984). Intentional action as a paradigm for developmental psychology: A symposium. *Human Development, 27*(3–4), 113–144.

Chapman, M., & Skinner, E. A. (1985). Action in development/development in action. In M. Frese & J. Sabini (Eds.), *Goal-directed behavior: The concept of action in psychology* (pp. 199–213). Hillsdale, NJ: Lawrence Erlbaum Associates.

Darwin, C. (1859). *The origin of species.* London: John Murray.

Deci, E. L. (1996). Making room for self-regulation: Some thoughts on the link between emotion and behavior. *Psychological Inquiry, 7,* 220–223.

Deci, E. L., & Ryan, R. M. (2000). The "what" and "why" of goal pursuits: Human needs and the determination of behavior. *Psychological Inquiry, 11,* 227–268.

Diener, E. (1984). Subjective well-being. *Psychological Bulletin, 95,* 542–575.

Elliot, A. J., & Covington, M. V. (2001). Approach and avoidance motivation. *Educational Psychology Review, 13,* 73–92.

Gottlieb, G. (1997). Commentary: A systems view of psychobiological development. In D. Magnusson (Eds.), *The lifespan development of individuals: Behavioral, neurobiological, and psychosocial perspectives: A synthesis* (pp. 76–103). New York: Cambridge University Press.

Graham, S., & Juvonen, J. (1998). Self-blame and peer victimization in middle school: An attributional analysis. *Developmental Psychology, 34*, 587–538.

Harter, S. (1999). *The construction of the self: A developmental perspective*. New York: Guilford.

Hawley, P. H. (1999). The ontogenesis of social dominance: A strategy-based evolutionary perspective. *Developmental Review, 19*, 91–132.

Hawley, P. H. (2003). Prosocial and coercive configurations of resource control in early adolescence: A case for the well-adapted Machiavellian. *Merrill-Palmer Quarterly, 49*, 279–309.

Hawley, P. H., & Little, T. D. (1999). On winning some and losing some: Social dominance in toddlers. *Merrill Palmer Quarterly, 45*, 185–214.

Hawley, P. H., & Little, T. D. (2002). Evolutionary and developmental perspectives on the agentic self. In D. Cervone & W. Mischel (Eds.), *Advances in personality science* (pp. 177–195). New York: Guilford.

Heider, F. (1944). Social perception and phenomenal relations. *Psychological Review, 51*, 358–374.

Heider, F. (1958). *The psychology of interpersonal relations*. New York: Wiley.

Heider, F. (1983). *The life of a psychologist: An autobiography*. Lawrence, KS: University Press of Kansas.

Kelley, H. H. (1983). Perceived causal structures. In J. Jaspars, F. D. Fincham, & M. Hewstone (Eds.), *Attribution theory research: Conceptual, developmental, and social dimensions* (pp. 343–369). London: Academic Press.

Laukkanen, M. (1990). Comparative cause mapping of organizational cognitions. *Organizational Science, 5*, 322–341.

Lerner, R. M. (1995). Developing individuals within changing contexts: Implications of developmental contextualism for human development research, policy, and programs. In T. A. Kindermann & J. Valsiner (Eds.), *Development of person-context relations* (pp. 13–37). Hillsdale, NJ: Lawrence Erlbaum Associates.

Lerner, R. M. (1996). Relative plasticity, integration, temporality, and diversity in human development: A developmental contextual perspective about theory, process, and method. *Developmental Psychology, 32*, 781–786.

Levenson, R. W. (1994). Human emotion: A functionalist view. In P. Ekman & R. J. Davidson (Eds.), *The nature of emotion: Fundamental questions* (pp. 123–126). New York: Oxford University Press.

Lewin, K. (1917). Die psychische tätigkeit bei der hemmung von willensorgängen und das grundgesetz der assoziation [The psychological activity when inhibiting deliberate processes and the fundamental law of association]. *Zeitschrift für Psychologie, 77*, 212–247.

Lewin, K. (1926). Vorsatz, wille und bedürfnis [Intention, will, and need]. *Psychologische Forschung, 7*, 330–385.

Lewin, K. (1935). *A dynamic theory of personality*. New York: McGraw-Hill.

Lewin, K. (1938). *The conceptual representation and the measurement of psychological forces*. Durham, NC: Duke University Press.

Lewin, K. (1951). *Field theory in social science* (D. Cartwright, Ed.). New York: Harper & Brothers.

Little, T. D. (1998). Sociocultural influences on the development of children's action-control beliefs. In J. Heckhausen & C. S. Dweck (Eds.), *Motivation and self-regulation across the life span* (pp. 281–315). New York: Cambridge University Press.

Little, T. D. (2002). Agency in development. In W. H. Hartup & R. K. Silbereisen (Eds.), *Growing points in developmental science: An introduction* (pp. 223–240). East Sussex, England: Psychology Press.

Little, T. D., Hawley, P. H., Henrich, C. C., & Marsland, K. (2002). Three views of the agentic self: A developmental synthesis. In E. L. Deci & R. M. Ryan (Eds.), *Handbook of self-determination research* (pp. 389–404). Rochester, NY: University of Rochester Press.

Little, T. D., & Lopez, D. F. (1996). Children's action-control beliefs and emotional regulation in the social domain. *Developmental Psychology, 32*, 299–312.

Little, T. D., Lopez, D. F., & Wanner, B. (2001). Children's action-control behaviors (Coping): A longitudinal validation of the behavioral inventory of strategic control. *Anxiety, Stress, and Coping, 14*, 315–336.

Little, T. D., Oettingen, G., Stetsenko, A., & Baltes, P. B. (1995). Children's action-control beliefs and school performance: How do American children compare with German and Russian children? *Journal of Personality and Social Psychology, 69,* 686–700.

Little, T. D., & Wanner, B. (1997). *The Multi-CAM: A multidimensional instrument to assess children's action-control motives, beliefs, and behaviors* (Materialen aus der Bildungsforschung, No. 59, ISBN #3-87985-064-x). Berlin: Max Planck Institute for Human Development.

Magnusson, D., & Cairns, R. B. (1996). Developmental science: Toward a unified framework. In R. B. Cairns, G. H. Elder, Jr., & J. E. Costello (Eds.), *Developmental science* (pp. 7–30). New York: Cambridge University Press.

Mithaug, D. (1996). *Equal opportunity theory.* Thousand Oaks, CA: Sage.

Mischel, W., & Shoda, Y. (1995). A cognitive-affective system theory of personality: Reconceptualizing situations, dispositions, dynamics, and invariance in personality structure. *Psychological Review, 102,* 246–268

Oettingen, G., Little, T. D., Lindenberger, U., & Baltes, P. B. (1994). Causality, agency, and control beliefs in East versus West Berlin children: A natural experiment on the role of context. *Journal of Personality and Social Psychology, 66,* 579–595.

Ovsiankina, M. (1928). Die wiederaufnahme und unterbrochenen handlungen [The resumption of interrupted action]. *Psycholgische Forschung, 11,* 302–389.

Ricklefs, R. E. (1979). *Ecology.* Portland OR: Chiron Press.

Ryan, R. M. (1993) Agency and organization: Intrinsic motivation, autonomy, and the self in psychological development. In J. E. Jacobs (Ed.), *Nebraska symposium on motivation, 1992: Developmental perspectives on motivation* (Vol. 40, pp. 1–56). Lincoln, NE: University of Nebraska Press.

Ryan, R. M., & Deci, E. L. (2000). Self-determination theory and the facilitation of intrinsic motivation, social development, and well-being. *American Psychologist, 55,* 68–78.

Ryan, R. M., & Deci, E. L. (2002). An overview of self-determination theory: An organismic-dialectical perspective. In E. L. Deci & R. M. Ryan (Eds.), *Handbook of self-determination theory* (pp. 3–36). Rochester, NY: University of Rochester Press.

Ryan, R. M., Sheldon, K. M., Kasser, T., & Deci, E. L. (1996). All goals are not created equal: An organismic perspective on the nature of goals and their regulation. In P. M. Gollwitzer & J. A. Bargh (Eds.), *The psychology of action: Linking cognition and motivation to behavior* (pp. 7–26). New York: Guilford.

Skinner, E. A. (1995). *Perceived control, motivation, and coping.* Beverly Hills, CA: Sage.

Skinner, E.A. (1996). A guide to constructs of control. *Journal of Personality and Social Psychology, 71*(3), 549–570.

Skinner, E. A., Chapman, M., & Baltes, P. B. (1988). Children's beliefs about control, means-ends, and agency: Developmental differences during middle childhood. *International Jounral of Behavioral Development, 11,* 368–388.

Skinner, E. A., & Edge, K. (2002). Self-determination, coping, and development. In E. L. Deci and R. M. Ryan (Eds.), *Handbook of Self-Determination Research* (pp. 297–338). Rochester, NY: University of Rochester press.

Snyder, C. R. (1994). *The psychology of hope: You can get there from here.* New York: The Free Press.

Snyder, C. R. (2000). Hypothesis: There is hope. In C. R. Snyder (Ed.), *Handbook of hope: Theory, measures, and applications* (pp. 3–21). San Diego, CA: Academic Press.

Snyder, C. R. (2002). Hope theory: Rainbows of the mind. *Psychological Inquiry, 13,* 249–275.

Snyder, C. R., Harris, C., Anderson, J. R., Holleran, S. A., Irving, L. M., Sigmon, S. T., Yoshinobu, L., Gibb, J., Langelle, C., & Harney, P. (1991). The will and the ways: Development and validation of an individual-differences measure of hope. *Journal of Personality and Social Psychology, 60,* 570–585.

Snyder, C. R., Irving, L., & Anderson, J. R. (1991). Hope and health: Measuring the will and the ways. In C. R. Snyder & D. R. Forsyth (Eds.), *Handbook of social and clinical psychology: The health perspective* (pp. 285–305). Elmsford, New York: Pergamon.

Snyder, C. R., LaPointe, A. B., Crowson Jr., J. J., & Early, S. (1998). Preferences of high- and low-hope people for self-referential input. *Cognition and Emotion, 12,* 807–823.

Snyder, C. R., Sympson, S. C., Ybasco, F. C., & Borders, T. F., Babyak, M. A., & Higgins, R. L. (1996). Development and validation of the State Hope Scale. *Journal of Personality and Social Psychology, 70*, 321–335.

Smith, J. S., & Baltes, P. B. (1999). Trends and profiles of psychological functioning in very old age. In P. B. Baltes & K. U. Maier (Eds.), *The Berlin aging study: Aging from 70 to 100* (pp.197–226). New York: Cambridge University Press.

Sroufe, A. L. (1990). An organizational perspective on the self. In D. Cicchetti & M. Beeghly (Eds.), *The self in transition: Infancy to childhood* (pp. 281–307). Chicago: University of Chicago Press.

Stetsenko, A., Little, T. D., Gordeeva, T. O., Grasshof, M., & Oettingen, G. (2000). Gender effects in children's beliefs about school performance: A cross-cultural study. *Child Development, 71*, 517–527.

Vanlede, M., Little, T. D., & Card, N. A. (in press). Action-control beliefs and behaviors as predictors of change in adjustment across the transition to middle school. *Anxiety, Stress, and Coping.*

Watson, J. B. (1913). Psychology as the behaviorist views it. *Psychological Review, 20*, 158–277.

Wehmeyer, M. L. (1996). Self-determination as an educational outcome: How does it relate to the educational needs of our children and youth? In D. J. Sands & M. L. Wehmeyer (Eds.), *Self-determination across the life span: Independence and choice for people with disabilities* (pp. 17–36). Baltimore: Paul H. Brookes.

Wehmeyer, M. L. (1998). Self-determination and individuals with significant disabilities: Examining meanings and misinterpretations. *Journal of the Association for Persons with Severe Handicaps, 23*, 5–16.

Wehmeyer, M. L. (1999). A functional model of self-determination: Describing development and implementing instruction. *Focus on Autism and Other Developmental Disabilities, 14*, 53–61.

Wehmeyer, M. L. (2001). Self-determination and mental retardation. In L. M. Glidden (Ed.), *International review of research in mental retardation* (Vol.24, pp. 1–48). San Diego, CA: Academic Press.

Wehmeyer, M. L., & Mithaug, D. (in press). Self-determination, causal agency, and mental retardation. In H. Switzky, R. Schalock, & M. Wehmeyer (Eds.), *Current perspectives on individual differences in personality and motivation in persons with mental retardation and other developmental disabilities* (Vol. 1). San Diego, CA: Academic Press.

Weiner, B. (1972). *Theories of motivation: From mechanism to cognition.* Chicago: Markham.

Weisz, J. R. (1990). Development of control-related beliefs, goals, and styles in childhood and adolescence: A clinical perspective. In J. Rodin, C. Schooler, & W. Schaie (Eds.), *Self-directedness: Cause and effects throughout the life course* (pp. 19–49). Hillsdale, NJ: Lawrence Erlbaum Associates.

White, R. W. (1959). Motivation reconsidered: The concept of competence. *Psychological Review, 66*, 297–333.

Zeigarnik, B. (1927). über das behalten van erledigten und unerledigten handlungen [On the retention of completed and uncompleted actions]. *Psychologische Forschung, 9*, 1–85.

5

Behavior Genetics and Personality Development

Robert F. Krueger and Wendy Johnson
University of Minnesota

Kristen C. Kling
St. Cloud State University

This chapter discusses research at the intersection of behavior genetics and the study of the development of personality. These areas are often quite distinct, both conceptually and methodologically. Behavior genetics, in many cases, represents the study of the sources of individual differences at a specific point in time. Moreover, it is often assumed that documenting genetic effects at a specific time implies genetic effects on continuity across time. This is not necessarily the case: Both genetic and environmental forces can influence both change and continuity. Hence, the study of development may be incomplete without disentangling genetic and environmental influences; similarly, the study of genetic and environmental influences may be incomplete without an understanding of how those influences act, interact, and correlate over time.

The discussion focuses on these themes, and is divided into sections that roughly correspond to major parts of the life course: infancy and childhood, adolescence and adulthood, and older adulthood and later life. This review is not intended to be exhaustive; owing to limitations inherent in covering the entire life course in a single chapter, the focus is on major and representative findings and research directions from each stage of life. It also comments on some new developments and future directions in the study of genetic and environmental influences on personality and its development.

ORIGINS OF PERSONALITY:
TEMPERAMENT IN INFANCY AND CHILDHOOD

A common hypothesis or assumption in much personality research and theory is that the stable patterns of affect, behavior, and cognition that constitute adult personality traits originate early in life. Although reasonable, this hypothesis requires empirical scrutiny, and the relevant data are difficult and expensive to obtain. Fortunately, long-term longitudinal studies of personality development are beginning to bear fruit, and the evidence does indicate that early emerging temperamental differences adumbrate adult personality traits (Caspi et al., 2003a).

A behavior genetic perspective enhances and expands on hypotheses of continuity and change in personality development by asking how continuity and change come about. Are the sources of continuity and change genetic, environmental, or some interactive or correlational mix of the two? Addressing this fundamental question first requires examination of the genetic and environmental sources of individual differences in early emerging temperaments.

At this point, it is safe to say that genetic factors play a role in some aspects of temperament at specific ages. The basic findings have been in the literature for some time and have generally stood the test of constructive replication, emerging from both twin and adoption studies (see, e.g., Cyphers, Phillips, Fulker, & Mrazek, 1990; Matheny, 1989; Schmitz, Saudino, Plomin, Fulker, & DeFries, 1996; Stevenson & Fielding, 1985; but see also Plomin, Coon, Carey, DeFries, & Fulker, 1991, and Riese, 1990). The general conclusion that genetic factors are part of the reason for temperamental differences may not be too surprising, however, because temperament is defined by prominent theorists such as Buss and Plomin as heritable dispositions appearing in the first year of life (see Goldsmith et al., 1987, for a discussion of approaches to the definition of temperament). Indeed, the Buss and Plomin scheme for categorizing temperamental differences has played a major role in genetically informative research on childhood temperament. Specifically, Buss and Plomin (1984) categorized temperament into three primary dimensions: emotionality (is the child fearful and angry, or emotionally calm?), activity (does the child move around a lot, or does the child tend to stay still?), and sociability (does the child prefer to be around other people, or does the child instead prefer solitude?). These individual differences constitute the core traits of the Emotionality-Activity-Sociability (EAS) system of temperament classification.

A straightforward model of genetic influence on human individual differences such as the EAS traits proceeds from the idea that different forms of genes (alleles) at different locations on the genome (loci) "add up" in their contribution to continuous individual differences, such as temperamental differences. Under the assumption that genetic effects are additive in nature, dizygotic twin (DZ) correlations should be half the value of monozygotic twin (MZ) correlations. However, DZ correlations tend to be less than half MZ correlations on the EAS dimensions—often even zero or negative (see Pedersen, 1993).

Spinath and Angleitner (1998) provided a discussion of the three major potential (and not necessarily competing) explanations for these findings. First, genetic contributions to temperament might correspond to a more complex "epistatic" genetic model in which the relevant alleles are not additive, but rather are interactive in their influence on temperamental phenotypes. If the precise combination of alleles determines temperament, then it would indeed be predicted that MZ twins, who share the same exact pattern of alleles across loci, would be considerably more similar than DZ twins, who do not share the same exact pattern of alleles across loci.

Second, raters such as parents might "assimilate" MZ twins, regarding them as more similar in temperament than they actually are, perhaps because of other more obvious similarities, such as similarity in appearance. Third, along these same lines, raters such as parents might "contrast" DZ twins, regarding them as less similar in temperament than they actually are, perhaps because, in order to make comparisons of the two children, the parents compare one DZ twin with the other, rating them as more dissimilar than they "actually are" because they have no other frame of reference for making the ratings. We agree with Spinath and Angleitner (1998) that the contrast hypothesis probably has the best current support, based on evidence from both statistical modeling studies indicating significant contrast effects (Neale & Stevenson, 1989; Saudino et al., 1995), coupled with evidence that alternative and putatively more objective means of assessing temperament (e.g., actometers; Saudino & Eaton, 1991, 1995) result in DZ correlations more in line with genetic additivity (see also Saudino, 2002, for a similar conclusion and review of these issues).

Earlier, it was suggested that evidence for genetic influence on temperament was perhaps not surprising, as temperament is often defined as early emerging, genetically rooted differences in personality. Perhaps more provocative, therefore, is recent evidence that different aspects of temperament are influenced by genes and environment to different degrees. Behavioral geneticists typically divide environmental influences into two parts. Shared environmental influences represent those environmental effects that make people from the same families similar, whereas nonshared environmental effects are those that make people from the same families different.

Goldsmith, Buss, and Lemery (1997) studied toddler and preschool-age twins who were rated by their parents on the Toddler Behavioral Assessment Questionnaire (TBAQ) and the Children's Behavior Questionnaire (CBQ). These questionnaires contain more content related to positive affect when compared with other commonly used temperament schemes, such as the EAS scheme. Goldsmith et al. (1997) found significant genetic influence on most dimensions of temperament indexed by the TBAQ and CBQ, and also found DZ correlations more in line with genetic additivity. In addition, the pleasure dimension of the TBAQ showed notable shared environmental influence, as did CBQ scales that were most highly correlated with TBAQ pleasure (i.e., CBQ approach and smiling-laughter). Thus, this work suggests distinct biometrical architectures for distinct aspects of temperament, with notably larger shared environmental contributions to indices of positive affect (cf. Emde et al., 1992; Robinson, Emde, & Corley, 2001).

Goldsmith, Lemery, Buss, and Campos (1999) expanded on the Goldsmith et al. (1997) findings by measuring temperament using another distinct instrument that has been frequently used in temperament research, Rothbart's (1981) Infant Behavior Questionnaire (IBQ). Importantly, the IBQ also showed distinct biometrical architectures for distinct aspects of temperament, with notably larger shared environmental contributions to its higher order positive affect factor versus its negative affect factor. DZ correlations were again more in line with genetic additivity. Some of the infants in Goldsmith et al.'s (1999) study also participated in a laboratory assessment of reactions. Interestingly, genetic effects on stranger wariness in the laboratory assessment were correlated with genetic effects on parent reported stranger wariness, suggesting that the same genetic influence on wariness could be detected across multiple methods.

This work by Goldsmith and his colleagues is important because, generally speaking, personality differences in adulthood tend to show insignificant shared environmental variance. However, the domain that has shown the most evidence for shared environmental variance is the domain of positive social behaviors, such as altruism (see, e.g., Krueger, Hicks, & McGue, 2001). Thus, emerging evidence in both childhood and adulthood points toward significant shared environmental contributions to positive social behaviors, and challenges the notion of similar biometrical architectures for all aspects of temperament and personality. The findings of DZ correlations consistent with genetic additivity are also important, and likely resulted from the fact that the TBAQ, CBQ, and IBQ items specify the context and behaviors of interest in fairly specific ways (e.g., how often during a specific time period did your baby show behavior x when y happened?). These observations further bolster the hypothesis that contrast effects are at work on the EAS scales; they also underline the intimate link between psychometric and assessment considerations and resulting biometrical findings (cf. Krueger & Markon, 2002).

EMERGING DIRECTIONS IN GENETICALLY INFORMATIVE STUDIES OF TEMPERAMENT IN INFANCY AND CHILDHOOD

The previous review has illustrated how current research on the etiology of individual differences in childhood temperament has moved beyond basic questions of genetic influence, to documentation of distinct etiologies for distinct aspects of temperament. The discussion turns now to other recent extensions of basic research on the biometry of childhood temperament. The focus is on illustrative findings in each domain to show how genetically informative temperament research has been put to good use in addressing questions of broad importance to those interested in the origins of adult personality.

Multivariate Biometrical Modeling

One way in which biometrical research on temperament has extended beyond the basic question of the existence of genetic influence is in the area of multivariate biometrical analysis. Just as biometrical models can parse variance into genetic and environmental components, these models can also parse covariance into genetic and environmental components. The aforementioned study by Goldsmith et al. (1999) is a good example of this approach. In that study, the covariance among mother reports of stranger wariness, father reports of stranger wariness, and lab assessments of stranger wariness was mediated genetically. Thus, not only are genetic factors important in understanding stranger wariness, but these effects also explain the convergence among different methods of indexing stranger wariness.

This multivariate approach need not be limited to multiple indices of the same phenotype. For example, one fundamental way in which this approach has been extended is to examinations of measured indices of the environment (Plomin, Loehlin, & DeFries, 1985). A key finding from behavior genetic research has been that indices of the home environment are heritable. Why would indices of the home environment show genetic variation? This is likely because the "environment" is not independent of the genetically influenced characteristics of the child. For example, multivariate biometric research illustrates that genetic effects on temperamental measures (e.g., task orientation, encompassing measures such as attention span and responsiveness to test materials) can account for a portion of genetic effects on observational measures of the home environments of infants (e.g., availability of toys and interesting activities; Saudino & Plomin, 1997).

Linking Temperament With Behavioral Problems

Another area in which multivariate biometric modeling has become important concerns the link between temperament and behavior problems. Temperament could be associated with behavior problems for a variety of reasons, but one especially compelling hypothesis is that behavior problems represent the extremes of temperament. Multivariate biometric modeling provides one means for evaluating this hypothesis. For example, Gjone and Stevenson (1997) examined the longitudinal link between parent-reported EAS temperament traits at a first assessment wave and problem behavior syndromes assessed via the Child Behavior Checklist (CBCL; Achenbach, 1991) at a second assessment wave (2 years later) in a sample of Norwegian same-gender twins from age 7 to 17 at the second wave. They found a significant genetic contribution to the link between EAS emotionality and CBCL attention problems and aggressive behavior. In addition, Schmitz et al. (1999) examined genetic relations between mothers' reports of temperament measured at 14, 20, 24, and 36 months of age, and CBCL broad-band syndromes (internalizing, externalizing, and total problems) at age 4 years in a sample of twins from the United States. The emotionality dimension of temperament showed consistent and very strong genetic connections with behavior problems, in particular, the CBCL total behavior problems score; indeed, genetic factors explained from 89% to 100% of the observed correlations between emotionality at the four measurements and CBCL total problems. Similarly, Goldsmith and Lemery (2000) presented evidence for a genetic basis for the link between temperamental fearfulness and overanxiousness. Together, these findings underscore the fundamental role of negative emotionality in predicting behavior problems and psychopathology across the life course (cf. Krueger, Caspi, & Moffitt, 2000) by demonstrating that, even early in life, there is substantial genetic continuity between "normal range" excessive emotionality and a variety of more serious behavioral problems.

LONGITUDINAL TEMPERAMENT RESEARCH

The multivariate approach can also be extended to the same measures across multiple waves of a longitudinal study. For example, Plomin et al. (1993) examined change and continuity from 14 to 20 months of age in the MacArthur Longitudinal Twin Study (MALTS). On a variety of indices of temperament, genetic influences represented the primary contribution to continuity. Nevertheless, although genetic influences were the major source of the stability observed from 14 to 20 months on some measures, the analyses also indicated novel genetic influences at 20 months that were not observed at 14 months. Follow-up results at 24 and 36 months in the MALTS sample suggested, however, that the primary source of stability in temperament across time was genetic, with unique environmental influences largely accounting for change (Saudino & Cherny, 2001; Saudino, Plomin, & DeFries, 1996). There is further discussion of this pattern of findings during an examination of longitudinal studies of adult personality.

MOLECULAR GENETICS AND THE ENVIRONMENT

Molecular approaches to behavioral genetic inquiry complement quantitative approaches in a number of important ways. For example, such approaches can identify the specific genes underlying the genetic effects observed in twin and adoption studies. Along these lines, Schmidt, Fox, Rubin, Hu, and Hamer (2002) examined associations between three genetic polymorphisms (dopamine D4 receptor, serotonin transporter, and serotonin 2C receptor) and aggression and shyness in 4-year-olds. Although none of the polymorphisms was significantly associated with laboratory measures of behavior, variation in the dopamine D4 receptor was associated with mothers' reports of aggression.

Perhaps less widely recognized, molecular approaches also have great potential for sharpening understanding of environmental influences. Caspi et al. (2002), for example, examined the joint impact of childhood maltreatment and variations in the monamine oxidase A (MAOA) gene (a gene coding for MAOA, a substance that metabolizes major neurotransmitters) on antisocial behavior later in life in a birth cohort of men from New Zealand. An interaction was found between genotype and environment: Childhood maltreatment was a risk factor for antisocial behavior, but the impact of childhood maltreatment on antisocial behavior was conditional on MAOA genotype, as the genetic polymorphism coding for high MAOA activity protected men against the adverse effects of childhood maltreatment. Similarly, Caspi, Sugden, et al. (2003b) presented evidence that variation in the serotonin transporter (5-HTT) gene predicted whether or not people developed depression and suicidality in response to stressful life events. This kind of approach to characterizing gene by environment interactions has great potential to inform our understanding of the way specific genes and environmental stressors interact throughout the life course.

PERSONALITY DEVELOPMENT IN ADOLESCENCE AND ADULTHOOD: OVERVIEW OF WELL-ESTABLISHED FINDINGS

Traditional Twin Studies Based on Self-Report

The conceptual approach used in behavioral genetic studies has two interrelated characteristics that were immediately advantageous in the application of the technique to personality research in adolescence and adulthood. First, the conceptual approach makes it possible to disentangle the effects of nature and nurture. The results from the early behavioral genetic studies of personality characteristics were striking: From 40% to 60% of the variance in broadly construed self-reported personality characteristics is genetic in origin. The explanation of this much variance in personality research is a striking achievement. Behavior is determined by many factors, and any single factor is unlikely to explain more than about 10% of the variance (Caspi, 1998). The ability of behavioral genetic studies to accomplish this arose directly from the second advantage of their conceptual approach: It does so at a broad-brush components-of-variance level that separates the net effect of genetic and environmental influences regardless of their specific natures or how many there may be. These results directly imply that characteristics inherent in the individual bring as much to bear on the individual's consistent patterns of behavior as any environmental circumstances.

These results have been established most firmly for broadly construed traits such as Extraversion and Neuroticism (see Bouchard, 1997; Bouchard & Loehlin, 2001; Eaves, Eysenck, & Martin, 1989; Loehlin, 1992; and Sherman et al., 1997, for reviews), but it has also been established that more narrowly construed self-reported traits and even individual questionnaire items demonstrate substantial, although perhaps somewhat lower, genetic influence (e.g., Finkel & McGue, 1997; Heath, Eaves, & Martin, 1989; Heath, Jardine, Eaves, & Martin, 1989; Jang, McCrae, Angleitner, & Riemann, 1998; Tellegen et al., 1988). At this point, it is fair to say that no self-reported personality trait has reliably shown little or no genetic influence. In addition, the same results show little or no effect of the shared environment for most traits. The majority of the 40%–60% of variance attributed to environmental influence is generally nonshared, although there are some exceptions (e.g., altruism, see Krueger et al., 2001, for an example). The question that arises here, however, is whether this finding is somehow dependent on the use of self-report measures, which has tended to dominate behavior-genetic studies (Brody, 1993; Saudino, 1997).

Studies Including Peer and Observer Reports

This question of dependence on self-reports has been addressed in several studies from slightly different perspectives. Looking specifically for evidence that the rater's own personality contributed to ratings of the personality of the person being rated, Heath, Neale, Kessler, Eaves, and Kendler (1992) found correlations of from .45 to .63 between self and co-twin ratings for Extraversion and Neuroticism, with similar and substantial estimates of genetic influence whether based on the self- or co-twin report. Notably, estimates of genetic influence based on a composite of the two sets of ratings were considerably higher for both traits. This result was confirmed and extended by Riemann, Angleitner, and Strelau (1997) based on the Big Five personality traits in a sample of nearly 1,000 German and Polish twins. The twins each completed the NEO Five Factor Inventory (NEO-FFI), and two peers of each twin also completed a third-person version of the same instrument. Average correlations between the two peer ratings were .61, and average correlations between the self and peer ratings were .55, indicating substantial agreement. More importantly, the peer ratings showed slightly less univariate genetic influence than the self-reports, but multivariate genetic analyses indicated that the same genes were involved in both the self-reports and the peer ratings. In addition, the estimated genetic influence on the latent variables underlying the three reports ranged from 66% to 79%, considerably greater than the 40%–60% typically found. These higher estimates reflect the increased reliability associated with latent variable measurement—and likely the largest source of unreliability in such ratings is the specificity of the viewpoint of the rater. This suggests that when a personality trait is considered as a consensus of viewpoints, the genetic influences on it increase. The self- and peer reports in this sample also indicate that the genetic influences on personality are highly stable over time (Angleitner, 2002).

Higher estimates of genetic influence also resulted from consensus composite ratings in the Nonshared Environment in Adolescent Development study (Loehlin, Niederhiser, & Reiss, 2003; Reiss, Niederhiser, Heatherington, & Plomin, 2000), designed to detect specific nonshared environmental effects. This study made use of self-reports, mothers' and fathers' ratings, and ratings of videotaped interactions of antisocial behavior, depression, cognitive agency, sociability, autonomy, and social responsibility in a national U.S. sample of over 700 same-gender adolescent sibling pairs and their parents. The sibling pairs included MZ and DZ twin pairs, full siblings living with both biological parents, and full, half, and genetically unrelated siblings from step-families. Antisocial behavior, depression, cognitive agency, and social responsibility showed the typical pattern of little shared environmental influence, but the estimates of genetic influence ranged from 71% to 89%. Sociability and autonomy showed shared environmental effects of 31% and 47%, respectively, as well as genetic effects of 57% and 40%.

Although these results are reassuring in that they replicate findings from self-reports in twins, more behavioral genetic research that explicitly incorporates a range of sources of personality data including self, peer, teacher, and supervisor reports; interviews, official and family records; objective laboratory measurements; and observational assessments is needed. A recent example of the type of research needed is provided by Borkenau, Riemann, Angleitner, and Spinath (2001). Based on ratings of videotaped behaviors in 15 different situations by judges who had never met the adult subjects in the videotapes, Borkenau et al. estimated that about 40% of the variance in their personality measures was genetic, 25% shared environmental, and 35% nonshared environmental. Perhaps contradicting other results, however, they observed that extraversion was the only trait that seemed to exhibit no shared environmental influence. This is a provocative result, in the sense that, in general, the shared environment is not a significant source of variance in adult personality. It may be that the lack of shared environmental variance in adult personality is linked to the almost exclusive reliance on self-reports in behavior genetic studies of adult personality; this possibility deserves further study, using innovative assessment approaches, such as those employed by Borkenau et al. (2001).

Adoption and Family Studies

Adoption and family studies have typically produced lower estimates of genetic influence on personality measures than have twin studies. For example, Ahern, Johnson, Wilson, McClearn, and Vandenbergh (1982) found correlations of .16 for Extraversion and .13 for Neuroticism among biological parents and offspring, suggesting genetic influence of at most 30%. Adoptive parents and children correlate .01 for Extraversion and .05 for Neuroticism (Loehlin, 1992). The adoptive results are important because they provide additional evidence, complementary to the twin method, that shared family environment does not influence personality. The Colorado Adoption Project has reported similar familial and adoptive results (Plomin, Corley, Caspi, Fulker, & DeFries, 1998), with the additional observation of average correlations of .03 for sociability, a major component of Extraversion, and -.01 for emotionality, a major component of Neuroticism, between biological parents and their adopted-away offspring.

There are at least two possible reasons for the discrepancy between twin and adoptive and familial results (Plomin et al., 1998). The first is that some form of environmental effect makes MZ twins more similar than DZ twins, inflating estimates of genetic influence. The types of environmental effects involved could range from greater environmental sharing among twins than among other biological relatives of the same degree to more similar treatment by parents and others of MZ than DZ twins to rater bias effects that cause MZ twins to rate themselves more similarly and DZ twins to rate themselves more differently. This is a complicated issue, and most tests for such effects have found little to report (Plomin, DeFries, McClearn, & Rutter, 1997) based on evaluation of environmental similarities and comparisons of estimates of genetic influence resulting from twins reared apart and together (Loehlin, 1992; Tellegen, et al., 1988; but see Pedersen, Plomin, McClearn, & Friberg, 1998, for a contradictory finding). In addition, Lake, Eaves, Maes, Heath, and Martin (2000) found no evidence for twin-specific environmental influences on Neuroticism in a sample of 45,850 twins and other relatives from Australia and the United States, using models designed to make explicit provisions for them.

The second plausible reason for the discrepancy between twin and adoptive and familial results is that nonadditive genetic effects may play a larger role in personality development than suggested by the twin correlations alone. As already discussed in the context of childhood temperament, most twin studies have relied on the assumption that genes influence personality in an additive manner. Lake et al. (2000) addressed this possibility as well, finding evidence for nonadditive genetic effects on Neuroticism. Others have also found evidence for nonadditive genetic effects on personality (e.g., Tellegen et al., 1988), but these effects have been notoriously difficult to replicate (Bouchard & Loehlin, 2001).

At this writing, the presence of genetic influences explaining on the order of from 40% to 60% of individual differences in personality can be considered to be well established. Questions about differences in the extent of effects among groups such as men and women and over time, the stability of genetic influences over time, and genetic and environmental contributions to personality structure are now foci of behavioral genetic research involving personality.

GENETIC DIFFERENCES IN GENETIC INFLUENCES ON PERSONALITY

The extent to which there are gender differences in personality and their possible origins are major sources of controversy in contemporary psychology (e.g., Buss, Haselton, Shackleford, Bleske, & Wakefield, 1999; Eagly & Wood, 1999; Mealey, 2000). An obvious possible source of gender differences is genetic influence. Two recent studies are noteworthy in this regard. Finkel and McGue (1997) used Multidimensional Personality Questionnaire data (MPQ; Tellegen, 1982) from the Minnesota Twin Registry that included male and female sibling pairs, father–son, father–daughter, mother–son, and mother–daughter pairs, as well as MZ and same- and opposite-gender DZ twin pairs. They found some evidence for differences in the extent of genetic influence for some personality traits, notably Alienation, Control, and Absorption, but no evidence that different sets of genes influence personality in each gender. Using a much larger and more diverse sample but more general personality traits, Eaves, Heath, Neale, Hewitt, and Martin (1998) obtained similar results for Extraversion and Neuroticism based on 20,554 individuals (twins and their family members) from the United States, Australia, and Finland. Thus, there is reason to believe that genes and environment may exert their effects to differing extents for males and females, but no evidence for genetic effects of differing natures (but see Heath, Madden, Cloninger, & Martin, 1999, who found evidence that sex differences in personality may mediate genetic influences on psychopathology).

ASSORTATIVE MATING FOR PERSONALITY

People tend to marry partners who are similar to themselves at some level. Positive assortative mating has been documented for a range of traits, including physical characteristics (Epstein & Guttman, 1984), cognitive ability (Jensen, 1978), and attitudes (Eaves et al., 1999; Waller, Kojetin, Bouchard, Lykken, & Tellegen, 1990). When large, assortative mating for a trait strongly controlled by additive genes accounts for a substantive amount of the variation in the trait, and this must be taken into account when estimating genetic and environmental effects on the trait. The situation only becomes more complex when a trait is controlled by genes that operate nonadditively. Thus, it is important to determine to what extent the twin and other familial correlations for personality traits that are studied have been influenced by assortative mating.

Widespread popular beliefs notwithstanding, the coefficients for personality traits are often found to be rather low. For example, Lykken and Tellegen (1993) found an average correlation of .13 for 583 spousal pairs on the 10 MPQ scales excluding Traditionalism, which showed somewhat higher correlations and reflect religious and conservative political attitudes. Bouchard, McGue, Hur, and Horn (1998) reported an average correlation of .22 for the 20 scales of the California Psychological Inventory (Gough, 1975), and Eaves et al. (1999) found correlations near zero for Psychoticism, Extraversion, and Neuroticism in multiple large sample studies. Lykken and Tellegen (1993) argued that mate selection results from romantic infatuation, which in the modern world is largely random within a broad field of possibilities made eligible by propinquity. If true, then the low assortative mating correlations for personality should be expected. Most assortative mating studies have estimated the degree of similarity in partners who have been together for some period of time, leaving open the question concerning whether whatever similarity is observed is the result of reciprocal influences. However, Caspi, Herbener, and Ozer (1992), using longitudinal data on couples planning marriage and extending over the subsequent 20 years, concluded that couples do not become more similar over time. Rather, their marriage acts to maintain the original similarity.

GENETIC AND ENVIRONMENTAL STRUCTURE
UNDERLYING OBSERVED PERSONALITY

The conceptual approach used in behavioral genetic studies has more recently been applied to address questions about the structure of personality and its origins. The structure of personality has traditionally been studied using factor analysis of correlations among phenotypic personality traits to infer the existence of underlying latent personality factors. This has been successful in the sense that structures that can be consistently replicated have been identified. Different researchers have identified different structures, however, which is a reminder that factor analysis can only reveal common variance among variables included for analysis, and many aspects of factor analysis are subjective. It is not clear that the phenotypic correlations that form the input to factor analysis reveal underlying causal structures of theoretical importance. Behavior genetic studies can help to resolve this issue. To the extent that the genetic variance in one variable is correlated with the genetic variance in another variable, these variables can be considered to be genetically correlated, and it can be inferred that the same sets of genes are influencing each variable. The same observations can be made about shared and nonshared environmental variances. As suggested by Crawford and DeFries (1978), matrices of genetic and environmental correlations can be factor analyzed in the same manner as matrices of phenotypic correlations. Because these correlation matrices have a particular causal interpretation (though note that they do not pinpoint specific genes or environmental influences), the resulting factor structures can be considered to illuminate the structure of the etiology of personality covariation.

Several studies have applied this approach to different personality models. Loehlin (1987) found evidence for similar extraversion and neuroticism dimensions in the genetic and nonshared environmental correlation matrices for 31 clusters of correlated items from the CPI, using data from Loehlin and Nichols' (1976) National Merit Twin Study. Using Cloninger's (1986, 1987a, 1987b) model of personality, Stallings, Hewitt, Cloninger, Heath, and Eaves (1996) demonstrated that the posited phenotypic structure could be extracted from the genotypic correlations as well (at least for women, as they had a very small sample of male DZ twin pairs). Carey and DiLalla (1994) attempted to extend these conclusions to more specific personality traits using 20 scales from the CPI, with results at the genetic level generally consistent with the phenotypic factors of the CPI. Krueger (2000), using the MPQ in the Minnesota Twin Registry, obtained highly comparable phenotypic, genotypic, and nonshared environmental factor structures underlying the 11 facet-level MPQ scales. McCrae, Jang, Livesley, Riemann, and Angleitner (2001) extended this procedure using a combined German and Canadian sample and the Five Factor model. In addition to extracting the Five Factor model from the phenotypic and genotypic correlations, they used self and spouse ratings from a separate sample to divide the nonshared environmental covariance into portions due to implicit personality theories of the raters and truly nonshared environmental variance. They extracted a typical Five Factor structure from the implicit personality theory matrices, but only two factors related to conscientiousness and humaneness in the residual nonshared environmental matrix. Thus, it seems to be possible to extract parallel phenotypic and genetic structures using several different personality models. This seems to provide additional strong evidence for the role of genes in shaping personality.

To the extent that the latent variables identified in phenotypic factor analyses actually represent underlying personality traits, it is reasonable to expect that their subdomains should form coherent structures with identifiable genetic and environmental influences. The few studies that have taken this approach, however, have yielded mixed results. Heath, Eaves, and Martin (1989) found that single common and genetic structures could be extracted for Extraversion and Neuroticism items from the Eysenck Personality Questionnaire (EPQ; H. J. Eysenck & M. W. Eysenck, 1985), but the Psychoticism items required 2 factors. Jang, Livesley, Angleitner, Riemann, and Vernon (2002) applied a similar approach to the facets of the Five Factor model assessed using the NEO–PI–R in the same German and Canadian samples referenced earlier, fitting models with increasing degrees of structure to the data. The most highly structured models based on the assumption of unified latent Five Factor personality traits failed to fit adequately, and each Five Factor domain appeared to consist of more than one common genetic and environmental factor. In addition, there were substantial genetic and environmental influences specific to each facet. Johnson and Krueger (2004) obtained very similar results using an adjective descriptor version of the Five Factor model in a national sample of U.S. twins. Although this approach needs to be applied to other personality models, these results call into question the meaning of the concept of a higher order personality trait, at least for the traits unique to the Five Factor model and for Psychoticism (although Extraversion and Neuroticism may show better properties). It is possible that higher order personality traits do not exist as unitary psychological entities, but are simply useful heuristic devices that can be associated with the activity of many genes and multiple environmental factors.

EXTENT AND SOURCES OF STABILITY AND CHANGE IN PERSONALITY IN ADOLESCENCE AND ADULTHOOD

As the previous sections illustrate, much behavior genetic personality research is not explicitly developmental, particularly that dealing with adults. To some degree, this reflects the tendency of personality research on adults in general to focus on the coherence and stability of personality constructs over time (Caspi & Roberts, 2001). Nevertheless, behavior genetic studies are also in a position to make strong contributions to the understanding of the extent and sources of stability and change in personality in adolescence and adulthood. First, there is now an extensive body of data about changes in genetic and environmental contributions to Extraversion and Neuroticism during these years. McCartney, Harris, and Bernieri (1990) reported a meta-analysis of twin studies from 1967 to 1985. They found that twin correlations for personality traits tended to decrease with age, and the decreases were similar for MZ and DZ twins. This implies that it is shared environmental rather than genetic influences that are decreasing. Their sample included individuals up to 50 years, but the average age was 16. Thus, their findings might best be characterized as applying to adolescence and early adulthood. Large twin studies from three countries (Finland: Viken, Rose, Kaprio, & Koskenvuo, 1994; Sweden: Floderus-Myrhed, Pedersen, & Rasmussen, 1980; and Australia: Loehlin & Martin, 2001) have found that shared environmental influences on both traits were negligible in the adult years, and for ages after 28, the models with genetic parameters constrained equal fit reasonably well. There was, however, some evidence for decreases in genetic influence in young adulthood.

More importantly, however, longitudinal behavior genetic studies can be used to investigate the sources of personality stability and change across the life span. Only a few studies of this nature have been carried out to date, but their results contain two tantalizing clues to the mechanisms involved. The methodology used in these studies again makes use of the correlations between two or more measures of genetic influence, in these studies taken at different points in time. Viken et al. (1994) found that genetic influences on Extraversion and Neuroticism were completely correlated in a Finnish sample ranging in age from 18 to 53. These results have been replicated using other personality measures by Angleitner (2002) in a German adult sample using the Five Factor model, and by Johnson, McGue, and Krueger (2005) in a Minnesota sample primarily in late adulthood. The complete genetic correlation was also replicated by McGue, Bacon, & Lykken (1993) in a small Minnesota sample of young adults ranging in age from 20 to 30 years, but they also noted overall decreasing genetic influence with age.

The consistent finding of complete genetic correlation over time suggests that the same genes operate in the same way to influence personality throughout the life span, contributing substantially to the stability that has been observed (for a meta-analysis, see Roberts & DelVecchio, 2000). Interestingly, however, these studies have also found high nonshared environmental correlations—around .60. This suggests that the nonshared environment also contributes importantly to personality stability, probably because it consists of stable environmental influences. Likely key sources of nonshared environmental stability include long-term residence in the same community, continuing marriage to the same spouse, ongoing employment in the same occupation or even position, and long-term participation in the same activities or hobbies. Nonshared environmental variance has generally been considered to be little more than noise; thinking of it as systematic in this way opens new possibilities for investigation (Turkheimer & Waldron, 2000). In their longitudinal study of personality traits in married couples, Caspi, Herbener, and Ozer (1992) noted that environmental experiences shared by spouses may contribute substantially to personality development in adulthood, which provides some guidance as to how such investigations might proceed.

ENVIRONMENTAL INFLUENCES ON PERSONALITY

Behavior genetic studies continue to provide the best evidence for environmental influences in general, and in particular for personality. Estimates of genetic influence for personality rarely exceed 50%, which means that estimates of environmental influence are rarely less than 50%. As described earlier, understanding these environmental influences could provide important clues about the development of personality. For example, behavior genetic studies have been rather emphatic in revealing that shared environmental influences in general, and in particular for personality, are negligible, at least in the way such influences have traditionally been conceptualized. In addition, the search for specific nonshared environmental factors that do have significant influence on behavior has not been fruitful. Turkheimer and Waldron (2000) concluded, based on a meta-analysis of 43 such studies, that objectively nonshared environmental factors did not account for a substantial portion of the observed nonshared environmental variance.

To interpret this conclusion, it is important to clarify some definitions associated with environmental effects, attributable to Goldsmith (1993). Objective environmental factors refer to environmental factors observable from outside the family system, such as by a researcher, without regard to the ways these environmental factors affect individual family members. These were the factors Turkheimer and Waldron (2000) studied. In contrast, effective environments are defined by the outcomes they produce, regardless of their objective status. Thus, objective and effective environmental factors may be shared or nonshared. Shared environmental effects create sibling resemblance, regardless of whether or not they involve environmental factors that can be considered to be objectively or effectively shared. These distinctions are important because they provide the key to interpreting many recent research findings involving environmental influences: Many environmental factors that are objectively shared may be effectively nonshared; the same events or circumstances are perceived differently by different individuals, and the perceptions are mediated by personality.

This generality can be used to interpret findings that sibling differences in family experiences are related to sibling differences in personality (Vernon, Jang, Harris, & McCarthy, 1997), parents more commonly respond to genetic differences between their children than cause those differences environmentally (Pike, McGuire, Hetherington, Reiss, & Plomin, 1996), there is genetic influence on self-report as well as more direct measures of family environment (Plomin, 1994; Plomin, McClearn, Pedersen, Nesselroade, & Bergeman, 1988; O'Connor, Hetherington, Reiss, & Plomin, 1995), and genetic effects on retrospective reports of adopted-apart twins' rearing environments can be accounted for by genetic influence on personality (Krueger, Markon, & Bouchard, 2003). Although these examples of findings involve children as well as adolescents, the general process involved likely applies every bit as much in adulthood: Genes and environments are correlated and interact, as do phenotypes and environments. That is, as a result of their genotypes and the phenotypes they have developed over time as a result of both genetic and environmental influences (Turkheimer, 1999), individuals seek out and are shuffled by a responsive and transactive environment into sets of circumstances that tend to reinforce the ways in which their genes influenced their personality traits. As an example, the careful and achievement-oriented employee rises rapidly through a professional hierarchy in recognition of the high quality of work produced, reinforcing the employee's existing personality characteristics.

Another approach to evaluating environmental influences on personality is to consider the possibility of gene–environment interaction, or the genetic control of sensitivity to environmental influences, at the statistical level, without specifying the genes involved. For example, there has long been evidence that the characteristics of the home environment in which an individual is reared are correlated with later psychological functioning (e.g., Burbach & Borduin, 1986; Parker, 1990). In addition, studies of conduct and personality disorders among adoptive samples (e.g., Cadoret, Yates, Troughton, Woodworth, & Stewart, 1995; Riggins-Caspers, Cadoret, Knutson, & Langbehn, 2003) have suggested that those at greater genetic risk are more vulnerable to pathogenic rearing environments. Newly described statistical techniques relying on analysis of raw data (Purcell, 2002) now make assessment of such gene–environment interactions relatively straightforward in twin samples. For example, Kendler, Aggen, Jacobson, and Neale (2003) investigated the extent to which dysfunction in the family of origin moderated the extent of genetic influence on neuroticism. They found no evidence for such interactive effects in their data, but could not rule out lack of statistical power as the reason for the null finding. The amount of information about gene–environment interactions will likely increase dramatically over the next few years.

MOLECULAR GENETIC ANALYSIS IN ADOLESCENCE AND ADULTHOOD

Normal personality traits can be considered complex, meaning they may be influenced by both genetic and environmental factors and are likely approximately normally distributed, or at least continuously distributed. Ten years ago, many believed that the rapid advances in molecular genetics would make possible the rapid identification of the quantitative trait loci (QTLs), or specific gene location, responsible for the genetic influences on these traits. In fact, several studies have found effects, but there have also been many failures to replicate these findings. For example, Cloninger, Adolfsson, and Svravik (1996), among others, reported that a polymorphism of the D4 receptor gene could account for about 10% of the heritable variance in Novelty Seeking. This led to a flurry of attempts to replicate, including many failures, and the degree to which this is a real effect is still unclear (Plomin & Caspi, 1998). This lack of clarity is characteristic of the field in general and in particular with respect to possible genetic effects on personality. For example, Lesch, Bengal, Heils, et al. (1996) found an association between the serotonin transporter (5-HTTLPR) and neuroticism, but there have been at least five failures to replicate this finding (Flory et al., 1999). There are, however, continuing interesting results that, if replicated, could change the nature of personality psychology. For example, Cloninger et al. (1998) used a genomewide scan to test for QTL's on the TPQ Harm Avoidance scale and found a locus that explained 38% of the trait variance. In addition, there was significant evidence of epistatic interactions, increasing the amount of trait variance that could potentially be explained to 66%. Loehlin, Spurdle, Treloar, and Martin (1999) found a relation between number of CAG repeats (C, A, and G are the names of bases within the DNA molecule, standing for cytosine, adenine, and guanine) on the androgen receptor gene and an aspect of psychological femininity. These findings all require multiple replication, but it seems likely that persistence in this area of work will eventually lead to substantive findings. For example, as described earlier, the recent work of Caspi et al. (2002, 2003b) on gene–environment interactions suggests an important and novel avenue for understanding specific genetic-environmental transactions. Next consider genetic and environmental influences on personality development in later adulthood.

PERSONALITY DEVELOPMENT IN LATER ADULTHOOD

As revealed by the foregoing sections, much behavior genetic research has been concentrated in adolescent and adult samples, and approached from the perspective of relative stability of personality. Thus, one of the first questions to be addressed when behavior genetic studies were initially conducted using participants in the ter stages of life was whether or not the biometric estimates found in younger participants would replicate in older samples. Studies of older participants yield results that are generally consistent with those from younger samples. That is, genetic influences account for approximately 30% to 50% of variation in personality in older samples, with the remaining variance explained by nonshared environmental influences (for reviews, see Bergeman, 1997; Loehlin, 1992). These overall results may mask some age trends, however, as they may indicate slightly lower proportions of genetic influence on personality in old age.

Consistent with this possibility, when age is examined as an explicit moderator of genetic influence on personality, the results have been mixed. Two recent studies suggest that age does not impact biometric estimates. First, using data from the Australian Twin Registry, Loehlin and Martin (2001) examined Eysenckian Neuroticism, Extraversion, Psychoticism, and the Lie Scale in twins whose ages covered the adult life span (age 17–92). When examining age trends in the contribution of genes and environment to personality, Loehlin and Martin found that a model specifying no age or gender differences fit the data well for Neuroticism (genetic influences = 40%), Extraversion (genetic influences = 47%), and Psychoticism (genetic influences = 28%). This indicates that the relative magnitudes of genetic and environmental influences were constant across both genders and across age groups. Although the results for the Lie scale indicated there were both age and gender differences in the biometric estimates, the authors urged replication before interpreting their results regarding this scale.

A second recent study (Heiman et al., 2003) also showed no significant effects of age on the genetic and environmental influences on four traits from Cloninger's structural model of personality (Novelty Seeking, Harm Avoidance, Reward Dependence, and Persistence; Cloninger, 1987b). Using data from same-gender female twins from the American Association of Retired Persons sample, the researchers investigated cross-sectional age differences, using age as both a continuous (ranging from 50 to 89) and a dichotomous variable (older or younger than 65). In their biometric analyses, a model including only additive genetic and nonshared environmental influences fit the data best, and this model could be constrained to be equivalent across the younger and older age groups without compromising the fit. When the more stringent test of age differences was applied (i.e., using age as a continuous measure and searching for both linear and quadratic effects), again, age did not exert a significant influence on the biometric estimates.

In contrast to these studies that find no age difference, three twin studies have shown that age does influence genetic variance estimates. First, an early study using twins from the Swedish Twin Registry examined the influence of age on heritability estimates (Floderus-Myrhed et al., 1980). In this study, a sample of 12,898 twin pairs completed the Neuroticism and Extraversion scales of the Eysenck Personality Inventory. As in other studies, the genetic variance estimates suggested that genetic influences explained more than half of the variation in scale scores (estimates ranged from 50% to 66%). Using the same data, Eaves et al. (1989) conducted a formal test of whether or not age influenced the biometric estimates. Across the three age groups (i.e., 16–28, 29–38, and 39–48), Eaves et al. found significant effects for both age and gender on the genetic variance estimates. Genetic variance estimates declined with age for Neuroticism for both genders. The pattern for Extraversion was less clear, with an increase in genetic variance with age for females and a decrease followed by an increase for males.

Results of Viken et al. (1994) described more briefly earlier, also document age effects on biometric estimates for Extraversion and Neuroticism. Specifically, six different birth cohorts from the Finnish Twin Cohort study completed a short form of the Eysenck Personality Inventory in both 1975 and 1981. At the first testing, the participants ranged from age 18 to 53. Shared environment effects in the data were nonsignificant, and a series of analyses was undertaken to examine age and cohort differences in additive genetic and nonshared environmental effects. For Extraversion, the best fitting model indicated there were age differences in genetic variation, decreasing with age from 52% in the youngest group (aged 18–23) to 41% in the oldest group (age 54–59). For Neuroticism, genetic variance estimates also decreased with age, and this effect was larger for the men, for whom the estimates decreased from 54% to 17% across the same age span. Notably, planned comparisons showed that the genetic contributions to both traits declined after the early 20s for both men and women.

Finally, a third study examined personality stability and change in the Swedish Adoption/Twin Study of Aging (SATSA; Pederson & Reynolds, 1998, 2002). Participants in the SATSA completed measures of Neuroticism, Extraversion, and Openness to Experience at as many as four time points. In general, genetic influences explained stability in personality over time, though proportions of genetic variance decreased. Time-specific nonshared environmental influences explained most of the change in scale scores over time, with indications of both new and lasting influences. All three of the measures tended to decrease with age. The authors concluded that genetic influences are much more stable than environmental influences, but they provide only about half of the stability observed in phenotypic personality because they decrease in relative importance with time, whereas environmental effects grow.

Clearly, results from these studies have not been consistent and, even within studies, results have been somewhat inconsistent. The confusion probably has its origins in the high level of summary of underlying processes necessary to produce estimates of proportions of genetic and environmental influences over varying age groups. To make sense of the kinds of results already summarized, it will be necessary to disentangle the genetic and environmental influences on these underlying processes, each of which is an active area of research today. The next section turns to a discussion of these underlying processes and the ways that behavior genetic approaches can add valuable insight.

PROCESSES UNDERLYING PERSONALITY CHANGE IN LATE ADULTHOOD: GENETIC AND ENVIRONMENTAL IMPLICATIONS

Researchers are currently at the beginning stages of understanding mean-level personality changes with age. Although the studies described earlier show inconsistent results, and other recent studies not involving twins are not much more consistent (e.g., Helson, Kwan, John, & Jones, 2002; Srivastava, John, Gosling, & Potter, 2003), two other very recent studies are beginning to shed light on personality development in later life. Mroczek and Spiro (2003) used individual growth modeling to understand developmental changes in the personality traits of extraversion and neuroticism for a large sample of adult men (age 43–91) in the Normative Aging Study, who were followed over a period of 12 years. Although general trajectories for these traits could be discerned in the data (overall, extraversion was relatively stable and neuroticism declined), more striking was evidence of significant heterogeneity in patterns of change over time, and further evidence that individual differences in patterns of change could be traced meaningfully to events in the men's lives. For example, neuroticism tended to decline with age, yet marriage or remarriage was associated with an enhanced rate of decline, greater than the normative rate of decline in the sample. Similarly, Small, Hertzog, Hultsch, and Dixon (2003) studied each of the Big Five traits in both men and women age 55–85, studied over a 6-year period, and were able to document individual differences in reliable change, some of which could be linked to demographic characteristics of the research participants. For example, women were more likely than men to show decreases in neuroticism and increases in agreeableness.

Although these studies are groundbreaking, they were not in a position to study genetic and environmental contributions to change and stability in personality. This is an important area for continued research because understanding the nature of changes in genetic and environmental influences will help with understanding the processes underlying patterns of personality development. For example, McCrae, et al. (2000) argued that personality traits are genetically controlled dispositions for which the environment merely sets the stage for expression. They maintained that both continuity and systematic change in personality have their sources in genetic influences, with genetic influences on basic temperament contributing stability, and genetic influences on developmental processes contributing to systematic change. If this is correct, then researchers should be able to observe two patterns of data in behavior genetic studies. First, there should be relatively small individual differences in personality change over time, and second, the differences that do occur should be under primarily genetic influence. For example, there is evidence that Harm Avoidance increases in older age (Carmichael, 1993). It is possible that this increase could be a genetically controlled adaptive psychological response to increased physical fragility. If this is true, then there should be a relatively constant total genetic variance in older individuals as compared to those who are in middle age. It should be possible to allocate this relatively constant total genetic variance between stability and change, with the portion allocated to change explaining the majority of the total variance associated with change.

There is also only a rudimentary conception of how personality might be expected to change in old age. In the gerontological literature more generally, changes with age can be characterized, for the most part, as group-level declines in functioning over time. Thus, researchers have investigated declines in memory skills and cognitive and physical functioning (e.g., Begun, Iachine, & Yashin, 2000; Hartman, Bolton, & Fehnel, 2001; Hofer et al., 2002; Park et al, 2002; Wilson et al., 2002). Decline in function seems, however, less relevant to personality because it is not clear how personality is associated with functionality, nor is it clear how particular personality traits might be affected by declining functionality. For example, declines in neuroticism in older age could indicate reduced responsiveness to environmental stress that might reflect decline in function. On the other hand, declines in neuroticism could indicate better adaptation to environmental circumstances that might actually reflect improvement in function. This may have implications for the nature of the associated genetic and environmental influences as well. For example, genetic influences on the nature and timing of aging and decline in physical function may affect personality in certain ways, whereas environmental influences such as greater leisure time associated with retirement might have completely different effects.

Finally, studies of genetic and environmental influences have most commonly presented estimates of the relative proportions of variance that can be attributed to genetic and environmental sources. Such statistics, however, mask changes that may be taking place in the total amounts of variance. Thus, for example, declines in estimates of proportions of genetic influence over time could result from stable genetic variance but increasing environmental variance or from decreasing genetic variance but stable environmental variance. The ability to distinguish these two conditions has important implications for understanding the aging process in general, and the raw variance components are generally readily available from standard behavior genetic analyses. Genetic-evolutionary theories of aging predict that genetic variance will increase with age for traits associated with reproductive success due to weak natural selection in postreproductive life (Charlewood & Hughes, 1996). In contrast, epidemiological–gerontological theories of aging predict that environmental variance will increase with age due to "wear and tear" due to the accumulation over time of damage from oxidative molecular reactions, the effects of radiation, and so on, at the cellular level (Campisi, 2001). These theories are not mutually exclusive, but it is only through examination of raw components of genetic and environmental variance that researchers can begin to understand the extent to which such processes may be involved. The theories are, of course, clearly relevant to physical and cognitive functioning and possibly less clearly related to personality because of the difficulty of assessing and possible irrelevance of functional decline, but there is evidence for increasing variance in personality as well as health measures later in life as well (Nelson & Dannefer, 1992). Thus, the processes implied by the theories may be operating for personality as well.

Complicating the issue of increasing individual differences later in life is the concept of terminal decline (Berg, 1996; Jarvik & Falek, 1963). This refers to the proposition that individual trait trajectories over time show relative stability throughout late adulthood until some period of time (2–5 years?) prior to death, at which point there is a notable decline. Again, the proposition has received considerable empirical support in the areas of physical and cognitive functioning (Bosworth, Schaie, & Willis, 1999; Johansson & Berg, 1989; Small & Backman, 1997), but it is less clear what form terminal decline might take for personality. Still, the concept deserves consideration in the study of personality, and its possible existence complicates the analysis of changes in both mean levels and amounts of variance with age. This is because there are clear individual differences in longevity and there are likely individual differences in the length of the period of terminal decline as well. Because it is never known in advance when any individual will die, it is difficult to assess whether any group-level changes observed in personality result from normative and dynamic developmental processes associated with age or from increasing proportions of the group entering terminal decline. Still, behavior genetic approaches to the study of personality changes with age can potentially offer unique and important insights into the nature of the underlying processes involved.

CONCLUSIONS: CONNECTING GENETICALLY INFORMATIVE METHODS WITH DEVELOPMENTAL QUESTIONS

Clearly, extensive evidence can be mustered to support the role of genetic factors in personality across the entire life course. Key questions now focus not on whether or not genes matter, but on understanding the way genes and environments work together to influence myriad aspects of personality development. Nevertheless, much of the statistical methodology of behavior genetics has been concerned with explaining individual differences at given points in time—with understanding how much of a trait can be traced to genetic and environmental sources of variance. Yet many key questions about genetic and environmental influences on personality development do not map easily onto the variance decomposition paradigm. The factors that influence individual difference at one time, or even at multiple points in time, are not necessarily the factors that influence *patterns of change* over time. Consider evidence reviewed earlier from longitudinal twin studies of personality. This evidence indicates that, to a large extent and for most traits studied, genetic effects on personality variance at different time points are entirely in common; the same genes influence personality at multiple points in time. This is a fundamental and important finding, but it also leads to other questions not easily addressed using the variance decomposition framework. For example, if personality traits have specific normative patterns of development (as has been suggested by e.g., McCrae et al., 2000), then what are the genetic and environmental influences on these patterns?

Some recent methodological developments may prove useful in addressing these kinds of developmental questions. Neale and McArdle (2000) described an extension of structured latent growth curve analysis to data from twins. Growth curves can be thought of in terms of three basic components (asymptote, initial level, and rate of growth) that describe change over time. The Neale and McArdle (2000) approach models genetic and environmental influences on each of these parameters, and thus, could be quite useful in understanding genetic and environmental influences on personality change over time. Applications and extensions of this approach were discussed in a special issue of *Behavior Genetics* devoted to linking issues in aging with behavior genetic approaches (Harris, 2003).

Other recent developments pertain to the gene–environment interface. Gene by environment interaction is a concept that has often seemed conceptually appealing, but application of the idea has been somewhat limited, due to limitations in the ability to model genetic and environmental variance in a specific phenotype as a continuous function of a separate moderating phenotype. This situation is changing, thanks to the development of sophisticated models and associated software that can tackle this modeling problem (see Purcell, 2002). As noted earlier, Kendler et al. (2003) applied this model to personality data, finding no evidence that dysfunction in the family of origin moderated the extent of genetic influence on neuroticism. Nevertheless, a plethora of personality traits and potential moderating variables remain to be investigated using this promising approach.

Understanding environmental influences that make children in the same family different (nonshared environments) is another important area for continued investigation. MZ twins reared together, who share both their childhood rearing environments and their genes, differ in their personalities. This important observation suggests an important role for the environment in shaping personality. Nevertheless, identifying the relevant environmental influences implicated by MZ twin differences has proven to be exceedingly difficult (Krueger et al., 2003; Turkheimer & Waldron, 2000). Yet some progress on this front has been made recently by Caspi et al. (2004). Caspi et al. (2004) found that differences in maternal expressed emotion at age 5 predicted differences between MZ twins' antisocial behavior at age 7. Whether or not such differences persist and adumbrate adult personality remains to be seen, but the technique of studying the effects of differences in environmental circumstances on MZ twins, thus controlling for genetic influences, should prove valuable in the search to identify specific nonshared environmental influences on personality development.

Another novel approach worthy of note is the children of twins design. By studying both twins and their offspring, it becomes possible to estimate direct effects of parental (twin) phenotypes on child phenotypes, controlling for both genetic and shared environmental reasons for such associations. For example, D'Onofrio et al. (2003) presented evidence that smoking during pregnancy has a direct environmental effect on birthweight, controlling for both potential genetic and shared environmental contributions to the association. With respect to personality, such designs might reveal whether or not, for example, authoritative parenting has a direct effect on the development of conscientiousness and achievement orientation in offspring. Finally, consider the molecular genetic research reported by Caspi et al. (2002, 2003) in the context of personality development. Their findings suggest that particular genes influence personality-related behaviors only in certain environmental circumstances. To the extent that this situation is common, it may help to explain the difficulties that have been experienced in replicating molecular genetic findings involving personality and other traits.

In sum, behavior genetic and developmental concerns can be integrated and newer methods and ideas in both quantitative and molecular genetics are already proving helpful in this endeavor. Integrative research requires both substantive expertise in formulating developmental questions and complementary expertise in developing genetically informative models that map onto developmental questions. The time seems right for these kinds of collaborative endeavors to flourish, because the field is moving beyond timeworn dichotomies between nature and nurture and between method and substance. This chapter has commented on a number of studies that have taken this approach, and hopefully there will be more in the near future.

REFERENCES

Achenbach, T. M. (1991). Manual for the Child Behavior Checklist/4—18 and 1991 profile. Burlington: University of Vermont, Department of Psychiatry.

Ahern, F. M., Johnson, R. C., Wilson, J. R., McClearn, G. E., & Vandenberg, S. G. (1982). Family resemblances in personality. Behavior Genetics, 12(3), 261–280.

Angleitner, A. (2002, July). Personality in adulthood: Findings from the Bielefeld Longitudinal Study of Adult Twins (BiLSAT). Presentation at the 11th European Conference on Personality, Jena, Germany.

Begun, A. Z., Iachine, I. A., & Yashin, A. I. (2000). Genetic nature of individual frailty: Comparison of two approaches. *Twin Research, 3,* 51–57.

Berg, S. (1996). Aging, behavior, and terminal decline. In J. E. Burres & K. W. Shaie (Eds.), *Handbook of the psychology of aging* (pp. 323–337). San Diego, CA: Academic Press.

Bergeman, C. S. (1997). *Aging: Genetic and environmental influences.* Thousand Oaks, CA: Sage.

Borkenau, P., Riemann, R., Angleitner, A., & Spinath, F. M. (2001). Genetic and environmental influences on observed personality: Evidence from the German Observational Study of Adult Twins. *Journal of Personality and Social Psychology, 80,* 655–668.

Bosworth, H. B., Schaie, K. W., & Willis, S. L. (1999). Cognitive and sociodemographic risk factors for mortality in the Seattle Longitudinal Study. *Journal of Gerontological, Biological, Psychological Sciences and Social Sciences, 54,* P273–P282.

Bouchard, T. J. (1997). The genetics of personality. In K. Blum & E. P. Noble (Eds.), *Handbook of psychiatric genetics* (pp. 273–296). Boca Raton, FL: CRC Press.

Bouchard, T. J., & Loehlin, J. C. (2001). Genes, evolution, and personality. *Behavior Genetics, 31*(3), 243–273.

Bouchard, T. J., McGue, M., Hur, Y.-M., & Horn, J. M. (1998). A genetic and environmental analysis of the California Psychological Inventory using adult twins reared apart and together. *European Journal of Personality, 12,* 307–320.

Brody, N. (1993). Intelligence and the behavioral genetics of personality. In R. Plomin & G. E. McClearn (Eds.), *Nature, nurture, and psychology* (pp. 161–178). Washington, DC: American Psychological Association.

Burbach, D. J., & Borduin, C. M. (1986). Parent–child relations and the etiology of depression: A review of methods and findings. *Clinical Psychology Review, 6,* 133–153.

Buss, D. M., Haselton, M. G., Shackleford, T. K., Bleske, A. L., & Wakefield, J. C. (1999). Interactionism, flexibility, and inferences about the past. *Annual Review of Psychology, 53,* 533–548.

Buss, A. H., & Plomin, R. (1984). *Temperament: Early developing personality traits.* Hillsdale, NJ: Lawrence Erlbaum Associates.

Cadoret, R. J., Yates, W. R., Troughton, E., Woodworth, G., & Stewart, M. A. (1995). Gene-environment interaction in genesis of aggressivity and conduct disorders. *Archives of General Psychiatry, 103,* 103–111.

Campisi, J. (2001). From cells to organisms: Can we learn about aging from cells in culture? *Experimental Gerontology, 36,* 607–618.

Carey, G., & DiLalla, D. L. (1994). Personality and psychopathology: Genetic perspectives. *Journal of Abnormal Psychology, 103,* 32–43.

Carmichael, C. M. (1993). A cross-sectional examination of twin similarity in personality during adulthood. *Dissertation Abstracts, International, 54*(6-B), 3358. (UMI No.)

Caspi, A. (1998). Personality development across the life course. In W. Damon and N. Eisenberg (Eds.), *Handbook of child psychology: Vol. 3. Social, emotional, and personality development* (pp. 311–388). New York: Wiley.

Caspi, A., Harrington, H., Milne, B., Amell, J. W., Theodore, R. F., & Moffitt, T. E. (2003a). Children's behavioral styles at age 3 are linked to their adult personality traits at age 26. *Journal of Personality, 71,* 495–513.

Caspi, A., Herbener, E. S., & Ozer, D. J. (1992). Shared experiences and the similarity of personalities: A longitudinal study of married couples. *Journal of Personality and Social Psychology, 62,* 281–291.

Caspi, A., McClay, J., Moffitt, T. E., Mill, J., Martin, J., Craig, I. W., Taylor, A., & Poulton, R. (2002). Role of genotype in the cycle of violence in maltreated children. *Science, 297,* 851.

Caspi, A., Moffitt, T. E., Morgan, J., Rutter, M., Taylor, A., et al. (2004). Maternal expressed emotion predicts children's antisocial behavior problems: Using monozygotic-twin differences to identify environmental effects on behavioral development. *Developmental Psychology, 40,* 149–161.

Caspi, A., & Roberts, B. W. (2001). Personality development across the life course: The argument for change and continuity. *Psychological Inquiry, 12*(2), 49–66.

Caspi, A., Sugden, K., Moffitt, T. E., Taylor, A., Craig, I. W., Harrington, H., McClay, J., Mill, J., Martin, J., Braithwaite, A., & Poulton, R. (2003b). Influence of life stress on depression: Moderation by a polymorphism in the 5-HTT gene. *Science, 301,* 386–389.

Charlewood, B., & Hughes, K. A. (1996). Age-specific inbreeding depression and components of genetic variance in relation to the evolution of senescence. *Proceedings of the National Academy of Sciences, USA, 93,* 6140–6145.

Cloninger, C. R. (1986). A unified biosocial theory of personality and its role in the development of anxiety states. *Psychiatric Developments, 3,* 167–226.

Cloninger, C. R. (1987a). A systematic method for clinical description and classification of personality variants. *Archives of General Psychiatry, 44,* 573–588.

Cloninger, C. R. (1987b). *The Tridimensional Personality Questionnaire, Version 4.* St. Louis, MO: Washington University School of Medicine.

Cloninger, C. R., Adolfsson, R., & Svrakic, N. M. (1996). Mapping genes for human personality. *Nature Genetics, 12,* 3–4.

Cloninger, C. R., Van Eerdewegh, P., Goate, A., Edemberg, H. J., Blangero, J., et al. (1998). Anxiety proneness linked to epistatic loci in genome scan of human personality traits. *American Journal of Medical Genetics (Neuropsychiactric Genetics), 81,* 313–317.

Crawford, C. B., & DeFries, J. C. (1978). Factor analysis of genetic and environmental correlation matrices. *Multivariate Behavioral Research, 13,* 297–318.

Cyphers, L. H., Phillips, K., Fulker, D. W., & Mrazek, D. A. (1990). Twin temperament during the transition from infancy to early childhood. *Journal of the American Academy of Child and Adolescent Psychiatry, 29,* 392–397.

D'Onofrio, B. M., Turkheimer, E. N., Eaves, L. J., Corey, L. A., Berg, K., et al. (2003). The role of the Children of Twins design in elucidating causal relations between parent characteristics and child outcomes. *Journal of Child Psychology and Psychiatry, 44,* 1130–1144.

Eagly, A. H., & Wood, W. (1999). The origins of sex differences in human behavior: Evolved dispositions versus social roles. *American Psychologist, 54,* 408–423.

Eaves, L. J., Eysenck, H. J., & Martin, N. G. (1989). *Genes, culture, and personality: An empirical approach.* New York: Academic Press.

Eaves, L. J., Heath, A. C., Martin, N., Maes, H., Neale, M., Kendler, K., Kirk, K., & Corey, L. (1999). Comparing the biological and cultural inheritance of personality and social attitudes in the Virginia 30,000 study of twins and their relatives. *Twin Research, 2,* 62–80.

Eaves, L. J., Heath, A. C., Neale, M. C., Hewitt, J. K., & Martin, N. G. (1998). Sex differences and nonadditivity in the effects of genes on personality. *Twin Research, 1,* 131–137.

Emde, R. N., Plomin, R., Robinson, J., Corley, R., DeFries, J., Fulker, D. W., Reznick, J. S., Campos, J., Kagan, J., & Zahn-Waxler, C. (1992). Temperament, emotion, and cognition at fourteen months: The MacArthur Longitudinal Twin Study. *Child Development, 63,* 1437–1455.

Epstein, E., & Guttman, R. (1984). Mate selection in man: Evidence, theory, and outcome. *Social Biology, 31,* 243–278.

Eysenck, H. J., & Eysenck, M. W. (1985). *Personality and individual differences: A natural science approach.* New York: Plenum.

Finkel, D., & McGue, M. (1997). Sex differences and nonadditivity in heritability of the Multidimensional Personality Questionnaire scales. *Journal of Personality and Social Psychology, 72,* 929–938.

Floderus-Myrhed, B., Pederson, N., & Rasmuson, I. (1980). Assessment of heritability for personality, based on a short-form of the Eysenck Personality Inventory: A study of 12,898 twin pairs. *Behavior Genetics, 10*(2), 153–162.

Flory, J. D., Manuck, S. B., Ferrell, R. E., Dent, K. M., Peters, D. G., & Muldoon, M. F. (1999). Neuroticism is not associated with the serotonin transponder (5-HTTLPR) polymorphism. *Molecular Psychiatry, 4,* 93–96.

Gjone, H., & Stevenson, J. (1997). A longitudinal twin study of temperament and behavior problems: Common genetic or environmental influences? *Journal of the American Academy of Child and Adolescent Psychiatry, 36*(10), 1448–1456.

Goldsmith, H. H. (1993). Nature–nurture issues in the behavioral genetic context: Overcoming barriers to communication. In R. Plomin & G. McClearn (Eds.), *Nature, nurture, and psychology* (pp. 325–339). Washington, DC: American Psychological Association.

Goldsmith, H. H., Buss, K. A., & Lemery, K. S. (1997). Toddler and childhood temperament: Expanded content, stronger genetic evidence, new evidence for the importance of environment. *Developmental Psychology, 33*, 891–905.

Goldsmith, H. H., Buss, A. H., Plomin, R., Rothbart, M. K., Thomas, A., et al. (1987). What is temperament? Four approaches. *Child Development, 58*, 505–529.

Goldsmith, H. H., & Lemery, K. S. (2000). Linking temperamental fearfulness and anxiety symptoms: A behavior–genetic perspective. *Biological Psychiatry, 48*, 1199–1209.

Goldsmith, H. H., Lemery, K. S., Buss, K. A., & Campos, J. J. (1999). Genetic analyses of focal aspects of infant temperament. *Developmental Psychology, 35*, 972–985.

Gough, H. G. (1975). *Manual for the California Psychological Inventory* (Rev. ed.). Palo Alto, CA: Consulting Psychologists Press.

Harris, J. R. (2003). Introduction to special issue on aging. *Behavior Genetics, 33*, 79–82.

Hartman, M., Bolton, E., & Fehnel, S. E. (2001). Accounting for age differences on the Wisconsin Card Sorting Test: Decreased working memory, not inflexibility. *Psychology and Aging, 16*, 385–399.

Heath, A. C., Eaves, L. J., & Martin, N. G. (1989). The genetic structure of personality III. Multivariate genetic item analysis of the EPQ scales. *Personality and Individual Differences, 10*, 877–888.

Heath, A. C., Jardine, R. Eaves, L. J., & Martin, N. G. (1989). The genetic structure of personality II. Genetic Item Analysis of the EPQ. *Personality and Individual Differences, 10*(6), 615–624.

Heath, A. C., Madden, P. A., Cloninger, C. R., & Martin, N. G. (1999). Genetic and environmental structure of personality. In C. R. Cloninger (Ed.), *Personality and psychopathology* (pp. 343–367). Washington, DC: American Psychological Association.

Heath, A. C., Neale, M. C., Kessler, R. C., Eaves, L. J., & Kendler, K. S. (1992). Evidence for genetic influence on personality from self-reports and informant ratings. *Journal of Personality and Social Psychology, 63*(1), 85–96.

Heiman, N., Stallings, M. C., Hofer, S. M. & Hewitt, J. K. (2003). Investigating age differences in the genetic and environmental structure of the tridimensional personality questionnaire in later adulthood. *Behavior Genetics, 33*, 171–180.

Helson, R., Kwan, V. S. Y., John, O. P, & Jones, C. (2002). The growing evidence for personality change in adulthood: Findings from research with personality inventories. *Journal of Research in Personality, 36*, 287–306.

Hofer, S. M., Christensen, H., Mackinnon, A. J., Korten, A. E., Jorm, A. F., Henderson, A. S., & Easteal, S. (2002). Change in cognitive functioning associated with ApoE genotype in a community sample of older adults. *Psychology and Aging, 17*, 194–208.

Jang, K. L., Livesley, W. J., Angleitner, A., Riemann, R., & Vernon, P. A. (2002). Genetic and environmental influences on the covariance of facets defining the domains of the five-factor model of personality. *Personality and Individual Differences, 33*, 83–101.

Jang, K. L., McCrae, R. R., Angleitner, A., & Riemann, R. (1998). Heritability of facet-level traits in a cross-cultural twin sample: Support for a hierarchical model of personality. *Journal of Personality and Social Psychology, 74*, 1556–1656.

Jarvik, L. F., & Falek, A. (1963). Intellectual stability and survival in the aged. *Journal of Gerontology, 18*, 173–176.

Jensen, A. R. (1978). Genetic and behavioral effects of non-random mating. In C. E. Noble, R. T., Osborne, & N. Weyle, N. (Eds.), *Human variation: Biogenetics of age, race, and sex* (pp. 51–105). San Diego, CA: Academic Press.

Johansson, B., & Berg, S. (1989). The robustness of the terminal decline phenomenon: Longitudinal data from the digit-span memory test. *Journal of Gerontological and Psychological Science, 44*, P184–P186.

Johnson, W. J., & Krueger, R. F. (2004). Genetic and environmental structure of adjectives describing the domains of the Big Five Model of Personality: A nationwide US twin study. *Journal of Research in Personality, 38*, 448–472.

Johnson, W. J., Krueger, R. F., & McGue, M. (2005). Personality stability in late adulthood: A behavioral genetic analysis. *Journal of Personality, 73,* 523–551

Kendler, K. S., Aggen, S. H., Jacobson, K. C., & Neale, M. C. (2003). Does the level of family dysfunction moderate the impact of genetic factors on the personality trait of neuroticism? *Psychological Medicine, 33,* 817–825.

Krueger, R. F. (2000). Phenotypic, genetic, and nonshared environmental parallels in the structure of personality: A view from the Multidimensional Personality Questionnaire. *Journal of Personality and Social Psychology, 79,* 1057–1067.

Krueger, R. F., Caspi, A., & Moffitt, T. E. (2000). Epidemiological personology: The unifying role of personality in population-based research on problem behaviors. *Journal of Personality, 68,* 967–998.

Krueger, R. F., Hicks, B. M., & McGue, M. (2001). Altruism and antisocial behavior: Independent tendencies, unique personality correlates, distinct ideologies. *Psychological Science, 12,* 397–402.

Krueger, R. F., & Markon, K. E. (2002). Behavior genetic perspectives on clinical personality assessment. In J. N. Butcher (Ed.), *Clinical personality assessment: Practical approaches* (2nd ed., pp. 40–55). New York: Oxford University Press.

Krueger, R. F., Markon, K. E., & Bouchard, T. J., (2003). The extended genotype: The heritability of personality accounts for the heritability of recalled family environments in twins reared apart. *Journal of Personality, 71,* 809–834.

Lake, R. E. I., Eaves, L. J., Maes, H. H. M., Heath, A. C., & Martin, N. G. (2000). Further evidence against the environmental transmission of individual differences in neuroticism from a collaborative study of 45,850 twins and relatives on two continents. *Behavior Genetics, 30*(3), 223–233.

Lesch, K. P., Bengel, D., Heils, A., et al. (1996). Association of anxiety-related traits with a polymorphism in the serotonin transporter gene regulatory region. *Science, 274,* 1527–1531.

Loehlin, J. C. (1987). Heredity, environment, and the structure of the California Psychological Inventory. *Multivariate Behavioral Research, 22,* 137–148.

Loehlin, J. C. (1992). *Genes and environment in personality development.* Newbury Park, CA: Sage.

Loehlin, J. C., & Martin, N. G. (2001). Age changes in personality traits and their heritabilities during the adult years: Evidence from Australian twin registry samples. *Personality and Individual Differences, 30,* 1147–1160.

Loehlin, J. C., Neiderhiser, J. M., & Reiss, D. (2003). The behavior genetics of personality and the NEAD study. *Journal of Research in Personality, 37,* 373–387.

Loehlin, J. C., & Nichols, R. C. (1976). *Heredity, environment, and personality.* Austin, TX: University of Texas Press.

Loehlin, J. C., Spurdle, A., Treloar, S. A., & Martin, N. G. (1999). Number of X-linked androgen receptor gene CAG repeats and femininity in women. *Personality and Individual Differences, 27,* 887–899.

Lykken, D. T., & Tellegen, A. (1993). Is human mating adventitious or the result of lawful choice? A twin study of mate selection. *Journal of Personality and Social Psychology, 65,* 56–68.

Matheny, A. P., Jr. (1989). Children's behavioral inhibition over age and across situations: Genetic similarity for a trait during change. *Journal of Personality, 57,* 215–235.

McCartney, K., Harris, M. J., & Bernieri, F. (1990). Growing up and growing apart: A developmental meta-analysis of twin studies. *Psychological Bulletin, 107,* 226–237.

McCrae, R. R., Costa, P. T., Ostendorf, F., Angleitner, A., Hřebíčová, M., Avia, M. D., et al. (2000). Nature over nurture: Temperament, personality, and life span development. *Journal of Personality and Social Psychology, 78,* 173–186.

McCrae, R. R., Jang, K. L., Livesley, W. J., Riemann, R., & Angleitner, A. (2001). Sources of structure: Genetic, environmental, and artifactual influences on the covariation of personality traits. *Journal of Personality, 69,* 511–535.

McGue, M., Bacon, S., & Lykken, D. T. (1993). Personality stability and change in early adulthood: A behavioral genetic analysis. *Developmental Psychology, 29,* 96–109.

Mealey, L. R. (2000). *Sex differences: Developmental and evolutionary strategies*. New York: Academic Press.

Mroczek, D. K., & Spiro, A. (2003). Modeling intraindividual change in personality traits: Findings from the Normative Aging Study. *Journal of Gerontology: Psychological Sciences, 58B,* 153–165.

Neale, M. C., & McArdle, J. J. (2000). Structured latent growth curves for twin data. *Twin Research, 3,* 165–177.

Neale, M. C., & Stevenson, J. (1989). Rater bias in the EASI temperament scales: A twin study: Erratum. *Journal of Personality and Social Psychology, 56,* 845.

Nelson, E. A., & Dannefer, D. (1992). Aged heterogeneity: Fact or fiction? The fate of diversity in gerontological research. *Gerontologist, 32*(1), 17–23.

O'Connor, T. G., Hetherington, E. M., Reiss, D., & Plomin, R. (1995). A twin-sibling study of observed parent–adolescent interactions. *Child Development, 66,* 812–829.

Park, D. C., Lautenschlager, G., Hedden, T., Davidson, N. S., Smith, A. D., & Smith, P. K. (2002). Models of visuospatial and verbal memory across the adult life span. *Psychology and Aging, 17,* 299–320.

Parker, G. (1990). The parental bonding instrument: A decade of research. *British Journal of Medical Psychology, 52,* 1–10.

Pedersen, N. L. (1993). Genetic and environmental continuity and change in personality. In T. J. Bouchard, Jr. & P. Propping (Eds.), *Twins as a tool of behavior genetics* (pp. 147–162). New York: Wiley.

Pedersen, N. L., Plomin, R., McClearn, G. E., & Friberg, L. (1998). Neuroticism, extraversion and related traits in adult twins reared apart and reared together. *Journal of Personality and Social Psychology, 55,* 950–957.

Pedersen, N. L., & Reynolds, C. A. (1998). Stability and change in adult personality: Genetic and environmental components. *European Journal of Personality, 12,* 365–386.

Pedersen, N. L., & Reynolds, C. A. (2002). Stability and change in adult personality: Genetic and environmental components. *European Journal of Personality, 16,* 77–78.

Pike, A., McGuire, S., Hetherington, E. M., Reiss, D., & Plomin, R. (1996). Using MZ differences in the search for nonshared environmental effects. *Journal of Child Psychology and Psychiatry, 37,* 695–704.

Plomin, R. (1994). The Emanuel Miller Memorial Lecture, 1993: Genetic research and identification of environmental influences. *Journal of Child Psychology and Psychiatry, 35,* 817–834.

Plomin, R., & Caspi, A. (1998). DNA and personality. *European Journal of Personality, 12,* 387–407.

Plomin, R., Coon, H., Carey, G., DeFries, J. C., & Fulker, D. W. (1991). Parent-offspring and sibling adoption analyses of parental ratings of temperament in infancy and childhood. *Journal of Personality, 59,* 705–732.

Plomin, R., Corley, R., Caspi, A., Fulker, D. W., & DeFries, J. (1998). Adoption results for self-reported personality: Evidence for nonadditive genetic effects? *Journal of Personality and Social Psychology, 75,* 211–218.

Plomin, R., DeFries, J. C., McClearn, G. E., & Rutter, M. (1997). *Behavioral genetics* (3rd ed.). New York: Freeman.

Plomin, R., Emde, R. N., Braungart, J. M., Campos, J., Corley, R., Fulker, D. W., Kagan, J., Reznick, J. S., Robinson, J., Zahn-Waxler, C., & DeFries, J. C. (1993). Genetic change and continuity from fourteen to twenty months: The MacArthur Longitudinal Twin Study. *Child Development, 64,* 1354–1376.

Plomin, R., McClearn, G. E., Pedersen, N. L., Nesselroade, J. R., & Bergeman, C. S. (1988). Genetic influence on childhood family environment perceived retrospectively from the last half of the linesman. *Developmental Psychology, 24,* 738–745.

Plomin, R., Loehlin, J. C., & DeFries, J. C. (1985). Genetic and environmental components of "environmental" influences. *Development Psychology, 21,* 391–402.

Purcell, S. (2002). Variance component models for gene–environment interaction in twin analysis. *Twin Research, 5,* 554–571.

Reiss, D., Neiderhiser, J., Hetherington, E. M., & Plomin, R. (2000). *The relationship code: Deciphering genetic and social influence on adolescent development*. Cambridge, MA: Harvard University Press.

Riemann, R., Angleitner, A., & Strelau, J. (1997). Genetic and environmental influences on personality: A study of twins reared together using the self- and peer report NEO–FFI scales. *Journal of Personality, 65*, 449–475.

Riese, M. L. (1990). Neonatal temperament in monozygotic and dizygotic twin pairs. *Child Development, 61*, 1230–1237.

Riggins-Caspers, K. M., Cadoret, R. J., Knutson, J. F., & Langbehn, D. (2003). Biology–environment correlation: Contributions of harsh discipline and parental psychopathy to problem adolescent behaviors. *Behavior Genetics, 33*, 205–220.

Roberts, B. W., & DelVecchio, W. F. (2000). The rank-order consistency of personality traits from childhood to old age: A quantitative review of longitudinal studies. *Psychological Bulletin, 126*, 3–25.

Robinson, J. L., Emde, R. N., & Corley, R. P. (2001). Dispositional cheerfulness: Early genetic and environmental influences. In R. N. Emde & J. K. Hewitt (Eds.), *Infancy to early childhood: Genetic and environmental influences on developmental change* (pp. 163–177). New York: Oxford University Press.

Rothbart, M. K. (1981). Measurement of temperament in infancy. *Child Development, 52*, 569–578.

Saudino, K. J. (1997). Moving beyond the heritability question: New directions in behavior genetic studies of personality. *Current Directions in Psychological Science, 6*, 86–90.

Saudino, K. J. (2002). Parent ratings of infant temperament: Lessons from twin studies. *Infant Behavior and Development, 26*, 100–107.

Saudino, K. J., & Cherny, S. S. (2001). Sources of continuity and change in observed temperament. In R. N. Emde & J. K. Hewitt (Eds.), *Infancy to early childhood: Genetic and environmental influences on developmental change* (pp. 89–110). New York: Oxford University Press.

Saudino, K. J., & Eaton, W. O. (1991). Infant temperament and genetics: An objective twin study of motor activity level. *Child Development, 62*, 1167–1174.

Saudino, K. J., & Eaton, W. O. (1995). Continuity and change in objectively assessed temperament: A longitudinal twin study of activity level. *British Journal of Development Psychology, 13*(1), 81–95.

Saudino, K. J., McGuire, S., Reiss, D., Hetherington, E. M., & Plomin, R. (1995). Parent ratings of EAS temperaments in twins, full siblings, half siblings, and step siblings. *Journal of Personality and Social Psychology, 68*, 723–733.

Saudino, K. J., & Plomin, R. (1997). Cognitive and temperamental mediators of genetic contributions to the home environment during infancy. *Merrill-Palmer Quarterly, 43*(1), 1–23.

Saudino, K. J., Plomin, R., & DeFries, J. C. (1996). Tester-rated temperament at 14, 20 and 24 months: Environmental change and genetic continuity. *British Journal of Developmental Psychology, 14*, 129–144.

Schmidt, L. A., Fox, N. A., Rubin, K. H., Hu, S., & Hamer, D. H. (2002). Molecular genetics of shyness and aggression in preschoolers. *Personality and Individual Differences, 33*, 227–238.

Schmitz, S., Fulker, D. W., Plomin, R., Zahn-Waxler, C., Emde, R. N., et al. (1999). Temperament and problem behavior during early childhood. *International Journal of Behavioral Development, 23*(2), 333–355.

Schmitz, S., Saudino, K. J., Plomin, R., Fulker, D. W., & DeFries, J. C. (1996). Genetic and environmental influences on temperament in middle childhood: Analyses of teacher and tester ratings. *Child Development, 67*, 409–422.

Sherman, S. L., DeFries, J. C., Gottesman, I. I., Loehlin, J. C., Meyer, J. M., Pelias, M. Z., Rice, J., & Waldman, I. D. (1997). Recent developments in human behavioral genetics: Past accomplishments and future directions. *American Journal of Human Genetics, 60*, 1265–1275.

Small, B. J., & Backman, L. (1997). Cognitive correlates of mortality: Evidence from a population-based sample of very old adults. *Psychology and Aging, 12*, 309–313.

Small, B. J., Hertzog, C., Hultsch, D. F., & Dixon, R. A. (2003). Stability and change in adult personality over 6 years: Findings from the Victoria Longitudinal Study. *Journal of Gerontology: Psychological Sciences, 58B,* 166–176.

Spinath, F. M., & Angleitner, A. (1998). Contrast effects in Buss and Plomin's EAS questionnaire: A behavioral genetic study on early developing personality traits assessed through parental ratings. *Personality and Individual Differences, 25,* 947–963.

Srivastava, S., John, O. P., Gosling, S. D., & Potter, J. (2003). Development of personality in early and middle adulthood: Set like plaster or persistent change? *Journal of Personality and Social Psychology, 84,* 1041–1053.

Stallings, M. C., Hewitt, J. K., Cloninger, C. R., Heath, A. C., & Eaves, L. J. (1996). Genetic and environmental structure of the tridimensional personality questionnaire: Three or four temperament dimensions? *Journal of Personality and Social Psychology, 70,* 127–140.

Stevenson, J., & Fielding, J. (1985). Ratings of temperament in families of young twins. *British Journal of Developmental Psychology, 3,* 143–152.

Tellegen, A. (1982). *Brief manual for the Differential Personality Questionnaire.* Unpublished manuscript, Minneapolis, MN.

Tellegen, A., Lykken, D. T., Bouchard, T. J., Wilcox, K. J., Segal, N. L., & Rich, S. (1988). Personality similarity in twins reared apart and together. *Journal of Personality and Social Psychology, 6,* 1031–1039.

Turkheimer, E. (1999, June). *Will the real nonshared environment please stand up?* Paper presented at the meeting of the American Psychological Association, Denver, CO.

Turkheimer, E., & Waldron, M. (2000). Nonshared environment: A theoretical, methodological, and quantitative review. *Psychological Bulletin, 126,* 78–108.

Vernon, P. A., Jang, K. L., Harris, J. A., & McCarthy, J. M. (1997). Environmental predictors of personality differences: A twin and sibling study. *Journal of Personality and Social Psychology, 72,* 177–183.

Viken, R. J., Rose, R. J., Kaprio, J., & Koskenvuo, M. (1994). A developmental genetic analysis of adult personality: Extraversion and neuroticism from 18 to 59 years of age. *Journal of Personality and Social Psychology, 66,* 722–730.

Waller, N. G., Kojetin, B. A., Bouchard, T. J., Lykken, D. T., & Tellegen, A. (1990). Genetic and environmental influences on religious interests, attitudes, and values: A study of twins reared apart and together. *Psychological Science, 1,* 138–142.

Wilson, R. S., Beckett, L. A, Barnes, L. L. Schneider, J. A., Bach, J., Evans, D. A., & Bennett, D. A. (2002). Individual differences in rates of change in cognitive abilities of older persons. *Psychology and Aging, 17,* 179–193.

6

The Structure of Personality and Temperament

Gerard Saucier
Jennifer Simonds
University of Oregon

In this chapter we review progress on an important scientific issue—how attributes of personality and temperament can best be organized and structured. After explaining the rationale for doing so, we will discuss some insights that have been gained from studies of person descriptors in diverse languages. We discuss the degree to which one prominent structural model—the Big Five—is indeed an ideal model, and what other structural models are most complementary to this one in terms of strengths. Because inquiries into the structure of attributes depend significantly on how personality and temperament are defined, we begin there.

DEFINING "PERSONALITY" AND "TEMPERAMENT"

For Funder (2001), personality is "an individual's characteristic patterns of thought, emotion, and behavior, together with the psychological mechanisms—hidden or not—behind those patterns" (p. 2). Funder referred simultaneously to characteristics that are ascribed to individuals, stable over time, and psychological in nature. But this is not the only way to define personality. Allport (1937) reviewed definitions of the concept of personality. He catalogued 50 distinct meanings. The definition he proposed was a synthesis of several of the psychological meanings of concept: "Personality is the dynamic organization within the individual of those psychophysical systems that determine his unique adjustments to his environment" (p. 48).

Definitions make assumptions explicit. The way personality is defined is quite consequential: It affects how variables are selected when studying personality phenomena. Allport's definition highlights attributes that are seen as residing "within" the individual. Other ways of defining personality emphasize more external types of attributes, such as the role individuals assume or the status they have achieved in society, their external appearance (including their attractiveness), and the reactions of others to the individuals as a stimulus (i.e., their social stimulus value; see MacKinnon, 1944). Later, we will explore some structural models for personality that include rather than exclude such externally defined attributes.

"Temperament" has usually been defined more narrowly than personality. Allport (1937) defined temperament with reference to "the characteristic phenomena of an individual's emotional nature, including his susceptibility to emotional stimulation, his customary strength and speed of response, the quality of his prevailing mood, and all peculiarities of fluctuation and intensity of mood; these phenomena being regarded as dependent on constitutional makeup and therefore largely hereditary in origin" (p. 54). Some modern theories have retained Allport's emphasis on and limitation to emotional reactivity and activity in their conceptualization of temperament (Goldsmith & Campos, 1982, 1986). However, early influential temperament research emphasized the idea of behavioral "styles" (Thomas, Chess, Birch, Hertzig, & Korn, 1963). Later, Buss and Plomin (1984) placed emphasis on genetics, defining temperament as "inherited personality traits present in early childhood" (p. 84). Rothbart and Bates (1998) took a psychobiological approach, defining temperament as "constitutionally-based individual differences in emotional, motor, and attentional reactivity and self-regulation" (p. 109).

Disagreements about definitions of temperament surround the issue of whether temperament is a purely affective construct, or whether systems related to cognition may be included in the traits that make up the structure of temperament (Goldsmith & Campos, 1982), and on issues regarding the relative influence of biological processes on temperamental variables (Goldsmith, et al., 1987). But virtually all definitions of temperament focus on basic dispositions that underlie and modulate the expression of reactivity, physical activity, emotionality, and sociability; dispositions that are present early in life and influenced, directly or indirectly, by biological factors; and traits that are subject to change due to environment and maturation (McCall in Goldsmith et al., 1987).

The previous review indicates that temperament is a less broad concept than personality. Although aspects of behavior, thought, and affect are widely acknowledged to be reflected in temperament, the emphasis has more often been on the affective elements, and on biologically based traits. There are few recent conceptualizations of temperament that make reference to physique or external appearance.

PARSIMONY IN PERSONALITY MODELS

A survey of the scales in current personality inventories finds scale labels for a bewildering variety of constructs. And if single words potentially referring to personality attributes in modern world languages are the focus, then the situation becomes simply overwhelming: Allport and Odbert (1936), for example, catalogued nearly 18,000 words from *Webster's Second International Dictionary* referring to characteristics that might be used to distinguish one human being from another. There needs to be a more parsimonious summary of this vast domain of concepts.

In the field of personality, there has been a rising wave of interest in the search for a scientifically compelling taxonomy of the huge number of personality attributes. A taxonomy chunks things, systematically dividing phenomena into ordered groups or categories; in other words, it is a way of "chunking" things. A scientific taxonomy helps organize and integrate knowledge and research findings by providing a standard scientific nomenclature, which facilitates communication and aids in the accumulation of empirical findings.

In taxonomy construction, a variety of procedures might be used to divide (or group) the phenomena under study. The most useful is a class of statistical methods generically referred to as "factor analysis." As noted by Goldberg and Digman (1994), factor analysis can be considered as a variable-reduction procedure, in which many variables are organized by a few factors that summarize the interrelations among the variables.

WHAT MAKES A STRUCTURAL MODEL GOOD?

However, prior to employing factor analysis, one must make a crucial determination—which variables to include in the analysis. One cannot find a dimension or factor without including a domain of variables relevant to it. Variable selection is inevitably guided by the investigator's beliefs about what makes a structural model good. These beliefs involve criteria that can be applied both to variables and factors formed from variables, and tend to focus on criteria from among the following eight alternatives:

1. *Social importance* of the variables or factors, that is, whether they are "shown to interact powerfully with social activities widely regarded as important" (Eysenck, 1991, p. 785).
2. *Comprehensiveness* of the variables or factors (taken as a whole), so that they cover "a wide field, and [are] not restricted to a narrow segment of personality research" (Eysenck, 1991, p. 774).
3. *Reliability and cross-time stability* of the variables or factors. This criterion is important for personality characteristics because they are expected to be relatively consistent across time. However, it is possible that traits themselves have more stability over time than do the correlations between, and thus the structures of, those traits.
4. *Predictive power and validity* of the variables or the factors they form. This criterion is related to social importance, but relies more heavily on specific practical contexts in which personality measures have wide application.
5. *Generalizability across types of data* that one finds for the variables or factors. For example, there should be less interest in a variable or factor found only in self-report data, than in one found to be important also in ratings by knowledgeable others, or in observer data.
6. *Generalizability across cultures and languages* that one finds for the variables or factors. This criterion has often been termed "universality"(Costa & McCrae, 1992, p. 653), or independence of "national, racial and cultural differences" (Eysenck, 1991, p. 784).
7. *Biological or other causal basis* established for the variables or factors. Personality characteristics are known to be moderately heritable (Bouchard, 1994), and heritability indicates biological influences. Therefore, biological bases are prime candidates, but not the only candidates, for important causal factors.
8. *A theory*, plausible and logically consistent, related to personality functioning or dynamics, that is linked to the model. Such a theory might enable researchers fruitfully to derive testable deductions and hypotheses to explain known

phenomena and predict phenomena that are not yet known, without contradicting well-established findings (cf. Eysenck, 1991, p. 774).

Developers of personality measures have long used a wide variety of criteria and combinations of criteria for variable selection. Because of the diversity of criteria employed, the long tradition of packaging structural models into multiscale personality inventories led to little agreement on the most important variables of personality. As of two decades ago, the literature on the structure of personality characteristics was a maelstrom of competing inventories, mostly proprietary, embedded in a mass of mutually isolated research measures. More order has been brought to the field by the lexical approach. This approach, although not perfectly combining or even involving all relevant criteria, has enabled the simultaneous application of most of the major criteria for the goodness of a structural model.

THE BASIS FOR THE LEXICAL APPROACH

Researchers have long recognized (e.g., Allport, 1937; Cattell, 1943; Goldberg, 1981; Norman, 1963) that some of the most basic personality attributes might be discovered from studying conceptions implicit in use of the natural language. If a distinction is highly represented in the lexicon, then it can be presumed to have practical importance. Folk concepts of personality (Tellegen, 1993) provide basic but not exhaustive (necessary but not sufficient) components for a science of personality attributes (Goldberg & Saucier, 1995).

This leads to a key premise of the lexical approach to taxonomy construction: The degree of representation of an attribute in language has some correspondence with the general importance of the attribute in real-world transactions. This premise links semantic representation directly with the *social importance criterion*.

An attribute represented by multiple terms in a language will likely appear as a factor in multivariate analyses. Moreover, if the factor includes terms used with high frequency, then the importance of the factor is underscored. Such factors are but a "starting point" because the lexicon could omit or underemphasize some scientifically important variables, and the meaning of single natural language terms can be vague, ambiguous, or context-dependent (John, Angleitner, & Ostendorf, 1988).

Many variables, and potential factors, might have rich semantic representation and thus satisfy a social importance criterion, so this should not be the sole criterion. Other criteria from among the eight might be fruitfully applied. In the lexical study paradigm, one particular additional criterion has taken on special importance, probably because it is the most demanding and therefore the most potentially efficient in rapidly reducing the field of candidates.

The *cross-cultural generalizability criterion* can adjudicate among competitor taxonomic structures. Structural models derived within one limited population, or a limited sample from that population, are prone to reflect the unique patternings found within that population or sample. Culture-specific patternings may be interesting in their own way. But models that transfer well across populations, and thus across languages and sociocultural settings, are more congruent with the scientific ideals of replicability and generalizability.

If cross-cultural generalizability is taken as a criterion for a good taxonomic structure, it can be applied in either a lenient or a stringent way. The lenient way is to export a set of variables (most often, those represented in a single personality inventory) for use in other populations, and then examine whether or not these preselected variables (after translation, if necessary) generate the same factor structure in each new language or culture. If the scales in a personality inventory generate similar factors across populations, it might be argued (McCrae & Costa, 1997) that the structure is widely generalizable. However, this is not a very challenging test. It shows only that when personality measures in a new language are made to conform to the Procrustean specifications of one model, that model can be recovered. A large number of models may be equally exportable and maintain their factor structures across many populations.

A more challenging test is to identify the most salient and important personality concepts within each linguistic/cultural context, derive an indigenous factor structure from those variables, and then examine the extent to which this new structure corresponds to any previously proposed models. A model that could meet this test in any language could be considered far more ubiquitous and universal than a structure that simply met the less demanding imposed test (i.e., showed a high degree of translatability).

The lexical approach involves such an indigenous research strategy. Analyses are carried out separately within each language, using a representative set of native language descriptors, rather than importing selections of variables from other languages (e.g., English). Generally, factors identified by the lexical approach have fared well with respect to the first six criteria, generating a relatively comprehensive set of socially important personality constructs that evidence consistency across time, good predictive validity, and generalizability across differing types of data as well as across cultures. Thus, these factors deserve in-depth consideration.

WHAT HAS BEEN LEARNED FROM NATURAL LANGUAGE PERSONALITY DESCRIPTIONS

The majority of lexical studies of personality descriptors have attempted to test the most widely influential personality model of the last two decades: the Big Five factor structure (Goldberg, 1990, 1993; John, 1990). The Big Five factors are customarily labeled Extraversion, Agreeableness, Conscientiousness, Emotional Stability (or its opposite, Neuroticism), and Intellect (or, in one inventory representation, Openness to Experience). There were signs of the Big Five structure in some studies from an earlier era (as detailed by Digman, 1990; Goldberg, 1993; John, 1990), but its identification in studies of natural language descriptors in English (e.g., Goldberg, 1990) was decisive.

If we value cross-cultural generalizability, however, applicability to one language is not enough. As detailed in more lengthy reviews (Saucier & Goldberg, 2001; Saucier, Hampson, & Goldberg, 2000), lexical studies have yielded structures resembling the Big Five most consistently in languages originating in northern Europe, including German (Ostendorf, 1990) and Polish (Szarota, 1996), as well as English. Although a study in Turkish (Goldberg & Somer, 2000) also found a structure with much resemblance to the Big Five, studies of other non-north-European languages (e.g., Di Blas & Forzi, 1998; Church, Katigbak, & Reyes, 1998; Church, Reyes, Katigbak, & Grimm, 1997; Szirmak & De Raad, 1994) have led to results that are less clearly supportive. And because a majority of studies have relied exclusively on self-report, the degree of generality of the Big Five in peer ratings is less certain than for self-ratings.

To this point, lexical studies have revealed a great deal about the relative robustness of the Big Five, as well as information about other less well-known candidate models, including some with fewer and some with more factors. The next section discusses the most consistent findings from lexical studies to date by describing models with successively more factors.

What If Only One Factor Is Allowed?

Several lexical studies have reported evidence about factor solutions containing only one factor (Boies, Lee, Ashton, Pascal, & Nicol, 2001; Di Blas & Forzi, 1999; Goldberg & Somer, 2000; Saucier, 1997, 2003b). The findings from these studies have been quite consistent. The single factor contrasts a heterogeneous mix of desirable attributes at one pole with a mix of undesirable attributes at the other pole. This unrotated factor can be labeled *Evaluation;* it involves the contrast between socially desirable and undesirable personal qualities. This one factor structure can be expected to be the most replicable one across languages and cultures based on two principles: (a) The more terms associated with a factor, the more replicable that factor should be, and (b) because the first unrotated factor will have the most terms associated with it, it should be the most ubiquitous factor.

Findings of a single large evaluative factor are no doubt related to a classic finding in psychology. In judgments about the meanings of diverse objects in a wide array of cultural settings, a global evaluation factor (good vs. bad) was typically found to be the single largest factor (Osgood, May, & Miron, 1975). Osgood hypothesized that the ubiquity of this evaluative factor was related to basic evolutionary principles: Our forebears would not have survived if they had not become adapted at a very basic level to any signals of good versus bad objects or events—those to approach versus those to avoid, those leading to pleasure versus those leading to pain (e.g., Can I eat it or will it eat me?). Hawley (chap. 8 in this volume) refers to the evolutionary value of evaluation as a tool for determining an individual's value to a group.

So evaluation may be evolutionarily the first factor. But it is also the first factor to emerge in the cognitions of young children. Whereas older children employ more differentiated trait concepts, younger children rely on global, evaluative inference (Alvarez, Ruble, & Bolger, 2001).

Are Two Factors Better Than One?

Two factor solutions from several lexical studies also suggest a consistent pattern: One factor includes attributes associated with positively valued dynamic qualities and individual ascendancy, whereas the other factor includes attributes associated with socialization, social propriety, solidarity, and community cohesion (Boies et al., 2001; Caprara, Barbaranelli, & Zimbardo, 1997; Di Blas & Forzi, 1999; Digman, 1997; Goldberg & Somer, 2000; Hřebíčková, Ostendorf, Osecká, & Čermák, 1999;

Paulhus & John, 1998; Saucier, 1997, 2003b; Shweder, 1972; White, 1980). Such a factor structure resembles that embodied in the theoretical model of Bakan (1966), who labeled the two factors Agency and Communion. In addition, these two factors may be aligned with some of the other sets of dual personological constructs reviewed by Digman (1997) and Paulhus and John (1998), including Hogan's (1983) distinction between "getting ahead" (Dynamism) and "getting along" (Social Propriety).

This constellation of two factors is also related to the three most ubiquitous dimensions of affective meaning, which include Potency (or Strength) and Activity in addition to Evaluation (Osgood et al., 1975). Whether this correspondence is due entirely to the imposition of universal tendencies in human cognition, or to the natural structure of phenomena "out in the world" remains an open question. In judgments about human targets, Potency and Activity tend to merge into a single dimension that Osgood and his associates called "Dynamism."

As is true of the Big One factor structure, no lexical study has presented evidence to contradict the view that this two factor structure is ubiquitous across languages and cultures. If both the one and two factor structures eventually turn out to be universal, the latter has some advantage, because two factors provide more information than one.

Regularities at the Five Factor Level

As already noted, lexical studies in languages originating in northern Europe (including English) have been supportive of the Big Five, and so has a study in Turkish. But studies in Italian (De Raad, Di Blas, & Perugini, 1997) and Hungarian (Szirmak & De Raad, 1994) found no counterpart to the Intellect factor in five factor solutions. Instead, there were two Agreeableness-related factors, one contrasting peacefulness with aggression and irritability, and the other contrasting humaneness with greed and egotism (cf. Deary, 1996). Extraction of additional factors was necessary to find a factor related to Intellect.

Several lexical studies have included a relatively broad selection of variables, each including terms that could be classified as referring to emotions and moods or as being unusually highly evaluative, and two of these studies included terms referring to physical appearance. Because none of these studies found the Big Five in a five factor solution, it is clear that the appearance of the Big Five as the first five factors is contingent on strictures in variable selection.

Lexical Seven Factor Models

Although not finding the Big Five in five factor solutions, studies with wide variable selection criteria in English and Turkish did find Big Five-like factors in a seven factor solution (Goldberg & Somer, 2000; Saucier, 1997; Tellegen & Waller, 1987). The two additional factors were "Negative Valence" (a factor emphasizing attributes with extremely low desirability and endorsement rates) found in all three studies and either "Positive Valence" (a factor emphasizing vague positive attributes like Impressive and Outstanding; found in Tellegen & Waller, 1987) or Attractiveness (found in the other two studies).

But studies in two other languages with broad variable selection criteria have led to an alternative seven factor structure. The convergences between these studies occurred despite their many differences in methodology. Lexical studies in Filipino (Church et al., 1997, 1998) and Hebrew (Almagor, Tellegen, & Waller, 1995)—languages from unrelated languages and cultures—yielded a highly convergent seven factor structure, although the similarity was obscured by discrepant labels. The English translations of marker adjectives for the Filipino and Hebrew factors have been shown to correspond in a one-to-one way (Saucier, 2003a).

One of these new factors resembles the Negative Valence factor just described. Two of them resemble the Big Five factors of Conscientiousness and Intellect. The other three Big Five factors—Extraversion, Agreeableness, and Emotional Stability—correlate substantially but complexly with the remaining four factors, which map an affective-interpersonal domain (cf. Saucier, 1992). These four can be labeled Gregariousness (or Liveliness), Self-Assurance (or Mettle or Fortitude), Even Temper (Tolerant vs. Temperamental), and Concern for Others (vs. Egotism). Big Five Extraversion is related to Gregariousness and Self-Assurance, Emotional Stability to Self-Assurance and Even Temper, and Agreeableness to Even Temper and Concern for Others.

Similar factors have been obtained from lexical data in English (Saucier, 2003a), and factors found in studies in Italian (e.g., Di Blas & Forzi, 1998) resemble the Multi-Language Seven. However, further replication tests are needed because few studies have used such broad variable selection criteria.

Ashton et al. (2001; cf., Saucier, 2002) presented evidence that more than half of the lexical studies conducted to date yield a consistent pattern in six factor solutions; the analyses involved presuppose removal of the most extremely evaluative terms. This six factor pattern resembles that of the Multi-Language Seven, with the following exceptions: (a) Even Temper is labeled Agreeableness, and Gregariousness is labeled Extraversion; (b) with a narrower variable selection, the three ML7 factors of Negative Valence, Concern for Others, and Self-Assurance become compressed into two (in Ashton and Lee's factors of Honesty and Emotionality).

Saucier's (2003a) analyses of convergences among Filipino, Hebrew, Italian, and English factors, taken together with Ashton and Lee's detection of related recurrent patterns in six factor solutions, suggest that a new competitor alternative to the Big Five is taking shape. There are three exciting features of this new model: Its origin is outside of northern European languages, its cross-cultural generalizability appears likely to exceed that for the Big Five, and it has incrementally greater comprehensiveness as compared to the Big Five.

Limitations

There are important limitations to the body of lexical studies carried out to date, and these can be related to any of the eight criteria. In terms of cross-cultural generalizability, more studies are needed in non-Western settings where the majority of the world's human population resides, and with non-European languages. In terms of generalizability across data types, lexical studies have focused almost entirely on those attributes represented in adjectives, although some attributes may be represented mainly as type nouns (e.g., Hick, Nerd, Slavedriver, Tease) or as attribute nouns (e.g., Integrity, Mettle); more studies that include attributes represented in nonadjectival forms are needed. In addition, most lexical studies to date have relied exclusively on self-descriptions, a methodology whose use should be supplemented with descriptions by knowledgeable informants.

Are sets of lexical factors comprehensive? Certainly they are more comprehensive than the structural models that came before. The extra content coverage in the NEO inventory after the grafting of two lexical factors (Agreeableness and Conscientiousness) into its structural model (Costa & McCrae, 1985) is a prime reason for its rapid gain in popularity. But, there are clearly dimensions of individual differences that are beyond the Big Five, particularly if we widen the taxonomy to include abilities, social attitudes, or appearance-related characteristics (Saucier & Goldberg, 1998).

Because of their derivation in commonly referenced attribute concepts, lexical factors are guaranteed strong *social importance*, although there is no guarantee that all socially important factors will be richly represented in the lexicon. Lexical factors have already performed a service to the field in enhancing the *comprehensiveness* of personality models; prior to the Big Five, there was little attention to Agreeableness or Conscientiousness. Lexical factors have shown good evidence of *cross-time stability*, and their *predictive validity* (e.g., in work settings) has been a major force behind their rising popularity. As the review indicates, their generalizability across types of data and across cultures has been impressive, and not matched by alternative models. On these six criteria, lexically based factors like the Big Five can be judged as something between adequate and superb. Structural models might be developed that are incrementally better on one or more of these criteria, but improvements are unlikely to be huge. It is the last two criteria that reveal limits of lexical factors.

One of these criteria is biological or other causal basis. The Big Five shows evidence of heritability for all factors in the model, but it is not clear that the factors actually maximize heritability. It may be possible, for example, through analyses of genetic and environmental correlations in suitable data sets, to locate factors whose causal clarity is maximized, located or rotated so as to yield the maximum heritability, or the maximum basis in shared environmental effects. The result would be a model with superior causal clarity. There is no clear evidence that the Big Five correspond closely to the primary lines of genetic or biological influence, or provide the optimal beachhead for inserting personality variables into studies of the brain.

The other criterion is theory. The Big Five (and any other lexical structural model) is inductively and empirically derived, and lacks theoretical underpinnings. There have been attempts to transplant the Big Five into some body of preexisting or ad hoc theory (e.g., McCrae & Costa, 1996; MacDonald, 1995), but it is not clear that these operations have been particularly successful.

Thus, structural models like the Big Five are vulnerable to being superseded by some model with a clearer basis in biology or in some other causal element, and by a model with a stronger basis in theory. There are a number of models that meet this description. Unfortunately, many of them contain only one or two factors, giving them little in the way of comprehensiveness, and have been measured exclusively via self-report methodologies with little attention paid to cross-cultural generalizability. Models that are lacking in so many respects give up more than they gain in comparison with a lexical model like the Big Five.

There are, however, models of temperament that are more comprehensive than this and are not limited to self-report. These models beneficially introduce a longitudinal perspective that is missing from structural models based on ratings of adult targets.

COMPLEMENTARY CONTRIBUTIONS FROM THE STUDY OF TEMPERAMENT

Temperament may be conceptualized as the early-in-a-life framework from which personality develops (Digman, 1994; Rothbart, Ahadi, & Evans, 2000). The nature of temperament as early-appearing dimensions underlying behavior presents challenges different from those faced by personality researchers. Expressions of temperament change during development. The systems that underlie temperament are, like the behavioral indicators of temperament, in the process of development and subject to change throughout the life span (Rothbart, 1989). New systems come "on line" at different stages. For example, the capacity to inhibit approach to new objects does not develop until later in the first year in infants, and once it is in place individual differences in this type of inhibition remain relatively stable (Rothbart & Bates, 1998). As another example, there are differences in elicitors of fear at different ages. Measurement of fear in infancy and early childhood is accomplished through determination of reaction to novel, unusual, or sudden presentation of stimuli (Rothbart, Derryberry, & Hershey, 2000). This type of fear goes away for nearly all children by school age, by which point going to the doctor, sleeping over at another child's house, being in dark rooms, and watching scary movies become major fear-evoking events (Rothbart, Ahadi, Hershey, & Fisher, 2001; Simonds & Rothbart, 2005). But for early adolescents and adults, better indicators of a fearful temperament are anticipation of negative events and possible failures (Capaldi & Rothbart, 1992; Rothbart, Ahadi, & Evans, 2000).

Measurement of temperament relies on different types of data at different ages. In order to measure temperament in infancy and early childhood, parent report is a valuable source of information. At this age assessment through laboratory measurement of behavioral and physiological indicators of underlying temperament is another potential method. But infants and younger children are unable to provide self-reports. Beyond age 4 or 5 years, it is possible for children to report on their own temperament with a fair degree of reliability, and there is some correspondence with parent reports of temperament in the self-reports of children from preschool age to early adolescence (Ellis & Rothbart, 2002; Hwang, 2002; Simonds & Rothbart, 2003). Once children have entered school, teachers become sources of information on temperament and emerging personality (Bramlett, Scott, & Rowell, 2000; Digman & Inouye, 1986; Digman & Shmelyov, 1996) and temperament (e.g., Kurdek & Lillie, 1985). Each rater provides information about a child in a different context: parents in the home, teachers in the school, peers in the social realm, and self-reports provide unique information about a child's internal states. Laboratory measures remain relevant at all ages.

Each method of measurement is controversial because of potential biases unique to it, imperfect agreement between raters, and between questionnaire data and objective laboratory measures (Teglasi, 1998), and the well-known limitations of self-report data, which apply to self-reports of children as well as adults. Despite arguments that parents are not reliable raters of their own children's temperament (Kagan, 2001), parent report data has shown substantial validity (Rothbart & Bates, 1998) and is the most frequently used method of measuring temperament in infants and children.

An important unresolved problem in temperament research stems from the variety of measurement methods. Although these methods show agreement, much disagreement between methods remains. It is unclear to what degree findings and key models are contingent on utilization of certain methods of measurement and not others. As is true in personality research, the use of a wide variety of measurement instruments makes it difficult to compare results; temperament research has not settled on a consensual structural model.

THE STRUCTURE OF TEMPERAMENT

There are several influential structural models of temperament, each involving a particular way of defining temperament and selecting variables (or creating items). These different theories have given rise to different ideas about the structure of temperament, with some marked similarity, and some remaining differences.

Thomas and Chess' Model of Behavioral Styles

Current models of temperament are strongly influenced by findings from the New York Longitudinal Study (NYLS; Thomas et al., 1963). Through interviewing parents about the behaviors of their 2- to 6-month-old infants, Thomas et al. identified nine dimensions of behavioral styles, or early-appearing patterns of behavior, to describe the observed differences: Activity Level, Approach/Withdrawal (responses to novel stimuli), Adaptability (ease of modification of response to new or altered situations), Mood (negative or positive), Threshold, Intensity (energy level of reaction), Distractibility, Rhythmicity (regularity of sleep, hunger, feeding, and elimination), and Attention Span/Persistence. Martin, Wisenbaker, and Huttunen (1994) conducted a factor analysis of large samples on NYLS-based measures and found five factors: Activity Level, Negative Emotionality, Task Persistence, Adaptability, and Inhibition. Two other factors were found, Rhythmicity and Threshold, but were determined to suffer from lack of relevance past infancy (Rhythmicity) or lack of internal consistency (Threshold).

Questionnaire measures based on the NYLS model have been developed for most age groups (Fullard, McDevitt, & Carey, 1984; Hegvik, McDevitt, & Carey, 1982; McDevitt & Carey, 1978; Windle & Lerner, 1986). NYLS-based infant and child questionnaires use parent reports for measuring temperament.

The NYLS model is based in observable behaviors that appear very early in child development and so have a strong temperament (as contrasted with adult personality) flavor. However, the scales are conceptually overlapping and lack discriminant validity, and there has been difficulty with replicating its nine factors (Martin, Wisenbaker, & Huttunen, 1994; Sanson, Prior, Garino, Oberklaid, & Sewell, 1987). Given these limitations of the NYLS model, other models have attracted attention.

Buss and Plomin's Emotionality-Activity-Sociability (EAS) Model

Buss and Plomin (1975) developed a model of temperament based on heritable dimensions believed to appear in early life: Emotionality, Activity, and Sociability, and Impulsivity (thus, the EASI model). Due to lack of support for the heritability of impulsivity, that dimension was later dropped (Buss & Plomin, 1984).

The EAS model is currently reflected in two measures of temperament: the EAS–III, and the EAS- and NYLS-based parent report Colorado Child Temperament Inventory, which includes a shyness scale in addition to the EAS factors (Buss & Plomin, 1984; Rowe & Plomin, 1977). The dimensions have a theoretical basis as well as evidence of stability (Rende, 1993). However, the model excludes the useful dimension of Positive Affect, and there is doubt about whether the EAS dimensions are actually more heritable than dimensions in other models.

Rothbart and Derryberry's Psychobiological Approach

Rothbart and Derryberry's (1981) model of temperament was influenced by the NYLS dimensions as well as characteristics identified as indicating temperamental variability in animal species (Diamond, 1957) and characteristics identified as heritable in human behavioral genetics research (Rothbart & Bates, 1998). The model was first empirically represented in the Infant Behavior Questionnaire (IBQ; Rothbart, 1981), which included a set of six scales that showed substantial internal consistency and lack of construct overlap: Activity Level, Smiling and Laughter, Fear, Distress to Limitations (Crying or fussing while confined, subject to caretaking actions, or unable to perform desired actions), Duration of Orienting, and Soothability. The IBQ provided the basis for further questionnaires: the revision of the IBQ (IBQ-R; Gartstein & Rothbart, 2003), the Children's Behavior Questionnaire (CBQ; Rothbart et al., 2001), the Temperament in Middle Childhood Questionnaire (TMCQ; Simonds & Rothbart, 2005), Early Adolescent Temperament Questionnaire, Revised (EATQ-R; Capaldi & Rothbart, 1992; Ellis & Rothbart, 2002), and the Adult Temperament Questionnaire (Evans & Rothbart, 2005).

Laboratory assessments can elicit temperament-based behaviors. For instance, latency to, intensity of, and duration of positive reaction (smiling, laughter, positive vocalization) to novel stimuli have been used as laboratory measures of Smiling and Laughter in infancy, a behavioral scale that indicates underlying positive affect. Rothbart, Derryberry, et al. (2000) found low to moderate correspondence between laboratory measures and parent report for a number of scales in infancy, and found that scores on laboratory measures in infancy predict (with medium to large effect sizes) parent ratings of 7-year-old activity and frustration.

Studies using these measures have found two factors that are present from infancy to adulthood: Extraversion/Surgency and Negative Affectivity. Effortful Control appears as a third factor from early childhood through adulthood. Recent evidence indicates that Affiliative tendencies form a factor that is present in infancy (Affiliation/Orienting) and in early adolescence (Affiliation; Putnam, Ellis, & Rothbart, 2001). Moreover, in adulthood, a separate Orienting Sensitivity factor is present (Rothbart, Ahadi, et al., 2000).

Compared to the NYLS and EASI models, this psychobiological model appears to be more comprehensive (Shiner, 1998). It is also more linked to theory regarding physiological mechanisms, and more inclusive of self-control mechanisms. One limitation is the dearth of clear evidence on the stability of its scores across long spans of time; the use of behavioral indicators distinct to each age group on inventories tailored to that age group have so far created some limitations to studying cross-time stability with these measures.

How does this psychobiological model stand with respect to the eight criteria for good structural models? The stability of three main factors from early childhood to adulthood (Extraversion/Surgency, Negative Affectivity, and Effortful Control) indicates some cross-time stability and reliability of these factors of temperament. Evidence for links between temperament factors of Negative Affectivity and Effortful Control and psychopathology (Lonigan & Phillips, 2001; Posner & Rothbart, 2000) indicate some predictive validity and, assuming that psychopathology is a major social problem, also some degree of social importance for the temperament factors. Moderate to strong correspondence between laboratory measures and questionnaire data indicates generalizability across types of data (Rothbart, Derryberry, et al., 2000). Temperament factors of Extraversion/Surgency, Negative Affectivity, and Effortful Control have been found in numerous studies examining temperament across cultures, although some lower level scales were related to different factors in different cultures (Ahadi, Rothbart, & Ye, 1993).

Relative to natural language-based models of the structure of personality, the greatest strengths of this model are on the last two of the eight criteria: biological basis and theory. This model has a theory-driven emphasis on biological systems that underlie the behavioral expression of temperament. It is likely that different genetic alleles predispose to the neural and neurochemical differences that underlie temperament (Rothbart & Bates, 1998). On the other hand, the psychobiological temperament model may not be as strong as lexicon-derived models on criteria like comprehensiveness, predictive validity, and generalizability across cultures and languages.

Generality of Structures of Temperament

Some studies have sought to determine the structure of temperament through use of multiple instruments (Anthony, Lonigan, Hooe, & Phillips, 2002; Lemery, Goldsmith, Klinnert, &Mroczek, 1999; Lonigan & Dyer, 2000). Combining the Children's Behavior Questionnaire (CBQ; Rothbart et al., 2001), Emotionality-Activity-Sociability questionnaire (EAS; Buss & Plomin, 1984), and the Positive Affect Negative Affect Scale (PANAS; Watson, Clark, & Tellegen, 1988), Lonigan and Dyer (2000) found three relatively independent factors, similar to findings of Rothbart et al. (2001): Positive Affectivity/Surgency, Negative Affectivity/Neuroticism, and Effortful Control.

Constructs similar to three main factors of temperament have been identified in models of adult personality. Eysenck's (1967) original model of personality consisted of the two factors of Extraversion and Neuroticism, to which Psychoticism, considered to be a measure of disinhibition (Watson & Clark, 1993), was later added (Eysenck & Eysenck, 1975). Tellegen (1985) put forth a three factor model consisting of Negative Emotionality, Positive Emotionality, and Constraint. Combining models of Eysenck and Tellegen, Clark and Watson (1999) identified three main superfactors of N/NE (Neuroticism/Negative Emotionality), E/PE (Extraversion/Positive Emotionality), and DvC (Disinhibition vs. Constraint). These three factors share similarities with the Extraversion/Surgency, Negative Affectivity, and Effortful Control factors (Rothbart, et al. 2001), although Constraint has fear as a component construct whereas Rothbart et al. group fear with Negative Affectivity and not with Effortful Control. The same three temperament factors correspond to three of the Big Five personality factors: Positive Affectivity/Surgency to Extraversion, Negative Affectivity to Neuroticism/Emotional Stability, and Effortful Control to Conscientousness (Rothbart, Ahadi, et al., 2000).

Thus, there is considerable overlap between structural models of personality and temperament. Overall, however, important questions remain about the relation of temperament factors to personality factors. Although lexical studies converge with respect to the factors in one and two factor solutions, it is not clear whether these lexical factors converge with one and two factor solutions from temperament measures. Approach (temperament) and Dynamism (lexical) are probably related. As for the lexically emphasized Social Propriety factor, these are attributes related to the effects of socialization, that is, whether a person is relatively well-behaved (e.g., considerate, polite, punctual, patient, honest) or ill-mannered (e.g., thoughtless, rude, negligent, careless, deceitful). Such attributes are certainly important in judgments made about the behavior of children (e.g., by teachers), but have conventionally been thought of as primarily effects of socialization, and perhaps of moral development, not primarily effects of temperament. In other words, Social Propriety (or Morality) has been assumed to be an effect from the outside, whereas Negative Affectivity or even Effortful Control are assumed to be effects from the inside. It appears that this difference in content representation between personality and temperament models may be a direct effect of variable selection: Attributes related to social propriety and morality have not been included in temperament studies, and consequences for structural results follow from this exclusion.

Cloninger, Svrakic, and Przybek (1993) proposed a psychobiological model for adult individual differences that separates temperament from character, with character assumed to represent "effects from outside" (i.e., environment) to a greater degree than temperament. That is, the theory supposes that temperament reflects mainly genetic effects, but character represents mainly environmental effects. However, heritability for the character dimensions (Cooperativeness, Self-directedness, Self-transcendence) does not seem to be markedly lower than that for temperament dimensions (Harm-avoidance, Novelty-seeking, Reward-dependence, Persistence) (Ando et al., 2002). This provides an interesting puzzle for the psychology of personality and temperament: Present psychobiological models have difficulty accounting for individual differences in certain forms of social behavior (i.e., character) that may have analogues in other social species, are important in human societies, and have some degree of genetic basis.

CONCLUSIONS

Recent decades have seen important progress in discerning the structure of personality attributes. At the very broadest level—too broad for many purposes—this structure appears to have much in common with Osgood's (1962) classic dimensions of affective meaning, which were found in studies of the ways that diverse objects (not just persons) are judged and perceived. At a slightly less broad but more informative level are the well-known Big Five factors. The extent to which the Big Five is optimal at its level in the hierarchy is not fully determined, there being promising new competitor models (Ashton et al., 2004; Saucier, 2003a), with the competitions not really yet begun. It is also not clear whether current models of child temperament structure, which correspond largely but imperfectly with personality structure models derived by studying adults, are ultimately the optimal ones. Factorial equivalence over groups is at present better established for lexically derived factor structures in adults. However, including both childhood and adulthood, factorial equivalence over time is better established for the structure of temperament. Hopefully, in the next decades, research on personality and temperament will converge on a common framework. To enable such a common framework, it is vital that personality and temperament researchers become and remain aware of the strong homologies between the domains they study.

Much remains unresolved, leaving potential for petty disputes about differences between structural models. So it is important to remember that scientific models are, by definition, set out tentatively, subject to the judgment of subsequent evidence. Researchers should bear in mind the criteria by which structural models can be compared—in other words, what makes a structural model "good." By focusing on these criteria, researchers might keep their eye on the prize—an ultimately optimal structural model—and generate increasing evidence related to overall optimality of structural models.

Future models of temperament and personality will be more comprehensive and more widely generalizable across languages and cultures. These models will not only provide improved prediction of a wide array of useful criteria, but will also include more explicit linkage to the psychological mechanisms that underlie individual differences. The ultimately optimal structural model, in other words, will have both basic science foundations and real-world applications.

ACKNOWLEDGMENTS

Work on this chapter was supported by Grant MH-49227 from the National Institute of Mental Health, U.S. Public Health Service. Some portions of this chapter are derived from a previous contribution (Saucier & Goldberg, 2003) by the first author.

REFERENCES

Ahadi, S. A., Rothbart, M. K., & Ye, R. (1993). Children's temperament in the U.S. and China: Similarities and differences. *European Journal of Personality, 7,* 359–378.

Allport, G. W. (1937). *Personality: A psychological interpretation.* New York: Holt.

Allport, G. W., & Odbert, H. S. (1936). Trait names: A psycho-lexical study. *Psychological Monographs, 47* (1, Whole No. 211).

Almagor, M., Tellegen, A., & Waller, N. (1995). The Big Seven model: A cross-cultural replication and further exploration of the basic dimensions of natural language of trait descriptions. *Journal of Personality and Social Psychology, 69,* 300–307.

Alvarez, J. M., Ruble, D. N., & Bolger, N. (2001). Trait understanding or evaluative reasoning? An analysis of children's behavioral predictions. *Child Development, 72,* 1409–1425.

Ando, J., Ono, Y., Yoshimura, K., Onoda, N., Shinohara, M., Kanba, S., & Asai, M. (2002). The genetic structure of Cloninger's seven-factor model of temperament and character in a Japanese sample. *Journal of Personality, 70*, 583–609.

Anthony, J. L., Lonigan, C. J., Hooe, E. S., & Phillips, B. M. (2002). An affect-based hierarchical model of temperament and its relations with internalizing symptomatology. *Journal of Clinical Child and Adolescent Psychiatry, 31*, 480–490.

Ashton, M. C., Lee, K., Perugini, M., Szarota, P. De Vries, R. E., Di Blas, L., Boies, K., & De Raad, B. (2004). A six-factor structure of personality-descriptive adjectives: Solutions from psycholexical studies in seven languages. *Journal of Personality and Social Psychology, 86*, 356–366.

Bakan, D. (1966). *The duality of human existence: Isolation and communion in Western man.* Boston: Beacon.

Boies, K., Lee, K., Ashton, M. C., Pascal, S., & Nicol, A. A. M. (2001). The structure of the French personality lexicon. *European Journal of Personality, 15*, 277–295.

Bouchard, T. J. (1994). Genes, environment, and personality. *Science, 264*, 1700–1701.

Bramlett, R. K., Scott, P., & Rowell, R. K. (2000). A comparison of temperament and social skills in predicting academic performance in first graders. *Special Services in the Schools, 16*, 147–158.

Buss, A. H., & Plomin, R. (1975). *A temperament theory of personality.* New York: Wiley.

Buss, A. H., & Plomin, R. (1984). *Temperament: Early developing personality traits.* Hillsdale, NJ: Lawrence Erlbaum Associates.

Capaldi, D. M., & Rothbart, M. K. (1992). Development and validation of an early adolescent temperament measure. *Journal of Early Adolescence, 24*, 153–173.

Caprara, G. V., Barbanelli, C., & Zimbardo, P. G. (1997). Politicians' uniquely simple personalities. *Nature, 385*, 493.

Cattell, R. B. (1943). The description of personality: Basic traits resolved into clusters. *Journal of Abnormal and Social Psychology, 38*, 476–506.

Church, A. T., Katigbak, M. S., & Reyes, J. A. S. (1998). Further exploration of Filipino personality structure using the lexical approach: Do the Big Five or Big Seven dimensions emerge? *European Journal of Personality, 12*, 249–269.

Church, A. T., Reyes, J. A. S., Katigbak, M. S., & Grimm, S. D. (1997). Filipino personality structure and the Big Five model: A lexical approach. *Journal of Personality, 65*, 477–528.

Clark, L. A., & Watson, D. (1999). Temperament: A new paradigm for trait psychology. In L. A. Pervin & O. P. John (Eds.), *Handbook of personality: Theory and research* (2nd ed., pp. 399–423). New York: Guilford.

Cloninger, C. R., Svrakic, D. M., & Przybeck, T. R. (1993). A psychobiological model of temperament and character. *Archives of General Psychiatry, 50*, 975–990.

Costa, P. T., & McCrae, R. R. (1985). *The NEO Personality Inventory manual.* Odessa, FL: Psychological Assessment Resources.

Costa, P. T., & McCrae, R. R. (1992). Four ways five factors are basic. *Personality and Individual Differences, 13*, 653–655.

Deary, I. J. (1996). A (latent) Big Five personality model in 1915? A reanalysis of Webb's data. *Journal of Personality and Social Psychology, 71*, 992–1005.

De Raad, B., Di Blas, L., & Perugini, M. (1997). Two independent Italian trait taxonomies: Comparisons with Italian and between Italian Germanic languages. *European Journal of Personality, 11*, 167–185.

Diamond, S. (1957). *Personality and temperament.* New York: Harper.

Di Blas, L., & Forzi, M. (1998). An alternative taxonomic study of personality descriptors in the Italian language. *European Journal of Personality, 12*, 75–101.

Di Blas, L., & Forzi, M. (1999). Refining a descriptive structure of personality attributes in the Italian language: The abridged Big Three circumplex structure. *Journal of Personality and Social Psychology, 76*, 451–481.

Digman, J. M. (1990). Personality structure: Emergence of the five-factor model. In M. R. Rosenzweig & L. W. Porter (Eds.), *Annual review of psychology* (Vol. 41, pp. 417–440). Palo Alto, CA: Annual Reviews.

Digman, J. M. (1994). Child personality and temperament: Does the five-factor model embrace both domains? In C. F. Halverson, Jr., G. A. Kohnstamm, & R. P. Martin (Eds.), *The developing structure of temperament and personality from infancy to adulthood* (pp. 323–338). Hillsdale, NJ: Lawrence Erlbaum Associates.

Digman, J. M. (1997). Higher order factors of the Big Five. *Journal of Personality and Social Psychology, 73,* 1246–1256.

Digman, J. M., & Inouye, J. (1986). Further specification of the five robust factors of personality. *Journal of Personality and Social Psychology, 50*(1), 116–123.

Digman, J. M., & Shmelyov, A. G. (1996). The structure of temperament and personality in Russian children. *Journal of Personality and Social Psychology, 71,* 341–351.

Ellis, L. K., & Rothbart, M. K. (2002). *Revision of the Early Adolescent Temperament Questionnaire.* Manuscript in preparation.

Evans, D. E., & Rothbart, M. K. (2005). *A hierarchical model of temperament and the Big Five.* Manuscript submitted for publication.

Eysenck, H. J. (1967). *The biological basis of personality.* Springfield, IL: Thomas.

Eysenck, H. J. (1991). Dimensions of personality: 16, 5, or 3? Criteria for a taxonomic paradigm. *Personality and Individual Differences, 12,* 773–790.

Eysenck, H. J., & Eysenck, S. B. G. (1975). *The Eysenck Personality Questionnaire.* London: Hodder & Stoughton.

Fullard, W., McDevitt, S. C., & Carey, W. B. (1984). Assessing temperament in one- to three-year old children. *Journal of Pediatric Psychology, 9,* 205–217.

Funder, D. C. (2001). *The personality puzzle* (2nd ed.). New York: Norton.

Gartstein, M. A., & Rothbart, M. K. (2003). Studying infant behavior via the Revised Infant Behavior Questionnaire. *Infant Behavior and Development, 26,* 64–86.

Goldberg, L. R. (1981). Language and individual differences: The search for universals in personality lexicons. In L. W. Wheeler (Ed.), *Review of personality and social psychology* (Vol. 2, pp. 141–165). Beverly Hills, CA: Sage.

Goldberg, L. R. (1990). An alternative "description of personality": The Big-Five factor structure. *Journal of Personality and Social Psychology, 59,* 1216–1229.

Goldberg, L. R. (1993). The structure of phenotypic personality traits. *American Psychologist, 48,* 26–34.

Goldberg, L. R., & Digman, J. M. (1994). Revealing structure in the data: Principles of exploratory factor analysis. In S. Strack & M. Lorr (Eds.), *Differentiating normal and abnormal personality* (pp. 216–242). New York: Springer.

Goldberg, L. R., & Saucier, G. (1995). So what do you propose we use instead? A reply to Block. *Psychological Bulletin, 117,* 221–225.

Goldberg, L. R., & Somer, O. (2000). The hierarchical structure of common Turkish person-descriptive adjectives. *European Journal of Personality, 14,* 497–531.

Goldsmith, H. H., Buss, A., Plomin, R., Rothbart, M. K., Thomas, A., Chess, S., Hinde, R. A., & McCall, R. B. (1987). Roundtable: What is temperament? Four approaches. *Child Development, 58,* 505–529.

Goldsmith, H. H., & Campos, J. J. (1982). Toward a theory of infant temperament. In R. N. Emde & R. J. Harmon (Eds.), *The development of attachment and affiliative systems* (pp. 161–193). New York: Plenum.

Goldsmith, H. H., & Campos, J. J. (1986). Fundamental issues in the study of early temperament: The Denver Twin Temperament Study. In M. E. Lamb, A. L. Brown, & B. Rogoff (Eds.), *Advances in developmental psychology* (pp. 231–283). Hillsdale, NJ: Lawrence Erlbaum Associates.

Hegvik, R. L., McDevitt, S. C., & Carey, W. B. (1982). The Middle Childhood Temperament Questionnaire. *Developmental and Behavioral Pediatrics, 3,* 197–200.

Hogan, R. (1983). A socioanalytic theory of personality. In M. M. Page (Ed.), *Nebraska symposium on motivation* (pp. 336–355). Lincoln: University of Nebraska Press.

Hřebíčová, M., Ostendorf, F., Osecká, L., &Cermák, I. (1999). Taxonomy and structure of Czech personality-relevant verbs. In I. Mervielde, I. J. Deary, F. De Fruyt, & F. Ostendorf (Eds.), *Personality psychology in Europe* (vol. 7, pp. 51–65). Tilburg, The Netherlands: Tilburg University Press.

Hwang, J. (2002). *Development of a temperament self-report measure for young children.* Unpublished doctoral dissertation, University of Oregon.

John, O. P. (1990). The "Big Five" factor taxonomy: Dimensions of personality in the natural language and in questionnaires. In L. A. Pervin (Ed.), *Handbook of personality: Theory and research* (pp. 66–100). New York: Guilford.

John, O. P., Angleitner, A., & Ostendorf, F. (1988). The lexical approach to personality: A historical review of trait taxonomic research. *European Journal of Personality, 2,* 171–203.

Kagan, J. (2001). The structure of temperament. In R. N. Emde & J. K. Hewitt (Eds.), *Infancy to early childhood: Genetic and environmental influences on developmental change* (pp. 45–51). New York: Oxford University Press.

Kurdek, L. A., & Lillie, R. (1985). The relation between classroom social status and classmate likeability, compromising skill, temperament, and neighborhood social interactions. *Journal of Applied Developmental Psychology, 6*(1), 31–41.

Lemery, K. S., Goldsmith, H. H., Klinnert, M. D., & Mrazek, D. A. (1999). Developmental models of infant and childhood temperament. *Developmental Psychology, 35*(1), 189–201.

Lonigan, C. J., & Dyer, S. M. (2000). *Toward a hierarchical affective model of temperament in early childhood.* Unpublished manuscript.

Lonigan, C. J., & Phillips, B. M. (2001) Temperamental influences on the development of anxiety disorders. In M. W. Vasey & M. R. Dadds (Eds), *The developmental psychopathology of anxiety* (pp. 60–91). New York: Oxford University Press.

MacDonald, K. (1995). Evolution, the five-factor model, and levels of personality. *Journal of Personality, 63,* 525–566.

MacKinnon, D. W. (1944). The structure of personality. In J. McV. Hunt (Ed.), *Personality and the behavior disorders* (Vol. 1, pp. 3–48). New York: Ronald.

Martin, R. P., Wisenbaker, J., & Huttenen, M. (1994). Review of factor analytic studies of temperament measures based on the Thomas–Chess structural model: Implications for the Big Five. In C. F. Halverson, Jr., G. A. Kohnstamm, & R. P. Martin (Eds.), *The developing structure of temperament and personality from infancy to adulthood* (pp. 323–338). Hillsdale, NJ: Lawrence Erlbaum Associates.

McCrae, R. R., & Costa, P. T. (1996). Toward a new generation of personality theories: Theoretical contexts for the five-factor model. In J. S. Wiggins (Ed.), *The five-factor model of personality: Theoretical perspectives* (pp. 51–87). New York: Guilford.

McCrae, R. R., & Costa, P. T. (1997). Personality trait structure as a human universal. *American Psychologist, 52,* 509–516.

McDevitt, S. C., & Carey, W. B. (1978). The measurement of temperament in 3-7 year old children. *Journal of Child Psychology and Psychiatry, 19,* 245–253.

Norman, W. T. (1963). Toward an adequate taxonomy of personality attributes: Replicated factor structure in peer nomination personality ratings. *Journal of Abnormal and Social Psychology, 66,* 574–583.

Osgood, C. E. (1962). Studies on the generality of affective meaning systems. *American Psychologist, 17,* 10–28.

Osgood, C. E., May, W., & Miron, M. (1975). *Cross-cultural universals of affective meaning.* Urbana: University of Illinois Press.

Ostendorf, F. (1990). *Sprache und persönlichkeitsstruktur: Zur Validität des Fünf-Faktoren-Modells der Persönlichkeit* [Language and personality structure: Toward the validation of the Five-Factor model of personality]. Regensberg, Germany: S. Roderer Verlag.

Paulhus, D. L., & John, O. P. (1998). Egoistic and moralistic biases in self-perception: The inter-play of self-descriptive styles with basic traits and motives. *Journal of Personality, 66,* 1025–1060.

Posner, M. I., & Rothbart, M. K. (2000). Developing mechanisms of self-regulation. *Development and Psychpathology, 12,* 427–441.

Putnam, S. P., Ellis, L. K., & Rothbart, M. K. (2001). The structure of temperament from infancy through adolescence. In A. Eliasz & A. Angleitner (Eds.), *Advances/proceedings in research on temperament* (pp. 165–182). Germany: Pabst Scientist Publisher.

Rende, R. D. (1993). Longitudinal relations between temperament traits and behavioral syn-dromes in middle childhood. *Journal of the American Academcy of Child and Adolescent Psychia-try, 32,* 287–290.

Rothbart, M. K. (1981). Measurement of temperament in infancy. *Child Development, 52,* 569–578.

Rothbart, M. K. (1989). Temperament and development. In G. A. Kohnstamm, J. E. Bates, & M. K. Rothbart (Eds.), *Temperament in childhood* (pp. 187–247). West Sussex, England: Wiley.

Rothbart, M. K., Ahadi, S. A., & Evans, D. E. (2000). Temperament and personality: Origins and outcomes. *Journal of Personality and Social Psychology, 78,* 122–135.

Rothbart, M. K., Ahadi, S. A., Hershey, K., & Fisher, P. (2001). Investigations of temperament at three to seven years: The children's behavior questionnaire. *Child Development, 72,* 1394–1408.

Rothbart, M. K., & Bates, J. E. (1998). Temperament. In W. Damon (Series Ed.) & N. Eisenberg (Vol. Ed.), *Handbook of child psychology: Vol. 3. Social, emotional and personality development* (5th ed., pp. 105–176). New York: Wiley.

Rothbart, M. K., & Derryberry, D. (1981). Development of individual differences in tempera-ment. In M. E. Lamb & A. L. Brown (Eds.), *Advances in developmental psychology* (Vol. 1, pp. 37–86). Hillsdale, NJ: Lawrence Erlbaum Associates.

Rothbart, M. K., Derryberry, D., & Hershey, K. (2000). Stability of temperament in childhood: Laboratory infant assessment to parent report at seven years. In V. J. Molfese & D. L. Molfese (Eds.), *Temperament and personality development across the life span* (pp. 85–119). Hillsdale, NJ: Lawrence Erlbaum Associates.

Rowe, D. C., & Plomin, R. (1977). Temperament in early childhood. *Journal of Personality Assess-ment, 41,* 150–156.

Sanson, A., Prior, M., Garino, E., Oberklaid, F., & Sewell, J.(1987). The structure of infant tem-perament: Factor analysis of the Revised Infant Temperament Questionnaire. *Infant Behavior and Development, 10,* 97–104.

Saucier, G. (1992). Benchmarks: Integrating affective and interpersonal circles with the Big-Five personality factors. *Journal of Personality and Social Psychology, 62,* 1025–1035.

Saucier, G. (1997). Effects of variable selection on the factor structure of person descriptors. *Jour-nal of Personality and Social Psychology, 73,* 1296–1312.

Saucier, G. (2002). Gone too far—or not far enough? Comments on Ashton and Lee (2001). *Euro-pean Journal of Personality, 16,* 55–62.

Saucier, G. (2003a). An alternative multi-language structure of personality attributes. *European Journal of Personality, 17,* 179–205.

Saucier, G. (2003b). Factor structure of English-language personality type-nouns. *Journal of Per-sonality and Social Psychology, 85,* 695–708.

Saucier, G., & Goldberg, L. R. (1998). What is beyond the Big Five? *Journal of Personality, 66,* 495–524.

Saucier, G., & Goldberg, L. R. (2001). Lexical studies of indigenous personality factors: Premises, products, and prospects. *Journal of Personality, 69,* 847–879.

Saucier, G., & Goldberg, L. R. (2003). The structure of personality attributes. In M. Barrick & A. M. Ryan (Eds.), *Personality and work* (pp. 1–29). New York: Jossey-Bass-Pfeiffer.

Saucier, G., Hampson, S. E., & Goldberg, L. R. (2000). Cross-language studies of lexical personality factors. In S. E. Hampson (Ed.), *Advances in personality psychology* (Vol. 1, pp. 1–36). East Sussex, England: Psychology Press.

Shiner, R. L. (1998). How shall we speak of children's personalities in middle childhood: A preliminary taxonomy. *Psychological Bulletin, 124,* 308–332.

Shweder, R. A. (1972). *Semantic structure and personality assessment.* Unpublished doctoral dissertation, Harvard University.

Simonds, J., & Rothbart, M. K. (2005). *Temperament in Middle Childhood Questionnaire.* Manuscript in preparation.

Szarota, P. (1996). Taxonomy of the Polish personality-descriptive adjectives of the highest frequency of use. *Polish Psychological Bulletin, 27,* 342–351.

Szirmák, Z., & De Raad, B. (1994). Taxonomy and structure of Hungarian personality traits. *European Journal of Personality, 8,* 95–118.

Teglasi, H. (1998). Temperament constructs and measures. *School Psychology Review, 27,* 564–585.

Tellegen, A. (1985). Structures of mood and personality and their relevance to assessing anxiety with an emphasis on self-report. In A. H. Tuma & J. D. Maser (Eds.), *Anxiety and the anxiety disorders* (pp. 681–706). Hillsdale, NJ: Lawrence Erlbaum Associates.

Tellegen, A. (1993). Folk concepts and psychological concepts of personality and personality disorder. *Psychological Inquiry, 4,* 122–130.

Tellegen, A., & Waller, N. G. (1987). *Re-examining basic dimensions of natural language trait descriptors.* Paper presented at the 95th annual convention of the American Psychological Association.

Thomas, A., Chess, S., Birch, H. G., Hertzig, M. E., & Korn, S. (1963). *Behavioral individuality in early childhood.* New York: New York University Press.

Watson, D., & Clark, L. A. (1993). Behavioral disinhibition versus constraint: A dispositional perspective. In D. M. Wenger & J. W. Pennebaker (Eds.), *Handbook of mental control* (pp. 506–527). Englewood Cliffs, NJ: Prentice-Hall.

Watson, D., Clark, L. A., & Tellegen, A. (1988). Development and validation of brief measures of positive and negative affect: The PANAS scales. *Journal of Personality and Social Psychology, 54,* 1063–1070.

Windle, M., & Lerner, R. M. (1986). Reassessing the dimensions of temperamental individuality across the life span: The Revised Dimensions of Temperament Survey (DOTS—R). *Journal of Adolescent Research, 1*(2), 213–229.

White, G. M. (1980). Conceptual universals in interpersonal language. *American Anthropologist, 82,* 759–781.

7

Cross-Cultural Perspectives on Adult Personality Trait Development

Robert R. McCrae
Paul T. Costa, Jr.
National Institute on Aging

Most research on personality and aging has been conducted in the United States, where longitudinal studies can be traced back to the pioneering work of Strong (1951) and Kelly (1955). Major advances occurred in the late 1970s when a series of longitudinal studies matured. Those studies suggested that personality, at least in adults over age 30, was predominantly stable (McCrae & Costa, 1984). That claim included two components: First, individual differences were preserved over long periods of time, and second, mean levels showed little change. Together, these suggested that the absolute scores of most individuals were more-or-less fixed over much of the adult life span.

At the time, this was a revolutionary idea. Many psychologists were skeptical that traits existed at all, let alone that they endured a lifetime. Adult developmentalists were busy generating theories of the midlife crisis and predictable phases of adult development (e.g., D. J. Levinson, Darrow, Klein, M. L. Levinson, & McKee, 1978). Almost everyone assumed that life events like marriage, parenting, retirement, and chronic illnesses would profoundly affect personality.

Two decades and many longitudinal studies later, the notion of predominant stability in personality traits is no longer in doubt. Psychologists have been persuaded that traits are, indeed, enduring dispositions, and research today focuses on the details of the relatively subtle changes that do occur. The interpretation of the observed age effects also remains controversial. In this chapter we will summarize current American research on mean-level changes in personality as a background for cross-cultural comparisons and exploit the power of cross-cultural designs in interpreting age effects.

ASSOCIATIONS OF AGE WITH PERSONALITY TRAITS

It might appear that the description of age trends in personality trait development would be a simple and straightforward research endeavor. How difficult can it be to chart changes in a personality variable across the life span? In fact, it is fiendishly difficult. Cross-sectional studies can be done quickly, but their results may reflect cohort differences or sampling biases rather than aging. Longitudinal studies take time, and they were all designed to answer yesterday's questions, not those that might be asked today. Like cross-sectional studies, longitudinal studies are ambiguous, because they inevitably confound aging with secular change. Because the effects of aging on personality are small in magnitude, they require large samples and powerful designs, and even then a host of artifacts like practice effects or selective mortality may obscure them. Longitudinal studies are an essential component of a suite of study designs containing cross-sectional, time-sequential, and cohort-sequential designs that are needed for a proper understanding of apparent age effects (Costa & McCrae, 1982). Determining that age effects are true maturational changes requires consistent results across these three types of research designs. Our early generalization that "personality is stable after age 30" (Costa & McCrae, 1988, p. 853) was based not on an absence of significant age effects, but on the absence of a consistent pattern of age effects across different research designs.

Subsequent studies have suggested to us that there are some consistent patterns that can be interpreted as true maturational change, although they are rather subtle. In brief, it appears that *Neuroticism (N) and Extraversion (E) decline from late adolescence on, that Agreeableness (A) and Conscientiousness (C) increase, and that Openness (O) increases in the teens and 20s, and thereafter declines. Most of the change occurs in late adolescence and early adulthood, and the total change across the lifetime is relatively small in magnitude, amounting in total to from one half to one full standard deviation* (Costa & McCrae, 2002). However, these generalizations are by no means universally accepted among adult developmentalists (e.g., Helson, Jones, & Kwan, 2002), and before proceeding further it is wise to re-evaluate them in light of recent findings.

Three recent studies must be considered. Mroczek and Spiro (2003) examined changes in N and E in a sample of over 1,600 men initially from age 43 to age 91 and followed for up to 12 years. Overall, N declined from age 40 to age 80, and then rose slightly. The general decline is consistent in direction with our summary, but considerably larger in magnitude than we would predict. Indeed, if extrapolated back to age 18, the Mroczek and Spiro linear effect would suggest a change of 1.2 SD by age 80, which could certainly not be called relatively small.

In sharp contrast, E was completely flat in this sample, showing no decline at all between age 40 and age 100. This finding would be consistent with our summary if these men had declined in E between age 18 and age 40, although our expectation would be for continued slow and relatively small change after age 40 (Costa & McCrae, 2002).

Srivastava, John, Gosling, and Potter (2003) reported a large-scale, Internet-based cross-sectional study that included women as well as men, and that assessed all five factors. It covered the range from age 21 to age 60. In many respects, their results are consistent with our summary: N and O declined with age, whereas A and C increased. The effect sizes were relatively small in magnitude, ranging from about .25 SD for N and O to about .5 SD for C. As in Mroczek and Spiro (2003), E showed little age effect.

However, because of their very large sample size ($N = 132,515$), Srivastava et al. (2003) were able to ask much more fine-grained questions. In particular, they were interested in testing two hypotheses: First, that there was no change after age 30 (a hypothesis we would have offered 20 years ago), and second, that the rate of change was higher between age 21 and age 30 than thereafter, as suggested by our summary. The first hypothesis was not supported; the second was supported for C, but not for the other four factors. In fact, in the case of A, the cross-sectionally estimated rate of change was higher after age 30. It is unfortunate that these authors did not include data from respondents from age 18 to age 20, because it is known that change occurs in that age range (Robins, Fraley, Roberts, & Trzesniewski, 2001), and it is likely that the estimated rate of change from age 18 to age 30 would have been greater for all factors.

In computing slopes before and after age 30, Srivastava et al. (2003) found one consistent instance of a reversal of direction: In both men and women, O increased slightly from age 21 to age 30, and decreased thereafter. This mid-20s peak had been suggested by previous findings of increasing O in high school (McCrae et al., 2002) and college (Robins et al., 2001), and many cross-sectional studies showing lower O scores in later life (e.g., McCrae & Costa, 2003, chap. 5).

Srivastava et al. (2003) noted significant gender differences in estimated rates of change for all the factors except C, but the effect was sizable only for N: Women declined about one third standard deviation on that factor, whereas men did not change. The authors interpreted this as evidence of the sociocultural influence of women's roles, but before such an interpretation is entertained, the data themselves must be evaluated. How can the flat curve of N for men in this cross-sectional study be reconciled with the steep longitudinal decline in N reported by Mroczek and Spiro (2003)? A mini-meta-analysis averaging those two studies would show a relatively small decline in N for men, which would be consistent with other longitudinal results. Costa, Herbst, McCrae, and Siegler (2000) reported a 9-year study of 40-year-olds and showed relatively small declines in N for both men and women. If there were consistent gender differences in developmental curves, then there might be some question about their environmental origins—but so far such differences have not been demonstrated.

Indeed, cross-sectional data, even from vast samples, is often of limited utility in explaining or even describing age changes. The developmental curves estimated from cross-sectional studies are actually composed of data from different people born at different times, and there is no assurance that any individual ever followed these courses. Cohort effects are a well-known danger in cross-sectional studies, but there are other problems as well. For example, A is thought to be associated with lower risk of coronary disease (Costa, Stone, McCrae, Dembroski, & Williams, 1987), so the higher levels of A in older populations may be the result of selective mortality, not maturational increase in the trait level. That interpretation would be consistent with the longitudinal findings of Costa et al. (2000), who found no change in A over a 6-year interval. Sampling bias is another problem, particularly troubling in Internet studies, where respondents are self-selected.

Many of the problems posed in interpreting cross-sectional data can be solved by longitudinal studies that assess the same individuals on two or more occasions. Roberts, Walton, & Viechtbauer (2006) reported a meta-analysis of studies covering the range from age 10 to age 70+. The studies used a variety of personality measures, which Roberts et al. assigned to one of the five factors, or, in the case of E-related scales, to subfactors of Social Vitality and Dominance. N decreased at a steady rate from age 10 on, at a rate that would suggest a drop of nearly 1 full *SD* over the full life span; generally similar patterns were seen for men and women. Social Vitality showed small increases and subsequent declines.

Roberts et al. (2006) reported that Dominance increased from age 10 to age 40. Considered as an aspect of *E*, that finding is inconsistent with our expectation that *E* ought to decline in this time period. However, scales like California Psychological Inventory Dominance are also related to facets of C (McCrae, Costa, & Piedmont, 1993) that would be expected to increase with age.

O increased from age 10 to age 22, and declined in the decade of the 60s; these findings are consistent with the reversal of direction seen in Srivastava et al. Agreeableness increased from age 10 to age 30 and again from age 50 to age 60; C increased from age 18 to age 40 and from age 50 to age 70 in the Roberts et al. meta-analysis. The authors concluded that change was most marked in young adulthood rather than in adolescence or later life, although most traits showed some evidence of continued change after age 30.

These three studies are generally consistent with previous findings, but all differed in some details from our summary. The most striking divergence is with regard to E. None of the new studies showed the decline in E we have come to expect, and one aspect of E, Dominance, appeared to increase during young adulthood. The moral of all this is that new studies and new approaches are still needed to describe reliably the relation of traits to age.

As mentioned earlier, some of the discrepancies between studies may have to do with the personality measures used. So far personality has been discussed only at the level of broad factors, which are known to be composed of more narrow, specific traits or facets. The Revised NEO Personality Inventory (NEO–PI–R; Costa & McCrae, 1992) provides scales to measure six facets for each factor, and facets defining the same factor sometimes have different developmental courses (McCrae et al., 1999). For example, the Excitement Seeking facet of E shows a sharp decline with age, whereas the Warmth facet does not show this decline. If the Social Vitality scales reviewed by Roberts et al. (2006) were chiefly related to warmth and sociability, then the general lack of age changes is more understandable. Unfortunately, it is not clear from their description of Social Vitality which facets of E are included.

INTERPRETATION OF THE EFFECTS

There are two major problems in interpreting age associations. The first is to distinguish true maturational change from various artifacts that mimic change, such as sampling bias in cross-sectional studies and practice effects in longitudinal studies (McCrae & Costa, 2003). In general, the most convincing way to demonstrate maturational change is by convergence across different research designs, which are susceptible to different artifacts (Costa & McCrae, 1982). Effects that appear in both longitudinal and cross-sectional studies are more likely to be real changes, and the patterns we have summarized are supported by both kinds of research.

The second problem concerns the causal origin of changes. Why does N decline from adolescence on? The possible causes fit within the general rubrics of nature and nurture, intrinsic maturation and common experience. Perhaps N declines in the same way that visual acuity does, a simple result of wear-and-tear in an aging psychological mechanism.

Perhaps it is genetically programmed to decline as an evolved mechanism for promoting emotional stability in parents and the elders who lead human groups. However, it is also possible that it has purely psychological causes, such as accumulated wisdom in coping with stress. In general, if the causes of personality change are environmental, the nature of the changes can be expected to vary across different environments.

Most psychologists prefer to hypothesize environmental causes of change, in part because they imply that psychological interventions may be feasible. If N declines because people eventually learn how to cope, couldn't instruction in effective coping lead to lowered N and better mental health earlier in life? In Five-Factor Theory (FFT; McCrae & Costa, 1999) we have taken a less popular view, attributing traits and their developmental course exclusively to biological bases. We have done so in part because that view fits well with findings from behavior genetics (Bouchard & Loehlin, 2001), and in part because we are painfully aware of the limitations (Ellis, 1987) of the deliberate psychological interventions that have so far been devised for changing personality traits (as opposed to symptoms or problem behaviors). It is, of course, likely that there are also environmental influences on trait development in some circumstances, although in FFT, environmental influences operate on Characteristic Adaptations rather than Basic Tendencies. Thus, for the present, FFT adopts a parsimonious position that recognizes only biological influences. Cross-cultural studies offer important tests of the theory.

Within any one culture, environmental effects are most convincingly shown in longitudinal designs, in which people who experience an event or circumstance change in trait level relative to people who did not experience it. For example, Costa et al. (2000) reported that women who were divorced between baseline and follow-up assessments increased in E and O relative to women who were married. In that case, however, it was not clear how transient or durable the personality changes were, or whether the change in marital status preceded or followed the change in personality—it was only certain that both occurred some time between first and final test administration. A better design was employed by Mroczek and Spiro (2003), who related intraindividual change to life events in the year preceding the initial personality assessment. Among other things, they found that men who had been bereaved in the year before assessment initially scored higher than others on N, but also declined faster on N, suggesting recovery from a depressed or bereaved state. Such findings, if replicated, would suggest environmental causes of personality change.

One can—at least indirectly—test hypotheses about environmental influences on personality development in cross-sectional studies by comparing groups with different life histories. The danger in that approach is that any observed differences may have preceded and caused the life event. If we found that people who had been incarcerated scored lower on C than those who had not, we probably would not conclude that prison has deleterious effects on character; instead, we might suspect that low C led to crime and incarceration (cf. Brooner, Schmidt, & Herbst, 2002). Nevertheless, cross-sectional data contrasting groups with different environmental histories can at least be suggestive. Srivastava et al. (2003) did not have such data, except for social class and ethnicity, and they reported that controlling for those variables had little effect on results. But variation in environmental histories is the stock-in-trade of cross-cultural studies, and cross-cultural studies of age differences have made major contributions to the understanding of personality development.

THE LOGIC OF CROSS-SECTIONAL,
CROSS-CULTURAL COMPARISONS

What can be learned by comparing cross-sectional age differences across different cultures? The answer depends very much on what is found. Suppose, for example, it was found that C increased in the United States, but it declined with age in the People's Republic of China. Taken together, those facts would allow researchers to conclude almost nothing. The opposite trends might be due to different paths of development in the two countries that might, in turn, be attributed to differences in language, or diet, or economic system, or ethnicity. Or they might be due to cohort effects—perhaps the long-term demoralizing effects of the Cultural Revolution among the generation of Chinese that lived through it, or the secular demise of moral standards among successive generations of Americans. Because any two cultures differ in an endless number of ways, the possible causes for observed differences are also endless.

The situation improves considerably when a range of cultures is studied, because culture-level correlations can be statistically evaluated. If a significant correlation was found between the association of age with C in a country and that country's Gross Domestic Product, there would be reason to believe that the developmental course of C is somehow tied to national prosperity. Many explanations are still possible, but the field would have been substantially narrowed.

Cross-cultural differences in age patterns can potentially be interpreted if a large sample of cultures is considered. But cross-cultural *similarities* in age patterns are much more readily interpreted, and strongly suggest that effects observed are true maturation rather than birth cohort effects. Recent studies show that patterns of age differences are actually very similar in the United States and the People's Republic of China (Yang et al., 1999). This is remarkable in some respects, because these two cultures are very different, and their citizens have had markedly different life histories (Yang, McCrae, & Costa, 1998). If personality retains the imprint of earlier life experience, then it should appear in different patterns of age differences. Conversely, no differences suggest no imprint, no cohort effects.

The idea that a similar pattern of age differences across cultures rules out cohort effects is, of course, an oversimplification, for two reasons. First, it is possible that similar age profiles may appear as the result of a complex set of causes that include cohort effects. Perhaps the Chinese who endured the Cultural Revolution were indeed demoralized, but the effect is masked by selective mortality: Only those very high in C survived. Such compound explanations are possible, but not parsimonious. Second, it is possible that effects are due to generational influences that are shared by the two cultures. Both the United States and the China were involved in World War II and the Korean Conflict; both have seen the growth of mass communications and improvements in medicine; both have lived under the threat of nuclear war. Conceivably, such shared influences might give rise to the same pattern of age differences in these two nations. That argument remains when similarities are noted across more than two cultures, although the number of shared influences declines as the number of cultures increases. Portugal was not directly involved in either World War II or the Korean conflict, so similar age differences among the Portuguese could not be attributed to those events.

Cross-cultural studies, then, can assist in the first problem in interpreting age associations, distinguishing true change from cohort effects and other artifacts. In principle, cross-cultural studies can also be useful in distinguishing intrinsic maturation from common environmental effects. As noted earlier, culture-level correlates might be used to explain differing courses of development in different nations. Increasing N might be found in countries with oppressive regimes, suggesting that sustained political oppression leads to chronic malaise; increasing O might be characteristic of nations with high literacy rates, suggesting that O can be learned. Hologeistic methods (R. Naroll, Michik, & F. Naroll, 1980) can be used to formally assess such hypotheses.

When age patterns are similar, however, the most straightforward interpretation is that the effects are not merely maturation; they are intrinsic maturation. Environmental influences surely vary immensely across cultures, and these differences have been shown to have profound effects on many aspects of psychological functioning (Markus & Kitayama, 1991). When we began cross-cultural research on adult personality development a few years ago, no one would have been surprised to find vastly different developmental paths in different cultures. In fact, the first comparison we did appeared to show that Croatian adolescents were better adjusted, less sociable, more conservative, more generative, and higher in self-discipline than their parents—the exact opposite of the American pattern. Was something in the recent experience of war in the Balkans the cause of this striking cultural difference? As it turned out, the explanation was more prosaic: The adolescent scales had mistakenly been reverse scored. Properly keyed, Croatians showed the same age differences as Americans (McCrae & Costa, 2003).

Similarity of age patterns across cultures does not guarantee that the causes are rooted in the biology of the species, because similarity might also result from cultural universals. In every culture, parents (or members of the parental generation) are obliged to raise, educate, and nurture their children, and to earn a livelihood. For these universal tasks, it would be advantageous to be high in A and C, and it might be argued that all cultures have devised means to socialize young adults in these directions. Neyer and Asendorpf (2001) have begun to tease apart these possibilities by tracing development in young adults who do and do not have children, establish relationships, and so on. At issue is whether personality change is more pronounced in those individuals who adopt the roles hypothesized to require more mature personality traits.

CROSS-CULTURAL FINDINGS

Until recently, there was essentially no literature comparing age differences in personality traits across cultures. Although there have been several studies of aging outside North America (e.g., Thomae, 1976), few comparisons of age differences using the same instruments had been made. Perhaps the best-known were reports by Gutmann (1974) that men moved from active to passive to magical mastery styles in TAT responses with increasing age in the United States, Mexico, and among the Highland Druze of Israel. Two of the first comparisons using self-report inventories were, by chance, presented at the same Gerontology Society of America symposium (McCrae et al., 1996; Tarnowski, Shen, Diehl, & Labouvie-Vief, 1996). Since that time, the growing use of the NEO–PI–R in translation (McCrae & Allik, 2002) has made many comparisons possible.

The Five Factors

In the first of these (McCrae et al., 1999), NEO–PI–R factor scores from Germany, Italy, Portugal, Croatia, and South Korea were examined in four age groups: 18–21, 22–29, 30–49, and 50+. There were significant age effects in all five cultures for E, O, A, and C; significant effects for N were found in German and Korean samples. Regression analyses showed that the effects were consistent in direction with American findings and generally relatively small in magnitude: Average B weights for N, E, O, A, and C, respectively, were –0.56, –1.73, –2.08, 1.70, and 2.20 T-score points per decade. At that rate, if effects are linear, C would increase a full standard deviation from age 18 to age 65. There was evidence, however, that age differences were more pronounced in early adulthood. There were significant differences between the youngest and the two oldest groups in 22 of 25 comparisons, but differences between the two oldest groups in only 10. The rate of change appears to slow down with age.

Data from Russia, Estonia, and Japan (as well as the United States) were examined next (Costa, McCrae et al., 2000). N was not related to age in the Russian and Estonian samples, but all other factors showed the expected pattern in all three cultures. Data were available from the short version of the NEO–PI–R, the NEO Five Factor Inventory (NEO–FFI; Costa & McCrae, 1992) in German, British, Spanish, Czech, and Turkish samples (McCrae et al., 2000). That study included a fifth age group, 14 to 17. Analyses showed significant cross-sectional declines in N and E and increases in C in all five samples. Agreeableness increased in German, Czech, and Turkish samples, and O declined in Spanish, Czech, and Turkish samples. The German and British data provided the first evidence of a curvilinear effect for O: Respondents from age 18 to age 29 scored higher in O than either younger or older participants.

Two of the cultures mentioned earlier, Czech and Russian, were later studied more intensively in larger samples using the full NEO–PI–R (McCrae et al., 2004). All five factors showed significant age regressions in the expected direction in both cultures when self-reports were analyzed; seven of these effects were replicated when observer ratings of the same respondents were analyzed. Five of the 20 analyses showed significant curvilinear effects, with more pronounced change in early adulthood. Age was examined only incidentally in studies of Zimbabweans (Piedmont, Bain, McCrae, & Costa, 2002) and psychiatric patients in the People's Republic of China (Yang et al., 1999). In both cultures, N, O, A, and C were significantly related to age in the expected directions, whereas (as in recent American studies) it was not related to E.

The 30 Facets

In 12 of the cultures already mentioned, data were also available on the individual facet scales that define the five factors. Not surprisingly, most facets showed age differences that paralleled the factor they defined: N, E, and O facets generally declined, whereas A and C facets increased with age. However, the strength of the age associations varied considerably. In the first study, E5: Excitement Seeking declined at a rate of nearly 1.5 SDs over the adult life span, 18 to 75, whereas E1: Warmth showed less than .25 SDs change. Again, O1: Fantasy dropped by 1.5 SDs across adulthood, whereas O2: Aesthetics declined by only 0.5 SDs. Generalizations at the factor level conceal consistent variation within factor definers, and future studies and reviews of personality and aging need to take more systematic account of facet-level information.

Facet scores can be decomposed into three portions: That which is common to the factor or factors they define, that which is specific to each facet, and error. Warmth and Gregariousness are not interchangeable measures of E; they measure different, if related, constructs. The difference is attributable to specific variance, and the specific variance of NEO–PI–R facets has been shown to be reliable over time, modestly heritable (Jang, McCrae, Angleitner, Riemann, & Livesley, 1998), and consensually validated (McCrae & Costa, 1992). Two studies (Costa et al., 2000; McCrae et al., 1999) examined the association of age with residual facet scores, net of the five factors. These correlations were quite small, but they tended to be consistent in direction across cultures. For example, the specific variance associated with N2: Angry Hostility increased with age in Germany, Italy, Portugal, Croatia, South Korea, Japan, and Estonia; the specific variance in N4: Self-Consciousness decreased with age in Germany, Italy, Portugal, Croatia, South Korea, and Estonia. These very subtle influences on personality traits are apparently universal.

Age Differences in Eight European Countries

Previous research has examined correlations of age with domains and facets, which is an analytic approach that requires data on age and personality for each individual case. In a number of cultures, the only data available are summary scores. McCrae (2001, 2002) analyzed data from 36 cultures, working with means and standard deviations on the 30 NEO–PI–R facet scales. Separate values were available for men and women, and for college age (roughly 17–21, but varying somewhat across cultures) and adult subsamples. Note that the adult subsamples differed in mean age and age range, but those data were not generally available. Half the cultures provided data from both college age and adult subsamples, and analysis of variance in these cultures showed that adult subsamples scored lower in N, E, and O, and higher in A and C than college age subsamples. Ten of the 18 cultures with age difference data had already been examined in previous studies, using the more informative correlational approaches. But (aside from a personal communication on Belgian age trends reported in Costa, McCrae, & Jónsson, 2002) there have been no previous reports of adult age differences on the NEO–PI–R in Austria, Belgium, Denmark, France, Hungary, Norway, Serbia, or Sweden, and even summary data are worth examining.

We defined domain score values for college age and adult samples as the unweighted mean of men's and women's domain scores. The pattern of age differences at the domain level was consistent with previous results: Adults scored lower in N, E, and O and higher in A and C in 37 of the 40 comparisons. (Adults in Belgium and Norway scored higher than college age respondents on O, and adults in Serbia scored lower on A.) When examined separately for men and women, results were generally similar. In particular, only in Hungary were age differences in N confined to women, as Srivastava et al. (2003) reported in their American sample.

More detailed information on the 30 facet scales of the NEO–PI–R is offered in Table 7.1. For this table, scores for adult and college age subsamples were calculated

TABLE 7.1

Estimated ds for Adult Versus College Age Subsamples in Eight European Cultures

Facet	Austria 138/306	Belgium 102/1017	Denmark 92/1121	France 392/674	Hungary 92/220	Norway 92/692	Serbia 619/501	Sweden 51/669	Mean	12 Cultures[a]
N1: Anxiety	-.39	-.23	-.20	-.35	-.18	-.03	-.22	-.24	-.23	down (5)
N2: Angry Hostility	-.21	-.43	-.35	-.31	-.15	.12	.02	-.13	-.18	down (6)
N3: Depression	-.35	-.45	-.30	-.47	-.33	.04	-.17	-.12	-.27	down (7)
N4: Self-Consciousness	-.27	-.20	-.35	-.31	-.28	-.30	-.09	-.17	-.25	down (7)
N5: Impulsiveness	-.24	-.29	-.48	-.47	-.34	-.24	-.18	-.64	-.36	down (12)
N6: Vulnerability	-.53	-.48	-.25	-.54	-.23	-.04	-.08	-.24	-.30	down (9)
E1: Warmth	-.13	-.03	.00	.10	-.27	.22	-.09	-.30	-.06	down (2)
E2: Gregariousness	-.35	-.31	-.42	-.07	-.53	-.14	-.23	-.78	-.35	down (8)
E3: Assertiveness	.15	.17	-.01	-.08	.04	.33	.18	-.06	.09	down (4)
E4: Activity	.29	.24	.13	.34	.20	.31	.10	.29	.24	down (2)
E5: Excitement Seeking	-.52	-.61	-.96	-.33	-.55	-.67	-.34	-1.05	-.63	down (11)
E6: Positive Emotions	-.11	-.09	-.39	-.12	-.31	-.02	-.19	-.43	-.21	down (10)
O1: Fantasy	-.33	-.13	-.82	-.67	-.57	-.05	-.38	-.63	-.45	down (12)
O2: Aesthetics	-.07	.05	-.02	-.40	-.01	.18	-.41	-.10	-.10	down (9)
O3: Feelings	-.14	.05	-.17	-.37	-.30	.33	-.25	-.19	-.13	down (12)

138

										Trend[a]
O4: Actions	−.08	.36	.00	−.04	.11	.21	−.17	.32	.09	down (10)
O5: Ideas	.07	.29	−.23	−.37	.00	.17	−.33	−.03	−.05	down (10)
O6: Values	−.03	.27	.02	−.13	.13	.33	−.03	.07	.08	down (11)
A1: Trust	.12	.05	.39	.44	.21	.32	.18	.08	.22	up (9)
A2: Straightforwardness	.20	.15	.49	.30	.06	.26	−.06	.51	.24	up (12)
A3: Altruism	.04	.24	.05	.05	.14	.16	−.04	−.05	.07	up (8)
A4: Compliance	.14	.32	.31	.30	−.02	.09	−.11	.35	.17	up (11)
A5: Modesty	−.08	−.02	.39	.01	−.06	.16	−.05	.58	.12	up (12)
A6: Tender-Mindedness	−.12	.07	.13	.08	.10	.20	−.13	.05	.05	up (11)
C1: Competence	.40	.39	.43	.47	.30	.25	.00	.25	.31	up (10)
C2: Order	.22	.44	.33	.24	.21	.13	.02	.43	.25	up (9)
C3: Dutifulness	.40	.88	.74	.64	.34	.09	.27	.78	.51	up (12)
C4: Achievement Striving	.14	.38	.07	.36	.21	.13	−.01	.36	.21	up (8)
C5: Self-Discipline	.31	.69	.56	.70	.37	.33	.13	.70	.47	up (12)
C6: Deliberation	.16	.57	.41	.41	.17	.02	.06	.15	.24	up (12)

Note. Ns for college age/adult subsamples given in the second row.

[a]Trend shows the direction and net number of significant age associations in 12 cultures: Germany, Italy, Portugal, Croatia, South Korea, U.S., Russia, Japan, Estonia, China, Zimbabwe, and Czech Republic (Sample A).

as the unweighted means of men's and women's facet scores; the raw age difference was divided by the mean within-subsample standard deviation. Thus, the tabled values can be roughly interpreted as standardized *d* scores. The mean of the eight effects is given in the ninth column. For comparison, the last column summarizes results from previous research in other cultures. For example, in 12 earlier comparisons, E4: Activity had small but significant negative correlations with age in four cultures, and small positive correlations in two, giving a net trend down by two cultures.

Note first that there is considerable agreement across the eight cultures. One way to quantify that agreement is to correlate the values for each pair of countries across the 30 facet scales. There are 28 pairs of cultures, and correlations range from .44 to .91, all $p < .05$, with a median value of .76. Second, note that these mean age differences generally parallel the results of earlier correlational studies. The last column can be coded from −12 to +12, and the correlation of this 12-culture summary score with the mean of the eight European cultures is .79. Patterns of facet-level age differences are consistent in Europe and around the world.

Third, age differences are generally small. In absolute magnitude, they range from 0 to 1.05; the median value, .23, is less than one quarter standard deviation. However, the interpretation of these values is unclear, because the age of the adults is unspecified. If most of the adults are in their 20s and 30s, then small age differences would not be unexpected. If, however, most of the adults are in their 70s and 80s—and if the effect is linear across the life span—then these are small age differences indeed.

Fourth, it is worth noting that some of the findings do not fit the general trend. E3: Assertiveness and E4: Activity usually show no age differences or small declines. In these eight European countries, however, there is a trend toward higher scores in the older groups for these facets of E. Even more striking is the overall upward trend for Openness to Actions and Values, which have almost uniformly shown age-related declines in previous studies. One possibility is that the preponderance of the adults in these samples are in their 20s, a time in which O apparently continues to increase. Studies of the full age range are clearly needed in these countries.

Finally, the mean values across the eight cultures confirm that age differences are most pronounced for certain traits. The largest effects here are for E5: Excitement Seeking and O1: Fantasy, which decline, and for C3: Dutifulness and C5: Self-Discipline, which increase. By contrast, there are relatively minor age differences for E1: Warmth and O2: Aesthetics. These results confirm previous findings and underscore the conclusion that generalizations at the factor level must be qualified by results at the facet level.

THE CONTRIBUTION OF CROSS-CULTURAL STUDIES

What can be concluded from this review of cross-cultural studies of age differences? First, the pattern of age differences is remarkably similar across vastly different cultures. It might be argued that most studies involved college students and their families, who may be among the most Westernized members of most cultures. In that respect, the effects of culture may be attenuated. Conversely, it must be recalled that investigators in different cultures used different methods of sampling that may have introduced unique biases into results; the fact that much the same age effects emerged in all of them attests to their strength relative to other effects.

Second, it seems increasingly likely that the effects are maturational rather than generational. Common cohort effects would demand common causes, and although there are events and circumstances common to the recent histories of such diverse cultures as Russia, Turkey, Portugal, and South Korea, it is hard to understand how they would have produced the observed effects. Why would growing up in the 1950s anywhere on Earth lead to higher A and lower N scores than growing up the 1970s? And if life experiences shared across cultures shape personality traits, then why don't life experiences unique to specific cultures? Why should a common experience such as watching television (including the state-run television of the former Soviet Union) be more formative than the unique experiences of living through the end of colonialism in Zimbabwe or growing up in the peaceful neutrality of Sweden? These studies do not rule out cohort effects, but they make the hypothesis of maturation—of true age change—far more plausible.

Third, and by a similar logic, these studies seem to point to intrinsic, species-wide, and thus biologically based causes for age changes. It may be true that there are certain age role requirements that are common to every culture, most directly dealing with the need for adults to nurture and educate children. These cultural dictates might encourage the development of similar traits at similar ages in all cultures. But it is also true that there are profound cultural differences in age role expectations. Power is concentrated in old age in many Asian cultures, but in middle adulthood in the United States. In some cultures, 20-year-olds are routinely saddled with the responsibilities of supporting their families; in other cultures, 20 is an age of freedom from responsibility. Why are such cultural differences not apparent in different developmental curves? Perhaps because trait development is biologically fixed. Incidentally, the hypothesis of intrinsic maturation is also bolstered by similar age trends in chimpanzees (King, Landau, & Guggenheim, 1998), and by evidence of a modest genetic influence on differences in personality change in humans (McGue, Bacon, & Lykken, 1993).

However, even if these cross-cultural comparisons make it likely that most age differences are due to intrinsic maturational changes, they do not rule out the possibility that there are other effects on trait development in adults that might be superimposed on the basic pattern. That hypothesis could account for the occasional failures to conform to the basic pattern, such as the fact that adults in Serbia score lower on A than adolescents. However, as discussed earlier, cultural differences in single cultures are essentially uninterpretable. What is required is a pattern of cultural differences across a group of cultures. A possible pattern is seen in Table 7.1, where all eight samples showed increases with age in E4: Activity. The fact that all these cultures are European suggests that there may be some shared features of European culture that promote higher activity levels in middle-aged, in comparison to college-age, adults. That hypothesis can be tested by examining effects on Activity in the 12 cultures previously studied. Six of these showed significant age effects on Activity, and Germany was one of two that showed increases. The other, however, was Zimbabwe; and three of the cultures in which Activity declined significantly with age—Portugal, Estonia, and the Czech Republic—were European. The pattern in Table 7.1 is not confirmed in other samples. At present, it seems unlikely that any persuasive case could be made for systematic age differences attributable to culture, but that conclusion can be reexamined as the number of cultures studied increases.

FUTURE DIRECTIONS

We have argued that cross-cultural studies are uniquely informative about the interpretation of age differences, but this does not diminish the need for longitudinal studies to confirm or quality conclusions. The first 5-year follow-up of a German sample has recently been reported (Angleitner, 2002); even over this brief interval, a significant decline in N and increase in C were found, especially for those under age 30. Plans are also underway for a Russian longitudinal study of couples and siblings (Martin, Costa, Oryol, Rukavishnikov, & Senin, 2002). In addition to offering a new kind of data on changes in mean levels, these studies will provide some of the first cross-cultural information on the stability of individual differences. Ideally, new longitudinal studies will also be begun in a more diverse sample of cultures. We know the broad outlines of human trait development, but there are still many details to resolve. Researchers should know that the labor of conducting longitudinal research in Latin America, Africa, and Asia is likely to be richly rewarded.

Certainly, future research should include personality assessments at the facet level. Some of the most dramatic age changes are seen with particular facets, such as Excitement Seeking and Openness to Fantasy. Studies that seek to determine the causes of age changes in personality may be most successful when focused on these facets, where statistical power is increased by larger effect sizes.

Finally, future studies should include not only self-reports, but also observer ratings of personality. An ongoing cross-cultural study in which college students rate college-age or adult targets has suggested both similarities and differences with self-report results (McCrae et al., 2005). Future cross-cultural studies should include raters from a broader age range, and should explicitly measure cultural expectations for age-graded behavior and traits. Such studies can help illuminate how personality changes—and is perceived to change—across the life span.

ACKNOWLEDGMENT

For data used in Table 7.1, we thank Fritz Ostendorf, Filip de Fruyt, Erik L. Mortensen, Jean-Pierre Rolland, Zsófia Szirmák, Hilmar Nordvik, Goran Knežević, and Hans Bergmann.

REFERENCES

Angleitner, A. (2002, July). *Personality in adulthood: Findings from the Bielefeld Longitudinal Study of Adult Twins.* Keynote address presented at the 11th European Conference on Personality, Jena, Germany.

Bouchard, T. J., & Loehlin, J. C. (2001). Genes, evolution, and personality. *Behavior Genetics, 31,* 243–273.

Brooner, R. K., Schmidt, C. W., & Herbst, J. H. (2002). Personality trait characteristics of opioid abusers with and without comorbid personality disorders. In P. T. Costa, Jr. & T. A. Widiger (Eds.), *Personality disorders and the Five-Factor Model of personality* (2nd ed., pp. 249–268). Washington, DC: American Psychological Association.

Costa, P. T., Jr., Herbst, J. H., McCrae, R. R., & Siegler, I. C. (2000). Personality at midlife: Stability, intrinsic maturation, and response to life events. *Assessment, 7,* 365–378.

Costa, P. T., Jr., & McCrae, R. R. (1982). An approach to the attribution of age, period, and cohort effects. *Psychological Bulletin, 92, 238–250.*

Costa, P. T., Jr., & McCrae, R. R. (1988). Personality in adulthood: A six-year longitudinal study of self-reports and spouse ratings on the NEO Personality Inventory. *Journal of Personality and Social Psychology, 54, 853–863.*

Costa, P. T., Jr., & McCrae, R. R. (1992). *Revised NEO Personality Inventory (NEO–PI–R) and NEO Five-Factor Inventory (NEO–FFI) professional manual.* Odessa, FL: Psychological Assessment Resources.

Costa, P. T., Jr., & McCrae, R. R. (2002). Looking backward: Changes in the mean levels of personality traits from 80 to 12. In D. Cervone & W. Mischel (Eds.), *Advances in personality science* (pp. 219–237). New York: Guilford.

Costa, P. T., Jr., McCrae, R. R., & Jónsson, F. H. (2002). Validity and utility of the Revised NEO Personality Inventory: Examples from Europe. In B. De Raad & M. Perugini (Eds.), *Big Five Assessment* (pp. 61–77). Göttingen, Germany: Hogrefe & Huber.

Costa, P. T., Jr., McCrae, R. R., Martin, T. A., Oryol, V. E., Senin, I. G., Rukavishnikov, A. A., Shimonaka, Y., Nakazato, K., Gondo, Y., Takayama, M., Allik, J., Kallasmaa, T., & Realo, A. (2000). Personality development from adolescence through adulthood: Further cross-cultural comparisons of age differences. In V. J. Molfese & D. Molfese (Eds.), *Temperament and personality development across the life span* (pp. 235–252). Hillsdale, NJ: Lawrence Erlbaum Associates.

Costa, P. T., Jr., Stone, S. V., McCrae, R. R., Dembroski, T. M., & Williams, R. B., Jr. (1987). Hostility, agreeableness—antagonism, and coronary heart disease. *Holistic Medicine, 2, 161–167.*

Ellis, A. (1987). The impossibility of achieving consistently good mental health. *American Psychologist, 42, 364–375.*

Gutmann, D. L. (1974). Alternatives to disengagement: The old men of highland Druze. In R. LeVine (Ed.), *Culture and personality: Contemporary readings.* Chicago: Aldine.

Helson, R., Jones, C., & Kwan, V. S. Y. (2002). Personality change over 40 years of adulthood: Hierarchical linear modeling analyses of two longitudinal samples. *Journal of Personality and Social Psychology, 83, 752–766.*

Jang, K. L., McCrae, R. R., Angleitner, A., Riemann, R., & Livesley, W. J. (1998). Heritability of facet-level traits in a cross-cultural twin sample: Support for a hierarchical model of personality. *Journal of Personality and Social Psychology, 74, 1556–1565.*

Kelly, E. L. (1955). Consistency of the adult personality. *American Psychologist, 10, 659–681.*

King, J. E., Landau, V. I., & Guggenheim, C. B. (1998, May). *Age-related personality changes in chimpanzees.* Paper presented at the 10th annual convention of the American Psychological Society, Washington, DC.

Levinson, D. J., Darrow, C. N., Klein, E. B., Levinson, M. L., & McKee, B. (1978). *The seasons of a man's life.* New York: Knopf.

Markus, H. R., & Kitayama, S. (1991). Culture and the self: Implications for cognition, emotion, and motivation. *Psychological Review, 98, 224–253.*

Martin, T. A., Costa, P. T., Jr., Oryol, V. E., Rukavishnikov, A. A., & Senin, I. G. (2002). Applications of the Russian NEO–PI–R. In R. R. McCrae & J. Allik (Eds.), *The Five-Factor Model of personality across cultures* (pp. 253–269). New York: Kluwer Academic/Plenum.

McCrae, R. R. (2001). Trait psychology and culture: Exploring intercultural comparisons. *Journal of Personality, 69, 819–846.*

McCrae, R. R. (2002). NEO–PI–R data from 36 cultures: Further intercultural comparisons. In R. R. McCrae & J. Allik (Eds.), *The Five-Factor Model of personality across cultures* (pp. 105–125). New York: Kluwer Academic/Plenum.

McCrae, R. R., & Allik, J. (Eds.). (2002). *The Five-Factor Model of personality across cultures.* New York: Kluwer Academic/Plenum.

McCrae, R. R., & Costa, P. T., Jr. (1984). *Emerging lives, enduring dispositions: Personality in adulthood.* Boston: Little, Brown.

McCrae, R. R., & Costa, P. T., Jr. (1992). Discriminant validity of NEO–PI–R facets. *Educational and Psychological Measurement, 52, 229–237.*

McCrae, R. R., & Costa, P. T., Jr. (1999). A Five-Factor Theory of personality. In L. A. Pervin & O. P. John (Eds.), *Handbook of personality: Theory and research* (2nd ed., pp. 139–153). New York: Guilford.

McCrae, R. R., & Costa, P. T., Jr. (2003). *Personality in adulthood: A Five-Factor Theory perspective* (2nd. ed.). New York: Guilford.

McCrae, R. R., Costa, P. T., Jr., de Lima, M. P., Simões, A., Ostendorf, F., Angleitner, A., Marušić, I., Bratko, D., Caprara, G. V., Barbaranelli, C., Chae, J. H., & Piedmont, R. L. (1999). Age differences in personality across the adult lifespan: Parallels in five cultures. *Developmental Psychology, 35*, 466–477.

McCrae, R. R., Costa, P. T., Jr., Hřebíčková, M., Urbánek, T., Martin, T. A., Oryol, V. E., Rukavishnikov, A. A., & Senin, I. G. (2004). Age differences in personality traits across cultures: Self-report and observer perspectives. *European Journal of Personality, 18*, 143–157.

McCrae, R. R., Costa, P. T., Jr., Ostendorf, F., Angleitner, A., Hřebíčková, M., Avia, M. D., Sanz, J., Sánchez-Bernardos, M. L., Kusdil, M. E., Woodfield, R., Saunders, P. T., & Smith, P. B. (2000). Nature over nurture: Temperament, personality, and lifespan development. *Journal of Personality and Social Psychology, 78*, 173–186.

McCrae, R. R., Costa, P. T., Jr., Piedmont, R. L., Chae, J.-H., Caprara, G. V., Barbaranelli, C., Marušić, I., & Bratko, D. (1996, November). *Personality development from college to midlife: A cross-cultural comparison.* Paper presented at the annual convention of the Gerontological Society of America, Washington, DC.

McCrae, R. R., Costa, P. T., Jr., Terracciano, A., Parker, W. D., Mills, C. J., De Fruyt, F., & Mervielde, I. (2002). Personality trait development from 12 to 18: Longitudinal, cross-sectional, and cross-cultural analyses. *Journal of Personality and Social Psychology, 83*, 1456–1468.

McCrae, R. R., Terracciano, A., & 78 Members of the Personality Profiles of Cultures Project. (2005). Universal features of personality traits from the observer's perspective: Data from 50 cultures. *Journal of Personality and Social Psychology, 88*, 547–561.

McGue, M., Bacon, S., & Lykken, D. T. (1993). Personality stability and change in early adulthood: A behavioral genetic analysis. *Developmental Psychology, 29*, 96–109.

Mroczek, D. K., & Spiro, A., III. (2003). Modeling intraindividual change in personality traits: Findings from the Normative Aging Study. *Journal of Gerontology: Psychological Sciences, 58B*, P153–P165.

Naroll, R., Michik, G. L., & Naroll, F. (1980). Holocultural research methods. In J. W. Berry (Ed.), *Handbook of cross-cultural psychology: Vol. 2. Methodology* (pp. 479–521). Boston: Allyn & Bacon.

Neyer, F. J., & Asendorpf, J. B. (2001). Personality-relationship transaction in young adulthood. *Journal of Personality and Social Psychology, 81*, 1190–1204.

Piedmont, R. L., Bain, E., McCrae, R. R., & Costa, P. T., Jr. (2002). The applicability of the Five-Factor Model in a Sub-Saharan culture: The NEO–PI–R in Shona. In R. R. McCrae & J. Allik (Eds.), *The Five-Factor Model of personality across cultures* (pp. 155–173). New York: Kluwer Academic/Plenum.

Roberts, B. W., Walton, K. E., & Viechtbauer, W. (2006). Patterns of mean-level change in personality traits across the life course: A meta-analysis of longitudinal studies. *Psychological Bulletin, 132*, 3–25.

Robins, R. W., Fraley, R. C., Roberts, B. W., & Trzesniewski, K. H. (2001). A longitudinal study of personality change in young adulthood. *Journal of Personality, 69*, 617–640.

Srivastava, S., John, O. P., Gosling, S. D., & Potter, J. (2003). Development of personality in early and middle age: Set like plaster or persistent change? *Journal of Personality and Social Psychology, 84*, 1041–1053.

Strong, E. K., Jr. (1951). Permanence of interest scores over 22 years. *Journal of Applied Psychology, 35*, 89–91.

Tarnowski, A., Shen, J., Diehl, M., & Labouvie-Vief, G. (1996, November). *Adult age differences in personality: Similarity of U.S. and Chinese patterns.* Paper presented at the 49th annual scientific meeting of the Gerontological Society of America, Washington, DC.

Thomae, H. (Ed.). (1976). *Patterns of aging: Findings from the Bonn Longitudinal Study of Aging.* Basel: S Karger.

Yang, J., McCrae, R. R., & Costa, P. T., Jr. (1998). Adult age differences in personality traits in the United States and the People's Republic of China. *Journal of Gerontology: Psychological Sciences, 53B,* P375–P383.

Yang, J., McCrae, R. R., Costa, P. T., Jr., Dai, X., Yao, S., Cai, T., & Gao, B. (1999). Cross-cultural personality assessment in psychiatric populations: The NEO–PI–R in the People's Republic of China. *Psychological Assessment, 11,* 359–368.

8

Evolution and Personality:
A New Look at Machiavellianism

Patricia H. Hawley
University of Kansas

Evolutionary approaches to personality offer novel insights into human behavior and social development. Although evolutionary revelations have long been found in fields as diverse as biology, anthropology, economics, and embryology, to name a few, a growing body of work can be found in psychology in the domains of social, developmental, cognitive, and clinical. Yet, this growing field of "evolutionary psychology" is not of one mind. Some refer to it as a revolution in psychology (Buss, 1999) in its inspired and righteous pursuit of the psychic unity of mankind (Tooby & Cosmides, 1990). Others (e.g., Hogan, 1998; Scher & Rauscher, 2003; Wilson, 2003) are concerned that the most vocal "evolutionary psychologists" are narrow in both their views and questions and, moreover, overestimate the originality of evolutionary reasoning to human behavior.

An example of this growing dissent over the standing of evolutionary psychology as its own unified domain is the disagreement about the relation between individual differences and human evolution. That is, do personality characteristics represent insignificant noise, variability in adaptation to local conditions, or variegated genetically encoded morphs? This chapter explores these three views and exemplifies the application of evolutionary theory to human personality with a new approach to Machiavellianism (Hawley, 1999). Additionally, this chapter highlights the need for explicitly considering contextual variables and interpersonal relationships when discussing adaptive stable behavior patterns (i.e., traits).

EVOLUTIONARY VIEWS ON INDIVIDUAL DIFFERENCES

Nonessential Noise

How can evolution by natural selection account for individual differences? One argument suggests that there would be no variability in the population if a trait was adaptive (Tooby & Cosmides, 1990). Indeed, one commonly accepted criterion for winning the label of "adaptation" is reliability; that is, does the quality or behavior develop consistently across all members of a species in normal environments and does it perform dependably the functions for which it was designed (Williams, 1966)? From biological perspectives, phenotypic (and thereby genotypic) variability is the raw material on which natural selection acts to homogenize a population or cull less optimal variants in favor of those that foster differential reproductive success (Williams, 1966). Individual differences are thus often considered "noise," which results from nonselective mechanisms such as mutation, recombination, and genetic drift. Accordingly, many evolutionary psychologists focus on species-typical behavior patterns and preferences (e.g., "a universal human nature"; Tooby & Cosmides, 1990, p. 17; but see Mealey, 1995) within domains such as mate selection and standards of physical beauty, with little consideration for individual difference variables (e.g., Cosmides & Tooby, 1995) with the possible exception of broad classifications such as gender, stage in the life span, or socioeconomic status (e.g., Buss, 1994).

Phenotypic Plasticity. In so far as personality reflects an individual's unique pattern of traits (e.g., Guilford, 1959), the prevailing evolutionary psychology paradigm (e.g., Tooby and Cosmides, 1990) recognizes that proximally adaptive stable behavior patterns can result from common-to-all gene suites that are differentially triggered by environmental cues (phenotypic plasticity; Wilson, 1994). In terms of "aggressiveness," for example, Tooby and Cosmides argued that every individual in a social group has inherited a complex aggression regulation mechanism (i.e., an adaptation), but with heritable variation in its activation threshold (i.e., nonessential noise). Activation of this "aggression mechanism" may be transitory (states), or may lead to enduring individual differences (traits) if activation conditions persist or if early activations permanently calibrate the system. Calibrations may be set in response to early environmental conditions such as family milieu or parenting variables (e.g., Bowlby, 1969; Draper & Harpending, 1982, 1987; Sulloway, 1996), win–loss experiences in the peer group (Hawley & Little, 1999), and/or in response to physical or behavioral characteristics of the self (e.g., activation threshold may be high in an individual who is small and weak, highly agreeable, or anxious).

Whereas Tooby and Cosmides did not consider these individual differences as adaptations per se in the classic sense, early calibrations can clearly be construed as adaptive responses to present-day environmental contexts. As an example of this process, Draper and Harpending (1982) explored the relation between reproductive strategy and early environmental cues (here, the absence of the father). Their argument rests on the assumption that what is adaptive for the individual is highly dependent not only on genotype, but also on the local environment in which the individual is raised. In the case of an absent father, the developing child may adopt a life history strategy characterized by early onset of sexual maturity and sexual activity, low parental investment, and high aggressiveness. Whereas traditional approaches may consider aggressiveness and sexual impulsivity as "maladjustment," these behaviors may compensate for suboptimal environments characterized by abbreviated life spans, intense competition for few resources, and low paternal investment.

Frequency-Dependent Selection and Game Theoretic Models

An additional line of reasoning maintains that physical or psychological individual differences may be more significant than nonessential noise and, furthermore, may reflect considerably more than variability in activation threshold (e.g., Wilson, 1994). For example, game theoretic models (e.g., Lewontin, 1961) have been usefully employed to draw inferences about various naturally selected strategies and the conditions under which they would be favored. Such an analysis assumes that payoff outcomes of one player's strategy depends on the strategies employed by the other players in the population. With respect to animal contests, for example, a population of players behaving according to either cautious (Dove) or escalating (Hawk) strategies can achieve a point at which the proportion of players adopting each strategy stabilizes to a population equilibrium (an evolutionary stable composition; Colman, 1999; Maynard Smith, 1974; Maynard Smith & Price, 1973). In other words, if hawks were to flood a population, there is a point at which costly hawk–hawk encounters increase the cost of hawkish behavior beyond its benefits. As a result, the benefits of caution increase, and so too does the relative frequency of doves. The number of hawks and doves thusly fluctuates until the function stabilizes. In more complex scenarios, optimal strategies may be "mixed" rather than "pure"; that is, overall payoffs may be maximized if a player flexibly responds to the behavior of its competitor as well as to the player's own win–loss history (e.g., pursue if a win is likely, defer if it is not). It should be noted that "strategy" is used in the sense of life history strategy and as such need not imply conscious calculation or forethought on the part of the behaving organism.

Game theoretic models have demonstrated that the fitness of any phenotype (and underlying genotype) depends on the phenotypic composition of the population (hence, *frequency-dependent selection*). In contrast to traditional models of natural selection that pit individual against nature, frequency-dependent selection highlights the behavioral variability expected in a population arising as a response to the behavior of others. Such models furthermore suggest that strategies that appear suboptimal (e.g., escalation) may in fact lead to optimal payoffs depending on other strategies adopted in the group.

Frequency-dependent selection, more so than the phenotypic plasticity model, views sociality as a stream of competitive contests and behavior as inherently strategic: Individuals strive to maximize gains in the presence of others who are also attempting to do so. Frequency-dependent selection permits variegated behavioral phenotypes to coexist and, moreover, to have correspondingly distinct genotypes. But frequency-dependent selection and phenotypic plasticity models need not be mutually exclusive; strategies can feasibly be calibrated by environmental cues that carry information about important aspects of the competitive landscape. As a theoretical example, parenting styles together with early experiences with competitive contests with peers may effectively communicate to the developing "player": "The world is full of hawks and doves. To thrive, it is best to play both." Deciding what to do under what conditions is the topic of the next section, the social function of intellect and Machiavellian intelligence.

THE SOCIAL FUNCTION OF INTELLECT
AND MACHIAVELLIAN INTELLIGENCE

The evolution of intelligence has been the source of controversy and discussion for several decades. Traditional models (i.e., pre-1970s) focused primarily on problem solving, creativity, and inventiveness (Gallup, 1970; Koehler, 1925). In step with game theoretic models, but developing independently from them, alternate views began to trickle in during the 1960s and 1970s from those studying monkeys and apes (e.g., Humphrey, 1976; Jolly, 1966). These primatological models suggested that the social domain was an equally important, if not more important, contributor to the evolution of primate intelligence. According to Humphrey (1976),

> "social primates are required by the very nature of the system they create and maintain to be calculating beings; they must be able to calculate the consequences of their own behaviour, to calculate the likely behaviour of others, to calculate the balance of advantage and loss—and all this in a context where the evidence on which their calculations are based is ephemeral, ambiguous and liable to change, not least as a consequence of their own actions." (p. 309).

This work and related others gave rise to the notion of *Machiavellian intelligence*, which embodies the idea that the advanced cognitive processes of primates are primarily adaptations to the special complexities of their social lives (e.g., Byrne & Whiten, 1988). The term *Machiavellian* was invoked because self-interested behavior[1] is best pursued by appearing "and, actually, to be merciful, faithful, humane, frank, religious. But he should preserve a disposition which will make a reversal of conduct possible in case the need arises" (Machiavelli, 1513/1966, p. 63).

Machiavellianism and Psychology

The term *Machiavellianism* was also invoked in psychology in the mid-1960s. Elizabethan literary references likely shaped the way Machiavelli is currently viewed and therefore heavily influenced what is meant when someone is referred to as *Machiavellian*. Shakespeare portrayed the Machiavellian as an unscrupulous villain, a soulless diabolical amoral creature excessively concerned with personal power and glory (see, e.g., *Henry VI*, *Richard III*). Richard Christie's reading of Machiavelli led him to describe the Machiavellian personality characterized by the lack of concern with conventional morality, emotional detachment from others, and greater concern for the manipulation itself over the goals of the manipulation (i.e., low ideological commitment; Christie, 1970a). Three measurable dimensions resulted; endorsement of deception and manipulation in interpersonal interactions, a cynical view of human nature (seeing others as weak and untrustworthy), and a disregard for conventional morality (Fehr, Samson, & Paulhus, 1992). "High-Machs" are considered to be goal oriented rather than person oriented, and yet often appear to be charming and cool (Christie & Geis, 1970). To a large extent, this conceptualization of Machiavellianism is considered a subclinical manifestation of sociopathy that

---

[1]Machiavelli was not giving advice about self-serving personal goals per se, but rather goals that would best serve the state under certain circumstances. In this sense, Machiavelli might be considered a group selectionist.

Christie casually observed in contexts rife with highly competent yet ambitious people (e.g., prestigious academic departments; Christie, 1970a).

Despite criticism that this work was largely atheoretical (e.g., Wilson, Near, & Miller, 1996) and the scale itself was weak (i.e., its facets were not highly intercorrelated; Hunter, Gerbin, & Boston, 1982), Christie's initial papers gave rise to a flood of studies relating his published scales to other constructs (e.g., intelligence, emotional sensitivity, underhandedness, internal/external locus of control, achievement motivation, anxiety, occupational choice and success, to name a few; see Christie, 1970b; Fehr et al., 1992; Wilson et al, 1996, for reviews). Aside from the finding that high-Machs are more effective liars than low-Machs (Kraut & Price, 1976), few clear and consistent patterns emerged from this literature. McHoskey and colleagues argued, however, that the most consistent of correlate of Machiavellianism is primary psychopathy, with high-Machs being more likely to be dominant, narcissistic, duplicitous, effectively manipulative, and emotionally shallow, and less likely to be guilt prone and empathetic (e.g., McHoskey, Worzel, & Szyarto, 1998). McHoskey and colleagues additionally described convergences between Machiavellianism and secondary psychopathy where there are positive associations with anxiety and emotional disturbance. Perhaps due to theoretical inadequacies, lack of clear empirical support, or both, one sees few studies on Christie's and Geis's Machiavellianism presently being conducted.

Integrating Biological and Psychological Views on Machiavellianism

Wilson and colleagues (1996) readdressed and reformulated the Machiavellianism construct into evolutionary terms and suggested reducing it to its key component of manipulation. Applying the logic of game theoretic models, Wilson et al. (1996) aligned Machiavellianism with the willingness to "defect" in multistrategic games (e.g., maximizing payoff for the self at the expense of another in a non-zero sum game). Populations composed of individuals using various strategies would theoretically stabilize after multiple "generations" in terms of the resultant numbers of cooperators and defectors. As already discussed, this frequency-dependent selection can account for the existence of various strategies in populations, even though some strategies in some contexts are clearly not as adaptive as others. Wilson, furthermore, correctly pointed out that Machiavelli's advice entails acting humanely and mercifully while at the same time being ready to behave inconsistently with conventional morality should the need arise. Thus, in terms of game theoretic models, high-Machs may use cooperative and defection strategies more flexibly than others or may be more willing to exploit those using cooperative strategies as a first strike option. Wilson et al. speculated that this willingness to defect or exploit others would lead to faring poorly in long-term interactions because others would avoid further contact after having been exploited. In contrast, low-Machs would be cooperators and as such would outperform high-Machs in contexts calling for coordinated interaction.

Wilson's and Christie's conceptualizations of the Machiavellianism construct differ in important ways. First, Christie's approach is moralistic in that it assumes Machiavellianism—indeed defines Machiavellianism—in terms of amorality and characteristics deemed undesirable and perhaps even pathological (e.g., manipulating for manipulation's sake). Wilson et al. adopted a more neutral stance and permitted high-Machs to enjoy a certain amount of success due to their behavioral flexibility. Their behavior as such is a competitive strategy and is honestly cooperative until the cost of doing so surpasses some threshold beyond that defection is chosen. Wilson's approach is consistent with the notion of "skill" or social competence and in this respect is in agreement with the perspective presented in this chapter (see also Hawley, 2002, 2003a).

As distinct as these approaches are, they are similar in terms of one limitation. Both constructs comprise several lower order traits or subfacets that may or may not be highly related. For Christie's Machiavellianism, this amalgamation has led to the curious situation that his construct is related to both high and low anxiety (McHoskey et al., 1998). For Wilson's approach, it is not clear what a measurement scale might look like. If being high on Machiavellianism implies behavioral flexibility and the willingness to defect and cooperate, then what is "scoring" low on this scale? Wilson suggested low Machiavellianism is distinguished by the tendency to cooperate only, a characterization that appears to assume that two behavioral morphs exist at opposite ends on some unidimensional scale (cooperation and defection). One can also imagine a low-Mach defecting only or neither cooperating nor defecting (a combination not considered from strictly game theoretic framings). In the latter case, those scoring low on Machiavellianism would not pursue personal goals but would instead defer repeatedly to others regardless of the strategy encountered. In contrast, various combinations of cooperation, coercion, and deference have been addressed by resource control theory.

Resource Control Theory

Resource control theory (Hawley, 1999) draws heavily on the work of evolutionary thinkers (e.g., Charlesworth, 1996; Trivers, 1971) and embraces the concepts of life history strategy (discussed earlier) and the dualism intrinsic to human functioning (e.g., balancing egoistic desires with needs of others; Bakan, 1966; Freud, 1930). From this perspective, goal attainment is a fundamental if not universal human value (e.g., effectance motivation, White, 1959; competence, Deci & Ryan, 1985). From an evolutionary standpoint, many goals include the acquisition of material resources and status (the two presumably being strongly intertwined; see also Hogan, 1983, and Wright, 2000). Consistent with game theoretic perspectives, various strategies of resource control presumably emerged and persist in human social groups. Some of these strategies, like the aggressive hawk strategy, are agonistic and aversive to others (i.e., coercive strategies of resource control; taking, threatening, deceiving). Prosocial strategies, in contrast, gain access to resources indirectly via reciprocity, cooperation, and friendship formation (Charlesworth, 1996; Trivers, 1971; Wright, 2000).

The relative employments of prosocial and coercive strategies of resource control are a source of important individual differences, and presumably derive from different sources intrinsic to the individual. For example, the ability and motivation to employ prosocial strategies conceivably are associated with an affinity toward others, interpersonally attractive characteristics such as agreeableness, and, because material rewards are not instantaneous with prosocial strategies, a degree of impulse control. In contrast, coercive strategies would be expected in those with less ability to delay gratification, a more negative approach to others (e.g., hostility), and a willingness to engage in aversive behaviors (e.g., aggression). In fact, these individual difference variables may very well underlie strategy employment (Hawley, 1999).

How would individual differences in these strategic proclivities in principle emerge and persist over time? It would happen in the same way other personality characteristics arise and maintain. That is, individuals come into the world with the above referenced temperament orientations, which, evidence suggests, may be heritable (e.g., Emde et al., 1992; Plomin et al., 1993). A child's environment plays an important role as well. Environmental contingencies, parenting practices, and sibling and peer relationships all presumably influence the degree to which behavioral strategies emerge and solidify (Bowlby, 1969; Harris, 1995; Patterson & Dishion, 1985; Sulloway, 1996). It is well known that the family constellation is a training ground for aggressive as well as prosocial orientations (Howes & Eldredge, 1985; Patterson, Littman, & Bricker, 1967; Zahn-Waxler, Radkey-Yarrow, & King, 1979) and peers reward some strategies whereas other strategies are punished or prove to be ineffective (Bandura, 1991; Harris, 1995; Patterson et al., 1967).

Research in the developmental domain has demonstrated that children and adolescents pursue material rewards, some are more successful than others, and children employ both prosocial and coercive behaviors to this end (e.g., Hawley, 2002, 2003a; LaFreniere & Charlesworth, 1987). To the degree one is successful at competition for resources, one is referred to as socially dominant (Hawley, 1999). Depending on the age of the children and other factors, prosocial and coercive strategies can be measured by self-report, other report, or behavior observations. Prosocial strategies are indicated when a child pursues control of resources (toys, for example) with socially acceptable behavior. In an experimental scenario, these behaviors include requests, promises of future favor, item trades, or unsolicited help (which generally leads to effective commandeering of the play material; Hawley, 2002). Teacher questionnaire items include "this child gets what he or she wants by reciprocating," "by being nice," or "... promising friendship" (Hawley, 2003a). Accordingly, coercive strategies are indicated by items such as "this individual gets what he or she wants by taking," "... threatening," or "... bullying."

Our program has utilized a person-centered approach; that is, we have focused on *types* of resource controlling individuals as well as relationships among variables (e.g., Hawley, 2002; Hawley & Little, 1999). Resource control types can be derived by dividing the distributions of prosocial and coercive strategies into thirds (i.e., 33rd percentile, 66th percentile). By dividing the distributions of the two variables in this way, we have derived five resource control subgroups: (a) bistrategic controllers score high on both prosocial and coercive strategies, (b) prosocial controllers score high on prosocial control only, (c) coercive controllers score high on coercive control only, (d) noncontrollers score low on both coercive and prosocial control, and (e) typical controllers, the largest group, are average on each and as such, serve as a useful comparison group. We invoke Machiavelli's name to apply to bistrategic controllers because his philosophy describes well the behavior of these very socially dominant individuals who seem to balance effectively prosociality and coercion, are consequently highly successful resource controllers, and as a result command a great deal of attention from the group.

We have studied strategies of resource control and their correlates in preadolescents (via self and peer report; Hawley, 2003; Hawley, Little, & Card, 2005; Hawley, Little, & Pasupathi, 2002) and preschoolers (via observations, interviews, and teacher ratings; Hawley, 2002, 2003c; Hawley, Napientek, Mize, & McNamara, 2005). An intriguing picture is beginning to coalesce of the Machiavellian as an aggressive and deceptive individual with bona fide social skills who is highly motivated to seek personal goals and obtain high status. In contrast to traditional developmental approaches that suggest that such "antisocial" behavior would repel others and be associated with an underdeveloped morality, these recent studies show that, on the contrary, bistrategic individuals appear to attract the attention of others and they may in fact fully understand moral norms and values (their self-interested behavior notwithstanding; Hawley, 2003c).

Bistrategic adolescents, for example, describe themselves as more aggressive than their peers in terms of both physical and relational forms of aggression (e.g., social exclusion and gossip; Crick & Grotpeter, 1995). They admit to being hostile and endorse cheating in school. Peers also report bistrategic controllers to be the most aggressive children in the schoolyard. At the same time, bistrategic controllers claim themselves to be socially skilled in terms of being able to detect their effect on the emotions of others (Hawley, 2003a). Although this claim sounds suspiciously self-aggrandizing and narcissistic, teachers see these youths as socially skilled as well, suggesting that there may be some validity to these adolescents' self-views (Hawley, 2003c; cf. Lochman & Dodge, 1994; Underwood, 2003). They are the most effective resource controllers from their own perspectives and that of peers and, despite their aggressive behavior, they are socially central (i.e., of high status), well-liked, and the focus of others' friendship aspirations (Hawley, 2004; Hawley, Little, & Card, 2005).

In terms of positive attributes and social success, bistrategic controllers are similar to the highly skilled prosocial controllers. At the same time, bistrategic controllers resemble coercive controllers in terms of negative characteristics such as aggression, hostility, and cheating. Yet coercive controllers are more impulsive than bistrategic controllers and lack their evident perspective taking ability. As a consequence, coercive controllers are socially repellent and disliked. Due to the differential evaluation of these two groups by their peers (even in preschool; Hawley, Napientek, et al., 2005), and to the fact that bistrategics are highly effective at resource control, it should come as no surprise that bistrategic children enjoy a higher than average social self-concept and positive well-being (Hawley et al., 2002).

Bistrategic controllers are certainly thought provoking due at least in part to their extreme relative standing on both prosocial and coercive strategies of resource control and all benefits that ensue. But none of these benefits are enjoyed by the other group also extreme on the two strategies; namely, noncontrollers. As predicted by resource control theory, these youths seem to be especially at risk. Though they as a group are rated as the least aggressive by peers and teachers, they are also described (by the self and others) as unable to pursue resources in the presence of peers, socially unskilled, anxious, and unhappy. To make matters worse, they are rejected by their peers (e.g., Hawley, 2003a). Thus the social centrality hypothesis of resource control theory (i.e., that social dominants are socially appealing) holds much to the benefit of the bistrategic controllers, but to the clear detriment of the noncontrollers.

The distinct behavioral and personality profiles of the resource control groups add to the discussion that interfaces Machiavellianism with game theoretic models. In the parlance of game theory, we can construe the bistrategic resource controller as effectively employing a mixed strategy of prosociality and coercion. Resource control theory views this behavioral flexibility more in line with social skill than with psychopathology. Unlike Christie's original Machiavellians, the bistrategic controllers of resource control theory do not appear to be manipulating for manipulation's sake, nor do their profiles suggest that they view others with excessive contempt. On the contrary, they appear to be highly extraverted and intrinsically motivated to pursue relationships with others (e.g., for joy and pleasure). Their profile is admittedly complicated, however, by the fact that this extraversion is accompanied by hostility and intrinsic social motives are balanced by extrinsic social motives (e.g., power and status; Hawley et al., 2002).

Also consistent with the logic of economic models and frequency dependent selection, effective strategies do not necessarily reduce the benefits of alternate strategies to zero. When an introverted and socially anxious child finds himself/herself in a population with effective bistrategic (a mixed strategy), prosocial (cooperative strategy), and coercive controllers (defect strategy), the wisest strategy in terms of minimizing costs and maximizing benefits may simply be to stay out of the fray. Indeed, deference appears to be the strategy adopted by the noncontrollers.

Because competition for resources is evident in the earliest social groups (e.g., already by the age of 3; Hawley & Little, 1999), and because some children habitually defer to others when their relative ranks are known (a matter of experience and familiarity), resource-related encounters in stable social groups can be powerful sculptors of personality. Accordingly, dominance and personality is the topic of the next section.

SOCIAL DOMINANCE AND PERSONALITY

The Language of Personality

Personality theoreticians have observed that the most critical features across which humans differ likely have evolutionary importance. For example, Cattell (1957) noted that natural language pertaining to personality reflects verbal symbols signaling important aspects of individual behavior patterns that are only evident in social contexts; that is, personality descriptions convey how individuals influence each other and adjust to each other's behavior (F. H. Allport & G. W. Allport, 1921). An evolutionary framing can illuminate why certain personality dimensions repeatedly arise in personality theories throughout the century (e.g., surgency/extraversion, agreeableness/sociability, emotional stability, conscientiousness, intellect/openness to experience; Buss 1997). These terms are consistently evaluative (Peabody, 1985) and as such communicate who will make a good alliance partner, who is no threat, who may cheat us, who will not return a favor, who is of high status, and so on. In short, individuals' personalities communicate their value as a group member and "summarize the most important features of the social landscape" (Buss, 1997, p. 334). More specifically, and especially germane to the discussion of social dominance, Hogan (1983) suggested that trait terms summarize observers' evaluations about who will contribute to the group's resources and who will exploit them.

Evolutionary psychologists and personality psychologists share the common goal of understanding the structure of human nature. For example, the representation of resource control types emerging from scores on two independently measured but functionally similar variables (i.e., prosocial strategies and coercive strategies) is reminiscent of several recurring themes in 20th-century personality psychology involving a balance of needs for aggression/ascension with needs for affiliation (e.g., Adler, 1929; Freud, 1930; Horney, 1945; Murray, 1938) as well as later interpersonal circumplex models (e.g., Leary, 1957; Wiggins, 1996). To the extent that bistrategic controllers are effectively meeting their own goals while at the same time attracting others securing status, they are quite effectively balancing "agency" and "communion" (Wiggins, 1991), meeting their competence and relatedness needs (Deci & Ryan, 1985), and "getting along" while "getting ahead" (R. Hogan & J. Hogan, 1991).

A Special Role for Extraversion. Machiavellians as described here appear to be "keenly attuned to the ways others are reacting, and so are able to continually fine-tune their social performance, adjusting it to make sure they are having the desired effect" (Goleman, 1995, p. 119). That is, they appear to be "emotionally intelligent." Social skills, including those of nonverbal decoding, also characterize classic descriptions of extraversion (e.g., G. W. Allport, 1924; Jung, 1923), where extraverts (in contrast to introverts) are especially attuned to the demands of the external social world. The social decoding skills of extraverts are especially evident in situations requiring the balance of multiple social goals that are inherent to a rich and complex social environment (Lieberman & Rosenthal, 2001). Not surprisingly, extraversion is generally associated with social competence and bistrategic controllers tend to score high on extraversion (Hawley, 2003b).

The Role of Context

Early applications of evolution to behavior (e.g., sociobiology) sometimes elicit negative reactions due to their genetically deterministic connotations. In contrast, contextual factors cannot be ignored in the present theoretical approach to social dominance (and Machiavellianism). First, aggressiveness alone does not ensure ongoing success at resource control. The bistrategic profile encourages broadening understanding of context to include other characteristics of the individual. That is, aggression coupled with more positive qualities, skills, and behavior tendencies make for social and material success in a way that aggression alone does not.

Second, and equally critical, individuals cannot be "socially dominant" alone. The presence of others is a necessary condition for a person to prevail. Thus, social dominance, or competitive superiority, is an aspect of a relationship, the asymmetry of which can be predicted by the interpersonal characteristics and win–loss histories of the individuals involved (see also Bernstein, 1981). Whereas this point may seem self-evident, it has long been overlooked in ethological studies that failed to explore social dominance within a complex system of interpersonal relationships. That is, social behavior, including that involving a contested resource is highly dependent on the identities of the interactants, their personal characteristics, and the unique history of their interactions (see Hawley & Little, 1999, for an application of the Social Relations Model of Kenny & La Voie, 1985).

Thus, because competition is inherent to relationships, social dominance cannot be a genetically encoded trait per se. As such, it makes no sense to speak of a "gene for dominance." More appropriately, the genetic underpinnings of several traits known to predict social dominance can be considered (e.g., persistence, extraversion). Without doubt, there is a conditioned component to relative success or failure at competition and therefore also the form and intensity of future attempts. If resources are constrained (which they generally are), then interactions may be characterized by a certain zero-sumness. For example, if "resources" to preschoolers include access to recreational/learning material, very often these materials are effectively monopolized. Unavoidably then, if there are consistent winners of competition, then there must also be losers. Experiencing early loss repeatedly in competitive interactions could intensify (indeed cause) individual differences in persistence (e.g., learned helplessness; Peterson, Maier, & Seligman, 1993). Because the noncontrolling strategy can be created experientially (e.g., learning that control attempts will be ineffective or punished), genetic mechanisms need not be invoked for explaining losing strategies. Accordingly, it makes little sense to propose selective mechanisms for a genome designed to lose in competitive contexts. Deferring to others can be considered simply making the best of a bad situation.

More likely, natural design endows organisms with the desire to win competitive contests as well as cognitive mechanisms designed to discriminate contexts in which a loss is probable. Additionally, organisms would be expected to be endowed with the ability to gravitate toward contexts where wins are more promising. In the case of preschoolers, this may entail the careful choosing of playmates (other weak competitors) or pursuing resources more vigorously in the presence of a teacher who is likely to enforce equity. The context specificity of behavior is easy to observe; behavior changes are striking in withdrawn or anxious children when an optimal niche is found. Such "niche picking" is not limited to preschoolers; presumably, adults also choose contexts where control attempts are rewarded.

CONCLUSIONS

Evolutionary approaches to personality should optimally incorporate issues of heritability, social and ecological contexts, and development. It is important to keep in mind that evolutionary theory itself is seldom under scrutiny, but rather some specified lower level theory is evaluated within an evolutionary metatheoretical framework. Here, resource control theory was described. As a (developing) formalized theory, it gives rise to fully testable and falsifiable predictions regarding the development of social dominance relationships, resource directed behavior, and strategy employment.

As an evolutionary theory, it makes some rather strong claims, namely, that interpersonal relationships are contexts rife with competition, however subtle. It suggests that some individuals, regardless of context, will come out on top due to the flexibility with which they employ various strategies of control. It also suggests that if there are consistent winners of interpersonal competition, then there will most assuredly be consistent losers. The costs and benefits associated with winning and losing extend well beyond the competition itself; the social group appears to be attracted to winners of competition and repelled by losers. Important questions for future inquiry may include those addressing the potential for physical health outcomes to win–loss experiences (Sapolsky, Alberts, & Altmann, 1997; Virgin & Sapolsky, 1997). If a loss experience is accompanied by an endocrine response, then is it not plausible that a lifetime of collected losses incurs some real physiological insult?

Work in social dominance lost its luster in the 1980s mostly due to its reliance on strictly ethological models (see Vaughn, 1999, for comment). As exemplified here, revised approaches that integrate strengths from modern evolutionary thinking (cf. genetically deterministic models), acknowledge the complexities of human interaction, and recognize the development of essential individual differences, may rejuvenate interest in the fundamental importance of power hierarchies as an inevitable aspect of group life.

REFERENCES

Adler, A. (1929). *The science of living.* London: G. Allen.

Allport, G. W. (1924). The study of the undivided personality. *Journal of Abnormal and Social Psychology, 19,* 132–141.

Allport, F. H., & Allport, G. W. (1921). Personality traits: Their classification and measurement. *Journal of Abnormal and Social Psychology, 16,* 6–40.

Bakan, D. (1966). *The duality of human existence.* Boston: Beacon Press.

Bandura, A. (1991). Social cognitive theory of moral thought and action. In W. M. Kurtines & J. L. Gewirtz (Eds.), *Handbook of moral behavior and development* (Vol. 1, pp. 45–103). Hillsdale, NJ: Lawrence Erlbaum Associates.

Bernstein, I. S. (1981). Dominance: The baby and the bathwater. *Behavioral and Brain Sciences, 4,* 419–457.

Bowlby, J. (1969). *Attachment and loss: Vol 1. Attachment.* New York: Basic Books.

Buss, D. M. (1994). The strategies of human mating. *American Scientist, 82,* 238–249.

Buss, D. M. (1997). Evolutionary foundations of personality. In R. Hogan, J. Johnson, & S. Briggs (Eds.), *Handbook of personality psychology* (pp. 317–344). San Diego: Academic Press.

Buss, D. M. (1999). *Evolutionary psychology: The new science of the mind.* Boston: Allyn & Bacon.

Byrne, R. W., & Whiten, A. (Eds.). (1988). *Machiavellian intelligence: Social expertise and the evolution of intellect in monkeys, apes, and humans.* Oxford, England: Clarendon Press.

Cattell, R. B. (1957). *Personality and motivation: Structure and measurement.* Yonkers on Hudson, NY: World Book.

Charlesworth, W. R. (1996). Co-operation and competition: Contributions to an evolutionary and developmental model. *International Journal of Behavioral Development, 19,* 25–39.

Christie, R. (1970a). Why Machiavelli? In R. Christie & F. Geis (Eds.), *Studies in Machiavellianism* (pp. 1–9). New York: Academic Press.

Christie, R. (1970b). Relationships between Machiavellianism and measures of ability, opinion, and personality. In R. Christie & F. Geis (Eds.), *Studies in Machiavellianism* (pp 35–52). New York: Academic Press.

Christie, R., & Geis, F. (1970). *Studies in Machiavellianism.* New York: Academic Press.

Colman, A. M. (1999). *Game theory and its applications in the social and biological sciences.* New York: Routledge.

Cosmides, L., & Tooby, J. (1995). From evolution to adaptations to behavior: Toward an integrated evolutionary psychology. In R. Wong (Ed.), *Biological perspectives on motivated activities* (pp. 11–74). Westport, CT: Ablex.

Crick, N. R., & Grotpeter, J. K., (1995). Relational aggression, gender, and social-psychological adjustment. *Child Development, 66,* 710–722.

Deci, E. L., & Ryan, R. M. (1985). *Intrinsic motivation and self-determination in human behavior.* New York: Plenum.

Draper, P., & Harpending, H. (1982). Father absence and reproductive strategy: An evolutionary perspective. *Journal of Personality, 58,* 255–273.

Draper, P., & Harpending, H. (1987). Parent investment and the child's environment. In J. B. Lancaster, J. Altmann, A. S. Rossi, & L. Sherrod (Eds.), *Parenting across the life span: Biosocial dimensions* (pp. 207–235). Hawthorne, NY: Aldine.

Emde, R. N., Plomin, R., Robinson, J., Reznick, J. S., Campos, J., Corley, R., DeFries, J. C., Fulker, D. W., Kagan, J., & Zahn-Waxler, C. (1992). Temperament, emotion, and cognition at 14 months: The MacArthur Longitudinal Twin Study. *Child Development, 63,* 1437–1455

Fehr, B., Samson, D., & Paulhus, D. L. (1992). The construct of Machiavellianism: Twenty years later. In C. D. Speilberger & J. N. Butcher (Eds.), *Advances in personality assessment* (pp. 77–116). Hillsdale, NJ: Lawrence Erlbaum Associates.

Freud, S. (1930). *Civilization and its discontents.* New York: J. Cape & H. Smith.

Gallup, G. G. (1970). Chimpanzees: Self-recognition. *Science, 167,* 86–87.

Goleman, D. (1995). *Emotional intelligence.* New York: Bantam Books.

Guilford, J. P. (1959). *Personality.* New York: McGraw-Hill.

Harris, J. R. (1995). Where is the child's environment? A group socialization theory of development. *Psychological Review, 102,* 458–489.

Hawley, P. H. (1999). The ontogenesis of social dominance: A strategy-based evolutionary perspective. *Developmental Review, 19,* 97–132.

Hawley, P. H. (2002). Social dominance and prosocial and coercive strategies of resource control in preschoolers. *International Journal of Behavioral Development, 26,* 167–176.

Hawley, P. H. (2003a). Prosocial and coercive configurations of resource control in early adolescence: A case for the well-adapted Machiavellian. *Merrill-Palmer Quarterly, 49,* 279–309.

Hawley, P. H. (2003b). *Machiavellian preschoolers: The personalities and moral reasoning of aggressive children.* Paper presented at the biennial meeting of Society for Research in Child Development, Tampa, FL.

Hawley, P. H. (2003c). Strategies of control, aggression, and morality in preschoolers: An evolutionary perspective. *Journal of Experimental Child Psychology, 85,* 213–235.

Hawley, P. H. (2004). *The myth of the alpha male: Gender differences and similarities in beliefs about social dominance and resource control in adolescents.* Paper presented at the biennial meeting of Society for Research in Adolescence, Baltimore, MD.

Hawley, P. H., Card, N. E., & Little, T. D. (2005). *The allure of a mean friend: Relationship quality and processes of aggressive adolescents.* Manuscript submitted for review.

Hawley, P. H., & Little, T. D. (1999). On winning some and losing some: A social relations approach to social dominance in toddlers. *Merrill-Palmer Quarterly, 43,* 185–214.

Hawley, P. H., Little, T. D., & Card, N. E. (2005). *The myth of the alpha male: A new look at dominance-related beliefs and behaviors among adolescent males and females.* Manuscript submitted for review.

Hawley, P. H., Little, T. D., & Pasupathi, M. (2002). Winning friends and influencing peers: Strategies of peer influence in late childhood. *International Journal of Behavioral Development, 26,* 466–473.

Hawley, P. H., Napientek, S. E., Mize, J. A., & McNamara, K. A. (2005). Beauty and power: The social and physical appeal of aggressive social dominants. Manuscript submitted for review.

Hogan, R. T. (1983). A socioanalytic theory of personality. In M. M. Page (Ed.), *Nebraska symposium on motivation: Personality-current theory and research* (pp. 58–89). Lincoln: University of Nebraska Press.

Hogan, R. T. (1998). New wine for the old bottle. *Contemporary Psychology, 43,* 401–402.

Hogan, R., & Hogan, J. (1991). Personality and status. In D. G. Gilbert & J. Connolly (Eds.), *Personality, social skills, and psychopathology: An individual differences approach* (pp. 137–154). New York: Plenum.

Horney, K. (1945). *Our inner conflicts.* New York: Norton.

Howes, C., & Eldredge, R. (1985). Responses of abused, neglected, and non-maltreated children to the behaviors of their peers. *Journal of Applied Developmental Psychology, 6,* 261–270.

Humphrey, N. K. (1976). The social function of intellect. In P. P. G. Bateson & R. A. Hinde (Eds.), *Growing points in ethology* (pp. 303–317). Cambridge, England: Cambridge University Press.

Hunter, J. ., Gerbin, D. W., & Boston, F. J. (1982). Machiavellian beliefs and personality: Construct validity of the Machiavellianism dimension. *Journal of Personality and Social Psychology, 43,* 1293–1305.

Jolly, A. (1966). Lemur social behaviour and primate intelligence. *Science, 153,* 501–506.

Jung, C. (1923). *Psychological types.* New York: Harcourt Brace.

Kenny, D. A., & La Voie, L. (1985). Separating individual and group effects. *Journal of Personality and Social Psychology, 48*, 339–348.

Koehler, W. (1925). *The mentality of apes*. New York: Harcourt, Brace

Kraut, R. E., & Price, J. D. (1976). Machiavellianism in parents and their children. *Journal of Personality and Social Psychology, 33*, 782–786.

LaFreniere, P. J., & Charlesworth, W. R. (1987). Dominance, attention, and affiliation in a preschool group: A 9-month longitudinal study. *Ethology and Sociobiology, 4*, 55–67.

Leary, T. (1957). *Interpersonal diagnosis of personality*. New York: Ronald.

Lewontin, R. C. (1961). Evolution and the theory of games. *Journal of Theoretical Biology, 1*, 382–403.

Lieberman, M. D., & Rosenthal, R. (2001). Why introverts can't always tell who likes them: Multitasking and nonverbal decoding. *Journal of Personality and Social Psychology, 80*, 294–310

Lochman, J. E., & Dodge, K. A. (1994). Social-cognitive processes of severely violent, moderately aggressive, and nonaggressive boys. *Journal of Consulting and Clinical Psychology, 62*, 366–374.

Machiavelli, N. (1513/1966). *The Prince*. New York: Bantam.

Maynard Smith, J. (1974). The theory of games and the evolution of animal conflict. *Journal of Theoretical Biology, 47*, 202–221.

Maynard Smith, J., & Price, G. R. (1973). The logic of animal conflict. *Nature, 246*, 15–18.

McHoskey, J. W., Worzel, W., & Szyarto, C. (1998). Machiavellianism and psychopathy. *Journal of Personality and Social Psychology, 74*, 192–210.

Mealey, L. (1995). The sociobiology of sociopathy: An integrated evolutionary model. *Behavioral and Brain Sciences, 18*, 523–599.

Murray, H. A. (1938). *Explorations in personality: A clinical and experimental study of fifty men of college age*. New York: Oxford University Press.

Patterson, G. R., & Dishion, T. J. (1985). Contributions of families and peers to delinquency. *Criminology, 23*, 63–79.

Patterson, G. R., Littman, R. A., & Bricker, W. (1967). Assertive behaviour in children: A step toward a theory of aggression. *Monographs of the Society for Research in Child Development, 35* (5, Serial No. 113).

Peabody, D. (1985). *National characteristics*. Cambridge, England: Cambridge University Press.

Peterson, C., Maier, S. F., & Seligman, M. E. P. (1993). *Learned helplessness: A theory for the age of personal control*. London: Oxford University Press.

Plomin, R., Emde, R. N., Braungart, J. M., Campos, J., Corley, R., Fulker, D. W., Kagan, J., Reznick, J. S., Robinson, J., Zahn-Waxler, C., & Defries, J. C. (1993). Genetic change and continuity from 14 to 20 months: The MacArthur Longitudinal Twin Study. *Child Development, 64*, 1354–1376.

Sapolsky, R. M., Alberts, S. C., & Altmann, J. (1997). Hypercortisolism associated with social subordinance or social isolation among wild baboons. *Archives of Genera Psychiatry, 54*, 1137–1143.

Scher, S. J., & Rauscher, F. (2003). Nature read in truth or flaw: Locating alternatives in evolutionary psychology. In S.J. Scher & F. Rauscher (Eds.), *Evolutionary psychology: Alternate approaches* (pp. 1–29). Boston: Kluwer Academic.

Sulloway, F. (1996). *Born to rebel*. New York: Pantheon.

Tooby, J., & Cosmides, L. (1990). On the universality of human nature and the uniqueness of the individual: The role of genetics and adaptation. *Journal of Personality, 58*, 17–68.

Trivers, R. L. (1971). The evolution of reciprocal altruism. *Quarterly Review of Biology, 46*, 35–57.

Underwood, M. K. (2003). The comity of modest manipulation, the importance of distinguishing among bad behaviors. *Merrill-Palmer Quarterly, 49*, 373–389.

Vaughn, B. E. (1999). Power is knowledge (and vice versa): A commentary on "On winning some and losing some: A social relations approach to social dominance in toddlers." *Merrill-Palmer Quarterly, 45*, 215–225.

Virgin, C. E., & Sapolsky, R. M. (1997). Styles of male social behavior and their endocrine correlates among low-ranking baboons. *American Journal of Primatology, 42*, 25–39.

White, R.W. (1959). Motivation reconsidered: The concept of competence. *Psychological Review*, 66, 297–333.

Wiggins, J. S. (1991). Agency and communion as conceptual coordinates for the understanding and measurement of interpersonal behavior. In D. Ciccheti & W. Grove Eds.), *Thinking critically in psychology: Essays in honor of Paul E. Meehl* (pp. 89–113). New York: Cambridge University Press.

Wiggins, J. S. (1996). An informal history of the interpersonal circumplex tradition. *Journal of Personality Assessment, 66*, 217–233.

Williams, G. C. (1966). *Adaptation and natural selection*. Princeton, NJ: Princeton University Press.

Wilson, D. S. (1994). Adaptive genetic variation and human evolutionary psychololgy. *Ethology and Sociobiology, 15*, 219–235.

Wilson, D. S. (2003). Evolution, morality, and human potential. In S. J. Scher & F. Rauscher (Eds.), *Evolutionary psychology: Alternate approaches* (pp. 55–70). Boston: Kluwer Academic.

Wilson, D. S., Near, D., & Miller, R.R. (1996). Machiavellianism: A synthesis of the evolutionary and psychological literatures. *Psychological Bulletin, 119*, 285–299.

Wright, R. (2000). *Non-zero: The logic of human destiny*. New York: Pantheon.

Zahn-Waxler, C., Radke-Yarrow, M., & King, R. A. (1979). Child rearing and children's prosocial initiations towards victims of distress. *Child Development, 50*, 319–330.

9

Modeling Intraindividual Stability and Change in Personality

Daniel K. Mroczek
Purdue University

David M. Almeida
Pennsylvania State University

Avron Spiro III
Boston VA Healthcare System

Christine Pafford
Fordham University

The question of stability and change is one of the most important in personality and is perhaps the most fundamental question in the area of personality development. Over the past 25 years, researchers have established that rank-order stability is high for most traits (Costa & McCrae, 1988, 1994; Roberts & DelVecchio, 2000), although mean-level stability varies by trait (McCrae & Costa, chap. 7 in this volume). In other types of personality variables (self-efficacy, goals, motives), there is less rank-order and mean-level stability (Helson, Soto, & Cate, chap. 17 in this volume). However, the techniques typically employed to estimate rank-order and mean-level stability in personality variables (or any other type of variable) conceal important information on individual differences. Personality psychology is strongly identified with the science of individual differences, yet it has overlooked the possibility of individual differences in stability and change. Almost 30 years ago, life-span developmentalists advocated the idea of individual differences in intraindividual change (Baltes, Reese, & Nesselroade, 1977), but it remained a largely theoretical notion until statistical techniques were invented in the 1980s that permitted adequate testing of this concept (Bryk & Raudenbush, 1992; Rogosa, Brandt, & Zimowski, 1982). As a result, a much more complex, and more accurate, way of conceptualizing stability and change in personality is now available. This chapter discusses these techniques and how they can advance the conceptual science of personality development.

INDIVIDUAL DIFFERENCES IN INTRAINDIVIDUAL STABILITY AND CHANGE

The dominance of older methods, such as repeated analysis of variance measures (ANOVA), narrowed the focus of early research on personality development. Despite research that utilized intraindividual methods as far back as the 1940s (Baldwin, 1946; Henry, 1941), scholars were trained to think in terms of either change in means or in relative positioning in a distribution (rank orders). Much of the important early work on personality stability and change concentrated on one or both of these forms (Conley, 1984, 1985; Costa & McCrae, 1988; Finn, 1986), and much of it has now been synthesized via meta-analysis (Roberts & DelVecchio, 2000). Means and correlations, however, do not allow the study of personality stability as an individual differences phenomenon. Rather, they tell if a trait increases or decreases over time, or if people maintain the same rank order over time, in a sample or population. Repeated measures means and correlation, as valuable as they are, largely conceal individual differences in stability and change (Aldwin, Spiro, Levenson, & Bosse', 1989; Lamiell, 1981). As a result of overreliance on these statistics and the preponderance of them in the literature, many researchers have concluded that personality is stable for all or most individuals, without actually evaluating the extent of the individual differences in stability. Do some individuals remain stable and others change? Do some change in one direction, whereas others change in the opposite direction?

Recent studies indicate that researchers in adult personality development are now using techniques that can estimate individual differences in stability and change (these techniques are described later; Helson, Jones, & Kwan, 2002; Jones, Livson, & Peskin, 2003; Jones & Meredith, 1996; Mroczek & Spiro, 2003a, 2003b; Roberts & Chapman, 2000; Small, Hertzog, Hultsch, & Dixon, 2003). Each of these studies has demonstrated that for many personality variables (although not all), individual differences in stability and change exist. Jones et al. (2003) termed this *heterogenous change*, meaning that some people change, others do not, and the direction or pattern of change (e.g., linear, quadratic) varies across people. Half a dozen studies on at least four different longitudinal samples have now shown that there are indeed individual differences in personality change. Put more simply, there is a range of change.

These empirical demonstrations of individual differences in change are consistent with a long-standing theoretical concept originating from life-span developmental theory, which holds that not everyone is characterized by the same developmental trajectory. This idea is embodied in the concept of *individual differences in intraindividual change*, which implies that some people change whereas others remain stable (Alwin, 1994; Baltes, 1987; Baltes & Nesselroade, 1973; Baltes, Reese, & Nesselroade, 1977; Wohlwill, 1973). The term *individual* signals that this is a form of differences among persons, and the term *intraindividual change* denotes within-person stability and change. The notion of such within-person change was introduced by Stephenson (1936) and elaborated on by Cattell (1950, 1966; see also McArdle & Woodcock, 1997; Mehta & West, 2000; Nesselroade, 1988, 1991). Individuals can and do differ from one another in whether they are stable or changing on various personality dimensions. Thus, as has been pointed out previously (Mroczek & Spiro, 2003a), the mutual exclusivity of the often-used phrase "stability *or* change," although sensible in some contexts, is less tenable with respect to the issue of personality development. The phrase *stability and change* better describes how personality develops, at least in the adult years. Some people change whereas others remain stable.

Although the principle of individual differences in intraindividual change has been in the social scientific literature for more than 30 years, it was not tested empirically until relatively recently. The main reason was that adequate statistical models were unavailable until the mid-1980s. Even then, it took time for these techniques to diffuse from the statistical to the psychological community. The next section describes some of these statistical models.

MODELS FOR ESTIMATING STABILITY AND CHANGE: MLM AND SEM

A variety of methods is now available that allow modeling of change over time (McArdle, 1991; Meredith & Tisak, 1990; Muthen, 2002; Raudenbush & Bryk, 2002; Rogosa et al., 1982; Singer & Willett, 2003; von Eye & Nesselroade, 1992). Some of these techniques are based on structural equation models (e.g., McArdle, 1991; Meredith & Tisak, 1990), whereas others are grounded in a multilevel modeling (MLM) framework. The latter type of model goes by many names (increasing confusion in the literature): random coefficient or random effects models, generalized estimating equations, mixed models, and hierarchical linear models (e.g., Raudenbush & Bryk, 2002; Singer & Willett, 2003). One method, however, bridges SEM and MLM approaches: growth mixture modeling (Muthen, 2002). No study of personality change has used the Muthen (2002) technique yet, although Small et al. (2003) and Jones and Meredith (1996) employed SEM techniques. All of the other studies in the literature have used MLM approaches to growth curves in personality (Helson, Jones, & Kwan, 2002; Jones, Livson, & Peskin, 2003; Mroczek & Spiro, 2003a; Roberts & Chapman, 2000). Therefore, this discussion describes in greater detail growth curve estimation within a MLM modeling framework (Singer & Willett, 2003; Willett & Sayer, 1994). First, there is a brief comparison of MLM versus SEM approaches to analyzing change.

When MLM modeling techniques for estimating change are employed, they are often called individual growth, or individual trajectory, models. The reason is because individual-level trajectories are estimated, as opposed to modeling data primarily from sample-based variances and covariances, as is done in structural equation modeling (SEM) approaches to the analysis of change. When SEM is used, the term *latent growth curve* (LGC) is usually employed. However, the advantage gained in using LGC over MLM is that the former permits measurement models that allow superior estimation of error via latent variables; another is that mediation can be examined more directly via path models. However, the advantage gained in using MLM over LGC is flexibility in handling missing data and unequal spacing between measurement occasions. In many longitudinal studies, the intervals between measurements are often unequal across participants, either by circumstance or design, creating spacing between measurement occasions that are of varying length. MLM approaches have no problem with such data (Singer & Willett, 2003). Researchers should weigh the relative importance of flexibility in handling missing data versus superior estimation of measurement error in making a decision about whether to use MLM- or SEM-based approaches to growth curves. However, the available data may make this decision for the researcher (e.g., Mroczek & Spiro, 2003a).

GROWTH CURVES IN A MULTILEVEL MODELING FRAMEWORK

The MLM modeling approach to growth curves is described in this section in a more formal way. Yet, before applying such a model, the researcher must obtain data of a particular quality. Growth curve models require longitudinal data that contain at least three measurement occasions for all or most persons. Over 40 years of commentary has made clear that two measurement occasions are suboptimal for estimating change, in particular prohibiting the accurate estimation of rate of change, or slope (Raudenbush & Bryk, 2002; Rogosa et al., 1982; Singer, 1998; Singer & Willett, 2003). To carry out growth modeling adequately, the minimum number of measurement occasions required is three, although for estimation of curvilinear models (e.g., quadratic, cubic) more waves are required.

Once at least three measurement occasions have been obtained, the data must be arranged in "person-time" (or "person-period"; Singer & Willett, 2003). This requires nesting measurements within persons. Each measurement occasion for a person must be placed on a separate row in the data matrix, with the participant ID serving to identify the multiple observations on a single individual during the analysis. In essence, individuals have their own data matrix that is nested within the larger data matrix. In this type of data arrangement, participants can vary not only with respect to length of measurement interval, but also with regard to number of measurements. Some people may have three measurements, others four, still others five or more, and some individuals may have only one or two (incidentally, this is not a problem if data are missing at random). This reflects the reality of longitudinal studies, where participants are often not available at the desired times of measurement, or drop out during the follow-up period. This kind of variability in spacing of measurements, common in long-term studies, present no data analytic problem for growth curves estimated in a MLM modeling framework. However, it violates key assumptions in the repeated measures ANOVA model, and also poses some difficulties for latent growth models estimated via SEM.

Fixed Effects

The MLM approach to individual growth models yields fixed and random effects. *Fixed effects* are parameters (coefficients) that characterize the overall trajectory for the sample. *Random effects* are parameters that characterize the variability around the fixed effects (i.e., interindividual differences). In a simple linear growth curve model, where there is no quadratic (curvature) term, there are two fixed effects, an intercept and a slope.

The intercept is the average amount of outcome (e.g., extraversion, conscientiousness) where the temporal metameter (time, age, etc.) equals zero. If the temporal metameter is years passed since an event (e.g., birth, baseline assessment, intervention), then the intercept defines the leftmost point of the trajectory. It is where the growth curve or trajectory passes through the y-axis. However, if age is the temporal metameter, then the intercept is the amount of that personality dimension when age equals zero, and it obviously makes little sense to think of a newborn having developed a psychological construct such as extraversion or conscientiousness.

Therefore, it is often desirable to re-center the temporal variable in order to place the zero point at a more conceptually meaningful spot (Biesanz, Debb-Sossa, Papadukis, Bollen, & Curran, 2004). This could be the mean entry age of people in a longitudinal study, the mean overall age across all time points, or even the mean age at study exit. The temporal metameter could also be person centered, in which each participant's personality measurements over time are centered at a value specific to each person, for example, their mean age across all occasions. In such a model, change in personality is interpreted as change from an individual's own average. It is the amount that individuals vary from themselves over time. By contrast, re-centering age around the grand mean for all people in the study has the effect of placing the intercept in the middle of the entire age distribution. As a result, the intercept is the predicted amount of the personality dimension at a fixed age. Grand mean and person mean centering are the most commonly used re-centering techniques in growth modeling, and each has its advantages and disadvantages. Regardless of the choice a researcher makes, re-centering should have the effect of improving interpretation of the intercept or average level (Biesanz et al., 2004).

The fixed effect for slope is the amount of change in the personality dimension of interest, per unit of time. If time is clocked in years, then the slope represents amount of personality change per year. The fixed effect for slope quantifies rate of change. Together, the intercept and slope define the shape of the overall trajectory, if it is purely linear. This tells if a personality variable increases, decreases, or remains stable over a period of time. It also tells if personality increases quickly, or decreases slowly. These fixed effects for intercept and slope, however, define only the overall, sample-level trajectory; but MLM models yield more than this. They also estimate the individual differences around the intercept and slope. These are the random effects, and lead some to label these techniques "random coefficient models."

Random Effects

Random effects estimate individual variability around a growth parameter. The random effect for the intercept is the estimate of variance around the intercept parameter. It simply captures individual differences in the level of the personality variable that is examined. This is usually not very interesting because, at least in the case of personality dimensions, researchers usually know that they differ significantly across people. What is typically much more interesting is the random effect for slope, because it reveals if rate of change varies by person. Imagine change in neuroticism over a 20-year period. Some people may have trajectories that rise or fall steeply; these individuals possess large slopes. Others display less steep slopes. Others still may show no change, and possess flat (zero) slopes over time. A slope of zero implies stability. What this illustrates is a range of slopes—some large, some small, some zero, some positive, and some negative. Such individual differences in rate of change exemplify the aforementioned life-span principle of interindividual differences in intraindividual change (Baltes et al., 1977).

Linear and Quadratic Growth Models in Personality

The initial model to be estimated in an analysis of change is an unconditional means model (Singer & Willett, 2003), also known as an intercept-only model (Raudenbush & Bryk, 2002). This model fits only an overall mean and the variance around that mean across all persons and measurement occasions. The time variable is not included in the equation at this step (Singer & Willett, 2003). The fixed effect in the unconditional means model is simply the grand mean across all measurements. One random effect, the variance around the intercepts, is estimated as well. This captures the between-person differences in intercept, or simply, the individual differences in level of the personality variable of interest, irrespective of measurement occasion. The remaining variability is the within-person variance, plus error. These estimates of between- and within-person variances are useful in that the former tells how much of the variability is due to between-person differences, whereas the latter represents how much people vary from themselves. The unconditional means model also provides a benchmark that the researcher can use to evaluate successive models (e.g., by comparing a measure of model fit such as the log likelihood or the Akaike information criterion; Raudenbush & Bryk, 2002).

The next step is to add the time variable into the equation. This is the *linear growth model*. If time is clocked via age, then a formal definition of the model using extraversion can be expressed as:

$$\text{Extraversion}_{ij} = \pi_{0i} + \pi_{1i}(age_{ij}) + \epsilon_{ij} \qquad (1)$$

The amount of extraversion for individual i at measurement occasion j, is a function of the person's age at that measurement occasion (age_{ij}). The intercept, p_{0i}, is the predicted amount of extraversion where age = 0 (or if recentered, at some age). The linear coefficient, p_{1i}, is the rate of change (slope); it is the predicted annual amount of change in extraversion for person i. ϵ_{ij} represents the errors on each person i at occasion j. In a sample, each participant's trajectory is described by this equation. Together, these intercepts and slopes define the overall, sample-level intercept and slope, that is, the fixed effects. The variability in intercepts and slopes across i persons are the random effects.

The linear growth model may prove adequate for characterizing change in some personality variables, but it is possible that a more complex model is required for others. Adding a squared function of the temporal variable to the linear growth model creates the *quadratic growth model*, which estimates curvilinearity. More formally, and again using extraversion, the quadratic model is expressed as:

$$\text{Extraversion}_{ij} = \pi_{0i} + \pi_{1i}(age_{ij}) + \pi_{2i}(age^2_{ij}) + \epsilon_{ij} \qquad (2)$$

The quadratic coefficient, π_{2i}, estimates amount of curvature for person i. Note that three fixed effect parameters are estimated in the quadratic model: intercept, slope, and curvature. Due to the estimation of an extra term, it is recommended that four or more measurement occasions be used, a number larger than the usual minimum of three. A researcher can fit a MLM model with at least two or three observations on some subjects, as long as some portion of the subjects have four or more occasions to permit estimation of the Level 1 model. Four occasions, at minimum, are required for the quadratic model. Similarly, if cubic functions of time are estimated, then to test for a second bend in the curve, at least five measurement occasions are required. In any case, the usual progression in growth curve modeling is to test simpler models first, and then gradually move toward more complex models, if higher order models are conceptually justified. An unconditional means model should be estimated first, then a linear growth model, then a quadratic growth model (Singer & Willett, 2003). As argued elsewhere (Mroczek & Griffin, in press) in the behavioral sciences, complex phenomena such as cubic growth are rare, and it is rarer still to find theory that predicts such phenomena.

EXPLAINING INDIVIDUAL DIFFERENCES IN PERSONALITY CHANGE: LEVEL 2 MODELS

The linear and quadratic growth models described in the prior section are Level 1 models (Raudenbush & Bryk, 2002). In the language of multilevel modeling, they reside at the first level; fundamentally, they describe within-person the temporal pattern of a personality variable (although certain between-person parameters are estimated as well). Even the fixed effects, which reflect sample-level parameters, are nevertheless based on the within-person relation between time or age and a personality dimension. If the slope or curvature variance (random effects) is significant at Level 1, then the investigator may go on to Level 2 models. Level 2 models introduce predictors or other explanatory variables to account for the observed individual differences in personality change. These models can potentially explain why some people change on a personality dimension whereas others remain stable.

The use of Level 2 models is illustrated in a recent study that applied individual growth models to personality trait data (Mroczek & Spiro, 2003a). Death of spouse was used to predict change in neuroticism over a 12-year period in older adults. The Level 1 model determined that there was statistically significant variability among persons in neuroticism slopes over 12 years. At Level 2, death of spouse was introduced into the model as a between-person variable. In the sample of older men, some had experienced the death of their spouse within the 2 years prior to the 12-year longitudinal period, and others had not. This dichotomous variable significantly predicted both intercept and slope of neuroticism. People whose spouses had died started out higher on neuroticism than those who had not endured this tragic life experience, but then displayed slopes that went down at a faster rate over the next 12 years. In other words, neuroticism was temporarily elevated immediately after the death of a spouse, but then reverted back in the years following. The between-person variable "death of spouse" accounted for some, but not all, of the individual variability in neuroticism slopes over a 12-year period. This finding indicates that rates of change in traits can be modified depending on life circumstances. It also speaks to the possibility that certain traits, like neuroticism, may have components that are sensitive to context, in addition to components that are stable over time.

WHAT GIVES RISE TO INDIVIDUAL DIFFERENCES IN INTRAINDIVIDUAL PERSONALITY CHANGE?

Various factors can bring about differences among people in personality trajectories. People differ with respect to the environments to which they are exposed, their genetic makeup, and the active ways they bring about change in themselves or their environments (Caspi & Roberts, 2001; Lerner & Busch-Rossnagel, 1981; Levenson & Crumpler, 1996; Roberts & Wood, chap. 2 in this volume). These individual differences in external and internal factors, as well as interactions between them, may produce individual differences in the developmental trajectories of personality dimensions.

A number of contextual variables have been shown to influence personality change. Cramer (2003) found that defense mechanisms predict change in Big Five traits over long-term periods (several years). Roberts and Chapman (2000) documented that role quality influences personality change. Clausen and Jones (1998) hinted that disorderly careers and divorce may disrupt personality stability and bring about trait change. Martin and Mroczek (in press) indicated that work and family overload in adults at midlife are associated with mean differences in Big Five traits when compared to younger or older adults. Additionally, personality trajectories may vary due to environmental-based variability associated with history-graded normative influences that may be indicated by birth cohort (Baltes, 1987; Nesselroade & Baltes, 1974). Indeed, evidence has suggested that there are birth cohort differences in level of (Twenge, 2000, 2001) and rate of change in extraversion and neuroticism (Mroczek & Spiro, 2003a).

Additionally, age-graded life events, especially relationship events, can alter personality trajectories (Neyer & Asendorpf, 2001). In older adulthood, death of spouse or remarriage are relationship events that can influence personality trajectories (Mroczek & Spiro, 2003a). Age-graded changes in health may also affect personality trajectories. If individuals' health deteriorates to the point where they are unable or unwilling to socialize with others, then this could create a shift toward less extraversion, greater neuroticism, and perhaps less agreeableness.

The previous findings and hypotheses illustrate the life-span developmental tenet of plasticity or adaptability (Alwin, 1994; Baltes, 1987; Roberts, 1997), which states that developmental constructs such as personality retain some degree of suppleness and malleability throughout the life span. Roberts (1997) argued that personality is an "open system" that remains sensitive to contextual life experiences and socialization processes through the life span, and the aforementioned studies have borne this out to some extent. The notion of plasticity, however, should not be taken too far, lest researchers make the claim that personality dimensions are as malleable as mood. Indeed, some personality dimensions may be more changeable than others, and Hooker and McAdams (2003) offered a model that makes explicit predictions about what types of personality constructs should be more likely to remain stable and what types should show change over the life span. For example, they argued that social-cognitive personality constructs such as mastery, goal strivings, and coping styles are more likely to change than traits constructs such as extraversion or neuroticism.

Most of the theoretical and empirical work on what predicts personality change has focused on environmental or contextual explanations. Biological influences have generally been ignored. This is unfortunate, because there is now evidence that individual differences in genes (whether or not a person possesses a particular variant), and individual differences in exposure to particular contexts (whether or not one was abused as a child), as well as their interaction, give rise to individual differences in certain personality outcomes, such as antisocial behavior and tendency toward depression (Caspi et al., 2002, 2003). Similar combinations of genetic and contextual factors may predict individual differences in long-term personality trajectories as well.

Explaining variability in personality trajectories, especially in rates of change, is an important task facing personality development researchers. Yet those who have attempted to account for such individual differences in change have often run into difficulties. Frequently, the hypothesized predictors do not predict well. One reason for this may be that personality trajectories are more responsive to idiosyncratic factors such as genetic makeup or nonnormative life events than normative or age-graded biological or contextual events (Baltes et al., 1977). Variability in personality trajectories may reflect, to some degree, very specific circumstances in individual lives, or individually distinct interventions, such as psychotherapy, pharmacologic therapy, or personal traumas. One way around this is to identify people whose trajectories show either great change or stability, and determine what environmental or biological factors may have promoted such high stability or change. Another possibility is to incorporate time-varying covariates into personality growth curve models. This refers to variables with values that may change over time, and are entered into the growth curve model at Level 1 as a covariate. Such models have been used in modeling change in well-being over time (Lucas, Clark, Georgellis, & Diener, 2003). Life events or health events are placed in the model when they occur, allowing for more proximal prediction. These kinds of models eventually could prove superior to static-predictor (between-person, or Level 2) models in accounting for individual differences in personality trajectories, because they mimic the vicissitudes of life more accurately.

SHORTER-TERM CHANGE IN PERSONALITY: PROCESS APPROACHES

Up to this point, the focus has been on prior research and theory relevant to long-term personality stability and change. Work in this area has focused on durations that last years. Yet, many other areas of personality conceptualize change that occurs over week, days, or even within a single day. The process approach to personality focuses on these shorter durations. Although it often assesses change, it is not change in the sense of trajectories declining over periods of years. The type of change assessed in the process approach is dynamic action. This is in part a remnant of the process approach's lineage in classic behaviorism, with its emphasis the unfolding of behavior over short periods of time (e.g., studies of learning curves and reinforcement schedules). One of the hallmarks of the process approach, daily diary and experience sampling studies, similarly seek to determine the characteristic ways that people respond to different situational stimuli. The trait approach, with its emphasis on structure, is less concerned with reactions to situations, and in some ways, the structure (trait) and process approaches to personality reflect the distinction immortalized in Cronbach's (1957) "two disciplines of scientific psychology" (Mroczek & Spiro, 2003b).

The two approaches, structure and process, are like the structural and dynamic components of an automobile. Cars have structural components that do not contain any moving parts, such as the chassis, frame, headlights, windshield, and windows. These make up the basic structure of a vehicle, and are analogous to basic structural features of personality such as the Big Five traits (Goldberg, 1993). Cars also have dynamic components that either contain moving parts or involve a chemical or physical process. Examples of dynamic components include the transmission, the steering and braking systems, and the internal combustion engine. These parts have structural elements, of course, but they differ from purely structural elements in that they involve processes that unfold over time. To brake a car takes time and invokes a dynamic process as calipers are engaged, friction is applied, and wheels are slowed down gradually. Braking is a process (governed by physical principles) in this sense. Other dynamic components involve chemical processes. Inside an internal combustion engine, gasoline is fed into cylinders where the dynamic action of pistons explodes the fuel, creating heat and energy that powers and propels the vehicle. Although this process involves structures, such as the engine block itself, it is in essence a chemical reaction. The burning of fuel to create energy and motion is not structural, but a process that occurs over a period of time, in this case, over a period of seconds. In essence, there is a stimulus (fuel), action (explosion of fuel), and a response (energy). This also implies a time element; a stimulus occurs first, some action happens, and there is a response—this takes some time, even if it is just seconds.

Personality also involves stimulus-response processes such as those occurring inside a car. Coping styles are processes invoked by stressors and unfold over time (Lazarus & Folkman, 1984). The stimulus (stressor) leads to action (the feeling of stress or threat) and a response (negative affect, problem-solving behavior). This is not a structure, but structural elements of personality, such as trait neuroticism, certainly influence this reaction to stimuli that encompass coping, as well as reactivity to stress (Almeida, in press; Bolger & Schilling 1991; Mroczek & Almeida, 2004; Tennen, Affleck, Armeli, & Carney, 2000). Defense mechanisms also involve stimuli that invoke a response (Cramer, 2003). The response is the defense itself, and the process of stimulus invoking response unfolds over time, although usually a short period of time. Goal attainment and goal-focused behaviors, a popular set of variables among social-cognitive personality researchers, involve processes that occur over longer periods of time, usually days or weeks, making daily diary and experience sampling methods common in this area (Christensen, Feldman-Barrett, Bliss-Moreau, Lebo, & Kaschub, 2003; Fleeson, 2001, 2004; Fleeson & Jolley, chap. 3 in this volume). In all these examples, the process is dynamic, involving a sequence of events. Just as the physical and chemical processes that power a car are not discrete events but rather a sequence of events, personality processes involve particular sequences of events over some period of time.

Cattell (1966) recognized this distinction between structure and process, and incorporated these ideas in his concept of the data box. In the three-dimensional data box, persons make up one dimension, occasions (or situations) a second, and variables a third. Pairs of data box dimensions can be combined to represent a distinct type of data and a unique way of conceptualizing personality. For example, R-technique focuses on variability across persons on a set of variables, holding occasion constant. *R-technique* is the essence of the structure approach to personality. It concentrates on variability across persons, or between-person variance. Or, the researcher may choose to focus on within-person variability across occasions (or situations), on a single variable; Cattell called this S-technique. *S-technique* is the essence of the process approach to personality. It concentrates on variability within persons. The data box, although 40 years old, is an invaluable tool for understanding how structure and process approaches to personality relate to one another (Mroczek & Almeida, 2004; Mroczek & Spiro, 2003b; Nesselroade, 1988). Despite this value, few have used the Cattellian data box to understand personality development, although Ozer (1986) made the most thorough and notable attempt thus far.

Long-Term Change in Personality Processes

An important issue in personality development concerns how structure variables such as traits and process variables, such as goal-focused behavior, change over time (Hooker & McAdams, 2003). Over the past 25 years, there have been many studies examining stability and change in structure variables, in particular, traits (Costa & McCrae, 1988, 1994). Yet, personality processes have never been examined longitudinally. This reason for this is fairly simple. Traits are relatively easily assessed at a given measurement occasion. Processes are not so easily assessed at a given time point because they usually involve several variables that act in a sequence. For example, stress reactivity is a process. A person reacts to a stressor with some level of negative emotion, which varies with the severity of the stressor as well as with the person's characteristic sensitivity to stressors (Bolger & Schilling, 1992; Lazarus & Folkman, 1984; Mroczek & Almeida, 2004). This process is somewhat involved, and usually involves daily, or multiple daily, measurements for a period of a week or more (Eizenman, Nesselroade, Featherman, & Rowe, 1997; Tennen et al., 2000). Such daily diary or experience sampling studies are difficult and expensive to carry out, and once completed, samples are rarely followed up to go through the ordeal once again. As a result, there are no long-term longitudinal studies of processes in personality (e.g., over many months or years).

However, this is changing. About 15 years ago, Nesselroade (1988, 1991) recognized that processes do not necessarily remain stable over time, and indicated the need to invent methodologies to deal with them over the long term. He proposed a "measurement burst" design, in which intensive periods of measurements (hourly, daily, or weekly assessments) are nested within long-term longitudinal studies (Nesselroade & Boker, 1994). In recent years, a few investigators (including ourselves) have begun deploy measurement burst designs, but it is too early for this work to have borne fruit.

MACRO AND MICRO LINKAGES

One of the interesting possibilities of such measurement burst designs are macro–micro linkages. Is variability at the daily or weekly level related to variability at the yearly level? To take an example, is daily variation in positive affect over the course of a week related to variability in positive affect over the course of a year? Are people who display high affect variability over the course of a week the same people who display high affect variability over the course of a year or a decade? Such symmetry has been labeled *ergodicity* (Molenaar, Huizenga, & Nesselroade, 2003). Ergodicity is a concept from physics indicating that a process that holds for a given entity (e.g., a molecule) holds for a much larger grouping of entities. For example, if the speed at which a particular molecule travels through the air is the same as the speed that a whole group of these molecules travel through air, then ergodicity holds. If the two levels—individual and group—act in dissimilar ways, then it is nonergotic. Molenaar et al. (in press) argued that there are parallels in life-span development. Some variables or processes in human development behave in an ergotic fashion, whereas others do not.

An example of ergodicity may be useful here. Take exercise and blood pressure. At the between-person level, individuals who exercise more have lower blood pressure than people who exercise less (a negative correlation). At the within-person level, on occasions when individuals exercise their blood pressure is higher than occasion when they are not exercising (a positive correlation). In fact, this within-person process usually leads to between-person differences in the case of exercise and blood pressure. It may be the case that personality traits and personality processes display similarly ergotic processes. Perhaps the process of handling stress over and over again (e.g., coping processes) actually alters individual differences in certain traits over time (e.g., neuroticism).

The findings of long-term personality growth curves may mimic some of the findings of short-term personality processes and dynamics. Fleeson (2004) argued that within-person variability provides a new frontier for personality psychologists. He spoke mainly of short-term variability, especially in terms of responses to situations. However, such short-term variability may be related to long-term variability. Such studies would bring together traditional personality psychologists interested mainly in structure or process (or both), with those studying long-term personality development. As covered earlier, there is a nascent literature on growth curve models of personality dimensions. There is a maturing literature on dynamic processes, using daily diary and experience sampling designs, but such processes have not been modeled in long-term longitudinal studies.

Two types of designs bring together long- and short-term models. The first is a design in which a single daily diary or experience sampling study is nested within a multiyear longitudinal study. Variability at the daily level can be used to predict (or be predicted by) variability at the annual level. The second is one in which multiple daily studies are nested within the multiyear longitudinal study (e.g., Nesselroade & Boker's measurement burst design). Then, daily variation is modeled on two levels, short term and long term; then the latter results are used to predict (or be predicted by) long-term change in nonprocess variables such as traits. In such designs, structure and process variables can be modeled simultaneously. Researchers could look at how structures influence processes and repeated processes may affect structures. Modeling of both in the same study would allow structure and process approaches to come together.

However, statistical challenges await those who make the first attempts at these new types of analyses. It means modeling change on both the left- and right-hand sides of the equation, and in some cases, multilevel change on one side of the equation. If short-term dynamics (as assessed in an experience sampling design) are used to predict long-term change (in a growth curve design), then change is being modeled on both the independent and dependent variable sides. Certain structural equation models can handle such complex data structures, but often have unrealistic assumptions or restrictions. For example, multiple diary studies would almost necessarily be collected at different times from measurements of nonprocess variables such as traits. This would create variable spacing problems that could present difficulties for structural models. On the other hand, the modeling of such complex change would likely create challenges in an MLM framework. Substantive investigators will have to work closely with developmental methodologists and statisticians to formulate adequate models for answering these interesting but complicated research questions.

FUTURE DIRECTIONS

Longitudinal studies that model intraindividual personality stability and change are increasing in number, and will become more common. As more longitudinal databases accumulate, and as statistical techniques for analyzing these data diffuse more widely, the area of personality development will see many more sophisticated studies in the future. Specifically, four types of studies will be particularly valuable.

First, researchers have applied growth curve and latent growth models to only a handful of personality dimensions so far (Helson et al., 2002; Jones et al., 2003; Jones & Meredith, 1996; Mroczek & Spiro, 2003a; Roberts & Chapman, 2000; Small et al., 2003.) Most have been traits, although growth models of certain major traits (e.g., impulsivity) have not yet been carried out. Nevertheless, the trait domain has seen the largest number of long-term longitudinal studies and application of growth models of change. Other nontrait areas of personality have been very slow to carry out long-term studies of the constructs of interest, let alone apply modern techniques for analyzing change.

Second, personality development researchers need to continue examining potential predictors of change. For some personality dimensions, undoubtedly change occurs in lockstep, that is, everyone changes in the same direction and at the same rate. Yet these dimensions will likely be in the minority, and most will be governed by the life-span principle of individual differences in intraindividual change (Baltes et al., 1977). Among dimensions that show individual differences in change, with some people changing at various rates (and some not changing at all), such individual variability must be accounted for.

Further, both environmental and biological predictors need to be investigated and time-varying predictors must be utilized. Some predictors will be static and unchanging over time, such as gender or ethnicity. These static variables may prove to be valuable predictors, accounting for some of the individual differences in a personality dimensions pattern of change (e.g., women may rise faster on conscientiousness than men). However, more interesting is the possibility that time-varying covariates shift either level or rate of change in personality dimensions. Perhaps the best recent examples, using a well-being dimension, are two studies by Lucas, Clark, Georgellis, and Diener (2003, 2004). In Lucas et al. (2003), marital status, which varies over time as many people slip in and out of marriage (and often back again), was used to predict changes in long-term life satisfaction. Lucas et al. (2004) used employment status, which also can vary over time, to predict changes in life satisfaction over a 15-year period. Use of time-varying covariates are an exciting new vista for the analysis of change in personality. Another exciting new technique is the coupled-change growth model (MacCallum, Kim, Malarkey, & Kiecolt-Glaser, 1997; Sliwinski, Hofer, & Hall, 2003), which can permit the personality development researcher to examine if change in one dimension is related to change in another dimension. For example, Mroczek and Spiro (2003a) documented significant individual differences in the rate at which extraversion and neuroticism change. These were done in separate growth curve models, but an interesting further question is whether changes in one are related to changes in the other. A coupled-change model could answer this question.

A second future direction is concerned with potential predictors of personality change. The third future direction proposes the use of personality change as a predictor itself. As noted in several studies (Helson et al., 2002; Jones et al., 2003; Jones & Meredith, 1996; Mroczek & Spiro, 2003a; Small et al., 2003), some personality dimensions display individual differences in rate of change. Are these differences in rate of change themselves predictive of important outcomes? For example, it is known that levels of some personality traits at a given point in time predict subsequent mortality (Friedman et al., 1993; Wilson, Mendes de Leon, Bienas, Evans & Bennett, 2004). However, does change in these traits (impulsivity, neuroticism) also predict how long a person will live? Also, decline in particular cognitive dimensions predict later mortality. This is the well-known gerontological finding of terminal decline (Small & Backman, 1998). Are there similar effects for decreases or increases in personality dimensions? Does a sharp decline in extraversion signal impending death? Future studies of change in personality should take up these questions, although there are certain statistical challenges that must be overcome. The suggested analyses would involve a combination of growth curve with proportional hazards models (Cox, 1972). Such a combination would require a less desirable two-step process, or some innovative mixing of the two models to allow simultaneous estimation. There has been some developmental work on integrating latent variable models with proportional hazards models, but it has not addressed the specific issue of using change parameters (e.g. slopes) as predictors of mortality (Masyn, 2003). Nevertheless, there is promise that, eventually, researchers will be able to estimate change and use parameters of change to predict mortality and other discrete events in a simultaneous model.

Fourth, and finally, what is the relation, if any, between microlevel change (daily level variation) and macrolevel change (long-term growth curves)? This will also help to bring together structure and process (person and situational) approaches to personality. The statistical challenges inherent in such models have already been discussed, but they are well worth solving, as they will provide a wealth of valuable results that could transform not only the area of personality development, but of personality psychology itself. Indeed, each of the four areas of future direction have such potential.

ACKNOWLEDGMENT

This work was supported by grants from the National Institute on Aging (R01-AG18436 and P01-AG020166).

REFERENCES

Almeida, D. M. (in press). Resilience and vulnerability to daily stressors assessed via diary methods. *Current Directions in Psychological Science.*

Aldwin, C. M., Spiro, A. III, Levenson, M. R., & Bossé, R. (1989). Longitudinal findings from the Normative Aging Study: 1. Does mental health change with age? *Psychology and Aging, 4,* 295–306.

Alwin, D. F. (1994). Aging, personality, and social change: The stability of individual differences over the adult span. In D. L. Featherman, R. M. Lerner, & M. Perlmutter (Eds.), *Life-span development and behavior* (Vol. 12, pp.135–185). Hillsdale, NJ: Lawrence Erlbaum Associates.

Baldwin, A. L. (1946). The study of individual personality by means of the intraindividual correlation. *Journal of Personality, 14,* 151–168.

Baltes, P. B. (1987). Theoretical propositions of life-span developmental psychology: On the dynamics between growth and decline. *Developmental Psychology, 23,* 611–626.

Baltes, P. B., & Nesselroade, J. R. (1973). The developmental analysis of individual differences on multiple measures. In J.R. Nesselroade & H.W. Reese (Eds.), *Life-span developmental psychology: Methodological issues* (pp. 219–251). New York: Academic Press.

Baltes, P. B., Reese, H. W., & Nesselroade, J. R. (1977). *Lifespan developmental psychology: Introduction to research methods.* Monterey, CA: Brooks/Cole.

Biesanz, J. C., Debb-Sossa, N., Papadukis, A. A., Bollen, K. A., & Curran, P. J. (2004). The role of coding time in estimating and interpreting growth curve models. *Psychological Methods, 9,* 30–52.

Bolger, N., & Schilling, E. A. (1991). Personality and problems of everyday life: The role of neuroticism in exposure and reactivity to daily stressors. *Journal of Personality, 59,* 356–386.

Bryk, A. S., & Raudenbush, S. W. (1992). *Hierarchical linear models in social and behavioral research: Applications and data analysis methods.* Newbury Park, CA: Sage.

Caspi, A., McClay, J., Moffitt, T., E., Mill, J., Martin, J., Craig, I. W., Taylor, A., & Poulton, R. (2002). Role of genotype in the cycle of violence in maltreated children. *Science, 297,* 851.

Caspi, A., & Roberts, B. W. (2001). Personality development across the life: The argument for change and continuity. *Psychological Inquiry, 12,* 49–66.

Caspi, A., Sugden, K., Moffitt, T., Taylor, A, Craig, A. S., Harrington, H., McClay, J., Mill, J., Martin, J., Braithwaite, A., & Poulton, R. (2003). Influence of life stress on depression: Moderation by a polymorphism in the 5-HTT gene. *Science, 301,* 386–389.

Cattell, R. B. (1950). *Personality: A systematical theoretical and factual study.* New York: McGraw-Hill.

Cattell, R. B. (1966). The data box: Its ordering of total resources in terms of possible relational systems. In R. B. Cattell (Ed.), *Handbook of multivariate experimental psychology* (pp. 78–97). Chicago: Rand-McNally.

Christensen, T. C., Feldman-Barrett, L., Bliss-Moreau, E., Lebo, K., & Kaschub, C. (2003). A practical guide to experience-sampling procedures. *Journal of Happiness Studies, 4,* 53–78.

Clausen, J. A., & Jones, C. J. (1998). Predicting personality stability across the life span: The role of competence and work and family commitments. *Journal of Adult Development, 5,* 73–83.

Conley, J. J. (1984). The hierarchy of consistency: A review and model of longitudinal findings on adult individual differences in intelligence, personality, and self-opinion. *Personality and Individual Differences, 5,* 11–26.

Conley, J. J. (1985). Longitudinal stability of personality traits: A multitrait–multimethod–multioccasion analysis. *Journal of Personality and Social Psychology, 49,* 1266–1282.

Costa, P. T., & McCrae, R. R. (1988). Personality in adulthood: A six-year longitudinal study of self-reports and spouse ratings on the NEO Personality Inventory. *Journal of Personality and Social Psychology, 54,* 853–863.

Costa, P. T., & McCrae, R. R. (1994). Set like plaster? Evidence for the stability of adult personality. In T. F. Heatherton & J. L. Weinberger (Eds.), *Can personality change?* (pp. 21–40). Washington, DC: American Psychological Association.

Cox, D. R. (1972). Regression models and life tables (with discussion). *Journal of the Royal Statistical Society, Series B, 74,* 187–220.

Cramer, P. (2003). Personality change in adulthood is predicted by defense mechanism use in early adulthood. *Journal of Research in Personality, 37,* 76–104.

Cronbach, L. J. (1957). The two disciplines of scientific psychology. *American Psychologist, 12,* 671–684.

Eizenman, D. R., Nesselroade, J. R., Featherman, D. L., & Rowe, J. W. (1997). Intraindividual variability in perceived control in an older sample: The MacArthur successful aging studies. *Psychology and Aging, 12,* 489–502.

Finn, S. E. (1986). Stability of personality self-ratings over 30 years: Evidence for an age/cohort interaction. *Journal of Personality and Social Psychology, 50,* 813–818.

Fleeson, W. (2001). Toward a structure- and process-integrated view of personality: Traits as density distributions of states. *Journal of Personality and Social Psychology, 80,* 1011–1027.

Fleeson, W. (2004). Moving personality beyond the person-situation debate: The challenge and opportunity of within-person variability. *Current Directions in Psychological Science, 13,* 83–87.

Friedman, H. S., Tucker, J. S., Tomlinson-Keasey, C., Schwartz, J. E., Wingard, D. L., & Criqui, M. H. (1993). Does childhood personality predict longevity? *Journal of Personality and Social Psychology, 65,* 176–185.

Goldberg, L. R. (1993). The structure of phenotypic personality traits. *American Psychologist, 48,* 26–34.

Helson, R., Jones C. J., & Kwan, V. S. Y. (2002). Personality change over 40 years of adulthood: Hierarchical linear modeling analyses of two longitudinal samples. *Journal of Personality and Social Psychology, 83,* 752–766.

Henry, C. E. (1941). Electroencephalographic individual differences and their constancy: II. During waking. *Journal of Experimental Psychology, 29,* 236–247.

Hooker, K., & McAdams, D. P. (2003). Personality reconsidered: A new agenda for aging research. *Journal of Gerontology: Psychological Sciences, 58B,* 296–304.

Jones, C. J., Livson, N., & Peskin, H. (2003). Longitudinal hierarchical linear modeling analyses of California Psychological Inventory data from age 33 to 75: An examination of stability and change in adult personality. *Journal of Personality Assessment, 80,* 294–308.

Jones, C. J., & Meredith, W. (1996). Patterns of personality change across the life-span. *Psychology and Aging, 11,* 57–65.

Lamiell, J. T. (1981). Toward an idiothethic psychology of personality. *American Psychologist, 36,* 276–289.

Lazarus, R. S., & Folkman, S. (1984). *Stress, appraisal and coping.* New York: Springer.

Lerner, R. M., & Busch-Rossnagel, N. (1981). *Individuals as producers of their development: A life-span perspective.* New York: Academic Press.

Levenson, M. R., & Crumpler, C. A. (1996). Three models of adult development. *Human Development, 39,* 135–149.

Lucas, R. E., Clark, A. E., Georgellis, Y., & Diener, E. (2003). Reexamining adaptation and the set point model of happiness: Reactions to changes in marital status. *Journal of Personality and Social Psychology, 84,* 527–539.

Lucas, R. E., Clark, A. E., Georgellis, Y., & Diener, E. (2004). Unemployment alters the set point for life satisfaction. *Psychological Science, 15*(1), 8–13.

MacCallum, R. C., Kim, C., Malarkey, W. B., & Kiecolt-Glaser, J. (1997). Studying multivariate change using multilevel models and latent curve models. *Multivariate Behavioral Research, 32,* 215–253.

Martin, M., & Mroczek, D. K. (in press). Are personality traits across the lifespan sensitive to environmental demands? *Journal of Adult Development.*

Masyn, K. E. (2003). *Discrete time survival mixture analysis for single and recurrent events using latent variables.* Unpublished doctoral dissertation, School of Education, University of California, Los Angeles, CA.

McArdle, J. J. (1991). Structural models of development theory in psychology. *Annals of Theoretical Psychology, 7,* 139–159.

McArdle, J. J., & Woodcock, R. W. (1997). Expanding test–retest designs to include developmental time-lag components. *Psychological Methods, 2,* 403–435.

Mehta, P. D., & West, S. G. (2000). Putting the individual back into individual growth curves. *Psychological Methods, 5,* 23–43.

Meredith, W., & Tisak, J. (1990). Latent curve analysis. *Psychometrika, 55,* 107–122.

Mroczek, D. K., & Almeida, D. M. (2004). The effects of daily stress, personality, and age on daily negative affect. *Journal of Personality, 72,* 355–378.

Mroczek, D. K., & Griffin, P. (in press). Growth-curve modeling in positive psychology. In A. Ong (Ed.), *Handbook of methods in positive psychology.* Thousand Oaks, CA: Sage.

Mroczek, D. K., & Spiro, A., III. (2003a). Modeling intraindividual change in personality traits: Findings from the Normative Aging Study. *Journals of Gerontology: Psychological Sciences, 58B,* 153–165.

Mroczek, D. K., & Spiro, A., III (2003b). Personality structure and process, variance between and within: Integration by means of developmental framework. *Journals of Gerontology: Psychological Sciences, 58B,* 305–306.

Molenaar, P. C. M., Huizenga, H. M., & Nesselroade, J. R. (2003). The relationship between the structure of inter-individual and intra-individual variability: A theoretical and empirical vindication of developmental systems theory. In U. M. Staudinger & U. Lindenberger (Eds.), *Understanding human development* (pp. 339–360). Boston: Kluwer.

Muthen, B. O. (2002). Beyond SEM: General latent variable modeling. *Behaviormetrika, 29,* 81–117.

Nesselroade, J. R. (1988). Sampling and generalizability: Adult development and aging issues examined within the general methodological framework of selection. In K. W. Schaie, R. T. Campbell, W. M. Meredith, & S. C. Rawlings (Eds.), *Methodological issues in aging research* (pp. 108–121). New York: Springer.

Nesselroade, J. R. (1991). Interindividual differences in intraindividual change. In L. M. Collins & J. L. Horn (Eds.), *Best methods for the analysis of change* (pp. 92–105). Washington, DC: American Psychological Association.

Nesselroade, J. R., & Baltes, P. B. (1974). Adolescent personality development and historical changes: 1970–1972. *Monographs of the Society for Research in Child Development, 39* (1, Serial No. 154).

Nesselroade, J. R., & Boker, S. M. (1994). Assessing constancy and change. In T. F. Heatherton & J. L. Weinberger (Eds.), *Can personality change?* (pp. 121–148). Washington, DC: American Psychological Association.

Neyer, F. J., & Asendorpf, J. B. (2001). Personality-relationship transaction in young adulthood. *Journal of Personality and Social Psychology, 81,* 1190–1204.

Ozer, D. J. (1986). *Consistency in personality: A methodological framework.* Berlin: Springer.

Raudenbush, S. W., & Bryk, A. S. (2002). *Hierarchical linear models: Applications and data analysis methods* (2nd ed.). Thousand Oaks, CA: Sage.

Roberts, B. W. (1997). Plaster or plasticity: Are adult work experiences associated with personality change in women? *Journal of Personality, 65,* 205–232.

Roberts, B. W., & Chapman, C. N. (2000). Change in dispositional well-being and its relations to role quality: A 30-year longitudinal study. *Journal of Research in Personality, 34,* 26–41.

Roberts, B. W., & DelVecchio, W. F. (2000). The rank order consistency of personality traits from childhood to old age: A quantitative review of longitudinal studies. *Psychological Bulletin, 126,* 3–25.

Rogosa, D. R., Brandt, D., & Zimowski, M. (1982). A growth curve approach to the measurement of change. *Psychological Bulletin, 92,* 726–748.

Singer, J. D. (1998). Using SAS Proc Mixed to fit multilevel models, hierarchical models, and individual growth models. *Journal of Educational and Behavioral Statistics, 23,* 323–355.

Singer, J. D., & Willett, J. B. (2003). *Applied longitudinal analysis: Modeling change and event occurrence.* New York: Oxford University Press.

Sliwinski, M. J., Hofer, S. M., & Hall, C. (2003). Correlated and coupled change in older adults with and without preclinical dementia. *Psychology and Aging, 18,* 672–683.

Small, B. J., & Backman, L. (1997). Cognitive correlates of mortality: Evidence from a population-based sample of very old adults. *Psychology and Aging, 12,* 309–313.

Small, B. J., Hertzog, C., Hultsch, D. F., & Dixon, R. A. (2003). Stability and change in adult personality over 6 years: Findings from the Victoria Longitudinal Study. *Journals of Gerontology: Psychological Sciences and Social Sciences, 58B,* 166–176.

Stephenson, W. (1936). Correlating persons instead of tests. *Character and Personality, 4,* 17–24.

Tennen, H., Affleck, G., Armeli, S., & Carney, M. A. (2000). A daily process approach to coping: Linking theory, research and practice. *American Psychologist, 55,* 626–636.

Twenge, J. M. (2000). The age of anxiety? The birth cohort change in anxiety and neuroticism, 1952–1993. *Journal of Personality and Social Psychology, 79,* 1007–1021.

Twenge, J. M. (2001). Birth cohort changes in extraversion: A cross-temporal meta-analysis, 1966–1993. *Personality and Individual Differences, 30,* 735–748.

von Eye, A., & Nesselroade, J. R. (1992). Types of change: Application of configural frequency analysis in repeated measurement designs. *Experimental Aging Research, 18,* 169–183.

Willett, J. B., & Sayer, A. G. (1994). Using covariance structure analysis to detect correlates and predictors of individual change over time. *Psychological Bulletin, 116,* 363–381.

Wilson, R. S., Mendes de Leon, C. F., Bienas, J. L., Evans, D. A., & Bennett, D. A. (2004). Personality and mortality in old age. *Journal of Gerontology: Psychological Sciences, 59B,* 110–116.

Wohlwill, J. F. (1973). *The study of behavioral development.* New York: Academic Press.

10

Methods for the Analysis
of Change

Todd D. Little
James A. Bovaird
David W. Slegers
University of Kansas

Throughout the social and behavioral sciences, researchers have increased their reliance on longitudinal designs to address questions about the potential change relations among various dimensions of behavior, including personality. One problem that researchers face as they embark on a longitudinal study is the lack of a roadmap to help inform important design decisions. Particularly with longitudinal investigations, understanding the interface between research question, study design, and analytic technique is crucial. This chapter offers a broad overview of the analytic techniques that can be used with longitudinal data and discusses important developmental design considerations. The goal is to provide a guide for researchers that will help clarify the strengths and weaknesses of the various techniques and the types of answer that the techniques can provide.

For the most part, few developmental questions can be addressed with a single analytic approach because each approach is geared to address only certain aspects of the data. This overview describes the basic features of the techniques and discusses their merits with regard to the nature of the question they can address and the quality of the answer that they provide. In general, longitudinal techniques can be categorized into those that address changes in group means (e.g., repeated measures analysis of variance, ANOVA), those that address changes in the individual differences standings among a sample of individuals (i.e., modeling between-person relations with procedures such as regression, path analysis, or structural equation modeling, SEM), and those that address changes intraindividually (i.e., modeling within-person change relations with procedures such as growth curve and multilevel modeling).

The focus of this chapter is primarily on the techniques derived from the general class of latent variable methods (i.e., SEM) for the analysis of change because of the various limitations with the classical (least squares) general linear model approach. Specifically, the advent of SEM brought with it a number of features that make it an ideal technique for modeling longitudinal data. First, the problems of unreliability are remedied by the use of multiple indicators of latent constructs. Second, the inherent need to represent indirect paths is easily accommodated. Third, the problem of correlated "errors" (i.e., item uniquenesses) is no longer seen as a violated assumption, but rather as effects that can and should be estimated. Fourth, classical approaches rely on a set of distributional assumptions related to normality or multivariate normality. Although the most popular estimation procedure in SEM, maximum likelihood, makes similar assumptions, SEM programs have numerous ways of dealing with mild to moderate violations of the classical distributional assumptions (e.g., robust standard errors, bootstrapping capabilities, and alternative estimation methods such as weighted least squares). Finally, measurement invariance of the constructs across time, which is an assumption of classical methods, can be tested and evaluated in the SEM framework.

Although SEM procedures possess numerous advantages, some disadvantages of longitudinal SEM include the need for large sample sizes and the assumption that the sample is homogeneous with regard to the underlying change processes or mechanisms. Mixture distribution modeling, however, attempts to address this latter assumption empirically (see later), or theoretically derived subgroups (who are then assumed to be homogeneous with regard to the change process) can be modeled separately using the multiple group capability of SEM procedures.

LATENT VARIABLE LONGITUDINAL METHODS

Two-Wave Difference and Residual Score Approaches

The simplest form of a longitudinal study is a two-occasion measurement design. Although most developmentalists would argue that two waves do not sufficiently constitute a longitudinal design, the two-occasion approach can, in fact, inform developmental questions (Hertzog, Dixon, Hultsch, & MacDonald, 2003). However, the two-occasion approach does carry with it significant disadvantages for answering questions about change. Bereiter (1963) outlined three basic problems with using a simple difference score to indicate change: the paradoxical relation between the test–retest correlation and the reliability of the change score, the negative correlation between initial status and the change score, and the lack of consistency in interpretability of the change score at different points in the distribution. In addition, when two-occasion data is analyzed using classical approaches (e.g., difference scores, gain scores, residual change scores, repeated measures ANOVA, etc.), quite restrictive assumptions must be met (e.g., sphericity of variances), and the effects of the ever-present problem of unreliability are significantly heightened (Rogosa & Willett, 1983). Problems related to measurement error include Type II errors associated with elevated variance estimates, underestimates of stability, and regression-to-(and-from)-the-mean effects—these problems can become exacerbated with time-dependent longitudinal data (McArdle & Nesselroade, 2002).

As already mentioned, methodologists have remedied many of these problems by taking a latent variable SEM approach. McArdle (2001), for example, outlined how to calculate a latent difference or latent residual score that does not suffer from the issues associated with measurement error or highly restrictive assumptions. Figure 10.1 provides a sketch of two alternative latent variable approaches to modeling change scores across two measurement occasions. The key to the latent variable approach is that constructs are assessed by multiple indicators at each time point. This process produces variance in each latent construct that is error free and, as a result, the change in variance, Δ, is also measured without error.

As seen in Fig. 10.1, both approaches decompose the variance of the Time 2 construct into two components (note that the Time 2 disturbance factor is fixed at 0.0 to identify the model's parameters as well as force the two-way decomposition). For the difference score model (Fig. 10.1, Panel A) the two components are variance associated with one's absolute standing at Time 1 and variance associated with the absolute difference from Time 1. For the residual score model (Fig. 10.1, Panel B), the two components are one's relative standing at Time 1 (i.e., the degree of correlation) and the change in relative standing at Time 2. Note that the graphic representation of the change scores in Fig. 10.1 can also be modeled as depicted in Fig. 10.2. Here, the disturbance factor represents the change variance but would also carry the indirect effects of Time 1 if predicting to an outcome construct.

Three features distinguish these two different approaches to representing change. First, both models are equivalent in terms of their ability to reproduce the observed variance-covariance matrix (although degrees of freedom differ). Second, because the difference score model assumes a perfect linear relation, the Time 1 construct and the difference at Time 2 will be correlated to some degree depending on how much the relation between the two constructs is not a perfect 1.0 correlation. Third, because the residual score model estimates the degree of relation between the two time points, the Time 1 construct and the residual at Time 2 are orthogonal. Fourth,

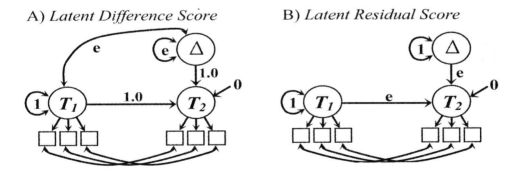

A) *Latent Difference Score*   B) *Latent Residual Score*

FIG. 10.1.   Latent difference and residual scores. The variances of the exogenous factors T_1 and Δ are fixed at 1. T_1 and T_2 are measured with multiple indicators that are invariant over Time.

A) *Latent Difference Score*   B) *Latent Residual Score*

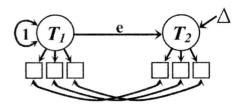

FIG. 10.2.   Latent difference and residual scores. The variances of the exogenous factor T_1 is fixed at 1. In these simplified drawings, the disturbance factor reflects the latent change variance Δ.

the mean of the difference factor in Fig. 10.1, Panel A is the absolute group-wise change. This mean-level change is similar to what would be estimated by repeated measures ANOVA with the exception that the mean difference is corrected for measurement error and does not assume homogeneity of the variances over time.

Given the differences in the information captured and modeled, the two approaches address different types of question. The latent difference score is most useful to model mean change over time and the individual differences around that mean change, whereas the latent residual score model is most useful to examine issues related to stability of individual differences and the individual differences around that stability. As outlined in the next section, the latent residual score model forms the basis for standard individual differences models whereas the latent change model forms the basis for recently proposed alternative individual differences models (McArdle, 2001; McArdle & Bell, 2000; McArdle & Nesselroade, 2002).

Standard Individual Differences SEM Models

Figure 10.3 displays a simple cross-lagged panel design for assessing change. This figure extends the graphical representation to include three waves of data with two constructs at each wave. The two constructs at Time 1 are said to be exogenous because no other variables or constructs are assessed prior to them (although, this model can easily be expanded to include covariate influences that could predict to Time 1). The four constructs at Times 2 and 3 are endogenous constructs because they are assessed "down stream" and the variance-covariance information among these constructs would have the different effects of the prior time points accounted for in the lagged regression estimation process. In this case, the relation between the two constructs at Time 1 is interpreted as an exogenous covariance (or correlation, depending on the scaling method), whereas the within-time associations among the constructs at Time 2 and Time 3 are interpreted as endogenous or residual covariances (or residual correlations when standardized).

The lines that link the corresponding constructs between each time point are termed auto-regressions and account for the individual differences stability of the constructs across each time point. If the change process is at a constant rate, then the between-time stability coefficients are sufficient to capture the rate of change over time (i.e., no direct effects from Time 1 to Time 3 are required). Such an idealized pattern of change results in what is referred to as a simplex covariance structure. If direct paths from Time 1 to Time 3 are required by the data, the change process no longer conforms to a simplex structure. A nonsimplex structure indicates that one or more factors has influenced the change process making the association between Time 1 and Time 3 either stronger or weaker than would be expected if the change process progressed at a constant linear rate. Factors that can influence the rate of change include contextual/environmental influences or nonlinear maturational processes that speed up or slow down the rate of change.

The paths that cross-link the constructs over time are referred to as cross-lagged effects. These effects, when significant, indicate that change in one variable is related to prior status in the other variable. Because of the time-ordered relations among the variables, such effects have a "causal" flavor about them, but cannot be considered causal because of the ever-present unmeasured variable problem and the exogeniety assumption. The unmeasured variable problem applies to any modeling endeavor and simply means that some other unmeasured variable may be the causal mechanism driving the observed pattern of influences. The exogeniety assumption also applies to any modeling endeavor and simply highlights the idea that the Time 1 constructs, which are assumed to be exogenous, are likely not representing the true beginning of the time-ordered sequence of relations among the constructs.

This being said, the primary research questions that can be asked and answered by the standard individual differences approach to longitudinal data concern the constructs measurement invariant over time (i.e., are the measures tapping in to the same thing at different points in time?), the stability of the constructs over the observed time

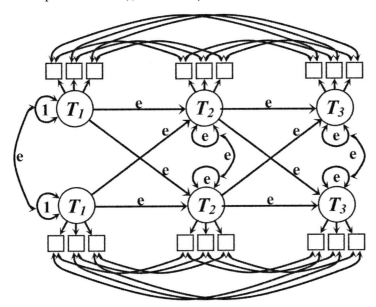

FIG. 10.3.   Traditional SEM model of individual differences change relationships. The variances of the exogenous factors at T_1 are fixed at 1 to set the scale and identify the constructs. T_1, T_2, and T_3 are measured with multiple indicators that are invariant over Time and each corresponding residual is allowed to correlate to account for the potential dependencies in the unique factors.

span (i.e., to what degree do the individual differences standings get shuffled over the time intervals assessed?), the relative mean-level differences in the constructs over time, whether the change process is adequately captured by a simplex process (i.e., is the rate of change linearly constant and unaffected by other sources of influence?), if there is any evidence of cross-lagged influences that are predictive of the cross-time changes, if the cross-time changes are reciprocal or predominantly unidirectional, and if the cross-time effects are consistent between each adjacent time point.

In addressing these basic concerns about the change process, the modeling steps typically begin with a longitudinal confirmatory factor analysis (CFA) wherein all constructs are allowed to correlate with one another (i.e., no directed paths are estimated). This model is used to explain and answer the first three questions regarding measurement invariance (which should include invariance of both the intercepts and loadings and allow all corresponding residuals to correlate over time; see Little & Slegers, 2005; Meredith, 1993), the general level of individual differences stabilities over time (i.e., the estimated latent correlations from the CFA model), and the relative mean-level changes over time.

The next step of the modeling process would then specify the expected pattern of cross-time influences (e.g., as depicted in Fig. 10.3). This model is typically more restricted than the CFA (i.e., fewer parameters are estimated), but should achieve a similar level of fit to be deemed adequate in capturing the change relations over time. This model would be used to evaluate and answer the latter four questions regarding the possible simplex structure of the change process, the existence of cross-lagged effects, their relative strengths, and their consistency over time.

As can be seen, the standard individual differences approach is useful for answering a number of relevant developmental questions (Burkholder & Harlow, 2003). Such models are also important to assess the adequacy and invariance of each construct's indictors over time and across groups (Little, 1997; Little, Lindenberger, & Nesselroade, 1999) and the potential for selectivity between continuers and dropouts (Little, Lindenberger, & Maier, 2000); however, the change dynamics are not fully examined in a standard individual differences model. A complementary procedure for modeling change over time is to analyze the data using growth curve methodology.

Growth Curve Modeling

This section presents univariate and multivariate change models as structural equation models and, in particular, latent growth curve models. These models are described in a variety of sources, including Aber and McArdle (1991), T. E. Duncan, S. C. Duncan, Strycker, Li, and Alpert (1999), McArdle (1988), Meredith and Tisak (1990), Raykov and Marcoulides (2000), and Willett and Sayer (1994). They could easily be conducted using any of the modern SEM programs, such as Mplus, EQS, LISREL, Amos, Mx, or SAS PROC CALIS, and most of the models presented in this section can also be implemented using multilevel modeling software such as SAS PROC NLMIXED (see, e.g., Ferrer, Hamagami, & McArdle, 2004).

Latent growth curve modeling is a procedure that allows modeling of individual differences in the changes over time by implementing a random coefficient or multilevel framework within the SEM framework (Bauer, 2003; Curran, 2004). In a multilevel model, of which the hierarchical linear model is a type, a population of lower level units (Level 1) are "nested" within a higher level population of units (Level 2). In the traditional HLM classroom example, the population of students (Level 1) are nested within classrooms (Level 2). Nesting is necessary when clustering (and statistical nonindependence) of observations occurs due to a higher level influence. In this case, assessments of students within a classroom are considered to be correlated to some degree because of their shared within-classroom experience (see Bryk & Raudenbush, 1987, 1992; Hox, 2000; Raudenbush & Bryk, 2002).

Just as student assessments within a classroom may be correlated, repeated observations (Level 1) on an individual student may be nested within the individual student (Level 2). More specifically, growth curve models attempt to represent the dynamic nature of change as a "mixed" combination of fixed and random coefficients or effects, hence the term *mixed model*, which is sometimes used to describe this type of analysis. In the mixed model, the basic components of change for a sample of individuals are the *fixed average intercept*, or starting point; the *fixed average slope*, or degree of change over time; the *random individual variability around the average starting point*; and the *random individual variability around the average shape of change* (Cudeck & du Toit, 2001). The examples to follow make the key assumption that the sample is homogeneous with regard to the change process being modeled. That is, the assumption is made that the data follows a two-level hierarchy (observations within individuals) and there is not a higher level of sampling present in the data (i.e., a "Level 3") whether observed or latent. This assumption is also true of SEM in general. It is possible to conduct a three-level multilevel growth curve analysis within an SEM framework (i.e., observations nested within persons and persons nested within schools; see T. E. Duncan, S. C. Duncan, Okut, Strycker, & Li, 2002; Heck & Thomas, 2000; Hox, 2000, 2002), but that type of analysis is beyond the scope of this chapter.

Latent growth modeling and multilevel modeling, as mentioned, can be specified such that they are identical approaches. However, modeling growth models in the SEM framework has two notable advantages over traditional multilevel approaches. First, latent growth modeling in the SEM context can easily be expanded to include distinct growth curves for multiple variables to examine the dynamic interplay among them (McArdle & Nesselroade, 2002). For example, growth curves for each of the Big Five personality factors can be estimated simultaneously to examine the potential change dynamics among them. Second, in conjunction with the multiple-group processing capabilities of SEM programs, complex (i.e., nonmonotonic) nonlinear effects can be specified (McArdle & Nesselroade, 2002). Third, latent growth curve modeling allows for the modeling of change in a latent construct, with all the benefits related to latent variables versus manifest variables described earlier.

Turning back to the basic specification of a latent growth curve model, if the assumption of sample homogeneity is warranted, then the specific nature of the change can be modeled in a number of ways. The model begins with the SEM alternative to the standard longitudinal mixed model assuming a linear trend over time and then extends to more complex, and more interesting, specifications.

Figure 10.4 provides a series of alternate (unconditional) growth curve models that can be fit to four waves of data. Note that growth curve models can also be fit to just three waves of data, but the nature of the shape of change that can be modeled is more limited. For all the models depicted in Fig. 10.4, the first construct represents the intercept or starting level of the curve that is being modeled. The loadings of

A) *Level and Linear Slope*

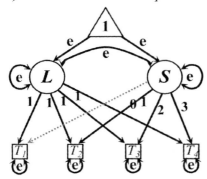

B) *Level and Quadratic Slope*

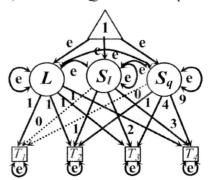

C) *Level and Shape Model I*

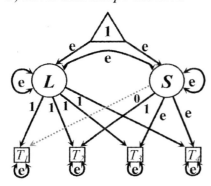

D) *Level and Shape Model II*

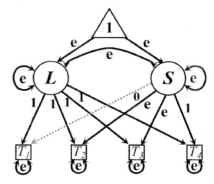

FIG. 10.4.   Various forms of latent growth curve models.

each variable on this construct are all fixed at 1.0 representing the regression of the repeated outcome measures on a constant in order to capture the mean intercept, or starting point of the curve. The estimated variance of this construct reflects the individual variability around the grand mean and the estimated latent mean of this construct is the estimated value of the mean intercept. These parameters are equivalent to the random individual variability around the average starting point and the fixed average intercept, or starting point in the mixed model described earlier. The means of the latent constructs are represented in these diagrams as the regression of the constructs on to the unit constant "factor" (e.g., Kappa and Alpha matrices of LISREL and V999 of EQS), which is depicted as a triangle in these diagrams (for more details of modeling means, see Browne & Arminger, 1995; Little & Slegers, 2005; Little et al., in press). The remaining latent constructs, labeled with an S_x, represent the change that occurs relative to the intercept and differs by model.

Simple Polynomial Models.   First consider an illustration of a simple linear relation between the dependent variable and time that provides a direct test of the actual linear slope of the growth trend using simple polynomial contrasts. A first polynomial model depicted in Fig.10.4, Panel A, is one in which the expected growth pattern is expected to be linear. In this model, all four loadings from the "shape" factor are fixed to values that reflect the proportional relation between time points (e.g., 0, 1, 2, 3 or 0, .33, .66, 1 if the observations are equally spaced; or say 0, 1, 3, 5 or 0, .20, .60, 1 if the observations are unequally spaced). Note that the factor loading for the first variable is zero and is denoted in Fig. 10.4 as a dashed line. The estimates are said to be centered on the first measurement occasion with this pattern of specified loadings. Specifically, the loading of the first variable is fixed at zero so that the intercept would take on the value of the starting point of the curve at the first occasion of measurement. If this value were fixed at 1, for example, then the intercept would then take on the value of the starting point at some point prior to the first occasion of measurement (McArdle & Nesselroade, 2002). If the loading for the last variable were fixed at zero and the loadings for the other three variables were negative (e.g. –3, –2, –1, 0), then the intercept would take on the value of the last measurement occasion and change would be interpreted as change leading up to a particular event rather than change since an event. See Kreft, de Leeuw, and Aiken (1995) or Rovine and Molenaar (1998) for additional discussions of centering.

The estimated variance of the shape construct reflects the individual variability around the average linear change in the sample, and the estimated latent mean of this construct is an estimate of the average slope. These parameters are equivalent to the random individual variability around the average shape of change and the fixed average slope, or degree of change over time, in the mixed model described earlier. The remaining model parameters are the residual error terms for the four variables, which are commonly constrained to be nonzero but equal, and the covariance between the intercept and slope factors. It is reasonable to assume that the initial status on a variable is related to, or correlated with, the subsequent change or growth on that variable. This assumption is commonly included in formulating a latent growth curve model, but it is not always required (Raykov & Marcoulides, 2000). Other specifications might include a specific directional relation between the level and shape factors such that the initial status on a variable directly impacts the nature of the subsequent change that occurs. As a result, instead of estimating the simple covariance between the level factor and the shape factor, a directional path may be modeled.

The residual terms are constrained to be equal under an assumption of homoscedasticity and are equivalent to the Level 1 residual in a multilevel or mixed model. The equality constraint on the residual terms can easily be relaxed and subsequently reflect a heteroscedastic situation. The residual variances are estimated to account for the deviation of scores from the individual trend curves. The constraint of homoscedasticity (or stationarity) keeps the error impact equal at all time points and preserves model parsimony (Raykov & Marcoulides, 2000). A residual variance represents unexplainable or unaccountable error or individual differences in measurement. By assuming a common residual variance, the implication is that the unexplainable variance at each time point is constant and the remaining variance is due to the initial status of the trait measured by a particular variable and subsequent change in the trait over time.

This method is more parsimonious than the heteroscedastic case because it allows for additional degrees of freedom (i.e., fewer estimated parameters). For example, consider each of the variables measured at all four time points. Instead of estimating four parameters (one residual variance for each time point), it is only necessary to estimate one common residual variance parameter thus saving three model degrees of freedom. Within the context of SEM models, the assumption of homoscedasticity can be evaluated by examining both global and local model fit and relaxing the constraints if so warranted.

If the linear slope model fits the data well, then it could be concluded that the growth pattern is readily captured by a linear trend. If this linear model does not fit, however, then the linear trend is not warranted and a quadratic or more complex function may be a better representation of the change over time. Figure 10.4, Panel B, depicts a growth curve model to estimate a quadratic function. Here, the fixed loadings for the linear construct are the same as they were for the linear slope model, and the fixed loadings for the quadratic construct are the squares of the corresponding linear loadings (e.g. 0^2, 1^2, 2^2, 3^2), just as x^2 in addition to x might be used to represent a quadratic relation between predictor and criterion in regression. The variance of the intercept, or level (L), construct still represents the individual variability at the intercept, the variance of the linear slope construct (S_l) still represents the variability in change over the range of time, and the variance of the quadratic construct (S_q) represents variability in the acceleration or deceleration of the growth over time. The latent means of each of these constructs represent the average status at the intercept, the average growth over time, and the average acceleration or deceleration. Residual error terms are still included in the model as are covariances between latent factors.

Because there are four measurement periods in this example, the polynomial growth function may be extended through a cubic component (i.e., the number of possible components is equal to the number of measurement periods minus 1).

Optimal Level and Shape Models. The next two models in Fig. 10.4 (Panels C and D) depict two alternative models that represent variations of the latent growth curve model previously presented. In both level and shape models, the second construct captures the shape of the change over time, but the shape of change over time is not specifically modeled as a particular function (i.e., linear, quadratic, etc.) as it was in the simple polynomial approach. Instead, this flexible approach to growth curve modeling allows for the parsimonious capture of nonlinear change over time without the need for additional latent factors beyond the intercept (level) and shape factors, regardless of the order of curvature.

In both Panel C and Panel D of Fig. 10.4, following the same consideration for centering discussed previously, the loading of the first variable is fixed at zero so that the intercept would take on the value of the starting point of the curve at the first occasion of measurement. As already mentioned, if this value were fixed at 1, for example, the intercept would then take on the value of the starting point at some point prior to the first occasion of measurement (McArdle & Nesselroade, 2002). In order to set the scale or change units of the shape of change, a second loading must be fixed to some nonzero value. In Panel C, the loading of the second variable on the shape construct is fixed at 1.0. The loadings for the variables at Time 3 and Time 4 are then freely estimated to capture the unrestricted shape of the change over time. The metric of the loadings at Time 3 and Time 4 are standardized as proportional change units relative to the magnitude of the change between the first and second measurement occasion.

In Panel D, the loading of the last variable on the shape construct is fixed at 1.0, and the middle two time points are estimated. Here, the values of the middle two time points would be proportional to the overall change between Time 1 and Time 4. Both of these models are identical in terms of their fit. The only difference is in the scaling of the estimates (e.g., the loadings, the mean of the shape construct, and the variability around the estimated slope). The model in Panel D provides roughly standardized values, so it is relatively easier to interpret. Plotting the estimated factor loadings for the given time points describes the shape of the nonlinear relation over time.

The loadings for the shape construct are termed *basis weights* because they reflect the basis by which the shape of the change can be interpreted and they provide the basis by which the change influences on the variances and covariances of the variables is evaluated (T. E. Duncan et al., 1999; McArdle & Nesselroade, 2002). Specifically, the mean of the shape factor reflects the expected amount of change, weighted by the estimated loading at each time point. The variance of the shape construct reflects the individual differences variability around the grand slope value. The variance of a variable at any given point in time is therefore decomposed into three sources: a part that is related to variability around the grand mean (i.e., intercept or level), a part that is related to variability around the grand slope (as determined by the basis weight for the time point in question), and a residual error component. Because a residual variance component is estimated for each variable at each time point, the unreliability and uniqueness of each measured variable is accounted for and thus these models can be referred to as being *latent* growth curve models (McArdle & Nesselroade, 2002).

Piece-Wise Models. The previous examples used the passage of time as the index of change in the growth curve model. Another approach to conceptualizing time may be to extend the two-wave difference score models discussed previously to multiple waves. For the piece-wise model shown in the top panel of Fig. 10.5, a factor is needed for every measurement occasion. The first factor for this type of model represents the initial status rather than intercept as in previous growth curve models, but the factor loadings are still fixed at 1.0 for all occasions. The remaining factors represent differences in the scores of a measure between adjacent occasions (differences in scores between Time 1 and Time 2, between Time 2 and Time 3, and between Time 3 and Time 4). The weights for a factor representing differences in scores between occasion t and occasion $t + 1$ are fixed to zero for the first t occasions and -1 for the remaining occasions. Means and the variances of the first factor reflect means and variances of measures on the first occasion, whereas the means and variances of the remaining factors reflect means and variances of differences in scores between adjacent occasions.

Covariances between factors can also be estimated that reflect the extent to which initial and difference scores on adjacent occasions covary. When all covariances among factors are included in the model, the piece-wise model becomes saturated and fits the data perfectly. Accordingly, the residual variances are unnecessary and must be fixed to zero. Restrictions can be imposed on such a saturated piece-wise model, allowing for estimation of the residual variances and allowing degrees of freedom for model fit assessments. For example, the covariances between nonadjacent difference scores

A) *Piece-wise Model*   B) *Spline Model*

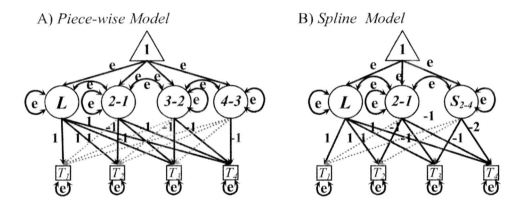

FIG. 10.5.   Various forms of latent growth curve models.

might be essentially zero. Accordingly, only covariances between adjacent factors might be estimated along with the residual variances allowing for two degrees of freedom with four measurement occasions.

Spline Models.   The simple polynomial, the level and shape, and the piece-wise models can be combined into a fourth class of model referred to as spline models. In a spline model, a focal point, sometimes referred to as a "knot," is determined where the growth process is expected to change in a meaningful way. A spline model allows the researcher to model the growth process up to the knot in a different manner than growth after the knot. For instance, Panel B of Fig. 10.5 illustrates a spline model where rapid change is expected between the first two time points but a much slower rate of change is expected from Time 2 through Time 4. In this model, a restriction on the factors is imposed so that the slope would be constant between Time 1 and Time 2 (up to the knot at Time 2) and constant (linear) from Time 2 and Time 4 (after the knot located at Time 2) but at a different rate. The first factor is an initial status factor representing scores at Time 1, the second factor is a piece-wise factor that represents the difference between scores at Time 1 and Time 2, and the third factor represents a linear pattern of change from Time 2 through Time 4. In addition, a common residual variance and the covariances among all three factors are estimated. The second factor represents the difference score between Time 1 and Time 2 but also can be interpreted as the linear rate of change between those time points as well.

Although the example presented reflects linear growth both prior to the knot and after the knot, any combination of the previous models could have been used as long as there are a sufficient number of time points to both support the model structure and preserve some degrees of freedom for model fit tests.

The No-Change or No-Growth Model.   A common baseline model that can be fit is one that assumes no change and simply estimates the variance around a grand, time invariant mean level. In this model, there is only a single intercept or level factor. Models of the possible change relations are then fit and compared to this baseline model to evaluate whether or not there is evidence for (significant) change in the time-ordered data. Evidence of change will emerge if the change process has effected any of the basic descriptive moments of the time-order variables (i.e., variances and covariances as well as mean-level differences; McArdle & Nesselroade, 2002).

Latent Growth Curve Models With Covariates.   The models discussed thus far can be considered as comprising the first of two stages. This initial stage illustrated various approaches to conceptualizing the change or growth process within individual over repeated measurements. The potential second stage of modeling to be considered is to predict the individual growth curve parameters in the same manner as researchers might attempt to predict a factor score in a confirmatory factor analysis model. As latent variables, the level and shape factors can easily be treated as independent or dependent variables in an expanded model. For instance, a variable such as "age" may be used to predict the initial status of a trait, and subsequent change in status over time may be a predictor of some other trait or behavior.

Multivariate Growth Curve Models.   In the univariate growth curve modeling contexts previously described, a primary objective is to understand how changes over time occur for a single outcome measure. Univariate growth curve modeling can be extended to multivariate growth modeling, where the primary objective is to model univariate growth in the context of multiple parallel measures and relate those multiple outcomes to each other. Regardless of whether the goal of the analysis is a univariate model or a multivariate model, the initial stage is to investigate the models of change for all variables separately and treat these univariate models as building blocks for creating the more complex multivariate models.

The first type of multivariate model to be presented is often referred to as an *associative* LGM (T. E. Duncan et al., 1999). Like the previous discussion of LGMs with covariates, the univariate growth curve is determined in Stage 1. An appropriate conceptualization of growth is determined for each developmental variable that is repeatedly observed over time. Once the univariate growth structure is determined, Stage 2 entails modeling the covariances between all latent constructs in the model as shown in Panel A of Fig. 10.6. This type of model is applicable when multiple constructs or processes are measured over time and the researcher is interested in how the latent aspects of one construct relates to the latent aspects of another construct. For instance, presume that the two constructs in Panel A of Fig. 10.6 represent the traits of conscientiousness (1) and perfectionism (2). The associative LGM could be used to determine whether initial status in perfectionism is related to initial status in conscientiousness, whether initial status on one variable is related to the change that occurs over time in the other variable, and whether change in both constructs are related to each other. A simple extension is to replace the certain correlations with structural relations and address if initial status in perfectionism predicts change in conscientiousness or if initial status in conscientiousness predicts change in perfectionism. In these models, the direction of the structural relation is critical in that change over time cannot predict initial status.

A second type of multivariate LGM is the *factor-of-curves model* suggested by McArdle (1988) to determine whether higher-order factors can adequately represent the relation between several univariate growth functions. In the factor-of-curves model shown in Panel B of Fig. 10.6, a simple linear slope univariate

A) *Associative LGM*

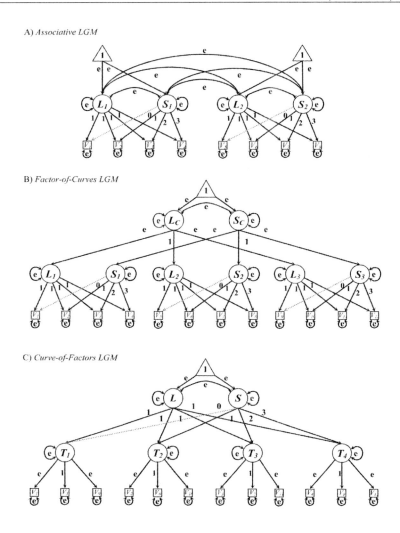

FIG. 10.6.   Various forms of multivariate latent growth curve models.

growth function is developed for each of three measures. The only difference between the linear slope functions at the lower level of the factor-of-curves model and the model presented in Fig. 10.4 is the absence of the covariance between intercept and slope (which is now implied by the higher order factor) and the latent construct means (which are reproduced as a function of the higher order factor means). Two higher order latent factors are then included that represent the common intercept (L_c) and common linear slope (S_c). In this case, the higher order latent variances are estimated and one factor loading per construct is fixed at a value of 1.0 for identification purposes; however, the variances could just have easily been constrained to 1.0 and all loadings freely estimated. It is often the case that additional constraints, such as equating the loadings, are needed to fully identify the model parameters. Extending the example from the previous paragraph, presume that the third construct (3) is dutifulness. The factor-of-curves model may answer the question of whether consci-entiousness, perfectionism, and dutifulness have a common initial status (L_C) and a common pattern of change over time (S_C).

The third type of multivariate LGM, the *curve-of-factors* LGM, can be used when modeling the growth function of a trait that has multiple indicators available at each measurement occasion. In Panel C of Fig. 10.6, the latent factors $T_1 - T_4$ are mea-surement models for a trait with three indicators that has been assessed over four time points. The trait then is modeled as a higher order LGM where the growth func-tion is determined for the change in the construct over time rather the change in the observed variables. For example, presume that the diagram in Panel C of Fig. 10.6 represents three aspects of perfectionism (self-oriented $[V_1 - V_4]$, other-oriented $[V_5 - V_8]$, and socially prescribed $[V_9 - V_{12}]$, which are measured using the Multidimen-sional Perfectionism Scale (MPS; Hewitt & Flett, 1991) on a sample of participants over four time periods. The curve-of-factors LGM allows researchers to determine the nature of change in the truly latent construct of perfectionism over time where the observation of perfectionism at each time point is itself a latent construct $(T_1 - T_4)$ with multiple indicators.

The final type of multivariate model to be presented is an extension of the two-wave difference and residual score approaches discussed in an earlier section. Figure 10.7 presents a bivariate *latent difference score* model (LDS: McArdle & Hamagami, 2001; McArdle & Nesselroade, 1994). This type of model assumes that

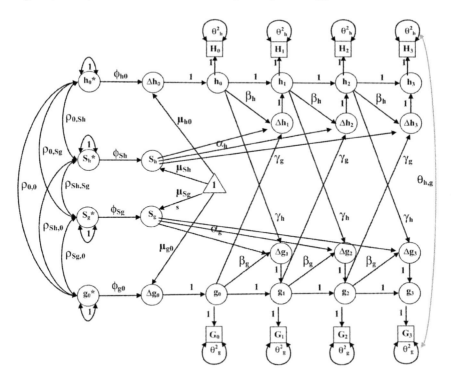

FIG. 10.7. A bivariate latent difference score (LDS) model (based on McArdle & Hamagami, 2001).

there is an underlying dynamic process that has been observed over a well-defined period of time. In the bivariate example in Fig. 10.7, there are two processes measured by single indicators over four time periods each ($h_0 - h_3$, $g_0 - g_3$). In this model, changes in a process (h and/or g) as a function time ($\Delta y_{[t|n]}/\Delta_{[t]}$) are both constantly related to a fixed slope and proportional to the previous measurement ($y_{[t-1]}$). The α and β parameters are the group or fixed coefficients, and variances on the latent variables Δy_n and S_y (represented in the model by $h_0{}^*$, $S_h{}^*$, $g_0{}^*$, $S_g{}^*$) allow for individual differences. The γ_y parameters represent the dynamic coupling, or lead-lag relation, between the two processes h and g. For instance, the parameter γ_h reflects the influence of process h at time $t-1$ on the change in process g from time $t-1$ to time t (Δg_n) and the parameter g_g reflects the opposite influence. As in the previous growth curve examples, there are common residual error terms ($\Theta^2{}_y$) and covariances (r) between the exogenous latent variables ($h_0{}^*$, $S_h{}^*$, $g_0{}^*$, $S_g{}^*$). The first three multivariate models described in this section consider change as a whole over the entire length of the time series of observations. The LDS model addresses the relation between processes between successive time points. Returning to the initial example in this section involving just concientiousnesss (h) and perfectionism (g), suppose that a researcher is interested in the role of concientiousness in predicting change in perfectionism, but the researcher is interested at a more specific level than just "initial status predicts change." Interpretation of the γ_h parameter addresses whether concientiousness serves as a leading indicator of perfectionism, whereas the γ_g parameter reflects the opposing influence. That is, does change in concientiousness from one observation to another serve as an antecedent event to change in perfectionism during the next successive interval?

Growth Mixture Distribution Modeling

A relatively new and increasingly popular branch of methodological approaches to longitudinal modeling seeks to investigate possible heterogeneity among individual patterns of growth (Li, T. E. Duncan, & S. C. Duncan, 2001; Muthén & Shedden, 1999; Nagin, 1999). Known generally as growth mixture modeling, these techniques seek to identify clusters of similar growth patterns across time. Because both the number of groups and their composition are unknown, these models are somewhat exploratory in nature. Traditional growth curve models that rely on structural equation modeling (and random coefficients modeling) can account for differences in the form of growth only for the sample as a whole or for subgroups if they are known a priori. Growth mixture modeling is useful to capture phenomenon that should have distinct subgroups of individuals who are defined by their common patterns of intraindividual change. For example, some individuals may never display any substance use, others may exhibit moderate use that decreases with time, and a third group may display high use that continues across time.

Growth mixture modeling is a general class of technique that includes latent trajectory analysis (Nagin, 1999). A mixture model makes use of a mixture distribution, which is merely a distribution of responses that is assumed to be comprised of more than one different distribution. These component distributions may be of the same shape but differ only in location, or they can vary in shape, or both. For example, the distribution of height among college students may be thought of as a mixture of two normal distributions, one for male students and the second for female students (see Rindskopf, 2003). In extreme cases, the unique parameters describing the component distributions results in a mixture distribution that is multimodal; however, such obvious potential markers of a mixture distribution are not common (Bauer & Curran, 2003). Growth mixture modeling has been developed for use with four unique distributions: the *normal* distribution used for multivariate normal data; the *zero-inflated Poisson* used for low frequency count data; *censored Normal* used for skewed and truncated data; and *logit* used for binary data (Nagin, 1999; Nagin & Tremblay, 2001). Applications to other forms of distribution are possible but as yet have not been developed.

In a particular model, all groups are assumed to arise from the same distribution being only distinguished by unique parameter estimates for each group. Like most other latent curve approaches, latent trajectory analysis uses a basic polynomial form for each mean group trajectory. Thus, actual growth within a group may take the form of a linear, quadratic, or cubic curve, for example. The model does allow testing for similarities across the group's trajectories. One very valuable attribute of the growth mixture approach is that it allows examination of the relationship between individual manifest variables and an estimate of the probability of group membership. Although individuals are assigned to a latent group based on their highest probability of group membership, the uncertainty of categorizing individuals into unobserved groups is accounted for in estimating other parameters of the model (Nagin, 1999).

There are a few limitations in the growth mixture modeling approach. The first centers on deciding on the optimal number of groups (Bauer & Curran, 2003a, 2003b; Muthén, 2003; Rindskopf 2003). Typically, information criterion methods such as the Bayesian Information Criterion (BIC) and the Akaike Information Criterion (AIC) have been used. However, these methods do not yield formal statistical tests and only measure relative fit.

Second, it is possible that a single skewed distribution can be interpreted as a mixture of distinct distributions (Bauer & Curran, 2003a). One limiting assumption of Nagin's approach is that it sets the variance of the group trajectories to zero, although other versions of the model make the variance identical across groups (Muthén, 2001). This assumption means that any individual differences apart from group membership are not accounted for by the model.

A similar technique known as latent transition analysis (Collins, 1991; Collins & Wugalter, 1992) is an example of a latent Markov chain model (Meiser & Ohrt, 1996) and can be viewed as an extension of latent class analysis (LCA). Traditional factor analysis is theoretically similar to LCA. Whereas factor analysis relates several continuous observed variables to a set of continuous unobserved variables, latent class analysis uses information from several categorical observed variables to classify individuals into two or more unobserved groups. Because it uses information from multiple indicators, latent transition analysis takes measurement error into account.

Estimation of latent transition models is based on the expectation-maximization (EM) algorithm (Dempster, Laird, & Rubin, 1977). Parameters of the model that can be estimated include the proportion in a particular latent status at Time t, the probability of a response to an item given membership in a status, and the probability of membership in a status at Time $t + 1$ given membership in a particular status at Time *t*. This final set of parameters forms the latent transition probability matrix that lists the probability of switching to a different status at each measurement occasion. These attributes make latent transition analysis well-suited for examining models of stage development. One key difference between latent transition analysis and growth mixture modeling is that in latent transition analysis the number of unobserved groups must be specified. In this context, an unobserved group is referred to as a latent status.

At least three general criteria can be applied to verify the validity of the classes that these techniques indicate. The first criterion is *replicability*. Are the same classes or groups identified when the analyses is conducted a number of times, either using new samples or randomly dividing large samples into smaller samples (i.e., the basic cross-validation approach; see Cudeck & Henley, 2003)? The second criterion is *interpretability*; that is, do the growth patterns that typify each class make theoretical sense? The third criterion is *predictability*. Given the identified classes or groups, is there a set of unique predictions that can be derived about the behavior of each class or group on a set of variables that are independent of the variables used to identify the classes?

Time Series Analysis

The methods for the analysis of change discussed thus far, including growth curve modeling and growth mixture distribution modeling, are generally implemented in designs involving a sample of participants and a smaller but adequate number of repeated observations where the number of participants is greater than the number of observations made on each participant. Increasingly, longitudinal research designs in the social sciences are resulting in analytic situations where individuals are measured repeatedly over a large number of intervals where 50 or more observations provide reasonable parameter estimates (Box & Pierce, 1970). Such time series designs can be considered as the ideal longitudinal design (Velicer & Fava, 2003). For instance, tracking mood states in hourly intervals can be made possible through technological advances such as the use of pagers, cell phones, or hand-held computers, resulting in the ability to collect a long series of behavioral observations. The goal of a time series analysis is to identify time-related patterns in the sequence of numbers where the patterns are correlated, but offset in time. Researchers could also assess the impact of one or more independent variables on the time series or perform forecasting. Generally, time series designs involve single subjects or a small number of subjects that are aggregated in some manner.

The need for a time series analysis arises when considering the appropriateness of classical methods such as multiple regression. The primary criteria for use of time series procedures rather than multiple regression analysis is the inherent dependency that results from making repeated observations of the same participant or group of participants, referred to as an autocorrelation. Analysis of time series data in the presence of an autocorrelation using multiple regression techniques is an explicit violation of the assumption of independence of errors. As a result, Type I error rates would be substantially increased. In addition, "false" patterns may either obscure or spuriously enhance intervention effects unless the autocorrelation is accounted for in the model.

There are two primary classes of time series analysis differing by the domain in which they are applied. Time series in the time domain are conducted using the Box–Jenkins Auto-Regressive Integrated Moving Average (ARIMA: Box, Jenkins, & Reinsel, 1994) class of models where the pattern of change in a dependent variable is assessed over time. Analyses in the spectral domain, such as Fourier spectral analyses, decompose a time series into its sine wave components. The ARIMA model has become the most common time series application in behavioral research (Velicer & Flava, 2003), providing a means of modeling the serial dependency in repeated measures data and thus provide valid statistical inference.

The basic properties of an ARIMA model are characterized by three parameters. The key elements of an ARIMA (p, d, q) time series analysis are the lingering effects of preceding scores called *auto-regressive* elements (p), trends in the data called *integrated* elements (d), and the lingering effects of preceding shocks called the *moving average* element (q). All ARIMA models also have random process error terms called *shocks*, but differ in the order (how many preceding observations must be considered when determining the dependency) of the p, d, and q parameters. A time series analysis consists of three steps: identifying which mathematical model best represents the data, focusing on the autocorrelation function, potential cyclic patterns, auto-regressive components (p), and moving-average components (q); reconfiguring the dependent observed variable into a serially independent variable through a transformation appropriate for the identified model; and estimating the model parameters through generalized least squares and examining the residuals for unaccounted patterns.

Time series can be used to answer research questions involving autocorrelation patterns ("Are there linear or quadratic trends?" or "Do previous scores/shocks have an effect?"), cycles and trends ("Are longer trends separate from 'local' patterns?" or "Are there seasonal, periodic, or cyclic patterns over time?"), forecasting ("What is the predicted value of observations in the near future?"), or covariates ("Are there predictors?"). Time series can also be used to assess interventions. Is there an impact of an intervention/treatment after accounting for patterns? Is the impact abrupt and permanent (e.g., man-made or natural disasters) or abrupt but temporary (e.g., New Year's resolutions).

Although time series analyses are typically performed on single-subject data, they can also be used to incorporate data from multiple participants or compare across individuals or groups to assess the degree of similarity in the patterns for different variables or populations. In *pooled* time series analysis (Dielman, 1989; Hsiao, 1986), all observations for all participants are included in a single vector, and a patterned transformation matrix is utilized to convert the serially dependent variable into a serially independent variable. Another alternative is meta-analysis, where individual participant time series are combined rather than individual studies. However, the meta-analytic approach is difficult in that there is a lack of statistical time series information in the published literature (many reports still rely on visual analysis) and an appropriate definition of effect size is needed for time series data.

Multilevel, or mixed modeling, as described in the previous sections, can be considered as a means of utilizing data from multiple participants, where the elements of the time series are nested within individuals, resulting in a two-level hierarchy. A multilevel approach to time series analysis is more difficult in the SEM context due to the necessary length of the time series (> 50), but can easily be conducted using traditional multilevel software (e.g., HLM or SAS PROC MIXED).

Multivariate time series models are then models where there are multiple measures at each time point for the same individual and each variable is a time series. A basic approach can be to determine the cross-lagged correlational structure between the multiple variables, where *lag* refers to the time relation between two variables. If one variable can be conceptualized as a dependent variable and the remaining variables can be considered covariates, then a *concomitant variable time series analysis* (Glass, Willson, & Gottman, 1975) can be conducted as a direct analog to the analysis of covariance.

Whereas the use of an SEM program to perform a time series analysis is not generally recommended (Velicer & Flava, 2003; cf. dynamic *p*-technique SEM later), both univariate (single variable) and multivariate time series data can also be represented as special cases of SEM (van Buuren, 1997). A related approach is *dynamic factor analysis*, an extension of p-technique factor analysis (Cattell, 1952, 1963, 1988). Nondynamic *p*-technique factor analysis has major concerns regarding the serial dependency inherent in the time series and can result in substantially underestimated factor loadings (i.e., due to positive autocorrelations; Wood & Brown, 1994), and dynamic factor analysis permits the serial dependency (Hershberger, 1998). Nesselroade and Molenaar (1999) proposed combining pooled time series techniques with dynamic factor analysis to overcome the limitation of the number of observations in the time series needed for stable estimation of the population covariance matrices. The next section describes a further extension of dynamic factor analysis.

Dynamic Single-Subject Repeated Measures Designs: p-Technique

A powerful, yet relatively underutilized technique to model developmental phenomena is the dynamic single-subject repeated-measures design, or *p*-technique. Dynamic *p*-technique factor analysis has seen some application in the field of psychology in, for example, the domains of mood, personality, and locus of control (see Jones & Nesselroade, 1990, for review); however, the technique, as yet, has not been fully exploited as a potentially powerful research tool. Nesselroade and Molenaar (1999) argued that the intensive study of a single individual allows modeling the truly dynamic interplay among variables. Such designs are ideally suited to examine questions regarding topics such as the person-fit debate (Fleeson & Jolley, chap. 3 in this volume) and the social-personality nexus. Dynamic p-technique SEM has the additional advantage of modeling change relations as latent constructs (i.e., error free) with varying degrees of potential lagged influences. Although dynamic p-technique SEM models can be fit to a single individual, the broader usefulness of this approach emerges when the resulting dynamic models of change are compared across a sample of individuals. With this approach, the key sample size issue is insuring sufficient data points for each individual to establish a well-conditioned model for each individual. The number of persons needed to make reasonably sound nomothetic generalizations is, therefore, relatively small.

The basic idea behind dynamic p-technique SEM is that a set of indicators measured repeatedly over time will yield a covariance structure that can be modeled using SEM (Cattell, 1963). Indicators of a construct will ebb and flow over time in a uniform manner such that they will reflect an underlying latent construct defined on the basis of the ebb and flow of change. The relations among multiple constructs can then be assessed and compared on the basis of their cross-time changes with one another. Such a time-order data matrix easily captures contemporaneous dynamic processes, but does not capture lagged dynamic influences. To address this limitation, dynamic p-technique SEM utilizes the inherent time-ordered information of such a data matrix to create a lagged covariance matrix wherein the effects of the constructs at time t can be evaluated for their impact on the latent constructs at time $t +$ 1 (Hawley & Little, 2003). Figure 10.8 depicts a basic block Toeplitz covariance matrix that is modeled in a dynamic p-technique SEM.

The structure of such a lagged covariance matrix contains three distinct elements. The simultaneous or synchronous relations among the three variables are represented twice, at Lag 0 and again at Lag 1, in the triangles directly below the major diagonal. At each lag, the variances of the variables are located along the major diagonals and covariances are located off the diagonals. For the most part, the corresponding elements between these two sections would be nearly or exactly identical (see Hawley & Little, 2003). The lower quadrant of the lagged covariance matrix contains the lagged information among the variables, which reflects two sources of lag information. The first source of information is the auto-regressive lagged relations between each variable. This information is represented along the diagonal of this lower quadrant ($AR_{1,1*}$, $AR_{2,2*}$, and $AR_{3,3*}$), that is, a variable's correlation with it-

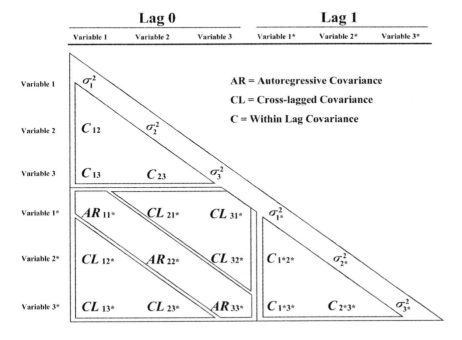

FIG. 10.8.   Example of a lagged covariance structure (from Hawley & Little, 2003).

self between Lag 0 and Lag 1. Cross-lagged relations among the variables are represented in the upper and lower triangles of this quadrant (e.g., $CL_{1,2*}$, $CL_{1,3*}$, and $CL_{2,3*}$) which represent, for example, covariation between Variable 1 at Lag 0 (V_1) and Variable 2 at Lag 1 (V_{2*}), V_1 and V_{3*}, V_2 and V_{3*}, and so on (see, e.g., Molenaar, 1985, 1994; Molenaar, De Gooijer, & Schmitz, 1992; Nesselroade, McArdle, Aggen, & Meyers, 2001; Wood & Brown, 1994).

Both time series and dynamic p-technique SEM are particularly useful for intensive repeated measures designs that are geared to understand dynamic change processes. Like time series analyses, key advantages of the dynamic p-technique include accounting for the auto-correlation among indicators as well as cross-lagged influences. Further advantages of dynamic p-technique include the inherent correction for measurement error (i.e., multiple indicators of latent variables are employed) and nearly limitless expandability of the model to incorporate static covariates, time-varying effects, and static outcomes (see survival analysis later). With multiple-group capabilities of SEM programs, comparing models across groups of individuals allows nomothetic assessments of the similarities and differences in the dynamic patterns among individuals.

Survival Analysis

Often in longitudinal research the outcome variable of interest is the absence or presence of a specific event. In this context, an event is defined as a qualitative change in state that occurs at a precise moment in time, including such occasions as incarceration, graduation, divorce, or death. Techniques to deal with such events fall under the rubric of survival analysis, and are primarily concerned with the length of time before the event occurs. The term *survival analysis* comes from biostatistics, but in other fields is also known as event history analysis, lifetime analysis, and reliability analysis (Allison, 1984). One unique circumstance with this type of data is when an event has not occurred for an individual by the end point of data collection. Such data is considered to be censored. Presumably, if the study had gone on indefinitely, then the event would have (or could have) taken place for the individual. Because of the censoring issue, standard regression models predicting the time to an event will be biased. Remedial measures, such as deleting or assigning the maximum time to the censored cases, may only exacerbate the problem. Models are typically instantiated for events that are not repeatable, or the case in which only the first occurrence is of interest (for models of repeatable events, see Blossfeld, Hammerle, & Mayer, 1989; Klein & Moeschberger, 1997)

There are two basic functions that are central to survival analysis, the survivor function and the hazard function. The survivor function is the probability of survival through a certain time period, say t. The survivor function for Time t is the probability that an individual lasts at least past Time t, consequently the survivor rate cannot increase. The hazard function, more commonly known as the hazard rate, is directly related to the survivor function. For the special case in which events take place in discrete time periods, the hazard rate is simply the probability that the event occurs for an individual at a specific time given the event had not yet occurred for the individual. For continuous models, the basic idea remains the same but is not as mathematically simple.

Some events, such as graduation, can only occur at certain points in time. Although other events can take place at any given instant, they are often only measured in discrete time periods, such that the researcher only knows the month or year of event occurrence. For data such as these a discrete time survival model is necessary (Allison, 1982; Willett & Singer, 1993; Yamaguchi, 1991). A typical discrete time survival analysis utilizes a person-period data set in which each individual has a separate record for each time period. The event variable is dummy-coded and listed with each person-period record.

Historically, most survival analysis models treat the hazard rate as a continuous function of time (Allison, 1995). These continuous survival models can be classified into two types, parametric models such as the accelerated failure time model (Kalbfleisch & Prentice, 2002) and semiparametric models such as the proportional hazards model, sometimes referred to simply as a Cox model (Cox, 1972). The key difference between the two models is in the function of time. Parametric models assume a known distribution for survival time whereas semiparametric models do not. The basic form of both discrete and continuous models is a regression equation predicting the log of the time until event occurrence. Accelerated failure time models are similar to censored normal models. Several other types of distributions may be specified for time including log-logistic and Gompertz and Weibull (Blossfeld & Rowher, 2002). In the semiparametric Cox model, for the case where none of the predictor variables vary with time, the ratio of the hazard for any individual compared to any other individual is a constant. This fixed ratio is termed the proportional hazards assumption. However, this assumption does not hold when dealing with time-varying covariates. Unfortunately, most semiparametric models are still referred to as a proportional hazards model even when the hazards no longer meet this assumption. Additional models that may be useful include models of competing risks in which the type of event must be distinguished (Klein & Moeschberger, 1997).

GENERAL MEASUREMENT AND DESIGN ISSUES

Appropriate Calibration of Time

A crucial design issue in the study of development is the choice of time unit calibration to index change. At least five categories of time unit calibration can be used. A first calibration point is *birth*. Indexing change as a function of age in years, months, or days is clearly the most common metric used to examine developmental changes. For most studies of the development of temperament and personality that focus on childhood and adolescence, this time unit is likely a sufficiently sensitive index of time. However, particularly during middle-age, years since birth may not be an appropriate index of life age (see Helson, Soto, & Cate, chap. 7 in this volume).

A second calibration point is *death*. Time from death can be a very powerful index of change for many developmental phenomena, particularly those related to physical and mental functioning. For example, the steep decline in functioning approximately 5 years prior to death (i.e., terminal drop) can only be adequately indexed as time from death.

A third calibration point, which may be termed *episodic time,* is the time before and after a particular event such as puberty, marriage, first-job, firstborn child, last promotion, retirement, and so on. Such normative life events are particularly relevant for developmentalists who wish to understand the developmental impact of these important milestones along the life course. Critical developmental questions related to the onset (early, on-time, late) of these milestones can be addressed directly using this form of calibration.

A fourth calibration point is *experiential time.* Experiential time is related to episodic time, but the focus is strictly forward in time. Here, change is indexed by the amount of time that a particular individual has experienced a particular status, influence, or context-related impact. Grade in school is a classic example of experiential time. A group of children who has experienced only 2 full years of elementary curriculum can be expected to be developmentally different than a group of children matched on the same age but who has experienced 2½ or more years of elementary curriculum.

A fifth calibration metric is *biological time.* McArdle and Nesselroade (2002) provided a nice example of biological time calibration based on the peak of the growth spurt across a set of individuals. Related to event time (i.e., the peak of growth), this approach to calibration allows researchers to examine the degree to which the shape of the growth pattern is invariant across individuals even though the intercept or onset of the growth curve can vary across individuals.

An important consideration is that these different calibration points are not exclusive. For example, a study of the effects of marriage could use the age since birth at which a person was married as well as the number of years that a person has been married. In one set of analyses, experiential time (years of marriage) could be used to index developmental changes but chronological age could be used as a covariate, mediator, or moderator of the developmental growth functions. Similarly, for other developmental questions, chronological age could be used to index developmental change while using experiential time as a covariate, mediator, or moderator.

Appropriate Interval of Time

In addition to the issue of calibrating time is the selection of time interval and the time duration needed to accurately capture the developmental process of interest. The issue of time interval relates to the frequency and distance between measurement occasions. For some developmental processes, the expected rate of change may be quite rapid, whereas for others the process may be quite slow in its progression. Too often, however, developmental processes are measured at intervals of convenience rather than intervals of sufficiency. For example, many developmental studies of childhood and adolescence conduct yearly assessments. Such a time interval would clearly be insufficient to capture inherent differential effects related to changes within a school year as opposed to changes that occur between school years (i.e., school effects vs. summer effects).

In terms of time duration, a proper longitudinal design must assess individuals over a sufficient time span such that the expected change period is captured (Nesselroade & Boker, 1994). A 2- or 3-year study of temperament in infancy and toddlerhood, for example, may be quite sufficient to track a nonlinear unfolding of such phenomena. On the other hand, the period of time needed to capture change in higher order personality constructs such as agreeableness in adulthood may require a decades-long study. In other words, because most developmental phenomena are globally nonlinear, in order to have the fidelity to capture the curvature, the data collection period must begin well before and extend well beyond the expected bend points. Otherwise, more often than not, the data will appear to be well represented as a locally linear trend.

Appropriate Scaling of the Construct

Three basic problems with simple change scores were briefly discussed in an earlier section of this chapter. The third basic problem, the lack of consistency in interpretability of the change score at different points in the distribution, warrants additional discussion here. Unless true interval level of measurement is attained, the meaning of change depends on the initial score level. That is, a small change from an extreme score may imply a different degree of change than the same small change from a moderate score. This problem can be solved or at least alleviated by using another latent variable approach called item response theory (IRT) to obtain justifiable interval scale properties. Lord and Novick (1968) is the classic resource, but Embretson and Reise (2000) and Hambleton, Swaminathan, and Rogers (1991) are more recent texts.

Suppose, for example, that two participants are given a 25-item stress checklist with successive items increasing in degree of stressfulness. Through analysis, the researcher finds that both participants indicated that they had experienced 15 out of the 25 stressors. Now suppose that Participant A indicated experiencing the first 15 stressors, and Participant B reported experiencing the last 15 stressors, thus Participant A experienced the least stressful events and Participant B experienced the most stressful events. Traditionally, scale scores are a combination of items checked or a sum of responses on a Likert scale, so in this example, both participants would be equally stressed. Under item response theory, however, the participants would receive different stress scores, with Participant B experiencing a higher degree of stress than Participant A. Under IRT an individual's trait level is inferred from the individual's responses on a measurable instrument by considering the characteristics of the responses themselves rather than solely determined by the number of items responded to. Thus, in this example, to assess a participants stress level, IRT scoring weights the experience of the stressor with the stressfulness of the event, such that more stressful events are potentially "worth more."

One of the defining characteristics of IRT is the property of invariance—that scale items and the sample of respondents are independent of each other (Hambleton et al., 1991). Unbiased estimates of item properties may be obtained from unrepresentative samples, but under traditional methods, an item determined to be low on a trait for a sample of high trait individuals would appear to be higher on the trait for a low trait sample. That is, under traditional methods, relatively low stress events experienced by a sample of very high stress individuals will appear to be more high stress than it would when experienced by a low stress sample. In such cases, it is highly likely that a greater proportion of the high stress individuals have experienced the low stress event, whereas fewer of the low stress individuals will have experienced the low stress event. Under IRT, the stress level of the item would be unbiased and invariant (generalizable) whether it was administered to high stress individuals or low stress individuals. In fact, IRT allows items with the same properties and mean trait levels to be administered to any population by use of Rasch model scaling and by placing items and persons on a common scale (Embretson & Reise, 2000). For an explanation of the differences in discrimination between classical test theory and IRT, see Embretson and Reise (2000).

Under traditional methods, meaningful change scores can only be compared when initial score levels are equivalent (Embretson & Reise, 2000). In other words, if two participants have different initial scores, any change score representing the difference in performance between two test conditions is meaningless. A small deviation from a high initial score does not mean the same thing as a small score change from an average score unless a true interval scale level of measurement is achieved. If interval scaling is achieved through transformations, then it is still specific to that particular test administration. However, in IRT, change scores can be meaningfully compared even when the initial scores are unequal. This comparability is largely due to the interval scale nature of item trait-level parameters and individual trait-level parameters.

Bereiter (1963) indicated three basic problems with using a simple classical test theory difference score to indicate change as previously described. A fourth problem, not indicated by Bereiter, is whether the change score actually reflects change due to a condition or is simple error (Embretson, 1998). This issue relates to the problems with standard errors inherent in classical testing. Assuming that the standard error applies to all individuals and a test is focused toward the "average" individual, then the task does not provide a basis to assess individuals at the extremes in the trait because there will be fewer items at their trait level. In addition, the standard error also depends on the specific population being tested, so comparisons across populations are inaccurate.

A special Rasch family model, the multidimensional Rasch model for learning and change (MRMLC; Embretson, 1991) deals with the four difficulties of classical test theory by resolving the scaling and reliability problems found with standard "change" scores and removing some of the confounds that occur with initial status. Two of the problems are addressed by IRT in general. First, the Rasch model achieves interval scale properties (see Andrich, 1985; Fischer, 1995), and as an interval scale model, it is distribution free. Second, the MRMLC, as an IRT model, provides individual standard error of measurement estimates. The MRMLC specifically focuses on two of Bereiter's (1963) dilemmas with change scores. The issue of paradoxical reliabilities is satisfied by modeling individual change directly in a model that explains changing test correlations. Bereiter's problem of the correlation between the initial score and the change score is also resolved by achieving interval scale properties (Embretson, 1998).

In summary, although there are several problems that have been observed with classical test theory approaches to static measurement and dynamic change, item response theory is able to adequately address such issues. This is done by achieving interval scale properties and by making items, tests, and trait measures platform independent and population independent.

Calibrating Developmentally Appropriate Measures

In a longitudinal study, it is sometimes necessary to use different measures of the same trait depending on the developmental stage of the participants. For instance, an attitude measure given to a toddler or preschool-age child must necessarily differ from a measure of the same construct given to an adolescent or young adult, but a study of the development of such a construct over a broad age range may necessitate the use of multiple age-appropriate measures. Likewise, studies across ethnicities, languages, or cultures may also require some ability to meaningfully combine multiple group-appropriate measures of the same construct. Assuming the construct validity of the multiple measures is assured, it becomes necessary to equate or calibrate the different measures. Equating requires that each measure have the same reliability and tap the same construct, which is often unrealistic in practice. Calibration, including *vertical equating* techniques, requires the same construct to be tapped but reliability and scale information may differ, and is a weaker form of equating. This discussion focuses on two common IRT-based methods of linking utilizing a vertical equating approach.

In *common item equating*, items are shared across multiple forms. For example, two forms are created—one appropriate for the younger portion of the age range of interest and the other appropriate for the older age range. Both forms would then include a subset of common items called *linking items* that would be appropriate for both age ranges. Responses to the linking items form the basis for equating the two forms and placing all responses across the age range on a comparable metric. In *common person equating*, respondents are shared across test forms. That is, a random subsample of study participants would be given both forms, where the forms do not include linking items, and the subsample's responses to both forms provide the basis for comparability. For additional explanations of item equating, see Wright and Stone (1979), Mislevy (1992), Linn (1993), Kolen and Brennan (1995), or Thissen and Wainer (2001).

REFERENCES

Aber, M. S., & McArdle, J. J. (1991). Latent growth curve approaches to modeling the development of competence. In M. Chandler & M. Chapman (Eds.), *Criteria for competence: Controversies in the conceptualization and assessment of children's abilities* (pp. 231–258). Hillsdale, NJ: Lawrence Erlbaum Associates.

Allison, P. D. (1982). Discrete-time methods for the analysis of event histories. *Sociological Methodology, 13,* 61–98.

Allison, P. D. (1984). *Event history analysis.* Beverly Hills, CA: Sage.

Allison, P. D. (1995). *Survival analysis using the SAS System: A practical Guide.* Cary, NC: SAS Institute.

Andrich, D. (1985). *Rasch measurement models.* Newbury Park, CA: Sage.

Bauer, D. (2003). Estimating multilevel linear models as structural equation models. *Journal of Educational and Behavioral Statistics, 28,* 135–167.

Bauer, D. J., & Curran P. J. (2003a). Distributional assumptions of growth mixture models: Implications for overextraction of latent trajectory classes. *Psychological Methods, 8,* 338–363.

Bauer, D. J., & Curran P. J. (2003b). Overextraction of latent trajectory classes: Much ado about nothing? Reply to Rindskopf (2003), Muthén (2003), and Cudeck and Henly (2003). *Psychological Methods, 8,* 384–393.

Bereiter, C. (1963). Some persisting dilemma in the measurement of change. In C. Harris (Ed.), *Problems in measuring change* (pp. 3–20). Madison, WI: University of Wisconsin Press.

Blossfeld, H. P., Hamerle, A., & Mayer, K. U. (1989). *Event history analysis.* Hillsdale, NJ: Lawrence Erlbaum Associates.

Blossfeld, H. P., & Rohwer, G. (2002). *Techniques of event history modeling: New approaches to casual analysis* (2nd ed.). Mahwah, NJ: Lawrence Erlbaum Associates.

Box, G. E. P., Jenkins, G. M., & Reinsel, G. C. (1994). *Time series analysis: Forecasting and control* (3rd ed.). Englewood Cliffs, NJ: Prentice-Hall.

Box, G. E. P., & Pierce, D. A. (1970). Distribution of residual autocorrelations in autoregressive-integrated moving average time series models. *Journal of the American Statistical Association, 65,* 1509–1526.

Browne, M. W., & Arminger, G. (1995). Specification and estimation of mean- and covariance-structure models. In G. Arminger, C. C. Clogg, & M. E. Sobel (Eds.), *Handbook of statistical modeling for the social and behavioral sciences* (pp. 311–359). New York: Plenum.

Bryk, A. S., & Raudenbush, S. W. (1987). Application of hierarchical linear models to assessing change. *Psychological Bulletin, 101,* 147–158.

Bryk, A. S., & Raudenbush, S. W. (1992). *Hierarchical linear models: Applications and data analysis methods.* Newbury Park, CA: Sage.

Burkholder, G. J., & Harlow, L. L. (2003). An illustration of a longitudinal cross-lagged design for larger structural equation models. *Structural Equation Modeling, 10,* 465–486.

Cattell, R. B. (1952). The three basic factor-analytic research designs—their interrelations and derivatives. *Psychological Bulletin, 49,* 499–551.

Cattell, R. B. (1963). The structuring of change by P- and incremental R- technique. In C. W. Harris (Ed.), *Problems in measuring change* (pp. 167–198). Madison: University of Wisconsin.

Cattell, R. B. (1988). The data box. In J. R. Nesselroade & R. B. Cattell (Eds.), *Handbook of multivariate experimental psychology* (pp. 67–128). New York: Plenum.

Collins, L. M. (1991). The measurement of dynamic latent variables in longitudinal aging research: Quantifying adult development. *Experimental Aging Research, 17,* 13–20.

Collins, L. M., & Wugalter, S. E. (1992). Latent class models for stage-sequential dynamic latent variable. *Multivariate Behavioral Research, 27,* 131–157.

Cox, D. R. (1972). Regression models and life tables. *Journal of the Royal Statistical Society, 34,* 187–202.

Cudeck, R., & du Toit, S. (2001). Mixed-effects models in the study of individual differences with repeated measures data. *Multivariate behavioral research, 31,* 371–403.

Cudeck, R., & Henley, S. J. (2003). A realistic perspective on pattern representation in growth data: Comment on Bauer and Curran (2003). *Psychological Methods, 8,* 378–383.

Curran, P. (2004). Have multilevel models been structural equation models all along? *Multivariate Behavioral Research, 38,* 529–569.

Dielman, T. E. (1989). *Pooled cross-sectional and time series data analysis.* New York: Marcel-Dekker.

Dempster, A. P., Laird, N. M., & Rubin, D. B. (1977). Maximum likelihood from incomplete data via the EM algorithm. *Journal of the Royal Statistical Society, Series B, 44,* 1–38.

Duncan, T. E., Duncan, S. C., Okut, H., Strycker, L.A., & Li, F. (2002). An extension of the general latent variable growth modeling framework to four levels of the hierarchy. *Structural Equation Modeling, 9,* 303–326.

Duncan, T. E., Duncan, S. C., Strycker, L. A., Li, F., & Alpert, A. (1999). *An introduction to latent variable growth curve modeling.* Mahwah, NJ: Lawrence Erlbaum Associates.

Embretson, S. E. (1991). A multidimensional latent trait model for measuring learning and change. *Psychometrika, 56,* 495–516.

Embretson, S. E. (1998, August). *Modifiability in lifespan development: Multidimensional Rasch model for learning and change.* Paper presented at the meeting of the American Psychological Association, San Francisco, CA.

Embretson, S.E., & Reise, S.P. (2000). *Item response theory for psychologists.* Mahwah, NJ: Lawrence Erlbaum Associates.

Ferrer, E., Hamagami, F., & McArdle, J. (2004). Modeling latent growth curves with incomplete data using different types of structural equation modeling and multilevel software. *Structural Equation Modeling, 11,* 452–483.

Fischer, G. (1995). Derivations of the Rasch model. In G. H. Fischer & I. W. Molenar (Eds.), *Rasch models: Foundations, recent developments and applications* (pp. 15–30). New York: Springer-Verlag.

Glass, G. V., Willson, V. L., & Gottman, J. M. (1975). *Design and analysis of time series experiments.* Boulder, CO: Colorado Associate University Press.

Hambleton, R. K., Swaminathan, H., & Rogers, H. J. (1991). *Fundamentals of item response theory.* Newbury Park, CA: Sage.

Hawley, P. H., & Little, T. D. (2003). Modeling intraindividual variability and change in bio-behavioral developmental processes. In B. Pugesek, A. Tomer, & A. von Eye (Eds.), *Structural equations modeling: Applications in ecological and evolutionary biology research* (pp. 143–170). Cambridge, England: Cambridge University Press.

Heck, R. H., & Thomas, S. L. (2000). *An introduction to multilevel modeling techniques* (pp. 154–180). Mahwah, NJ: Lawrence Erlbaum Associates.

Hershberger, S. L. (1998). Dynamic factor analysis. In G. A. Marcoulides (Ed.), *Modern methods for business research* (pp. 217–249). Mahwah, NJ: Lawrence Erlbaum Associates.

Hertzog, C., Dixon, R. A., Hultsch, D. F., & MacDonald, S. W. (2003). Latent change models of adult cognition: Are changes in processing speed and working memory associated with changes in episodic memory? *Psychology and Aging, 18,* 755–769.

Hewitt, P. L., & Flett, G. L. (1991). Perfection in the self and social contexts: Conceptualization, assessment and association with psychopathology. *Journal of Personality and Social Psychology, 60,* 456–470.

Hox, J. J. (2000). Multilevel models of grouped and longitudinal data. In T. D. Little, K. U. Schnabel, & J. Baumert (Eds.), *Modeling longitudinal and multilevel data: Practical issues, applied approaches and specific examples* (pp. 219–240). Mahwah, NJ: Lawrence Erlbaum Associates.

Hox, J. (2002). *Multilevel analysis: Techniques and applications* (pp. 225–262). Mahwah, NJ: Lawrence Erlbaum Associates.

Hsiao, C. (1986). *Analysis of panel data.* Cambridge, England: Cambridge University Press.

Jones, J. C., & Nesselroade, J. R. (1990). Multivariate, replicated, single-subject, repeated measures designs and P-technique factor analysis: A review of intraindividual change studies. *Experimental Aging Research, 16,* 171–183.

Kalbfleisch, J. D., & Prentice, R. L. (2002). *The statistical analysis of failure time data* (2nd ed.). Hoboken, NJ: Wiley.

Klein, J. P., & Moeschberger, M. L. (1997). *Survival analysis: Techniques for censored and truncated data.* New York: Springer-Verlag.

Kolen, M. J., & Brennan, R. L. (1995). *Test equating methods and practices.* New York: Springer-Verlag.

Kreft, I. G. G., de Leeuw, J., & Aiken, L. A. (1995). The effect of different forms of centering in hierarchical linear models. *Multivariate Behavioral Research, 30,* 1–21.

Li, F., Duncan, T. E., & Duncan, S. C. (2001). Latent growth modeling of longitudinal data: A finite growth mixture modeling approach. *Structural Equation Modeling, 8,* 493–530.

Linn, R. L. (1993). Linking results of distinct assessments. *Applied Measurement in Education, 6,* 83–102.

Little, T. D. (1997). Mean and covariance structures (MACS) analyses of cross-cultural data: Practical and theoretical issues. *Multivariate Behavioral Research, 32,* 53–76.

Little, T. D., Lindenberger, U., & Maier, H. (2000). Selectivity and generalizability in longitudinal research: On the effects of continuers and dropouts. In T. D. Little, K. U. Schnabel, & J. Baumert (Eds.), *Modeling longitudinal and multilevel data: Practical issues, applied approaches and specific examples* (pp. 187–200). Mahwah, NJ: Lawrence Erlbaum Associates.

Little, T. D., Lindenberger, U., & Nesselroade, J. R. (1999). On selecting indicators for multivariate measurement and modeling with latent variables: When "good" indicators are bad and "bad" indicators are good. *Psychological Methods, 4,* 192–211.

Little, T. D., & Slegers, D. W. (2005). Factor analysis: Multiple groups. In B. S. Everitt & D. C. Howell (Eds.), *Encyclopedia of statistics in behavioral science* (pp. 617–623). Wiley.

Little, T. D., Card, N. A., Slegers, D. W., & Ledford, E. C. (in press). Modeling contextual effects with multiple-group MACS models. In T. D. Little, J. A. Bovaird, & N. A. Card (Eds.), *Modeling ecological and contextual effects in longitudinal studies of human development* (pp. 000–000). Mahwah, NJ: Lawrence Erlbaum Associates.

Lord, F. M., & Novick, M. R. (1968). *Statistical theories of mental test scores.* Reading, MA: Addison-Wesley.

McArdle, J. J. (1988). Dynamic but structural equation modeling of repeated measures data. In R. B. Cattell & J. Nesselroade (Eds.), *Handbook of multivariate experimental psychology* (2nd ed., pp. 561–614). New York: Plenum.

McArdle, J. J. (2001). A latent difference score approach to longitudinal dynamic structural analyses. In R. Cudeck, S. du Toit, & D. Sörbom (Eds.), *Structural equation modeling: Present and future* (pp. 342–380). Lincolnwood, IL: Scientific Software International.

McArdle, J. J., & Anderson, E. (1990). Latent variable growth models for research on aging. In J. E. Birren & K. W. Schaie (Eds.), *Handbook of the psychology of aging* (3rd ed., pp. 21–44). New York: Academic Press.

McArdle, J. J., & Bell, R. Q. (2000). An introduction to latent growth models for developmental data. In T. D. Little, K. U. Schnabel, & J. Baumert (Eds.), *Modeling longitudinal and multilevel data: Practical issues, applied approaches and specific examples* (pp. 69–108). Mahwah, NJ: Lawrence Erlbaum Associates.

McArdle, J. J., & Hamagami, E. (2001). Latent difference score structural models for linear dynamic analyses with incomplete longitudinal data. In L. Collins & A. Sayer (Eds.), *Methods for the analysis of change* (pp. 139–175). Washington, DC: American Psychological Association.

McArdle, J. J., & Nesselroade, J. R. (1994). Structuring data to study development and change. In S. H. Cohen & H. W. Reese (Eds.), *Life-span developmental psychology: Methodological innovations* (pp. 223–267). Mahwah, NJ: Lawrence Erlbaum Associates.

McArdle, J. J., & Nesselroade, J. R. (2002). Growth curve analysis in contemporary psychological research. In J. Schinka & W. Velicer (Eds.), *Comprehensive handbook of psychology: Volume 2. Research methods in psychology* (pp. 447–480). New York: Wiley.

Meiser, T., & Ohrt, B. (1996). Modeling structure and chance in transitions: Mixed latent partial Markov-chain models. *Journal of Educational and Behavioral Statistics, 21,* 91–109.

Meredith, W. (1993). Measurement invariance, factor analysis and factorial invariance. *Psychometrika, 58,* 525–543.

Meredith, W., & Tisak, J. (1990). Latent curve analysis. *Psychometrika, 55,* 107–122.

Mislevy, R. J. (1992). *Linking educational assessments: Concepts, issues, methods, and prospects.* Princeton, NJ: ETS Policy Information Center.

Molenaar, P. C. M. (1985). A dynamic factor model for the analysis of multivariate time series data. *Psychometrika, 57,* 333–349.

Molenaar, P. C. M. (1994). Dynamic latent variable models in developmental psychology. In A. von Eye & C. C. Clogg (Eds.), *Latent variables analysis* (pp. 155–180). Thousand Oaks, CA: Sage.

Molenaar, P. C. M., De Gooijer, J. G., & Schmitz, B. (1992). Dynamic factor analysis of nonstationary multivariate time series. *Psychometrika, 57,* 333–349.

Muthén, B. (2001). Latent variable mixture modeling. In G. A. Marcoulides & R. E. Schumacker (Eds.), *New developments and techniques in structural equation modeling* (pp. 1–33). Mahwah, NJ: Lawrence Erlbaum Associates.

Muthén, B. (2003). Statistical and substantive checking in growth mixture modeling: Comment on Bauer and Curran (2003). *Psychological Methods, 8,* 369–377.

Muthén, B., & Shedden, K. (1999). Finite mixture modeling with mixture outcomes using the EM algorithm. *Biometrics, 55,* 463–469.

Nagin, D. S. (1999). Analyzing developmental trajectories: A semi-parametric, group-based approach. *Psychological Methods, 4,* 139–157.

Nagin, D. S., & Tremblay, R. E. (2001). Analyzing developmental trajectories of distinct but related behaviors: A group-based method. *Psychological Methods, 6,* 18–34.

Nesselroade, J. R., & Boker, S. M. (1994). Assessing constancy and change. In T. F. Heatherton &
J. L. Weinberger (Eds.), *Can personality change?* (pp. 121–147). Washington, DC: American
Psychological Association.

Nesselroade, J. R., McArdle, J. J., Aggen, S. H., & Meyers, J. (2001). Dynamic factor analysis models for representing process in multivariate time-series. In D. M. Moskowitz & S. L.
Hershberger (Ed.), *Modeling intraindividual variability with repeated measures data: Methods and
applications* (pp. 235–265). Mahwah, NJ: Lawrence Erlbaum Associates.

Nesselroade, J. R., & Molenaar, P. C. M. (1999). Pooling lagged covariance structures based on
short, multivariate time series for dynamic factor analysis. In R. H. Hoyle (Ed.), *Statistical strategies for small sample research* (pp. 224–251). Thousand Oaks, CA: Sage.

Raudenbush, S. W., & Bryk, A. S. (2002). *Hierarchical linear models: Applications and data analysis
methods* (2nd ed.). Newbury Park, CA: Sage.

Raykov, T. Y., & Marcoulides, G. A. (2000). *A first course in structural equation modeling.* Mahwah,
NJ: Lawrence Erlbaum Associates.

Rindskopf, D. (2003). Mixture or homogeneous: Comment on Bauer and Curran (2003). *Psychological Methods, 8,* 364–368.

Rogosa, D. R., & Willett, J. B. (1983). Demonstrating the reliability of the difference score in the
measurement of change. *Journal of Educational Measurement, 20,* 335–343.

Rovine, M. J., & Molenaar, P. C. M. (1998). The covariance between level and shape in the latent
growth curve model with estimated basis vector coefficients. *Methods of Psychological Research
Online, 3*(2), 95–107.

Thissen, D., & Wainer, H. (Eds.). (2001). *Test scoring.* Mahwah, NJ: Lawrence Erlbaum Associates.

van Buuren, S. (1997). Fitting ARMA time series by structural equation models. *Psychometrika,
62,* 215–236

Velicer, W. F., & Fava, J. L. (2003). Time series analysis. In W. F. Velicer & J. A. Schinka (Ed.),
Handbook of psychology: Research methods in psychology (Vol. 2, pp. 581–606). New York: Wiley.

Willett, J. B., & Sayer, A. G. (1994). Using covariance structure analysis to detect correlates and
predictors of individual change over time. *Psychological Bulletin, 116,* 363–381.

Willett, J. B., & Singer, J. D. (1993). Investigating onset, cessation, relapse, and recovery: Why you
should, and how you can, use discrete-time survival analysis to examine event occurrence.
Journal of Consulting and Clinical Psychology, 61, 952–965.

Wright, B. D., & Stone, M. H. (1979). *Best test design: Rasch measurement.* Chicago: Mesa Press.

Wood, P., & Brown, D. (1994). The study of intraindividual differences by means of dynamic factor
models: Rationale, implementation, and interpretation. *Psychological Bulletin, 116,* 166–186.

Yamaguchi, K. (1991). *Event history analysis.* Newbury Park, CA: Sage.

III

Personality Development in Childhood and Adolescence

11

Temperament and Personality in Childhood

Rebecca L. Shiner
Colgate University

Children are remarkably different from one another from the earliest months of life. Some infants cry loudly and often, whereas others peer at the world in a state of contentment. Some infants laugh with delight at a new, noisy toy; others shrink in fear from new experiences. Even in the womb, some children appear to be more active than others. Over time, as children mature, they display an increasingly differentiated, complex range of individual differences. Older children vary in their capacities to control their impulses, exert leadership among peers, approach new situations creatively, and inhibit aggression when provoked. Parents, educators, physicians, mental health workers, and policymakers all ask important questions about these early emerging differences in children: Do early traits forecast children's later personalities and life outcomes? To what extent do children's personalities change and through what processes? Do parents, schools, and the broader community make a difference in the formation of children's personalities? During the last several decades, research on early personality development has begun to yield answers to these questions.

This chapter reviews four aspects of research on early emerging individual differences during the years from infancy through middle childhood. First, it provides a historical overview of how temperament and personality have been conceptualized. It then describes what is known about the structure or form of individual differences in childhood. Next, there is a review of evidence for later outcomes of early individual differences: To what extent does childhood personality show continuity and predict later adaptation? A description of the processes underlying continuity and change follows, and research examples of each process are provided; this section also addresses the issue of "goodness-of-fit" between children's temperaments and their environments. The chapter concludes with suggestions for future work in this area. Throughout, the intention is to demonstrate the vibrancy of this research and its potential to answer crucial questions asked by a variety of adults who care about children's individual development and adult outcomes.

HISTORICAL OVERVIEW

The contemporary empirical study of early temperament was spurred largely by Thomas and Chess, who initiated the New York Longitudinal Study to examine the significance of biologically based temperament in infancy and childhood (Thomas, Chess, Birch, Hertzig, & Korn, 1963). Thomas and Chess viewed temperament as "the stylistic component of behavior—that is, the *how* of behavior as differentiated from motivation, the *why* of behavior, and abilities, the *what* of behavior" (Goldsmith et al., 1987, p. 508). Thomas and Chess challenged the way that social development was studied at the time, because they emphasized the interplay of biological and environmental processes in shaping children's outcomes, rather than the dominant influence of children's rearing environments.

In the last several decades, other models of temperament have appeared (Goldsmith et al., 1987), and the idea of temperament as "style" has been critiqued as vague and unnecessarily narrow. Rothbart and Derryberry (2002) have provided an alternative definition of temperament: "We have defined temperament as constitutionally based individual differences in emotional and attentional reactivity and self-regulation, influenced over time by heredity and experience" (p. 19). Like the ancient Greek view of temperament, this one highlights the central role of emotional processes; it includes differences in attention and regulation as well. Further, the definition is broad enough to include the temperament traits often studied in adults.

Personality is typically seen as including a wider range of individual differences in feeling, thinking, and behaving than does temperament. In the last 15 years or so, the field of adult personality research has undergone a resurgence of interest; this revitalization has occurred in part because of the resolution of some longstanding thorny issues, including debates about personality versus situations and about the structure of personality (Caspi & Shiner, 2006; Funder, 2001). Paralleling this renewed vigor in the field of adult personality have been new attempts to study personality structure and development in children and adolescents (Caspi & Shiner, 2006; Funder, Parke, Tomlinson-Keasey, & Widaman, 1993; Graziano, 2003; Halverson, Kohnstamm, & Martin, 1994; Kohnstamm, Halverson, Mervielde, & Havill, 1998; Rothbart, Ahadi, & Evans, 2000; Shiner, 1998; Shiner & Caspi, 2003). From the point of view of this emerging developmental science of personality, children's personalities should be conceptualized with an eye toward adult personality structure, and adult personality should be understood in light of its childhood antecedents.

A TAXONOMY OF INDIVIDUAL DIFFERENCES IN INFANCY AND CHILDHOOD

Research on personality structure has as its goal the identification of the most robust patterns of covariation of traits across individuals. The identification of a personality taxonomy has the potential to hasten progress in understanding personality development. Researchers can focus their attention on a consensual set of traits and thereby avoid the "jingle-jangle" problems of studying the same trait under different names ("jingle") or using the same name to describe different traits ("jangle"; Block, 1996). Further, research on adult personality structure has revealed that personality is organized hierarchically (Markon, Krueger, & Watson, 2005). Covariation among specific behavioral descriptors (e.g., talkative, friendly) is explained by lower order traits, and the covariation among these more narrow lower order traits (e.g., sociability, social potency) is explained by broad higher order traits (e.g., extraversion). Children's individual differences appear to share such a hierarchical structure (Goldberg, 2001; Halverson et al., 2003; Putnam, Ellis, & Rothbart, 2001).

Structure of Individual Differences in Infancy and Early Childhood

During infancy and early childhood, children display a more limited range of traits. Much of the early research on temperament in these developmental periods was derived from Thomas and Chess's nine-trait model (Thomas et al., 1963). Thomas and Chess identified a number of traits that have proven to have great clinical significance, particularly children's tendencies toward the intense expression of anger and frustration and toward fearful withdrawal from new situations (Maziade et al., 1990). More recent research has uncovered some limitations of the Thomas and Chess model (for a summary, see Rothbart & Derryberry, 2002; Shiner & Caspi, 2003), and other models are increasingly used in research instead.

Current models of temperament in infancy and early childhood typically include at least the following traits (Caspi & Shiner, 2006; Rothbart & Bates, 1998): positive emotions/pleasure (expression of positive emotions and pleasure and excitement in social interactions); fear/inhibition (withdrawal and expressions of fear in stressful or novel situations); irritability/anger/frustration (fussing, anger, and poor toleration of frustration and limitations); discomfort (negative emotional reactions to irritating or painful sensory stimulation); attention/persistence (attentiveness to environmental stimuli and, in toddlers, ability to sustain attention over time and persist at a task); and activity level.

Rothbart and colleagues also explored the structure of higher order temperament traits in infancy and during the toddler years by examining the factor structure of two newly expanded parent-report temperament questionnaires (Putnam et al., 2001; Rothbart & Derryberry, 2002). In both infancy and the toddler years, three factors emerged. At both time periods, a Surgency factor tapped children's tendencies toward high activity, a rapid approach style, and expression of positive affect, and a Negative Affectivity factor tapped children's ability to be quieted after high arousal (reversed) and their tendencies toward sadness, irritability and frustration, and fear. The third factor differed in the two periods. In infancy, the third factor measured soothability, cuddliness, ability to sustain attention, and pleasure in low intensity situations, whereas in the toddler years this factor (labeled Effortful Control) also included more sophisticated self-regulatory abilities. During both time periods, the third factor appeared to tap young children's emerging behavioral constraint and regulation. As is described in the next section, this three-factor higher order trait structure is highly similar to temperament and personality structure observed among older children.

Structure of Individual Differences in the Preschool-Age and Middle Childhood Years

Over the last decade, a number of parent and teacher questionnaire studies from a range of (mostly Western) countries have pointed consistently to a higher order structure of individual differences in preschool-age and school-age children; this structure has turned out to look remarkably similar to the structure observed in adolescents and adults. Many of these factor analytic studies have yielded the Big Five traits—Extraversion, Neuroticism, Conscientiousness, Agreeableness, and Openness to Experience—although the evidence for Openness is weaker than that for the other four traits (Caspi & Shiner, 2006; Shiner, 1998; Shiner & Caspi, 2003). In children ages 3 through 7, Rothbart and colleagues (Rothbart, Ahadi, Hershey, & Fisher, 2001) found evidence for the three higher order traits previously described as characterizing temperament in toddlers: Surgency, Negative Affectivity, and Effortful Control. Taken together, these questionnaire studies provide convincing evidence that even fairly young children exhibit traits similar to the Big Five traits manifested by adults. The nature of each of these higher order traits in older children is described and the lower order traits that are likely to be subsumed within them are noted. Developmental research provides a particularly rich source of information about the lower order traits because these traits have been studied through a variety of methods, including observational and lab studies (Shiner, 1998). A more complete description of the lower order traits can be found in Caspi and Shiner (2006) and in Shiner and Caspi (2003); instruments assessing individual differences in childhood and adolescence can be found in Shiner and Caspi (2003).

Extraversion measures children's tendencies to engage the world in an energetic, vigorous, emotionally positive fashion. Extraverted children are described in the Big Five studies as sociable, lively, physically active, socially potent, and expressive. Extraversion encompasses the lower order traits of sociability and energy/activity level. Another lower order trait—social inhibition—is related to both extraversion and neuroticism. *Sociability* involves preferences for being with others, as well as tendencies to be vigorously and actively involved in social interactions (e.g., talkativeness, expressiveness). Sociability can be distinguished conceptually and empirically from *social inhibition*, feelings of discomfort and reluctance to act in novel situations. Social inhibition appears to be a more complex blend of both low extraversion and high fear or anxiety (Asendorpf & van Aken, 2003b), most likely with the degrees of low extraversion and high fear varying among different inhibited children. Kagan and colleagues (Kagan, 1998) have studied extensively a related broad temperament of inhibition to the unfamiliar, which includes inhibition to social and nonsocial novel stimuli. *Energy/activity level* includes energetic, active physical engagement with pleasurable tasks. Poorly controlled, impulsive activity is more likely to be associated with low conscientiousness and low agreeableness than with extraversion in children (Goldberg, 2001).

In Big Five studies, children and adolescents who are high on *Neuroticism* are described as anxious, vulnerable, tense, easily frightened, "falling apart" under stress, guilt-prone, moody, low in frustration tolerance, and insecure in relationships with others. Fewer descriptors define the low end of this dimension; these include traits such as stability, being "laid back," adaptability in novel situations, and the ability to "bounce back" after a bad experience. The lower order traits associated with neuroticism in children are somewhat unclear. Research on negative emotions suggests that neuroticism may include at least three distinct but related lower order traits in youths: fear, anxiety, and sadness (Muris, Schmidt, Merckelbach, & Schouten, 2001). *Fear* represents negative affect and bodily symptoms arising from exposure to an actual or an imagined object or situation; it is not yet clear to what extent fear overlaps with the social inhibition trait described previously. *Anxiety* taps tendencies toward nervous apprehension, general distress, worry, and physical tension when there is no imminent threat. *Sadness* involves lowered mood, hopelessness, and dejection arising from experiences of disappointment and loss.

Two lower order traits are likely to be related to both neuroticism and (low) agreeableness: anger/irritability and alienation/mistrust. *Anger/irritability* taps outer-directed, hostile emotions such as anger, jealousy, frustration, and irritation; in children, such hostility is often evoked by limits set by adults. In some studies, anger/irritability combines with aspects of neuroticism to form an overarching *Negative emotionality* trait (Shiner & Caspi, 2003). However, as noted in the section on infant and toddler temperament, it is possible to distinguish children's tendencies toward irritable, hostile emotions from their tendencies toward fear beginning in infancy (Rothbart & Bates, 1998). *Alienation/mistrust* indexes tendencies to mistrust others and to feel mistreated. Individual differences in interpersonal alienation and mistrust have been identified in research on social information processing in youths (Crick & Dodge, 1994) and in the attachment literature (Sroufe, Carlson, Levy, & Egeland, 1999).

In Big Five studies, *Conscientiousness* includes tendencies to be responsible, attentive, persistent, orderly, and planful, and to possess high standards and think before acting. Children who are low on this trait are depicted as irresponsible, unreliable, careless, distractible, and quitting easily. Based on parental descriptions of children from a number of countries, parents rarely describe their children in terms of traits linked with conscientiousness at age 3 years but do use such descriptors more often by age 6 years (Slotboom, Havill, Pavlopoulos, & De Fruyt, 1998). There is evidence from at least one study, however, that some of these more complex manifestations of self-control can be measured with moderate reliability in children as young as ages 3 and 4 years (Halverson et al., 2003). Conscientiousness appears to include a number of lower order components in childhood: *attention* (the ability to focus and regulate attention and persist at tasks); *self-control* (tendencies to be planful, cautious, deliberate, and behaviorally controlled); *achievement motivation* (tendencies to strive for high standards, to work hard, and to pursue goals over time); *orderliness* (a propensity to be neat, clean, and organized); and *responsibility* (tendencies to be reliable and dependable).

Agreeableness includes a variety of traits seen as very important by developmental psychologists; yet, these traits historically have been left out of temperament models. The high end of agreeableness includes descriptors such as considerate, empathic, generous, gentle, protective of others, and kind, whereas the low end includes tendencies toward being aggressive, rude, spiteful, stubborn, bossy, cynical, and manipulative. Childhood agreeableness also includes being willing to accommodate others' wishes rather than forcing one's own desires and intentions on others; for children, this aspect of the trait also involves how manageable the child is for parents and teachers. Whereas Conscientiousness taps self-control in task-related domains, Agreeableness appears to measure self-control in interpersonal relationships (Tobin, Graziano, Vanman, & Tassinary, 2000), and it more generally seems to assess individuals' motivation to maintain harmonious relationships with others (Graziano & Eisenberg, 1997).

Agreeableness includes several lower order components. *Prosocial tendencies* (also potentially called helpfulness or nurturance) encompasses children's individual differences in being empathic, kind, and nurturing, whereas *antagonism* ranges from the tendency to be peaceful and gentle to the tendency to be aggressive, spiteful, quarrelsome, and rude. Although prosocial tendencies and antagonism may tend to covary negatively, they also appear to co-occur in some individuals and, when combined, may confer social benefits in some "Machiavellian" children (Hawley, 2003; chap. 8 in this volume). *Willfulness* involves proclivities to be bossy, overbearing, and defiant, rather than accommodating and flexible.

In Big Five studies, children who are high on *Openness to Experience*, or *Intellect*, are described as eager and quick to learn, clever, knowledgeable, perceptive, imaginative, curious, and original. It appears that openness can be measured reliably by at least age 6 or 7 years, but the childhood trait does not appear to be as broad as some adult conceptualizations of openness (Caspi & Shiner, 2006). The lower order components of openness in childhood are not yet clear, but 1) intellect and 2) curiosity and creativity have received some support (Mervielde, De Clercq, De Fruyt, & Van Leeuwen, 2005).

DO EARLY INDIVIDUAL DIFFERENCES MATTER?: THE PREDICTION OF LATER PERSONALITY AND ADAPTATION

Continuity of Children's Individual Differences Over Time

To what extent do children's early traits exhibit continuity? Rank-order consistency refers to the consistency of individuals' relative standing within a group on particular personality traits across time. Following the first few months of life, is there convincing evidence of continuity? A meta-analysis by Roberts and DelVecchio (2000) provided a comprehensive answer to this question. This meta-analysis included studies from birth through old age that reported correlations between dispositional measures taken at least 1 year apart; the average time between assessments for all the studies was 6.8 years. Measures for children ranged widely and included parent and teacher questionnaires and q-sorts, self-ratings, observations, peer ratings, interviews, and performance on tasks. The following estimated population cross-time correlations for dispositional measures were obtained: 0 – 2.9 years = .35; 3 – 5.9 years = .52; 6 – 11.9 years = .45; and 12 – 17.9 years = .47. These results suggest that individual differences show more modest continuity during infancy and toddlerhood and then show a rather large increase in stability during the preschool years. Surprisingly, continuity does not appear to increase during middle childhood and adolescence but remains at a moderate level, comparable to that seen in the preschool years.

Roberts and DelVecchio (2000) also examined trait consistency for specific traits. Among the temperament traits described previously, adaptability showed the highest consistency (.47); approach, task persistence, and negative emotionality ranged in consistency from .35 to .41; and activity level demonstrated the lowest stability (.28). The Big Five traits were assessed in many of the studies including older children, adolescents, and adults, and these traits showed fairly similar levels of consistency, ranging from .50 to .54. Taken together, the results of this meta-analysis demonstrate that individual differences are indeed stable enough to be considered trait-like during childhood, but change is still an important part of the picture.

Early Individual Differences and Later Adaptation

One of the questions that has fueled scholarly and popular interest in temperament is this: Are children with particular temperaments at greater risk of negative outcomes, including psychopathology? Much of the early interest in temperament traits was generated by Thomas and Chess's (Thomas, Chess, & Birch, 1968) suggestion that children's early individual differences could help set off a chain of transactions between the child and the environment that could lead eventually to the development of clinical disorders. It is equally important to understand whether certain early individual differences foreshadow children's positive life outcomes. A substantial number of studies have demonstrated direct, linear relationships between temperament and adjustment (Rothbart & Bates, 1998); however, there are limitations to many of these studies, including the use of parent reports to measure both temperament and adjustment, the concurrent assessment of both temperament and adjustment, and the relatively rare focus on children's positive outcomes. In the last several years, a profusion of studies has documented links between children's individual differences and various aspects of their adaptation. These newer studies have often included methodological improvements over the earlier studies, including different sources for assessing temperament and adaptation, longitudinal methods, the control of possible third variables that could cause spurious correlations between individual differences and adjustment, and the prediction of changes in adaptation across time.

This chapter reviews findings linking each of the Big Five traits with adaptation. In general, studies are cited that include at least one of the methodological improvements previously listed. The positive outcomes included are those that are considered to be salient developmental tasks in childhood and adolescence—academic achievement, social competence with peers, and rule-abiding conduct—and two others that are added in adulthood—the development of romantic relationships and work competence (Masten et al., 1995). Children's internalizing and externalizing behaviors are also frequently assessed as developmental outcomes, so these are included as well. The studies point to two important conclusions: Children's traits are differentially linked with specific outcomes and these patterns are often replicated across studies, and there is convincing evidence for the reality and consequential nature of children's individual differences. Typically, the prediction afforded by children's temperament and personality traits is modest to moderate in size.

Children's differences in extraversion predict a complex set of outcomes. Not surprisingly, childhood extraversion is associated with positive peer relationships concurrently and across time into late adolescence and early adulthood and predicts positive changes in social competence across time as well (Shiner, 2000; Shiner, Masten, & Roberts, 2003). Similarly, extraversion in early adolescence predicts growth in perceived social support from early adolescence to late adolescence (Asendorpf & van Aken, 2003a). More extraverted children are more likely than introverted children to have a history of having a stable, high quality romantic relationship by age 30 as well (Shiner et al., 2003). Higher childhood extraversion is also associated with lower levels of later internalizing symptoms (Chen et al., 2002).

Despite the many seemingly positive outcomes of extraversion, the picture for childhood extraversion is not entirely rosy: A wide variety of studies have linked early signs of extraversion with heightened risk of externalizing symptoms and aggression (Chen et al., 2002). It is not yet clear why extraverted children are more likely than introverted children to develop antisocial behavior; they may have stronger impulses that they must learn to regulate, or they may be more likely to engage in antisocial behavior with peers. Outcomes of shyness and inhibition essentially mirror those found for low extraversion, including lower social support (Newman, Caspi, Moffitt, & Silva, 1997) and higher rates of anxious symptoms (Kagan, Snidman, Zentner, & Peterson, 1999). Shy or socially inhibited boys may experience more negative life outcomes than shy girls, perhaps because shyness is more socially sanctioned for girls than for boys (Caspi, Bem, & Elder, 1989; Gest, 1997). Overall, extraversion appears to bolster the quality of social relationships and protect against internalizing symptoms, but puts children at risk of externalizing behaviors.

Neuroticism and the broader Negative Emotionality trait are associated with negative adaptation in a variety of domains. Eisenberg and colleagues documented in a series of studies that children high on negative emotionality trait are at risk for a wide variety of social difficulties (summarized in Eisenberg, Fabes, Guthrie, & Reiser, 2000, and in Shiner, 1998). Negative emotionality in children also predicts both internalizing and externalizing behaviors (Lengua, 2002; Rothbart & Bates, 1998). It is important to consider the outcomes for anxiety and fear separately from the outcomes for irritability. In some cases, the lower order traits predict similar outcomes but may do so for quite different reasons. For example, higher anxiety or fear and higher irritability both predict greater social difficulties (Asendorpf & van Aken, 2003a; Eisenberg, Pidada, & Liew, 2001) and lower occupational attainment in adulthood (Caspi et al., 1989; Judge, Higgins, Thoresen, & Barrick, 1999). However, anxiety and fear may cause such difficulties by preventing children from fully engaging with their social and work worlds, whereas children's irritability may exert its ill effects through alienating youths from those around them. In other cases, these two aspects of negative emotionality may predict different outcomes altogether. For example, anxiety and fear are associated with greater risk of internalizing symptoms and irritability with greater risk of externalizing symptoms (Rothbart & Bates, 1998).

Lest it appear that high negative emotionality portends across-the-board negative outcomes, it is important to recognize that higher fearfulness, at least, may actually predispose children toward some positive outcomes. For example, more fearful children experience greater guilt when they believe they have done something wrong, and this guilt-proneness in turn appears to mediate the link between children's fearfulness and their later compliance with rules (Kochanska, Gross, Linn, & Nichols, 2002). These findings are consistent with other research documenting that childhood fearfulness appears to protect against the development of externalizing behavior problems such as aggression (Raine, Reynolds, Venaldes, Mednick, & Farrington, 1998). Like high extraversion, high fear predicts a complex mixture of both positive and negative outcomes.

Empirical work on children's Conscientiousness documents what thinkers about the moral life have argued for centuries: Greater self-control appears to promote many good outcomes. First, children's attention, carefulness, and self-control predict their later academic achievement, even when controlling for earlier measures of academic ability or IQ (Martin, Olejnik, & Gaddis, 1994; Shiner, 2000; Shiner et al., 2003). Childhood conscientiousness, in fact, predicts positive changes in academic achievement from childhood to adulthood (Shiner, 2000; Shiner et al., 2003). Conscientiousness in adolescence likewise foreshadows adult career success in terms of income and occupational status, as well as job satisfaction (Judge et al., 1999). Children's self-control and attention, whether measured with behavioral tasks, parent interviews, or questionnaires, also appear to promote the development of rule-abiding behavior versus externalizing, antisocial behavior; in other words, children who are impulsive, inattentive, or careless are at risk for developing externalizing behaviors (Ackerman, Brown, & Izard, 2003; Olson, Schilling, & Bates, 1999; Shiner, 2000). These links between early self-control and lower risk of externalizing problems may be mediated in part by more self-controlled children's tendencies to develop stronger consciences (Kochanska & Knaack, 2003). Finally, components of Conscientiousness in childhood, including effortful attention, self-control, and carefulness, have predicted children's concurrent and later social competence with peers in several studies (Lamb et al., 2002; Shiner, 2000).

Like conscientiousness, childhood Agreeableness foreshadows many different positive life outcomes. Not surprisingly, greater childhood agreeableness is associated with better peer relationships concurrently and across time (Graziano, Jensen-Campbell, & Finch, 1997; Shiner, 2000). However, the name of this trait is somewhat misleading if it suggests that its importance is confined to interpersonal relationships. Childhood agreeableness is also linked with greater academic attainment and a reduced risk of externalizing behaviors and delinquency (Laursen, Pulkkinen, & Adams, 2002; Shiner, 2000; Shiner et al., 2003). In one study, childhood agreeableness also predicted positive work competence 20 years later, when childhood academic achievement and IQ were controlled (Shiner et al., 2003).

As noted previously, agreeableness includes at least two major lower order traits—prosocial tendencies and antagonism (which includes aggressiveness). Findings for children's prosocial tendencies mirror those for agreeableness; for example, a stronger prosocial orientation in childhood predicts positive social adjustment and academic achievement, as well as fewer externalizing behaviors over time (Chen, Li, Li, Li, & Liu, 2000). In contrast, findings for antagonism or aggression typically are like those found for low agreeableness. More antagonistic, aggressive children are at a higher risk of a number of negative outcomes, including academic failure, job difficulties and unemployment, peer rejection, and later conflictual romantic relationships (Kokko & Pulkkinen, 2000; Moffitt & Caspi, 1998; Rubin, Bukowski, & Parker, 1998). Boys who are chronically physically aggressive are at a heightened risk of serious delinquency and violence (Nagin & Tremblay, 1999).

Thus, the traits underlying both conscientiousness and agreeableness promote positive adaptation in many different domains. As noted previously, these two higher order traits appear to share a common core of behavioral constraint or self-control, with conscientiousness focused on task-related behavior and with agreeableness focused on interpersonal behavior. It is interesting to note, however, that the positive outcomes of conscientiousness are not confined to the domains of achieving and striving, nor are the positive outcomes of agreeableness confined to interpersonal relationships. High compliance, an aspect of agreeableness, may be a risk factor for negative outcomes for girls (Pulkkinen, 2002); it will be important for future work to address whether extremely high behavioral control or agreeableness poses adaptive risks for children. More detailed research on how highly conscientious and agreeable children approach a variety of situations will help to clarify why the two traits share such similar adaptive profiles.

Research on the links between Openness to Experience or Intellect and Adaptation is more limited than for the other four traits; however, the findings generally are consistent. In a number of studies, these traits have shown concurrent correlations with academic achievement in samples of school-age children and young adolescents (Graziano et al., 1997; John, Caspi, Robins, Moffitt, & Stouthamer-Loeber, 1994). The size of the correlations varies from modest to strong, perhaps because the trait descriptors for this dimension sometimes emphasize intellectual characteristics and sometimes do not. Because openness/intellect in childhood is moderately associated with IQ or other measures of intellectual ability (Lamb et al., 2002), it is not clear to what extent these traits predict academic achievement because of their association with children's intellectual abilities. In most studies, the adaptive correlates of openness or intellect are limited to academic achievement; thus, these traits differ from the other Big Five Traits in that they show more narrowly focused importance for adaptation.

PROCESSES UNDERLYING CONTINUITY AND CHANGE IN PERSONALITY DEVELOPMENT

Children's early temperament and personality traits show both substantial continuity and substantial change. As noted previously, by the preschool years, individual differences are moderately stable. And, as described earlier, children's individual differences modestly to moderately foreshadow many aspects of their adaptation. Thus, early personality traits do meaningfully predict later personality and life outcomes for some children, but other children appear to undergo significant change over time. These data require explanation: What are the processes that underlie both continuity and change in children's early personality development? The issue of personality continuity and change was raised by Thomas and Chess (Thomas et al., 1963) in their early theoretical work on temperament. Thomas and Chess argued that each early temperamental trait could yield a variety of later outcomes, depending on the "goodness-of-fit" between the children's temperament and the context in which the child grew. For example, some infants with a "difficult" temperament may continue to exhibit irritable, hard-to-manage behavior as children, whereas other infants with similarly challenging early temperaments may learn to manage their intense negative emotions if their parents can successfully adapt their parenting style.

Researchers, parents, and authors of popular parenting books have readily embraced the idea that a variety of intervening processes can play an important role in determining the eventual outcomes of children's early individual differences. These differences may promote personality continuity by shaping children's experience of and engagement with the environment; the processes through which personality promotes its own stability are discussed in detail elsewhere (Caspi & Shiner, 2006; Shiner & Caspi, 2003) and are not reviewed here. Other processes promoting continuity and change range from genetic or biological processes to more broad, contextual processes involving classrooms and neighborhoods. Next some examples of recent research in this area are presented. They are organized into four levels at which the processes have been studied, ranging from the lowest level of analysis to the highest: genetic or other biological variables, intra-individual variables, family variables, and broader contextual variables.

Genetic and Other Biological Processes

Genetic influences may play a role in shaping the continuity versus discontinuity of early individual differences. It is possible to use a longitudinal twin design to examine the genetic and environmental influences on the stability of a trait across two or more time periods and to examine the influences on change. A recent example of this method derives from the MacArthur Longitudinal Twin Study (Saudino & Cherny, 2001). Aspects of the twins' temperaments—activity, task orientation, affect-extraversion, shyness at home, and behavioral inhibition in the lab—were observed several times from the ages of 14 months through 24 or 36 months. For all of the traits except shyness, the stability of the traits derived from genetic influences; for shyness, both genetic and shared (family-wide) environmental factors contributed to stability. Sources of change varied for the traits. For example, changes in shyness across time derived from both shared and nonshared (child-specific) environmental influences, whereas change in affect-extraversion was due to nonshared environmental influences only. The results from this study dovetail with other research on children and adults suggesting that, whereas personality stability appears to be due to genetic factors, change is due to environmental influences (Saudino & Plomin, 1996). However, research emanating from the Louisville Twin Study has found evidence for genetic influences on change in temperament in the first 4 years of life (summarized in Loehlin, 1992). More work is needed to establish more definitively the genetic influences on continuity and change in children's individual differences; such studies would be strengthened by larger sample sizes, more robust measurement of temperament and personality, and a wider range of ages and traits studied. Twin studies can also be used to examine the genetic and environmental influences mediating the links between children's early individual differences and their later adaptive outcomes.

Intraindividual Characteristics

Children's intraindividual characteristics are another potential source of stability and change for particular personality traits. Personality theorists have recognized for many years that the implications of particular personality traits can only be fully understood within the context of a person's other individual differences. Allport's (1937) classic definition of personality assumes the importance of intraindividual psychological organization: "Personality is the dynamic organization within the individual of those psychophysical systems that determine his unique adjustment to his environment" (p. 48). Researchers have recently attempted to understand how the "dynamic organization within the individual" may shape the stability and change in youths' personalities. Three types of intraindividual characteristics have been investigated as potential moderators of personality stability and change: other personality traits, IQ, and life adaptation.

First, children's other personality traits may influence the outcome of a particular personality trait. One of the best documented examples involves the interaction between negative emotionality and conscientiousness. In a series of studies, Eisenberg and colleagues (summarized in Eisenberg at al., 2000) demonstrated that children's negative emotionality often moderates the links between aspects of conscientiousness (attention and behavioral regulation) and children's social behavior, such that children with poor attentional and behavioral control have poorer quality social functioning when they are also high on negative emotionality. In addition, poor self-control is particularly associated with later externalizing, antisocial behavior for children with higher levels of negative emotionality (Henry, Caspi, Moffitt, & Silva, 1996).

Second, children's intelligence may moderate the stability and outcomes of their personalities. Brighter children may find it easier to handle challenging aspects of their personalities. For example, a longitudinal study of children from age 4 to age 10 demonstrated that IQ predicted the stability and change in behavioral inhibition or shyness; more intelligent children became increasingly less inhibited over the 6-year span (Asendorpf, 1994).

Third, children's relative success or failure in important developmental domains (e.g., academic achievement, social competence with peers) may influence personality development. Research previously reviewed makes clear that childhood personality shapes later adaptation in work, school, and relationships. But, indeed, the converse may occur: Life adaptation may influence children's typical ways of feeling, thinking, and behaving (Shiner & Masten, 2002). One example of this process derives from a longitudinal study of children from age 10 to age 20; poorer academic achievement and higher antisocial behavior in childhood predicted increased negative emotionality over the 10-year span (Shiner, Masten, & Tellegen, 2002). Clearly, it will be important to examine the patterning of children's individual differences in personality, IQ, and adaptation in order to understand the circumstances leading to stability versus change.

Family Processes

As noted previously, Thomas and Chess's (Thomas et al., 1963) early work on temperament highlighted the potential role of the family environment in moderating the outcomes of children's early individual differences; this idea was at the core of their goodness-of-fit model of personality development. Although this notion was intuitively appealing, it proved difficult to substantiate with data. More recent work, however, has demonstrated several replicable patterns of interactions between childhood temperament and parenting in the prediction of various outcomes (for reviews, see Bates & McFadyen-Ketchum, 2000; Gallagher, 2002; Putnam, Sanson, & Rothbart, 2002).

An example will serve to illustrate this recent research on the interaction of temperament and family processes. Researchers have been particularly interested in temperamental traits that put children at risk of developing externalizing problems; such traits include high levels of irritability and other early markers of low agreeableness (e.g., temper tantrums, high unmanageability, aggressiveness). In several studies, it has been found that parenting moderates the links between these temperament traits and later externalizing problems. Specifically, when children are high on irritability or low on agreeableness, several maternal parenting variables predict higher externalizing behaviors: unskilled disciplining tactics, negativity toward the child, and a lack of restrictive control over the child (Bates, Pettit, Dodge, & Ridge, 1998; Belsky, Hsieh, & Crnic, 1998; Rubin, Burgess, Dwyer, & Hastings, 2003; Stoolmiller, 2001). It appears that skillful, warm parenting may protect highly negative and hard-to-manage children from developing externalizing problems. Identification of other family moderators of temperamental outcomes should be a high priority for research on children's individual differences; such research may potentially yield insights into how to modify outcomes for children who are temperamentally at-risk. Because it is possible that genetic factors can account for the covariance of children's temperaments and family variables, future work on goodness-of-fit would benefit from the use of genetically informative research designs. The use of twin or adoption studies would help to clarify whether genes can account for the moderating role of family processes or whether the family processes are a true environmental cause of children's outcomes.

Broader Contextual Processes

A final source of children's personality continuity and change involves the broader context in which children develop. Children's school environments, peer relationships, and neighborhoods could all have important impacts on whether children's personalities remain stable and on whether their personalities lead to poor or good outcomes. Although these broad contextual factors have received less research attention than more proximal family processes, a number of recent studies have found evidence of moderating effects of children's contexts on their personality development. For example, with regard to peer relationships, there is evidence that peer exclusion and rejection in early elementary school predict increases in aggression among already aggressive children (Dodge et al., 2003) and greater continuity in anxious solitude among already anxious solitary children (Gazelle & Ladd, 2003). Teacher warmth within middle school classrooms appears to moderate the effects of children's withdrawal and aggression on peer acceptance; warmer teachers appear to have a positive effect on the peer acceptance of children with such potentially risky social behaviors (Chang, 2003). Similarly, neighborhood wealth and staying in school both moderate the links between poor self-control and criminal involvement; highly impulsive youth who live in better-off neighborhoods or who stay in school show lesser criminal behavior than similarly impulsive youth who live in poor neighborhoods or who drop out of school prematurely (Henry, Caspi, Moffitt, Harrington, & Silva, 1999; Lynam et al., 2000). Taken together, these studies provide clues that broader contexts are, in fact, important moderators of personality development.

FUTURE DIRECTIONS

Despite the substantial progress made in the decades since Thomas and Chess' (Thomas et al., 1963) earliest work on temperament, some aspects of knowledge about childhood personality development remain limited. Following are suggestions for potentially fruitful avenues of work on early personality structure, the long-term outcomes of childhood personality, and the processes shaping personality continuity and change from childhood to adulthood.

Although the higher order structure of personality in older children appears clear, the structure of individual differences from infancy to age 8 warrants special attention, because developmental changes during this period are rapid and wide ranging. Future work should measure individual differences during this period in as broad a way as possible, making few a priori assumptions about what traits truly represent "temperament." Much more work is also needed to specify lower order traits that can be identified in children. Many lower order traits examined in adults may prove to exist in children (e.g., positive emotions, humility, integrity, unconventionality, and talent). The field could benefit from continued creative measures of individual differences (Caspi, Roberts, & Shiner, 2005), such as implicit measures of self-views, physiological measures, and puppet interviews (Measelle, John, Ablow, Cowan, & Cowan, 2005). More research is needed about the cross-cultural generalizability of the taxonomic systems reviewed here for children and adolescents.

As described previously, many of the findings for the long-term outcomes of children's personalities are robust and consistent. Future work should examine the pathways linking personality and adaptation (Shiner & Masten, 2002). Researchers need to understand more about the mediating processes. As Funder (2001) noted in a review of adult personality research, more data are needed about how personality traits are expressed through behavior in context. A particularly promising avenue may be linking children's traits with social-cognitive constructs, such as mental representations and encoding processes. Observational studies could also be used to examine the expressions of traits in different contexts (e.g., Markey, Markey, & Tinsley, 2004). Many studies linking early personality with later outcomes span long periods of time; more short-term longitudinal studies could provide a closer glimpse of the processes at work.

Currently, one of the most exciting areas of research involves the study of the genetic, intraindividual, family, and contextual factors promoting personality continuity and change in children. Some promising new data have pointed to moderators of the links between childhood personality and later outcomes. Again, it will be important to explore the processes that actually mediate stability and change; simply identifying a moderator does not establish the mediating processes through which it has its effect. The continuing search for moderators should be guided by theory about the relevant temperament and personality traits and about the relevant moderators. This area of research is particularly important because it may lead to interventions to help children with challenging temperaments. Although certain temperamental profiles do appear to put children at risk of negative outcomes, extant data suggest that many children with difficult personalities still manage to thrive and reach adulthood as happy, productive adults. Future work may serve to enrich understanding of how such resilience emerges across development.

REFERENCES

Ackerman, B. P., Brown, E., & Izard, C. E. (2003). Continuity and change in levels of externalizing behavior in school of children from economically disadvantaged families. *Child Development, 74,* 694–709.

Allport, G. W. (1937). *Personality: A psychological interpretation.* New York: Holt.

Asendorpf, J. B. (1994). The malleability of behavior inhibition: A study of individual developmental functions. *Developmental Psychology, 30,* 912–919.

Asendorpf, J. B., & van Aken, M. A. G. (2003a). Personality-relationship transaction in adolescence: Core versus surface personality characteristics. *Journal of Personality, 71,* 629–666.

Asendorpf, J. B., & van Aken, M. A. G. (2003b). Validity of Big Five personality judgments in childhood: A 9 year longitudinal study. *European Journal of Personality, 17,* 1–17.

Bates, J. E., & McFadyen-Ketchum, S. (2000). Temperament and parent–child relations as interacting factors in children's behavioral adjustment. In V. J. Molfese & D. L. Molfese (Eds.), *Temperament and personality development across the life span* (pp. 141–176). Mahwah, NJ: Lawrence Erlbaum Associates.

Bates, J. E., Pettit, G. S., Dodge, K. A., & Ridge, B. (1998). Interaction of temperamental resistance to control and restrictive parenting in the development of externalizing behavior. *Developmental Psychology, 34,* 982–995.

Belsky, J., Hsieh, K., & Crnic, K. (1998). Mothering, fathering, and infant negativity as antecedents of boys' externalizing problems and inhibition at age 3: Differential susceptibility to rearing influence? *Development and Psychopathology, 10,* 301–319.

Block, J. (1996). Some jangly remarks on Baumeister & Heatherton. *Psychological Inquiry, 7,* 28–32.

Caspi, A., Bem, D. J., & Elder, G. H. (1989). Continuities and consequences of interactional styles across the life course. *Journal of Personality, 57,* 375–406.

Caspi, A., Roberts, B. W., & Shiner, R. L. (2005). Personality development: Stability and change. *Annual Review of Psychology, 56,* 453–484.

Caspi, A., & Shiner, R. L. (2006). Personality development. In W. Damon & R. Lerner (Series Eds.) & N. Eisenberg (Vol. Ed.), *Handbook of child psychology: Vol. 3. Social, emotional, and personality development* (6th ed., pp. 300–365). New York: Wiley.

Chang, L. (2003). Variable effects of children's aggression, social withdrawal, and prosocial leadership as functions of teacher beliefs and behaviors. *Child Development, 74,* 535–548.

Chen, X., Li, D., Li, Z., Li, B., & Liu, M. (2000). Sociable and prosocial dimensions of social competence in Chinese children: Common and unique contributions to social, academic, and psychological adjustment. *Developmental Psychology, 36,* 302–314.

Chen, X., Liu, M., Rubin, K. H., Cen, G., Gao, X., & Li, D. (2002). Sociability and prosocial orientation as predictors of youth adjustment: A seven-year longitudinal study in a Chinese sample. *International Journal of Behavioral Development, 26,* 128–136.

Crick, N. R., & Dodge, K. A. (1994). A review and reformulation of social information processing mechanisms in children's social adjustment. *Psychological Bulletin, 115,* 74–101.

Dodge, K. A., Lansford, J. E., Burks, V. S., Bates, J. E., Pettit, G. S., Fontaine, R., & Price, J. M. (2003). Peer rejection and social information-processing factors in the development of aggressive behavior problems in children. *Child Development, 74,* 374–393.

Eisenberg, N., Fabes, R. A., Guthrie, I. K., & Reiser, M. (2000). Dispositional emotionality and regulation: Their role in predicting quality of social functioning. *Journal of Personality and Social Psychology, 78,* 136–157.

Eisenberg, N., Pidada, S., & Liew, J. (2001). The relations of regulation and negative emotionality to Indonesian children's social functioning. *Child Development, 72,* 1747–1763.

Funder, D. C. (2001). Personality. *Annual Review of Psychology, 52,* 197–221.

Funder, D. C., Parke, R. D., Tomlinson-Keasey, C., & Widaman, K. (Eds.). (1993). *Studying lives through time: Personality and development.* Washington, DC: American Psychological Association.

Gallagher, K. C. (2002). Does child temperament moderate the influence of parenting on adjustment? *Developmental Review, 22,* 623–643.

Gazelle, H., & Ladd, G. W. (2003). Anxious solitude and peer exclusion: A diathesis-stress model of internalizing trajectories in childhood. *Child Development, 74,* 257–278.

Gest, S. D. (1997). Behavioral inhibition: Stability and associations with adaptation from childhood to early adulthood. *Journal of Personality and Social Psychology, 72,* 467–475.

Goldberg, L. R. (2001). Analyses of Digman's child-personality data: Derivation of Big Five factor scores from each of six samples. *Journal of Personality, 69,* 709–743.

Goldsmith, H. H., Buss, A., Plomin, R., Rothbart, M. K., Thomas, A., Chess, S., Hinde, R. A., McCall, R. B. (1987). Roundtable: What is temperament? *Child Development, 58,* 505–529.

Graziano, W. G. (2003). Personality development: An introduction toward process approaches to long-term stability and change in persons. *Journal of Personality, 71,* 893–903.

Graziano, W. G., & Eisenberg, N. (1997). Agreeableness: A dimension of personality. In R. Hogan, J. Johnson, & S. Briggs (Eds.), *Handbook of personality psychology* (pp. 795–824). San Diego, CA: Academic.

Graziano, W. G., Jensen-Campbell, L. A., & Finch, J. F. (1997). The self as a mediator between personality and adjustment. *Journal of Personality and Social Psychology, 73,* 392–404.

Halverson, C. F., Havill, V. L., Deal, J., Baker, S. R., Victor, J. B., Pavlopoulos, V., Besevegis, E., & Wen, L. (2003). Personality structure as derived from parental ratings of free descriptions of children: The Inventory of Child Individual Differences. *Journal of Personality, 71,* 995–1026.

Halverson, C. F., Kohnstamm, G. A., & Martin, R. P. (Eds.). (1994). *The developing structure of temperament and personality from infancy to adulthood.* Hillsdale, NJ: Lawrence Erlbaum Associates.

Hawley, P. H. (2003). Prosocial and coercive configurations of resource control in early adolescence: A case for the well-adapted Machiavellian. *Merrill-Palmer Quarterly, 49,* 279–309.

Henry, B., Caspi, A., Moffitt, T. E., Harrington H., & Silva, P. A. (1999). Staying in school protects boys with poor self-regulation in childhood from later crime: A longitudinal study. *International Journal of Behavioral Development, 23,* 1049–1073.

Henry, B., Caspi, A., Moffitt, T. E., & Silva, P. A. (1996). Temperamental and familial predictors of violent and nonviolent criminal convictions: Age 3 to age 18. *Developmental Psychology, 32,* 614–623.

John, O. P., Caspi, A., Robins, R. W., Moffitt, T. E., & Stouthamer-Loeber, M. (1994). The "Little Five": Exploring the nomological network of the Five-Factor model of personality in adolescent boys. *Child Development, 65,* 160–178.

Judge, T. A., Higgins, C. A., Thoresen, C. J., & Barrick, M. R. (1999). The Big Five personality traits, general mental ability, and career success across the life span. *Personnel Psychology, 52,* 621–652.

Kagan, J. (1998). Biology and the child. In W. Damon (Series Ed.) & N. Eisenberg (Vol. Ed.), *Handbook of child psychology: Vol. 3. Social, emotional, and personality development* (5th ed., pp. 177–235). New York: Wiley.

Kagan, J., Snidman, N., Zentner, M., & Peterson, E. (1999). Infant temperament and anxious symptoms in school age children. *Development and Psychopathology, 11,* 209–224.

Kochanska, G., Gross, J. N., Lin, M., & Nichols, K. E. (2002). Guilt in young children: Development, determinants, and relations with a broader system of standards. *Child Development, 73,* 461–482.

Kochanska, G., & Knaack, A. (2003). Effortful control as a personality characteristic of young children: Antecedents, correlates, and consequences. *Journal of Personality, 71,* 1087–1112.

Kohnstamm, G. A., Halverson, C. F., Mervielde, I., & Havill, V. (1998). *Parental descriptions of child personality: Developmental antecedents of the Big Five?* Mahwah, NJ: Lawrence Erlbaum Associates.

Kokko, K., & Pulkkinen, L. (2000). Aggression in childhood and long-term unemployment in adulthood: A cycle of maladaptation and some protective factors. *Developmental Psychology, 36,* 463–472.

Lamb, M. E., Chuang, S. S., Wessels, H., Broberg, A. G., & Hwang, C. P. (2002). Emergence and construct validation of the Big Five factors in early childhood: A longitudinal analysis of their ontogeny in Sweden. *Child Development, 73,* 1517–1524.

Laursen, B., Pulkkinen, L., & Adams, R. (2002). The antecedents and correlates of Agreeableness in adulthood. *Developmental Psychology, 38,* 591–603.

Lengua, L. J. (2002). The contribution of emotionality and self-regulation to the understanding of children's responses to multiple risk. *Child Development, 73,* 144–161.

Loehlin, J. C. (1992). *Genes and environment in personality development.* Newbury Park, CA: Sage.

Lynam, D. R., Caspi, A., Moffitt, T. E., Wikstrom, P. H., Loeber, R., & Novak, S. (2000). The interaction between impulsivity and neighborhood context on offending: The effects of impulsivity are stronger in poorer neighborhoods. *Journal of Abnormal Psychology, 109,* 563–574.

Markey, P. M., Markey, C. N., & Tinsley, B. J. (2004). Children's behavioral manifestations of the Five-Factor model of personality. *Personality and Social Psychology Bulletin, 30,* 423–432.

Markon, K. E., Krueger, R. F., & Watson, D. (2005). Delineating the structure of normal and abnormal personality: An integrative hierarchical approach. *Journal of Personality and Social Psychology, 88,* 139–157.

Martin, R. P., Olejnik, S., & Gaddis, L. (1994). Is temperament an important contributor to
schooling outcomes in elementary school? Modeling effects of temperament and scholastic
ability on academic achievement. In W. B. Carey & S. C. McDevitt (Eds.), *Prevention and early
intervention: Individual differences as risk factors for the mental health of children: A festschrift for
Stella Chess and Alexander Thomas* (pp. 59–68). New York: Brunner/Mazel.

Masten, A. S., Coatsworth, J. D., Neemann, J., Gest, S. D., Tellegen, A., & Garmezy, N. (1995).
The structure and coherence of competence from childhood through adolescence. *Child Development, 66,* 1635–1659

Maziade, M., Caron, C., Cote, R., Merette, C., Bernier, H., Laplante, B., Boutin, P., & Thivierge, J.
(1990). Psychiatric status of adolescents who had extreme temperaments at age 7. *American
Journal of Psychiatry, 147,* 1531–1536.

Measelle, J. R., John, O. P., Ablow, J. C., Cowan, P. A., & Cowan, C. P. (2005). Can children provide coherent, stable, and valid self-reports on the Big Five dimensions? A longitudinal study
from ages 5 to 7. *Journal of Personality and Social Psychology, 89,* 90–106.

Mervielde, I., De Clercq, B., De Fruyt, F., & Van Leeuwen, K. (2005). Temperament, personality
and developmental psychopathology as childhood antecedents of personality disorders. *Journal of Personality Disorders, 19,* 171–201.

Moffitt, T. E., & Caspi, A. (1998). Implications of violence between intimate partners for child
psychologists and psychiatrists. *Journal of Child Psychology and Psychiatry, 39,* 137–144.

Muris, P., Schmidt, H., Merckelbach, H., & Schouten, E. (2001). The structure of negative emotions in adolescents. *Journal of Abnormal Child Psychology, 29,* 331–337.

Nagin, D., & Tremblay, R. E. (1999). Trajectories of boys' physical aggression, opposition, and hy-
peractivity on the path to physically violent and nonviolent juvenile delinquency. *Child Development, 70,* 1181–1196.

Newman, D. L., Caspi, A., Moffitt, T. E., & Silva, P. A. (1997). Antecedents of adult interpersonal
functioning: Effects of individual differences in age 3 temperament. *Developmental Psychology,
33,* 206–217.

Olson, S. L., Schilling, E. M., & Bates, J. E. (1999). Measurement of impulsivity: Construct coherence, longitudinal stability, and relationship with externalizing problems in middle childhood
and adolescence. *Journal of Abnormal Child Psychology, 27,* 151–165.

Pulkkinen, L. (2002). Social development and its risk factors. In C. von Hofsten & L. Backman
(Eds.), *Psychology at the turn of the millennium: Vol. 2. Social, developmental, and clinical perspectives* (pp. 53–76). New York: Taylor & Francis.

Putnam, S. P., Ellis, L. K., & Rothbart, M. K. (2001). The structure of temperament from infancy
through adolescence. In A. Eliasz & A. Angleitner (Eds.), *Advances in research on temperament*
(pp. 165–182). Miami, FL: Pabst Science Publishers.

Putnam, S. P., Sanson, A. V., & Rothbart, M. K. (2002). Child temperament and parenting. In M.
H. Bornstein (Ed.), *Handbook of parenting: Vol. 1. Children and parenting* (2nd ed., pp. 255–277).
Mahwah, NJ: Lawrence Erlbaum Associates.

Raine, A., Reynolds, C., Venables, P. H., Mednick, S. A., & Farrington, D. P. (1998). Fearlessness,
stimulation-seeking, and large body size at age 3 years as early predispositions to childhood aggression at age 11 years. *Archives of General Psychiatry, 55,* 745–751.

Roberts, B. W., & DelVecchio, W. F. (2000). The rank-order consistency of personality traits from
childhood to old age: A quantitative review of longitudinal studies. *Psychological Bulletin, 126,*
3–25.

Rothbart, M. K., Ahadi, S. A., & Evans, D. E. (2000). Temperament and personality: Origins and
outcomes. *Journal of Personality and Social Psychology, 78,* 122–135.

Rothbart, M. K., Ahadi, S. A., Hershey, K. L., & Fisher, P. (2001). Investigations of temperament
at three to seven years: The Children's Behavior Questionnaire. *Child Development, 72,*
1394–1408.

Rothbart, M. K., & Bates, J. E. (1998). Temperament. In W. Damon (Series Ed.) & N. Eisenberg (Vol. Ed.), *Handbook of child psychology: Vol. 3. Social, emotional, and personality development* (5th ed., pp. 105–176). New York: Wiley.

Rothbart, M. K., & Derryberry, D. (2002). Temperament in children. In C. von Hofsten & L. Backman (Eds.), *Psychology at the turn of the millennium: Vol. 2. Social, developmental, and clinical perspectives* (pp. 17–35). New York: Taylor & Francis.

Rubin, K. H., Bukowski, W., & Parker, J. G. (1998). Peer interactions, relationships, and groups. In W. Damon (Series Ed.) & N. Eisenberg (Vol. Ed.), *Handbook of child psychology: Vol. 3. Social, emotional, and personality development* (5th ed., pp. 619–700). New York: Wiley.

Rubin, K. H., Burgess, K. B., Dwyer, K. M., & Hastings, P. D. (2003). Predicting preschoolers' externalizing behaviors from toddler temperament, conflict, and maternal negativity. *Developmental Psychology, 39,* 164–176.

Saudino, K. J., & Cherny, S. S. (2001). Sources of continuity and change in observed temperament. In R. N. Emde & J. K. Hewitt (Eds.), *Infancy to early childhood: Genetic and environmental influences on developmental change* (pp. 89–110). New York: Oxford University Press.

Saudino, K. J., & Plomin, R. (1996). Personality and behavior genetics: Where have we been and where are we going? *Journal of Research in Personality, 30,* 335–347.

Shiner, R. L. (1998). How shall we speak of children's personalities in middle childhood?: A preliminary taxonomy. *Psychological Bulletin, 124,* 308–332.

Shiner, R. L. (2000). Linking childhood personality with adaptation: Evidence for continuity and change across time into late adolescence. *Journal of Personality and Social Psychology, 78,* 310–325.

Shiner, R. L., & Caspi, A. (2003). Personality differences in childhood and adolescence: Measurement, development, and consequences. *Journal of Child Psychology and Psychiatry, 44,* 2–32.

Shiner, R. L., & Masten, A. S. (2002). Transactional links between personality and adaptation from childhood through adulthood. *Journal of Research in Personality, 36,* 580–588.

Shiner, R. L., Masten, A. S., & Roberts, J. M. (2003). Childhood personality foreshadows adult personality and life outcomes two decades later. *Journal of Personality, 71,* 1145–1170.

Shiner, R. L., Masten, A. S., & Tellegen, A. (2002). A developmental perspective on personality in emerging adulthood: Childhood antecedents and concurrent adaptation. *Journal of Personality and Social Psychology, 83,* 1165–1177.

Slotboom, A.-M., Havill, V. L., Pavlopoulos, V., & De Fruyt, F. (1998). Developmental changes in personality descriptions of children: A cross-national comparison of parental descriptions of children. In G. A. Kohnstamm, C. F. Halverson, I. Mervielde, & V. L. Havill (Eds.), *Parental descriptions of child personality: Developmental antecedents of the Big Five?* (pp. 127–153). Mahwah, NJ: Lawrence Erlbaum Associates.

Sroufe, L. A., Carlson, E. A., Levy, A. K., & Egeland, B. (1999). Implications of attachment theory for developmental psychopathology. *Development and Psychopathology, 11,* 1–13.

Stoolmiller, M. (2001). Synergistic interaction of child manageability problems and parent-discipline tactics in predicting future growth in externalizing behavior for boys. *Developmental Psychology, 37,* 814–825.

Thomas, A., Chess, S., & Birch, H. (1968). *Temperament and behavior disorders in children.* New York: New York University Press.

Thomas, A., Chess, S., Birch, H., Hertzig, M., & Korn, S. (1963). *Behavioral individuality in early childhood.* New York: New York University Press.

Tobin, R. M., Graziano, W. G., Vanman, E. J., & Tassinary, L. G. (2000). Personality, emotional experience, and efforts to control emotions. *Journal of Personality and Social Psychology, 79,* 656–669.

12

Agency to Agentic Personalities: The Early to Middle Childhood Gap

Theodore A. Walls
University of Rhode Island

Sarah H. Kollat
Pennsylvania State University

This chapter considers the course of agentic development beginning with the emergence of infant *intentionality and agency*. There is speculation about ways in which this developmental progression could be linked to the development of *agentic personality* characteristics that begin to emerge in middle childhood (around age 7). The discussion selectively traces early life-span cognitive developmental findings in order to characterize the developmental trajectory of intentionality and agency in infancy and early childhood. It considers ways in which this trajectory may lead to the development of metacognitive abilities and suggests that these abilities may mediate the relation between early agency and agentic personality. In addition, specific empirical study designs and related prospective analyses that could contribute meaningfully to the understanding of the developmental progression of agency to agentic personality characteristics are described briefly.

INTENTIONALITY AND AGENCY

Agentic personalities are important because agentic views and many other views in the perceived control family of constructs have been associated with positive life outcomes across studies and contexts (Little, 1998; Skinner, 1995; Walls & Little, 2005). The study of infant and early childhood intentionality and agency has been a prominent activity in cognitive psychology for the last decade. The cognitive developmental progression of intentional behavior over infancy and early childhood may in part comprise the developmental roots of agentic personality characteristics exhibited during middle childhood. In this chapter, the viability of an early life-span theory of agency that spans the developmental progression of early cognitive achievements through the emergence of durable beliefs about an individual's agency in middle childhood and adolescence is considered. Relevant empirical findings from the literature are reviewed with a particular focus on the possible theoretical congruence of metacognition and agentic personality.

COGNITIVE ACHIEVEMENTS IN AGENCY DURING INFANCY AND EARLY CHILDHOOD

A selective review of developmental milestones of agentic development in infancy is provided in this section. Figure 12.1 portrays these milestones over developmental time.

Agency, as considered in cognitive developmental literatures, is the ability to select and take actions toward goals of a person's own choosing. In the early months of life, the emergence of agency has been attributed to either innate sources or experience. For example, Leslie (1995) suggested that infants have a modular device for agency that begins to mature more fully at age 2 and that earlier indications of the component parts of such a device suggest it may be part of human biological endowment. By contrast, Russell (1995) suggested that this claim would require too prodigious a mental parser of propositional content, hence, the presence of such a device may be nominally necessary but functionally insufficient. For example, although infants can encode representations and find inconsistencies, they likely do not mentally reverse these representations until they have acquired more experience. Such a feat would imply the presence of a novel intention rather than simple reactions to inconsistent representations. In a complementary position, Gelman and Lucariello (2002) suggested that the child is inherently an agent owing to an individual consciousness that affords intentions and that manifestations of agency appear very early in the sensorimotor period. They argued that it is clear that infants begin to demonstrate an understanding of agency as a principle early in development. In keeping with this notion, Russell (1995, 1996) suggested that repeated attempts despite failures in early grasping behaviors and search for hidden objects in occlusion

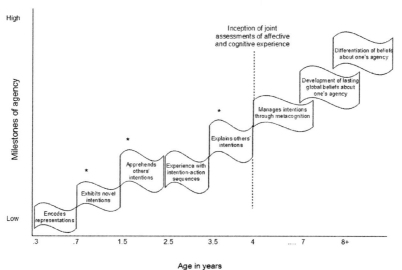

FIG. 12.1. The developmental progression of agency into agentic characteristics.

experiments are perhaps the earliest indications of intentional states (around 4–6 months). The infant's understanding of what can and cannot be reversed in a world composed of physical objects as propositional content develops most quickly—on attempts at manipulation, some objects are reversible (manipulation is self-determined), whereas others are irreversible (manipulation is impossible because the properties are world-determined). Such an interaction-based view of intentionality is elaborated by Russell to later include the central role of social interactions as propositional content subject to the same types of properties.

As the infant matures from the early weeks to about 10 months, representations become increasingly durable and differentiated; more sophisticated occlusion experiments produce surprise and a nascent understanding that humans uniquely possess the ability to act with intention develops (Gelman & Lucariello, 2002; Legerstee, 1992; Russell, 1995; Wynn, 1992). At 9–11 months, as indicated by frequently replicated findings across joint attention activities with adults, infants demonstrate that they know what another person is trying to do with an object and can imitate and improvise on behaviors that they are shown (Carpenter, Nagell, & Tomasello, 1998; Tomasello, 1999). This age, then, is the first watershed period of agency, reflecting two critical developmental milestones. First, in early infancy, the act of imitating what another does indicates that the first step from an egocentric viewpoint toward a more allocentric view of the world has been traversed (Russell, 1995). At this time, however, the infant begins to reflect the ability to be selective about its actions, either coadopting actions of others in social interactions or independently adopting similar or novel actions. Second, and more importantly, these novel actions often demonstrate that the infant can now develop novel *intentions* (see Fig. 12.1). Tomasello (1999) further argued that this period reflects the domain general appearance of intentionality. This notion is further elaborated by Bruner (1991, 1999), who claimed that a "theory of mind in world" evolves out of the behaviors manifested in joint attention studies and this provides the foundation for intentional (volitional) acts as manifested in various types of sign use (see also, Sperber, D. Premack & J. Premack, 1995).

From 9 to 18 months, comprehension of others' actions, and to a limited extent their intentions as well, appears to solidify through more use of imitation and joint attention. Apparent in the infant's social interaction are intentional communication, referencing of objects through signs, being aware of multiple perspectives, early use of language to communicate intentions, and social referencing (Baldwin, 1993; Baldwin & Moses, 1994; Gelman & Lucariello, 2002; Spelke & Newport, 1998). For example, Repacholi (1998) demonstrated that at 14 months, infants have adopted understanding of directed actions of others based on emotional cues, as evidenced by their attending to objects for which an adult expresses joy more than those for which disgust is expressed. In general, MacTurk, McCarthy, Vietze, and Yarrow (1987) argued that this period reflects a transition from mainly exploratory behavior to goal-directed behavior, which may contribute to the child's overall sense of efficacy. Further, Wertsch (1985) suggested that during this period these goal-directed intentional patterns can be internalized just as physical objects in logical development. This period appears to reflect a more incremental development of the concept of an intention and apprehension of an intention in others. This apprehension emerges concomitantly with more frequent imitation of actions and improvisation on actions themselves than was apparent prior to the 9- to 11-month watershed.

A second watershed in the development of agency appears to occur at around 18 months, when infants begin to reflect early forms of a so-called folk psychology; that is, persons are seen as intentional beings (Meltzoff, Gopnik, & Repacholi, 1999). For example, infants at this age can detect the intentions of an adult through observation of a failed attempt at an action (Meltzoff, 1995). Likewise, infants take into account the intentions of another person in their attempts to determine the referent of a novel word (Baldwin & Moses, 1994; Tomasello, 1995). Repetition of sequences of apprehension and enactment of both actions and intentions in a social context appears to be the early machine of learning that may enable a later understanding of what it is to be agentic (Bloom & Tinker, 2001; Russell, 1995; Shweder, 1990; Wertsch, 1984, 1985). Accordingly, Meacham (1984) argued that "intentions are based in shared meanings and expectations, so that they can be communicated. Intentions become important in a social, multi-person context, where possibilities arise for misreading of intentions, and also, more importantly, for cooperative action based on shared intentions, on one mind affecting another" (p. 121).

Although this period from 18 to 36 months is still not understood well and has been referred to as the "dark ages" of intentional development, experience with intention-action sequences with others appears to accrue in a "constant process of revision, like the process of theory change in science" (Meltzoff et al., 1999, p. 38). As such, Meltzoff and colleagues indicated that the "terrible twos" can be seen as a time of testing the limits of one's own intentions and those of others. Around 36 months, however, a third watershed of agentic characteristics commences. A more advanced folk psychology begins to emerge in which children can explain human actions and reactions in terms of actors' mental states, rather than attributing them to undirected movements (Flavell, 1999; Gelman & Lucariello, 2002). This achievement may be the earliest harbinger of a child's "theory of mind" that has been extensively documented using false-belief tasks at age 4 to 4½ (Wellman, Cross, & Watson, 2001; see also, Sperber et al., 1995). Children's successful performance on false-belief tasks indicates that children can ascribe beliefs that they know to be logically false to be held by others (Wimmer & Perner, 1983). Note that an issue of considerable interest and some debate about this period involves to what extent these abilities commence through or are constrained by the maturation of executive function working in tandem with social interaction versus developing from early conceptual understanding of intentions and actions (Norman & Shallice, 1986; Perner, Stummer, & Lang, 1999).

METACOGNITION

After age 4, both theoretical and empirical literatures are much less decisive about the course of development of cognitive agency. Flavell (1999) explained that children begin to combine beliefs and desires to determine actions jointly. In order for this to occur, children need some way to balance beliefs about how things in the world operate and desires for what they want (i.e., to act on desires and intentions). This may come of being able to reflect on the outcomes of many diverse intention-action sequences, rather than simply acting on a localized belief in relation to a desire. The intention-action sequences and their results in effect need a general manager to evaluate which actions tend to be or not be successful in a given domain. This next developmental phase of agency is enabled by *metacognition* (Flavell,

1979), or "using knowledge and cognition about cognitive phenomena" (p. 906). Brown and Campione (1977) similarly described a process that involves monitoring cognitive activity and performance through planning, checking, and making inferences. Consistently, Keating (1990) indicated that this thinking explicitly involves looking for consistency, gaps, and accuracy in one's thinking and suggests that the ability may commence with respect to a particular domain of inquiry. The concept of metacognition was a "fuzzy concept" from its earliest roots (Flavell, 1981, p. 37). Years of study using a diversity of approaches have yielded a variety of definitions and theoretical descriptions of metacognition; most of these early definitions reduce easily to something as trite as "thinking about the quality of one's thinking."

However, the field has made some progress in giving form to this rather amorphous idea over the last two decades. Flavell's (1999) now more robust definition reads: "Metacognition includes knowledge about the nature of people as cognizers, about the nature of different cognitive tasks, and about possible strategies that can be applied to the solution of different tasks" (p. 2). A recent symposium on metacognition reflected continued challenges in developing a comprehensive theory of metacognition (Schraw & Impara, 2000). A compendium stemming from the symposium on issues in the measurement of metacognition by Schraw and Impara (2000) provides a valuable starting place for future work as a consolidated resource on the construct. Challenges include defining the role of metacognition amidst motivation, attribution, strategy use, and other complementary constructs, as well as distinguishing among subcomponents of metacognition, such as metacognitive knowledge and metacognitive regulation.

Despite theoretical ambiguities, some recurrent themes and representative findings about metacognition have accrued from studies conducted over the middle childhood period. Studies of phenomena indicating that children become more reflective about the contents of their thought are widely available. For example, Mischel (1984) argued that some amount of metacognitive activity was apparent when children around age 6 evaluated diverse ways of planning to delay gratification in contrast to what they expected to experience through delay of gratification (e.g., waiting to eat marshmallows) as a result of each strategy. These explanations differed from those of 4 year-olds in that they involved more cognitive versatility than simply stating a plan. Similarly, Gopnik, Capps, and Meltzoff (2000) purported that an understanding of interpretation, inference, and ambiguity begins to develop from age 5 to age 7 years based on children's performance on more complex tasks involving the interpretation of others' beliefs (see Chandler & Helm, 1984). This metacognitive ability is only beginning to develop at this time, however. Evidence indicating that children between age 6 and age 8 lack sufficiently robust "counter-scripts" to explain idiosyncratic events suggests that a more skeptical metacognition is needed than children of this age possess (Lucariello & Mindolovich, 1995). Similarly, other conceptions of metacognitive skill in a range of childhood and early adolescent literatures reflect dramatically lower explanatory ability about an individual's own actions (e.g., those involving learning strategies; Chan, 1994), motivation for learning (Dweck,1986), and self-regulation (Pintrich & DeGroot, 1990; Schwanenflugel, Fabricius & Alexander, 1994). In general, these studies indicate a similar age-graded increase in differentiation of specific metacognitive skills beginning around age 8 or age 9 and progressing well into early adolescence, when manifestations of formal operational abilities emerge prominently (Graham & Wiener, 1996).

As these literatures extend over childhood and into adolescence, researchers have asked whether the apparent ability to hold several complex mental representations simultaneously and evaluate them spontaneously distinguishes the metacognitive ability of older and younger children (Keating, 1990; Klayman, 1985). Another proposed hallmark of metacognition after age 5 for normally developing children may be the independence of "this thinking about one's thinking" with respect to consciousness (Russell, 1995). Perner and Clements (1997) suggested that such a consciousness involves simultaneous awareness of a state of affairs and the implicit recognition that a mental state reflects this state of affairs. Gelman and Lucariello (2002) integrated these two conceptions and suggested that children bring order to all of the representations they have accrued through the process of metacognition, reflecting the manifestation of an individual consciousness reviewing its own contents. Consistent with this view, Russell (1996) suggested that "agents" do not just self-monitor and control their actions, but are also "disposed to exercise these powers because they desire certain outcomes" (p. 90). Despite the obvious theoretical attractiveness of this concept as a key linkage between early and later childhood metacognition, few studies have operationalized designs to study the role of consciousness as part of metacognition.

Metacognition to Agentic Characteristics

The notion of metacognition is appealing as a developmental framework that may help to explain the course of agency as it may lead to the emergence of agentic personality characteristics. Four conceptual issues may confront those who endeavor to pursue this line of inquiry. First, there is little explicit empirical information documenting the linkage between the feat of understanding other's beliefs as distinct and becoming truly reflective about one's own beliefs and actions. Although successful performance on false-belief tasks constitutes an advancement in a folk psychology beyond that apparent in joint attention behaviors, how these nascent folk psychological skills then molt into a metacognitive awareness that transcends activities or domains is not clear.

Second, assuming that such a transition takes place, as it likely does, the milestones of this process are not well understood at the most crucial ages after early childhood; there appears to be a gap of about 3 years (from roughly age $4\frac{1}{2}$–$7\frac{1}{2}$) that is fairly devoid of theory and empirical findings that suggest how early agency progresses into metacognitive awareness. Several literatures, however, may provide insights on how to study the types of cognitive reflection that may occur in this period, for example, the everyday (situated) cognition literature provides a diverse sampling of some techniques that could tap reasoning at this age (e.g., Rogoff & Lave, 1984; see also Schliemann & Nunes, 1990, for an adolescent example). Greenfield and Lave (1982) contended that cross-cultural studies may reflect different cognitive processes and more studies need to focus on the analysis of a particular skill found in a given culture (as several of their studies have endeavored to do). Also, Vinden and Astington (2000) argued that Western culturally determined conceptions of what "thinking" is—or more generally, what it is to be a "person"—may simply not exist in other cultures. Hence, new methodological approaches, such as those that may consider action itself as an expression of thought, may be needed to understand the course of metacognition from a cross-cultural standpoint. In this view, "rather than forming a 'Western' psychological theory as to the relation of thought and behavior, children in other cultures may simply learn that an agent is someone who acts in expectable ways under expectable circumstances" (p. 514). Similarly, the "theory theory" perspective, which embraces a notion of the mind developing from an everyday or "foundational" framework that is ontologically coherent, is very compatible with these cross-cultural perspectives (Flavell, 1999).

Third, assuming the presence of a kind of metacognition in the early grade school years, how this thought compares with the concept of agentic personality as a belief-based trait studied through self-report is not established. As mentioned earlier and to be discussed in greater detail later, work by Skinner and colleagues and Little and colleagues considers children in grade two (approximately age 8) and older. In this area, the notion of agency is much more generalized. The issues under primary consideration include how the reports (of oneself or of others) of control or agency beliefs change over time, how internal constituent parts of the beliefs interrelate, and what these beliefs indicate in relation to various outcomes in a diversity of domains.

Hence, little consideration of how (or if) agency evolves from intentions and action sequences in infancy and early childhood into agentic personality in later childhood has been undertaken. A key topic for consideration, then, is how the conversion of metacognitive thought processes into lasting beliefs within a domain proceeds and whether such a conversion process results in domain specific or domain general agentic beliefs.

Fourth, the sources of agentic behavior after early childhood may not be exclusively cognitive or even social cognitive. Henderson and Dweck (1990) argued that many kinds of constraints in reasoning and higher order thinking may not be narrowly cognitive, but derive from motivations and dispositions. Similarly, different concepts of a self or of self as a learner may lead to different types of metacognitive processes (Harter, 1988, 1990a, 1990b; Markus & Kitayama, 1991). Consistent with Lewin's (1946) position on the role of peer groups and the notion of learned helplessness (e.g., Dweck, 1986), theoretical views offered by Hawley and Little (2002) suggest that successive win–loss experiences beginning in toddlerhood may eventually lead to agentic characteristics. Consistently, Flavell (1999) explained that the concept of developing an intention in early childhood is important because it leads to an understanding of morality and personal responsibility, both of which clearly require a prominent role of beliefs. In fact, a diversity of social and affective theories could potentially contribute to explanations of middle childhood and adolescent metacognition and/or agentic personality.

The Case for Mapping Early Agency to Agentic Personality

Agentic individuals recognize their own volitional power to manipulate the system of goals, means, and ends. Agentic characteristics can be seen as part of the personality; this construct is reviewed elsewhere in this volume, so it will only be treated briefly here. In recent years, researchers have forwarded more general stances about how agentic behavior may be rooted in a generalized sense of personal agency. Reviews covering aspects of these theories can be found in Stipek and Weisz (1981),

Skinner, Chapman, and Baltes (1988), Eccles (1983), and Walls (2002). One model, originally outlined in Chapman (1984), provides useful distinctions among a few beliefs that are likely to be related to intentional action. The model was intentionally inexplicit about many requisite characteristics of a "complete" action theory or system surrounding such beliefs. It has supported fruitful inquiry into the inner workings of various dimensions of action-related beliefs for over a decade. The model involves three interrelated belief components and has been referred to as a tripartite action-control theory model of psychological control (Little, 1998; Skinner, 1995). The first component is *agency* or *capacity* beliefs, which reflect personal judgments about one's own potential to perform based on possession of or access to specific sources of potential such as effort, ability, luck, or teachers (e.g., when it comes to learning something new in school can you work hard enough—i.e., expend effort—at it?). The effort, ability, and luck sources of potential are often categorized in the literature as being more personal sources (intra-self). Conversely, teachers, powerful others, and unknown sources are often thought of as being tied to possible causes of performance outside of the self (extra-self). The second component is *means–ends* (or *causality*) beliefs, which are generalized judgments about the importance of specific sources of potential, such as effort, ability, luck, or teachers, as needed to attain a given performance level (e.g., "when other kids learn something new in school, is it because they can keep trying enough to get it?"). In this case, the sources of potential are typically called means or causes and, analogous to agency belief sources of potential, can be seen as falling into personal (e.g., one's own effort and ability as a means) or conversely, nonpersonal categories (e.g., luck, others, or something intangible other than the self is the means). Finally, *control-expectancy* beliefs regard one's general potential to perform in a certain way, independent of any specific sources of potential (e.g., "when it comes to learning something new in school, can you do it?").

An understanding of how an individual becomes agentic with regard to their control beliefs and related action behavior requires consideration of the fundamental questions of development: What are the specific components, such as types of goals, beliefs, or actions, that develop over ontogeny? How do these individual components and the system of components in which they reside develop? How does this development vary among diverse individuals living in diverse contexts? A major limitation of the current developmental theory is the specificity with which these developmental questions are rendered in light of an action-control system, as a whole, and with respect to the developmental course of earlier agency beliefs, in particular. We have tried to redress this situation by tracing the empirical literature by depicting the course of agency (as shown in Fig. 12.1 and described earlier). This body of work characterizes cognitive achievements that over many daily repetitions in early childhood may lead to the emergence of characteristics.

Prospective Study Designs for Joint Consideration of Early Agency and Agentic Personality

As the theoretical and empirical work reviewed in this chapter suggests, the potential association between agency in infancy and early childhood and the later development of agentic qualities in middle childhood and adolescence warrants further examination. In order to better understand the relation between these two factors, it is also necessary to investigate the role of metacognition. Although cognitive developmental theory and much empirical literature have considered metacognition, whether agency follows a developmental trajectory toward agentic personality and whether metacognition plays an important mediational role in facilitating the emergence of these agentic qualities are important possibilities for empirical consideration. A vital next step in furthering understanding of agency is to explore the middle childhood gap and assess the role that metacognition may play in linking early agency with agentic personality during this developmental period.

In particular, the influence of metacognition as a possible mediator between early agency and later agentic personality must be examined. In order to pursue this goal, several possible research objectives should be considered. First, more detailed theoretical propositions about specific age ranges and the relation of these propositions to the developmental course of agentic personality traits must be developed. Second, in order to pursue questions about these populations, new designs will need to be developed in order to assess the three constructs in question—agency, metacognition, and agentic personality. For example, multimodal longitudinal research designs that consider microlevel changes in cognition via experimental means and molar changes in personality via self-report means may be useful. Third, because studies of metacognition have been almost comprehensively cross-sectional in nature and often involve very small samples, longitudinal designs assessing both early agency or agentic personality over the "early to middle childhood gap" when metacognition may play a role, would be very informative. Studies that track and consider analytically intraindividual change will be particularly important in determining how microlevel agency processes may relate to personality development.

In addition, extension of self-report and peer/observer-report designs covering agentic personality to earlier developmental periods-(i.e., before the current measurement starting point of around age 6). Specifically, if future studies extend the experimental measurement models of cognitive agency forward to later developmental periods and the self-report measurement models of agentic personality backward in developmental time, it would be possible to employ both models of measurement on a sample simultaneously. If these methods were applied before the middle childhood gap (e.g., 3½ years old) and continued longitudinally on the same sample beyond the gap (e.g., 8½ years old), then it would be possible to track the developmental transformation of agency, the emergence of agentic personality, and to assess the mediational role of metacognition.

In consideration of these methodological modifications for both agency and agentic personality research paradigms, one potential experimental design is depicted in Fig. 12.2. Data could be collected on both the micro-level (typically in clock time increments) for agency and metacognition and the molar-level (typically in calendar time increments) for agentic personality over the course of an extended longitudinal design (cf. Cook & Campbell, 1979). Beginning in infancy, study participants could be measured for both agency and agentic personality qualities. Regarding agency, study participants could be measured using a *multiple measurement burst* design, with assessments occurring multiple times over the course of several minutes using currently predominant experimental protocols (e.g., those used in joint attention: Moore & Dunham, 1995; Tomasello, 1995; false-belief tasks: Wimmer & Perner, 1983). As shown in Fig. 12.2, the

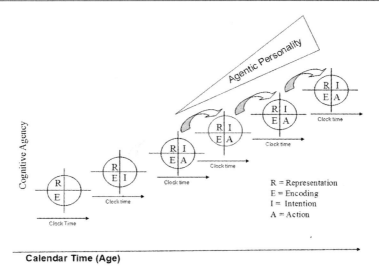

FIG. 12.2.   Microlevel and molar changes in the developmental course of agency and agentic personality.

agency variables of representation, encoding, intention, and intention-action sequences could be measured, although the sequencing of these variables would depend on the developmental level of the subjects. Initially, due to their limited cognitive abilities, infants would only be measured on their representations and encodings. With age, however, subjects' intentions and intention-action sequences could also be measured as they become developmentally observable. Following a clock time protocol, these measurements could be repeated twice a week for 6-month periods, with 3-month spacings separating measurement periods. Simultaneously, subjects' agentic personality traits could also be assessed globally, using a calendar time paradigm of two measurements over the 6-month measurement period. This data collection protocol could continue from infancy, through the middle childhood gap, and on into late adolescence. Such a comprehensive examination of agency and agentic personality would provide a promising approach to clarify the relation between these two complementary constructs. By carrying the experimental, micro-measurement of cognitive agency into adolescence and extending the molar, self-report measurement of agentic personality into early childhood, elucidation of the developmental trajectories of these two constructs could be pursued meaningfully.

This empirical approach could elucidate the middle childhood gap in agentic development and promote longitudinal investigation of early childhood agentic development. The use of longitudinal designs would also enable the use of advanced statistical techniques that describe micro-intraindividual change well (Walls & Schafer, 2006). For example, structural equation modeling could enable researchers to test the fitness of a model incorporating agency, metacognition, and agentic personality, ultimately allowing statistical assessment of the potential mediating role of metacognition between early agency and later agentic personality characteristics. Likewise, multilevel modeling and latent growth models could potentially be used to evaluate and compare the developmental trajectories of agency, metacognition, and agentic personality and to explain the heterogeneity of these trajectories with important contextual covariates.

Although these methodological and theoretical issues and the relation between early agency, later agentic personality, and metacognition have been adequately defined within a given culture, cross-cultural experiments could also be conducted in order to determine the universality of agency's developmental course. As discussed earlier, previous work proposes that members of different cultures may not perceive the process of thinking about what one is doing (metacognition) at all or in the same way (e.g., Greenfield & Lave, 1982; Vinden & Astington, 2000), suggesting that developmental trajectories of agency and agentic personality may differ among cultures in important ways.

In summary, cognitive developmental agency in early childhood provides a starting point for thinking about how agency and its various requisite components may develop. This proposed source of the roots of agency advances specificity over earlier psychological theories that have not devoted specific attention to either the early development of the cognitive system as a source of later agentic characteristics or to the likely influential role of metacognition. On the other hand, a countervailing view is that perhaps the developmental course of agency beliefs in the later childhood years does not source to the early agency developmental course at all. It may be a qualitatively distinct phenomenon that begins in the school-age years, is domain-specific, and is composed of different domain-specific social and educational experiences with different accordant cognitive processes than those which the early agency literature considers. Some work in advancing the specificity of theory and research in the early life-span study of agentic development has begun in this chapter. In the future, longitudinal studies should emerge that can bear on the assessment of these proposals.

ACKNOWLEDGMENTS

Portions of this chapter were pursued as part of the first author's dissertation work at Boston College and during his participation in research activities at the Yale University Agency Lab (Todd D. Little, Director). During the preparation of this work, the first author also received support from the National Institute of Drug Abuse, grant P50 DA10075 at the Methodology Center, Pennsylvania State University. The authors express gratitude for comments on earlier versions of the chapter from Penny Hauser-Cram, Joan Lucariello, and Ulrich Mueller.

REFERENCES

Baldwin, D. A. (1993). Early referential understanding: Infant's ability to recognize referential acts for what they are. *Child Development, 62,* 460–467.

Baldwin, D. A., & Moses, L. J. (1994). Early understanding of referential intent and attentional focus: Evidence from language and emotion. In C. Lewis & P. Mitchell (Eds.), *Children's early understanding of mind: Origins and development* (pp. 133–156). Hillsdale, NJ: Lawrence Erlbaum Associates.

Bloom, L., & Tinker, E. (2001). The intentionality model and language acquisition. *Monographs of the Society for Research in Child Development, 66*(4, Serial No. 267) Boston: Blackwell Publishers.

Brown, A. L., & Campione, J. C. (1977). Training strategic study time apportionment in educable retarded children. *Intelligence, 1,* 94–107.

Bruner, J. (1991). *Acts of meaning.* Cambridge, MA: Harvard University Press.

Bruner, J. (1999). The intentionality of referring. In P. D. Zelazo, J. W. Astington, & D. R. Olson, (Eds.), *Developing theories of intention: Social understanding and self-control* (pp. 329–339). Mahwah, NJ: Lawrence Erlbaum Associates.

Carpenter, M., Nagell, K., & Tomasello, M. (1998). Social cognition, joint attention, and communicative competence from 9-15 months of age. *Monographs of the Society for Research in Child Development, 63*(4, Serial No. 255).

Chan, L. K. S. (1994). Relationship of motivation, strategic learning, and reading achievement in grades 5, 7, 9. *Journal of Experimental Education, 62*(4), 319–339.

Chandler, M., & Helm, D. (1984). Developmental changes in the contribution of shared experience to role-taking competence. *International Journal of Behavioral Development, 7,* 145–156.

Chapman, M. (1984). Intentional action as a paradigm for developmental psychology: A symposium. *Human Development, 27*(3–4), 113–144.

Cook, T. D., & Campbell, D. T. (1979). *Quasi-experimentation: Design and analyses issues for field settings.* Chicago: Rand McNally.

Dweck, C. S. (1986). Motivational processes affecting learning. *American Psychologist, 41,* 1040–1048.

Eccles, J. (1983). Expectancies, values and academic behaviors. In J. T. Spence (Ed.), *Achievement and achievement motives* (pp. 75–146). San Francisco: Freeman.

Flavell, J. H. (1979). Metacognition and cognitive monitoring. A new area of cognitive-developmental inquiry. *American Psychologist, 34,* 906–911.

Flavell, J. H. (1981). Cognitive monitoring. In W. P. Dickson (Ed.), *Children's oral communication skills* (pp. 35–60). New York: Academic.

Flavell, J. H. (1999). Cognitive development: Children's knowledge about the mind. *Annual Review of Psychology, 50* (Annual, 1999), 21–45.

Gelman, R., & Lucariello, J. (2002). Learning in cognitive development. In H. Pashler (Ed.). *Steven's handbook of experimental psychology* (Vol. 3, pp. 395–443). New York: Wiley.

Gopnik, A., Capps, L., & Meltzoff, A. N. (2000). Early theories of mind: What the theory theory can tell us about autism. In S. Baron-Cohen, H. Tage-Flusberg, & D. Cohen (Eds.), *Understanding other minds: Perspectives from developmental cognitive neuroscience* (2nd ed., pp. 52–72). Oxford, England: Oxford University Press.

Graham S., & Wiener, B. (1996). Theories and principles of motivation. In D. C. Berliner & R. C. Calfee, (Eds.), *Handbook of educational psychology* (pp. 85–113). New York: Simon & Schuster Macmillan.

Greenfield, P. M., & Lave, J. (1982). Cognitive aspects of informal education. In D. Wagner & H. Stevenson (Eds.), *Cultural perspectives on child development* (pp. 181–207) New York: Freeman.

Harter, S. (1988). Developmental processes in the construction of the self. In T. D. Yawkey & J. E. Johnson (Eds.), *Integrative processes and socialization: Early to middle childhood* (pp. 45–78). Hillsdale, NJ: Lawrence Erlbaum Associates.

Harter, S. (1990a). Causes, correlates and the functional roles of global self-worth: A life-span perspective. In J. Kolligian, Jr. & R. Sternberg (Eds.), *Competence considered* (pp. 67–98). New Haven, CT: Yale University Press.

Harter, S. (1990b). *Self-and identity development.* In S. Feldman & G. Elliott (Eds.), *At the threshold: The developing adolescent* (pp. 352–387). Cambridge, MA: Harvard University Press.

Hawley, P. H., & Little, T. D. (2002). Evolutionary and developmental perspectives on the agentic self. In D. Cervone & W. Mischel (Eds.), *Advances in personality science* (pp. 177–195). New York: Guilford.

Henderson, V., & Dweck, C. S. (1990). Adolescence and achievement. In S. Feldman & G. Elliott (Eds.), *At the threshold: The developing adolescent* (pp. 308–329). Cambridge, MA: Harvard University Press.

Keating, D. P. (1990) Adolescent thinking. In S. Feldman & G. Elliott (Eds.), *At the threshold: The developing adolescent* (pp. 55–89). Cambridge, MA: Harvard University Press.

Klayman, J. (1985). Children's decision strategies and their adaptation to task characteristics. *Organizational Behavior and Human Decision Process, 35,* 179–201.

Legerstee, M. (1992). A review of the animate-inanimate distinction in infancy. *Early Development and Parenting, 1*, 59–67.

Leslie, A. (1995). A theory of agency. In D. S. Sperber, D. P. Premack, & A. J. Premack (Eds.), *Causal cognition: A multidisciplinary approach* (pp. 121–141). New York: Clarendon.

Lewin, K. (1946). Behavior and development as a function of the total situation. In L. Carmichael (Ed.), *Manual of child psychology* (pp. 791–802). New York: Wiley.

Little, T. D. (1998). Sociocultural influences on the development of children's action-control beliefs. In J. Heckhausen & C. S. Dweck (Eds.), *Motivation and self-regulation across the life span* (pp. 281–315). New York: Cambridge University Press.

Lucariello, J., & Mindolovich, C. (1995). The development of complex metarepresentational reasoning: The case of situational irony. *Cognitive Development, 10*, 551–576.

MacTurk, R. H., McCarthy, M. E., Vietze P., & Yarrow, L. J. (1987). Sequential analysis of mastery behavior in 6 to 12 month old infants. *Developmental Psychology, 23*, 199–203.

Markus, H., & Kitayama, S. (1991). Culture and the self: Implications for cognition. Psychological Review, 98, 224–253.

Meacham, J. A. (1984). The social basis of intentional action. *Human Development, 27,* 119–124.

Meltzoff, A. N. (1995). Understanding the intentions of others: Re-enactment of intended acts by 18-month-old children. *Developmental Psychology, 31,* 838–850.

Meltzoff, A. N., Gopnik, A., & Repacholi, B. M. (1999). Toddler's understanding of intentions, desires, and emotions. In P. D. Zelazo, J. W. Astington, & D. R. Olson, (Eds.), *Developing theories of intention: Social understanding and self-control* (pp. 17–41). Mahwah, NJ: Lawrence Erlbaum Associates.

Mischel, H. N. (1984). From intention to action: The role of rule knowledge in the development of self-regulation. *Human Development, 27,* 193–196.

Moore, C., & Dunham, P. (Eds.). (1995). *Joint attention: Its origins and role in development.* Hillsdale, NJ: Lawrence Erlbaum Associates.

Norman, D. A., & Shallice, T. (1986). Attention to action: Willed and automatic control of control of behavior. In R. J. Davidson, G. E. Schwartz, & D. Shapiro (Eds.), *Consciousness and self-regulation.* (Vol. 4, pp. 1–18). New York: Plenum.

Perner, J., & Clements, W. A. (1997). From and implicit to an explicit "theory of mind." In Y. Rossetti & A. Revonsuo (Eds.), *Dissociation BUT interaction between conscious and nonconscious processing.* Amsterdam, John Benjamins.

Perner, J., Stummer, S., & Lang, B. (1999). Executive functions and theory of mind: Cognitive complexity or functional dependence? In P. D. Zelazo, J. W. Astington, & D. R. Olson, (Eds.), *Developing theories of intention: Social understanding and self-control* (pp. 133–152) Mahwah, NJ: Lawrence Erlbaum Associates.

Pintrich, P. R., & De Groot, E. V. (1990). Motivational and self-regulated learning components classroom academic performance. *Journal of Educational Psychology, 82*, 33–40.

Repacholi, B. M. (1998). Infant's use of attentional cues to identify the referent of another person's emotional expression. *Developmental Psychology, 34,* 12–21.

Rogoff, B., & Lave, J. (Eds.). (1984). *Everyday cognition: Its development in social context.* Cambridge, MA: Harvard University Press.

Russell, J. (1995). At two with nature: Agency and the development of self-world. In J. L. Bermudez, A. Marcel, & N. Eilan (Eds.), *The body and the self* (p. 326). Cambridge, MA: MIT Press.

Russell, J. (1996). *Agency: Its role in mental development.* East Sussex, England: Lawrence Erlbaum Associates.

Schliemann, A. D., & Nunes, T. (1990). A situated schema of proportionality. *British Journal of Developmental Psychology, 8,* 259–268.

Schraw, G., & Impara, J. (Eds.). (2000). *Issues in the measurement of metacognition.* Lincoln, NE: Buros Institute of Mental Measurements, University of Nebraska.

Schwanenflugel, P., Fabricius, W., & Alexander, J. (1994). Developing theories of mind: Understanding concepts and relations between mental activities. *Child Development, 65,* 1546–1563.

Shweder, R. A. (1990). Cultural psychology—what is it? In J. W. Stigler, R. A. Shweder, & G. Herdt (Eds.), *Cultural psychology: Essays on comparative human development* (pp 1–43). Cambridge, England: Cambridge University Press.

Skinner, E. A. (1995). *Perceived control, motivation, and coping.* Beverly Hills, CA: Sage.

Skinner, E. A., Chapman, M., & Baltes, P. B. (1988). Children's beliefs about control, means-ends, and agency: Developmental differences during middle childhood. *International Journal of Behavioral Development, 11,* 369–388.

Spelke E. S., & Newport, E. (1998). Nativism, empiricism, and the development of knowledge. In W. Damon (Series Ed.) & R. M. Lerner (Vol. Ed.), *Theoretical models of human development: Vol. 1. Handbook of child psychology* (5th ed., pp. 807–863) New York: Wiley.

Sperber, D., Premack, D., & Premack, A. J. (Eds.). (1995). *Causal cognition: A multidisciplinary debate.* Oxford, England: Oxford University Press.

Stipek, D. J., & Weisz, J. R. (1981). Perceived personal control and academic achievement. *Review of Educational Research, 51*(1), 101–137.

Tomasello, M. (1995). Joint attention as social cognition. In C. Moore & P. Dunham (Eds.), *Joint attention: Its origins and role in development* (pp. 103–130). Hillsdale, NJ: Lawrence Erlbaum Associates.

Tomasello, M. (1999). Having intentions, understanding intentions, and understanding communicative intentions. In P. D. Zelazo, J. W. Astington, & D. R. Olson (Eds.), *Developing theories of intention: Social understanding and self-control* (pp. 63–75). Mahwah, NJ: Lawrence Erlbaum Associates.

Vinden, P. G., & Astington, J. W. (2000). Culture and understanding other minds. In S. Baron-Cohen, H. Tage-Flusberg, & D. Cohen (Eds.), *Understanding other minds: Perspectives from developmental cognitive neuroscience* (2nd ed., pp. 503–520). Oxford, England: Oxford University Press.

Walls, T. A. (2002). *Relations among agency beliefs, motivational self-regulation, and academic performance in adolescence.* Doctoral dissertation, Lynch School of Education, Boston College. (UMI No. AAT 3043419)

Walls, T. A., & Little, T. D. (2005). Personal agency, motivation, and school adjustment in early adolescence. *Journal of Educational Psychology, 97*(1), 23–31.

Walls, T. A. & Schafer, J. L (Eds.). (2006). *Models for intensive longitudinal data.* New York: Oxford University Press.

Wellman, H. M., Cross, D., & Watson, J. (2001). Meta-analysis of theory of mind development: The truth about false belief. *Child Development, 72*(3), 655–684.

Wertsch, J. V. (1984). The multiple levels of analysis in a theory of action. *Human Development, 27,* 193–196.

Wertsch, J. V. (1985). *Vygotsky and the social formation of mind.* Cambridge, MA: Harvard University Press.

Wimmer, H., & Perner, J. (1983). Beliefs about beliefs: Representation and constraining function of wrong beliefs in young children's understanding of deception. *Cognition, 13,* 103–128.

Wynn, K. (1992). Addition and subtraction by human infants. *Nature, 358,* 749–750.

13

Emotion Regulation and Personality Development in Childhood

Carolyn Saarni
Sonoma State University

The construct emotion regulation has links both to individual temperament and to attachment style. These, in turn, are associated with personality development in childhood. The discussion of these theoretical and empirical linkages also includes a brief overview of the kinds of research that have investigated how emotion regulation contributes to individual differences in social competence.

THE CONSTRUCT OF EMOTION REGULATION

Emotion regulation has almost as many definitions as it has researchers studying the phenomena that are thought to be evidence of emotion regulation. The following definition is used here:

> The ability to manage one's subjective experience of emotion, especially its intensity and duration, and to manage strategically one's expression of emotion in communicative contexts. Optimal emotion regulation also contributes to a sense of well-being, a sense of self-efficacy, and a sense of connectedness to others. (See also Thompson, 1994; Walden & Smith, 1997.) (Saarni, 1999, p. 220)

What is important to note about this definition is that there are two components to emotion regulation: The first has to do with how the subjective experience of emotional arousal is modulated (intensity, duration), which will generally be a more covert process, although a flushed neck or face, trembling hands, respiration rate, and perspiration are all visible indicators of the individual's emotional arousal. The second part has to do with the way a person manages the external or overt expression of emotion, particularly when engaged in a social exchange. Social psychologists studying nonverbal behavior in interpersonal contexts have referred to this as self-presentation (e.g., Baumeister, 1993). The second sentence in this definition might at first glance appear to imply that adaptive emotion regulation entails only positive emotional experience. This would be far too simplistic, because being able to experience negative emotions such as empathy with another's distress, grief, guilt, morally justified anger, and so forth are also part of adaptive emotion regulation. These "negative" emotions allow individuals to connect with others through seeking and providing support when they experience loss and sadness, to protest injustice with morally justified anger, and to amend and repair those actions that have injured others when they feel guilt. As this chapter elaborates under links between emotion regulation and social functioning, there are a number of studies that suggest *effective* emotion regulation is associated with enhanced social competence, well-being, and self-confidence.

An issue not included in the previous definition, but that I think does need to be addressed, is another way individuals regulate emotion. They avoid those situations from past learning that will likely evoke aversive emotions (shame, anxiety) or seek out those situations in which they can anticipate pleasurable outcomes (happiness, tranquility). Thus, basic approach/avoidance preferences that individuals acquire function as regulators of what they are exposed to, thereby reducing or enhancing the likelihood of experiencing various emotions. More on this subject will be included in the discussion of temperament and developmental contributors to emotion regulation.

It is important to distinguish two related constructs from emotion regulation: *emotional reactivity* and *emotion generation*. The former is best defined as a biological bias relative to the threshold for emotion elicitation, and the discussion of temperament elaborates on how emotional reactivity may have its source in early patterns of temperament. Emotion generation is more complex. This discussion takes Gross' perspective on emotion generation (Gross & John, 2003), which is that emotion unfolds over time (albeit very short), and thus emotion regulation strategies can be applied at different points during that temporal dimension. Gross also emphasized the appraisal processes that occur during the temporal unfolding of emotion, with the result that it is possible to regulate the experience of emotion (e.g., its intensity, duration) by modifying the meanings attributed to potentially emotion-evoking situations. Gross referred to this as antecedent-focused emotion regulation. Alternatively, it is possible to focus on the second part of emotion regulation in the definition noted previously and attempt to suppress, minimize, maximize, or substitute the expressive display of an individual's emotion. Gross called this response-focused emotion regulation. (Note: Gross and his colleagues investigated only the suppression of expressive response, not whether one minimizes or maximizes the emotion expression or substitutes another emotion expression, such as smiling when feeling socially anxious).

HOW DOES EMOTION REGULATION FUNCTION?

To make matters even more complicated, researchers have used the construct of emotion regulation to study how something else is modified as a function of emotion regulation. For example, individuals might choose a problem-solving strategy to cope with some stressful situation as opposed to simple avoidance, depending on whether they have reduced the intensity of their felt emotion. If the intensity of their emotional arousal is too great, then they are more likely to flee the stress-inducing situation; by regulating one's emotional intensity such that they are not overwhelmed by it, they can scan the situation, their resources, and their support system for strategies that might resolve the source of distress. In this example, emotion regulation plays a *mediating* role in how individuals cope with a particular taxing situation: Modulation of one's emotional response allows for a different sort of coping behavior than simple flight or avoidance. However, emotion regulation might in other contexts play a *moderating* role; for example, sustaining the duration of the expressive display of happiness (a genuine smile) influences the likelihood that individuals' interactant will respond positively in kind. In other words, regulation of emotional-expressive behavior often increases or decreases the sorts of social interaction one desired with another (see, e.g., discussion of emotion communication in interpersonal negotiation, relationship repair, enhancement of intimacy, etc. in Saarni & Buckley, 2002).

Lastly, a number of studies have examined how emotion *regulates* other behaviors (e.g., anxiety facilitates self-protective behaviors), processes (attention deployment, effortful control, e.g., Eisenberg et al., 2004), or even other people's responses (e.g., a child's fear elicits protective behavior in her caregiver; for relevant reviews, see Thompson, 1995; Walden & Smith, 1997). This body of research should be distinguished from the aforementioned discussion focusing on the regulation of emotion. To illustrate this distinction, consider how a fearful child withdraws from a scary situation, but her frightened expressive behavior and wariness is noted by her father, and he reaches out supportively and with appropriate "scaffolding" helps his daughter to tolerate the fearful situation until she can feel more masterful toward it. Subsequently, she is able to regulate her arousal sufficiently to approach the formerly feared situation with curiosity and even a sense of adventure. Her emotion, fear, regulates her behavior such that she withdraws, but her fear also influences her father's behavior toward her, and he responds with encouragement as he reframes how to make sense of the situation. The father's behavior exerts a reciprocal influence on her emotional response such that she becomes able to risk approaching the formerly feared situation, finds out that it can be pleasurable, and her appraisal of what was once scary is replaced by positive anticipation. Mutually regulating behaviors that involve the exchange of emotional signals has a long history of research, for the most part with infants and their caregivers (for relevant reviews, see Trevarthen, 1984, 1993). Less research has been undertaken with school-age children, but a number of studies suggest that children are well-aware that their expressive displays (self-presentation) influence their peers' subsequent responses to them (e.g., Carlson Jones, Abbey, & Cumberland, 1998; Gottman, Guralnick, Wilson, Swanson, & Murray, 1997; Halberstadt, Denham, & Dunsmore, 2001; Hubbard, 2001; Parker et al., 2001; Saarni, 1984, 1988; Saarni & Weber, 1999; Underwood & Hurley, 1999; von Salisch, 1996; Zeman & Shipman, 1997).

EMOTION REGULATION AND TEMPERAMENT

Temperament is broadly defined as a biologically based disposition of reactivity to stimuli and concomitantly the degree of likelihood in modulating that reactivity. Furthermore, investigators of temperament believe that there are relatively stable individual differences in temperament, such individual differences are observable early in a child's life, and there is moderate continuity in temperamental dispositions from one age period to the next, although not necessarily across multiple age periods except for extreme temperament patterns (e.g., Bates, 2000; Goldsmith, 1993; Rothbart & Bates, 1998). Investigators of temperament also tend to view regulation of emotional arousal (intensity, duration) as a component of temperament, and some might argue that there is little difference between temperamental *traits* (i.e., reliably observed disposition of reactivity and modulation of that reactivity) and emotion regulation *styles* (i.e., the preferred propensity for how to manage emotional arousal and expression). However, temperament is relatively global, both in its conceptualization and its assessment, when applied to how a specific instance of emotion regulation unfolds in an individual's experience. More specifically, temperament is a general proclivity within an individual to approach or withdraw from a novel situation and to react strongly or not to a novel situation; temperament is not the same as the emotional response elicited in the individual that requires regulation, rather temperament can be thought of as the background on which the emotion plays out. Emotions are also highly contextualized and dependent on the individual's goals and motives of the moment (J. J. Campos, Mumme, Kermoian, & R. G. Campos, 1994; Lewis, 1997); their nuances and variety are captured by the huge number of emotion-related words in the English language (White, 2000).

Metaphorically, temperament is rather like a season of the year, whereas emotions are the mercurial weather conditions that shift from day to day, demanding adjustment and accommodation on a frequent basis. Within this metaphor, the season provides constraints on the daily weather, just as temperament may provide some degree of limitation on the experience of emotional response. Temperament influences emotion regulation as in figure-ground relations; it is the "ground," whereas emotions and their regulation are the "figure." Thus, the child who is relatively inhibited in temperament (prone to withdrawal from novel situations) and who tends to react strongly to novel situations (less likely to modulate intensity) may be the child who will more often experience emotions of anxiety, fear, and shame. But this same child may also be more likely to respond to familiar situations with pleasure, sympathy, and caring. Indeed, the more inhibited child is also the one who is more compliant with parents and internalizes a moral conscience more readily than those young children characterized as more bold and active (reviewed in Kochanska & Thompson, 1997).

A cautionary note should be made at this point about the reliability over time and across situations in the assessment of temperament. Different raters of a given child's temperamental characteristics often do not correlate well (e.g., mothers vs. teachers; Eisenberg, Fabes, Nyman, Bernzweig, & Pinuelas, 1994), and using the same rater to evaluate a child's temperament in different contexts may yield disappointing results as well. For example, Goldsmith and Campos (1982) found that toddlers' fearfulness as they approached a visual cliff bore little relation to the toddlers' fearfulness when a stranger approached them. Lewis (2001) argued for a "strong" contextualist position and noted that until researchers measure continuity in environments, there will be only a limited understanding of how temperament, emotion regulation, and personality may be related because a critical part of the equation is being left out, that is, behavior does not occur in a vacuum; it occurs in highly nuanced situations. Children, their families, and their peers may also jointly create consistencies in environments, thereby also contributing to coherence in functioning at the individual level (see further contextual arguments by Lerner, 1998). Indeed, most developmental research addressing "context" primarily examines rather broad environmental influence such as poverty, ethnicity, or culture (e.g., Cole, Brushi, & Tamang, 2002; Garner & Spears, 2000). Less frequently examined are how the same children's emotion regulation strategies vary across different situations (but see Saarni, 1989, 1991, 1995; Underwood, Coie, & Herbsman, 1992; Zeman & Garber, 1996).

Lastly, it bears mentioning that the cultural context and its folk theories and beliefs about how emotion "works" is relevant to how people think of emotion regulation and temperament. The following four rather facetious metaphors for North American folk beliefs about emotion regulation have been described elsewhere:

- The volcano theory ("if you don't vent your emotions, you'll explode");
- The tidal wave theory ("don't lose control, or your feelings will build up until they overwhelm you");
- The out-of-sight/out-of-mind theory ("if you don't think about your feelings, they'll go away");
- The Vulcan theory from the *Star Trek* television series ("your emotions are irrational and illogical, surely they get in the way of solving problems"). (Saarni, 1999, p. 58)

These folk beliefs are similar to scripts (e.g., Abelson, 1981) and are acquired by children in the socializing milieus in which they live (Lillard, 1998; Lock, 1981; Lutz, 1985). Indeed, all four of the previous facetious scripts or beliefs can be supported at one time or another, but it would be interesting to know which contexts tend to elicit which belief as a more salient script and which contexts do not. There is very little research that has systematically explored children's beliefs about *emotional arousal regulation* relative to contexts, although one exception is a study by Harris and Lipian (1989), who did find that hospitalized children seemed to believe that negative emotions were pervasive and unyielding, whereas children newly arrived at boarding school did acknowledge that with time they would feel less homesick if they distracted themselves and/or did not think about their distress. On the other hand, there is a substantial body of work that has examined children's and youth's understanding of when to express their emotions (e.g., Gnepp & Hess, 1986; Saarni, 1979, 1989, 1991, 1997; Saarni & Weber, 1999; Underwood et al., 1992; von Salisch, 1996; Zeman & Garber, 1996; Zeman & Shipman, 1997, 1998).

DEVELOPMENTAL CONTRIBUTORS TO EMOTION REGULATION

A rich literature has emerged over the last 20 years that provides considerable descriptive detail about how children's emotion regulation (both arousal modulation and expression management) is influenced by parents, peers, traumatic events, and even at the more macrolevel by media, community, and culture (for reviews, see Calkins, 1994; Cicchetti, Ackerman, & Izard, 1995; Coates, Feldman, & Philippot, 1999; Denham, 1999; Fabes, 2002; Fox, 1994; Garner & Spears, 2000; Halberstadt et al., 2001; Saarni, 1999). My comments are restricted to several key sources of influence on children's emotion regulation and to how emotion regulation changes as a function of these influences: caregiver scaffolding, parental coaching and meta-emotion, and trauma exposure.

Caregiver Scaffolding

Infants and young children rely heavily on their caregivers to provide safe environments, that is, situations in which distress is limited and the young child's ability to cope is assured (e.g., Denham, 1999). The young child's caregivers can be thought of as gatekeepers: They limit what their child is exposed to and they also channel the child toward situations considered to be desirable. Obviously, caregivers also support and comfort their children when they are distressed or encourage them to approach a situation that the caregiver views as desirable but the children do not (e.g., the earlier example of the father who encourages his daughter to approach a feared situation). Ratner and Stettner's (1991) term "intersubjectivity" is useful when describing how parents and their children mutually influence one another's emotional responses due to their shared history of repeated emotion-laden interactions with one another. When children experience a particular emotion, for example, fear, their prior interactions with their parents when they felt fear previously are also evoked as representations accompanying the present fear response. Thus, if the parents typically responded with reassurance and support, their child's experience of fear is buffered by that set of representations or shared meanings. On the other hand, if their experience of fear with their parents was chronically reacted to with negative judgment or derogation, then their current experience of fear is not buffered but may become blended with shame, withdrawal, and anxiety about the self's integrity. Needless to say, the former child can probably better cope with the fear-inducing situation without becoming overwhelmed, whereas the latter child may well feel demoralized and diminished.

Caregiver influence of infants' and toddlers' emotional experience has also been heavily researched from the standpoint of social referencing: When in an ambiguous and potentially arousing situation, the infant looks to its caregiver for emotional-expressive cues that will define the emotional meaning of this interpersonal encounter. The caregiver's expressive response helps the infant to regulate both its arousal and its behavior (e.g., Feinman, 1992; Walden, 1991). Obviously, social referencing is something that people do when in an emotionally and/or socially ambiguous situation, but it becomes particularly noticeable toward the end of the first year when infants intentionally use their caregivers as sources of information, thereby activating and elaborating an intersubjectively shared set of emotion meanings. Dix (1991) also persuasively argued for the importance of understanding how caregivers' emotions are managed in so far as they influence care-giving behaviors directed at their children. This is undoubtedly of critical importance when it is the children's emotional displays that elicit caregivers' emotional responses, but it is also significant in caregivers' pervasive mood disturbances, most notably depression (e.g., Field, 1994).

As an illustration of the sort of research that appropriately appreciates the complexity and reciprocity involved in parent–infant emotion communication, I shall briefly comment on Spinrad and Stifter's (2002) short-term longitudinal research on 87 mother–infant pairs. They adapted their study from Lewis, Allessandri, and Sullivan (1990), who undertook a cross-sectional design investigating infants' expectancies about their caregivers' behaviors and their subsequent anger reactions. Spinrad and Stifter followed the 87 mother–infant pairs from when the infants were 5 months until they were 10 months, a period during which significant development occurs (e.g., crawling, stranger awareness, separation anxiety). When the infants were 5 months old, the mothers were told to restrain their baby's arm while maintaining a neutral face. At age 10 months, mothers played with their infants briefly with a very attractive toy, then the mothers removed the toy while keeping it visible, again maintaining a neutral facial expression. Not surprisingly, most infants were frustrated by these events, displaying expressions that were coded as angry or distressed, although from 6% to 7% of expressions coded at the two ages were positive. Cluster analyses yielded three patterns of infant emotional response that were similar at both ages: an angry-distressed combination, an intensely angry response with few distress and low positive expressions, and a positive affect response.

However, the stability of whether an infant would be in the same cluster from 5 to 10 months was not evident in that as many as from 40% to 60% of the infants changed clusters. But this is where there is dynamic interplay of emotion communication and caregiver scaffolding: How does one account for 41% of the infants in the first two negative reactivity clusters at 5 months becoming classified as displaying positive reactivity at 10 months? Their mothers had figured out that if they have a cranky baby, they should be prepared to actively distract them from the source of their distress. Although the authors coded such distracting behavior as "intrusive," they acknowledged that this maternal behavior may be effective in providing an avenue for frustrated infants to modulate their initial response by changing their attention to the distraction provided by their mothers, thereby attenuating their initial negative reaction. A fascinating longitudinal follow-up study to undertake would be to see if such infants at later ages began to internalize their mothers' regulatory efforts such that they learned to distract themselves from sources of distress or frustration.

Somewhat parallel research has been undertaken with toddlers judged to be temperamentally inhibited (based on their fearful reactions to an automated robot and clown), who subsequently at age 7 were judged to have moved toward an average degree of sociability (Fox, Sobel, Calkins, & Cole, 1996). In this study, the judgment of degree of inhibition at age 7 was based on observations of the children's social withdrawal when playing with a same-gender quartet of children and on an extensive interview with the children after they had watched a videotape of themselves at age 2 having to deal with the robot and clown. The largest proportion (45%) of children at age 7 were those who had changed from being inhibited at age 2 to being relatively uninhibited at age 7. Interestingly, these children were girls. Among 7-year-old boys, 31% also changed, but this time from having been uninhibited at age 2 to becoming inhibited at age 7. Fox et al. suggested that this latter shift may be due to acquiring self-conscious shyness as opposed to the earlier fearful shyness that was assessed at age 2, which had been elicited by the approaching robot and clown. For those children who changed temperament groups, Fox et al. found that they were unusually self-reflective about their change, and those children who became relatively uninhibited at age 7 frequently attributed their change to responsive care-giving, such as their parents introducing them gently to new or stressful situations. The children (largely boys) who became inhibited at age 7 attributed their change to concerns about the way their peers perceived them, and they tended to be self-critical. It is unknown whether that self-criticalness is a quality that they internalized from parental criticalness or derogation (see discussion of parental coaching in the next section).

Parental Coaching and Meta-Emotion

Gottman, Katz, & Hooven (1997) defined parental coaching of emotion in the following way: (a) Parents are aware of their child's emotion, (b) they see their child's emotional experience as a learning opportunity, (c) they help their child to label or verbalize feelings, (d) they empathize and validate their child's emotions, and (e) they assist their child in dealing with the distressing circumstances. Gottman, et al. (1997) followed a number of families for 3 years, beginning when the target children were 5 years old, and examined how the children changed during this time in how they regulated emotion and deployed their attention. If the parents were effective emotion-coaches, they helped their children learn to engage "with the world cognitively or affectively by self-soothing, inhibiting negative affect and focusing attention" (Gottman et al., 1997, p. 105). This ability to regulate emotional reactions and to focus attention translated into the children successfully negotiating the many transitions associated with school entry. By age 8, these children were functioning well socially and academically.

Gottman et al. argued that effective parent coaching of emotion is part of a *meta-emotion system*, which is essentially a complex network of beliefs and feelings about how emotions "work," especially the emotions anger and sadness. They interviewed the parents extensively about their own experience of negative emotions, including how such emotions were elicited, coped with, and given meaning. In a sense, they determined what the parents' implicit emotion theories were, similar to the folk theories of emotion mentioned previously. Based on the parents' meta-emotion beliefs, Gottman et al. were also able to predict which children would not be faring so well at age 8: These children had parents who were prone to derogate and provided insufficient scaffolding/praising in the preschool years.

Similar results have been obtained by other investigators. For example, Denham and her associates (reviewed in Denham, 1999) conducted a number of studies with preschool-age children and their parents, typically their mothers. The overall pattern they found has been that mothers who talked about emotions with their young children, expressed predominantly positive emotions, responded to their children's emotion calmly and reassuringly, and used emotion-laden explanations in their discipline tactics tended to have children whose emotional-expressive behavior was better regulated and who were socially more competent with peers. In short, such mothers had children who were both happier and more self-confident.

Attachment and Emotion Regulation

Eisenberg and her associates (Eisenberg, Cumberland, & Spinrad, 1998) undertook an extensive literature review on the socialization of emotion, and similar to the preceding discussion, they also concluded that the negative emotionality of parents in conjunction with their negative reaction to their children's emotional experience were key features that predicted their children's own negative emotionality and impoverished social competence in preschool and early elementary school grades. Relative to the earliest effects that parents have on their infants' emotional experience, Eisenberg et al. further examined the attachment literature for how infants and toddlers' emotion regulation was influenced. Their review suggests that sensitive and

responsive parents have infants who in the first months of life show a decrease in crying in contrast to relatively insensitive parents whose infants increase their crying.
The former infants have presumably learned ways to sooth themselves or become
less reactive to stimuli. Eisenberg et al. cautioned the reader that an infant's attachment status (secure vs. insecure) may be just as much determined by the young infant's temperament qualities of irritability, intensity of reactivity, and soothability as
by the parents' contingent sensitivity (e.g., Calkins, 1994).

Thompson (1998) also exhaustively reviewed the attachment literature relative
to early social and personality development. Paramount in his view is that infants
learn to expect *social responses* to their emotional cues, particularly to distress. The
social response is ideally coming from a responsive caregiver, who provides support,
comfort, and distraction. But the social response may be from a caregiver who is distant or uninvested in the infant. Then the social response may be hostile, evasive, intrusive, or inappropriate to the infant's emotional display and situation.

Thompson addressed a dilemma within the attachment literature in which some
investigators endorse a very broad view of attachment and others take a more narrow
view of attachment. The broad view argues that infant attachment experience is robust and continuous, despite later changes in caregiving quality, and attachment status profoundly affects early personality development, including such features as
self-representations, interpersonal orientation, and social skills. On the other hand,
proponents of the narrow view of attachment contend that attachment status can
vary with subsequent changes in care-giving quality and attachment should be considered in the context of other kinds of social interaction the infant experiences.
Cultural context and variable meaning of parent–infant interactions would also be
taken into account. Discontinuity would therefore be far more likely from the latter
standpoint, particularly if caregiving quality and consistency changes.

If we ask how does attachment experience affects personality development, depending on one's perspective, broad or narrow, our conclusion would be either all encompassing (e.g., Sroufe, 1996) or more contextually defined (e.g., Lamb, 1987).
The view herein leans toward a more contextually influenced position: Individuals'
early social experiences do influence them, but not with fixity or easy predictability.
To the degree that children's experience within their family is fairly consistent, there
is more likely to be continuity in those children's representations of self and others,
growth of social skills, and ability to regulate emotional arousal and emotional expressiveness, depending on their goals and incentives at the moment. But research
that takes into account contextual influence and discontinuity suggests that there
may be less predictability in ways of regulating emotional arousal and expression,
particularly when looking across large chunks of time as in longitudinal studies. For
example, Lewis (2000) found in a longitudinal study that children who had initially
been rated as securely attached as toddlers were—subsequent to their parents'
divorce—more likely to be evaluated as insecurely attached in adolescence.

A landmark longitudinal study that also dramatically demonstrated discontinuity
in emotional development (attachment per se was not assessed) was carried out by
Murphy and Moriarty (1976). They followed a number of children from birth to early
adulthood. What they repeatedly found was that a number of seemingly vulnerable
infants (due to difficult temperaments, prematurity, inadequate parenting, etc.) began to develop abilities in the preschool years such that they could persist in the face

of pressures or threats. Those children who were effective tended to progress through their childhood and adolescence with resilience. They were the "good copers," and in many respects what they demonstrated was adaptive emotional regulation: Even when faced with serious setbacks and episodes of very distressing emotional experience, they were able to "ride out the storm," handle anxiety and tolerate frustration, seek help when needed, and adapt flexibly to alternatives.

Exposure to Trauma and Its Effects on Emotion Regulation

To begin with, *crisis* needs to be differentiated from *trauma*. Both refer to catastrophic events, but crises require individuals to reorganize their coping style, supports, and even personality structure such as following the "developmental crises" proposed by Erickson (1968). To quote Lazarus (1999): "The disturbances generated by the crisis have demonstrated that the previous [personality] structure is not equal to the task of managing life without this personality reorganization" (p. 162). Trauma, on the other hand, is a catastrophe for which the individual cannot find meaning (Lazarus, 1999), at least not for a significant period of time. If individuals cannot appraise the catastrophe as at all meaningful, then their flood of emotions overwhelms their ability to cope, with the result they feel little or no control over the crisis-producing circumstances or of the self. Parenthetically, psychotherapy treatment for posttraumatic reactions often involves developing meaning for the traumatic event (e.g., Janoff-Bulman & Frantz, 1997). To some extent, this difference in "meaning-attribution" is an important source of individual differences in reactions to catastrophes: one person's crisis is another person's trauma. In the first case, the motivational effects of crises tend to mobilize people, their resources, and their supports for coping, whereas in the second situation the numbing effects of trauma tend to leave people feeling immobilized when overwhelmed by trauma.

There is an immense body of literature on the maltreatment of children and its posttraumatic effects (e.g., hypervigilance, internalizing and/or externalizing behavior patterns, dissociation, truncated problem-solving coping skills, deficits in understanding emotional experience both in oneself and in others, deficits in accessing an emotion lexicon and the concomitant representation of emotional experience, deficits in empathy, maladaptive patterns of emotional interpersonal communication, and, not surprisingly, low self-regard). A comprehensive review of child maltreatment and appropriate psychosocial interventions is found in the *APSAC Handbook on Child Maltreatment* (Briere & Berliner, 1996). Elsewhere there are summaries of empirical studies on how children respond to maltreatment, serious loss, and exposure to family violence in so far as these crises become traumatizing experiences when the children involved cannot meaningfully manage or cope with the catastrophic circumstances; such victimized children are likely to have problems in acquiring the skills of emotional competence (Saarni, 1999).

This chapter highlights the more specific effects of serious and chronic traumatizing experience that a child may be forced to endure and how such a child might be expected to develop an emotion regulation style that works—after a fashion—to protect the child while the traumatizing crisis is current, but is likely to prove maladaptive when the child is in nontraumatizing settings. In terms of understanding personality development, it is important to recognize how events that happen to children can shape their future personality traits, but this "shaping" is probably medi-ated and moderated by a variety of cognitive, social, and emotional changes in the child, including emotion regulation. Again, from a contextualist perspective, it is also important to differentiate a single episode of acute crisis versus chronic and per-sistent exposure to traumatizing events, with the latter more often being maltreat-ment and/or witnessing family violence. Furthermore, maladaptive emotional and behavioral sequelae in the child, who suffers maltreatment, is undoubtedly influ-enced by what happened before the abuse occurred and by what happens after the abusive incident (Alexander, 1992; Cole & Putnam, 1992).

When a person is extremely stressed and intensely emotionally reactive, a cre-scendo of neurohormones is released, including cortisol, epinephrine, vasopressin, oxytocin, and endogeous opioids, among others (Van der Kolk & Saporta, 1991). These neurohormones mobilize the individual to deal with the stressor, but when the stressor becomes chronic (as in prolonged military combat or on-going child mal-treatment), desensitization or numbing also paradoxically develops along with hyperarousal to "triggering" stimuli that are similar to those initially associated with the traumatic stressor (Bradley, 2000). At the moment of the acute, overwhelming, and uncontrollable catastrophic event, such desensitization may be adaptive, just as the subsequent hypervigilance for cues suggestive of a recurrence of such traumatizing events may also be adaptive. But maladaptive problems develop when the catastrophic/traumatizing events recur episodically, resulting in chronically traumatized individuals developing a biased perception of the world and disturbed information processing. Not surprisingly, their ability to cope by using resourceful problem solving becomes limited in part due to difficulties in effective attention de-ployment: If a person is only looking for cues of threat, it is hard to see anything else that might be strategically useful for dealing with distress. Even the ability to linguis-tically represent one's internal affective states may become problematic ("alexithymia"; see Krystal, 1988). Thus, exposure to chronic stressors that are expe-rienced by individuals as traumatizing impairs their ability to cope effectively or to seek appropriate support from others who can exert control over the acute stressors.

A number of studies have indicated that maltreated children also have different patterns of neuroendocrine activity (see Bradley, 2000, for a review). One intriguing study found that cortisol levels in maltreated children appeared associated with im-paired social competence, particularly high incidence of externalizing behavior (Hart & Gunnar, 1995). Interestingly, these investigators found that maltreated pre-schoolers showed reduced cortisol reactivity ("blunted cortisol distributions") in contrast to a comparison sample of young children drawn from a similarly low socio-economic community. The maltreated children also showed reduced cortisol reac-tivity during periods of peer or teacher conflict, again in contrast to the comparison children, whose cortisol levels increased when social conflicts erupted in their class-rooms. It was not clear what the blunted cortisol reactivity means for these mal-treated children; the authors suggested that it might shield the children from some of the negative effects of chronically high levels of cortisol, in that some sort of neuroendocrine accommodation to repeated exposure to extreme stressors may have occurred. However, it is also interesting to speculate on whether or not some of these maltreated children grow up to exhibit what has been referred to as "callous personality traits" (e.g., Frick et al., 2003). Such research remains to be done, but a suggestive connection has been found in research done with juvenile delinquents exhibiting both conduct disorder and high callous traits, who showed a significant negative correlation between degree of callousness and trait anxiety when degree of behavioral disturbance was controlled for (Frick & Ellis, 1999).

Research on maltreated children and children exposed to family violence shows that many develop problems of behavioral control and aggressive, externalizing behavior (particularly boys); regrettably, some go on to develop conduct disorder (e.g., McCloskey, Figueredo, & Koss, 1995) and in adulthood may demonstrate antisocial personalities (Frick et al., 2003). Chronically traumatized girls, often due to repeated sexual abuse, appear to develop more often internalizing disorders, characterized by depression and anxiety; however, impulsivity and distractibility are also noteworthy in these girls as well (e.g., Feiring, Taska, & Lewis, 1996; Peters, 1988). Whether it is chronic exposure to family violence or chronic maltreatment, children's emotion regulation strategies are sorely taxed, and the developmental sequelae include representations of self that are often characterized by shame and stigma whereas their representations of others are characterized by distrust and fear (Briere & Berliner, 1996; Feiring et al., 1996).

PERSONALITY DEVELOPMENT AND INDIVIDUAL DIFFERENCES IN EMOTION REGULATION

There are further ways to investigate how emotion regulation plays a significant role in personality development. It is important to recall that the theoretical emphasis here is on the importance of context in how emotion regulation plays out in the immediate experience of the individual; therefore, I do not emphasize "enduring" individual differences in personality development, relative to emotion regulation. I also support a person-centered approach to personality development rather than a variable-focused approach, because the former emphasizes the dynamic organization of personality attributes rather than simply bundling together an assortment of traits. A program for future research should address how personality attributes are moderated and mediated by the emotion regulation strategies available to the individual, at a given point in time and relative to the contexts eliciting emotional responses. (Again, this refers to both facets of emotion regulation: arousal regulation and expression management.) Because individuals can also change very substantially over time, as suggested by several of the studies mentioned earlier (notably Fox et al., 1996, and Lewis, 2000), it becomes important for personality theorists to consider discontinuity in the organization of personality attributes; that is, the organization of personality itself changes with development.

Emotion Regulation as a Mediator of Personality

To illustrate how personality attributes might be mediated by emotion regulation strategies, assume that several kindergarten children are well-known to one another and are playing together under conditions of no distress. They all demonstrate to the observing personality researcher moderate levels of outgoingness, prosocial behavior, and imaginativeness. Then suddenly a much older child, a bully, walks up to them and while yelling various threats at them, kicks to pieces their cooperatively built tower of Lego blocks. Now, under conditions of distress, the children's attachment security is threatened, and there may be different emotion regulation strategies evoked depending on their attachment status and past experience in coping with bullies. Child A, securely attached, may be quite provoked and angry about the attack; the child calls over the yard teacher to intervene. Child B, insecurely and anxiously attached, starts to wail and clutch at the yard teacher. Child C, insecurely and avoidantly attached, withdraws. If the personality researcher now tried to evaluate these children's personality attributes, the result would be a different set of profiles of personality functioning as compared to those drawn based on the observations of these children prior to the experience with the bully: Child A would now be seen as assertive and resourceful; Child B would be seen as dependent and emotionally vulnerable, and Child C would be seen as inhibited and perhaps emotionally overcontrolled.

Zimmermann (1999) did something analogous to the previous scenario when he asked adolescents to respond to several questions about five hypothetical social rejection vignettes, about which they were to imagine that the various incidents of social rejection happened to them. He evaluated their open-ended responses in terms of how flexible their appraisal of the distressing social rejection was, how flexible and variable their behavioral strategies were for coping with the social rejection, and how clearly they could articulate how they would feel as well as what sort of rationale they provided for why they would feel that way. The resulting scores were transformed and aggregated to provide a score indicative of "adaptive emotion regulation." The adolescents were also rated by their best friend, their parents, and by two psychologists with the California Adult Q-sort (J. Block & J. Block, 1980) for degree of ego resiliency, which is often used as a personality prototype. The adolescents also responded to the Adult Attachment Interview (George, Kaplan, & Main, 1985). The results showed that the securely attached teens obtained a robustly positive correlation between "adaptive emotion regulation" and ego resiliency ($r = .57$), whereas for dismissing (insecure-avoidant) teens the correlation coefficient was $-.32$ and for preoccupied (insecure-preoccupied) teens it was $-.41$ (both significant). This research study suggests that personality organization, defined as ego resiliency, is likely mediated by style of emotion regulation, which in turn may be mediated by attachment history. The small sample size prohibited this kind of analysis, but Zimmermann's work is seminal in helping point the way in how theoretical models can be built for how personality organization changes as a function of emotion regulation style and attachment status. A more narrow view of attachment status (i.e., that it can vary with changes in the individual's significant relationships) requires including the situational influence on Zimmermann's youth: What if the two latter groups who obtained negative correlations between their regulation style and ego resilience also happened to include a number of teens whose parents had divorced in the preceding years (cf. Lewis, 2000)? Or what if these two groups included not only those with recent parental divorces but also some who had been rejected by their first "loves"? So now the mediational model would have to include the contextual influence of significant relationship change on personality organization.

Emotion Regulation as a Moderator of Personality

Relevant to how emotion regulation might moderate personality organization, that is, enhancement or diminishment of how personality attributes are manifested in behavior, are studies on children's and adolescents' understanding and use of self-presentational strategies and their capacity for self-monitoring relative to the demands of the immediate social transaction. Another rich area for research would be to create naturalistic scenarios in which children/youth interact with confederates whose behavior systematically varies so as to elicit different emotional expression management strategies. For example, Underwood's ingenious use of the insulting same-age confederate in a rigged computer game could be adapted to include additional interactions with a cooperative and socially responsive same-age confederate and subsequently with a whining, dependent, "poor-me" same-age confederate (Underwood, Hurley, Johanson, & Mosley, 1999). In their investigation, they found that boys and girls did not reveal angry expressions to any great degree when having to deal with the insulting confederate. Neutral expressions increased with age whereas sadness and the rare anger expressions decreased with age. The participating children (8–12 years) in Underwood's study had also been rated as popular, rejected, or aggressive, and to the investigators' surprise, the children nominated as aggressive by their peers behaved no differently with the provoking confederate child than non-aggressive children. These children also did not differ from the popular children. Interestingly, the rejected children were significantly more likely than other children to ask the researchers to stop the computer game before it came to an end, and these might have been the children who would have become very upset or angry if they had been forced "to stick it out" with the insulting confederate (Underwood & Hurley, 1999). In short, what Underwood's study suggests for organization of personality and emotion expression management is that context is very powerful indeed: An unfamiliar peer who behaves provocatively in a university lab facility elicits controlled and tightly managed expressive behavior in school-age children, regardless of whether an individual's personality is organized according to an aggressive trajectory or a socially adept trajectory. Thus, personality organization as observed in behavior can be moderated, given the right social circumstances.

CONCLUSIONS: FUTURE RESEARCH DIRECTIONS

Given that emotion regulation has two major components, the regulation of emotional arousal and the management of emotional expression, personality research should consider individual differences in these two facets separately. The former is likely to show up more in studies on "emotionality," and the latter more often in studies on "agreeableness" and "conscientiousness." Given my contextual bias, I would also like to see more research that systematically varies the situation in which personality organization or personality attributes are examined. For example, the social contextual dimensions of degree of affiliation and degree of dominance in conjunction with the dimension of how much control over a situation a person possesses profoundly influence individuals' coping strategies and emotional expressions (e.g., Aldwin, 1994; Lazarus, 1991). A program of studies could be designed that examines these contextual variables, including pervasive environmental variables such as culture and poverty, relative to how emotion regulation mediates and/or moderates personality organization as manifested in behavior or in attributions. Lastly, more research is needed that earnestly takes on the theoretical task of what exactly develops (as opposed to simple changes) in personality organization as children mature into adolescents and then become adults.

REFERENCES

Abelson, R. (1981). Psychological status of the script concept. *American Psychologist, 36,* 715–729.

Aldwin, C. (1994). *Stress, coping, and development.* New York: Guilford.

Alexander, P. C. (1992). Application of attachment theory to the study of sexual abuse. *Journal of Consulting and Clinical Psychology, 60,* 185–195.

Bates, J. E. (2000). Temperament as an emotion construct: Theoretical and practical issues. In M. Lewis & J. Haviland (Eds.), *Handbook of emotions* (2nd ed., pp. 382–396). New York: Guilford.

Baumeister, R. (1993). Self-presentation: Motivational, cognitive, and interpersonal patterns. In G. v. Heck, P. Bonaiuto, I. J. Deary, & W. Nowack (Eds.), *Personality psychology in Europe* (Vol. 4, pp. 257–280). Tilburg, The Netherlands: Tilburg University Press.

Block, J., & Block, J. (1980). The role of ego-control and ego-resiliency in the organization of behavior. In W. A. Collins (Ed.), *Development of cognition, affect, and social relations: The Minnesota Symposia on Child Psychology* (Vol. 13, pp. 39–101). Hillsdale, NJ: Lawrence Erlbaum Associates.

Bradley, S. J. (2000). *Affect regulation and the development of psychopathology.* New York: Guilford.

Briere, J., & Berliner, L. (Eds.). (1996). *The APSAC handbook on child maltreatment. (American Professional Society on the Abuse of Children).* Thousand Oaks, CA: Sage.

Calkins, S. D. (1994). Origins and outcomes of individual differences in emotion regulation. *Monographs of the Society for Research in Child Development, 59,* 53–72.

Campos, J. J., Mumme, D., Kermoian, R., & Campos, R. G. (1994). A functionalist perspective on the nature of emotion. *Monographs of the Society for Research in Child Development,* 284–303.

Carlson Jones, D., Abbey, B. B., & Cumberland, A. (1998). The development of display rule knowledge: Linkages with family expressiveness and social competence. *Child Development, 69,* 1209–1222.

Cicchetti, D., Ackerman, B., & Izard, C. (1995). Emotions and emotion regulation in developmental psychopathology. *Development and Psychopathology, 7,* 1–10.

Coates, E. J., Feldman, R. S., & Philippot, P. (1999). The influence of television on children's nonverbal behavior. In P. Philippot, R. S. Feldman, & E. J. Coats (Eds.), *The social context of nonverbal behavior* (pp. 156–181). Cambridge, England: Cambridge University Press.

Cole, P. M., Brushi, C., & Tamang, B. (2002). Cultural differences in children's emotional reactions to difficult situations. *Child Development, 73,* 983–996.

Cole, P. M., & Putnam, F. (1992). Effect of incest on self and social functioning: A developmental psychopathology perspective. *Journal of Consulting and Clinical Psychology, 60,* 174–184.

Denham, S. A. (1999). *Emotional development in young children.* New York: Guilford.

Dix, T. (1991). The affective organization of parenting: Adaptive and maladaptive processes. *Psychological Bulletin, 110,* 3–25.

Eisenberg, N., Cumberland, A., & Spinrad, T. (1998). Parental socialization of emotion. *Psychological Inquiry, 9,* 241–273.

Eisenberg, N., Fabes, R., Nyman, M., Bernzweig, J., & Pinuelas, A. (1994). The relations of emotionality and regulation to children's anger-related reactions. *Child Development, 65,* 109–128.

Eisenberg, N., Spinrad, T., Fabes, R., Reiser, M., Cumberland, A., Shepard, S., Valiente, C., Losoya, S., Guthrie, I., & Thompson, M. (2004). The relations of effortful control and impulsivity to children's resiliency and adjustment. *Child Development, 75,* 25–46.

Erikson, E. H. (1968). *Identity, youth, and crisis.* New York: Norton.

Fabes, R. (Ed.). (2002). *Emotions and the family.* New York: Haworth Press.

Feinman, S. (Ed.). (1992). *Social referencing and the social construction of reality in infancy.* New York: Plenum.

Feiring, C., Taska, L., & Lewis, M. (1996). A process model for understanding adaptation to sexual abuse: The role of shame in defining stigmatization. *Child Abuse and Neglect, 20,* 767–782.

Field, T. (1994). The effects of mother's physical and emotional unavailability on emotion regulation. *Monographs of the Society for Research in Child Development,* 208–227.

Fox, N. E. (1994). The development of emotion regulation: Behavioral and biological considerations. *Monographs of the Society for Research in Child Development, 59*(Serial No. 240).

Fox, N., Sobel, A., Calkins, S., & Cole, P. (1996). Inhibited children talk about themselves: Self-reflection on personality development and change in 7-year-olds. In M. Lewis & M. W. Sullivan (Eds.), *Emotional development in atypical children* (pp. 131–147). Mahwah, NJ: Lawrence Erlbaum Associates.

Frick, P. J., Cornell, A. H., Bodin, S. D., Dane, H. E., Barry, C. T., & Loney, B. R. (2003). Callous-unemotional traits and developmental pathways to severe conduct problems. *Developmental Psychology, 39,* 246–260.

Frick, P. J., & Ellis, M. L. (1999). Callous-unemotional traits and subtypes of conduct disorder. *Clinical Child and Family Psychology Review, 2,* 149–168.

Garner, P. W., & Spears, F. M. (2000). Emotion regulation in low-income preschool children. *Social Development, 9,* 246–264.

George, C., Kaplan, N., & Main, M. (1985). *The Attachment Interview for Adults.* Unpublished manuscript, University of California, Berkeley.

Gnepp, G., & Hess, D. L. R. (1986). Children's understanding of verbal and facial display rules. *Developmental Psychology, 22,* 103–108.

Goldsmith, H. (1993). Temperament: Variability in developing emotion systems. In M. Lewis & J. Haviland (Eds.), *Handbook of emotions* (pp. 353–364). New York: Guilford.

Goldsmith, H. H., & Campos, J. (1982). Toward a theory of infant temperament. In R. Emde & R. Harmon (Eds.), *The development of attachment and affiliative systems* (pp. 161–193). New York: Plenum.

Gottman, J., Katz, L. F., & Hooven, C. (1997). *Meta-emotion.* Hillsdale, NJ: Lawrence Erlbaum Associates.

Gottman, J. M., Guralnick, M., Wilson, B., Swanson, C., & Murray, J. (1997). What should be the focus of emotion regulation in children? A nonlinear dynamic mathematical model of children's peer interaction in groups. *Development and Psychopathology, 9,* 421–452.

Gross, J. J., & John, O. P. (2003). Individual differences in two emotion regulation processes: Implications for affect, relationships, and well-being. *Journal of Personality and Social Psychology, 85,* 348–362.

Halberstadt, A., Denham, S., & Dunsmore, J. (2001). Affective social competence. *Social Development, 10,* 79–119.

Harris, P., & Lipian, M. S. (1989). Understanding emotion and experiencing emotion. In C. Saarni & P. Harris (Eds.), *Children's understanding of emotion* (pp. 241–258). Cambridge, England: Cambridge University Press.

Hart, J., & Gunnar, M. (1995). Salivary cortisol in maltreated children: Evidence of relations between neuroendocrine activity and social competence. *Development and Psychopathology, 7,* 11–26.

Hubbard, J. (2001). Emotion expression processes in children's peer interaction: The role of peer rejection, aggression, and gender. *Child Development, 72,* 1426–1438.

Janoff-Bulman, R., & Frantz, C. (1997). The impact of trauma on meaning: From meaningless world to meaningful life. In M. Power & C. Brewer (Eds.), *The transformation of meaning in psychological therapies* (pp. 91–106). London: Wiley.

Kochanska, G., & Thompson, R. (1997). The emergence and development of conscience in toddlerhood and early childhood. In J. Grusec & L. Kuczynski (Eds.), *Parenting and children's internalization of values: A handbook of contemporary theory* (pp. 53–77). New York: Wiley.

Krystal, H. (1988). *Integration and self-healing: Affect, trauma, and alexithymia.* Hillsdale, NJ: Analytic Press.

Lamb, M. E. (1987). Predictive implications of individual differences in attachment. *Journal of Consulting and Clinical Psychology, 55,* 817–824.

Lazarus, R. S. (1991). *Emotion and adaptation.* New York: Oxford University Press.

Lazarus, R. S. (1999). *Stress and emotion: A new synthesis.* New York: Springer.

Lerner, R. M. (1998). Theories of human development: Contemporary perspectives. In R. M. Lerner (Ed.), *Handbook of child psychology: Vol. 1. Theoretical models of human development* (5th ed., pp. 1–24). New York: Wiley.

Lewis, M. (1997). *Altering fate: Why the past does not predict the future.* New York: Guilford.

Lewis, M. (2000). Attachment over time. *Child Development, 71,* 707–720.

Lewis, M. (2001). Issues in the study of personality development. *Psychological Inquiry, 12,* 67–83.

Lewis, M., Alessandri, S., & Sullivan, M. (1990). Expectancy, loss of control, and anger in young infants. *Developmental Psychology, 25,* 745–751.

Lillard, A. (1998). Ethnopsychologies: Cultural variations in theories of mind. *Psychological Bulletin, 123,* 3–32.

Lock, A. (1981). Indigenous psychology and human nature: A psychological perspective. In P. Heelas & A. Lock (Eds.), *Indigenous psychologies: The anthropology of the self* (pp. 183–201). London: Academic Press.

Lutz, C. (1985). Cultural patterns and individual differences in the child's emotional meaning system. In M. Lewis & C. Saarni (Eds.), *The socialization of affect* (pp. 37–53). New York: Plenum.

McCloskey, L. A., Figueredo, A. J., & Koss, M. P. (1995). The effects of systemic family violence on children's mental health. *Child Development, 66,* 1239–1261.

Murphy, L., & Moriarty, A. (1976). *Vulnerability, coping, and growth.* New Haven, CT: Yale University Press.

Parker, E. H., Hubbard, J., Ramsden, S., Relyea, N., Dearing, K., Smithmyer, C., & Schimmel, K. (2001). Children's use and knowledge of display rules for anger following hypothetical vignettes versus following live peer interaction. *Social Development, 10,* 528–557.

Peters, S. D. (1988). Child sexual abuse and later psychological problems. In G. Wyatt & G. Powell (Eds.), *Lasting effects of child sexual abuse* (pp. 101–117). Newbury Park, CA: Sage.

Ratner, H., & Stettner, L. (1991). Thinking and feeling: Putting Humpty Dumpty together again. *Merrill-Palmer Quarterly, 37,* 1–26.

Rothbart, M., & Bates, J. E. (1998). Temperament. In N. Eisenberg (Ed.), *Social, emotional and personality development* (5th ed., Vol. 3, pp. 105–176). New York: Wiley.

Saarni, C. (1979). Children's understanding of display rules for expressive behavior. *Developmental Psychology, 15,* 424–429.

Saarni, C. (1984). An observational study of children's attempts to monitor their expressive behavior. *Child Development, 55,* 1504–1513.

Saarni, C. (1988). Children's understanding of the interpersonal consequences of dissemblance of nonverbal emotional-expressive behavior [Special issue: Deception]. *Journal of Nonverbal Behavior, 12* (4, Pt. 2), 275–294.

Saarni, C. (1989). Children's understanding of strategic control of emotional expression in social transactions. In C. Saarni & P. Harris (Eds.), *Children's understanding of emotion* (pp. 181–208). New York: Cambridge University Press.

Saarni, C. (1991, April). *Social context and management of emotional-expressive behavior: Children's expectancies for when to dissemble what they feel.* Paper presented at the biennial meeting of the Society for Research in Child Development, Seattle, WA.

Saarni, C. (1995, April). *Children's coping strategies for aversive emotions.* Paper presented at the biennial meeting of the Society for Research in Child Development, Indianapolis, IN. (ERIC, Document Reproduction Service No. PS 023-350)

Saarni, C. (1997). Coping with aversive feelings. *Motivation and Emotion, 21,* 45–63.

Saarni, C. (1999). *The development of emotional competence.* New York: Guilford.

Saarni, C., & Buckley, M. (2002). Children's understanding of emotion communication in families. In R. A. Fabes (Ed.), *Emotions and the family. Special issue of the Marriage and Family Review* (pp. 213–242). New York: Haworth.

Saarni, C., & Weber, H. (1999). Emotional displays and dissemblance in childhood: Implications for self-presentation. In P. Philippot, R. S. Feldman, & E. Coats (Eds.), *The social context of nonverbal behavior* (pp. 71–105). Cambridge, England: Cambridge University Press.

Spinrad, T., & Stifter, C. (2002). Maternal sensitivity and infant emotional reactivity: Concurrent and longitudinal relations. In R. A. Fabes (Ed.), *Emotions and the family* (pp. 243–263). New York: Haworth.

Sroufe, A. (1996). *Emotional development.* Cambridge, England: Cambridge University Press.

Thompson, R. (1995). Emotional regulation: Its relations to attachment and developmental psychopathology. In D. Cicchetti & S. Toth (Eds.), *Emotion, cognition, and representation. Roch-*

ester symposium on developmental psychopathology (Vol. 6, pp. 261–299). Rochester, NY: University of Rochester Press.

Thompson, R. A. (1994). Emotion regulation: A theme in search of definition. *Society for Research in Child Development Monographs, 59*(Serial No. 240), 25–52.

Thompson, R. A. (1998). Early sociopersonality development. In W. Damon & N. Eisenberg (Eds.), *Handbook of child psychology: Vol. 3. Social, emotional, and personality development* (5th ed., pp. 25–104). New York: Wiley.

Trevarthen, C. (1984). Emotions in infancy: Regulators of contact and relationships with persons. In K. Scherer & P. Ekman (Eds.), *Approaches to emotion* (pp. 129–157). Hillsdale, NJ: Lawrence Erlbaum Associates.

Trevarthen, C. (1993). The function of emotions in early infant communication and development. In J. Nadel & L. Cumaioni (Eds.), *New perspectives in early communicative development* (pp. 48–81). London: Routledge.

Underwood, M., Coie, J., & Herbsman, C. (1992). Display rules for anger and aggression in school-age children. *Child Development, 63,* 366–380.

Underwood, M., & Hurley, J. (1999). Emotion regulation and peer relationships during the middle childhood years. In C. Tamis-LeMonda & L. Balter (Eds.), *Child psychology: A handbook of contemporary issues* (pp. 237–258). Philadelphia: Psychology Press.

Underwood, M., Hurley, J., Johanson, C., & Mosley, J. (1999). An experimental, observational investigation of children's responses to peer provocation: Developmental and gender differences in middle childhood. *Child Development,* 1428–1446.

Van der Kolk, B., & Saporta, J. (1991). The biological response to psychic trauma: Mechanisms and treatment of intrusion and numbing. *Anxiety Research, 4,* 199–212.

von Salisch, M. (1996, April). *What boys and girls expect when they express their anger toward a friend.* Paper presented at the biennial meeting of the Society for Research on Emotions, Toronto.

Walden, T. (1991). Infant social referencing. In J. Garber & K. Dodge (Eds.), *The development of emotion regulation and dysregulation* (pp. 69–88). Cambridge, England: Cambridge University Press.

Walden, T., & Smith, M. C. (1997). Emotion regulation. *Motivation and Emotion, 21,* 7–25.

White, G. M. (2000). Representing emotional meaning: Category, metaphor, schema, discourse. In M. Lewis & J. Haviland-Jones (Eds.), *Handbook of emotions* (2nd ed., pp. 30–44). New York: Guilford.

Zeman, J., & Garber, J. (1996). Display rules for anger, sadness, and pain: It depends on who is watching. *Child Development, 67,* 957–973.

Zeman, J., & Shipman, K. (1997). Social-contextual influences on expectancies for managing anger and sadness: The transition from middle childhood to adolescence. *Developmental Psychology, 33,* 917–924.

Zeman, J., & Shipman, K. (1998). Influence of social context on children's affect regulation: A functionalist perspective. *Journal of Nonverbal Behavior, 22,* 141–165.

Zimmermann, P. (1999). Structure and functions of internal working models of attachment and their role for emotion regulation. *Attachment and Human Development, 1,* 291–306.

14

Development of Regulatory Processes Through Adolescence: A Review of Recent Empirical Studies

Renée M. Tobin
Illinois State University

William G. Graziano
Purdue University

Thompson (1994) observed that implicit notions of emotional regulation are so powerful that many pieces dealing with the topic do not offer a clear explicit definition of the phenomenon. He then offered this working definition: "Emotion regulation consists of the extrinsic and intrinsic processes responsible for monitoring, evaluating, and modifying emotional reactions, especially their intensive and temporal features, to accomplish their goals" (pp. 27–28). Thompson's definition did not mention developmental processes per se. Ultimately, Thompson suggested that emotional regulation is not easily defined because it refers to a range of dynamic processes, "each of which may have its own catalysts and control processes" (p. 52). Given this state of affairs, it is not surprising that operational definitions of regulation include such diverse items as spontaneous heart rate fluctuations, adrenal secretions in blood, gaze aversion, proximity seeking to mother, and even look-backs during reading.

In its common usage, "regulation" refers to a process in which a system is brought into compliance with a standard. These processes may be external to the system, as in legal regulation of property transfers. The law prescribes the standard and when deviations are identified they are challenged by the legal system. When systems are "self-regulating," the system is assumed to contain two additional components beyond the standard. These two elements are a mechanism for detecting deviation from the standard, and a mechanism for bringing a system back from deviation toward the standard. It is important to differentiate systems that are regulated externally from systems that are self-regulating, especially for biological and psychological systems. A self-regulated child with a strong conscience (internal standard) will not steal or cheat even when authority figures are absent, whereas an externally regulated child will refrain from deviation only when authority figures are present to sanction the deviation. Both children are regulated, but the former is self-regulated.

A wide range of psychological systems is assumed to be regulated, and a subset is assumed to become self-regulating as part of normal development, including control of emotions, reactions to failure and disappointment, and most forms of moral and achievement activities. Indeed, when certain systems fail to show self-regulation, it is often assumed that normal development has been disrupted, as in the case of the school-age child who steals or cheats when adults are not watching (Graziano, Jensen-Campbell, & Finch, 1997; Graziano & Waschull, 1995; Kochanska & Knaack, 2003; Metcalf & Mischel, 1999).

OPERATIONAL DEFINITIONS OF REGULATION

In their now-classic edited volume entitled *The Development of Emotional Regulation and Dysregulation*, Dodge and Garber (1991) offered a comprehensive conceptual analysis and summary of empirical work available at that time. They noted that emotion regulation is an ambiguous term, with at least three different meanings. First, the term may refer to processes external to the emotion that influence emotion. In this sense, emotional regulation processes are inherently relational, and involve at least two components, namely, self-contained and interrelational (i.e., affect and cognition). A second meaning reverses the flow of relational influence, suggesting that emotions regulate some component external to emotion, such as cognition. A third meaning implies that emotions have both regulated and unregulated aspects, and some forms of regulation are internal to emotion, whereas other forms are external. Dodge and Garber (1991) proposed a general conceptual scheme of emotional regulation system that involved three domains to reduce ambiguity. In *intradomain* regulation, modulation of one aspect of responding occurs as a result of processes in another aspect of the same domain. An example is the regulation of vagal tone by means of respiratory activity. In *interdomain* regulation, modulation of one aspect of responding occurs as a result of processes in another domain. An example is the inhibition of impulsive behavior by means of distraction from the goal. The process of emotional regulation through *interpersonal* processes involves the modulation of emotion in one person through the activity of another. An example is an infant's use of mother to regulate the infant's emotional responses to strange, ambiguous objects.

CONCEPTUAL BASE FOR REGULATION

The Dodge–Garber scheme is useful conceptually, but it has some potential shortcomings. For example, the intrapersonal domains cover a wide variety of processes, and it is not clear how to define boundaries among them. Intuitively, vagal tone and respiration patterns seem to be within the same domain of physiological processes, but are EMG-assessed motor behaviors within the same domain with them as a physiological process or in a different domain as a perceptual/cognitive process? Furthermore, because emotional regulation processes may be qualitatively different in infants relative to older persons (Kagan, 1994; Kochanska & Knaack, 2003), it is also useful to segregate studies by the general age groups of the participants in the studies (infants, toddlers, preschoolers, school-age children, adolescents). It is possible to expand the Dodge-Garber scheme to generate a more precise classification in terms of content area and developmental level of research participants.

Following Graziano and Tobin (2002), this chapter takes an approach somewhat different from Dodge and Garber in organizing work on regulation. Accordingly, portions of this chapter were adapted and updated from Graziano and Tobin (2002). Without denying the merits of the top-down conceptual scheme, the focus is on patterns emerging across empirical studies, with an eye to the bottom-up construction of "empirical concepts" through the "upward seepage of meaning" (Campbell, 1988; Feigl, 1970). Specifically, this review searched for all empirical studies dealing with regulation in infants, children, and adolescents published in refereed journals from 1986 to March 2004. These were categorized based on the age of the child and the substantive topic of the research (the coding system is described subsequently). The research studies analyzed here were identified by searching citations in earlier reviews and computerized searches of PsycINFO (1986–2004). Key words used in the searches included "regulation," "emotion control," and "self-control." A number of a priori decisions were made about selection and presentation of findings from the research literature. The review is limited to articles that offer data and are primarily empirical contributions, focus on populations living in the United States, are written in English, appear in peer reviewed journals or their equivalent, and focus on positive development (as opposed to a deficit-based criteria). Outcomes are reported on Table 14.1.

Of the 413 potential studies, 107 (25.91%) studies were not classified further because they did not meet the inclusion criteria. An additional 16 publications presented theory, but were not classified because they did not present data. The remaining research studies that met criteria were then classified into a 6 (content) × 5 (developmental level) matrix. To provide a rough indication of trends in the literature, studies were also subclassified within each cell for publication year: 1986–1994 and 1995–March 2004.

The *content area* refers to the main process or substantive focus of the research. These areas were physiological processes, perceptual/cognitive processes, individual-centered social/personality processes, interpersonal processes, and applied issues. Due to their special importance in developmental sciences, a category was added for longitudinal studies and these studies were treated as a separate, superordinate category. *Developmental level* refers to age of the research participants, and consists of infants, toddlers, preschoolers, school-age children, and adolescents. Assignment to categories was difficult for some studies, and forced the development of clarification of conceptual ambiguities. For example, some studies included wide ranges of ages with no differentiation (e.g., participants were described as being 8–25 years), or were cross-sectional with different developmental levels. For another example, some studies were interdomain (in Garber–Dodge terms) and involved prediction across domains, such as interpersonal behavior predicted from physiological processes, or behavior as predicted by variables from multiple categories. The study

TABLE 14.1
Numbers of Empirical Publications on Regulation by Age Group and Content Area for 1986–March 2004

Content	Infants			Toddlers			Preschool			School			Adolescents			Totals		
	A	B	Total	A	B	Total	A	B	Total	A	B	Total	A	B	Total	A	B	Total
Physiological	12	10	22	0	1	1	0	3	3	1	6	7	0	0	0	13	20	33
Perception/Cognition	3	2	5	0	1	1	7	2	9	8	5	13	0	1	1	18	11	29
Social/Personality	1	3	4	2	3	5	7	11	18	9	25	34	2	5	7	21	47	68
Interpersonal	12	13	25	3	7	10	12	14	26	2	15	17	1	3	4	30	52	82
Applied	0	0	0	1	0	1	1	1	2	11	7	18	0	9	9	13	17	30
Longitudinal	1	15	16	2	3	5	1	8	9	2	7	9	0	4	4	6	37	43
Totals	29	43	72	8	15	23	28	39	67	33	65	98	3	22	25	101	184	285

Note. The A Column represents the time period between 1986 and 1994. The B column represents the time period between 1995 and March, 2004.

allowed assignment of studies to only one category. In cases where a study included participants from more than one age group, the studies were categorized by the age group of the youngest participants. In cases where a study crossed content areas, placement priority was given to interpersonal processes over within-child processes. For purposes of exposition, the literature is described by content domain, noting qualifications that are necessary depending on the developmental level of the participants in the research. Additional considerations are described as needed.

In terms of frequency of published regulation research studies, across all age groups the largest domain by far during 1986 through March 2004 was interpersonal relations (overall 82/285 = 28.77%), followed by social/personality processes (23.86%), longitudinal studies (15.09%), physiological processes (11.58%), applied studies (10.53%), and perceptual/cognitive processes (10.18%). The interpersonal relations classification was the largest single category for the three youngest age groups, but not for school-age and adolescent persons.

This outcome seems not to be an artifact of base rate differences in studies by developmental level. In the period from 1986 to March, 2004, the largest number of regulation studies was conducted on school-age children (34.39% of total studies), followed by infants (25.26%), preschoolers (23.51%), adolescents (8.77%), and toddlers (8.07%). Within this general pattern, there appears to be a time trend. The frequency of interpersonal studies on school-age children's self-regulation appears to be increasing from 1986 to March 2004. Within other age groups, however, there appeared to be no time trend for an increase in frequency of interpersonal studies.

These general patterns will help frame the assessment of the quality of evidence supporting claims about regulatory processes within each domain. For example, the number of recent studies in certain domains, with participants of certain developmental levels, may be too small to justify firm conclusions. Within each domain, a few representative or especially illustrative studies are described. Space limitations preclude comprehensive descriptions. Conclusions about physiological and perceptual-cognitive aspects of regulation in toddlers must be tentative, given the small number of recent studies devoted specifically to them.

INSTRUMENTS AND MEASURES OF REGULATION

Physiological Measures of Regulation

Regulation has been assessed based on physiological measures such as vagal tone (Porges, 1991) and electroencephalography (EEG) activity (Fox et al., 1996). Vagal tone is an index of the influence of the parasympathetic nervous system on the heart, as measured by the magnitude of respiratory sinus arrhythmia (RSA). It has been used as an indicator of regulation in infants (Field, Pickens, Fox, Nawrocki, & Gonzalez, 1995; Portales et al., 1997) and toddlers (Calkins, 1997).

Other-Ratings

Regulation often is assessed based on the reports of individuals who know the child well. One of the most common methods is to obtain parental reports of a child's regulatory abilities. Carter, Little, Briggs-Gowan, and Kogan (1999) conducted a multimethod examination of emotional regulation in infants. In this study, parents completed the Infant-Toddler Social and Emotional Assessment (ITSEA; Carter, Briggs-Gowan, Jones, & Little, 2003) and the Infant Behavior Questionnaire (IBQ; Rothbart & Derryberry, 1981). The ITSEA provides ratings for 7 competence scales and 3 problem domains: Externalizing, Internalizing, and Dysregulation. The IBQ is a 94-item instrument completed by parents using a 7-point Likert-type scale.

Rothbart and colleagues (Ahadi, Rothbart, & Ye, 1993; Derryberry & Rothbart, 1988) generated several other temperamental measures of regulation in older children (e.g., preschoolers, school-age children), including an Effortful Control factor on the Children's Behavior Questionnaire. This measure is a 195-item questionnaire yielding 15 scale scores. Parents complete the instrument based on the child's behavior over the last 6 months using a 7-point Likert-type scale. Derryberry and Rothbart (1988) presented another parent report measure of temperamental differences in regulation that Eisenberg and Fabes (1995) adapted in their study examining social competence, regulation, and emotionality. In addition, Eisenberg and Fabes presented parents with vignettes to which parents reported their expectations for their children's behavior. These responses to the vignettes then were used as indicators of emotional regulation.

J. H. Block and J. Block (1980) generated another type of parent report instrument that has been used as a measure of regulation. The Block and Block measure assesses Ego Control and Ego Resiliency using a Q-sort method.

Another measure of regulation, Lack of Control, has been used to assess regulation in preschool children (Caspi, Henry, McGee, Moffitt, & Silva, 1995). Henry, Caspi, Moffitt, Harrington, and Silva (1999) found that the relation between preschool measures of Lack of Control and criminal behavior in adolescence was moderated by school attendance.

Following up on their earlier work (e.g., Lopez & Little, 1996), Little, Lopez, and Wanner (2001) took a somewhat different approach. They examined the validity of the Behavioral Inventory of Strategic Control (BISC) for children with unstable social networks. In particular, Little et al. examined a multidimensional model of strategic control in 318 second- through sixth-grade students of military families. They completed the BISC on three occasions during a 3-month period. Coping strategies were classified as avoidance, emotional support seeking, social exploitation, social cooperation, aggressive individualism, or hostility. Results showed that the BISC discriminated between social, antisocial, direct, and indirect behaviors, and these four primary dimensions mediated well-being and adjustment. Findings support multidimensional conceptualizations of coping and regulation.

Behavioral/Observational Ratings

Behavioral observations also have been used as measures of emotional regulation in children of all ages, including infants. Along with two parent report measures, Carter et al. (1999) presented measures of infant reactivity, regulation, and coping behaviors. Using this method, measures of reactivity and regulation are coded in real time using a computer–videotape-linked system. Ratings of swaddling, regulation, and maternal reunion episodes were coded on a 6-point Likert-type scale.

One of the earliest and best known measures of regulation is delay of gratification tasks (Mischel & Baker, 1995; Mischel & Ebbesen, 1970; Shoda, Mischel, & Peake,

1990). During these tasks, children's ability to wait for a desirable object (e.g., candy) is recorded and coded. Regulation methods (e.g., looking away, distraction) also are examined. According to Metcalfe and Mischel (1999), the ability to shift attention from the tempting object and delay gratification is a measure of emotional regulation.

Kochanska and colleagues (Kochanska & Knaack, 2003; Kochanska, Murray, & Harlan, 2000; Kochanska, Tjebkes, & Forman, 1998) examined regulation among children between age 12 months and 52 months. The Kochanska measures of effortful control involve a series of activities the child is asked to perform, such as moving an animal at various speeds across a game board, whispering, walking a straight line, and resisting the temptation of candy. Children's behaviors are recorded and coded as indicators of effortful control, a type of regulation reflecting the ability to shift and focus attention voluntarily.

Van der Meere and Stemerdink (1999) presented another behavioral measure of state regulation. They examined the impulse control of 7- to 12-year-old boys using a go–no go task used in previous research (van der Meere, Stemerdink, & Gunning, 1995). It involves presenting children with letters and symbols on a video monitor. Children are instructed to press a response button when a certain letter (e.g., *P*) appears on the screen. The experimenters record the total number of omissions (correct stimulus is presented, but child does not press button) and commissions (incorrect stimulus is presented and child presses button).

Although it may not be intuitively obvious, attachment measures also may be considered interpersonal measures of emotional regulation. Attachment initially was assessed in childhood, but it now is measured across the life span. Numerous methods have been established to assess attachment. The widely used methodology is the Ainsworth Strange Situation procedure (Ainsworth, Blehar, Waters, & Wall, 1978). Attachment also has been assessed using parental Q-sort methodology (Waters & Deane, 1985) and various other methods. In 1985, the *Monographs of the Society for Research in Child Development* dedicated an entire issue to the topic of attachment theory and measurement (Bretherton & Waters, 1985).

Another way to examine regulation is to observe interpersonal processes and code them. Feldman, Greenbaum, Yirmiya, and Mayes (1996) assessed mother–child regulation during videotaped play sessions. Their ratings of maternal regulation reflected the parent's adjustment in amount of stimulation to the infant. These ratings were related to later positive outcomes.

EMPIRICAL EVIDENCE BY DOMAIN

Physiological Processes

In terms of frequency, the largest number of studies of regulation within the physiological domain was focused on infancy (22/33 studies, 66.67%). Of all the regulation studies of infants, physiological studies represent 30.56% of the total. Physiological studies of regulation examine the following domains: vagal tone, adrenocortical activity, blood composition, sleep patterns, and psychophysiological measures (e.g., EEG, EKG, EMG). Typically, this category involves small numbers of participants.

Vagal tone may be related to individual differences in capabilities for physiological reactivity and self-regulation (Porges, 1991). RSAs decrease during bottle-feeding for

33- to 42-week-old infants (Portales et al., 1997), suggesting that the gustatory-vagal response system can be systematically elicited during feeding. Porges, Doussard-Roosevelt, Portales, and Greenspan (1996) measured vagal activity in 7- to 9-month-old infants ($N = 24$) during various attention-demanding tasks. Subsequently, the mothers rated their infants for behavioral/emotional problems at age 3. The data support a psychobiological model of social behavior hypothesizing that infants with difficulties in regulating the "vagal brake" (decreasing cardiac vagal tone) during attention tasks have later difficulties in social interactions that require reciprocal engagement. Calkins, Dedmon, Gill, Lomax, and Johnson (2002) examined easily frustrated and less easily frustrated infants and their physiological and attentional responding. These researchers found that infants classified as easily frustrated (particularly male infants) were more reactive physiologically in terms of RSA. This finding is consistent with previous work reported by Stifter and Fox (1990).

Calkins (1997) measured vagal tone in toddlers ($N = 41$), and exposed them to emotion-eliciting episodes. She found that baseline vagal tone was related to reactivity to positive and negative tasks (but not to delay tasks), and children who consistently suppressed vagal tone began with higher vagal baselines. Field et al. (1995) found that infants of depressed mothers showed lower vagal tone than their peers, and did not show the developmental increase in vagal tone occurring from 3 to 6 months for infants of nondepressed mothers. With a sample of 91 school-age children and adolescents, Allen, Matthews, and Kenyon (2000) found that decreased vagal tone was related to increased impulse control problems, but only in male participants.

Blood chemistry also may provide information about regulation. Gunnar, Mangelsdorf, Larson, and Hertsgaard (1990) found that 9- and 13-month-old infants who were more prone to distress than their peers during laboratory tests showed greater adrenocortical activity. Adrenocortical activity was not associated with attachment classification. Gunnar, Isensee, and Fust (1987) compared normal newborns (Group 1) from 32 to 222 hours old with neonates with perinatal complications (Group 2), and found few correlations between behavioral responding and levels of plasma cortisol. However, Group 1 neonates who were more competent in behavioral control and state regulation had higher levels of plasma cortisol. In Group 2, neonates who showed the greater adrenocortisol response to the examination also showed more behavior indicative of behavioral arousal and distress. Spangler and Scheubeck (1993) found inconsistent correlations with infant adrenocortical response and newborn irritability, but Spangler, Schieche, Ilg, Maier, and Ackerman (1994) observed mothers and infants during play, and collected measures of behavioral and adrenocortical activity. Elevated cortisol was more frequently observed among children of highly insensitive mothers, suggesting a role for maternal behavior in infant behavioral regulation.

Regulation of sleep–wake cycles has also been examined. Burnham, Goodlin-Jones, Gaylor, and Anders (2002) revealed that high levels of quiet time at birth, longer parental response times to awakenings, and less amount of time spent out of the crib were significant predictors of self-soothing at one year.

Physiological processes associated with regulation in preschool children have been examined by Cole, Zahn-Waxler, Fox, Usher, and Welsh (1996). Emotion regulation was assessed during a negative mood induction, and used to categorize preschoolers ($N = 79$) into three groups: inexpressive, modulated expressive, and highly expressive. Inexpressive preschoolers had the highest heart rate, lowest vagal tone, and smallest ANS change during induction. Inexpressive preschoolers appeared to have more depressive and anxious symptoms at follow-up in first grade.

Perceptual and Cognitive Processes

In terms of frequency, the largest number of studies of self-regulation or emotion regulation within the perceptual and cognitive domain was focused on school-age children (13/29 studies, 44.83%). Of all the regulation studies of school-age children, perceptual and cognitive studies represent 13.27% of the total. Perceptual and cognitive studies of regulation examine the following domains: metacognitive monitoring, private speech, sensory stimulation, and temporal regulation. This category varies greatly in terms of participant numbers, although larger participant numbers appear in the older children categories.

Perceptual and cognitive researchers working with infants have focused on basic processes like attention, sensory stimulation, distraction from distress, motor control, and crying. Feldman and Mayes (1999) examined cyclic oscillations of attention and nonattention in 3- and 6-month olds ($N = 40$). Patterns of oscillations were related to recognition memory, suggesting that regulation of attention in recurrent patterns is a correlate of efficient processing in the early stages of perceptual development. Ashmead and McCarty (1991) examined the self-regulation of posture in the light and dark for 12- to 24-month-old infants, in comparison with adults. Infants, unlike adults, did not sway more in the dark than in the light. Outcomes suggest that infants' regulation of early standing posture is adequate in the absence of visual surroundings (cf. Nougier, Bard, Fleury, & Teasdale, 1998, with school-age children). Buss and Goldsmith (1998) examined the regulation of emotional distress in 6-, 12- and 18-month-olds ($N = 148$). Outcomes suggest that certain putative self-regulatory behaviors like distraction are effective for reducing the observed intensity of some emotions (e.g., anger), but not others (e.g., fear). The results suggested caution in assuming that postulated regulatory behavior actually has general distress-reducing effects, and "distress" is too general a construct for research on emotional regulation.

Private speech, which has been linked to self-regulation in theory, has continued to be examined in the play of toddlers and preschoolers over the last 15 years. Krafft and Berk (1998) found that children in a Montessori preschool program showed lower incidence of private speech than children in a traditional preschool. Structural aspects of instruction and contextual factors also contributed to the drop in private speech for children at age 5.

Regulation research on school-age children focuses on school-related tasks like reading and memory for written material. Bossert and Schwantes (1995) examined "looking back" at previously read material as a form of regulatory behavior in fourth graders. Children trained to look back produced more correct responses than children in a control group. Allexander and Schwanenflugel (1994) examined metacognitive attributions for a sort-recall task in first and second graders. Knowledge base was a powerful predictor of strategic looking behavior, whereas metacognitive attributions were influential in the low knowledge base condition.

D. C. Miller and Byrnes (1997) examined self-regulation during risk-taking decisions in third through eighth graders. Inappropriate risk taking was associated with overconfidence, falling prey to potential deregulatory influences (e.g., impulsivity, peer presence), and insensitivity to outcomes. In addition, risk taking was correlated with ability beliefs, preferences for thrill seeking, peer status, and competitiveness.

Social and Personality Differences

In terms of frequency, the largest number of studies of self-regulation or emotion regulation within the social and personality differences domain was focused on school-age children (34/68 studies, 50.00%). Of all the regulation studies of school-age children, social and personality difference studies represent 34.69% of the total. Studies of social and personality differences in regulation examine the following domains: temperament, SES, socialization, attachment, conscience, social-cognitive expectancies, social support, and parenting stress. This category centers on predictors/correlates of regulatory activity in individual children. It differs from the subsequent interpersonal category in that it focuses on activity in an individual person, not on interacting persons.

Regulation research examining social and personality differences in infants often focused on temperament and emotional reactivity. Goldsmith, Buss, and Lemery (1997) examined heritable influences on temperament dimensions in toddlers and preschoolers. Positive affect revealed substantial shared environmental influence, whereas emotion regulation revealed additive genetic influence. Stifter and Braungart (1995) examined differences in the regulation of negative arousal in 5- and 10-month olds. Self-comforting behaviors were exhibited most often during periods of decreasing negative arousal. Avoidance and communicative behavior were exhibited most often during increasing distress. Stifter and Spinrad (2002) found that excessive criers, relative to typical criers, were more negatively reactive, but only excessive male criers showed less regulation than their peers.

Cournoyer and Trudel (1991) classified 33-month-olds ($N = 48$) on patterns of self-control behavior in two delay-of-gratification tasks. Low delay children looked at and touched the forbidden toy often, medium delay children engaged in more social referencing, and high delay children were more likely to reference nonforbidden objects, and to use self-distracting tactics. The observed delay tactics were stable from task to task. Kochanska, DeVet, Goldman, Murray, and Putnam (1994) studied the emergence of conscience and its link to temperament in two studies. For most aspects of conscience, major developmental shifts occurred around 3 years. Two components of early conscience were *affective discomfort* (guilt, apology, concern for good feelings following wrong-doing, and empathy) and *active moral regulation/vigilance* (confession, reparation for wrongdoing, internalization of rules of conduct). Low impulsivity and high inhibitory control were associated with active moral regulation for both genders. Kochanska et al. (2000) indicated that individual differences in effortful control as a toddler were related to regulation of anger and joy and to stronger restraint (see also Kochanska & Knaack, 2003). Kieras et al. (2005) found that behavioral measures of effortful control in preschool-age children predicted the regulation of positive affect following the receipt of desirable and undesirable gifts.

Grolnick, Bridges, and Connell (1996) examined the expression of negative emotion, and strategies to reduce or change them, in 2-year-olds ($N = 37$). Active engagement was most commonly used and was negatively associated with child distress. Strategies varied with task context. Eisenberg et al. (1996) found that for second graders, vagal tone was related positively to boys' self-reported sympathy, whereas the pattern was reversed for females. In general, sympathy was related to high levels of self-regulation, teacher-reported positive emotionality, and physiological reactivity to stress.

Denham et al. (2003) examined the relations among emotion regulation, emotional expressivity, emotion knowledge, and social competence among preschoolers. These researchers found that the emotional competence indicators at age 3 and age 4 predicted social competence concurrently and in kindergarten. Shields et al. (2001) purported that emotion regulation at the beginning of the school year predicted better classroom adaptation in low-income preschoolers. Gumora and Arsenio (2002) found that mood and emotion regulation, emotionality, and academic affect were all unique predictors of academic performance as measured by students' grade point averages.

Grolnick and Ryan (1989) used a structural interview to assess parental style, autonomy support, involvement, and provision of structure on self-regulatory behavior of third to sixth graders. Parental autonomy support was related to children's self-report of autonomous self-regulation, teacher-rated competence, school grades, and achievement. The structure dimension was primarily related to children's understanding of control.

Interpersonal Processes

In terms of frequency, this category represents the largest single domain of recent research on regulation (82/285 total studies or 28.77%). Within the interpersonal domain, infants and preschool-age children are about equally represented and generate the largest numbers of studies of regulation (25/82 studies, 30.49%, and 26/82 studies, 31.71%, respectively). Of the regulation studies of infants, interpersonal studies represent 34.72% of the total. Of the regulation studies of preschoolers, interpersonal studies represent 38.81% of the total. These studies examined the domains of attachment, referencing, and parent–infant affect synchrony. This category differs from the social/personality category in that it reports data for at least two persons who are interacting.

In general, this literature is large enough to justify several conclusions. Studies show that infants' interpersonal processes and emotional regulation are influenced reliably by both temperament and attachment-related presence of others (e.g., Manglesdorf, Shapiro, & Marzolf, 1995). The need for qualifications of these general patterns also is reported (see Gottman, Guralnick, Wilson, Swanson, & Murray 1997). Walden and Baxter (1989) examined infant social referencing during parental expressions. They showed that younger infants (6–40 months) looked more often when parents expressed positive reactions, whereas older infants (24–40 months) looked equally at fearful and positive expressions. Only older infants showed regulation. Braungart and Stifter (1991) indicated that infants ($N = 80$) who were overtly upset in the Strange Situation oriented less toward people, more toward objects, and engaged in less toy exploration than their peers. Infants' attachment classification was related to self-regulation, but the pattern was complex, and not consistent with attachment theory. Zach and Keller (1999) studied the connection between infant attachment patterns and emotional regulation in the United States and Germany. In novel situations, infants regulated emotional reactions but referred to their mothers more, and explored less, than they did in familiar situations. U.S. infants conformed more closely to attachment theory prediction than did German infants, whose age-appropriate exploration was not related to physical contact, but significantly and negatively to visual referencing. Blackford and Walden (1998) showed that temperament is more closely associated with regulation and responsiveness to differences in parent messages, but not to child looking at parents per se.

Diener, Mengelsdorf, McHale, and Frosch (2002) found that infants who were securely attached to both parents showed greater levels of parent-oriented regulation relative to their peers who were less securely attached to one or both parents. Based on a sample of 223 children, Vondra, Shaw, Swearingen, Cohen, and Owens (2001) concluded that attachment classification, although not always stable between infancy and preschool, gives the most useful information about child functioning. Braungart-Rieker, Garwood, Powers, and Wang (2001) examined the still-face procedure and parent sensitivity as predictors of attachment to mother and father. Attachment classification at 12 months was related to maternal sensitivity at 4 months. Rosenblum, McDonough, Muzik, Miller, and Sameroff (2002) also used the still-face procedure to examine the relation between maternal representations and affect displays. Researchers classified mother–infant dyads into three maternal representation categories: balanced, distorted, and disengaged. After controlling for maternal depression, only infants in the balanced representation category resumed high levels of positive emotional displays following the still face procedure.

Calkins, Smith, Gill, and Johnson (1998) examined the link between physiological processes and maternal interactive style on the behavior of toddlers. Negative maternal behavior was related to poor physiological regulation (vagal tone), less adaptive emotional regulation, and noncompliant behavior. Fabes et al. (1999) found that preschoolers high in the temperamental dimension of effortful control were unlikely to experience high levels of negative emotional arousal in response to peer interactions. When interactions were of high intensity, highly regulated preschoolers were likely to show socially competent responses. Rubin, Coplan, Fox, and Calkins (1995) reported similar links between temperament and peer relations.

A program of research by A. L. Miller, Volling, and McElwain (2000) examined family relations between toddlers, preschoolers, and their parents. A. L. Miller et al. looked at the relation between jealousy and sibling rivalry with toddlers who had older preschool-age siblings. They found parental responses differed based on whether the child was an older or younger sibling. Older siblings were generally better able to regulate their jealousy and showed greater behavioral consistency across parents, suggesting that emotion regulation abilities were developing. Volling, McElwain, and A. L. Miller (2002) revealed that younger sibling jealousy was related to temperamental differences, whereas older sibling jealousy was related to the older siblings' emotional understanding when paired with their mothers.

Research on regulation among school age children and adolescents echoes themes found in research with younger children. Regulation is not a single process or set of processes. The data suggest that regulation processes in which children engage are probably moderated by the relation with the interaction partners and by the types of emotion (Collins, Laursen, Mortensen, Luebker, & Ferreira, 1997; Dearing et al., 2002; Eisenberg et al., 1996; Jensen-Campbell & Graziano, 2000; McDowell, O'Neil, & Parke, 2000; Zeman & Shipman, 1996, 1997).

Applied Studies

These studies represent 30/285 (10.53%) regulation studies in the recent literature. Most of the applied studies are based on school-age children, and generally examine school-related activities. For example, Wentzel, Weinberber, Ford, and Feldman (1990) investigated the concurrent effects of motivational, affective, and self-regulatory processes on sixth graders' GPA and school motivation. Student self-report and teacher's ratings both suggested that self-restraint is an important contributor to success in school. Jensen-Campbell and Graziano (2001) collected daily diary records of interpersonal conflicts from sixth-, seventh-, and eighth-grade adolescents and found that individual differences in Agreeableness were closely related to self-regulatory processes during interpersonal conflicts (See also Graziano & Eisenberg, 1997; Hair & Graziano, 2003).

Most intervention studies were not included in this review because they involved children and adolescents from disordered populations. A few interventions, however, were implemented for at-risk children and adolescents and include training such as anger management, problem solving, and violence prevention. With a sample of 84 preschool children, Serna, Nielsen, Lambros, and Forness (2000) indicated that a problem-solving intervention improved or maintained the social and emotional functioning of participants following intervention.

Longitudinal Studies

Because prospective longitudinal studies have the potential to be especially informative about developmental antecedents and processes of transformation, they are presented here as a separate section. The developmental level used to describe these studies refers to the focus or the age of first assessment. Of the recent regulation studies, 43/285 used longitudinal assessments. Within the longitudinal studies, the distribution was 16 (infancy), 5 (toddlers), 9 (preschoolers), 9 (school-age children), and 4 (adolescents). These studies provide incomparable data relevant to the developmental stability of regulation over the life span.

Do physiological processes associated with regulation show a developmental pattern? Bornstein and Suess (2000) measured infant vagal tone and heart rate at 2 months and at 5 years in both children ($N = 81$) and their mothers. Assessments were taken at rest and during an environmental task. Children reached the adult baseline for vagal tone by age 5 years, and did not differ from their mothers in baseline-to-task change in vagal tone or heart rate. Baseline-to-task change in vagal tone showed consistent mother–child concordance. These researchers interpreted their data to suggest that experiential or environmental influences shape children's developing characteristic physiological response style.

Doussard-Roosevelt, Porges, J. W. Scanlon, Alemi, and K. B. Scanlon (1997) examined heart rate (HR) and RSA, neonatal ECG beginning at 48 hours after birth, and followed up 3 years later. RSA measures predicted 3-year outcomes beyond the effects of birthweight, medical risks, and SES. A measure of joint RSA and heart rate was associated with better behavioral regulation at age 3, as measured by the Child Behavior Checklist and Parenting Stress Index scores. Generalizing these outcomes must be done with caution, however, in that the sample consisted of 41 very low birthweight infants.

Stifter, Spinrad, and Braungart-Rieker (1999) investigated early emotional regulation, as indexed by vagal tone, and later compliance. Heart rate measures were assessed at 5, 10, and 18 months of age during a frustration task. At age 30 months, children were given several compliance tasks. Infants who showed low levels of regulatory behavior were less compliant as toddlers. Vagal tone bore an inconsistent, contradictory relation to compliance across tasks.

Lewis, Koroshegyi, Douglas, and Kampe (1997) investigated emotional responses to infant separation at 2, 6, and 10 months, and related them to sensorimotor coordination at 4, 8, and 13 months. Separation distress at 2 months predicted lower sensorimotor scores. Emotional responses and cognitive performance may be linked by individual differences in self-regulation and attention management. Attention management is an aspect of regulation, and may have antecedents that can be discovered in longitudinal research. Feldman et al. (1996) videotaped infant attentive states at 3 and 9 months during free-play with their mothers. Patterns in the early synchrony between mothers and infants predicted verbal and general IQ at age 2. How these processes map onto regulation is not yet clear.

Building on Kochanska's (1991) earlier work on temperament and regulation, Kochanska et al. (1998) examined children's restraint and attention in multiple settings at ages 8 and 10 months, and children's compliance to mother and internalization of prohibitions at ages 13 and 15 months. Committed compliance had different developmental antecedents than did situational compliance, with girls surpassing boys in committed compliance. The internalization of maternal prohibition was related to committed compliance, but not to situational compliance (cf. Gralinski & Kopp, 1993).

Eisenberg et al. (1997) followed children from early to middle childhood, collecting parents' and teachers' reports of children's social behavior, emotionality, and regulation. In addition, children engaged in puppet-based analog "peer conflicts." High-quality social functioning was predicted by earlier high regulation, negative emotionality, and general emotional intensity. Eisenberg et al. (1999) explored the relations between self-reported parental reactions to children's early (age 4) negative emotions and children's later (age 12) appropriate/problem behavior. Evidence suggests that parents' reported reactions to children's negative emotions, especially punitive reactions, affect children's regulation and externalizing negative emotions. The evidence also suggested bidirectional influence (i.e., child to parent, as well as parent to child). In a related study, Eisenberg et al. (1998) found that earlier regulatory abilities and emotionality predicted later teacher-rated dispositional sympathetic tendencies in school-age children. Eisenberg et al. (2000) looked at the relations among behavioral emotion regulation, attentional control, and externalizing problems in kindergarten and then again in third grade. These researchers found that behavioral emotion regulation was predictive of externalizing problems regardless of the emotionality level of the school-age child; however, attentional control was predictive of problematic externalizing behavior only for children higher in negative emotionality.

Nelson, Marin, Hodge, Havill, and Kamphaus (1999) used parental ratings of temperament at age 5 to predict school performance problems, behavior problems, and positive social behavior as rated by teachers at age 8. Early parental rating of negative emotionality predicted later externalizing behavioral problems, and was a modest (inverse) predictor of positive social behavior. Katz and Gottman (1995) examined the hypothesis that a child's ability to regulate emotions (as indexed by vagal tone) could buffer children from the effects of marital hostility. They measured vagal tone in children when they were 5 years old, and teachers completed the Child Adaptive Behavior Inventory 3 years later. Outcomes suggest that high vagal tone can buffer children from the negative effects of parental hostility.

OVERALL SUMMARY AND FUTURE DIRECTIONS

Self-regulation and emotional regulation are complex processes that have been examined in many domains, age groups, and at many levels of abstraction. The empirical evidence is not perfectly clear, but some patterns are emerging from the data. Recent research suggests that basic biobehavioral processes associated with cardiovascular function index some basic regulatory processes, and appear to contribute to the development of subsequent regulatory processes in other domains. The biobehavioral processes associated with cardiovascular function (e.g., vagal tone) have been established most clearly in infancy. The presence of strong biological precursors of regulation does not exclude social and interpersonal forces. Even in infancy, social networks and interpersonal relations, especially with caregivers, can influence developing regulatory systems.

During development, basic biobehavioral processes come into contact with cognitive and social forces. These forces may be conceptualized as a three-legged stool. Each of the three legs contributes to the stability of the system, and none are independent of each other, although different processes may be more active than others at certain developmental periods. At the least, these data point to increasing interest in process-oriented approaches to development (Graziano, 2003; Graziano & Bryant, 1998; Richards, 2004). More speculatively, they point to a view of normal development in which separate process modules come to communicate with each other with increasing efficiency. Disruptions in intermodular communication may appear as problems of regulation, and in some cases, the disruption of basic skills in acquiring culturally appropriate skills in achievement and in social and interpersonal relationships (Cole et al., 1996; Fabes et al., 1999; Hair & Graziano, 2003; Kochanska & Knaack, 2003). Clearly, these are processes worthy of careful empirical attention in the future.

Two other avenues for future research show promise. First, past research emphasized only two cells in a 2×2 conceptual matrix (regulation, lack of regulation $\times$ positive/negative consequences). Until recently, researchers focused on the connection between regulation and positive outcomes, and lack of regulation and negative outcomes. Almost no attention was directed toward the other two less intuitive cells, namely, the connection between regulation and negative outcomes and lack of regulation and positive outcomes. However, researchers have become increasingly aware that regulatory processes may bring negative as well as positive consequences (e.g., Ainslie, 2001; Baumeister, Bratslavsky, Muraven, & Tice, 1998; Wegner, 2002). Overregulation phenomena are just beginning to be investigated, and these may provide intriguing information about basic processes (e.g., Richards, 2004). This work is a reminder that regulation, per se, is less important as an adaptive tool than the appropriate deployment of regulatory processes depending on circumstances.

A second avenue involves individual differences in regulatory process, but as they interact with contexts and settings. It seems as if future research will move beyond simplistic main effects models assuming common processes underlie regulation in all persons in the same way; the development of regulatory processes proceed in the same pattern and at the same rate for all persons; and that individual differences are noise, or at best, inert contributors to regulatory effects. More complex interactive models of regulation will situate individual differences in context, and outcomes of this work will suggest new ways of conceptualizing regulatory processes. These two new avenues have the potential to show multiple pathways for the development of valuable regulatory processes within the larger goal of adaptation.

REFERENCES

Ahadi, S. A., Rothbart, M. K., & Ye, R. (1993). Children's temperament in the US and China: Similarities and differences. *European Journal of Personality, 7*(5), 359–377.

Ainslie, G. (2001). *Breakdown of will.* Cambridge, England: Cambridge University Press.

Ainsworth, M. D. S., Blehar, M. C., Waters, E., & Wall, S. (1978). *Patterns of attachment: A psychological study of the Strange Situation.* Hillsdale, NJ: Lawrence Erlbaum Associates.

Allen, M. T., Matthews, K. A., & Kenyon, K. L. (2000). The relationships of resting baroreflex sensitivity, heart rate variability and measures of impulse control in children and adolescents. *International Journal of Psychophysiology, 37*(2), 185–194.

Allexander, J. M., & Schwanenflugel, P. J. (1994). Strategy regulation: The role of intelligence, metacognitive attributions, and knowledge base. *Developmental Psychology, 30,* 709–723.

Ashmead, D. H., & McCarty, M. E. (1991). Postural sway of human infants while standing in light and dark. *Child Development, 62,* 1276–1287.

Baumeister, R. F., Bratslavsky, E., Muraven, M., & Tice, D. M. (1998). Ego depletion: Is the self a limited resource? *Journal of Personality and Social Psychology, 74,* 1252–1265.

Blackford, J. U., & Walden, T. A. (1998). Individual differences in social referencing. *Infant Behavior and Development, 21*(1), 89–102.

Block, J. H., & Block, J. (1980). The role of ego-control and ego-resiliency in the organization of behavior. In W. A. Collins (Eds.), *Development of cognition, affect, and social relations. The Minnesota symposium on child psychology* (Vol. 13, pp. 39–101). Hillsdale, NJ: Lawrence Erlbaum Associates.

Bornstein, M. H., & Seuss, P. E. (2000). Child and mother cardiac vagal tone: Continuity, stability, and concordance across the first 5 years. *Developmental Psychology, 36,* 54–65.

Bossert, T. S., & Schwantes, F. M. (1995). Children's comprehension monitoring: Training children to use rereading to aid comprehension. *Reading Research and Instruction, 35*(2), 109–121.

Braungart, J. M., & Stifter, C. A. (1991). Regulation of negative reactivity during the strange situation: Temperament and attachment in 12-month-old infants. *Infant Behavior and Development, 14,* 349–364.

Braungart-Rieker, J. M., Garwood, M. M., Powers, B. P., & Wang, X. (2001) Parental sensitivity, infant affect, and affect regulation: Predictors of later attachment. *Child Development, 72,* 252–270.

Bretherton, I., & Waters, E. (1985). Growing points of attachment theory and research. *Monographs of the Society for Research in Child Development, 50*(1–2, Serial No. 209).

Burnham, M. M., Goodlin-Jones, B. L., Gaylor, E. E., & Anders, T. F. (2002). Nighttime sleep–wake patterns and self-soothing from birth to one year of age: A longitudinal intervention study. *Journal of Child Psychology and Psychiatry and Allied Disciplines, 43*(6), 713–725.

Buss, K. A., & Goldsmith, H. H. (1998). Fear and anger regulation in infancy: Effects on the temporal dynamics of affective expression. *Child Development, 69,* 359–374.

Calkins, S. D. (1997). Cardiac vagal tone indices of temperamental reactivity and behavioral regulation in young children. *Developmental Psychobiology, 31,* 125–135.

Calkins, S. D., Dedmon, S. E., Gill, K. L., Lomax, L. E., & Johnson, L. M. (2002). Frustration in infancy: Implications for emotion regulation, physiological processes, and temperament. *Infancy, 3,* 175–197.

Calkins, S. D., Smith, C. L., Gill, K. L., & Johnson, M. C. (1998). Maternal interactive style across contexts: Relations to emotional, behavioral, and physiological regulation during toddlerhood. *Social Development, 7*(3), 350–369.

Campbell, D. T. (1988). Descriptive epistemology: Psychological, sociological, and evolutionary. In E. S. Overman (Ed.), *Methodology and epistemology for the social sciences: Selected papers* (pp. 435–486). Chicago: University of Chicago Press.

Carter, A. S., Briggs-Gowan, M., Jones, S. M., & Little, T. D. (2003). The infant toddler social and emotional assessment: Factor structure, reliability, and validity. *Journal of Abnormal Child Psychology, 31,* 495–514.

Carter, A. S., Little, C., Briggs-Gowan, M. J., & Kogan, N. (1999). The infant-toddler social and emotional assessment (ITSEA): Comparing parent ratings to laboratory observations of task mastery, emotion regulation, coping behaviors, and attachment status. *Infant Mental Health Journal, 20*(4), 375–392.

Caspi, A., Henry, B., McGee, R., Moffitt, T. E., & Silva, P. A. (1995). Temperamental origins of child and adolescent behavior problems: From age three to age fifteen. *Child Development, 66,* 55–68.

Cole, P. M., Zahn-Waxler, C., Fox, N. A., Usher, B. A., & Welsh, J. D. (1996). Individual differences in emotion regulation and behavior problems in preschool children. *Journal of Abnormal Psychology, 105,* 518–529.

Collins, W. A., Laursen, B., Mortensen, N., Luebker, C., & Ferreira, M. (1997). Conflict processes and transitions in parent and peer relationships: Implications for autonomy and regulation. *Journal of Adolescent Research, 12,* 178–198.

Cournoyer, M., & Trudel, M. (1991). Behavioral correlates of self-control at 33 months. *Infant Behavior and Development, 14,* 497–503.

Dearing, K. F., Hubbard, J. A., Ramsden, S. R., Parker, E. H., Relyea, N., Smithmyer, C. M., & Flanagan, K. D. (2002). Children's self-reports about anger regulation: Direct and indirect links to social preference and aggression. *Merrill-Palmer Quarterly, 48*(3), 308–336.

Denham, S. A., Blair, K. A., DeMulder, E., Levitas, J., Sawyer, K., Auerbach-Major, S., & Queenan, P. (2003). Preschool emotional competence: Pathway to social competence. *Child Development, 74,* 238–256.

Derryberry, D., & Rothbart, M. K. (1988). Arousal, affect, and attention as components of temperament. *Journal of Personality and Social Psychology, 55,* 958–966.

Diener, M. L., Mengelsdorf, S. C., McHale, J. L., & Frosch, C. A. (2002). Infants' behavioral strategies for emotion regulation with fathers and mothers: Associations with emotional expressions and attachment quality. *Infancy, 3,* 153–174.

Dodge, K. A., & Garber, J. (1991). Domains of emotion regulation. In J. Garber & K. A. Dodge (Eds.), *The development of emotion regulation and dysregulation* (pp. 3–14). New York: Cambridge University Press.

Doussard-Roosevelt, J. A., Porges, S. W., Scanlon, J. W., Alemi, B., & Scanlon, K. B. (1997). Vagal regulation of heart rate in the prediction of developmental outcome for very low birth weight preterm infants. *Child Development, 68,* 173–186.

Eisenberg, N., & Fabes, R. A. (1995). The relation of young children's vicarious emotional responding to social competence, regulation, and emotionality. *Cognition and Emotion, 9(2–3)*, 203–228.

Eisenberg, N., Fabes, R. A., Murphy, B., Karbon, M., Smith, M., & Maszk, P. (1996). The relations of children's dispositional empathy-related responding to their emotionality, regulation, and social functioning. *Developmental Psychology, 32*, 195–209.

Eisenberg, N., Fabes, R. A., Shepard, S. A., Guthrie, I., Murphy, B. C., & Reiser, M. (1999). Parental reactions to children's negative emotions: Longitudinal relations to quality of children's social functioning. *Child Development, 70*, 513–534.

Eisenberg, N., Fabes, R. A., Shepard, S. A., Murphy, B. C., Guthrie, I. K., Jones, S., Friedman, J., Poulin, R., & Maszk, P. (1997). Contemporaneous and longitudinal prediction of children's social functioning from regulation and emotionality. *Child Development, 68*, 642–664.

Eisenberg, N., Fabes, R. A., Shepard, S. A., Murphy, B. C., Jones, S., & Guthrie, I. (1998). Contemporaneous and longitudinal prediction of children's sympathy from dispositional regulation and emotionality. *Developmental Psychology, 34*, 910–924.

Eisenberg, N., Guthrie, I. K., Fabes, R. A., Shepard, S., Losoya, S., Murphy, B. C., Jones, S., Poulin, R., & Reiser, M. (2000). Prediction of elementary school children's externalizing problem behaviors from attention and behavioral regulation and negative emotionality. *Child Development, 71*, 1367–1382.

Fabes, R. A., Eisenberg, N., Jones, S., Smith, M., Guthrie, I., Poulin, R., Shepard, S., & Friedman, J. (1999). Regulation, emotionality, and preschoolers' socially competent peer interactions. *Child Development, 70*, 432–442.

Feigl, H. (1970). The "Orthodox" view of theories: Remarks in defense as well as critique. In M. Radner & S. Winokur (Eds.), *Minnesota studies in the philosophy of science: Analyses of theories and methods of physics and psychology* (pp. 3–16). Minneapolis: University of Minnesota Press.

Feldman, R., Greenbaum, C. W., Yirmiya, N., & Mayes, L. C. (1996). Relations between cyclicity and regulation in mother-infant interaction at 3 and 9 months and cognition at 2 years. *Journal of Applied Developmental Psychology, 17*, 347–365.

Feldman, R., & Mayes, L. C. (1999). The cyclic organization of attention during habituation is related to infants' information processing. *Infant Behavior and Development, 22*, 37–49.

Field, T., Pickens, J., Fox, N. A., Nawrocki, T., & Gonzalez, J. (1995). Vagal tone in infants of depressed mothers. *Development and Psychopathology, 7*, 227–231.

Fox, N. A., Schmidt, L. A., Calkins, S. D., Rubin, K. H., & Coplan, R. J. (1996). The role of frontal activation in the regulation and dysregulation of social behavior during the preschool years. *Development and Psychopathology, 8*, 89–102.

Goldsmith, H. H., Buss, K. A., & Lemery, K. S. (1997). Toddler and childhood temperament: Expanded content, stronger genetic evidence, new evidence for the importance of environment. *Developmental Psychology, 33*, 891–905.

Gottman, J. M., Guralnick, M. J., Wilson, B., Swanson, C. C., & Murray, J. D. (1997). What should the focus of emotion regulation in children be? A nonlinear dynamic mathematical model of children's peer interaction in groups. *Development and Psychopathology, 9*, 421–452.

Gralinski, J. H., & Kopp, C. B. (1993). Everyday rules for behavior: Mothers' requests to young children. *Developmental Psychology, 29*, 573–584.

Graziano, W. G. (2003). Personality development: An introduction toward process approaches to long-term stability and change in persons. *Journal of Personality, 71*, 893–903.

Graziano, W. G., & Bryant, W. H. (1998). Self-monitoring and the self-attribution of positive emotions. *Journal of Personality & Social Psychology, 74*, 250–261.

Graziano, W. G., & Eisenberg, N. (1997). Agreeableness: A dimension of personality. In R. Hogan, J. Johnson, & S. Briggs (Eds.), *Handbook of personality psychology* (pp. 795–824). San Diego: Academic Press.

Graziano, W. G., Jensen-Campbell, L. A., & Finch, J. F. (1997). The self as a mediator between personality and adjustment. *Journal of Personality and Social Psychology, 73*, 392–404.

Graziano, W. G., & Tobin, R. M. (2002). Emotional regulation from infancy through adolescence. In M. H. Bornstein, L. Davidson, C. L. M. Keyes, K. A. Moore, & The Center for Child

Well-being (Eds.), *Well-being: Positive development across the life course* (pp. 139–154). Mahwah, NJ: Lawrence Erlbaum Associates.

Graziano, W. G., & Waschull, S. (1995). Social development and self-monitoring. *Review of Personality and Social Psychology, 15,* 233–260.

Grolnick, W. S., Bridges, L. J., & Connell, J. P. (1996). Emotion regulation in two-year-olds: Strategies and emotional expression in four contexts. *Child Development, 67,* 928–941.

Grolnick, W. S., & Ryan, R. M. (1989). Parent styles associated with children's self-regulation and competence in school. *Journal of Educational Psychology, 81,* 143–154.

Gumora, G., & Arsenio, W. F. (2002). Emotionality, emotion regulation, and school performance in middle school children. *Journal of School Psychology, 40,* 395–413.

Gunnar, M. R., Isensee, J., & Fust, L. S. (1987). Adrenocortical activity and the Brazelton Neonatal Assessment Scale: Moderating effects of the newborn's biomedical status. *Child Development, 58,* 1448–1458.

Gunnar, M. R., Mangelsdorf, S., Larson, M., & Hertsgaard, L. (1990). Attachment, temperament, and adrenocortical activity in infancy: A study of psychoendocrine regulation. *Developmental Psychology, 25,* 355–363.

Hair, E. C., & Graziano, W. G. (2003). Self-esteem, personality and achievement in high school: A prospective longitudinal study in Texas. *Journal of Personality, 71,* 971–994.

Henry, B., Caspi, A., Moffitt, T. E., Harrington, H., & Silva, P. A. (1999). Staying in school protects boys with poor self-regulation in childhood from later crime: A longitudinal study. *International Journal of Behavioral Development, 23,* 1049–1073.

Jensen-Campbell, L. A., & Graziano, W. G. (2000). Beyond the school yard: Relationships as moderators of daily interpersonal conflict. *Personality and Social Psychology Bulletin, 26,* 923–935.

Jensen-Campbell, L. A., & Graziano, W. G. (2001). Agreeableness as a moderator of interpersonal conflict. *Journal of Personality, 69,* 323–361.

Kagan, J. (1994). On the nature of emotion. *Monographs of the Society for Research in Child Development, 59*(2–3, Serial No. 240), 7–24, 250–283.

Katz, L. F., & Gottman, J. M. (1995). Vagal tone protects children from marital conflict. *Development and Psychopathology, 7,* 83–92.

Kieras, J. E., Tobin, R. M., Graziano, W. G., & Rothbart, M. K. (2005, May). You can't always get what you want: Effortful control and young children's responses to undesirable gifts. *Psychological Science, 16,* 391–396.

Kochanska, G. (1991). Socialization and temperament in the development of guilt and conscience. *Child Development, 62,* 1379–1392.

Kochanska, G., DeVet, K., Goldman, M., Murray, K., & Putnam, S. P. (1994). Maternal reports of conscience development and temperament in young children. *Child Development, 65,* 852–868.

Kochanska, G., & Knaack, A. (2003, December). Effortful control as a personality characteristic of young children: Antecedents, correlates, and consequences. *Journal of Personality, 71,* 1087–1112.

Kochanska, G., Murray, K. T., & Harlan, E. T. (2000). Effortful control in early childhood: Continuity and change, antecedents, and implications for social development. *Developmental Psychology, 36,* 220–232.

Kochanska, G., Tjebkes, T. L., & Forman, D. R. (1998). Children's emerging regulation of conduct: Restraint, compliance, and internalization from infancy to the second year. *Child Development, 69,* 1378–1389.

Krafft, K. C., & Berk, L. E. (1998). Private speech in two preschools: Significance of open-ended activities and make-believe play for verbal self-regulation. *Early Childhood Research Quarterly, 13,* 637–658.

Lewis, M. D., Koroshegyi, C., Douglas, L., & Kampe, K. (1997). Age-specific associations between emotional responses to separation and cognitive performance in infancy. *Developmental Psychology, 33,* 32–42.

Little, T. D., Lopez, D. F., & Wanner, B. (2001). Children's action-control behaviors (coping): A longitudinal validation of the Behavioral Inventory of Strategic Control. *Anxiety, Stress, and Coping, 14*(3), 315–336.

Lopez, D. F., & Little, T. D. (1996). Children's action-control beliefs and emotional regulation in the social domain. *Developmental Psychology, 32*, 299–312.

Mangelsdorf, S. C., Shapiro, J. R., & Marzolf, D. (1995). Developmental and temperamental differences in emotional regulation in infancy. *Child Development, 66*, 1817–1828.

McDowell, D. J., O'Neil, R., & Parke, R. D. (2000). Display rule application in a disappointing situation and children's emotional reactivity: Relations with social competence. *Merrill-Palmer Quarterly, 46*(2), 306–324.

Metcalfe, J., & Mischel, W. (1999). A hot-cool system analysis of delay of gratification: Dynamics of willpower. *Psychological Review, 106*, 3–19.

Miller, A. L., Volling, B. L., & McElwain, N. L. (2000). Sibling jealousy in a triadic context with mothers and fathers. *Social Development, 9*(4), 433–457.

Miller, D. C., & Byrnes, J. P. (1997). The role of contextual and personal factors in children's risk taking. *Developmental Psychology, 33*, 814–823.

Mischel, W., & Baker, N. (1995). Cognitive appraisals and transformations in delay behavior. *Journal of Personality and Social Psychology, 31*, 254–261.

Mischel, W., & Ebbesen, E. B. (1970). Attention in delay of gratification. *Journal of Personality and Social Psychology, 16*, 329–337.

Nelson, B., Marin, R. P., Hodge, S., Havill, V., & Kamphaus, R. (1999). Modeling the prediction of elementary school adjustment form preschool temperament. *Personality and Individual Differences, 26*, 687–700.

Nougier, V., Bard, C., Fleury, M., & Teasdale, N. (1998). Contribution of central and peripheral vision on the regulation of stance: Developmental aspects. *Journal of Experimental Child Psychology, 68*, 202–215.

Porges, S. W. (1991). Vagal tone: An autonomic mediator of affect. In J. Garber & K. A. Dodge (Eds.), *The development of emotion regulation and dysregulation* (pp. 111–128). New York: Cambridge University Press.

Porges, S. W., Doussard-Roosevelt, J. A., Portales, A. L., & Greenspan, S. I. (1996). Infant regulation of the vagal "brake" predicts child behavior problems: A psychobiological model of social behavior. *Developmental Psychobiology, 29*(8), 697–712.

Portales, A. L., Porges, S. W., Doussard-Roosevelt, J. A., Abedin, M., Lopez, R., Young, M. A., Beeram, M. R., & Baker, M. (1997). Vagal regulation during bottle feeding in low-birth weight neonates: Support for the gustatory-vagal hypothesis. *Developmental Psychobiology, 30*(3), 225–233.

Richards, J. M. (2004). The cognitive consequences of concealing feelings. *Current Directions in Psychological Sciences, 13*, 131–134.

Rosenblum, K. L., McDonough, S., Muzik, M., Miller, A., & Sameroff, A. (2002). Maternal representations of the infant: Associations with infant response to the Still Face. *Child Development, 73*, 999–1015.

Rothbart, M. K., & Derryberry, D. (1981). Development of individual differences in temperament. In M. E. Lamb, A. L. Brown, & B. Rogoff (Eds.), *Advances in developmental psychology* (Vol. 1, pp. 37–86). Hillsdale, NJ: Lawrence Erlbaum Associates.

Rubin, K. H., Coplan, R. J., Fox, N. A., & Calkins, S. D. (1995). Emotionality, emotion regulation, and preschoolers' social adaptation. *Development and Psychopathology, 7*, 49–62.

Serna, L., Nielsen, E., Lambros, K., & Forness, S. (2000). Primary prevention with children at risk for emotional or behavioral disorders: Data on a universal intervention for Head Start classrooms. *Behavioral Disorders, 26*(1), 70–84.

Shields, A., Dickstein, S., Seifer, R., Giusti, L., Magee, K. D., & Spritz, B. (2001). Emotional competence and early school adjustment: A study of preschoolers at risk. *Early Education and Development, 12*(1), 73–96.

Shoda, Y., Mischel, W., & Peake, P. K. (1990). Predicting adolescent cognitive and self-regulatory competencies from preschool delay of gratification: Identifying diagnostic conditions. *Developmental Psychology, 26*, 978–986.

Spangler, G., & Scheubeck, R. (1993). Behavioral organization in newborns and its relation to adrenocortical and cardiac activity. *Child Development, 64*, 622–633.

Spangler, G., Schieche, M., Ilg, U., Maier, U., & Ackermann, C. (1994). Maternal sensitivity as an external organizer for biobehavioral regulation in infancy. *Developmental Psychobiology, 27*, 425–437.

Stifter, C. A., & Braungart, J. M. (1995). The regulation of negative reactivity in infancy: Function and development. *Developmental Psychology, 31*, 448–455.

Stifter, C. A., & Fox, N. A. (1990). Infant reactivity: Physiological correlates of newborn and 5-month temperament. *Developmental Psychology, 26*, 582–588.

Stifter, C. A., & Spinrad, T. L. (2002). The effect of excessive crying on the development of emotion regulation. *Infancy, 3*, 133–152.

Stifter, C. A., Spinrad, T. L, & Braungart-Rieker, J. M. (1999). Toward a developmental model of child compliance: The role of emotion regulation in infancy. *Child Development, 70*, 21–32.

Thompson, R. A. (1994). Emotion regulation: A theme in search of definition. *Monographs of the Society for Research in Child Development, 59*(2–3, Serial No. 240).

van der Meere, J. J., & Stemerdink, N. (1999). The development of state regulation in normal children: An indirect comparison with children with ADHD. *Developmental Neuropsychology, 16*, 213–225.

van der Meere, J. J., Stemerdink, B. A., & Gunning, W. B. (1995). Effect of presentation rate of stimuli on response inhibition in ADHD children with and without tics. *Journal of Perceptual and Motor Skills, 81*, 259–262.

Volling, B. L., McElwain, N. L., & Miller, A. L. (2002). Emotion regulation in context: The jealousy complex between young siblings and its relations with child and family characteristics. *Child Development, 73*, 581–600.

Vondra, J. I., Shaw, D. S., Swearingen, L., Cohen, M., & Owens, E. B. (2001). Attachment stability and emotional and behavioral regulation from infancy to preschool age. *Development and Psychopathology, 13*(1), 13–33.

Walden, T. A., & Baxter, A. (1989). The effect of context and age on social referencing. *Child Development, 60*, 1511–1518.

Waters, E., & Deane, K. E. (1985). Defining and assessing individual differences in attachment relationships: Q-methodology and the organization of behavior in infancy and early childhood. *Monographs of the Society for Research in Child Development, 50*(1–2, Serial No. 209), 41–104.

Wegner, D. (2002). *The illusion of conscious will.* Cambridge, MA: MIT Press.

Wentzel, K. R., Weinberber, D. A., Ford, M. E., & Feldman, S. S. (1990). Academic achievement in preadolescence: The role motivational, affective, and self-regulatory processes. *Journal of Applied Developmental Psychology, 11*, 179–193.

Zach, U., & Keller, H. (1999). Patterns of the attachment-exploration balance of 1-year-old infants from the United States and Germany. *Journal of Cross-Cultural Psychology, 30*, 381–388.

Zeman, J., & Shipman, K. (1996). Children's expression of negative affect: Reasons and methods. *Developmental Psychology, 32*, 842–849.

Zeman, J., & Shipman, K. (1997). Social-contextual influences on expectancies for managing anger and sadness: The transition from middle childhood to adolescence. *Developmental Psychology, 33*, 917–924.

15

Personality and Self-Esteem Development in Adolescence

M. Brent Donnellan
Michigan State University

Kali H. Trzesniewski
Stanford University

Richard W. Robins
University of California, Davis

Classic accounts portray adolescence as a time of upheaval and turmoil, a period of "storm and stress" (Hall, 1904). Aristotle (trans. 1954), for example, described the youthful character as mercurial and subject to the whims of internal drives:

> Young men have strong passions, and tend to gratify them indiscriminately. Of the bodily desires, it is the sexual by which they are most swayed and in which they show absence of self-control. They are changeable and fickle in their desires, which are violent while they last, but quickly over: their impulses are keen but not deep-rooted, and are like sick people's attacks of hunger and thirst. (Rhetoric Book II, chap. 12)

Although contemporary researchers reject such strong views (e.g., Petersen, 1988; Steinberg, 2001, 2002), certain aspects of this storm and stress notion may have validity (e.g., Arnett, 1999). For example, rates of depression for girls tend to increase during early adolescence (Ge, Lorenz, Conger, Elder, & Simons, 1994) and the age-crime curve peaks at around age 17 (Moffitt, 1993). Arnett concluded that the "paradox of adolescence is that it can be at once a time of storm and stress and a time of exuberant growth" (p. 324). Accordingly, adolescence is a particularly interesting time to study personality and self-esteem development because transitional periods offer important opportunities for studying the processes that affect continuity and change in individual differences (Caspi & Moffitt, 1991).

This chapter summarizes what is known about personality and self-esteem development during adolescence. It also identifies several gaps in knowledge that limit the conclusions that can be reached from the existing literature. It then describes a framework for conceptualizing personality and self-esteem development during adolescence, drawing on theoretical perspectives from the adolescent development literature. Next, there is a discussion of how the mechanisms that facilitate stability and change in personality development may operate during adolescence. The final sections offers suggestions for future research on personality and self-esteem development during adolescence.

BASIC FINDINGS ABOUT PERSONALITY AND SELF-ESTEEM DEVELOPMENT IN ADOLESCENCE

The Big Five Capture the Range of Individual Differences in Adolescent Personalities

There is consensus among personality psychologists that the majority of personality traits used to describe adults can be meaningfully organized into five broad domains, referred to as the Big Five: Extraversion, Agreeableness, Conscientiousness, Neuroticism (or its opposite, Emotional Stability), and Openness to Experience (Digman, 1990; Funder, 2001; John & Srivastava, 1999; Ozer & Reise, 1994; McCrae, 2001; but see Block, 1995, 2001). Several investigators have now identified the Big Five in adolescents (e.g., Digman & Inouye, 1986; Graziano & Ward, 1992; John, Caspi, Robins, Moffitt, & Stouthamer-Loeber, 1994; Parker & Stumpf, 1998; Robins, John, & Caspi, 1994) and even children (Asendorpf & Van Aken, 2003; Kohnstamm, Halverson, Mervielde, & Havill, 1998; Lamb, Chuang, Wessels, Broberg, & Hwang, 2002). This downward extension of the Big Five is an important discovery because it facilitates the accumulation of a coherent picture of personality development across the life span by focusing on the same core set of personality traits at different phases of development.

Moreover, recent work suggests that many measures of the Big Five developed for adult samples provide reliable and valid measures of the Big Five in adolescent samples. For example, McCrae et al. (2002) found that the Neo Five Factor Inventory (NEO–FFI; Costa & McCrae, 1992) was suitable for assessing the personalities of both gifted and nongifted adolescents. De Fruyt, Mervielde, Hoeskstra, and Rolland (2000) indicated that the Neo Personality Inventory, Revised (NEO–PI–R; Costa & McCrae, 1992) can reliably and validly measure adolescent personality at the level of the primary scales (i.e., the Big Five). Jensen-Campbell et al. (2002) successfully adapted the Big Five Inventory (John & Srivastava, 1999) for use with children in the fifth and sixth grade. Collectively, these results suggest that most inventories designed to capture the Five Factor model are suitable assessment instruments for measuring adolescent personality. This is an important conclusion because it indicates that the same measures of the Big Five can be used to track personality development from adolescence through adulthood.

Individual Differences in Personality and Global Self-Esteem Become More Stable From Early Adolescence to Young Adulthood

The stability of individual differences is typically assessed by test–retest correlations, which reflect the degree to which people who are high (vs. low) at one point in time maintain their relative ordering over time. A recent meta-analysis found that personality traits become increasingly stable across the life span: test–retest correlations increase from .30 for children to .43 for adolescents from age 12 to 17.9 to .54 for young adults from age 18 to 21.9 to around .70 for adults from age 50 to 70 (Roberts & DelVecchio, 2000). Two studies highlight this same shift in stability from adolescence to early adulthood: McCrae et al. (2002) found that the average test–retest correlation for the Big Five was .41 in sample of 12- to 16-year-olds (Study 1), whereas Robins, Fraley, Roberts, and Trzesniewski (2001) found that the average test–retest correlation for the Big Five was .61 in their sample of 18- to 21-year-olds. A recent meta-analysis of global self-esteem reveals a similar pattern of increasing stability from early adolescence (mean test–retest correlation = .48) to young adulthood (mean test–retest correlation = .62; Trzesniewski, Donnellan, & Robins, 2003).

Why is stability lower during early adolescence than during late adolescence and early adulthood? Lower stability is expected when the individual is faced with dramatic environmental and/or maturational changes (Alsaker & Olweus, 1992; Ge & Conger, 1999; Stein, Newcomb, & Bentler, 1986; West & Graziano, 1989; Wiggins & Pincus, 1992). The transition to adolescence is perhaps the most volatile normative transition in the life span, entailing a coalescence of social, cognitive, and biological changes. It is associated with rapid maturational changes, shifting societal demands, exploration of new identities and roles, and the initiation of new peer and romantic relationships. These changes may differentially impact individuals, thus shifting the relative ordering of individual differences and reducing stability coefficients. Furthermore, as individuals make the transition into adulthood, maturational changes are reduced, environmental changes are increasingly subject to individual control, and a more stable sense of self is formed. This process would tend to promote continuity over time and thus increase stability coefficients. In summary, the findings on rank-order stability suggest that personality traits are more malleable in adolescence than in later developmental periods.

Normative Changes in the Big Five and Self-Esteem During Adolescence Are Not Well Understood

Normative trends in personality and self-esteem development are typically assessed by changes in mean levels. Mean-level changes can result from maturational processes or social-contextual factors that influence a population in a similar manner. A recent meta-analysis of mean-level personality change across the life span suggested that Social Dominance (aspects of Extraversion related to independence and dominance), Emotional Stability (the converse of Neuroticism), and Openness increased from ages 10 to 18 (Roberts, Walton, & Viechtbauer, in press). Even so, these mean-level changes were small—the d-metric effect size for Openness to Experience was the largest at .23. Agreeableness, Conscientiousness, and Social Vitality (aspects of Extraversion related to positive affect, activity level, and sociability) demonstrated rather negligible mean-level changes during this period (e.g., the largest of these effect sizes was .11 in the d-metric).

Additionally, McCrae et al. (2002) combined longitudinal, cross-sectional, and cross-national studies to examine normative changes in the Big Five during adolescence. These results are worth summarizing because they were not included in the Roberts et al. meta-analysis. McCrae et al. (2002) found that mean levels of Openness increased from ages 12 to 18 and that Neuroticism slightly increased for girls but not for boys during this period. They found no replicable evidence of changes in Extraversion, Agreeableness, or Conscientiousness. All told, the results from McCrae et al. (2002) and Roberts et al. (in press) generally converge, especially with respect to increases in Openness and generally negligible changes in Agreeableness and Conscientiousness during the adolescent years. As such, the best available evidence suggests that there are few robust normative changes in the Big Five during adolescence.

There is somewhat less clarity about mean-level change in global self-esteem given that researchers have long debated if self-esteem shows normative age changes during adolescence (e.g., Demo, 1992; McCarthy & Hoge, 1982; O'Malley & Bachman, 1983; Rosenberg, 1986; Twenge & Campbell, 2001; Wylie, 1979). Several recent studies, including a large, cross-sectional study of 326,641 individuals from age 9 to age 90, and a meta-analysis of 86 published articles may help shed light on this issue (Robins, Trzesniewski, Tracy, Gosling, & Potter, 2002; Trzesniewski, Donnellan, & Robins, 2001). These studies converge in showing that self-esteem begins to decline in late childhood and continues to decline throughout adolescence, producing a substantial cumulative drop. For example, the meta-analysis revealed a one full standard deviation drop when 7- and 8-year-olds were compared to 13- and 14-year-olds. The adolescent drop in self-esteem appears to be particularly robust because it replicates across gender, although it is much more pronounced for girls, across several ethnic groups and across U.S. and non-U.S. citizens. After dropping during adolescence, self-esteem begins to increase during the transition into young adulthood.

There is an absence of strong theory for predicting and interpreting these mean-level changes in personality and self-esteem. This absence is symptomatic of a larger problem in adolescent research as identified by Steinberg and Morris (2001): "No comprehensive theories of normative adolescent development have emerged to fill the voids created by the declining influence of Freud, Erikson, and Piaget" (p. 101). Thus, researchers typically rely on more narrow theoretical conceptualizations to explain mean-level trends. For example, cognitive changes occurring during adolescence, such as an increased understanding of abstract concepts and increased reasoning abilities, may explain the observed increases in Openness (McCrae et al., 2002).

All told, a consensus on the empirical reality and theoretical explanations for the normative trends in personality and self-esteem have yet to be reached. More research and theory development is badly needed. However, tentatively it can be concluded that adolescence is probably not a time of robust mean-level changes in personality, with the exception of perhaps an increase in Openness and a decrease in global self-esteem. Indeed, one of the most striking findings to emerge from Roberts et al. (in press) meta-analysis is that adolescence is not the time of greatest change in mean levels of personality; rather, the most substantive normative changes occur during young adulthood. Consistent with this finding, Jones and Meredith (2000) reported that there was no mean-level change in clinician reports of psychological health from age 14 to 18.

Why might there be a lack of normative personality change in adolescence? The adolescent period is sometimes conceptualized as a period of identity exploration (e.g., Erikson, 1950). The absence of clearly defined age-related role progressions may be responsible for the few normative personality changes during this period. It may be the case that adolescence is best characterized as a period of individual, rather than normative, change in personality. It is possible that some adolescents increase, some decrease, and some remain relatively consistent in the Big Five dimensions, but the net effect is to produce rather negligible mean-level changes. Thus, personality change in adolescence may be best characterized as a time of individual differences in change trajectories (e.g., Baltes, Reese, & Nesselroade, 1977; see Young & Mroczek, 2003, for a demonstration of the use of growth modeling to study individual differences in change during adolescence). Normative changes in personality may occur in subsequent developmental periods when there are stronger and more consistent societal influences on behavior such as young adulthood. Roberts et al. (in press) speculated that it is the acquisition of adult roles, such as entering the workforce and beginning a family, that produce more consistent findings for normative personality development in young adulthood.

TOWARD A FRAMEWORK FOR THINKING ABOUT PERSONALITY AND SELF-ESTEEM DEVELOPMENT DURING ADOLESCENCE

One of the central arguments in this chapter is that attention to developmental issues salient in adolescence will provide important insights into personality and self-esteem development during this phase of life. Research attention should focus on the contexts likely to have the most significant reciprocal relations with personality development because surprisingly little is known about the interplay of experiences in these contexts and the development of personality. The discussion builds on Hill's (1983; Steinberg, 2002) framework for studying adolescence because his approach offers a convenient way to organize a discussion of these issues. Indeed, Hill highlighted how developmental changes in the biological, cognitive, and social domains may directly and indirectly affect the development of individual differences in personality and self-esteem. Hill also emphasized the contexts that were most developmentally relevant for adolescents, such as peer relationships, schools, and extracurricular activities. Finally, using Hill's framework may facilitate greater cross-fertilization between the expanding literatures on personality development and the literature on adolescent development (for reviews, see Lerner & Galambos, 1998; Petersen, 1988; Steinberg & Morris, 2001).

Adolescence Is a Time of Transition

Adolescence is a time of relatively dramatic biological, cognitive, and social change. These changes tend to coalesce during early adolescence and therefore much attention has focused on the early adolescent transition (e.g., Eccles et al., 1993; Simmons & Blyth, 1987). A naïve view is that these transitions create dramatic changes in personality and self-esteem; however, life transitions that lack clear proscriptions for behavior may actually accentuate existing individual differences and promote continuity (Caspi & Moffitt, 1991). Consistent with this notion, Allport, Bruner, and Jandorf (1953) noted that even catastrophic social events can "select and reinforce traits that were already present" (p. 445). Thus, to the extent that adolescent transitions lack clearly defined behavioral norms and expectations for behavior, these events may accentuate rather than disrupt individual differences. In either case, adolescent transitions provide fertile ground for testing hypotheses regarding continuity and change.

Biological Transitions.   Changes in physical appearance are the most outwardly visible indications of the biological changes that occur during adolescence (Archibald, Graber, & Brooks-Gunn, 2003; Brooks-Gunn & Reiter, 1990). Biological changes that occur during adolescence include development in areas of the brain such as the prefrontal cortex and the limbic system (Spear, 2000), increases in hormones such as testosterone and estrogen (e.g., Susman et al., 1987; Susman & Rogol, 2004), and the maturation of primary and secondary sexual characteristics (e.g., Tanner, 1962). The study of the brain changes may someday provide a proximal explanation for many of the changes associated with adolescence, such as increases in peer affiliation, sensation seeking, risk taking, and negative affect in response to stress (Spear, 2000).

Indeed, the belief that the biological changes associated with adolescence are linked with changes in thoughts, feelings, and behaviors has an enduring history in psychology (e.g., Hall, 1904). For instance, neo-psychoanalytic writers linked pubertal changes with psychosocial upheaval (Blos, 1962; Erikson, 1950; Freud, 1958). Erikson (1950) believed that puberty and body growth caused the adolescent to "refight many of the battles of earlier years" (p. 261). Although the available evidence does not support such a dramatic viewpoint, contemporary research has established a connection between pubertal timing and psychosocial development (Alsaker, 1996; Caspi & Moffitt, 1991; Ge, Conger, & Elder, 1996). One well-replicated finding is that early maturing girls (i.e., girls who experience the onset of menstruation earlier than their peers) exhibit greater internalizing and externalizing symptoms during adolescence than their on-time or later maturing peers. The impact of pubertal timing on males is not as well established, but recent evidence hints that early maturing boys may also demonstrate increased psychological distress and problem behaviors relative to their on-time and later maturing peers (e.g., Ge, Conger, & Elder, 2001b). Although several hypotheses have been proposed to explain these findings, the stage-termination hypothesis is particularly compelling (e.g., Caspi & Moffitt, 1991; Ge et al., 1996).

The stage-termination explanation suggests that early maturing adolescents are not developmentally prepared for the new challenges and developmental tasks that accompany puberty (e.g., increasing social demands from peers and parents). Put simply, the unprepared (or underprepared) early maturing adolescent responds to new demands by manifesting increased psychological distress. Importantly, Caspi and Moffitt (1991) found that increased delinquency in connection with early puberty was most pronounced among girls with preexisting behavioral difficulties. This result nicely illustrated their accentuation hypothesis that stressful life events and transitions tend to intensify existing individual characteristics.

A handful of investigations also suggest that the impact of early maturation depends on features of the social ecology. These studies illustrate that the effects of biological changes on human development often involve a complicated interplay between physiological, psychological, and social processes. For example, Caspi, Lynam, Moffitt, and Silva (1993) demonstrated that the early maturing girls were more likely to exhibit delinquency in mixed-gender school settings rather than same-gender schools. Ge, Brody, Conger, Simons, and Murry (2002) found that the negative relation between early puberty and behavior problems was stronger in disadvantaged neighborhoods than in more socially advantaged neighborhoods. These findings suggests that the behavioral impact of biological changes during adolescence can be moderated by environmental factors. This work also highlights the possibility that the impact of biological factors on personality development will likely involve the interplay between individuals and their contextual circumstances.

The biological changes associated with the adolescent transition may have particular relevance for the study of gender differences in personality development. For example, there is a pressing need to explain why gender differences in self-esteem are more pronounced in adolescence (e.g., Kling, Hyde, Showers, & Buswell, 1999), and perhaps similarly why gender differences in depression first emerge during early adolescence (Ge, Conger, & Elder, 2001a). Of course, females and males are exposed to different hormonal influences during puberty (Brooks-Gunn & Reiter, 1990) and these gender-specific hormonal influences may produce gender differences in self-esteem and depression. However, it is unlikely that hormones will provide a complete explanation for these gender differences given that hormones typically explain only a small portion of the variance in behavioral outcomes (Buchanan, Eccles, & Becker, 1992).

It is more likely that the interplay between biological development and socialization factors plays a major role in the emergence of gender differences in self-esteem. For example, the development of secondary sex characteristics during puberty may make gender increasing salient to the individual and to those in their social environments. This outward change in appearance may trigger changes in the adolescent's self-concept and elicit socialization practices that are differentially associated with gender (i.e., the gender intensification hypothesis). For instance, Block and Robins (1993) speculated that adolescent self-esteem development is tied to the different socialization practices affecting girls and boys. They argued that the cultural press during adolescence emphasizes interpersonal connection and communion for girls (i.e., getting along) and personal autonomy and agency for boys (i.e., getting ahead). These cultural norms were linked to gender-specific correlates of self-esteem trajectories. Specifically, personality traits associated with an interpersonal orientation promoted self-esteem in adolescent females whereas personality traits associated with the management of social anxiety promoted self-esteem in adolescent males.

Cognitive Transitions.   Cognitive changes in adolescence are less visible than biological changes but are no less important for understanding personality and self-esteem development. There is little debate that adolescent cognitive abilities tend to be more advanced than those of children. Adolescents can understand possibility, reason deductively, think in multiple dimensions, and consider abstract notions (Byrnes, 2003; Keating, 1990, 2004). One of the most important implications of these changes for personality development is that adolescents are able to think about themselves in these new and complex ways. Elkind (1967) proposed that adolescents become temporally self-obsessed and egocentric in their thoughts once they apply these newfound cognitive abilities to understanding themselves. At the very least, cognitive changes should permit adolescents to "know" themselves well enough to provide valid answers on pencil-and-paper measures of personality.

The ability to think abstractly, think in multiple dimensions, and take the perspectives of others may have a profound impact on personality and self-esteem development during adolescence. For example, adolescents are able to develop notions of ideal versus actual selves (Harter, 1998, 1999), and are thus able to experience discrepancies between ideal and actual self-conceptualizations. Classic accounts argue that self-esteem is maximized as this difference is minimized (e.g., James, 1890). The emergence of the capacity to perform this complicated psychological algorithm may be linked to the decline in self-esteem that occurs during adolescence. More generally, this suggests that the cognitive underpinnings of self-esteem in adolescence may be somewhat different than the cognitive underpinnings of self-esteem in childhood.

Cognitive changes may also affect aspects of personality beyond self-esteem. Children may be conscientious, agreeable, and emotionally stable, and perhaps form simple self-representations related to these dimensions, but only adolescents can weave these representations into abstract narratives and life stories. Ultimately, according to McAdams (2001), changes in cognitive abilities enable the individual to formulate a life story that provides an evolving yet coherent and organized account of the self.

Increased self-understanding may have other important influences on personality development. Specifically, increased self-understanding may enable adolescents to seek out environments that are congruent with their own dispositions. For example, a shy and introverted adolescent may seek out activities and contexts that are consistent with these traits. This niche picking should promote continuity in personality development because life circumstances that are congruent with individual differences will likely reinforce individual tendencies and are unlikely to offer an impetus for dramatic change.

On the other hand, self-reflection and self-observation have also been suggested as one mechanism that may promote personality change (Caspi & Roberts, 2001). It could be that adolescents, for the first time in development, have the cognitive abilities to actually change their personalities. For example, adolescents may reflect on their behavior and interpersonal interactions and discover that they are relatively judgmental and unkind. These individuals may then make a concerted effort to change these tendencies to facilitate better peer relationships.

Social Transitions.   Adolescents experience a number of changes in their social world, including changes from primarily same-gender peer groups to more integrated peer groups (Brown, 1990), changes in the number of hours spent with peers (Brown, 2004), and greater autonomy in parent–child relationships (Steinberg, 1990). Perhaps the clearest and most well-known social transition during adolescence is the transition from elementary school to secondary school. This shift in the educational context is one of the first social markers of early adolescence (Elder, 1968) and has been characterized as a potentially difficult transition.

Simmons and Blyth (1987) argued that the change from the close community ties, or "gemeinschaft," of the elementary school to the larger, institutional ties, or "gesellschaft," of the secondary school environment can prove stressful and disruptive to the early adolescent. Eccles and her colleagues (e.g., Eccles & Midgley, 1989; Eccles et al., 1993) indicated that adolescents are at-risk for difficulties during the middle school transition because of increasingly negative relationships between students and teachers, changes in instructional practices and increasingly competitive grading practices, and general restrictions on autonomy. These changes in the social environment are a poor fit with the needs and strivings of the developing adolescent.

These social changes have been used to explain the decline in self-esteem that has been observed in early adolescence. For instance, Wigfield, Eccles, Mac Iver, Reuman, and Midgley (1991) found a dip in self-esteem following the transition to junior high in a large sample of adolescents from Michigan. Seidman, Allen, Aber, Mitchell, and Feinman (1994) replicated this drop using a diverse urban sample of low SES students. However, others have failed to replicate this drop (Hirsch & Rapkin, 1987; Nottlemann, 1987), so there may be a fair amount of heterogeneity in the experience of the transition to secondary education. Moreover, cross-national replications of the drop (e.g. Robins, Trzesniewski, et al., 2002) cast doubt on the possibility that school transitions are the sole explanation for normative changes in self-esteem, given that the educational context and the timing of school transitions differs across countries. Nonetheless, it is possible that school transitions play some role in the normative drop in self-esteem during early adolescence.

Shifts in the school environment provide good opportunities to test hypotheses about personality continuity and change (e.g., Does the middle school transition accentuate individual differences in personality?) and about basic personality processes (e.g., Do neurotic adolescents have more difficulties during these transitions?). Few studies have used these early adolescent social transitions to answer questions framed in these ways. Furthermore, given that secondary school success likely foretells future success, studies linking personality and self-esteem with school success may have significant applied value.

The last and perhaps least well understood adolescent social transition involves the relatively slow and ambiguous transition out of adolescence. In contemporary societies, it is relatively unclear when adolescence ends and adulthood begins (e.g., Arnett, 2000). This leads to an interesting asymmetry about adolescence; the transition into this phase of the life span is more clearly marked by biological, cognitive, and social changes than the transition out of this phase of the life span. Arnett (2000) argued that adolescence should be restricted to ages 12 through 18 when individuals are commonly enrolled in secondary schools, living with their parent(s), and grappling with the physical changes of puberty. He suggested that a relatively distinct phase of the life span labeled emerging adulthood occurs after adolescence, between age 18 and age 25, when individuals enjoy greater freedom and more diverse life experiences. However, the distinction between adolescence and emerging adulthood is as much a matter of identity as it is a matter of chronological age.

Given the ambiguity of the transition out of adolescence, its impact on personality and self-esteem development is not particularly well understood. Some existing evidence suggests that there are positive normative trends in personality and self-esteem development associated with the transition into emerging adult-

hood. For example, Roberts, Caspi, and Moffitt (2001) found declines in negative emotionality and increases in agentic positive emotionality from late
adolescence to young adulthood. Similarly, Robins et al. (2001) discovered normative increases in Agreeableness, Conscientiousness, and Openness and decreases in Neuroticism from age 18 to age 22. Self-esteem also tends to slightly
increase from late adolescence into emerging adulthood (e.g., Donnellan,
Trzesniewski, & Conger, 2005; Robins et al., 2002).

These normative changes in personality from adolescence to emerging adulthood
may indicate that leaving adolescence entails positive psychological development.
Adolescence may not be an absolute time of storm and stress but these trends suggest
that things do get "better" for the average individual after adolescence. Adolescence
may therefore be a relatively difficult period in the life span even if it is not terribly
difficult for the average individual. This recognition may help explain why adolescent storm and stress notions persist even without strong empirical support.

One explanation for any relative difficulties associated with adolescence is that
there are substantial limitations on an individual's freedom and autonomy stemming
from economic, educational, and legal constraints. A perhaps unfortunate consequence of modernization is that puberty occurs at a relatively early point in adolescence; the average age at menarche in the United States is between age 12 and age
13 (Brooks-Gunn & Reiter, 1990; Herman-Giddens et al., 1997), whereas the end of
adolescence is not until several years later. This creates a relatively lengthy period of
time where individuals are biologically and cognitively mature but have limited
opportunities to socially express this maturity. Moffitt (1993) identified this gap in
maturity as an explanation for involvement in transitory antisocial behavior. In addition to promoting adolescent-limited antisocial behavior, this difficult asynchrony in
development may also negatively affect self-esteem. Accordingly, exiting adolescence and experiencing the freedom, opportunities, and responsibilities of young
adulthood may facilitate positive development and psychological maturity.

Adolescent Adaptation and Important Contexts
of Adolescent Development

Individual differences in personality are likely to affect how well adolescents master
the most significant developmental tasks that they face, namely, making and keeping friends, succeeding in school, and following appropriate social norms for behavior and conduct (e.g., Masten & Coatsworth, 1998). Allport (1937) noted that
personality traits are "*modi vivendi [ways of living]*, ultimately deriving their significance from the role they play in advancing adaptation within, and mastery of, the
personal environment" (p. 137). Although the body of findings linking adolescent
personality to adjustment may not approach the size of the adult literature, it is likely
that the relations between personality and adjustment found in adult samples will
also be evident in adolescent samples. For example, Agreeableness and Conscientiousness are negatively associated with adolescent delinquency (John et al., 1994)
and with adult crime (Miller & Lynam, 2001). Similarly, traits related to
Neuroticism and low Conscientiousness are linked with adolescent substance use
(e.g., Shedler & Block, 1990; Shoal & Giancola, 2003; Wills & Stoolmiller, 2002)
and with adult substance use (e.g., Krueger, Caspi, & Moffitt, 2000).

In addition to the perspective that personality traits shape outcomes, it is important to recognize that individual lives are embedded within contextual settings that may also affect developmental trajectories of self-esteem and personality. It is likely that there are reciprocal links between personality and social contexts such that individual differences both influence and are influenced by experiences in these settings. Some of the important contexts of adolescent development include peers, romantic relationships, schools, and extracurricular activities.

Peers. It is nearly axiomatic in the adolescent development literature that peers play an increasingly important role in the lives of adolescents (e.g., Brown, 1990, 2004). Descriptive work suggests that the amount of time spent with peers increases during adolescence (Larson & Richards, 1991; Larson & Verma, 1999) accounting for around 29% of high school students time (Larson & Verma, 1999). Harris (1995) emphasized the important role that peers play in shaping personality development, although this point was largely ignored because so much attention was given to her claim that parenting practices have little long-term influence on development (but see Loehlin, 1997).

The link between peer influences and adolescent development is likely to be reciprocal. Kandel (1978) demonstrated that both selection effects and socialization effects are involved in the links between peer groups and adolescent substance use. This finding suggests that preexisting individual characteristics influenced peer group experiences and likewise that peer groups affected individual behavior at least with respect to substance use (for further evidence on this later point see Guo, Hill, Hawkins, Catalano, & Abbott, 2002; Hawkins, Catalano, & Miller, 1992).

With respect to individual differences in personality, there is evidence that personality traits affect the quality of peer relationships (e.g., Gest, 1997; Jensen-Campbell et al., 2002; Shiner, 2000; Shiner & Caspi, 2003). For example, Jensen-Campbell et al. (2002) found that Agreeableness and Extraversion predicted peer acceptance and the number of friends in a sample of fifth and sixth graders (Study 1). Moreover, Agreeableness helped prevent subsequent peer victimization illustrating its importance for interpersonal adaptation in early adolescence (Study 2). There is also evidence that individual differences in personality and self-esteem evoke different responses from the social environment during adolescence. For example, low self-regard invites greater peer victimization (Egan & Perry, 1998), whereas Agreeableness is associated with less peer victimization (Jensen-Campbell et al., 2002). Thus, differences in personality and self-esteem are linked with different environmental experiences in the peer context.

Only a few studies have examined how peer experiences shape personality and self-esteem development (e.g., Hartup & Stevens, 1997). For example, Harter (1998) reported that peer acceptance is positively associated with self-esteem, and Bagwell, Newcomb, and Bukowski (1998) indicated that peer experiences prior to adolescence affected self-esteem in young adulthood.

Romantic Relationships. It is estimated that between 69% and 76% of 18-year-olds have been involved in a romantic relationship within the past 18 months based on the National Longitudinal Study of Adolescent Health (Carver, Joyner, & Udry, 2003). The median length of romantic relationship for individuals age 16 or older was 20.5 months in this data set (Carver et al., 2003). These demographic findings suggest that involvement in romantic relationships is relatively common during adolescence and adolescent romantic relationships can be relatively enduring. Scholars who specialize in adolescent development have recently suggested that romantic relationships are an important influence on adolescents (e.g., Collins, 2003; Furman, 2002), although empirical research on this topic is sparse, particularly research linking the Big Five to adolescent romantic relationships.

In contrast, researchers have examined the impact of personality traits on romantic relationships for at least 70 years (Cooper & Sheldon, 2002). The most robust finding from this literature is that Neuroticism is negatively linked with relationship quality. Neuroticism has an adverse affect on both young adult romantic relationships (e.g., Donnellan, Larsen-Rife, & Conger, 2005; Robins, Caspi, & Moffitt, 2000, 2002) and more established relationships (Bouchard, Lussier, & Sabourin, 1999; Watson, Hubbard, & Wiese, 2000). The reciprocal relation may also hold. Robins et al. (2002) found that negative relationship experiences predicted increases in negative emotionality from age 18 to age 26. Consistent with this general notion, Larson, Clore, and Wood (1999) purported that adolescents involved in romantic relationships experienced more severe mood swings. This work suggests that romantic relationships may provide an important context for the development of personality in adolescence.

Schools and Extracurricular Activities.   Research supports the claim that personality traits and self-esteem influence academic achievement. In particular, Conscientiousness and Openness may be the most important traits for understanding success in achievement-related contexts (Digman, 1989; Graziano & Ward, 1992; Hair & Graziano, 2003). However, school-related experiences may reciprocally influence the development of personality and self-esteem. Adolescents spend, roughly, from 5 to 7 hours per day in school, which amounts to about 25% to 30% of their waking hours (Larson, 2000; Larson & Verma, 1999) and schools are an important context for the operation of peer culture (Brown, 1990). Thus, it is plausible that schooling would affect more than just intellectual characteristics (e.g., Eccles et al., 1993; Roeser, 1998; Roeser & Eccles, 1998).

Although there is little research that directly examines the influence of school experiences on personality trait development, Roberts, Caspi, and Moffitt (2003) found that positive experiences in the workplace predict personality changes in young adulthood. Given that work settings and school settings are both achievement-related contexts, it is possible that schools affect personality development similarly.

Another way that the school context may affect personality is through exposure to extracurricular activities. Larson (2000) suggested that these activities provide a context for the development of initiative because adolescents reported elevated levels of intrinsic motivation and concentration during sports and organized youth activities (e.g., Girl Scouts and Boy Scouts). It is quite possible that these extracurricular activities also facilitate the development of traits such as Conscientiousness and promote self-esteem. However, very little attention has focused on how these contexts impact personality trait development. Accordingly, researchers also need to explore how extracurricular activities and school settings affect the development of personality and self-esteem.

PROCESSES OF PERSONALITY AND SELF-ESTEEM DEVELOPMENT IN ADOLESCENCE

The previous section discussed the idea that individual differences in personality and self-esteem are reciprocally linked with adaptation. An important focus of developmental research is to specifically study how this process plays out during adolescence. Shiner and Caspi (2003; Shiner, chap. 11 in this volume) summarized the processes through which personality traits at one point in time influence later adaptation and personality development across the life span, such as evoking specific environmental experiences, shaping individualized interpretations of situations, and motivating individuals to seek out specific environments that are consistent with their individual dispositions (see also Buss, 1987; Scarr & McCartney, 1983). Caspi and Roberts (2001) described several mechanisms that may promote change in personality and self-esteem, including responding to environmental contingencies, self-reflection, observational learning, and changes in perceptions by significant others. An important insight from this work is that the mechanisms that promote continuity may differ from the mechanisms that promote change. This section illustrates how some of these mechanisms likely play out during adolescence.

Mechanisms That Promote Continuity

Environmental Elicitation. Personality traits "draw out," or elicit, particular responses from the social environment. This notion is similar to Scarr and McCartney's (1983) notion of evocative genotype–environment interactions, the process of evocation outlined by Buss (1987), and the general idea that individuals play active roles in shaping their own development (e.g., Lerner & Busch-Rossnagel, 1981). For instance, adolescents high in Agreeableness may evoke friendlier responses from their peers and this may contribute to more positive peer interactions. Adolescents lower in self-esteem may evoke peer victimization. In these cases, environmental stimuli become differentially associated with individual differences. The consequences of these evocative transactions likely follow the "correspondive principle" (Roberts et al., 2003), the proposition that life experiences accentuate the personality characteristics that were initially responsible for the environmental experiences in the first place. When agreeable adolescents evoke positive responses from their peers, it is likely to facilitate the future development of agreeableness. When low self-esteem invites victimization, it is likely that peer victimization will further depress self-esteem.

Environmental Construal. Personality traits shape how adolescents perceive and construe social situations. For example, Shiner and Caspi (2003) related this mechanism to social information processes (Crick & Dodge, 1994), such as the hostile attribution of intent or "hostile attribution bias." Adolescents with a hostile attribution bias interpret neutral social interactions negatively and often respond in kind. This attribution bias creates a kind of self-fulfilling prophecy whereby social interactions quickly turn hostile and negative after the individual responds with hostility to the initially neutral interaction.

A similar process may affect the perceptions of school transitions. For example, a neurotic adolescent may expect that the transition to secondary schooling is more threatening, more hostile, and more stressful than another adolescent. This construal will likely affect how the transition is experienced. The neurotic adolescent may inadvertently contribute to a more stressful transition to middle school by their perceptions of the transition. The upshot is that individual differences in personality and self-esteem affect how adolescents perceive and ultimately experience situations. This process is also likely to maintain individual differences in personality according to the corresponsive principle: Environmental construals will likely strengthen the traits that gave rise to the perceptions in the first place.

Environmental Selection and Environmental Manipulation.   Selection is similar to Scarr and McCartney's (1983) notion of active genotype–environment interactions, the process of environmental selection outlined by Buss (1987), and the concept of active individuals shaping their own development. The basic idea is that individuals seek out or create environments that are consistent with their individual characteristics. An adolescent high in Extraversion may run for class president, whereas an adolescent low in Extraversion may shun participation in school activities. An adolescent high in Openness may seek out intellectually challenging courses and opportunities whereas an adolescent low in Openness may opt for more traditional educational fare. In these cases, differences in personality traits motivate adolescents to select certain situations over others.

Environmental manipulation is when individuals actively change or modify their environments to fit their personalities (Buss, 1987). Selection and manipulation can also facilitate continuity by the corresponsive principle: Traits that influence adolescents to select one context over another and to modify their context will likely be accentuated in these new situations. Scarr and McCartney (1983) argued that these active person–environment transactions increase in frequency over the life span as the individual gains agency. Adolescence is a time of increasing autonomy and thus active person–environment transactions are likely to increase in importance across adolescence.

The increase in active-person environment transactions may explain the observed increases in stability coefficients from early adolescence to late adolescence. Across adolescence, individuals are given more freedom to seek out situations that are consistent with their individual characteristics. Continuity is facilitated as the person and the situation become increasingly synchronized. Adolescents are granted more freedom and autonomy than children, but their ability to select and manipulate environments is more constrained by social factors than adults. Moreover, as noted previously, adolescence may be stressful to the extent that social conditions (e.g., parental control, compulsory education, legal restrictions) place limits on the abilities of adolescents to fully select niches that are consistent with their individual characteristics.

Mechanisms that Promote Change

Responding to Contingencies.   Individuals are responsive to the rewards and punishments of a given setting. Clearly, these contingencies affect behavior in the short term and it is possible that long-term exposure may produce lasting changes. Responding to new contingencies is one reason why scholars have suggested behavior change is associated with "turning points" in the life course (e.g., Caspi, 1998; Caspi & Roberts, 2001). Many of these changes (e.g., military, marriage) launch individuals into more restricted and closely monitored environments that provide more salient reward and punishment structures for certain behaviors. Accordingly, this shift in contingencies may facilitate the observed changes associated with turning points in the life course.

Many contingencies are implicitly associated with particular social roles. In general, however, adolescents have fewer formal roles to play in society than adults and are not typically subjected to extremely restrictive environments such as the military. Nonetheless, adolescents are rewarded and punished for certain behaviors at school and at home. These different contingencies may help shape personalities. It is also likely that nonnormative shifts in family roles could shape personality. For example, following a parental divorce, an adolescent may have to assume greater responsibility for the care of younger siblings. This could lead to an increase in responsibility and self-control.

Self-Reflection. Self-reflection can be one avenue of personality change. As noted earlier, cognitive changes during adolescence lead to greater self-reflective abilities. Thus, adolescents now have one of the tools to change their own personalities. Even so, it is not clear how easy it is for people to willfully change their own personality or whether adolescents have a clear idea of a direction they would want to change their personalities. It may be the case that adolescents first use their abilities of self-reflection to simply figure out their own personalities before attempting to change them. Thus, self-reflection may be a more powerful influence on personality development in later phases of the life span.

Observation of Significant Others. Social learning theorists argue that observing others is one pathway to learn new behavior. Adolescents spend an increasing amount of time with peers and therefore have increased opportunities to observe the personalities of their friends and acquaintances. This observation may motivate change. For example, a more conscientious peer may do better in school and gain greater social approval from teachers and parents. An observant but less conscientious adolescent may decide to adopt new ways of interfacing with the world to gain similar levels of social approval.

Reflected Appraisals. Perceptions by others may shape personality. Caspi and Roberts (2001) termed this mechanism listening to others, and noted that this was most commonly known as *reflected appraisals*. Reflected appraisals have long been implicated in self-esteem development (Cooley, 1902; Rosenberg, Schooler, & Schoenbach, 1989; but see Shrauger & Schoeneman, 1979). For instance, being viewed as competent and liked by peers may promote self-esteem, whereas being viewed as incompetent and disliked by peers may diminish self-esteem. Shifts in reflected appraisals may affect personality and self-esteem development.

METHODOLOGICAL CONCERNS

There are several design virtues that future studies of adolescent personality and self-esteem development should strive to incorporate into their work. These issues are particularly important to consider when studying adolescent development, because they can have a profound impact on the ability to draw meaningful conclusions from adolescent research.

Longitudinal Data Collection.

Questions about personality and self-esteem development are best addressed by longitudinal studies. The timing and frequency of assessments is a major consideration when studying adolescent populations because it is especially useful to assess variables more frequently during key developmental phases when change is expected to be rapid, such as the transition into and out of adolescence. It is also important to note that two data points offer an impoverished dataset for the study of change (Bryk & Raudenbush, 1987; Willet, Singer, & Martin, 1998).

Multiwave longitudinal data should be analyzed by appropriate statistical techniques (reviewed by Little, Bovaird, & Slegers, chap. 10 in this volume). These include growth curve modeling in either the structural equation modeling framework (SEM; e.g., T. E. Duncan, S. C. Duncan, Strycker, Li, & Alpert, 1999; Muthén & Curran, 1997; Willet & Sayer, 1994) or the multilevel modeling/random-effects modeling framework (MLM; e.g., Raudenbush & Bryk, 2002; Singer & Willet, 2003). These techniques are useful for detecting normative patterns of change and for identifying correlates of individual differences in developmental trajectories. The SEM and MLM frameworks are formally equivalent (e.g., Hertzog & Nesselroade, 2003) and the decision to work in one or the other boils down to convenience. Put simply, some analyses are easier to conduct with SEM programs, whereas others are easier to conduct with MLM programs. For example, it easier to handle data structures where the ages of participants vary widely at each wave with MLM programs (e.g., Hertzog & Nesselroade, 2003), whereas it is easier to correlate growth parameters between two time-varying variables such peer victimization and self-esteem in SEM programs (e.g., Singer & Willet, 2003). Other techniques for analyzing longitudinal data include procedures for extracting "types" of individuals with similar growth trajectories (e.g., growth mixture modeling; B. M. Muthén and L. K. Muthén, 2000, and SAS Proc Traj; Nagin, 1999) and traditional autoregressive approaches (e.g., cross-lagged models; Kessler & Greenberg, 1981). All of these techniques are useful for maximizing the information gained from multiwave studies.

Multimethod Assessment

The ideal study of adolescent personality development uses multiple methods of assessment (e.g., parent, teacher, and self-reports) and multiple measures (e.g., the NEO, the BFI, and trait adjective measures). These design virtues help reduce measurement error and provide a closer approximation of true patterns of stability and change during the adolescent years.

Cohort-Sequential Designs

Developmental studies should strive to distinguish true maturational change from cohort effects and period effects. The cohort-sequential design is useful for disentangling these influences on development (e.g., Nesselroade & Baltes, 1974; Schaie, 1965). Anderson (1993) illustrated how short-term cohort-sequential designs can be linked together to provide developmental insights across a longer period of time. This procedure can increase the yield from longitudinal studies while also explicitly testing for cohort effects. This innovative technique is rarely applied to studies of adolescent personality and self-esteem development and we believe that it holds a good deal of promise.

Genetically Informed Designs

Investigators may quibble over heritability estimates and the differences that arise between twin versus adoption studies, but these "debates" should not obscure the basic message that genetic factors influence personality (e.g., Caspi, 1998; Plomin & Caspi, 1999). It is a safe bet that at least 30% to 50% of the variance in core personality traits can be attributed to genetic influences. Perhaps less well-known, recent behavioral genetics findings also indicate that individual differences in global self-esteem can be traced in part to genetic differences (Kendler, Gardner, & Prescott, 1998; McGuire et al., 1999; Roy, Neale, & Kendler, 1995; reviewed in Neiss, Sedikides, & Stevenson, 2002). Although genetically informed research affirms the importance of genetic factors, this research also clearly indicates that the environment has an important influence on personality development.

Indeed, understanding how genetic and environmental factors influence personality and self-esteem is a crucial developmental question. As Loehlin, Neiderhiser, and Reiss (2003) noted, genes "[initiate] processes that lead to individual differences during the adolescent period" (p. 386). For example, it is not clear how genetic influences on self-esteem are mediated. Is it that genes influence physical attractiveness, athletic ability, and/or personality, which in turn influence the successful mastery of the social world thereby generating greater self-acceptance and approval from peers, parents, and romantic partners? Genetically informed designs provide the best avenue for testing hypothesis about the environmental mediation of genetic influences (Rutter, Pickles, Murray, & Eaves, 2001).

CONCLUSION

There are two "poles" in current debates over the proper conceptualization of personality traits. The classical trait perspective asserts that personality traits are biologically based "temperaments" that are relatively impervious to the influence of the environment (McCrae et al., 2000). In contrast, the contextual perspective emphasizes that personality changes with role transitions and fluctuations in life experiences (Lewis, 1999). This later perspective suggests that personality traits are fluid and even ephemeral. There are similar "poles" in the conceptualization of global self-esteem as *state* or *trait* (summarized in Trzesniewski et al., 2003).

It appears that both extreme positions are incorrect (Caspi & Roberts, 2001; Roberts & Caspi, 2001; Trzesniewski et al., 2003). Retest correlations for personality and self-esteem are often substantial even if they do not approach unity. As Caspi and Roberts (2001) suggested, personality traits are properly conceptualized as developmental constructs because they exhibit both continuity and change across the life span. This notion fits nicely with Allport's (1937) law, which states that "every personality develops continually from the stage of infancy until death, and throughout this span it persists even though it changes" (p. 102). A developmental conceptualization of traits also focuses appropriate attention on processes responsible for continuity and change in individual differences across the life span.

Hopefully, researchers will take the developmental conceptualization of traits seriously and fully explore the processes underlying personality and self-esteem development during adolescence. Adolescence is an interesting time for studying the developmental nature of traits because it is a relative dynamic phase in the life span marked by changes in the biological, cognitive, and social domains. Adolescence is also an important time for studying the reciprocal links between individual differences and adaptation: How well individuals negotiate the developmental tasks of adolescence likely foreshadows adaptation throughout the life span.

REFERENCES

Allport, G. W. (1937). *Personality: A psychological interpretation.* New York: Holt.
Allport, G. W., Bruner, J. S., & Jandorf, E. M. (1953). Personality under social catastrophe. In C. Kluckhohn & H. A. Murray (Eds.), *Personality in nature, society, and culture* (2nd ed., pp. 436–455). New York: Knopf.
Alsaker, F. D. (1996). Annotation: The impact of puberty. *Journal of Child Psychology and Psychiatry, 37,* 249–258.
Alsaker, F. D., & Olweus, D. (1992). Stability of global self-evaluations on early adolescence: A cohort longitudinal study. *Journal of Research on Adolescence, 2,* 123–145.
Anderson, E. R. (1993). Analyzing change in short-term longitudinal research using cohort-sequential designs. *Journal of Consulting and Clinical Psychology, 61,* 929–940.
Archibald, A. B., Graber, J. A., & Brooks-Gunn, J. (2003). Pubertal processes and physiological growth in adolescence. In G. R. Adams & M. D. Berzonsky (Eds.), *Blackwell handbook of adolescence* (pp. 24–47). Malden, MA: Blackwell.
Aristotle. (1954). *Rhetorica* (W. R. Roberts, Trans.). New York: Random House.
Arnett, J. J. (1999). Adolescent storm and stress, reconsidered. *American Psychologist, 54,* 317–326.
Arnett, J. J. (2000). Emerging adulthood: A theory of development from the late teens through the twenties. *American Psychologist, 55,* 469–480.
Asendorpf, J. B., & Van Aken, M. G. (2003). Validity of the Big Five personality judgments in childhood: A 9 year longitudinal study. *European Journal of Personality, 17,* 1–17.
Bagwell, C. L., Newcomb, A. F., & Bukowski, W. M. (1998). Preadolescent friendship and peer rejection as predictors of adult adjustment. *Child Development, 69,* 140–153.
Baltes, P. B., Reese, H. W., & Nesselroade, J. R. (1977). *Life-span developmental psychology: Introduction to research methods.* Monterey, CA: Brooks/Cole.
Block, J. (1995). A contrarian view of the five-factor approach to personality description. *Psychological Bulletin, 117,* 187–215.
Block, J. (2001). Millennial contrarianism: The Five Factor approach to personality description 5 years later. *Journal of Research in Personality, 35,* 98–107.
Block, J., & Robins, R. W. (1993). A longitudinal study of consistency and change in self-esteem from early adolescence to early adulthood. *Child Development, 64,* 909–923.
Blos, P. (1962). *On adolescence: A psychoanalytic interpretation.* New York: The Free Press.
Bouchard, G., Lussier, Y., & Sabourin, S. (1999). Personality and marital adjustment: Utility of the Five-Factor model of personality. *Journal of Marriage and the Family, 61,* 651–660.
Brooks-Gunn, J., & Reiter, E. O. (1990). The role of pubertal processes. *At the threshold: The developing adolescent* (pp. 16–53). Cambridge, MA: Harvard University Press.

Brown, B. B (1990). Peer groups. In S. Feldman & G. Elliott (Eds.), *At the threshold: The developing adolescent* (pp. 171–196). Cambridge, MA: Harvard University Press.

Brown, B. B. (2004). Adolescents' relationships with peers. In R. M. Lerner & L. Steinberg (Eds.), *Handbook of adolescent psychology* (2nd ed., pp. 363–394). Hoboken, NJ: Wiley.

Bryk, A. S., & Raudenbush, S. W. (1987). Application of hierarchical linear models to assessing change. *Psychological Bulletin, 101,* 147–158.

Buchanan, C. M., Eccles, J. S., & Becker, J. B. (1992). Are adolescents the victims of raging hormones: Evidence for activational effects of hormones on moods and behavior at adolescence. *Psychological Bulletin, 111,* 62–117.

Buss, D. M. (1987). Selection, evocation, and manipulation. *Journal of Personality and Social Psychology, 53,* 1214–1221.

Byrnes, J. P. (2003). Cognitive development during adolescence. In G. R. Adams & M. D. Berzonsky (Eds.), *Blackwell handbook of adolescence* (pp. 227–246). Malden, MA: Blackwell.

Carver, K., Joyner, K., & Udry, J. R. (2003). National estimates of adolescent romantic relationships. In P. Florsheim (Ed.), *Adolescent romantic relations and sexual behavior: Theory, research and practical implications* (pp. 23–56). Mahwah, NJ: Lawrence Erlbaum Associates.

Caspi, A. (1998). Personality development across the life course. In W. Damon (Ed.), *Handbook of child psychology: Vol. 3. Social, emotional, and personality development* (5th ed., pp. 311–388). New York: Wiley.

Caspi, A., Lynam, D., Moffitt, T. E., & Silva, P. A. (1993). Unraveling girls' delinquency: Biological, dispositional, and contextual contributions to adolescent misbehavior. *Developmental Psychology, 29,* 19–30.

Caspi, A., & Moffitt, T. E. (1991). Individual differences are accentuated during periods of social change: The sample case of girls at puberty. *Journal of Personality and Social Psychology, 61,* 157–168.

Caspi, A., & Roberts, B. W. (2001). Personality development across the life course: The argument for change and continuity. *Psychological Inquiry, 12,* 49–66.

Collins, W. A., (2003). More than myth: The developmental significance of romantic relationships during adolescence. *Journal of Research on Adolescence, 13,* 1–24.

Cooley, C. H. (1902). *Human nature and the social order.* New York: Scribner's.

Cooper, M. L., & Sheldon, M. S. (2002). Seventy years of research on personality and close relationships: Substantive and methodological trends over time. *Journal of Personality, 70,* 783–812.

Costa, P. T., & McCrae, R. R. (1992). *Revised Neo Personality Inventory (NEO–PI–R) and NEO Five-Factor inventory (NEO–FFI) professional manual.* Odessa, FL: Psychological Assessment Resources.

Crick, N. R., & Dodge, K. A. (1994). A review and reformulation of social information processing mechanisms in children's social adjustment. *Psychological Bulletin, 115,* 74–101.

De Fruyt, F., Mervielde, I., Hoekstra, H. A., & Rolland, J. (2000). Assessing adolescents' personality with the NEO–PI–R. *Assessment, 7,* 329–345.

Demo, D. H. (1992). The self-concept over time: Research issues and directions. *Annual Review of Sociology, 18,* 303–326.

Digman, J. M. (1989). Five robust trait dimensions: Development, stability, and unity. *Journal of Personality, 57,* 195–214.

Digman, J. M. (1990). Personality structure: Emergence of the Five-Factor model. *Annual Review of Psychology, 41,* 417–440.

Digman, J. M., & Inouye, J. (1986). Further specification of the five robust factors of personality. *Journal of Personality and Social Psychology, 50,* 116–123.

Donnellan, M. B., Larsen-Rife, D., & Conger, R. D. (2005). Personality, family history, and competence in early adult romantic relationships. *Journal of Personality and Social Psychology, 88,* 562–576.

Donnellan, M. B., Trzesniewski, K. H., & Conger, R. D. (2005). Personality correlates of self-esteem during the transition from late adolescence to young adulthood. Unpublished manuscript, Department of Psychology, Michigan State University.

Duncan, T. E., Duncan, S. C., Strycker, L. A., Li, F., & Alpert, A. (1999). *An introduction to latent variable growth curve modeling: Concepts, issues, and applications*. Mahwah, NJ: Lawrence, Erlbaum Associates.

Eccles, J. S., & Midgley, C. (1989). Stage/environment fit: Developmentally appropriate classrooms for early adolescents. In R. E. Ames & C. Ames (Eds.), *Research on motivation in education* (Vol. 3, pp. 139–186). San Diego: Academic Press.

Eccles, J. S., Midgley, C., Wigfield, A., Buchanan, C. M., Reuman, D., Flanagan, C., & Mac Iver, D. (1993). Development during adolescence: The impact of stage-environment fit on young adolescents' experience in schools and in families. *American Psychologist, 48,* 90–101.

Egan, S. K., & Perry, D. G. (1998). Does low self-regard invite victimization? *Developmental Psychology, 34,* 299–309.

Elder, G. H. (1968). *Adolescent socialization and personality development.* Chicago: Rand McNally.

Elkind, D. (1967). Egocentrism in adolescence. *Child Development, 38,* 1025–1034.

Erikson, E. H. (1950). *Childhood and society.* New York: Norton.

Freud, A. (1958). Adolescence. *Psychoanalytic study of the child, 15,* 255–278.

Funder, D. C. (2001). Personality. *Annual Review of Psychology, 52,* 197–221.

Furman, W. (2002). The emerging field of adolescent romantic relationships. *Current Directions in Psychological Science, 11,* 177–180.

Ge, X., Brody, G. H., Conger, R. D., Simons, R. L., & Murry, V. M. (2002). Contextual amplification of pubertal transition effects on deviant peer affiliation and externalizing behavior among African American children. *Developmental Psychology, 38,* 42–54.

Ge, X., & Conger, R. D. (1999). Adjustment problems and emerging personality characteristics from early to late adolescence. *American Journal of Community Psychology, 27,* 429–459.

Ge, X., Conger, R. D., & Elder, G. H. (1996). Coming of age too early: Pubertal influences on girls' vulnerability to psychological distress. *Child Development, 67,* 3386–3400.

Ge, X., Conger, R. D., & Elder, G. H. (2001a). Pubertal transition, stressful life events, and the emergence of gender differences in adolescent depressive symptoms. *Developmental Psychology, 37,* 404–417.

Ge, X., Conger, R. D., & Elder, G. H., (2001b). The relation between puberty and psychological distress in adolescent boys. *Journal of Research on Adolescence, 11,* 49–70.

Ge, X., Lorenz, F. O., Conger, R. D., Elder, G. H., & Simons, R. L. (1994). Trajectories of stressful life events and depressive symptoms during adolescence. *Developmental Psychology, 30,* 467–483.

Gest, S. D. (1997). Behavioral inhibition: Stability and associations with adaptation from childhood to early adulthood. *Journal of Personality and Social Psychology, 72,* 467–475.

Graziano, W. G., & Ward, D. (1992). Probing the big five in adolescence: Personality and adjustment during a developmental transition. *Journal of Personality, 60,* 425–439.

Guo, J., Hill, K. G., Hawkins, J. D., Catalano, R. F., & Abbott, R. D. (2002). A developmental analysis of sociodemographic, family, and peer effects on adolescent illicit drug initiation. *Journal of the American Academy of Child and Adolescent Psychiatry, 41,* 838–845.

Hair, E. C., & Graziano, W. G. (2003). Self-esteem, personality, and achievement in high school: A prospective longitudinal study in Texas. *Journal of Personality, 71,* 971–994.

Hall, G. S. (1904). *Adolescence: Its psychology and its relation to physiology, anthropology, sociology, sex, crime, religion, and education* (Vols. 1 & 2). Englewood Cliffs: NJ: Prentice-Hall.

Harris, J. R. (1995). Where is the child's environment? A group socialization theory of development. *Psychological Review, 102,* 458–489.

Harris, J. R. (1998). *The nurture assumption: Why children turn out the way they do.* New York: The Free Press.

Harter, S. (1998). The development of self-representations. In W. Damon & N. Eisenberg (Eds.), *Handbook of child psychology: Vol. 3. Social, emotional, and personality development* (5th ed., pp. 553–617). New York: Wiley.

Harter, S. (1999). *The construction of the self: A developmental perspective.* New York: Guilford.

Hartup, W. W., & Stevens, N. (1997). Friendships and adaptation in the life course. *Psychological Bulletin, 121,* 355–370.

Hawkins, J. D., Catalano, R. F., & Miller, J. Y. (1992). Risk and protective factors for alcohol and other drug problems in adolescence and early adulthood: Implications for substance abuse prevention. *Psychological Bulletin, 112,* 64–105.

Herman-Giddens, M. E., Slora, E. J., Wasserman, R. C., Bourdony, C. J., Bhapkar, M. V., Koch, G. G., & Hasemeier, C. M. (1997). Secondary sexual characteristics and menses in young girls seen in office practice: A study from the Pediatric Research in Office Settings Network. *Pediatrics, 99,* 505–512.

Hertzog, C., & Nesselroade, J. R. (2003). Assessing psychological change in adulthood: An overview of methodological issues. *Psychology and Aging, 18,* 639–657.

Hill, J. P. (1983). Early adolescence: A research agenda. *Journal of Early Adolescence, 3,* 1–21.

Hirsh, B. J., & Rapkin, B. D. (1987). The transition to junior high school: A longitudinal study of self-esteem, psychological symptomology, school life, and social support. *Child Development, 58,* 1235–1243.

James, W. (1890). *The principles of psychology.* New York: Holt.

Jensen-Campbell, L. A., Adams, R., Perry, D. G., Workman, K. A., Furdella, J. Q., & Egan, S. K. (2002). Agreeableness, extraversion, and peer relations in early adolescence: Winning friends and deflecting aggression. *Journal of Research in Personality, 36,* 224–251.

John, O. P., Caspi, A., Robins, R. W., Moffitt, T. E., & Stouthamer-Loeber, M. (1994). The "little five": Exploring the nomological network of the Five-Factor model of personality in adolescent boys. *Child Development, 65,* 160–178.

John, O. P., & Srivastava, S. (1999). The Big Five trait taxonomy: History, measurement, and theoretical perspectives. In L. A. Pervin & O. P. John (Eds.), *Handbook of personality: Theory and research* (2nd ed., pp. 102–138). New York: Guilford.

Jones, C. J., & Meredith, W. (2000). Developmental paths of psychological health from early adolescence to later adulthood. *Psychology and Aging, 15,* 351–360.

Kandel, D. B. (1978). Homophily, selection, and socialization in adolescent friendships. *American Journal of Sociology, 84,* 427–436.

Keating, D. (1990). Adolescent thinking. In S. Feldman & G. Elliot (Eds.), *At the threshold: The developing adolescent* (pp. 54–89). Cambridge, MA: Harvard University Press.

Keating, D. (2004). Cognitive and brain development. In R. M. Lerner & L. Steinberg (Eds.), *Handbook of adolescent psychology* (2nd ed., pp. 45–84). Hoboken, NJ: Wiley.

Kendler, K. S., Gardner, C. O., & Prescott, C. A. (1998). A population-based twin study of self-esteem and gender. *Psychological Medicine, 28,* 1403–1409.

Kessler, R. C., & Greenberg, D. F. (1981). *Linear panel analysis: Models of quantitative change.* New York: Academic Press.

Kling, K. C., Hyde, J. S., Showers, C. J., & Buswell, B. N. (1999). Gender differences in self-esteem: A meta-analysis. *Psychological Bulletin, 125,* 470–500.

Kohnstamm, G. A., Halverson, C. F., Mervielde, I., & Havill, V. L. (1998). *Parental descriptions of child personality: Developmental antecedents of the big five?* Mahwah, NJ: Lawrence Erlbaum Associates.

Krueger, R. F., Caspi, A., & Moffitt, T. E. (2000). Epidemiological personology: The unifying role of personality in population-based research on problem behaviors. *Journal of Personality, 68,* 967–998.

Lamb, M. E., Chuang, S. S., Wessels, H., Broberg, A. G., & Hwang, C. P. (2002). Emergence and construct validation of the big five factors in early childhood: A longitudinal analysis of their ontogeny in Sweden. *Child Development, 73,* 1517–1524.

Larson, R. W. (2000). Toward a psychology of positive youth development. *American Psychologist, 55,* 170–183.

Larson, R. W., Clore, G. L., Wood, G. A. (1999). The emotions of romantic relationships: Do they wreak havoc on adolescents? In W. Furman, B. B. Brown, & C. Feiring (Eds.), *The development of romantic relationships in adolescence* (pp. 19–49). New York: Cambridge University Press.

Larson, R. W., & Richards, M. (1991). Daily companionship in late childhood and early adolescence: Changing developmental contexts. *Child Development, 62,* 284–300.

Larson, R. W., & Verma, S. (1999). How children and adolescents spend time across the world: Work, play, and developmental opportunities. *Psychological Bulletin, 125,* 701–736.

Lerner, R. M., & Busch-Rossnagel, N. (1981). *Individuals as producers of their development: A life-span perspective.* New York: Academic Press

Lerner, R. M., & Galambos, N. L. (1998). Adolescent development: Challenges and opportunities for research, programs, and policies. *Annual Review of Psychology, 49,* 413–446.

Lewis, M. (1999). On the development of personality. In L. A. Pervin & O. P. John (Eds.), *Handbook of personality theory and research* (pp. 327–346). New York: Guilford.

Loehlin, J. C. (1997). A test of J. R. Harris's theory of peer influences on personality. *Journal of Personality and Social Psychology, 72,* 1197–1201.

Loehlin, J. C., Neiderhiser, J. M., & Reiss, D. (2003). The behavior genetics of personality and the NEAD study. *Journal of Research in Personality, 37,* 373–387.

Masten, A. S., & Coatsworth, J. D. (1998). The development of competence in favorable and unfavorable environments: Lessons from research on successful children. *American Psychologist, 53,* 205–220.

McAdams, D. P. (2001). The psychology of life stories. *Review of General Psychology, 5,* 100–122.

McCarthy, J. D., & Hoge, D. R. (1982). Analysis of age effects in longitudinal studies of adolescent self-esteem. *Developmental Psychology, 18,* 372–379.

McCrae, R. R. (2001). 5 years of progress: A reply to Block. *Journal of Research in Personality, 35,* 108–113.

McCrae, R. R, Costa, P. T. Jr., Ostendorf, F., Angleitner, A., Hrebickova, M., Avia, M. D., et al. (2000). Nature over nurture: Temperament, personality, and life span development. *Journal of Personality & Social Psychology, 78,* 173–186.

McCrae, R. R., Costa, P. T., Terracciano, A., Parker, W. D., Mills, C. J., De Fruyt, F. D., et al. (2002). Personality trait development from age 12 to age 18: Longitudinal, cross-sectional, and cross-cultural analyses. *Journal of Personality and Social Psychology, 83,* 1456–1468.

McGuire, S., Manke, B., Saudino, K. J., Reiss, D., Hetherington, E. M., & Plomin, R. (1999). Perceived competence and self-worth during adolescence: A longitudinal behavioral genetic study. *Child Development, 70,* 1283–1296.

Miller, J. D., & Lynam, D. (2001). Structural models of personality and their relation to antisocial behavior: A meta-analytic review. *Criminology, 39,* 765–798.

Moffitt, T. E. (1993). Adolescence-limited and life course-persistent antisocial behavior: A developmental taxonomy. *Psychological Review, 100,* 674–701.

Muthén, B. M., & Curran, P. J. (1997). General longitudinal modeling of individual differences in experimental designs: A latent variable framework for analysis and power estimation. *Psychological Methods, 2,* 371–402.

Muthén, B. M., & Muthén, L. K. (2000). Integrating person-centered and variable-centered analyses: Growth mixture modeling with latent trajectory classes. *Alcoholism: Clinical and Experimental Research, 24,* 882–891.

Nagin, D. S. (1999). Analyzing developmental trajectories: A semiparametric, group-based approach. *Psychological Methods, 4,* 139–177.

Neiss, M. B., Sedikides, C., & Stevenson, J. (2002). Self-esteem: A behavioural genetic perspective. *European Journal of Psychology, 16,* 351–367.

Nesselroade, J. R., & Baltes, P. B. (1974). Adolescent personality development and historical change: 1970–1972. *Monographs of the Society for Research in Child Development, 39* (Serial No. 154).

Nottlemann, E. D. (1987). Competence and self-esteem during transition from childhood to adolescence. *Developmental Psychology, 23,* 441–450.

O'Malley, P. M., & Bachman, J. G. (1983). Self-esteem: Change and stability between ages 13 and 23. *Developmental Psychology, 19,* 257–268.

Ozer, D. J., & Reise, S. P. (1994). Personality assessment. *Annual Review of Psychology, 45,* 357–388.

Parker, W. D., & Stumpf, H. (1998). A validation of the Five-Factor model of personality in academically talented youth across observes and instruments. *Personality and Individual Differences, 25,* 1005–1025.

Petersen, A. C. (1988). Adolescent development. *Annual Review of Psychology, 39,* 583–607.

Plomin, R., & Caspi, A. (1999). Behavior genetics and personality. In L. A. Pervin & O. P. John (Eds.), *Handbook of personality: Theory and research* (2nd ed., pp. 251–276). New York: Guilford.

Raudenbush, S. W., & Bryk, A. S. (2002). *Hierarchical linear models: Applications and data analysis methods* (2nd ed.). Thousand Oaks, CA: Sage.

Roberts, B. W., & Caspi, A. (2001). Personality development and the person–situation debate: It's deja vu all over again. *Psychological Inquiry, 12,* 104–109.

Roberts, B. W., Caspi, A., & Moffitt, T. E. (2001). The kids are alright: Growth and stability in personality development from adolescence to adulthood. *Journal of Personality and Social Psychology, 81,* 670–683.

Roberts, B. W., Caspi, A., & Moffitt, T. E. (2003). Work experiences and personality development in young adulthood. *Journal of Personality and Social Psychology, 84,* 582–593.

Roberts, B. W., & DelVecchio, W. F. (2000). The rank-order consistency of personality from childhood to old age: A quantitative review of longitudinal studies. *Psychological Bulletin, 126,* 3–25.

Roberts, B. W., Walton, K. E., & Viechtbauer, W. (in press). Patterns of mean-level change in personality traits across the life course: A meta-analysis of longitudinal studies. *Psychological Bulletin.*

Robins, R. W., Caspi, A., & Moffitt, T. E. (2000). Two personalities, one relationship: Both partners' personality traits shape the quality of their relationship. *Journal of Personality and Social Psychology, 79,* 251–259.

Robins, R. W., Caspi, A., & Moffitt, T. E. (2002). It's not just who you're with, it's who you are: Personality and relationship experiences across multiple relationships. *Journal of Personality,* 925–964.

Robins, R. W., Fraley, R. C., Roberts, B. W., Trzesniewski, K. H. (2001). A longitudinal study of personality change in young adulthood. *Journal of Personality, 69,* 617–640.

Robins, R. W., John, O. P., & Caspi, A. (1994). Major dimensions of personality in early adolescence: The Big Five and beyond. In C. F. Halverson, G. A. Kohnstamm, & R. P. Martin (Eds.), *The developing structure of temperament and personality from infancy to adulthood* (pp. 267–292). Hillsdale, NJ: Lawrence Erlbaum Associates.

Robins, R. W., Trzesniewski, K. H., Tracy, J. L., Gosling, S. D., & Potter, J. (2002). Self-esteem across the lifespan. *Psychology and Aging, 17,* 423–434.

Roeser, R. W. (1998). On schooling and mental health: Introduction to the special issue. *Educational Psychologist, 33,*129–133.

Roeser, R. W., & Eccles, J. S. (1998). Adolescents' perceptions of middle school: Relation to longitudinal changes in academic and psychological adjustment. *Journal of Research on Adolescence, 8,* 123–158.

Rosenberg, M. (1986). Self-concept from middle childhood through adolescence. In J. Suls & A. G. Greenwald (Eds.), *Psychological perspectives on the self* (pp. 107–136). Hillsdale, NJ: Lawrence Erlbaum Associates.

Rosenberg, M., Schooler, C., & Schoenbach, C. (1989). Self-esteem and adolescent problems: Modeling reciprocal effects. *American Sociological Review, 54,* 1004–1018.

Roy, M. A., Neale, M. C., & Kendler, K. S. (1995). The genetic epidemiology of self-esteem. *British Journal of Psychiatry, 166,* 813–820.

Rutter, M., Pickles, A., Murray, R., & Eaves, L. (2001). Testing hypotheses on specific environmental causal effects on behavior. *Psychological Bulletin, 127,* 291–324.

Scarr, S., & McCartney, K. (1983). How people make their own environments: A theory of genotype → environment effects. *Child Development, 54,* 424–435.

Schaie, K. W. (1965). A general model for the study of developmental problems. *Psychological Bulletin, 64,* 92–107.

Seidman, E., Allen, L., Aber, J. L., Mitchell, C., & Feinman, J. (1994). The impact of school transitions on the self-system and perceived social context of poor urban youth. *Child Development, 65,* 507–522.

Shedler, J., & Block, J. (1990). Adolescent drug use and psychological health: A longitudinal inquiry. *American Psychologist, 45*, 612–630.

Shiner, R. L. (2000). Linking childhood personality with adaptation: Evidence for continuity and change across time into late adolescence. *Journal of Personality and Social Psychology, 78*, 310–325.

Shiner, R. L., & Caspi, A. (2003). Personality differences in childhood and adolescence: Measurement, development, and consequences. *Journal of Child Psychology and Psychiatry, 44*, 1–31.

Shoal, G. D., & Giancola, P. R. (2003). Negative affectivity and drug use in adolescent boys: Moderating and mediating mechanisms. *Journal of Personality and Social Psychology, 84*, 221–233.

Shrauger, S., & Schoeneman, T. J. (1979). Symbolic interactionist view of self-concept: Through the looking glass darkly. *Psychological Bulletin, 86*, 549–573.

Simmons, R. G., & Blyth, D. A. (1987). *Moving into adolescence: The impact of pubertal change and school context*. New York: Aldine De Gruyter.

Singer, J. D., & Willett, J. B. (2003). *Applied longitudinal data analysis: Modeling change and event occurrence*. New York: Oxford University Press.

Spear, L. P. (2000). The adolescent brain and age-related behavioral manifestations. *Neuroscience and Biobehavioral Reviews, 24*, 417–463.

Stein, J. A., Newcomb, M. D., & Bentler, P. M. (1986). Stability and change in personality: A longitudinal study from early adolescence to young adulthood. *Journal of Research in Personality, 20*, 276–291.

Steinberg, L. (1990). Autonomy, conflict, and harmony in the family relationship. In S. Feldman & G. Elliott (Eds.), *At the threshold: The developing adolescent* (pp. 255–276). Cambridge, MA: Harvard University Press.

Steinberg, L. (2001). We know some things: Parent–adolescent relationships in retrospect and prospect. *Journal of Research on Adolescence, 11*, 1–19.

Steinberg, L. (2002). *Adolescence* (6th ed.). New York: McGraw-Hill.

Steinberg, L., & Morris, A. (2001). Adolescent development. *Annual Review of Psychology, 52*, 83–110.

Susman, R. J., Inoff-Germain, G., Nottelmann, E.D., Loriaux, D. L., Cutler, G. B., Jr., & Chrousos, G. P. (1987). Hormones, emotional disposition, and aggressive attributes in young adolescents. *Child Development, 58*, 1114–1134.

Susman, E., & Rogol, A. (2004). Puberty and psychological development. In R. M. Lerner & L. Steinberg (Eds.), *Handbook of adolescent psychology* (2nd ed., pp. 15–44). Hoboken, NJ: Wiley.

Tanner, J. M. (1962). *Growth at adolescence*. New York: Lippincott.

Trzesniewski, K. H., Donnellan, M. B., & Robins, R. W. (2001, April). *Self-esteem across the life span: A meta-analysis*. Poster presented at the biannual meeting of the Society for Research on Child Development, Minneapolis, MN.

Trzesniewski, K. H., Donnellan, M. B., & Robins, R. W. (2003). Stability of self-esteem across the life span. *Journal of Personality and Social Psychology, 84*, 205–220.

Twenge, J. M., & Campbell, W. K. (2001). Age and birth cohort differences in self-esteem: A cross-temporal meta-analysis. *Personality and Social Psychology Review, 5*, 321–344.

Watson, D., Hubbard, B., & Wiese, D. (2000). General traits of personality and affectivity as predictors of satisfaction in intimate relationships: Evidence from self- and partner-ratings. *Journal of Personality, 68*, 413–449.

West, S. G., & Graziano, W. G. (1989). Long-term stability and change in personality: An introduction. *Journal of Personality, 57*, 175–193.

Wigfield, A., Eccles, J. S., Mac Iver, D., Reuman, D. A., & Midgley, C. (1991). Transitions during early adolescence: Changes in children's domain specific self-perceptions and general self-esteem across the transition to junior high school. *Developmental Psychology, 27*, 552–565.

Wiggins, J. S., & Pincus, A. L. (1992). Personality: Structure and assessment. *Annual Review of Psychology, 43*, 473–504.

Willet, J. B., & Sayer, A. G. (1994). Using covariance structure analysis to detect correlates and predictors of individual change over time. *Psychological Bulletin, 116*, 363–381.

Willett, J. B., Singer, J. D., & Martin, N. C. (1998). The design and analysis of longitudinal studies of development and psychopathology in context: Statistical models and methodological recommendations. *Development and Psychopathology, 10,* 395–426.

Wills, T. A., & Stoolmiller, M. (2002). The role of self-control in early escalation of substance use: A time-varying analysis. *Journal of Consulting and Clinical Psychology, 70,* 986–997.

Wylie, R. C. (1979). *The self-concept.* Lincoln, Nebraska: University of Nebraska Press.

Young, J. F., & Mroczek, D. K. (2003). Predicting intraindividual self-concept trajectories during adolescence. *Journal of Adolescence, 26,* 586–600.

16

Developmental and Individual Difference Perspectives on Self-Esteem

Susan Harter
University of Denver

This chapter begins with a brief historical overview of how interest in self-esteem or self-worth has waxed and waned over the last century (see Harter, 1999, for a more in-depth review). Then attention turns to the evidence on the emergence of self-esteem from a developmental perspective, charting the reasons for why the level of self-esteem is higher during the formative years of early childhood. This analysis is yoked to our own model of the determinants of self-esteem, as well as to cognitive-developmental processes among young children. Evidence is then provided that documents how, beginning in middle childhood, marked individual differences in level of self-esteem begin to emerge and will continue across the life span. A developmental analysis is provided. The focus then shifts to one controversy in this literature, namely, whether self-esteem, once established in childhood, remains stable over time or is susceptible to change. More recent literature on these issues is reviewed with regard to whether self-esteem should be viewed as a trait or a state. The chapter argues that this is a bogus question. Constructs such as self-esteem are not, in and of themselves, traits or states per se. Rather, for some individuals self-esteem is traitlike and for others it is more statelike. The goal then becomes finding a way to account for these individual differences. Three studies from our own laboratory are presented in support of this position.

BRIEF HISTORICAL OVERVIEW

Interest in global self-esteem or self-worth, namely, how much individuals value themselves as a person, has been granted mixed attention over the past century. One hundred years ago, historical scholars of the self, namely, William James (1890, 1892) and Charles Horton Cooley (1902; the father of symbolic interactionism), waxed eloquently about the nature of self-esteem and its causes. Their philosophical formulations became the models for the thoughtful consideration of self-processes. However, with the emergence of radical behaviorism during the 20th century, cognitions, in general, and self-constructs, in particular, were excised from the scientific vocabularies of many theorists, leaving the writings of James and the symbolic interactionists to gather dust on the shelf. The very cornerstone of the behaviorist movement rested on the identification of *observables*. Self-representations were deemed unmeasurable because they could not be operationalized as observable behavior. Self-report measures were also suspect because people were judged to be very inaccurate reporters of their own behavior. Finally, self-constructs were not satisfying to the behaviorist's palate because their functions were not clearly specified. The very essence of behavioral approaches rested on a functional analysis of behavior. In contrast, a focus on the self did little more that implicate self-representations as correlates of behavior, affording them little explanatory power as causes or mediators of behavior.

Several shifts in emphasis, beginning in the second half of the 20th century, have allowed self-constructs to regain center stage. Hypothetical constructs, in general, gained favor as parsimonious predictors of behavior, often far more economical in the theoretical model than a multitude of discrete observable behaviors. In addition, there was a cognitive revolution within the fields of child, adolescent, and adult psychology. For developmentalists, Piagetian models came to the forefront. For experimental and social psychologists, numerous cognitive models found favor. With the emergence of this revolution, self theorists jumped on the bandwagon, resurrecting the self as a *cognitive construction*, a mental representation that constitutes a theory of self (e.g., Brim, 1976; Case, 1985; Epstein, 1973, 1981; Fischer, 1980; Kelley, 1955; Markus, 1977, 1980; Sarbin, 1962). Finally, self-representations gained increasing legitimacy as behaviorally oriented therapists were forced to acknowledge that the spontaneous self-evaluative statements of their clients seemed powerfully implicated in their pathology as well as treatment.

Within the last three decades, self-constructs have once again taken center stage within all fields in the discipline, including social psychology, developmental psychology, clinical psychology, educational psychology, cognitive psychology, and neuropsychology. However, this reconsideration of the self has led to several controversies, one of which becomes a focus of this chapter, namely, the stability of self-representations (see Wylie, 1979, 1989). Does self-esteem become established in early childhood and remain immutable throughout a person's lifetime or, conversely, is it subject to change?

THE DEVELOPMENTAL EMERGENCE OF THE SELF

Certain cognitive limitations of young children (age 3–7) lead to their inability to create a verbalizable concept of their overall worth as a person, namely, a representation of their global self-esteem as a person (Harter, 1999). Such a self-representation requires a higher order integration of domain-specific evaluations that have first been differentiated. Young children do begin to describe themselves in terms of concrete cognitive abilities ("I can count"), physical abilities ("I can run fast"), how they behave ("I don't get in trouble"), how they look ("I'm pretty"), and their friendships

("I have a lot of friends"), however, these domains are not clearly differentiated as revealed through factor analytic procedures (Harter & Pike, 1984). Moreover, the mean levels of these domain-specific evaluations are highly skewed toward the positive end of the scale, indicating that the vast majority of young children tout their virtuosities in these domains. However, they cannot yet combine these into a higher order generalization about their overall worth as a person. They must first understand that they are a "person," not just a girl versus boy, or a child versus an adult—that is, they must first form this more basic higher order generalization. Once they have the concept that they are a "person," then they must come to appreciate that individuals have their own sense of overall worth or self-esteem.

However, the fact that young children cannot cognitively or verbally formulate a general concept of their worth as a person does not dictate that they lack some rudimentary experience of self-esteem. Rather, findings (see Haltiwanger, 1989; Harter, 1990b) reveal that young children manifest self-esteem in their behavior. In examining what is labeled "behaviorally presented self-esteem," it was determined, through Q-sorts to teachers, that young children exude positive self-esteem through displays of confidence, pride in their work, curiosity, initiative, and independence. Those failing to demonstrate these behaviors (by far in the minority) are identified by teachers as children with low self-esteem.

Why, however, should young children's own self-ratings of their adequacy in discrete domains and teachers' ratings of their overall self-esteem be so high? Why should there be so few individual differences in early childhood? Why is there a general decline in self-esteem between early and middle childhood, and why do marked individual differences in verbalizable self-esteem begin to emerge in middle childhood? To answer these questions, the discussion first considers a review of the formulations of James (1890, 1892) and Cooley (1902), who developed theories about the causes of adult self-esteem. Then, it addresses the cognitive limitations of the young child that make these models questionable during early childhood but more plausible during middle childhood and beyond when the cognitive processes demanded by these models emerge.

HISTORICAL PERSPECTIVES ON THE CAUSES OF GLOBAL SELF-WORTH: THE FORMULATIONS OF JAMES AND COOLEY

The contributions of James (1890, 1892) were legion. Central to this chapter is his formulation on the causes of global self-esteem or self-worth. For James, individuals' sense of their worth as a person is not merely the psychological aggregate of their perceived successes and failures or strengths and weaknesses. Rather, people need to weigh successes and failures against the backdrop of the importance of success in each life domain (e.g., intellectual, social, moral, occupational, etc.). According to James, individuals do not scrutinize their every action or attribute; rather, they focus primarily on their perceived adequacy in domains where they have pretensions, or aspirations (in less arcane language) for success. Thus, the individuals who perceive the self positively in domains where they aspire to excel will have high self-esteem. Those who fall short of their ideals, creating a discrepancy between perceived success and their pretensions, will experience low self-esteem (see literature in Harter,

1999b, on the convergence between James' formulation and the research on the disparity between a person's ideal and real self-image).

It is critical to appreciate that from a Jamesian perspective, perceived inadequacy in domains deemed unimportant to the self should not adversely affect global self-esteem. For example, an individual may judge the self to be unathletic. However, if athletic prowess is not an aspiration, then self-esteem will not be negatively affected. Thus, the high self-esteem individual is able to discount the importance of domains in which they are not competent, whereas the low self-esteem individual appears unable to devalue success in domains of inadequacy. Thus, individuals' sense of adequacy in domains that are judged to be important to them is what determines their level of global self-worth for James. There is considerable empirical support for this formulation beginning in middle childhood and across the life span (see reviews in Harter, 1990b, 1999).

For Cooley (1902) and the other symbolic interactionists to follow (e.g., Mead, 1925, 1934), the self was primarily a social construction crafted through linguistic exchanges (symbolic interactions) with significant others. Thus, the self develops within the crucible of interpersonal relationships. In his "looking-glass-self" formulation, Cooley postulated that significant others constituted social mirrors into which the child gazes in order to detect the opinions of these others toward the self. These perceived opinions, in turn, were incorporated into the evaluation of an individual's worth as a person. For Mead, the attitudes of different significant others toward the self were psychologically averaged across these individuals, resulting in the "generalized other" who represented a shared perspective on the self. For the symbolic interactionists, there was an implicit and gradual internalization process through which the child came to adopt and eventually to personally own the initial values and opinions of significant others. Thus, if individuals feel that they are well-regarded, valued for who they are as a person, by significant others, then high self-esteem will be the outcome. Conversely, if they feel denigrated by such others, devalued as a person, then low self-esteem will result.

THE APPLICATION OF OUR OWN MODEL
OF THE DETERMINANTS OF GLOBAL SELF-ESTEEM

Building on the formulations of both James (1892) and Cooley (1902), a model has been developed that integrates each of these formulations and predicts global self-esteem, namely, how much individuals value themselves as a person (Harter, 1990b, 1999). Initially, five domains of relevance in the lives of those between age 8 and age 14 were identified, domains in which children could evaluate their competence or adequacy in each domain as well as rate the importance of success in that domain, for them personally, to address James' formulation. These domains were physical appearance, likability by peers, athletic competence, academic competence, and behavioral conduct. Consistent with Cooley's formulation, several sources of approval or personal support from others were identified, determining that support from parents and support from peers were the most predictive of self-reported self-esteem. It was further specified that domains of competence and source of approval were linked in that the first three domains—physical appearance, likability, and athletic competence—were more highly predictive of peer support, whereas scholastic competence and behavioral conduct were more predictive of parental support. All of these components were predictive of self-reported global self-esteem with direct paths from competence/adequacy in domains of importance as well as indirect paths, where approval from peers and parents served as mediators to global self-esteem. This model is extremely robust in predicting global self-esteem from middle childhood through the life span (see Harter, 1990b, 1999). Later instruments increased the number of age-relevant domains further documenting the model.

The model is not as applicable to children younger than age 7 for reasons that also explain why their self-evaluations are extremely positive and why teacher ratings of self-esteem are relatively high. With regard to the construct of competence/adequacy in domains of importance, derived from James (1892), young children do not have the capacity to make this "real-ideal" distinction (Fischer, 1980; Higgins, 1991; Glick & Zigler, 1985; Leahy & Shirk, 1985; Rogers, 1951). That is, they cannot separate their judgments of the actual abilities and talents from ideally what they would like to be like. Their responses on questionnaires, therefore, are more likely to reflect their ideal self. This overestimation, for some children, is not a reflection of socially desirable response tendencies (they do not have the cognitive sophistication for that type of strategy), but rather a genuine normative inability to distinguish between their actual abilities and their desired qualities.

The fact that most young children jubilantly and unabashedly focus on their virtues is also in part a reflection of the fact that skills are developing so rapidly that they are focused on temporal comparisons within their own personal development rather than social comparisons with others. The ability to make social comparisons for the purpose of self-evaluation does not seriously emerge until middle childhood. Young children are powerfully aware of social comparison that provides information about issues of fairness (e.g., "you got more cookies than I did at snack time," "you got more turns on the swing," "the teacher let you lead the line to the lunch room more times than for me"). Yet, young children do not yet take these comparisons as evidence that they, their selves, are deficient (see Ruble & Frey, 1991). Thus, their high self-esteem is protected.

With regard to Cooley's contentions that global self-esteem is derived from the internalization of the positive or negative opinions of significant others, how does this component of the model help to explain why young children, on average, have such high evaluations of themselves in specific domains and why teachers rate their "observed or exuded" self-esteem so high? Research (see Harter, 1990, 1999) indicates that the primary sources of self-esteem for young children are their parents or parent surrogates. The majority of parental figures (including teachers) are typically benevolent, encouraging, supportive, and approving of their young children's accomplishments. This feedback is consistent with a positive affective response leading young children to feel positive about themselves. Thus, positive parental and other adult feedback will promote positive feelings about the self.

Many young children today go to day care and preschool prior to entering kindergarten and then formal school begins in first grade. Within this context there may be disputes, rejection, and bullying, which hopefully teachers will try to contain and discourage. These events are distressing to young children. However, Selman (1980) and others noted that young children do not have the perspective-taking skills to realize that these acts reflect judgments about them by other people, judgments about themselves as a person, that they should internalize. Their primary experience is feeling emotionally hurt.

MEAN DROP IN SELF-ESTEEM IN MIDDLE CHILDHOOD COUPLED WITH INCREASED INDIVIDUAL DIFFERENCES

From a developmental perspective, why should the mean level of verbalizable self-esteem that emerges in middle childhood drop, and why should greater individual differences emerge at this age level and continue throughout the life span? It has commonly been asserted, particularly in the adult social psychological and personality literature, that the self-concept is a theory, a cognitive construction, and its architecture, by evolutionary design, is extremely functional (see Allport, 1961; Brim, 1976; Damon & Hart, 1988; Epstein, 1973, 1981, 1991; Greenwald, 1980; Kelley, 1955; Markus, 1980; Rogers, 1951; Sarbin, 1962). These include organizational functions, motivational functions, and finally, most relevant to this chapter, the function of maintaining high self-esteem. Self-representations supposedly perform protective functions toward the goals of maintaining favorable impressions of individuals' attributes, including their global sense of worth as a person. Thus, why is it that self-processes do not always conform to this functional job description?

From a contemporary developmental perspective, many cognitive advances that come from the movement to new stages and skill levels bring with them inherent liabilities (Harter, 1999b; Leahy, 1985; Maccoby, 1980). This perspective contrasts sharply with Piaget's (1960) assumption that movement to higher stages increasingly leads to greater positive functioning toward the teleological endpoint at formal operations. Harter (1999b) argued that, across many different domains, the shift to new cognitive-developmental levels obviously, by definition, leads to the emergence of new and valuable skills, but this comes at a cost. That is, there are also psychological liabilities. How, then, does this framework inform the findings that the mean level of self-esteem drops in middle childhood and individual differences in self-esteem become much more marked from this age period on? Four developmental shifts are applied to these questions.

The Ability to Create a Discrepancy Between Adequacy and the Importance of Success

A central tenet of James' theory is that global self-esteem is derived from the ability of individuals to compare their adequacy (their real self) with the value placed on the success (their ideal self). This formulation is consistent with considerable later research on discrepancies between the real and ideal self, as noted earlier. During middle childhood, the ability to make this distinction emerges, allowing children to evaluate whether they are meeting their ideals, which may stem from the expectations of parents, teachers, coaches, and peers. At this developmental juncture, they begin to internalize these standards, gradually taking them on as their own (Harter, 1999b; Higgins, 1991; Connell & Wellborn, 1991). For children, in general, there will be discrepancies not present during early childhood when young children could not make these distinctions. Thus, the mean level of self-esteem declines because greater discrepancies, according to James, lead to more negative evaluations of worth as a person, as the empirical findings demonstrate.

With regard to greater individual differences in self-esteem, that is, greater variability in the distribution of scores, the discrepancies between individuals' evaluation of their real and ideal adequacies will vary from one individual to another. Some individuals will set very high standards that may be impossible to meet, given their own skill levels. For example, someone with high level computer skills in a school that values athletic ability may attempt, with little success at sports, to join a team. Another student with learning difficulties may aspire to his parents' desire that their child go to an Ivy League school, creating a tremendous discrepancy between the importance of academic success and poor academic performance, leading to low self-esteem. Other students, in contrast, will have only moderate discrepancies between their real and ideal self, or negligible discrepancies, leading to moderate or high levels of self-esteem, respectively. Thus, these different profiles will produce variability in self-esteem.

It should be noted that, theoretically, those who are able to assign very low importance to areas of extreme inadequacy should have high self-esteem. In point of fact, children in today's culture are socialized to value or tout the importance of most of the domains that appear on this and others' domain-specific instruments (e.g.,, scholastic competence, peer likability, behavioral conduct, physical attractiveness, and athletic competence). Thus, it is extremely rare for children to devalue or discount the importance of such domains.

Increase in Perspective-Taking Skills

In middle childhood, perspective-taking skills emerge, allowing children to realize that others are evaluating the self (Harter, 1999b; Selman, 1980). Considering the mean drop during this developmental period, children, in general, realize that others are evaluating them negatively or positively and for those perceiving negative evaluations, this will bring the mean level of self-esteem down. Peer evaluations become particularly important during this developmental period and beyond (Furman & Bierman, 1984; Harris, 1998; Rubin, Chen, & Hymel, 1993; Sroufe & Fleeson, 1986). Some of these messages are indirect, in the form of rejection (Rubin chapter, etc.). Other feedback will be more direct (e.g., teasing, bullying), leading to humiliation and low self-esteem. This type of extreme feedback, as in the case of the 11 high profile school shooting incidents, led to high levels of humiliation and low self-esteem, which in turn produced violence (Harter, Low, & Whitesell, 2003). Individual differences in negative feedback therefore will produce greater variability in self-esteem beginning in middle childhood.

The Emergence of Social Comparison Skills

Beginning in middle childhood, children develop the ability to compare themselves with others for the purposes of self-evaluation (Harter, 1999; Ruble & Frey, 1991). They are keenly aware of the skill hierarchies of everyone in their classroom or peer group, with regard to academic and athletic success, as well social acceptance. Unless they feel that they are high on the ladder in these skill arenas or at the top of the pecking order with regard to the social domain, their self-esteem will suffer. This will produce a drop in mean level of self-esteem as well as increased individual differences in self-esteem.

Changes in Parental Expectations and Evaluations

Once children become immersed in formal schooling, many parents (in this competitive society of which school is a microcosm) tend to become less effusive in their praise and more demanding of their children (see Harter, 1999b). Thus, they raise the bar with regard to standards of behavior and performance, that is, they increase their expectations for their children. Thus, this would contribute to a mean decline in self-esteem to the extent that some students would not be receiving the support or approval that they did during early childhood. However, parents also differ with regard to the level and type of support they provide (Harter, 1999b), and many are unrealistic in their expectations of the levels of success that their children can achieve. Consider the child with a learning disability whose parents expected him to eventually go to an Ivy League school. Such a child would not garner parental support that is a major determinant of self-esteem. Other parents may offer what has been termed "conditional approval" (Harter, Marold, & Whitesell, 1992), the opposite of Roger's (1951) concept of unconditional positive regard. Research has shown that conditional "approval" is actually a misnomer in that children and adolescents do not perceive it as approval. Rather, it specifies the psychological hoops through which middle childhood children must jump in order to try to please the parents. Research reveals that such conditionality undermines children's self-esteem and contributes to the individual differences in self-esteem that emerge (Harter, Marold, Whitesell, & Cobbs, 1996). In summary, cognitive-developmental advances represent new acquisitions; however, they also can carry with them liabilities that will result in a general decline in self-esteem during middle childhood, as well as an increase in individual differences or greater variability in self-esteem from this period on.

These cognitive-developmental advances that can result in liabilities with regard to lowered self-esteem include individuals' ability to create a discrepancy between their adequacy and the importance of success, increases in perspective-taking abilities, and the emergence of social comparison skills. The emergence of these skills will lead to a general decrease in self-esteem; however, they will interact with the child's actual skills levels as well as their socialization, leading to greater variability in self-esteem as well. A fourth cause of lowered self-esteem and greater variability stems from changes in parental expectations and evaluations. In general, parents raise the bar in terms of what they expect of their children, which can lead to a drop in self-esteem, affecting mean scores. Second, there are individual differences in the level of parental support and the conditionality of support, which contributes to greater individual differences or variability in child self-esteem.

CONTINUITY OR CHANGE IN SELF-ESTEEM

Against this developmental backdrop, once individuals' level of self-esteem has been established through these processes in early and middle childhood, does the future follow a continuous trajectory, such that self-esteem appears to be a relatively immutable trait, or is it subject to change of meaningful proportions? Following the structure of the chapter to date, are there normative-developmental changes in self-esteem during childhood and adolescence? Second, on the issue of individual differences in the stability or change in self-esteem, is self-esteem best viewed as a trait or state over time?

Developmental Analyses

Consistent with the analysis of early and middle childhood, there are those within the fields of developmental and educational psychology, who have argued that global self-esteem or self-worth will change as a function of development. Evidence, consistent with our analysis, reveals that self-evaluative judgments become less positive as children move into middle childhood (see Frey & Ruble, 1985, 1990; Harter, 1982; Harter & Pike, 1984; Stipek, 1981). Investigators attribute such a decline to the greater reliance on social comparison and external feedback, leading to more realistic judgments about an individual's capabilities (see also Marsh, 1989). An analysis points to better perspective-taking skills, ability to make distinctions between real and ideal self-evaluations, and changes in parental expectations. Studies suggest that there is another decline at early adolescence (age 11–13) after which self-esteem and domain-specific self-evaluations gradually become more positive over the course of adolescence (Dusek & Flaherty, 1981; Engel, 1959; H. W. Marsh, 1991; H. W. Marsh, Parker, & Barnes, 1985; H. W. Marsh, Smith, M. R. Marsh, & Owens, 1988; O'Malley & Backman, 1983; Piers & Harris, 1964; Rosenberg, 1986; Savin-Williams & Demo, 1984; Simmons, Rosenberg, & Rosenberg, 1973).

The normative decline in self-evaluations coincides with the educational transition to junior high school. Eccles and colleagues (Eccles & Midgley, 1989; Eccles, Midgley, & Adler, 1984) as well as Simmons and others (Blyth, Simmons, & Carlton-Ford, 1983; Nottleman, 1987; Simmons, Blyth, Van Cleave, & Bush, 1979; Simmons et al., 1973; Wigfield, Eccles, MacIver, Reuman, & Midgley, 1991) have postulated that differences in the school environments of elementary and junior high schools are in part responsible. Junior high school brings more emphasis on social comparison and competition, stricter grading standards, more teacher control, less personal attention from teachers, and disruptions in social networks, all of which lead to a mismatch between the structure of the school environment and the needs of young adolescents. The numerous physical, cognitive, social, and emotional changes further jeopardize the adolescent's sense of continuity, that may in turn threaten self-esteem (Leahy & Shirk, 1985).

The findings then reveal gradual gains in self-esteem over the high school years (see Harter, 1999a; McCarthy & Hoge, 1982). Gains in personal autonomy may provide more opportunity to select performance domains in which one is competent. Increasing freedom may allow more opportunities for support groups that will provide esteem-enhancing approval. Increased role-taking ability may also lead teenagers to behave in more socially acceptable ways that garner the acceptance of others. Hart, Fegley, and Brengelman (1993) provided some confirming evidence. In describing their past and present selves, older adolescents asserted that they have become more capable, mature, personable, and attractive, and they have shed undesirable cognitive, emotional, and personality characteristics.

INDIVIDUAL DIFFERENCES IN STABILITY VERSUS CHANGE

Many contributing to the adult social psychological literature have argued that self-representations are relatively stable. Swann (1995) provided evidence demonstrating individuals' elaborate and ingenious strategies for self-verification. People go to great lengths to seek information that confirms their self-concepts and are highly resistant to information that threatens their view of self (see also Epstein, 1991; Greenwald, 1980; Markus, 1977; Rosenberg, 1979). Epstein observed that "people have a vested interest in maintaining the stability of their personal theories of reality, for they are the only systems they have for making sense of their world and guiding their behavior" (p. 97). Those proposing hierarchical models of the self, where global self-esteem is at the apex of the hierarchy, have argued that higher order schemas are far more resistant to modification than lower order, situations-specific constructs (Epstein, 1991; Hattie, 1992). Epstein indicated that such higher order constructs have typically been derived from emotionally significant experiences in early development, to which the individual may have little conscious access, making the beliefs difficult to alter.

Other investigators have focused on more short-term changes in self-evaluation, demonstrating that situational factors produce such fluctuations (see Baumgardner, Kaufman, & Levy, 1989; Gergen, 1967, 1982, 1991; Heatherton & Polivy, 1991; Jones, Rhodewalt, Berglas, & Skelton, 1981; Kernis, 1993; Markus & Kunda, 1986; Rosenberg, 1986; Savin-Williams & Demo, 1983; Tesser, 1988). For example, different relational contexts (e.g., with parents, close friends, classmates, teachers, employers) where the people in question may evaluate a person differently, will produce different self-evaluations.

This brief overview of the literature reveals that there are those who believe that global self-esteem or self-worth is relatively stable over time, there are those who point to normative developmental changes in self-esteem, and there are still others who identify short-term fluctuations in self-esteem. How can these divergent perspectives be reconciled, given that there is a compelling database for each contention? Here, a return to James may provide a partial answer. James (1890) scooped more recent theorists in postulating that "there is a certain average tone of self-feeling which each one of us carries about with him, and which is independent of the objective reasons we may have for satisfaction and discontent" (p. 305). The implication is that the "average tone" (global self-esteem) is relatively stable. However, James also spoke to the issue of how on a day-to-day basis an individual's evaluation of self may fluctuate: "We ourselves know how the barometer of our self-esteem and confidence rises and falls from one day to another" (p. 307).

Building upon this thesis, Rosenberg (1986) made the distinction between "baseline" global self-esteem or worth (that he felt could be subject to gradual change over an extended period), and "barometric self-esteem," which represents short-term fluctuations over situation and time. Such volatility is particularly evident during adolescence. Markus and Kunda (1986), in a related attempt to reconcile the different positions, argued that individuals possess a stable universe of core self conceptions. However, they have also invoked the construct of the "working self-concept," a temporary structure of self-conceptions elicited by those situational factors that occur at any given point in time. Thus, self-representations are malleable, in the short run, to the extent that the content of this working self-concept changes. Others (see Kernis, 1993) make the distinction between "trait" and "state" self-esteem where trait self-esteem may be relatively stable, whereas state self-esteem reflects fluctuations around an individual's more stable average level of trait self-esteem, providing evidence with adults to identify the causes of each construct. Savin-Williams and Demo (1983) documented such a distinction among adolescents. They noted that "self-feelings are apparently global and context dependent. The largest number of our adolescents had a baseline of self-evaluation from which fluctuations rose or fell mildly, more likely dependent on features of the context" (p. 131).

Although these distinctions provide a framework for thinking about long-term stability versus short-term fluctuations, they do not reflect the complexity of self-esteem processes with regard to stability or change (see also DuBois, Reach, Tevendale, & Valentine, 2002). In particular, they do not address individual differences in the extent to which global self-esteem remains relatively immutable versus changes, nor do they speak to individual differences in the extent to which more statelike self-esteem fluctuates or remains relatively stable.

This chapter takes the stance that constructs like self-esteem or self-worth (these labels are interchangeable throughout the text), in and of themselves, are not traits or states per se. Rather, for some individuals self-esteem is stable, whereas for others self-esteem is subject to change. Among adolescents, there is evidence for this position with regard to (a) self-esteem over a school year period of time (Study A), (b) short-term fluctuations or stability in self-esteem (Study B), and (c) self-esteem as a function of relational context (e.g., with parents, classmates, etc.; Study C). Stated somewhat differently, over a relatively long time period, over short time periods, and across relational contexts, some individuals behave in a traitlike fashion whereas others behave in a statelike fashion. Three different strands of research are examined, with adolescents, in documenting these contentions. Approached from this standpoint, the goal of the research is twofold. First, it must demonstrate that for some individuals self-esteem changes whereas for others it does not. Second, it cannot merely demonstrate such individual differences but also must address what causes the patterns of individual differences. Why is it that self-esteem is relatively stable over time or situation for some adolescents but not for others?

STUDY A: THE EFFECTS OF STUDENTS' TRANSITION FROM ELEMENTARY TO JUNIOR HIGH SCHOOL ON SELF-ESTEEM

There is particular interest in change versus continuity in self-esteem as a function of educational transitions that coincide with numerous other changes in early adolescence. These include cognitive changes, movement into puberty, and potential shifts in social status, and related peer approval (relevant to Cooley's formulation), as individuals move from being the oldest in elementary school to the youngest in junior high school. The new school milieu may represent a different value system than in elementary school, such that self-evaluations of an individual's competence/adequacy and judgments of the importance of success in the various domains may well change. These shifts will have direct implications for self-esteem, as predicted by James' theory.

A number of investigators has documented the general effects of such changes on the self-esteem of adolescents, demonstrating that the mean level of self-esteem declines over this transition (see Blyth et al., 1983; Eccles & Midgley, 1989; Nottleman, 1987; Simmons et al., 1973; Wigfield et al., 1991). However, studies, for the most part, have not looked at patterns or change or continuity, identifying those whose self-esteem increases, decreased, and those whose self-esteem remains unchanged.

Thus, Study A, a dissertation by Riddle (1985), sought to examine self-esteem stability or change during the transition from elementary school to junior high school. It was the general expectation that this transition does not have a unilaterally devastating effect on all students. This 9-month longitudinal study led to administering a battery of self-report measures at Time 1, in the spring of their sixth-grade elementary year, and then 9 months later, in late winter of their seventh-grade year. Three elementary schools fed into one large junior high school resulting in the fact that two thirds of the students would be new to each individual. Thus, social comparison and perspective-taking processes would naturally be activated.

It was predicted that there would be three subgroups of adolescents: those whose self-worth remained stable, those whose self-worth decreased, and those whose self-worth increased over the 9-month period between elementary school and junior high school. It was also predicted that stability and change in self-worth would be related to stability or change in the causes of self-worth, namely, perceived success or adequacy in domains of importance (James) and the perceived opinions of significant others (Cooley).

Methods

The self-worth subscale from our Self-Perception Profile for Children (1985) was administered to tap how much individuals valued themselves as a person. A sample item is: Some students like themselves as a person but other students do not like themselves as a person. The participants first decide which kind of student they are like, and then indicate whether that description is Sort of True for them or Really True for them. Items are scored from 4 (the highest level of self-worth) to 1 (the lowest level of self-worth). Reliabilities have ranged from .86 to .90.

The Self-Perception Profile also contains subscales that tap domain-specific self-concepts across 12 life arenas relevant to the lives of students. These domains include Scholastic Competence, Athletic Competence, Physical Appearance, Peer Acceptance, and Behavioral Conduct. Alpha reliabilities across subscales ranges from .85 to .89. For each of these domains, there are parallel items that tap the importance of success in each domain, to test James' assertion that perceptions of adequacy/success in domains of importance determine the level of an individual's self-esteem.

In order to assess Cooley's contention that support in the form of approval from significant others impacts self-esteem, the Social Support Scale for Children and Adolescents was administered (Harter, 1985b), which taps approval from Parents, Teachers, Classmates, and Close Friends. A sample item from the Parents' subscale is: Some students feel that their parents are pleased with who they are as a person but Other students feel that their parents are disappointed with who they are as a person.

Students indicate which statement is more descriptive of them and whether that statement is Sort of True or Really True. Items are scored from 4 (highest support) to 1 (lowest support). Reliabilities across subscales ranged from .81 to .85.

Participants.   Two hundred seventy elementary school students (52% females, 48% males) filled out the scale in the spring of their sixth-grade elementary school and then again in the late winter of their seventh-grade junior high school. The sample was 90% European American, from primarily middle-class backgrounds.

Results

Global Self-Worth.   The mean self-worth scores for the entire sample at Time 1 was 3.03 and at Time 2 it was virtually identical at 3.06. Does this mean that global self-worth is stable during the transition to junior high school? Not necessarily. Next, three subgroups were identified whose self-worth did remain stable (within the standard error of measurement of .17) and represented 61% of the sample. At Time 1, their self-esteem score was 3.1 and at Time 2 it was 3.1. Another 20% reported statistically significant ($p < .0001$) gains in self-worth (from 3.2 to 3.6) and 19% reported equally significant decreases in self-worth (from 3.0 to 2.5) over this 9-month time period.

To examine the causes of the stability of the no-change group, as well as the increases and decreases in self-worth for the two change groups, the study turned to the causes identified by James (1892) and Cooley (1902). Recall that, for James, perception of success or adequacy in domains of importance was a major determinant of global self-worth. The findings revealed that for those in the no-change self-worth group, success in domains judged important did not change. For those whose self-worth decreased, success in domains of importance also decreased significantly. For the subgroup whose self-worth increased, success in domains of importance also increased, significantly. Thus, the results support the interpretation that if a *cause* of self-worth changes, self-worth will change, in tandem.

A similar pattern was obtained for approval from significant others, the primary cause of global feelings of worth from Cooley's perspective. For the group whose self-worth did not change, there was parallel stability in approval. Those whose self-worth increased between Time 1 and Time 2 reported significant increases in the level of approval that they were receiving from significant others. Those whose self-worth decreased across the two time periods reported a significant decrease in approval from others. Thus, if the predicted causes of global self-worth or esteem change, there should be corresponding changes in the level of self-worth.

What might be some cameos of students that would suggest why perceived success in domains of importance and level of approval might change as a function of their shift to junior high school? Consider a male elementary school student with reasonable, although not outstanding grades, who had been a soccer star in an elementary school that very much valued and rewarded its athletes. It represented a major source of peer approval. He shifts to a seventh-grade environment in which academic and computer skills are far more highly valued than sports skills. Here, scholastic success (not sports) represents the pathway to peer approval. Such a student may adopt the values of the new academic culture, however, as only an average student, his self-worth may become eroded because he is not competent in the new domain of importance.

Consider another male student from the same elementary school who was keenly interested in mathematics and computer programming and very academically talented, but not at all athletically gifted. Jocks were revered whereas computer nerds were not at this school. Such a student would be unlikely to receive approval from the majority of peers, leading to low self-worth because his talents and importance hierarchies were at variance with the school culture. However, in the new seventh-grade setting, with a strong emphasis on academics and computer skills, his talents are highly respected. He is extremely successful in this domain of importance and receives approval from peers and instructors alike. In fact, he is asked by instructors to tutor peers in computer skills. His global self-worth increases dramatically as a result of the transition to junior high school.

Consider a third student, a girl, who in a different elementary school was well-rounded, doing extremely well academically, and part of the popular crowd. Her talents in a school play were applauded by the student body. When she entered junior high, she found that not only did the school value academic success, but it also has a drama club that she joined immediately. She was accepted by this group, consistent with her elementary school experience, and was rewarded for her academic competence. In the new junior high school, her sense of adequacy in domains of importance remained high, as did her social support, and thus her high self-worth remained stable across the transition.

The findings and these three cameos suggest how changes or stability in students' sense of success, in their importance hierarchies, and in their level of approval are directly linked to their global self-worth. Stability in these causes will lead students to maintain their level of self-worth. Changes in these causes, be they increases or decreases, will be linked to corresponding changes in self-worth. Thus, to underscore a major theme in this chapter, self-esteem, as a construct, is not necessarily a trait. It will appear traitlike in some individuals if the causes remain stable, but it will be subject to changes if the causes are altered.

STUDY B: SHORT-TERM FLUCTUATIONS IN SELF-WORTH: THE LIABILITIES OF MAINTAINING A LOOKING-GLASS SELF ORIENTATION.

Study B targeted short-term fluctuations over time in middle school adolescents. Rosenberg (1986), in describing the "barometric" self, argued that such short-term fluctuations in global self-esteem or self-worth are particularly evident during adolescence, for several reasons. She cited considerable literature revealing that adolescents experience an increased concern with what their peers think of them, which is relevant to Cooley's looking glass self model. This heavy dependence on the perceptions of other's opinions tends to set the stage for volatility in individuals' assessment of the self. However, there is inevitable ambiguity about others' attitudes toward the self, because one person can never have direct access to the mind of another. Thus, attributions about others' thought processes may change from one time period to another. The second reason for fluctuating self-evaluations inheres in the fact that different significant others have different opinions of the self, depending on the situation or moment in time. Third, adolescents' concern with what others think of them leads to efforts at impression management, provoking variations in the self across relational contexts. Finally, at times, adolescents are treated as more adultlike (e.g., on a job) whereas at other times, they are treated as more childlike (e.g., with parents at home). Thus, the self fluctuates in tandem.

The construct of the barometric self has obvious appeal, particularly as applied to adolescent behavior. However, the position here is that there are individual differences in the extent to which adolescents engage in looking glass self behavior. Some are much more drawn to the social mirror than are others. Thus, not all adolescents demonstrate the rampant volatility in self-representations that the concept of the barometric self implies. Those who are not as dependent on the social feedback of others, who are far less concerned with contrived self-presentations, should report far fewer short-term fluctuations in self-worth.

Kernis (1993) made a similar argument in explaining individual differences in short-term fluctuations. He suggested that individuals whose self-esteem or self-worth is continually "on the line" will be more likely to display instability. Such individuals are highly dependent on the reactions of others toward the self, reactions that he noted can be quite variable from day to day. On some occasions, feedback may be positive (e.g., a compliment about one's appearance), whereas on another occasion it may be negative (e.g., in the face of task failure). In the absence of direct social feedback, such individuals may explicitly ask a question (e.g., how do I look today?) in an attempt to elicit others' opinions about the self. Thus, Kernis and colleagues argued that individuals who are so ego involved in what others think of them will report greater short-term fluctuation in self-esteem or worth than those who are much less ego involved and who rely more directly on their own internalized sense of self.

This topic sparked interest because of the findings that in correlating perceived approval with global self-esteem, to test Cooley's looking glass self formulation, a subgroup was found for whom the correlation was strong but there was another subgroup for whom it was much weaker. It was hypothesized that perhaps the former group might be harboring a metatheory that their self-worth is dependent on the approval of others. In contrast, the latter group, for whom the correlation was weaker, might turn the directionality of this link around, contending that their level of self-worth should impact whether others approved of them. Because these directionality issues are impossible to determine with correlational data, the task became to unravel this issue by asking middle school adolescents directly. A new and relatively straightforward methodology was devised in which adolescents were asked to endorse one of two orientations, thinking about their peers: (a) If others approve of me first, then I will like myself as a person, or (b) If I like myself as a person first, then others will like and approve of me (Harter, Stocker, & Robinson, 1996). It was found that 59% selected the looking glass self orientation, whereas 41% opted for the second sequence of attitudes about this link. Moreover, students provided examples that corroborated their choice, supporting the validity of the choice measure.

Sample responses from the looking glass self adolescents, for whom approval precedes self-worth, were: "When I meet new kids and they approve of me then I look at myself and say 'I'm not so bad,' and it makes me feel good about myself." "When other kids make you feel left out you don't feel good about yourself." "If other people don't like me as a person, then I wonder if I *am* a good person, I care about what people say about me."

Sample responses for those who believe in the metatheory that liking oneself precedes the approval of others, were: "I just like myself and then other people like me too." "The way I figure it, if you can't like the person you are first, then how do you expect other people to like you!" "You have to appreciate yourself first, as a person. If you wait for other people to make you feel good, you could be waiting a long time!"

The prediction was that those who endorsed the first looking glass self-metatheory (approval precedes self-worth) would report more fluctuations than would those endorsing the belief that self-worth precedes approval from others. It was reasoned, much as did Kernis (1993), that if individuals are so preoccupied with the opinions of others toward the self and more socially distracted (looking for social feedback) in the classroom, then small social cues may be signals that the approval of others shifts. One day, someone says "hi" to you in the hall but another day you are ignored. You get invited to one party but not to another. You are asked to join a lunchroom table one day but feel rebuffed on another day. To assess fluctuations, students were asked to indicate how frequently their liking of themselves (their self-esteem or worth) changed: (1) hardly ever changes, (2) changes about once a month, (3) changes several times a month, (4) changes about once a week, (5) changes several times a week, (6) changes about once a day, (7) changes several times a day.

The findings revealed that, as predicted, the looking glass self students, basing their self-worth on the perceived approval of others, reported significantly more fluctuations in self-worth, with mean scores between several times a week and once a week. Those endorsing the metatheory that their self-worth precedes approval from others reported far fewer fluctuations in self-worth, between once a month to several times a month. These differences were paralleled by perceptions of fluctuations of the perceived approval of others, as predicted. The looking glass self students reported more fluctuations (about once a week) than did the self-worth to approval group (about once a month). Thus, the looking glass self students reported greater fluctuations in perceived approval which would appear to be driving their greater fluctuations in self-worth, because by definition, they are basing their views of their worth on the opinions of others. Thus, the barometric self construct is more demonstrable in what has been labeled as the looking glass self students than those not endorsing such an orientation, for whom perceptions of self-worth are much more stable.

Finally, there are other liabilities associated with the adoption of a looking glass self metatheory. Such students reported that they were more preoccupied with the opinions of peers and teachers reported that such students were more socially distracted in the classroom, concentrating less on their schoolwork and more on how their peers were reacting to them. In addition, looking glass self adolescents reported lower levels of peer approval compared to the group for whom self-worth preceded perceived approval. Looking glass self adolescents, in their preoccupation with approval, may engage in behaviors that do not garner the support of their peers. For example, they may be trying too hard to obtain peer approval, or they may adopt inappropriate strategies to extract feedback from peers or to make friends, and in so doing, they may annoy or alienate their peers. Given that looking glass self adolescents, by definition, base their self-worth on perceived approval, their self-worth should also suffer. The findings supported this expectation in that the looking glass self participants reported lower self-worth than did those who felt that self-worth precedes approval.

There is only speculation on why some adolescents maintain a looking glass self perspective whereas others appear to have internalized the opinions of others. The former group may have experienced a socialization history characterized by inconsistent feedback (e.g., fluctuations in approval and disapproval), providing no clear message for what should be internalized. Greenier, Kernis, and Waschull (1995) suggested a related hypothesis, namely, that such individuals may experience feedback from significant others that is unreliable and thus lack clearly defined "reflected appraisals" of their self-worth. Also, looking glass self adolescents may have had a history of support that was conditional on meeting the demands of parents. An early history of conditionality would not provide the kind of validating support for who one is as a person, support that could be internalized as approval of the self. Kernis came to a similar conclusion in noting that feedback that is experienced as controlling, that is, "pressure to think, feel, or behave in specified ways" (Deci & Ryan, 1985, p. 95), is likely to contribute to an unstable sense of self-worth.

STUDY C: RELATIONAL SELF-WORTH AMONG ADOLESCENTS: DIFFERENCES IN PERCEIVED WORTH AS A PERSON ACROSS INTERPERSONAL CONTEXTS

The first two studies presented in this chapter dealt with self-worth change over time, both relatively long-term changes as well as short-term fluctuations. A major conclusion of both studies is that for some adolescents there is change over time, whereas for other adolescents there is relative stability. Therefore, the construct of self-worth, in and of itself, is neither traitlike nor statelike. Rather, certain individuals behave in more traitlike fashion over long or short periods of time, whereas others manifest change. The same can be said for a new construct to emerge in our work, namely, "relational self-worth" (Harter, Waters, & Whitesell, 1998). Relational self-worth refers to the fact that a person can have different perceptions of self-worth in different relational contexts, that is, relationship-specific self-worth. The four contexts initially investigated have been self-worth with parents, with teachers, with male classmates, and with female classmates. Relational self-worth was tapped by making global self-worth items specific to given relational contexts, for example: Some teenagers like the kind of person they are around their parents but other teenagers do not like the kind of person they are around their parents. As with other items written in this format, the participants first identify which description is most like them and then indicate whether that statement is Sort of True for Me or Really True for Me. Items are scored on a 4-point scale where a 4 designates the highest level of self-worth and a 1 reflects the lowest level of self-worth.

In an initial sample of 279 high school students (equal representation of males and females) from middle-class, primarily European-American ethnicity, the relational self-worth survey was administered (Harter et al., 1998). Internal consistencies across the four contexts ranged from .87 to .91.

Results

Initial interest was in the factor pattern, to determine whether items defining the four contexts (parents, teachers, male classmates, and female classmates) loaded on separate factors, employing an oblique rotation. Factor loadings are extremely high on the designated subscale, with negligible cross-loadings (see Harter et al., 1998). Thus, the findings provide evidence for the factorial validity of the relational self-worth measure.

Does this mean that all adolescents are making significant distinctions between their self-worth in different relational contexts? No, it does not. Consistent with the general thesis of this chapter, there was evidence that for some adolescents, self-worth across relational contexts is very stable whereas for other adolescents, there is significant variability. How do the findings bear on this conclusion?

The discrepancies were first examined between the highest and lowest relational self-worth scores across the four contexts. Two groups were identified. The first group consisted of those for whom self-worth was stable across contexts (26.5% of the sample) where stability was defined as lack of contextual differences within the standard error of measurement. This group, therefore, displayed more traitlike be-havior with regard to their level of self-worth. The second group, the remaining 73.5%, reported discrepancies in self-worth across relational contexts, displaying relationship specificity.

The goal of this research, as in the other two studies, was not merely to demonstrate that certain individuals report stability whereas others report variability, but to search for the determinants of each pattern. In an attempt to ascertain what might be the cause of individuals' relational self-worth in these different contexts, it was hypothe-sized, in keeping with a revisionist looking glass self model, that the level of approval from each source of self-worth may dictate the level of their self-worth in that context. Findings revealed that correlations between approval from each source and relational self-worth in each social context are much higher and more statistically significant than the correlations between approval and self-worth in different social contexts. Thus, the findings support a more situation-specific version of the looking glass self model in that approval in given contexts predicts relational self-worth.

Several caveats are worth pointing out. The previous study noted that the directionality of perceived approval from significant others and self-worth can vary according to the individual's metatheory about this link. Thus, the present study can not equivocally assert that it is the approval of significant others that is causing the individuals' level of self-worth in that context. It could be the case that their sense of self-worth in a given context is driving the approval that they perceive from those persons. Such an observation does not invalidate the construct of relational self-worth, because the correlations between approval in a given context and self-worth in the corresponding context are quite striking. Rather, the directionality methodology must be incorporated into the assessment of relational self-worth in order to provide future answers.

SPECIFIC CONCLUSIONS

Developmentally, self-esteem emerges during early childhood where it is first dis-played in behavior that can be reliably rated by others, for example, teachers. Cogni-tive-developmental processes and socialization practices together shape the content and structure of young children's self-evaluations. However, normative cognitive-developmental limitations prevent the young child from developing a verbalizable concept of their global self-worth as a person. Although young children can provide evaluations of their domain-specific competencies, these judgments are unrealistically positive, due to their cognitive limitations. Thus, mean scores are relatively high and there is low variability in scores demonstrating fewer individual differences than at later ages (Harter & Pike, 1984).

Beginning in middle childhood, three new cognitive skills emerge that cause self-judgments to be more realistic and therefore less positive for many children. These skills include (a) the ability to appreciate the distinction between a person's real and ideal self, leading to the construction of a discrepancy between these constructs. In general, the bigger the discrepancy, where the real self is judged more negatively than the ideal self, the lower the individual's self-esteem. Also, there is (b) the ability to take the perspective of others, realizing that they are evaluating the self. Perceived feedback from others may not always be as positive as the individual would wish, leading to lowered self-esteem. Finally, there is (c) the ability to make use of social comparison for the purpose of self-evaluation. Given older children's sensitivity to the performance of peers, many will feel that they fall short of the superstars in their peer group, which in turn can erode self-esteem. Thus, whereas movement to new cognitive levels represents many advances, with regard to the realm of self-evaluations, these three processes that emerge in middle childhood may, for some children, also introduce liabilities, leading them to evaluate themselves more negatively.

Finally, parents of those in middle childhood begin to raise the bar with regard to standards of performance as well as behavioral expectations. This can create the potential for lowered self-perceptions if the child is not meeting these expectations. Thus, all of these changes in middle childhood can lead to lower mean levels of self-esteem as well as greater variability or individual differences in self-esteem.

Once these individual differences have been established in middle childhood, what is the fate of children's self-esteem as they move into later childhood and beyond? Is it relatively immutable or is it subject to change? It has been argued that, phrased as such, this is not the question that should be asked. Rather, the question should ask: For whom is self-esteem stable and for whom is it malleable, and why?

The three strands of research have addressed a number of issues. During the transition from elementary school to junior high school, certain students show stability in global self-esteem or self-worth over a 9-month period, whereas other students do not. Among this latter group, certain students report decreases in global self-worth but others report increases. Further evidence reveals that the causes of global self-worth, perceived success in domains deemed important (from James, 1890) and the perceived approval of significant others (from Cooley, 1902), parallel changes in self-worth across the transition. With regard to short-term fluctuations in global self-worth, certain adolescents report short-term fluctuations, whereas others report greater stability. These differences are linked to adolescents' metatheories about the directionality of the relation between approval and self-worth. Those looking glass self adolescents who continue to base their self-worth on approval from others report that they are more preoccupied with the feedback of others, leading to fluctuations in perceived approval as well as parallel fluctuations in self-worth. Liabilities for these adolescents include greater social distraction in the classroom, less ability to concentrate on schoolwork, lower levels of perceived approval from peers and a lower level of self-worth, each of which can put students at risk.

Finally, in examining the construct of relational self-worth, namely, perceptions of worth in different relational contexts, there were group differences. Certain adolescents report very stable self-worth across the social contexts with parents, teachers, male classmates, female classmates. However, other students report variations in self-worth, from moderate to extreme, across these contexts. Level of self-worth in each context is highly correlated with the particular level of approval in that context, although, in light of Study B, the directionality of this link needs to be considered in future research.

GENERAL CONCLUSIONS

Constructs such as self-worth or self-esteem are not traits or states, in and of themselves. Rather, certain individuals behave in traitlike fashion over time as well as relational context, whereas others do not. Social processes such as approval from significant others contribute heavily to whether one behaves in a traitlike or more statelike manner, although the nature of these links is complex. In future efforts, energy should be put into research that examines the causes of these individual differences rather than remain rooted in the traditional controversy about whether constructs such as self-esteem are stable over time and situation or are changeable. The field of personality has clearly moved in this direction in recent years, providing a clearer understanding of the complexity of self-processes during childhood and adolescence, as well as adulthood.

However, there is considerably more work to be done. With regard to change over relatively long periods of time, there is a need to move to longitudinal designs that identify predictors, outcomes, mediators, and subsequent consequences at multiple time periods and provide the most meaningful data about whether, how, and why self-constructs change or remain stable over time. New statistical methodologies to measure more complicated trajectories over many more time periods are coming into favor as routes to uncovering more different pathways over time, addressing issues of both stability and change in self-worth (e.g., see DuBois et al., 2002; Hirsh & DuBois, 1991). With new tools in the armamentarium, researchers will be better able to map the multiple trajectories that identify stability as well as change, thereby doing justice to the complexities of the development of self-processes over time. With regard to short-term fluctuations, they need to determine precisely what leads certain adolescents to initially adopt the views of significant others and then gradually over the course of development internalize these attitudes of others toward the self, owning their self-evaluations. What discriminates these individuals from those who remain fixated on the social mirror, to define themselves, leading to psychological liabilities. The findings on the link between relational social support and relational self-worth demand further studies of the directionality of this link. Also, researchers need to examine the link between relational self-worth and global self-worth because the former construct does not dictate the demise of the latter but rather suggests the complexities of these processes. These define clear goals for future research.

ACKNOWLEDGMENT

Support for this research was provided by NICHD and the W. T. Grant Foundation.

REFERENCES

Allport, G. W. (1961). *Pattern and growth in personality.* New York: Holt, Rinehart & Winston.

Baumgardner, A. H., Kaufman, C. M., & Levy, P. E. (1989). Regulating affect interpersonally: When low self-esteem leads to greater enhancement. *Journal of Personality and Social Psychology, 56,* 907–921.

Blyth, D. A., Simmons, R. G., & Carlton-Ford, S. (1983). The adjustment of early adolescents to school transitions. *Journal of Early Adolescence, 3,* 105–120.

Brim, O. B. (1976). Life-span development of the theory of oneself: Implications for child development. In H. W. Reese (Ed.). *Advances in child development and behavior* (Vol. 11, pp. 82–103). New York: Academic Press.

Case, R. (1985). *Intellectual development: Birth to adulthood.* New York: Academic Press.

Connell, J.P., & Wellborn, J. G. (1991). Competence, autonomy, and relatedness: A motivational analysis of self-system processes. In M. R. Gunnar & L. A. Sroufe (Eds.), *Self processes and development: The Minnesota symposium on child development* (Vol. 23, pp. 43–78). Hillsdale, NJ: Lawrence Erlbaum Associates.

Cooley, C. H. (1902). *Human nature and the social order.* New York: Scribner's.

Damon, W., & Hart, D. (1988). *Self-understanding in childhood and adolescence.* New York: Cambridge University Press.

Deci, E. L., & Ryan, R. M. (1995). Human autonomy: The basis for true self-esteem. In M. H. Kernis (Ed.), *Efficacy, agency, and self-esteem* (pp. 31–46). New York: Plenum.

DuBois, D. L., Reach, K., Tevendale, H., & Valentine, J. (2002, April). Self-esteem in early adolescence: Trait, state, or both? In D. L. DuBois (Chair), *Change and stability in self-esteem during adolescence: The long and the short of it.* Symposium conducted at the biennial meeting of the Society for Research on Adolescence, New Orleans.

Dusek, J. B., & Flaherty, J. (1981). The development of self during the adolescent years. *Monograph of the Society for Research in Child Development, 46* (Whole No. 191), 1–61.

Eccles, J. S., & Midgley, C. (1989). Stage/environment fit: Developmentally appropriate classroom for early adolescents. In R. Ames & C. Ames (Eds.), *Research on motivation in education* (Vol. 3, pp. 139–181). San Diego: Academic Press.

Eccles, J. S., Midgley, C., & Adler, T. (1984). Grade-related changes in the school environment: Effects on achievement motivation. In J. G. Nicholls (Ed.), *The development of achievement motivation* (pp. 283–331). Greenwich, CT: JAI Press.

Engel, M. (1959). The stability of the self-concept in adolescence. *Journal of Abnormal and Social Psychology, 58,* 211–217.

Epstein, S. (1973). The self-concept revisited or a theory of a theory. *American Psychologist, 28,* 405–416.

Epstein, S. (1981). The unity principle versus the reality and pleasure principles, or the tale of the scorpion and the frog. In M. D. Lynch, A. A. Norem-Hebeisen, & K. Gergen (Eds.), *Self-concept: Advances in theory and research* (pp. 82–110). Cambridge, MA: Ballinger.

Epstein, S. (1991). Cognitive-experiential self theory: Implications for developmental psychology. In M. Gunnar & L. A. Sroufe (Eds.), *Self-processes and development: The Minnesota symposia on child development* (Vol. 23, pp. 111–137). New York: Guilford.

Fischer, K. (1980). A theory of cognitive development: The control and construction of a hierarchy of skills. *Psychological Review, 87,* 477–531.

Frey, K. S., & Ruble, D. N. (1985). What children say when the teacher is not around: Conflicting goals in social comparison and performance assessment in the classroom. *Journal of Personality and Social Psychology, 48,* 550–562.

Frey, K. S., & Ruble, D. N. (1990). Strategies for comparative evaluation: Maintaining a sense of competence across the life span. In R. J. Sternberg & J. Kolligian, Jr. (Eds.), *Competence considered* (pp. 167–189). New Haven, CT: Yale University Press.

Furman, W., & Bierman, K. (1984). Children's conceptions of friendships: A multimethod study of developmental changes. *Developmental Psychology, 20,* 925–931.

Gergen, K. J. (1967). To be or not to be the single self. In S. M. Journal (Ed.), *To be or not to be: Existential perspectives on the self* (pp. 104–132). Gainesville: University of Florida Press.

Gergen, K. J. (1982). From self to science: What is there to know? In J. Suls (Ed.), *Psychological perspectives on the self* (Vol. 1, pp. 129–149). Hillsdale, NJ: Lawrence Erlbaum Associates.

Gergen, K. J. (1991). *The saturated self.* New York: Basic Books.

Glick, M., & Zigler, E. (1985). Self-image: A cognitive-developmental approach. In R. Leahy (Ed.), *The development of the self* (pp. 1–54). New York: Academic Press.

Greenier, K. D., Kernis, M. H., & Waschull, S. B. (1995). Not all high or low self-esteem people are the same: Theory and research on the stability of self-esteem. In M. H. Kernis (Ed.), *Efficacy, agency, and self-esteem* (pp. 51–68). New York: Plenum.

Greenwald, A. G. (1980). The totalitarian ego: Fabrication and revision of personal history. *American Psychologist, 7,* 603–618.

Haltiwanger, J. (1989, April). *Behavioral referents of presented self-esteem in young children.* Paper presented at the meeting of the Society for Research in Child Development, Kansas City, MO.

Harris, J. (1998). *The nurture assumption.* New York: The Free Press.

Harris, P. L. (1983a). Children's understanding of the link between situation and emotion. *Journal of Experimental Child Psychology, 36,* 490–509.

Harris, P. L. (1983b). What children know about the situations that provoke emotion. In M. Lewis & C. Saarni (Eds.), *The socialization of affect* (pp. 162–185). New York: Plenum.

Hart, D., Fegley, S., & Brengelman, D. (1993). Perceptions of past, present, and future selves among children and adolescents. *British Journal of Development, 11,* 265–282.

Harter, S. (1982). The perceived competence scale for children. *Child Development, 53,* 87–97.

Harter, S. (1985a). *The Self-Perception Profile for Children.* Unpublished Manual, University of Denver, Denver, CO.

Harter, S. (1985b). *The Social Support Scale for Children.* Unpublished Manual, University of Denver, Denver, CO.

Harter, S. (1990a). Adolescent self and identity development. In S. S. Feldman & G. R. Elliot (Eds.), *At the threshold: The developing adolescent* (pp. 352–387). Cambridge, MA: Harvard University Press.

Harter, S. (1990b). Causes, correlates and the functional role of global self-worth: A life-span perspective. In R. Sternberg & J. Kolligian, Jr. (Eds.), *Competence considered* (pp. 67–98). New Haven, CT: Yale University Press.

Harter, S. (1990c). Developmental differences in the nature of self-representations: Implications for the understanding and treatment of maladaptive behaviors. *Cognitive Therapy and Research, 14,* 113–142.

Harter, S. (1990d). Issues in the assessment of the self-concept of children and adolescents. In A. La Greca (Ed.), *Childhood assessment: Through the eyes of a child* (pp. 292–335), New York: Allyn & Bacon.

Harter, S. (1993). Causes and consequences of low self-esteem in children and adolescents. In R. F. Baumeister (Ed.), *Self-esteem: The puzzle of low self-regard* (pp. 87–116). New York: Plenum.

Harter, S. (1999). *The construction of the self: A developmental perspective.* New York: The Guilford Press.

Harter, S., Low, S., & Whitesell, N. (2003). What have we learned from Columbine: The role of the self-system in understanding adolescent violent and suicidal ideation. *Journal of School Violence, 2,* 3–26.

Harter, S., Marold, D. B., & Whitesell, N. R. (1992). A model of psychosocial risk factors leading to suicidal ideation in young adolescents. *Development and Psychopathology, 4,* 167–188.

Harter, S., Marold, D. B., Whitesell, N. R., & Cobbs, G. (1996). A model of the effects of parent and peer support on adolescent false self behavior. *Child Development, 67,* 360–374.

Harter, S., & Pike, R. (1984). The pictorial scale of perceived competence and social acceptance for young children. *Child Development, 55,* 1969–1982.

Harter, S., Stocker, C., & Robinson, N. S. (1996). The perceived directionality of the link between approval and self-worth: The liabilities of a looking glass self orientation among young adolescents. *Journal of Research on Adolescence, 6,* 285–308.

Harter, S., Waters, P. L., & Whitesell, N. R. (1998). Relational self-worth: Differences in perceived worth as a person across interpersonal contexts. *Child Development, 69,* 756–766.

Hattie, J. (1992). *Self-concept.* Hillsdale, NJ: Lawrence Erlbaum Associates.

Heatherton, T. F., & Polivy, J. (1991). Development and validation of a scale for measuring state self-esteem. *Journal of Personality and Social Psychology, 60,* 895–910.

Higgins, E. T. (1991). Development of self-regulatory and self-evaluative processes: Costs, benefits, and tradeoffs. In M. R. Gunnar & L. A. Sroufe (Eds.), *Self processes and development: The Minnesota symposium on child development* (Vol. 23, pp. 125–166). Hillsdale, NJ: Lawrence Erlbaum Associates.

Hirsh, B. J., & DuBois, D. L. (1991). Self-esteem in early adolescence: The identification and prediction of contrasting longitudinal trajectories. *Journal of Youth and Adolescence, 20,* 53–72.

James, W. (1890). *Principles of psychology.* Chicago: Encyclopedia Britannica.

James, W. (1892). *Psychology: The briefer course.* New York: Henry Holt.

Jones, E. E., Rhodewalt, F., Berglas, S., & Skelton, J. A. (1981). Effect of strategic self-presentation in subsequent self-esteem. *Journal of Personality and Social Psychology, 41,* 407–421.

Kernis, M. H. (1993). The roles of stability and level of self-esteem in psychological functioning. In R. F. Baumeister (Ed.), *Self-esteem: The puzzle of low self-regard* (pp. 167–180). New York: Plenum.

Kelley, G. A. (1955). *The psychology of personal constructs.* New York: Norton.

Leahy, R. L. (1985). The costs of development: Clinical implications. In R. L. Leahy (Ed.), *The development of the self* (pp. 267–294). New York: Academic Press.

Leahy, R. L., & Shirk, S. R. (1985). Social cognition and the development of the self. In R. L. Leahy (Ed.), *The development of the self* (pp. 123–150). New York: Academic Press.

Maccoby, E. (1980). *Social development.* New York: Wiley.

Markus, H. (1977). Self-schemata and processing information about the self. *Journal of Personal and Social Psychology, 35,* 63–78.

Markus, H. W. (1980). The self in thought and memory. In D. M. Wegner & R. R. Vallacher (Eds.), *The self in social psychology* (pp. 42–69). New York: Oxford University Press.

Markus, H., & Kunda, Z. (1986). Stability and malleability of the self-concept. *Journal of Personality and Social Psychology, 51,* 858–866.

Marsh, H. W. (1989). Age and sex effects on multiple dimensions of self-concept: Preadolescence to early adulthood. *Journal of Educational Psychology, 81,* 417–430.

Marsh, H. W. (1991). *Self-Description Questionnaire–III.* San Antonio, TX: Psychological Corporation.

Marsh, H. W., Parker, J., & Barnes, J. (1985). Multidimensional adolescent self-concepts: Their relationship to age, sex, and academic measures. *American Educational Research Journal, 22,* 422–444.

Marsh, H. W., Smith, I. D., Marsh, M. R., Owens, L. (1988). The transition from single-sex to coeducational high schools: Effects on multiple dimensions of self-concept and on academic achievement. *American Educational Research Journal, 25,* 237–269.

McCarthy, J., & Hoge, D. (1982). Analysis of age effects in longitudinal studies of adolescent self-esteem. *Developmental Psychology, 18,* 372–379.

Mead, G. H. (1925). The genesis of the self and social control. *International Journal of Ethics, 35,* 251–273.

Mead, G. H. (1934). *Mind, self, and society from the standpoint of a social behaviorist.* Chicago: University of Chicago Press.

Nottlemann, E. D. (1987). Competence and self-esteem during the transition from childhood to adolescence. *Developmental Psychology, 23,* 441–450.

O'Malley, P., & Bachman, J. (1983). Self-esteem: Change and stability between ages 13 and 23. *Developmental Psychology, 19,* 257–268.

Piaget, J. (1960). *The psychology of intelligence.* Patterson, NJ: Littlefield-Adams.

Riddle, M. (1985). *The effect of the transition to junior high school on adolescent self-esteem.* Unpublished doctoral dissertation, University of Denver.

Piers, E. V., & Harris, D. B. (1964). Age and other correlates of self-concept in children. *Journal of Educational Psychology, 55*, 91–95.

Rogers, C. R. (1951). *Client-centered therapy.* Boston: Houghton Mifflin.

Rosenberg, M. (1979). *Conceiving the self.* New York: Basic Books.

Rosenberg, M. (1986). Self-concept from middle childhood through adolescence. In J. Suls & A. G. Greenwald (Eds.), *Psychological Perspectives on the self* (Vol. 3, pp. 107–135). Hillsdale, NJ: Lawrence Erlbaum Associates.

Rubin, K. H., Chen, X., & Hymel S. (1993). Socioemotional characteristics of withdrawn and aggressive children. *Merrill-Palmer Quarterly, 49*, 518–534.

Ruble, D. N., & Frey, K. S. (1991). Changing patterns of comparative behavior as skills are acquired: A functional model of self-evaluation. In J. Suls & T. A. Wills (Eds.), *Social comparison contemporary theory and research* (pp. 70–112). Hillsdale, NJ: Lawrence Erlbaum Associates.

Sarbin, T. R. (1962). A preface to a psychological analysis of the self. *Psychological Review, 59*, 11–22.

Savin-Williams, R. C., & Demo, P. (1993). Situational and transitional determinants of adolescent self-feelings. *Journal of Personality and Social Psychology, 44*, 820–833.

Selman, R. L. (1980). *The growth of interpersonal understanding.* New York: Academic Press.

Simmons, R. G., Blyth, D. A., Van Cleave, E. F., & Bush, D. (1979). Entry into early adolescence: The impact of school structure, puberty, and early dating on self-esteem. *American Sociological Review, 44*, pp. 948–967.

Simmons, R. G., & Rosenberg, M. (1973). Disturbances in the self-images at adolescence. *American Sociological Review, 38*, 553–568.

Simmons, R. G., Rosenberg, F., & Rosenberg, M. (1973). *American Sociological Review, 38*, 553–568.

Sroufe, L. A., & Fleeson, J. (1986). Attachment and the construction of relationships. In W. Hartup & Z. Rubin (Eds.), *Relationships and development* (pp. 51–71). New York: Cambridge University Press.

Stipek, D. (1981). Children's perceptions of their own and their classmates' ability. *Journal of Educational Psychology, 73*, 404–410.

Swann, W. B., Jr. (1995). *Self-traps: The elusive quest for higher self-esteem.* New York: Freeman.

Tesser, A. (1988). Toward a self-evaluation maintenance model of social behavior. In L. Berkowitz (Ed.), *Advances in experimental social psychology* (Vol. 21, pp. 181–227). New York: Academic Press.

Wigfield, A., Eccles, J. S., MacIver, D., Reuman, D. A., & Midley, C. (1991). Transitions during early adolescence: Changes in children's domain-specific self-perceptions and general self-esteem across the transition to junior high school. *Developmental Psychology, 27*, 555–562.

Wylie, R. C. (1979). *The self-concept: Theory and research on selected topics* (Vol. 2). Lincoln: University of Nebraska Press.

Wylie, R. C. (1989). *Measures of self-concept.* Lincoln: University of Nebraska Press.

IV

Personality Development
in Middle and Older Adulthood

17

From Young Adulthood Through the Middle Ages

Ravenna Helson
Christopher J. Soto
Rebecca A. Cate
University of California, Berkeley

Periods of life have underpinnings in the universals of biology and social life, but they are conceptualized differently in different cultures and historical periods (Menon, 2001; Shweder, 1998). Middle age is not recognized at all in some societies, but in ours estimates often stretch from age 35 or 40 to age 60 or 65—a span of 20 to 30 years. The question of whether or not personality should be expected to change or develop within this period has received little attention. This chapter begins with a brief and selective review of two background topics: (a) relations between age, roles, status, and personality, and (b) personality change in adulthood. Then after a brief consideration of middle age as a whole, the issue of making differentiations within this long expanse is discussed. Three phases of middle age are proposed, then longitudinal evidence supporting the conception along with divergent findings are presented. Finally, there are suggestions for further research.

BRIEF REVIEW OF RESEARCH AREAS

Relations between Age, Roles, Status, and Personality

Anthropologists and sociologists have linked age to roles and social status across a diverse range of societies (e.g., Linton, 1936; Riley, 1976). There are norms about what people of a certain age should be doing, and these norms may be internalized and help to guide or motivate behavior (Neugarten, 1977). In Western culture, the first half of adulthood has been described as a period of growth and expansion during which individuals seek to find and maximize their status in society, whereas security and threat-avoidance become more important in the second half (Kuhlen, 1968; Staudinger & Bluck, 2001). Middle age is described as a period of multiple roles and complex relationships among roles (Antonucci, Akiyama, & Merline, 2001). It is a time of competition between demands of work and family (Havighurst, 1972).

A number of social scientists have argued that age has lost potency as a determinant of adult life patterns in Western society (e.g., Neugarten, 1979; Riley, Kahn, Foner, & Mack, 1994). Life styles and schedules have become more diverse (Bumpass & Aquilino, 1995), and people have become more tolerant of this diversity (Settersten, 1998). However, age remains a major factor in people's adult lives and personality. Lachman, Lewkowicz, Markus, and Peng (1994) found that middle-age people (average age = 48) described themselves and were described by younger and older adults as experiencing physical decline, having many responsibilities, and enjoying little leisure, but also as showing a peak of competence, productivity, and social responsibility. Earlier studies reported similar results, describing middle-aged individuals as showing both gains and losses (Heckhausen, Dixon, & Baltes, 1989), and as peaking in dominance, status, effective intelligence, and integrative skills (Cameron, 1970, 1973; Neugarten, 1968; Schaie, 1977-78).

Contemporary family roles begin and change at heterogeneous times, but some changes are predictable. In middle age, children leave home and parents die (Bumpass & Aquilino, 1995). Some longitudinal studies support Gutmann's (1987) view that gender roles are most stringent during the early period of childrearing, and men become more feminine and women more masculine in later adulthood (e.g., Harker & Solomon, 1996; Helson, Pals, & Solomon, 1997), but this is a complex issue and findings vary with measures and study design as well as with sample, cohort, and social climate (Diehl, Owen, & Youngblade, 2004; Parker & Aldwin, 1997).

Several stage theorists have based their stages in part on the relation between age and social roles, conceptualized in terms of developmental tasks (e.g., Erikson, 1950; Havighurst, 1972) or life structures that change with phases in career development (D. J. Levinson, Darrow, Klein, M. H. Levinson, & McKee 1978; Vaillant, 1977). Research on Eriksonian constructs suggests that sense of identity becomes stronger from young adulthood to middle age (Stewart, Ostrove, & Helson, 2001), and number and quality of social roles is related to identity development and well-being (Vandewater, Ostrove, & Stewart, 1997). Generativity tends to peak in middle age, but the conditions associated with its peaking are not altogether clear (McAdams, 2001a) and some have argued that it is the felt capacity for generativity, as opposed to desire for or actual generative actions, that peaks in middle adulthood (Stewart & Vandewater, 1998). Several studies (e.g., Ryff & Heincke, 1983; Zucker, Ostrove, & Stewart, 2002) show that young adults expect to increase in identity certainty and generativity during middle age in the ways hypothesized by theorists.

Personality Change in Adulthood

Personality trait psychologists have traditionally emphasized continuity in adult personality, conceiving traits as largely genetic and unchanging (e.g., McCrae et al., 2000). Recently, a new consensus regarding adult personality change has developed, more in line with cognitive approaches and a perspective of adaptation to changing biological resources in a changing environment throughout the life span (Baltes, 1997; Heckhausen & Schulz, 1995). A meta-analysis showed that personality continues to increase in rank-order consistency until late middle age (Roberts & DelVecchio, 2000). Several large cross-sample or cross-national studies have shown relations between age and personality in both men and women over the adult years (see review in Helson, Kwan, John, & Jones, 2002). Most studies show increase with age in conscientiousness and agreeableness, and decrease with age in the social vitality aspect of extraversion. Although many studies have looked only for linear relations between personality and age, recent work provides much evidence of quadratic relationships (e.g., Cramer, 2003; Helson, Jones, & Kwan, 2002; Srivastava, John, Gosling, & Potter, 2003).

Researchers have also conceptualized and demonstrated relations of emotionality and coping styles with age (e.g., Carstensen, Pasupathi, Mayr, & Nesselroade, 2000; Diehl, Coyle, & Labouvie-Vief, 1996; Gross et al., 1997; Mroczek & Kolarz, 1998). People are said to increasingly avoid negative emotions and maintain positive states through improved emotional control, shifts in coping techniques, or lesser emotional reactivity. Older married couples are more skilled in affective relationships with each other than are those in early middle age (Levenson, Carstensen, & Gottman, 1994). As people age, they choose their social contacts less on the basis of the information these contacts provide and more for their emotional value (Carstensen, Isaacowitz, & Charles, 1999). Labouvie-Vief and Medler (2002) suggested that affect regulation involves two independent coping strategies: Affect optimization is the tendency to constrain affect to positive values, and affect complexity is the amplification of affect in the search for differentiation and objectivity. Based on this and earlier work (e.g., Labouvie-Vief, DeVoe, & Bulka, 1989), Labouvie-Vief and Márquez (2004) proposed that the former increases throughout adulthood, whereas the latter peaks in middle age and then declines.

Cognitive researchers say that perceptual speed begins to decline in the mid-20s, but that some higher order abilities, such as inductive reasoning, continue to increase in middle age and then decline very gradually with many individual differences (Willis & Schaie, 1999). Studies of wisdom as "expertise in the pragmatics of everyday life" do not show increase into the later years, but they also do not show the decline that might be expected from cognitive losses (Baltes, Staudinger, Maercker, & Smith, 1995; Pasupathi, Staudinger, & Baltes, 2001).

In other areas of research, motivation and values have been found to shift from tenacious goal pursuit (changing one's situation to meet one's goals) to flexible goal adjustment (changing one's goals to meet one's situation) over middle age (Brandtstaedter & Renner, 1990). Search for personal growth lessens after midlife (Ryff, 1991), but spirituality increases (Wink & Dillon, 2002).

It must be emphasized that most research on personality in relation to age has used cross-sectional designs. Because cultural and cohort effects make a difference (e.g., Roberts & Helson, 1997; Twenge, 2001), more longitudinal work is needed to demonstrate that the same individuals change or stay the same in the ways we have discussed. Nevertheless, there are many lines of evidence that personality changes within and across middle age.

MIDDLE AGE AND ITS PHASES

Middle Age

Research on personality and age in adulthood often contrasts young and old, omitting middle age altogether (Lachman & Bertrand, 2001). This may be done as a matter of convenience, with middle-aged individuals being busier and less likely to participate, but the latent implication is that midlife is merely an intermediary zone between young adulthood and old age. However, middle age is a unique period of life. In terms of roles, the distinctive content of middle age includes the middle stages of parenting, changing relations to one's own parents, transitions in employment in coordination with changing family responsibilities, and in later middle age the anticipation of relinquishing the employment role or the experience of actually retiring (Moen & Wethington, 1999). As Bumpass and Aquilino (1995) said, "The negotiation of ... changing roles and statuses constitutes, to a significant extent, the nature of midlife experience." (p. 52). Thus, middle age should be regarded not only as a period when certain conditions prevail, but also as a period during which certain changes take place. Although there may be variation across cultures and socioeconomic groups, here are the characteristics of midlife personality and experience that are most salient in the literature:

1. The individual has become a responsible member of society; there is pressure toward the coordination of multiple roles.
2. Most people attain their maximum status and widest responsibilities in the labor force and/or the community and family.
3. There is increasing physical decline, along with awareness of this decline and of the finiteness of opportunities, and of life itself.
4. Affect optimization increases and peak cognitive and affect complexity and integrative skills are in evidence.
5. Experience, power, and increased skills are used in personality development (e.g., achieving identity certainty; becoming an individual; becoming less egocentric and more generative, spiritual, and wise).

Phases of Middle Age

Ideas about what age range middle age encompasses vary considerably (Staudinger & Bluck, 2001). When a middle-aged sample is included in a study of age and personality, the average age of this subgroup may be 40 years, but it may also be 45 or 50 years. Differing results are hard to interpret, especially because very little research documents systematic change within middle age. In their conceptualization of male adulthood, D. J. Levinson et al. (1978) portrayed ages 35–40 as a period of peak achievement effort, and ages 40–45 as the midlife transition, a time of considerable tension and crisis for many men. There then follows a generally more stable period (with several parts) from ages 45–60, and after that the late adulthood transition from age 60 to age 65. Levinson's depiction of men's development, however, has been criticized as too universalistic and elitist (because the men interviewed were 10 workers, 10 executives, 10 biologists, and 10 novelists). Particular controversy has surrounded the midlife transition, with many researchers (e.g., Costa & McCrae, 1980; Thurnher, 1983; Wethington, 2000) failing to find evidence for a "midlife crisis."

Staudinger and Bluck (2001) suggested that distinguishing early and late middle age would reflect the very different preoccupations of the 40-year-old and the 60-year-old. They said that over the life course a person's goals direct resources into carrying out three kinds of functions: growth functions (e.g., growing, achieving, helping children develop), maintenance functions (e.g., balancing a career and family), and the management of loss (e.g., adjusting to chronic illness). Early in life most resources go into growth functions, maintenance functions in midlife peak, and late in life most resources go into the management of loss. Staudinger and Bluck suggested that this shift in allocation of resources could be used to differentiate early and late middle age. These authors may have suggested only two phases because they were working with the age range from 40 to 60 as the extent of middle age. Following the example of Lachman and James (1997), McAdams (2001b), Mroczek (2004), and others, middle age here is considered to begin in the mid-30s and extend to age 65, and in this longer period (if not in the shorter) early, middle, and late phases of middle age can be identified.

The idea of phases seems particularly compelling if it is true that important factors show peaks or troughs or change quality during middle age. The conceptualization offered here focuses on these changes: an increase in social commitments and status from young adulthood to early middle age followed by decrease in commitments and striving for status by late middle age; progressive increase in affect optimization along with increase followed by decrease in affect complexity; awareness of time constraints and aging, which differs in quality at different points in middle age. The following sketches of three phases of middle age suggest how these factors relate to the self and to different syndromes of middle age that have been identified by researchers.

The Ascendant Phase.   At this time, the individual is motivated (in part by internalized social norms) to find a route of upward mobility for self and family. Commitments to multiple roles and adherence to social schedules and expectations require discipline and personal sacrifices, but they also increase integration of personality, confidence, and assertiveness. The pinch between individual needs and the increased level of conformity, along with the excitement of status potential and awareness of the finiteness of time, lead to a focus on self and identity and an increase in complex coping. Although the individual now shows more successful affect optimization than the young adult, the ascendant phase is characterized by less positive and more negative emotionality than are subsequent phases of middle age. This phase shows predominance of the growth function described by Staudinger and Bluck (2001). It shows features of Levinson and colleagues' (1978) period of Becoming One's Own Man, assigned to the late 30s, and the Midlife Transition, assigned to the period from age 40 to age 45. The concept of the ascendant phase is also enriched by the demonstration of Labouvie-Vief, Chiodo, Goguen, Diehl, and Orwoll (1995) that the self-concept is particularly rich and dynamic near age 40, and by Jung's (1969) conception of age 40 as a turning point after which the dominance of the ego lessens, hitherto less conscious parts of the personality become more accessible, and the person in time becomes more of an individual.

The Executive Phase.   During this phase, the individual reaches maximum status and responsibility in a socially complex environment. Affective controls and cognitive skills and breadth continue to increase and to become increasingly integrated. However, the individual works under time constraints to meet the demands of the day and lacks leisure. In terms of Staudinger and Bluck (2001), maintenance functions are emphasized. The person in this phase has many features of Neugarten's executive personality (1968), such as increased mastery and competence, and resembles the middle-aged person as compared to young adults and older adults (e.g., Lachman et al., 1994, described in an earlier section).

The Acceptant Phase.   This phase finds the individual relaxing the effort to achieve future goals and higher status, being content with the present or beginning to lessen commitment to the public sphere and increase attention to private pursuits. Awareness of aging and of limited time ahead increases, but daily demands on time are reduced as the number of major roles drops. The individual becomes less affectively complex but sometimes more spiritual. This phase has features of Levinson et al.'s (1978) transitional period between age 60 and age 65, which he regarded as a major turning point of the life cycle, when the task is to "conclude the efforts of middle adulthood and to prepare oneself for the era to come" (p. 62). The understanding of it is informed by work on the shift in adaptational styles over middle age treated by Baltes (1997), Brandtstaedter and Renner (1990), Heckhausen and Schulz (1995), and others. Also relevant are Neugarten's (1968) idea of middle age as showing a shift in time frame from time since birth to time left to live, Karp's (1988) work on the interpersonal context of the increased awareness of aging throughout the 50s, and descriptions of preretirement consciousness (Ekerdt & DeViney, 1993; Super, 1990), during which ties to the work world loosen and more energy is invested in private undertakings.

Phases and Individual Differences in Change.   The phases of middle age described here are not conceived as universal in nature. There are certain to be individual differences in when, how, and why people progress through them. Nevertheless, previous findings in the literature and the work described later suggest that these phases capture important commonalities among people in modern cultures.

PHASES OF MIDDLE AGE IN THE MILLS LONGITUDINAL STUDY

Helson and Soto (2005) formulated hypotheses about how personality changes from young adulthood through middle age, and tested these hypotheses using data from the Mills Longitudinal Study. This study built on much previous work on personality change by the Mills study researchers, although the organizing constructs and the period covered were unique to this article. The Mills sample consists of a representative two thirds of the 1958 and 1960 graduating classes at a women's college in northern California (Helson, 1967). Follow-ups have been conducted at ages 27, 43, 52, and 61. At each of these ages, the women provided information about life events, social roles, status, and health, as well as inventory data including the California Psychological Inventory (CPI; Gough & Bradley, 1996) and the Adjective Checklist (ACL; Gough & Heilbrun, 1983). In addition to its standard scales, the CPI was used to score scales developed by Joffe and Naditch (1977) to assess Haan's (1977) constructs of coping and defending: Intellectuality and Tolerance of Ambiguity were used to measure affect complexity. To measure affect optimization, Positive and Negative Emotionality were scored (Gough, Bradley, & Bedeian, 1996; Helson & Klohnen, 1998), assessing Tellegen's (1985) constructs, from the ACL. At the age 43, 52, and 61 follow-ups, the women also rated a set of "Feelings About Life" items taken from theories of adult development. This chapter discusses how changes found in the Mills sample relate to the conceptualization of three phases in middle age.

During the transition from young adulthood (age 27) to the ascendant phase of early middle age (age 43), the Mills women typically came to occupy a peak number of social roles, as spouse, parent, and worker. Their status level in work increased, and they were anxious to reach their full potential and take advantage of opportunities (high ratings of the Feelings About Life items "Anxiety that I won't live up to opportunities" and "Excitement, turmoil, confusion about my impulses and potential"). They gained in purposiveness and confidence (higher CPI Dominance, lower CPI Femininity/Masculinity; see Fig. 17.1). They scheduled their lives in the interests of achievement (higher CPI Achievement via Conformance, lower CPI Flexibility). They increased in affect optimization (higher Positive Emotionality and lower Negative Emotionality; see Fig. 17.2), and also became more affectively complex, as assessed by the Joffe and Naditch (1977) scales (higher Intellectuality and Tolerance of Ambiguity; see Fig. 17.3).

In the executive phase of middle age (age 52), the Mills women occupied fewer social roles than they did during the ascendant phase, because in most cases their children had left home. This did not mean that their children were no longer sources of concern (Huyck, 1989), but it did give the women more time on a day-to-day basis, which they tended to devote to their careers. Not coincidentally, they attained their highest ratings on status level in work at this age. They remained purposive and confident (high Dominance) and adjusted to their confining schedules (high Achievement via Conformance, low Flexibility), and they dropped further in emotional vulnerability (lower Femininity/Masculinity). They again increased in affect optimization (higher Positive Emotionality and lower Negative Emotionality) and attained a peak level of affect complexity (Intellectuality and Tolerance of Ambiguity). They began to experience the passing of time less in relation to the achievement of their potential and more in terms of their place in the life course (lower ratings of the items "Anxiety that I won't live up to opportunities" and "Excitement, turmoil, confusion about my impulses and potential," and higher ratings of the item "Looking old").

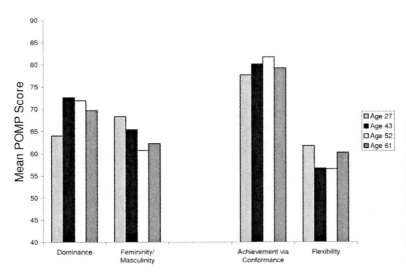

FIG. 17.1 Change in social competence, confidence, and norm adherence. Data are from Helson and Soto (2005, p. 199). Copyright 2005 by the American Psychological Association.

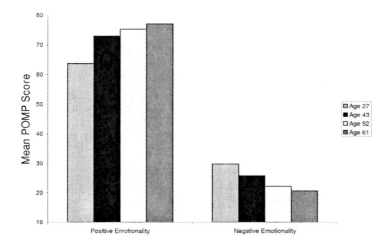

FIG. 17.2. Change in affect optimization. Data are from Helson and Soto (2005, p. 199). Copyright 2005 by the American Psychological Association.

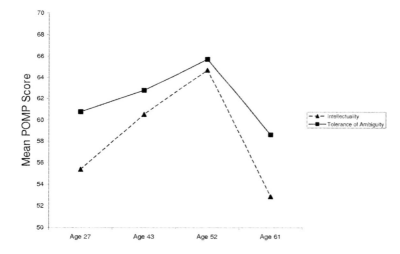

FIG. 17.3 Change in affect complexity. Data are from Helson and Soto (2005, p. 199). Copyright 2005 by the American Psychological Association.

In the acceptant phase of middle age (age 61), the Mills women began to relax their level of purposiveness and tension. About one half either had retired or were reducing their work hours or were preparing for retirement. Achievement strivings and the stringent organization of life decreased (lower Dominance and Achievement via Conformance, higher Flexibility). The women increased in affect optimization (higher Positive Emotionality, lower Negative Emotionality) while declining in affect complexity (lower Intellectuality and Tolerance of Ambiguity). Their consciousness of time shifted to a greater awareness of aging and death (higher ratings of the Feelings About life item "Thinking a lot about death"). In short, they prepared themselves for release from formal social roles and for old age.

The generality of these patterns of change was tested across subgroups within the Mills sample defined by level or change on various social role (e.g., parent or not, work status) and biosocial (e.g., general health) factors. Several examples were found of associations between these social and biosocial factors and personality change from one specific assessment time to the next (e.g., women whose children had not left home by age 52 did not gain as much in Intellectuality from age 43 to age 52 as other women did). There were, however, very few significant associations (no more than would be expected by chance) between the individual difference factors and overall change on each personality variable across young adulthood and the three phases of middle age.

ADDITIONAL EVIDENCE FOR AND AGAINST THE GENERALITY OF THE PHASES

The Mills study has followed the graduates of a particular women's college through a particular period of history. Is there any evidence for the generality of the pattern of change over middle age that was found in the Mills study, beyond its general consistency with the literature?

Supportive Longitudinal Findings From an Older Cohort

Cramer (2003) described personality change in 155 men and women of the combined Berkeley and Oakland samples studied at the Institute of Human Development (IHD) at average ages in the mid-30s, mid-40s, and late 50s. These men and women constitute a more representative sample than the Mills women in terms of social background, and having been born in the early or late 1920s, they had a different cohort experience. The women, for example, had less education, more children, and many fewer years in the labor force than did the Mills women (Helson, Jones, & Kwan, 2002).

Cramer (2003) used observer Q-sort data scored on the Big Five dimensions and a multivariate analysis of variance (MANOVA) design. From their mid-30s to late 50s, both men and women increased on Agreeableness and decreased on Neuroticism (a pattern resembling the changes in Mills women on affect optimization), and both groups increased on Openness from their mid-30s to mid-40s and then decreased by their late 50s (a pattern resembling change in the Mills sample on affect complexity). The women increased and then decreased on Extraversion and Conscientiousness, as the Mills women did on Dominance and Achievement via Conformance. On both of these scales, the men increased as the women had done from their mid-30s to mid-40s, but they did not change significantly from their mid-40s to late 50s, possibly because they did not consider themselves close to retirement. Although one would like to have information about roles and status, these findings are, nonetheless, strong evidence of similarity in personality change across gender, sample, and cohort.

Cohort and Sample Differences and Their Implications

When role histories vary, one often finds differences in personality change. Women in recent cohorts often put out strenuous career effort in young adulthood and then have children after they have made a place for themselves in the labor force, creating a period of very high stress in their late 30s or 40s. This stress is a serious social concern of the present time. Perhaps it is one reason that middle-aged women in the cross-sectional study of Mroczek and Kolarz (1998) scored lower on positive affect than did younger and older women, whereas the Mills women, most of whom began their families in their mid-20s, increased linearly in positive affect from young adulthood through middle age (Helson & Klohnen, 1998; Helson & Soto, 2005).

Another sample whose affect optimization did not increase from young adulthood to middle age were the male managers and foremen at AT&T studied by Howard and Bray (1988) over a 20-year period, which included institutional setbacks, extensive social change, and lowered expectations for advancement. From youth to middle age these men became "less affable with upsurges of autonomy desires accompanied by increased feelings of hostility and decreased needs for friendships or for understanding others" (Howard & Bray, 1988, p. 150). Unfortunately, there was no further follow-up of this sample.

Other studies suggest that features of life history may only temporarily accelerate or retard the development of a characteristic. Studying the Oakland and Berkeley IHD samples, Jones and Meredith (1996) found that Self-confidence increased from age 30 to age 40 in the Berkeley participants, born in the late 1920s, whereas in the Oakland participants, born in the early 1920s, it decreased somewhat from age 30 to age 40, then increased to the same level as the Berkeley sample between age 40 and age 50. The authors attributed this difference to the delayed parenting and career patterns of the Oakland sample. Most of the Oakland men served in World War II and most of the women had a more extended period of childrearing, along with less and later participation in the labor force, than did the Berkeley women.

Though these are distinctive changes related to role sequences and cohort experience, the generality of personality change should not be underestimated. It was reported earlier that, in the Mills study, whether or not a woman had children and the level of status she had obtained (among several other factors) showed very little relation to her change over middle age. The IHD women had patterns of roles and status very different from those of the Mills women, yet their personality change seems to have been similar. Miner-Rubino, Winter, and Stewart (2004) obtained retrospective questionnaire data from a sample of men and women in their 60s, both college educated and noncollege educated. Noncollege men reported the strongest concerns about aging, but there were no differences among the groups in their sense of having increased since their 20s in clarity of identity, sense of confident power, and generativity.

Why is personality change not more closely related to roles and status, to social class and ethnicity? A social variable may be related to some aspects of middle age but not to others. For example, upper-middle and working-class men were reported to have different ideas about how soon middle age began and whether it was a period of productivity or decline (Neugarten & Datan, 1974), but there are broad expectations that middle-aged people across class lines (except at the extremes of the social class continuum) should have married and started a family, and that men at least should have made some progress in an occupation (Krueger, Heckhausen, & Hundertmark, 1995).

It is important to recognize that distinct role behaviors can be functionally equivalent. People with little opportunity to gain status in work may seek it in family or community roles or relationships. Thus, an immigrant cab driver seeks status by helping his children to go to college. Those who are not parents themselves have younger relatives and coworkers by whom they are perceived and with whom they interact in ways that change their self-concept over middle age (Karp, 1988; Lachman et al., 1994; Zucker et al., 2002). This certainly does not mean that differences in gender, social class, and lifestyle are not important, but may help to explain why there is significant uniformity across these factors in development over middle age.

DIRECTIONS FOR FUTURE RESEARCH

There is now much evidence from many sources for normative personality change across adulthood. In some respects, change is unidirectional, but in others there are peaks or troughs during middle age. These peaks and troughs are the most direct evidence that middle age has qualitative characteristics that distinguish it from young adulthood and old age, and they also suggest the usefulness of making differentiations within middle age.

The term "phases" of middle age is used to call attention not only to systematic changes including the increase and decline in effortfulness related to multiple roles, responsibilities, and ambitions; shift in the pattern of coping styles; and shifts in time perspective between the mid-30s and mid-60s, but also to the patterning of these various characteristics in individuals at particular ages. Several portraits of middle-aged people that are prominent in the literature have contradictory features, but the recognition of phases resolves this tension by locating these differing portraits in distinct periods of middle age. Thus, it is the individual in the ascendant phase who is most likely to show turmoil and achievement-related identity conflicts and the individual in the executive phase who is most likely to show superior affect complexity and integrative skills. It is the individual in the acceptant phase who is making the transition from social centrality to a more private life.

As pointed out previously, every individual goes through middle age differently. The process of change is affected by more factors and patterns of factors than there is space here to describe. Nevertheless, the phases have sufficient generality to make them useful heuristic tools. The goal of future research is not to show that patterns of change through middle age are always the same, but to identify factors related to different ways of experiencing the phases and to the consequences of these differences in experience, and to look for differences in the phases themselves that have characterized particular cultures or may be developing in our own changing society.

What Should Be Studied?

One important topic is the causal network among factors that seem related to change to and through middle age. Do the social clock tasks expected of young adults (finding an occupation, finding a partner) lay a foundation for the confidence and dominance of middle age? How do different sequences of roles and role combinations affect the phases of middle age, within and across cohorts? Does having young children and a career in a person's early 40s increase stress for a few years without long-term effects, or does the expectation and experience of this pattern change that individual's adaptation more profoundly?

The late phase of middle age is an intriguing topic. As in Levinson and colleagues (1978), it is conceived of here as a transitional period, some of its features associated with the multiple changes that characterize the early 60s. For example, the increase in Flexibility shown by the Mills women from age 52 to age 61 may be temporary, because other studies show a general pattern of decrease with age into the 70s (e.g., Helson, Jones, & Kwan, 2002). The Mills women in their early 60s may have been experiencing a "honeymoon" period during which many enjoyed greater leisure or looked forward to a new lifestyle while still in good health. On the other hand, now that older people are healthier and expected to travel and do new things, perhaps flexibility will decline later in life and more slowly.

How should the decline in affect complexity combined with higher affect optimization be regarded? Is it the longer term trend labeled as "graceful degradation" (Labouvie-Vief & Márquez, 2004)? Is a lower level of complexity necessarily a loss? Think of the distinctive late-life style of creative older artists, characterized by less emphasis on centering (Arnheim, 1986) or more oceanic content when compared to younger artists (Maduro, 1974), or the Jungian idea that the last of the four personality functions can be integrated into consciousness only by a lowering of the level of consciousness as a whole (Von Franz, 1993).

How Should Middle Age Be Studied?

It seems obvious that a variety of approaches is necessary for studying middle age. Large cross-sectional studies give an invaluable breadth of coverage, but they find personality differences among age groups, not changes in personality with age. They have two serious weaknesses: They cannot separate age effects from cohort and sampling effects, and they usually do not obtain enough information about individuals to explain the differences (or lack of difference) that they report. Thus, longitudinal studies are essential. Sometimes cross-sectional samples are studied at repeated intervals, thus obtaining longitudinal data. However, they usually examine change over short periods of time, and they may not have sufficient data to explain what they find, or even to evaluate attrition biases. These problems are particularly serious in studies of middle age, where contextual factors are thought to be maximally influential (Mroczek, 2004).

Longitudinal studies of particular birth cohorts show how a sample of individuals change over a particular time period. They usually have enough information to provide some causal texture, but they are imprisoned within their particular historical and sample context. Sometimes longitudinal researchers compare or combine data across studies and show whether relationships hold across them, or whether they differ in hypothesized ways (e.g., Charles, Reynolds, & Gatz, 2001; Helson, Jones, & Kwan, 2002; Helson, Stewart, & Ostrove, 1995; Jones & Meredith, 1996). Although this approach is important and should be encouraged, it tends to be limited in that measures devised for one study may be less appropriate or not available in another. This necessarily narrows the focus and hypotheses. For this reason, it is important that longitudinal studies be encouraged to tell their unique stories, without having to take on the burden of establishing generality in every investigation. Between the extremes of cross-sample studies and uniqueness, however, intermediary strategies are useful, such as taking hypotheses from the literature and applying them to a particular body of longitudinal data.

Phases are important in providing a sense of the life narrative, a sense that one part of life leads to the next. Much of what people work and strive for is won or lost in middle age. If middle age is considered a patternless period of 30 years, just because no one pattern is universal, psychologists take meaning away from the life story.

REFERENCES

Antonucci, T. C., Akiyama, H., & Merline, A. (2001). Dynamics of social relationships in midlife. In M. E. Lachman (Ed.), *Handbook of midlife development* (pp. 571–598). New York: Wiley.

Arnheim, R. (1986). On the late style. In R. Arnheim (Ed.), *New essays on the psychology of art* (pp. 285–293). Berkeley, CA: University of California Press.

Baltes, P. B. (1997). On the incomplete architecture of human ontogeny: Selection, optimization, and compensation as foundation of developmental theory. *American Psychologist, 52*, 366–380.

Baltes, P. B., Staudinger, U. M., Maercker, A., & Smith, J. (1995). People nominated as wise: A comparative study of wisdom-related knowledge. *Psychology and Aging, 10*, 155–166.

Brandtstaedter, J., & Renner, G. (1990). Tenacious goal pursuit and flexible goal adjustment: Explication and age-related analysis of assimilative and accommodative strategies of coping. *Psychology and Aging, 5*, 58–67.

Bumpass, L. L., & Aquilino, W. S. (1995). *A social map of midlife: Family and work over the middle life course.* Vero Beach, FL: MacArthur Foundation Research Network on Successful Midlife Development.

Cameron, P. (1970). The generation gap: Which generation is believed powerful vs. generational members' self-appraisal of power? *Developmental Psychology, 3*, 403–404.

Cameron, P. (1973). Which generation is believed to be intellectually superior and which generation believes itself intellectually superior? *International Journal of Aging and Human Development, 7*, 143.

Carstensen, L. L., Isaacowitz, D. M., & Charles, S. T. (1999). Taking time seriously: A theory of socioemotional selectivity. *American Psychologist, 54*, 165–181.

Carstensen, L. L., Pasupathi, M., Mayr, U., & Nesselroade, J. R. (2000). Emotional experience in everyday life across the adult life span. *Journal of Personality and Social Psychology, 79*, 644–655.

Charles, S. T., Reynolds, C. A., & Gatz, M. (2001). Age-related differences and change in positive and negative affect over 23 years. *Journal of Personality and Social Psychology, 80*, 136–151.

Costa, P. T., Jr., & McCrae, R. R. (1980). Still stable after all these years: Personality as a key to some issues in adulthood and old age. In P. B. Baltes & O. G. Brim, Jr. (Eds.), *Life span development and behavior* (Vol. 3, pp. 65–102). New York: Academic Press.

Cramer, P. (2003). Personality change in later adulthood is predicted by defense mechanism use in early adulthood. *Journal of Research in Personality, 37*, 76–104.

Diehl, M., Coyle, N., & Labouvie-Vief, G. (1996). Age and sex differences in strategies of coping and defense across the life span. *Psychology and Aging, 11*, 127–139.

Diehl, M., Owen, S. K., & Youngblade, L. M. (2004). Agency and communion attributes in adults' spontaneous self-representations. *International Journal of Behavioral Development, 28*, 1–15.

Ekerdt, D. J., & DeViney, S. (1993). Evidence for a preretirement process among older male workers. *Journals of Gerontology, 48*, S35–S43.

Erikson, E. H. (1950). *Childhood and society.* New York: Norton.

Gough, H. G., & Bradley, P. (1996). *California Psychological Inventory manual.* Palo Alto, CA: Consulting Psychologists Press.

Gough, H. G., Bradley, P., & Bedeian, A.G. (1996). *ACL scales for Tellegen's three higher-order traits.* Unpublished manuscript.

Gough, H. G., & Heilbrun, A. B., Jr. (1983). *The Adjective Check List Manual.* Palo Alto, CA: Consulting Psychologists Press.

Gross, J. J., Carstensen, L. L., Pasupathi, M., Tsai, J., Skorpen, C. G., & Hsu, A. Y. C. (1997). Emotion and aging: Experience, expression, and control. *Psychology and Aging, 12,* 590–599.

Gutmann, D. L. (1987). *Reclaimed powers: Toward a new psychology of men and women in later life.* New York: Basic Books.

Haan, N. (1977). *Coping and defending.* New York: Academic Press.

Harker, L., & Solomon, M. (1996). Change in goals and values of men and women from early to mature adulthood. *Journal of Adult Development, 3,* 133–143.

Havighurst, R. J. (1972). *Developmental tasks and education* (3rd ed.). New York: David McKay.

Heckhausen, J., Dixon, R. A., & Baltes, P. B. (1989). Gains and losses in development throughout adulthood as perceived by different adult age groups. *Developmental Psychology, 25,* 109–121.

Heckhausen, J., & Schulz, R. (1995). A life-span theory of control. *Psychological Review, 102,* 284–304.

Helson, R. (1967). Personality characteristics and developmental history of creative college women. *Genetic Psychology Monographs, 76,* 205–256.

Helson, R., Jones, C., & Kwan, V. S. Y. (2002). Personality change over 40 years of adulthood: HLM findings in two longitudinal samples. *Journal of Personality and Social Psychology, 83,* 752–766.

Helson, R., & Klohnen, E. C. (1998). Affective coloring of personality from young adulthood to midlife. *Personality and Social Psychology Bulletin, 24,* 241–252.

Helson, R., Kwan, V. S. Y., John, O. P., & Jones, C. (2002). The growing evidence for personality change in adulthood: Findings from research with personality inventories. *Journal of Research in Personality, 36,* 287–306.

Helson, R., Pals, J. L., & Solomon, M. F. (1997). Is there adult development distinctive to women? In R. Hogan, J. Johnson, & S. Briggs (Eds.), *Handbook of personality psychology* (pp. 293–314). San Diego, CA: Academic Press.

Helson, R., & Soto, C. J. (2005). Up and down in middle age: Monotonic and nonmonotonic changes in roles, status, and personality. *Journal of Personality and Social Psychology, 89,* 194–204.

Helson, R., Stewart, A. J., & Ostrove, J. (1995). Identity in three cohorts of midlife women. *Journal of Personality and Social Psychology, 69,* 544–557.

Howard, A., & Bray, D. W. (1988). *Managerial lives in transition: Advancing age and changing times.* New York: Guilford.

Huyck, M. H. (1989). Midlife parental imperatives. In R. Kalish (Ed.), *Midlife loss: Coping strategies* (pp. 10–34). Thousand Oaks, CA: Sage.

Joffe, P., & Naditch, M. P. (1977). Paper and pencil measures of coping and defending processes. In N. Haan (Ed.), *Coping and defending* (pp. 280–294). New York: Academic Press.

Jones, C. J., & Meredith, W. (1996). Patterns of personality change across the life span. *Psychology and Aging, 11,* 57–65.

Jung, C. G. (1969). The stages of life. In *The structure and dynamics of the psyche* (Collected Works, 8). Princeton, NJ: Princeton University Press.

Karp, D. A. (1988). A decade of reminders: Changing age consciousness between fifty and sixty years old. *The Gerontologist, 28,* 727–738.

Krueger, J., Heckhausen, J., & Hundertmark, J. (1995). Perceiving middle-aged adults: Effects of stereotype-congruent and incongruent information. *Journals of Gerontology, 50B,* 82–93.

Kuhlen, R. G. (1968). Developmental changes in motivation during the adult years. In B. L. Neugarten (Ed.), *Middle age and aging* (pp. 115–136). Chicago: University of Chicago Press.

Labouvie-Vief, G., Chiodo, L. M., Goguen, L. A., Diehl, M., & Orwoll, L. (1995). Representations of self across the life span. *Psychology and Aging, 10,* 404–415.

Labouvie-Vief, G., DeVoe, M., & Bulka, D. (1989). Speaking about feelings: Conceptions of emotion across the life span. *Psychology and Aging, 4,* 425–437.

Labouvie-Vief, G., & Márquez, M. G. (2004). Dynamic integration: Affect optimization and differentiation in development. In D. Y. Dai & R. J. Sternberg (Eds.), *Motivation, emotion, and cognition* (pp. 237–272). Mahwah, NJ: Lawrence Erlbaum Associates.

Labouvie-Vief, G., & Medler, M. (2002). Affect optimization and affect complexity: Modes and styles of regulation in adulthood. *Psychology and Aging, 17,* 571–588.

Lachman, M. E., & Bertrand, R. M. (2001). Personality and the self in midlife. In M. E. Lachman (Ed.), *Handbook of midlife development* (pp. 279–309). New York: Wiley.

Lachman, M. E., & James, J. B. (1997). Charting the course of midlife development: An Overview. In M. E. Lachman & J. B. James (Eds.), *Multiple paths of midlife development* (pp. 1–17). Chicago: University of Chicago Press.

Lachman, M. E., Lewkowicz, C., Marcus, A., & Peng, Y. (1994). Images of midlife development among young, middle-aged, and older adults. *Journal of Adult Development, 1,* 201–211.

Levenson, R. W., Carstensen, L. L., & Gottman, J. M. (1994). Influence of age and gender on affect, physiology, and their interrelations: A study of long-term marriages. *Journal of Personality and Social Psychology, 67,* 56–68.

Levinson, D. J., Darrow, C. M., Klein, E. B., Levinson, M. H., & McKee, B. (1978). *The seasons of a man's life.* New York: Knopf.

Linton, R. (1936). *The study of man.* New York: Appleton-Century-Crofts.

Maduro, R. (1974). Artistic creativity and aging in India. *International Journal of Aging and Human Development, 5,* 303–329.

McAdams, D. P. (2001a). Generativity in midlife. In M. E. Lachman (Ed.), *Handbook of midlife development* (pp. 395–443). New York: Wiley.

McAdams, D. P. (2001b). When bad things turn good and good things turn bad: Sequences of redemption and contamination in life narrative and their relation to psychosocial adaptation in midlife adults and in students. *Personality and Social Psychology Bulletin, 27,* 474–485.

McCrae, R. R., Costa, P. T., Jr., Ostendorf, F., Angleitner, A., Hrebickova, M., Avia, M.D., Sanz, J., Sanchez-Bernardos, M. L., Kusdil, M. E., Woodfield, R., Saunders, P. T., & Smith, P. B. (2000). Nature over nurture: Temperament, personality, and life span development. *Journal of Personality and Social Psychology, 78,* 173–186.

Menon, U. (2001). Middle adulthood in cultural perspectives: The imagined and the experienced in three cultures. In M. E. Lachman (Ed.), *Handbook of midlife development* (pp. 40–74). New York: Wiley.

Miner-Rubino, K., Winter, D. G., & Stewart, A. J. (2004). Gender, social class, and the subjective experience of aging: Self-perceived personality change from early adulthood to late midlife. *Personality and Social Psychology Bulletin, 30,* 1599–1610.

Moen, P., & Wethington, E. (1999). Midlife development in a life course context. In S. L. Willis & J. D. Reid (Eds.), *Life in the middle* (pp. 3–23). San Diego, CA: Academic Press.

Mroczek, D. K. (2004) Positive and negative affect at midlife. In O. G. Brim, C. D. Ryff, & R. C. Kessler (Eds.), *How healthy are we? A national study of well-being at midlife.* Chicago: University of Chicago Press.

Mroczek, D. K., & Kolarz, C. M. (1998). The effect of age on positive and negative affect: A developmental perspective on happiness. *Journal of Personality and Social Psychology, 75,* 1333–1349.

Neugarten, B. L. (1968). The awareness of middle age. In B. L. Neugarten (Ed.), *Middle age and aging* (pp. 93–98). Chicago: University of Chicago Press.

Neugarten, B. L. (1977). Personality and aging. In J. E. Birren & K. W. Schaie (Eds.), *Handbook of the psychology of aging* (pp. 626–649). New York: Van Nostrand Reinhold.

Neugarten, B. L. (1979). Time, age, and the life cycle. *American Journal of Psychiatry, 136,* 887–894.

Neugarten, B.L., & Datan, N. (1974). The middle years. In S. Arieti (Ed.), *The foundations of psychiatry* (pp. 592–608). New York: Basic Books.

Parker, R. A., & Aldwin, C. M. (1997). Do aspects of gender identity change from early to middle adulthood? Disentangling age, cohort, and period effects. In M. E. Lachman & J. B. James (Eds.), *Multiple paths of midlife development* (pp. 67–107). Chicago: University of Chicago Press.

Pasupathi, M., Staudinger, U. M., & Baltes, P. B. (2001). Seeds of wisdom: Adolescents' knowledge and judgment about difficult matters of life. *Developmental Psychology, 37,* 351–361.

Riley, M. W. (1976). Age strata in social systems. In R. H. Binstock & E. Shanas (Eds.), *Handbook of aging and the social sciences* (pp. 189–217). New York: Van Nostrand-Reinhold.

Riley, M. W., Kahn, R. L., Foner, A., & Mack, K. A. (Eds.). (1994). *Age and structural lag: Society's failure to provide meaningful opportunities in work, family, and leisure.* Oxford, England: Wiley.

Roberts, B. W., & DelVecchio, W. F. (2000). The rank-order consistency of personality from childhood to old age: A quantitative review of longitudinal studies. *Psychological Bulletin, 126,* 3–25.

Roberts, B. W., & Helson, R. (1997). Changes in culture, changes in personality: The influence of individualism in a longitudinal study of women. *Journal of Personality and Social Psychology, 72,* 641–651.

Ryff, C. D. (1991). Possible selves in adulthood and old age: A tale of shifting horizons. *Psychology and Aging, 6,* 286–295.

Ryff, C. D., & Heincke, S. G. (1983). Subjective organization of personality in adulthood and aging. *Journal of Personality and Social Psychology, 44,* 807–816.

Schaie, K. W. (1977–78). Toward a stage theory of adult cognitive development. *International Journal of Aging and Adult Development, 8,* 129–138.

Settersten, R. A. (1998). Time, age, and the transition to retirement: New evidence on life-course flexibility? *International Journal of Aging and Human Development, 47,* 177–203.

Shweder, R. A. (Ed.). (1998). *Welcome to middle age (and other cultural fictions).* Chicago: University of Chicago Press.

Srivastava, S., John, O. P., Gosling, S. D., & Potter, J. (2003). Development of personality in adulthood: Set like plaster or persistent change? *Journal of Personality and Social Psychology, 84,* 1041–1053.

Staudinger, U. M., & Bluck, S. (2001). A view on midlife development from life-span theory. In M. E. Lachman (Ed.), *Handbook of midlife development* (pp. 3–39). New York, NY: Wiley.

Stewart, A. J., Ostrove, J. M., & Helson, R. (2001). Middle-aging in women: Patterns of personality change from the 30s to the 50s. *Journal of Adult Development, 8,* 23–37.

Stewart, A. J., & Vandewater, E. A. (1998). The course of generativity. In D. P. McAdams & E. de St. Aubin (Eds.), *Generativity and adult development: How and why we care for the next generation* (pp. 75–100). Washington, DC: American Psychological Association.

Super, D. E. (1990). A life-span, life-space approach to career development. In D. E. Brown & L. Brooks (Eds.), *Career choice and development* (2nd ed., pp. 179–261). San Francisco: Jossey-Bass.

Tellegen, A. (1985). Structures of mood and personality and their relevance to assessing anxiety with an emphasis on self-report. In A. H. Tuma & J. D. Maser (Eds.), *Anxiety and the anxiety disorders* (pp. 681–706). Hillsdale, NJ: Lawrence Erlbaum Associates.

Thurnher, M. (1983). Turning points and developmental change: Subjective and "objective" assessments. *American Journal of Orthopsychiatry, 53,* 52–60.

Twenge, J. M. (2001). Changes in women's assertiveness in response to status and roles: A cross-temporal meta-analysis, 1931–1993. *Journal of Personality and Social Psychology, 81,* 133–145.

Vaillant, G. E. (1977). *Adaptation to life.* Boston: Little, Brown.

Vandewater, E. A., Ostrove, J. M., & Stewart, A. J. (1997). Predicting women's well-being in midlife: The importance of personality development and social role involvements. *Journal of Personality and Social Psychology, 72,* 1147–1160.

Von Franz, M. (1993). The inferior function. In M. von Franz (Ed.), *Psychotherapy* (pp. 16–145). Boston: Shambhala.

Wethington, E. (2000). Expecting stress: Americans and the "midlife crisis." *Motivation and Emotion, 24,* 85–102.

Willis, S. L., & Schaie, K. W. (1999). Intellectual functioning in midlife. In S. L. Willis & J. D. Reid (Eds.), *Life in the middle* (pp. 234–250). San Diego, CA: Academic Press.

Wink, P., & Dillon, M. (2002). Spiritual development across the adult life course: Findings from a longitudinal study. *Journal of Adult Development, 9,* 79–94.

Zucker, A. N., Ostrove, J. M., & Stewart, A. J. (2002). College-educated women's personality development in adulthood: Perceptions and age differences. *Psychology and Aging, 17,* 236–244.

18

Goals as Building Blocks of Personality and Development in Adulthood

Alexandra M. Freund
Northwestern University

Michaela Riediger
Max Planck Institute for Human Development

Since its very conception, personality psychology has seen goals as the building blocks of personality (e.g., Allport, 1937). Personal goals are typically defined as consciously accessible cognitive representations of states an individual wants to attain or avoid in the future. They provide consistency across situations, and structure and organize behavior over time into meaningful action units. We submit that the concept of personal goals is particularly well suited for a developmental approach to personality. Integrating motivational processes into a life-span context furthers our understanding of both the direction of development and of interindividual differences in the level of functioning in various life domains. One of the basic assumptions of joining an action-theoretical perspective with a life-span perspective is that people actively shape their own development in interaction with a given physical, cultural, social, and historical context (see Little, Snyder, & Wehmeyer, chap. 4, this volume). In this chapter, we put forth the idea that goals link the person to these contexts and thus are central to—or building blocks of—personality and development in adulthood.

The chapter is organized as follows. In a first part, we discuss the notion of goals as "personality-in-context" (e.g., B. Little, 1989), and elaborate on the idea that personal goals reflect the proactive interaction between a person and his or her environment over time. In the second part, we briefly summarize *what* it is that adults of various ages typically strive to attain or avoid, and elaborate on mechanisms that may determine the content of goals at different points in the life span. In the third part, we turn to basic goal processes that specify *how* people interact with their environment and manage resources across the life span. In this context, we delineate the central ideas of the action-theoretical specification of a general model of developmental regulation: the model of selection, optimization, and compensation (SOC; P. Baltes & M. Baltes, 1990; Freund & P. Baltes, 2000). The SOC model posits that the kind of goals a person sets and pursues develops in close interaction with his or her context. We illustrate this with an example of research investigating age-related differences in the way people formulate their goals either in terms of acquiring new or preserving existing resources. Linking personal goals to early personality theories (Kelly, 1995), we follow our life-span perspective to address the importance of intergoal relations (i.e., of conflict and facilitation among a person's goals and how intergoal relations change with age). On the basis of this overview, we conclude that the concept of personal goals is valuable for understanding "personality-in-context" across adulthood, and that it may provide a fruitful approach toward a theory that can integrate motivation, emotion, cognition, and behavior into a developmental framework.

GOALS AS "PERSONALITY-IN-CONTEXT"

Personal goals can be viewed as dynamic aspects reflecting the interaction of a person with his or her environment over time. Following Hooker and McAdams (2003), goals ("personal action units") and motivational processes ("self-regulatory processes") constitute one level in a multiple-levels-of-analysis model of personality—besides personality traits (i.e., nonconditional dispositions that generalize across a variety of situations and show considerable stability over time) and life stories (i.e., people's narrations of their personal past, present, and future).

Similarly, Cantor (1990) proposed that goals or life tasks characterize personality on an intermediate level, the level between "being" (i.e., personality traits, basic dispositions) and "doing" (i.e., behavioral responses in a given situation). Goals are not as broad and comprehensive as traits, although they may be influenced by them, nor are they as specific as behaviors; instead, they *regulate* behavior. Drawing attention to the fact that goals are inherently oriented to a specific content or life domain and related to time (namely, the future), B. Little (1989) called this level of personality the "personality-in-context."

Context can be broadly defined as the set of circumstances that surround a person, such as culture, historical time, family, family relations, or geographical environment. Context does not only serve as a background for the behavioral *expression* of personality, but also plays an important role in *shaping* personality. The latter is a result of the constraints and possibilities for personality development that the context provides. Cultural, social, or geographical *constraints* may on the one hand exclude certain possibilities of how a person can express his or her basic personality traits. On the other hand, however, contextual constraints fulfill an important function; they specify boundaries without which focused personality development would be impossible. The space of possible developmental trajectories would be too vast and unstructured. Moreover, context provides possibilities for personality development, such as resources, defined as actual or potential means that help in achieving one's goals (Freund & Riediger, 2001; see also Hawley, chap. 8, this volume). Contextual resources are located outside the person, that is, in the material, social, cultural, historical, or biological environment (e.g., educational system). Such an understanding of context is reminiscent of the term *affordances* as introduced by Gibson (1997). Affordances denote possibilities for action resulting from the interaction between the context and the person. For possibilities to become actual *capabilities* and *competencies*, also Gibsonian terms, goals need to connect situational affordances with the more basic levels of personality reflecting traits, needs, and motives.

Addressing the contextual nature of goals, Freund (2003) distinguished two interacting levels of goal representation, namely social expectations and personal goals. Social expectations (level 1) are reflected in social norms that inform us about age-graded opportunity structures and goal-relevant resources. They define limitations for developmental trajectories in the individual life course and also indicate institutional or social opportunity structures, such as the age-dependent availability of resources (J. Heckhausen, 1999). Social expectations are also reflected in personal beliefs about the appropriate timing sequencing of goals. Setting personal goals (level 2) in accordance with social expectations may help to take advantage of available resources. Through social sanctions as well as societal approval or disapproval, social expectations serve as an orientation or standard for the development, selection, pursuit, and maintenance of personal goals (Cantor, 1994; Freund, 1997; Nurmi, 1992). In addition to consciously represented personal goals, automatized goals and (nonconscious) motives impact behavior and development.

In summary, the notion of goals as "personality-in-context" refers to the fact that a person's goals reflect the interface between a person's basic personality traits and the specific context in which he or she lives. In the remainder of this chapter, we take a developmental perspective to further elaborate on this idea. Specifically, we address two questions: *What* is it that people at various ages strive for in their goals? And *how* do goals impact behavior and development in adults of various ages?

ADDRESSING THE "WHAT" OF PERSONALITY: CONTENT OF GOALS ACROSS ADULTHOOD

The *content* of goals—which connect basic aspects of a personality, such as traits, with characteristics of the particular context in which this person lives—changes with age. Next, we illustrate the available empirical evidence with an example of some prototypical studies and discuss mechanisms that underlie these age-associated shifts.

Empirical Evidence of Age-Related Changes in the Content of Goals in Adulthood

Nurmi (1992, 1994) investigated age differences in the content of future-oriented *goals* (i.e., hopes, plans, and dreams about the future) and *concerns* (i.e., anxieties and worries about the future) in a large cross-sectional study of adults from 19 to 64 years old. Young adults reported *goals* related to their future *education, family/marriage* and concerns about *own self, friends,* and *occupation* significantly more frequently than order respondents. Middle-aged respondents frequently reported goals related to the *future of their children* and concerns about their *occupation.* Both young and middle-aged adults also frequently mentioned *property-related goals*. In the age group of 45- to 54-year-old participants, a high percentage of *health-related goals* were reported. This percentage was even higher in the older age group (55 to 64 years old). Furthermore, older adults reported goals relating to their *retirement, leisure activities*, and *world-related matters* more frequently than the other age groups.

Cross and Markus (1991), in an adult sample aged 18 to 86 years old, cross-sectionally investigated conceptually very similar future expectancies, namely, people's personal images of themselves in the future, their hoped-for or feared *possible selves*. Young adults tended to report extremely positive, idealized hoped-for selves that were often related to marriage, family, or career. Their feared selves typically reflected the concern that life may be disappointing and not measuring up to their hopes and expectations. Typically, these feared selves, were rather unspecific and often extreme. Young middle-aged adults' (25 to 39 years old) hoped-for selves tended to be comparatively more moderate, qualified, concrete, and more related to the participants' current lives. Their common themes were those of settling down and consolidating personal identity. The feared selves in that age group typically reflected concerns with not attaining personally and socially desired roles and status, particularly in the life domains of occupation, marriage, and family. Late middle-aged adults (40 to 59 years old) reported fewer hoped-for selves that indicated new beginnings or dramatic changes than did younger respondents. Rather, their hoped-for selves reflected a desire for enjoyment and achievement in the roles they already inhabited. Their feared selves strongly reflected concerns with the losses and decrements accompanying aging, and with financial insecurity. A common theme in the hoped-for selves of the participants aged 60 years and older was the maintenance of current states, although hoped-for selves in that age group also reflected a desire for further improvement or growth. Their feared selves reflected concerns with aging-associated losses in physical capacity and lifestyle.

Research by Staudinger (e.g., Staudinger, Freund, Linden, & Maas, 1999) on life investment—the investment of cognitive or behavioral resources into a specific life domain—provides additional evidence for the theoretical assumptions formulated by Havighurst (1948) and Erikson (1959) on the age-dependent relative importance of different life domains. Younger adults are primarily concerned with their profession, friends, and family, whereas older adults are more and more concerned with their health, family, and life review.

Regarding the adaptivity of setting goals in accordance with age-related expectations, Harlow and Cantor (1996) showed in a large sample of older Americans that life satisfaction was associated with the participation in life tasks of late adulthood, such as community service. Active participation in social life proved to be more important for retirees' life satisfaction compared to adults who still enjoyed active involvement in work. This difference was particularly pronounced for men. Harlow and Cantor interpreted this gender-related difference as support for the importance of shifting life tasks in accordance with age-related expectations and opportunities.

Taken together, there is evidence for age-related differences in the content of adults' goals. Education, partnership, friends, and career are particularly important for younger adults. Middle-aged adults are particularly interested in the future of their children, in securing what they have already established, and in property-related matters. Health, retirement, leisure, world-related matters, and issues related to their own aging process are salient in older adults' goals. What are the mechanisms and influences that underlie these age-associated differences in goals?

Influences on the Content of Goals in Adulthood

Influences on the content of goals include (a) non-normative, (b) normative history-graded, and (c) normative age-graded factors (Baltes, 1987). *Non-normative influences* are events that do not happen to everyone, or that have no predictable timing. Examples are chance encounters with ideas, people, or places; serious injuries; or job transfers. These events contribute to the increasing diversity among people as they get older. Because of those non-normative influences, future-oriented aspirations and their developmental trajectories are unique for each person. *Normative history-graded influences* are closely tied to the particular historical era in which an individual lives. Most members of a cohort experience these influences. Epidemics, wars, technological advances, or conceptions of what constitutes "normal" development are examples. *Normative age-graded influences* on future-oriented aspirations correlate closely with an individual's age and are highly similar for many individuals. They may be biological (e.g., biological clock for female fertility), societal (e.g., institutionally prescribed entry and exit ages in educational system), or psychological (e.g., extent of future time perspective). Next, we discuss age-graded opportunity structures and internalized age norms as well as age-associated changes in future time perspective as prominent influences on the development of personal goals in more detail.

The Role of Age-Graded Opportunity Structures and Age Norms for the Content of Goals in Adulthood

Modern societies have institutionalized age-related opportunities and constraints that regulate the amount of resources, support, and reinforcement a society provides for particular pursuits at particular ages. Thereby, societies provide age-dependent opportunity structures for certain life events and transitions and thus canalize future-oriented aspirations at different ages (Wrosch & Freund, 2001). Goals are much more difficult to attain if they deviate from institutionalized age-chronological constraints (e.g., the goal of starting out a new career in older versus younger adulthood). Age-graded opportunity structures for the attainment of future-oriented aspirations are not only societal, but may also be biological (e.g., childbearing).

Besides external and biological age-graded opportunity structures, internalized age-normative conceptions also fulfill an important function in the regulation of the content of people's goals. Internalized norms about the timing of life events and transitions are highly consensual within a given culture. They provide an age-graded agenda of "normal" development and influence future-oriented expectancies as guiding images of what one's life should be like at particular ages (cf. the concept of "developmental tasks," Havighurst, 1948).

J. Heckhausen (1999) in her Action-Phase Model of Developmental Regulation theoretically described the process of age-associated changes in the content of people's goals. This model is based on the idea that individuals encounter changes in the opportunities to realize certain goals as they move through their lives. It proposes that a developmental goal becomes activated during phases of increased opportunities. If the goal is attained, the individual turns to other developmental goals. Individuals who have not yet realized the goal are assumed to become increasingly motivated to invest effort into goal attainment as opportunities decline. The model also introduces the notion of *developmental deadline* to refer to the point at which opportunities have declined so much that goal attainment becomes unlikely. According to the model, if this deadline has been passed, the goal becomes deactivated, for example, through goal disengagement or goal substitution (see Wrosch, Heckhausen, & Lachman, chap. 20, this volume, for a more extensive discussion of this model and related empirical evidence).

Within the life-span literature, a number of theories and findings imply that a "recalibration" of one's future-oriented aspirations is indeed a key factor in successful adaptation to age-associated changes, particularly in old age (cf. the notions of loss-based selection, Freund, Li, & Baltes, 1999; flexible goal adjustment, Brandtstädter & Wentura, 1995; or secondary control, Heckhausen & Schulz, 1995; different kinds of control strivings, Grob, T. Little, & Wanner, 1999). Such revisions of goals likely occur gradually. Simply giving up important aspirations might result in a sense of loss or failure. Consistent with this view, Wrosch, Heckhausen, and Lachman (2000) found that simply lowering one's aspirations in the face of financial or health-related stress was negatively correlated with well-being across adulthood and into old age. Only for young adults, persistence showed a positive relationship with well-being. In contrast, middle-aged and older adults profited most from positive reappraisal. Throughout the life, future-oriented aspirations must be revised in such a way that the individual can maintain a sense that their goals are yet unachieved but in principle attainable, motivating him or her to strive for their accomplishment, but at the same time to feel good about his or her current life and future prospects (Cross & Markus, 1991).

The Role of Future Time Perspective for the Content of Goals in Adulthood

Another important age-graded aspect underlying developmental shifts in people's goals is the extent of future time perspective. Whereas younger adults may perceive the future as being full of limitless opportunities for exploration, older adults increasingly perceive their future as limited and finite (Lang & Carstensen, 2002). The role of future time perspective for the content of expectancies is particularly well researched in the domain of social motivation (for an overview of the role of social motivation in personality development, see Lang, Reschke, & Neyer, chap. 22, this volume). Socio-Emotional Selectivity Theory (Carstensen, Isaacowitz, & Charles, 1999) proposes that the perceived future time perspective regulates the type of social goals people have. The theory distinguishes two types of goals that underlie different forms of social contact. One goal, to *acquire new knowledge and information,* is most easily attained in the interaction with novel social partners. In contrast, the goal to *regulate one's emotions* (e.g., to feel good and socially embedded) is most easily achieved with familiar and close social partners. The central proposition of the model is that, when time is perceived as largely open ended (i.e., in younger age-groups), knowledge seeking is proposed to be of primary importance for social goals. In contrast, when time is perceived as limited (i.e., in old age), present-oriented goals (e.g., emotion regulation) are most important. Because age is associated with the time perspective people have in their lives, the model proposes changing configurations of knowledge and emotion regulation goals throughout the life span. There is ample empirical evidence supporting the proposed age-associated shifts in the social goals. A number of studies show that the shifts in the content of social goals occur in response to constrained time perspectives rather than age per se (for an overview, see Carstensen et al., 1999).

To summarize, there is cross-sectional empirical evidence of a shift in the content of personal goals from a primary interest in one's future education, partnership, friends, and career in younger adulthood, to a primary interest in one's future health and aging, leisure and retirement activities, and in world-related matters in older adulthood. These age-related changes emphasize the notion that goals reflect "personality-in-context" (B. Little, 1989): Non-normative, normative history-graded, and normative age-graded influences underlie these developmental shifts. The content of future expectancies is canalized through biological and societal opportunity structures that facilitate or hinder certain pursuits at particular ages. Internalized age norms of what is normal and desirable to strive for at a given age have a similar function. Furthermore, age-associated changes in the extent of future time perspective are associated with changing priorities in people's social motivation. When time is perceived as largely open-ended, knowledge acquisition is one of the prime motives underlying social contact. When the time perspective is limited, emotion regulation takes priority.

FROM CONTENT TO PROCESSES

So far, we have addressed how and why the content of goals changes across adulthood. Research on this topic shows how goals develop in close interaction with the context of a person, be it age-related social norms and expectations or future-time perspective. In the next section, we will turn to more *proactive* aspects of this interaction, namely, to the question of how a person sets and pursues his or her goals.

One of the central assumptions of life-span developmental psychology is that development is a dynamic process involving the interplay of proactively creating and reacting to one's environment (Baltes, 1987; Baltes, Lindenberger, & Staudinger, 1998; Brandtstädter, 1998; Lerner & Busch-Rossnagel, 1981). Thus, an adequate description of development needs to take into account that people, within the limits given by social, cultural, and biological constraints, actively shape their own environment and life course. In order to describe how this proactive interaction with the environment unfolds over time, a theory of development needs to include the notion of goal-related processes. Such processes are helpful in understanding both the *direction* and the *level* of development.

One of the basic distinctions in motivational psychology is that of goal setting and goal pursuit, which refer to the central questions of describing and explaining *what* it is that people want and *how* they go about attaining these goals (e.g., Atkinson, 1957). Heckhausen (1991) has elaborated on this distinction in his phase model of motivation, the Rubicon model. "Crossing the Rubicon," that is, committing to a goal and formulating concrete action plans for pursuing that goal, separates the predecisional phase from the actional phase. The predecisional phase is characterized by a deliberative mind-set of a ranking of various potential goals according to their short- and long-term desirability and the likelihood of their attainment. In contrast, in the actional phase people no longer engage in comparing different options, but rather focus on the realization of their intentions. The likelihood of actually pursuing one's goal depends on the volitional strength, that is, on how much the person wants to achieve the goal, and on available opportunities for action. Furthermore, the more precise and concrete the formulation of opportunities for action, the more likely that a person will actually engage in goal-relevant behavior (Gollwitzer, 1999).

Another important distinction is the absence or presence of a loss for setting and pursuing goals. Taking a life-span developmental perspective, this distinction is important because the ratio of gains to losses of resources becomes less favorable with increasing age. This is primarily due to two factors (P. Baltes, 1997): (1) Fewer resources are available in old age (e.g., decline of cognitive and physical abilities); (2) The efficiency of resources decreases (e.g., cognitive intervention shows less effect in older adults; e.g., Singer, Lindenberger, & P. Baltes, 2003). Consequently, more resources need to be invested into the maintenance of functioning or into counteracting losses rather than into growth (Freund & Ebner, 2005; Heckhausen, 1997; Staudinger, Marsiske, & P. Baltes, 1995).

Taking these broad motivational and developmental distinctions into account, Freund & P. Baltes (2000; Freund et al., 1999) elaborated on a general model of developmental regulation—the model of selection, optimization, and compensation (SOC model, P. Baltes & M. Baltes, 1990)—as an action-theoretical model of goal selection and pursuit. Next, we discuss this model in more detail.

THE MODEL OF SELECTION, OPTIMIZATION, AND COMPENSATION (SOC)

The SOC theory postulates that selection, optimization, and compensation are general mechanisms promoting successful development, which is defined as simultaneous maximization of gains and minimization of losses. *Selection* implies focusing one's resources on a subset of potentially available options, thereby giving development its direction. It functions as a precondition for developmental specialization. *Optimization* reflects the growth aspect of development. It is defined as the acquisition, refinement, and coordinated application of resources directed at the achievement of higher functional levels. *Compensation* addresses the regulation of loss in development. It involves efforts to maintain a given level of functioning despite decline in, or loss of, previously available resources.

As a meta-model, the SOC model can be applied to a variety of domains of functioning (e.g., social, cognitive, physical) and to different levels of analysis (e.g., individual, group). Consequently, selection, optimization, and compensation are proposed to have a multitude of possible phenotypic realizations (for various applications of the SOC model see, e.g., Abraham & Hansson, 1995; B. Baltes & Dickson, 2001; M. Baltes & Carstensen, 1998; M. Baltes & Lang, 1997; Freund, in press; Freund & Baltes, 2000; Lerner, Freund, DeStafanis, & Habermas, 2001; Li, Lindenberger, Freund, & P. Baltes, 2001; Marsiske, Lang, P. Baltes, & M. Baltes,

1995). The action-theoretical conceptualization of SOC (Freund & P. Baltes, 2000; Freund et al., 1999) addresses central processes of the development of "personality-in-context" over time.

Action-Theoretical Conceptualization of SOC

In the action-theoretical conceptualization of SOC, *selection* refers to the development, selection, and commitment to goals. It has been repeatedly shown in research on judgment and decision making (e.g., Tversky & Kahnemann, 1981) as well as in the motivational literature (e.g., Emmons, 1996; Higgins, 1997) that it is important to distinguish between a gain focus and a loss focus when investigating goal-related processes. Impending or actual losses seem to affect people stronger than gains (Hobfoll, 1998). The goal literature has also shown that the pursuit of avoidance rather than approach goals is detrimental for both well-being and actual attainment of goals (e.g., Coats, Janoff-Bulman, & Alpert, 1996; Elliot & Church, 1997). This fundamental distinction between a gain focus and a loss focus is captured in the SOC-model by distinguishing between two modes of selection, elective and loss-based selection. *Elective selection*—the delineation of goals to advance the match of a person's needs and motives with the given or attainable resources and opportunity structures—aims at higher levels of functioning. In contrast, *loss-based selection* occurs as a response to losses in previously available goal-relevant means. It involves focusing and redirecting resources when other means for the maintenance of positive functioning and/or substitution of a loss are either not available or would be invested at the expense of other, more promising goals. Prototypical examples are changes in goals or the goal system, such as reconstructing one's goal hierarchy, focusing on the most important goal(s), adapting standards, or searching for new goals (cf. assimilative coping, Brandtstädter & Wentura, 1995; compensatory secondary control, Heckhausen, 1999; shifts in different control strivings and goal importance, Grob et al., 1999). The SOC model posits that loss-based selection is an important process of successful development in general and of successful aging in particular, because older adulthood is a time in life when losses tend to outweigh gains.

Selection promotes positive development in a number of ways. For instance, to hold and feel committed to goals contributes to a feeling that one's life has a purpose and meaning (e.g., Klinger, 1977; B. Little, 1989). In addition, goals organize behavior into action sequences. They reduce the complexity of any given situation by guiding attention and behavior. In other words, goals can also be seen as chronically available decision rules ("implemental mind-set"; Gollwitzer, 1999), for directing attention (which of the numerous stimuli or information of a given situation are goal relevant?) and behavior (which of the many behavioral options in this situation are goal relevant?). In this sense, then, goals facilitate efficient interactions with the environment. Instead of deliberating about all of the possible alternatives they face in any given situation, people scan their environment for possibilities to pursue their goals. Goals do not necessarily need to be conscious in order to function as guides for attention and behavior. According to the auto-motive model by Bargh and Gollwitzer (1994), the repeated activation of a goal in a certain situation leads to an association between the respective goal and situational cues. Such situational features can then automatically trigger a goal and activate goal-relevant actions.

The actual implementation of goal-relevant actions (the "actional phase," Heckhausen, 1991) involves processes that in the SOC model are subsumed under the notion of optimization and compensation. *Optimization* involves the acquisition, application, and refinement of goal-relevant means in order to achieve desired outcomes in selected domains. Which means are best suited for achieving one's goals vary according to the specific goal domain (e.g., academic versus social domain), personal characteristics (e.g., gender), and the sociocultural context (e.g., institutional support systems). On the most general level, some sort of monitoring between the actual state and the desired state (goal) needs to take place (Carver & Scheier, 1999). This continuous monitoring, which might occur outside of conscious awareness (Wegner, 1992), allows for a constant adaptation of goal-related action. Progress toward the goal indicates that continuation of investment of the selected goal-relevant means is worthwhile, whereas no progress or even a greater distance from the goal indicates that other means might be better suited for achieving the respective goal (Boesch, 1991). Another example of a general process related to optimization is the ability to delay immediate gratification for the sake of a more long-term payoff (e.g., Mischel, Cantor, & Feldman, 1996). Long-term goals often require investing resources with no immediate gain (e.g., studying for good SAT scores instead of partying). Not giving in to temptations offering short-term gratifications is thus a precondition for persistently pursuing a goal over an extended period of time. The importance of the ability to delay gratification for positive functioning is also underscored by a finding reported by Mischel et al. (1996) showing that impulse control (delay of gratification) in children predicts academic performance about a decade later. Another general process of optimization is practice. As has been shown in the expertise literature, deliberate practice is a key factor for acquiring new skills and reaching peak performance (Ericsson, 1996). Repeated practice leads to the refinement of skill components, to their integration and automatization. As a result, goal pursuit becomes less resource demanding, so that free resources can be devoted to other goal-related means. Although the role of practice might be most obvious in domains with a clear achievement aspect, such as academic achievement, sports, or music (Ericsson, 1996), practice may also be important for domains with less clearly defined skills and criteria.

Compensation refers to processes aimed at maintaining functioning in the face of the losses with which people are inevitably confronted during their lives, and particularly in old age. Whereas loss-based selection refers to restructuring one's goals, compensation implies the maintenance of goals by using alternative means. Typical instances of compensation are the substitution of previously available goal-relevant means by acquiring new or activating unused internal or external resources (Carstensen, Hanson, & Freund, 1995; Bäckman & Dixon, 1992). From a life-span developmental perspective, the maintenance of functioning is as important for successful developmental regulation as achieving high levels of functioning. This is the case because development can be characterized as comprising both gains and losses throughout the entire life span (P. Baltes, 1997; Labouvie-Vief, 1981). With increasing age, the ratio of gains to losses becomes less positive (e.g., P. Baltes & Smith, 2003). This implies that with age, there is an increasing need to invest more and more resources into maintenance and resilience of functioning rather than into growth processes (P. Baltes, 1997; Staudinger et al., 1995). Compensation can thus be considered as a central process of developmental regulation. In summary, the action-theoretical conceptualization of the SOC model proposes that people actively and successfully shape their own development by setting and pursuing personal goals, even in the face of the loss of previously available goal-relevant resources. In the following section, we briefly review some empirical evidence of the adaptiveness of elective and loss-based selection, optimization, and compensation.

Individual Differences in Selection, Optimization, and Compensation

There is converging empirical evidence concerning the role of selection, optimization, and compensation for well-being. A number of studies found (e.g., Freund & P. Baltes, 1998, 2002; Wiese, Freund, and P. Baltes, 2000) that adults ranging in age from early to old and very old adulthood who report engaging in selection, optimization, and compensation also report higher well-being (e.g., frequency of experiencing positive emotions, having a purpose in life, life satisfaction). The pattern of correlations is stable across adulthood into old and very old age. In a longitudinal study focusing on younger adults, Wiese, Freund, and P. Baltes (2002) found that young adults reporting frequent use of SOC-related behaviors scored higher on multiple subjective indicators of well-being, positive emotions, as well as on subjective indicators of developmental success in the life domains of partnership and profession. Similarly, Wiese and Freund (2001) found that young adults who set priorities in one life domain over another (here: work and family) feel less conflicted about their goals, and are more satisfied with their lives in general and with their development in the prioritized life domain. These findings are consistent with those reported in studies of dual-career development (B. Baltes & Heydens-Gahier, 2003).

Cross-sectional evidence indicates that self-reported frequency in the use of SOC shows age-related differences across adulthood with a peak in middle adulthood (Freund & P. Baltes, 2002). In old age, use of SOC-related behaviors is less prevalent. Only elective selection continues to be prominent. Probably due to the decrease in resources, older adults continue to be pressured for high selectivity and have fewer resources at their disposal that they can invest into goal-pursuit (optimization and compensation). Optimization and compensation are effortful and therefore presumably become more and more taxing with age until they exceed the individual, social, and technical reserve capacities available to individuals in old age. This is especially relevant when people suffer from severe illnesses or enter very old age, the so-called Fourth Age (P. Baltes & Smith, 2003). As findings from the Berlin Aging study show, however, the decrease in self-reported use of SOC does not imply a decrease in the adaptivity of the SOC-processes—even in very old age, SOC is related to higher levels of subjective well-being Freund & P. Baltes, 1998).

In summary, there is empirical evidence supporting the main assumption of the SOC model. Selecting goals and investing into their pursuit and maintenance when faced with losses appear to be important processes in managing resources across adulthood. In the following sections, we elaborate in more detail on age-related differences in two aspects of the selection and pursuit of personal goals—goal focus (i.e., focus on gains versus losses) and intergoal relations (i.e., mutual facilitation and interference among goals).

GOAL-FOCUS IN ADULTHOOD

From a motivational perspective, compensation (i.e., the pursuit goals that focus on the *avoidance* of a loss) might have less positive consequences than optimization (i.e., the pursuit of approach goals). A number of studies with young adult participants (e.g., Coats et al., 1996; Elliot, & Church, 1997; Emmons, 1996) have shown that trying to achieve gains/growth is associated with a higher degree of self-efficacy and leads to more positive emotions and a sense of well-being whereas trying to avoid losses/decline is related to more negative emotions and distress.

The relative importance of focusing on gains/growth and on maintenance/avoidance of loss, however, might change across adulthood because the importance of attaining new resources might be more vital for younger than for older adults. Based on assumptions of evolutionary psychology, resources might be of particular importance in younger adulthood, as resources are essential for one's own survival and the survival of one's future offspring (see also Hawley, chap. 8, this volume, for an evolutionary approach to resources and personality). In addition, accumulation of resources is believed to enhance one's sexual attractiveness because it serves as an indicator of good genetic material to potential mates (Buss, 1999). Resource gain should be particularly motivating in younger adults because, from this evolutionary perspective, they are in a life stage when their primary motive is to reproduce. For middle-aged adults who have to care and provide for their off-spring, the acquisition and the maintenance of resources should also be very important.

In older adults, however, who are increasingly confronted with losses in resources, the motivation to maintain one's resources and thereby to avoid losses should become more important (Freund & P. Baltes, 2000; J. Heckhausen, 1999; Staudinger et al., 1995). In addition, because of declining efficiency of resources in older age, the pursuit of new goals focusing on gains/growth might be too resource intense for older adults. In contrast to maintaining goals, pursuing new goals requires additional means and strategies for goal-pursuit, which, in themselves, require resources. Thus, it might be more adaptive for the management of resources in old age to focus on the maintenance of functioning and on avoidance of losses rather than on the acquisition of new gains. Given that losses become more pervasive and normative in old age, avoiding losses might, psychologically, take on more of the meaning of gains. Therefore, the negative effects of loss orientation that has been documented for younger adults might not be present in old adulthood (see Freund & Ebner, 2005, for a more detailed discussion of the dynamics of gains and losses across adulthood with respect to goals)

There is some empirical evidence supporting the assumption that goal-focus changes across adulthood. Younger adults' goals are more oriented toward gains whereas older adults show a stronger orientation toward maintenance and avoidance of losses (Freund & Ebner, 2005; Heckhausen, 1997; Ogilvie, Rose, & Heppen, 2001). For instance, Ogilvie et al. (2001) showed that personal projects reflecting an orientation toward acquiring future positive outcomes declined across adulthood, although they are reported most often as a reason for goal involvement in all age groups. Goals of older adults more often reflected an orientation toward the maintenance of a given level of functioning than did the goals of adolescents or middle-aged adults. Contrary to expectations, however, there were no systematic age-related differences in the goal focus on compensation (here: curing an existing negative condition or preventing a negative outcome). Similarly, Freund and Ebner (2005) summarized a series of studies providing evidence that younger adults rated their personal goals primarily as oriented toward growth, whereas older adults' goals were equally oriented toward maintenance and loss prevention.

Regarding the differential adaptiveness of goal focus, there are a number of studies showing that for younger adults, a loss-avoidance focus is negatively related to subjective well-being (e.g., Coats et al., 1996; Elliot & Sheldon, 1997; Emmons, 1996). As expected, in older adulthood, however, a stronger goal focus on maintenance and loss avoidance was related to higher well-being (Ebner & Freund, 2003). In addition, younger adults appear to be more motivated to achieve higher levels of performance than to maintain performance when working on a task. In contrast, older adults are more persistent when working on overcoming losses than when striving to improve their performance (Freund, in press). This line of research shows the importance of taking a developmental perspective when conceptualizing the interaction of a person with his or her environment. As resources change, the processes of their management change as well. In the next section, we take a closer look at the question of how younger and older adults manage to pursue multiple goals in the face of limited resources.

INTERRELATIONS AMONG PERSONAL GOALS

Typically, people have multiple goals. For example, a person might have the goals to be an excellent student, to enjoy life, to spend more time with the family, and to exercise regularly. Such multiple goals are not necessarily independent. Exercising regularly and enjoying life might facilitate each other, as exercising might help one to relax and open up to the enjoyable sides of life. Being an excellent student and spending more time with family, on the other hand, might interfere with each other, as both goals draw on the same limited resource of time. In other words, multiple personal goals may influence each other in positive (facilitative) or negative (interfering) ways.

The importance of consistency among conceptions about oneself and the world, among which conceptions we place personal goals, has been stressed by personality theories since Kelly (1955; see also Lecky, 1969). According to these cognitive approaches to personality, only a consistent system of cognitive conceptions can fulfill the function of organizing experiences and guiding actions. As pointed out by Emmons (1989), this is also true for personal goals. Conflicting goals might lead to contradictory behavioral implications and tension within the person. One might experience this as stressful, hindering the positive experiences typically associated with successful goal pursuit. In contrast, goals that facilitate each other also facilitate engagement in goal pursuit, with two or more goals providing the same guides for actions (Riediger & Freund, 2005). Research on intergoal relations has typically investigated samples of college students. It has shown that interference among personal goals is a prevalent phenomenon in younger adulthood (e.g., Emmons & King, 1988; Palys & B. Little, 1983; Sheldon & Kasser, 1995). Riediger, Freund, and P. Baltes (2005) conducted two cross-sectional studies comparing the extent of intergoal facilitation and interference reported by younger and older adults. These studies show that goals of older adults tend to be organized into a more integrated structure than goals of younger adults. Older participants in both studies reported more mutual facilitation among their goals (due to instrumental intergoal relations and overlapping goal attainment strategies) and in one study also less intergoal interference (due to resource limitations and incompatible goal attainment strategies) than younger participants. In both studies, the observed age-group differences in intergoal relations were robust when controlling for various other person and goal characteristics (e.g., social desirability, personality traits). In these and an additional diary study, older adults were more engaged in the accomplishment of their goals than were the younger adults. As expected, this higher goal involvement of the older adults could be accounted for by the more highly integrated intergoal relations in that age group. Interestingly, goal conflict was unrelated to goal involvement but predicted lower emotional well-being.

Which processes underlie the observed age-group differences in intergoal relations? Life-span developmental psychology offers three interrelated theoretical explanations. First, the finding of more mutually facilitative personal goals in older as compared to younger adults is in line with developmental theories that emphasize the potential of continuing psychological growth in adulthood, characterized by an increased integration and differentiation of various aspects of the individual (Erikson, 1959; Labouvie-Vief & Blanchard-Fields, 1982; Werner, 1967). The improved ability to commit oneself to goals that are organized into a facilitative structure may reflect a higher life-management competence in older adulthood. As pointed out previously, the shifting dynamic of resource gains and losses make resource limitations increasingly salient in older adulthood (P. Baltes, 1997). One adaptive strategy for managing increasingly limited resources is to invest resources into harmonious rather than conflicting goals.

Intergoal facilitation could also be a possible expression of selection. In addition to holding *fewer* goals, the selection of goals pertaining to the same life domains and, thereby, converging in higher order goals, should help focus one's limited resources on a subset of highly important life domains (Riediger & Freund, in press). Similar goals might be more mutually facilitative because they can be pursued simultaneously more easily, whereas more dissimilar goals might be susceptible to mutual interference because their pursuit is more resource intensive.

A third perspective derived from life-span theory is that individuals might experience more choice in goal selection as they age. Specifically, in older adulthood, social expectations are less clear and roles less explicitly defined, regulating goal selection and pursuit to a lesser degree than in younger age groups (e.g., Freund et al., 1999; Wrosch & Freund, 2001). Older adults have in principle a larger freedom in deciding which goals to pursue and which one to abandon. Consequently, it might be easier for them to elect goals that are mutually enhancing.

In summary, there is cross-sectional empirical evidence that older adults tend to select more harmonious (i.e., more mutually facilitative, less interfering) personal goals than do younger adults. This appears to be among the protective factors contributing to the maintenance of high levels of goal involvement despite increasingly salient resource limitations in older adulthood. The question of which psychological mechanisms underlie these age-group differences remains open to future research.

SUMMARY

In this chapter, we mapped out an approach to personality that views motivational processes at the heart of what B. Little (1989) called "personality-in-context." This approach, according to the personality model of McAdams (1990, 1996), is located at an intermediate level of analyzing personality, between personality traits and personal identity or life stories. We proposed that personal goals represent the dynamic aspects of personality reflecting and shaping the interaction of a person with his or her environment over time (see also Cantor, 1990). Taking a life-span developmental view of personality, we argued that personal goals are a fruitful concept for understanding how behavior is organized over time and across situations, and that goal-related processes are important for describing and understanding both the direction and the level of adult development. We elaborated on this argument by discussing developmental shifts in the content of personal goals throughout adulthood (i.e., the "what" of "personality-in-context") and in the manifestation and adaptiveness of goal-directed processes through which people proactively influence and shape their own development (i.e., the "how" of "personality-in-context").

On the basis of the SOC model (P. Baltes & M. Baltes, 1990), three basic processes of managing internal and external resources can be distinguished: selection, optimization, and compensation. Developing and committing to personal goals (selection) provides the constraints that are essential for development. Moreover, selection addresses the fact that (internal and external) resources are limited throughout the life span. Committing to a subset of possible alternative options allows the concentration of resources and thereby enhances the likelihood of achieving higher levels of functioning as well as of accessing new resources. The process of selection is closely linked to the "what" of personality, that is, what kinds of situations a person seeks out and what a person typically tries to do (Emmons, 1989; B. Little, 1989). Studies on the content of personal goals show that adults set goals in areas that are in accordance with age-related social expectations, which might signal the availability of resources for a given age group (Cantor, 1994; Freund, 2003; J. Heckhausen, 1999).

The question of the level of functioning in a given life domain depends on the investment of resources in the service of achieving (optimization) or maintaining one's goals despite goal-relevant losses (compensation). Trying to achieve new outcomes or growth as compared to trying to maintain something in the face of loss or decline, although both important throughout adulthood, shift in their relative importance dependent on the availability of resources. Whereas optimization goals appear to play a more important role in young adulthood, maintenance or avoidance of loss goals become more prevalent and more adaptive in old adulthood, a phase in life when resources decline and their use becomes less effective (Freund & Ebner, 2005).

For a long time, personality theories have stressed the importance of consistency. According to Kelly (1955), individuals are motivated to create a system of conceptions about themselves and the world. This system has the function of organizing the otherwise chaotic experiences, and thereby allowing for meaningful actions (see also Lecky, 1969). Only a system of consistent conceptions that leads to clear predictions of means–ends relations and prescriptions for actions can fulfill this function. This is also true for personal goals (Emmons, 1989; Riediger & Freund, 2005): If a person's goals conflict with one another, they might lead to the dilemma that, whatever one does for one of one's goals, it is, for at least one of one's other goals, the wrong thing. People experience this as stressful and it hampers positive experiences typically associated with successful goal pursuit. In contrast, goals that facilitate each other also facilitate engagement in goal pursuit, with two or more goals providing the same guides for actions. There is first empirical evidence that older adults have more integrated (particularly more mutually facilitative) goals than do younger adults. This appears to be among the protective factors that contribute to the maintenance of high levels of goal involvement despite increasingly salient resource limitations in older adulthood.

Taken together, then, there is some empirical evidence supporting the theoretical claim that personal goals are important for understanding a person's interaction with his or her environment. In our view, this warrants the conclusion that personal goals are the central building blocks of a theory of "personality-in-context."

OUTLOOK: WHERE CAN THE RESEARCH GO FROM HERE?

We believe that the central future potential of the developmental perspective on personality outlined in this chapter is that it allows the bringing together of motivation, emotion, and cognition in a life-span context. The potential integration of these typically separate fields of psychology is clearly not yet realized. Originating in the "new look" movement (Bruner & Postman, 1947), social cognitive approaches to motivation help our understanding of how motivational states influence perception and cognition (Higgins & Sorrentino, 1990). Most goal theories link motivational processes to emotions, arguing that the attainment of goals (or failure thereof) leads to emotional reactions by which the very pursuit of goals might be motivated (Martin & Tesser, 1996), that emotions signal success or failure of the process of goal pursuit (e.g., Carver & Scheier, 1999), or that specific emotions are related to motivational states (e.g., Higgins, 1997). There is a large literature linking goals to behavior (e.g., Locke & Latham, 2002). Recently, Bargh (e.g., Bargh & Gollwitzer, 1994) has proposed an auto-motive model arguing for an automatic link between situational stimuli that activate goals that, in turn, automatically trigger certain goal-relevant behaviors. All of these approaches are very important for understanding certain aspects of motivation. They do not, however, situate the person into a context that changes over time and are typically not well integrated with another.

We therefore conclude that a theory of "personality in context" that integrates motivation, emotion, cognition, and behavior into a developmental framework would benefit psychology as a whole. It would provide the relatively fragmentized bodies of research and theory currently dominating psychology with a meaningful overarching framework toward which to work.

REFERENCES

Abraham, J. S., & Hansson, R. O. (1995). Successful aging at work: An applied study of selection, organization, optimization, and compensation through impression management. *Journal of Gerontology-Series B-Psychological Sciences and Social Sciences, 2,* 94.

Allport, G. W. (1937). *Personality: A psychological interpretation.* New York: Holt.

Atkinson, J. W. (1957). Motivational determinants of risk-taking behavior. *Psychological Review,* *64,* 359–372.

Bäckman, L., & Dixon, R. A. (1992). Psychological compensation: A theoretical framework. *Psychological Bulletin, 112,* 1–25.

Baltes, B. B., & Dickson, M. W. (2001). Using life-span models in industrial/organizational psychology: The theory of selective optimization with compensation. *Applied Developmental Science, 5,* 51–61.

Baltes, B. B., & Heydens-Gahir, H. A. (2003). Reduction of work–family conflict through the use of selection. *Journal of Applied Psychology,* 1005–1018.

Baltes, M. M., & Carstensen, L. L. (1998). Social psychological theories and their applications to aging: From individual to collective selective optimization with compensation. In V. L. Bengston & K. W. Schaie (Eds.), *Handbook of theories of aging.* New York: Springer.

Baltes, M. M., & Lang, F. R. (1997). Everyday Functioning and Successful Aging: The Impact of Resources. *Psychology and Aging, 12,* 433–443.

Baltes, P. B. (1987). Theoretical propositions of life-span developmental psychology: On the dynamics between growth and decline. *Developmental Psychology, 23,* 611–626.

Baltes, P. B. (1997). On the incomplete architecture of human ontogeny: Selection, optimization, and compensation as foundation of developmental theory. *American Psychologist, 52,* 366–380.

Baltes, P. B., & Baltes, M. M. (1990). Psychological perspectives on successful aging: The model of selective optimization with compensation. In P. B. Baltes & M. M. Baltes (Eds.), *Successful aging. Perspectives from the behavioral sciences* (pp. 1–34). New York: Cambridge University Press.

Baltes, P. B., Lindenberger, U., & Staudinger, U. M. (1998). Life-span theory in developmental psychology. In R. M. Lerner (Ed.), *Handbook of child psychology. Vol. 1: Theoretical models of human development* (5th ed., pp. 1029–1143). New York: Wiley.

Baltes, P. B., & Smith, J. (2003). New frontiers in the future of aging: From successful aging of the young old to the dilemmas of the fourth age. *Gerontology, 49,* 123–135.

Bangerter, A., Grob, A., & Krings, F. (2001). Personal goals at age 25 in three generations of the twentieth century: Young adulthood in historical context. *Swiss Journal of Psychology, 60,* 59–64.

Bargh, J. A., & Gollwitzer, P. M. (1994). Environmental control of goal-directed action: Automatic and strategic contingencies between situations and behavior. *Nebraska Symposium on Motivation, 41,* 71–124.

Boesch, E. E. (1991). *Symbolic action theory and cultural psychology.* Heidelberg: Springer.

Brandtstädter, J. (1998). Action theory in developmental psychology. In R. M. Lerner (Ed.), *Handbook of child psychology: Vol. 1. Theoretical models of human development* (pp. 807–866). New York: Wiley.

Brandtstädter, J., & Wentura, D. (1995). Adjustment to shifting possibility frontiers in later life: Complementary adaptive modes. In R. A. Dixon & L. Bäckman (Eds.), *Compensating for psychological deficits and declines: Managing losses and promoting gains* (pp. 83–106). Hillsdale, NJ: Lawrence Erlbaum Associates.

Bruner, J. S., & Goodman, C. C. (1947). Value and need as organizing factors in perception. *Journal of Abnormal Social Psychology, 42,* 33–44.

Bruner, J. S., & Postman, L. (1947). Emotional selectivity in perception and reaction. *Journal of Personality, 16,* 69–77.

Buss, D. M. (1999). *Evolutionary psychology: The new science of the mind.* Boston: Allyn & Bacon.

Cantor, N. (1990). From thought to behavior: "Having" and "doing" in the study of personality and cognition. *American Psychologist, 45,* 735–750

Cantor, N. (1994). Life task problem solving: Situational affordances and personal needs. *Personality and Social Psychology Bulletin, 20,* 235–243.

Carstensen, L. L., Hanson, K. A., & Freund, A. M. (1995). Selection and compensation in adulthood. In R. A. Dixon & L. Bäckman (Eds.), *Compensating for psychological deficits and declines: Managing losses and promoting gains* (pp. 107–126). Mahwah, NJ: Lawrence Erlbaum Associates.

Carstensen, L. L., Isaacowitz, D. M., & Charles, S. T. (1999). Taking time seriously: A theory of socioemotional selectivity. *American Psychologist, 54,* 165–181.

Carver, C. S., & Scheier, M. F. (1999). Themes and Issues in the self-regulation of behavior. In R. S. Wyer, Jr. (Ed.), *Perspectives on behavioral self- regulation* (pp. 1–105). Mahwah, NJ: Lawrence Erlbaum Associates.

Coats, E. J., Janoff-Bulman, R., & Alpert, N. (1996). Approach versus avoidance goals: Differences in self-evaluation and well-being. *Personality and Social Psychology Bulletin, 22,* 1057–1067.

Cross, S., & Markus, H. (1991). Possible selves across the life span. *Human Development, 34,* 230–255.

Ebner, N., & Freund, A. M. (2003, August). *Win or don't lose: On the differences in personal goal forms in early and late adulthood.* Poster presented at the 111th meeting of the American Psychological Association, Toronto, Canada.

Elliot, A. J., & Church, M. A. (1997). A hierarchical model of approach and avoidance motivation. *Journal of Personality and Social Psychology, 72,* 218–232.

Emmons, R. A. (1989). Exploring the relationship between motives and traits: The case of narcissism. In D. M. Buss & N. Cantor (Eds.), *Personality psychology: Recent trends and emerging directions* (pp. 32–44). New York: Springer.

Emmons, R. A. (1996). Striving and feeling: Personal goals and subjective well-being. In P. M. Gollwitzer & J. A. Bargh (Eds.), *The psychology of action: Linking cognition and motivation to behavior* (pp. 313–337). New York: Guilford.

Emmons, R. A., & King, L. A. (1988). Conflict among personal strivings: Immediate and long-term implications for psychological and physical well-being. *Journal of Personality and Social Psychology, 54,* 1040–1048.

Ericsson, K. A. (1996). *The road to excellence: The acquisition of expert performance in the arts and sciences, sports and games.* Mahwah, NJ: Lawrence Erlbaum Associates.

Erikson, E. H. (1959). Identity and the life cycle. *Psychological Issues, 1,* 1–171.

Freund, A. M. (1997). Individuating age-salience: A psychological perspective on the salience of age in the life course. *Human Development, 40,* 287–292.

Freund, A. M. (2003). Die Rolle von Zielen für die Entwicklung [The role of goals for development]. *Psychologische Rundschau, 54,* 233–242.

Freund, A. M. (in press). Differential motivational consequences of goal-focus in younger and older adults. *Psychology and Aging.*

Freund, A. M., & Baltes, P. B. (1998). Selection, optimization, and compensation as strategies of life-management: Correlations with subjective indicators of successful aging. *Psychology and Aging, 13,* 531–543.

Freund, A. M., & Baltes, P. B. (2000). The orchestration of selection, optimization, and compensation: An action-theoretical conceptualization of a theory of developmental regulation. In W. J. Perrig & A. Grob (Eds.), *Control of human behavior, mental processes and consciousness* (pp. 35–58). Mahwah, NJ: Lawrence Erlbaum Associates.

Freund, A. M., & Baltes, P. B. (2002). Life-management strategies of selection, optimization, and compensation: Measurement by self-report and construct validity. *Journal of Personality and Social Psychology, 82,* 642–662.

Freund, A. M., & Ebner, N. C. (2005). The aging self: Shifting from promoting gains and balancing losses. In W. Greve, D. Wentura, & K. Rothermund (Eds.), *The adaptive self: Personal continuity and intentional self-development* (pp. 185–202). Ashland, OH: Hogrefe & Huber Publishers.

Freund, A. M., Li, K. Z. H., & Baltes, P. B. (1999). Successful development and aging: The role of selection, optimization, and compensation. In J. Brandtstädter & R. M. Lerner (Eds.), *Action and self-development: Theory and research through the life span* (pp. 401–434). Thousand Oaks, CA: Sage.

Freund, A. M., & Riediger, M. (2001). What I have and what I do—the role of resource loss and gain throughout life. *Applied Psychology, 50,* 370–380.

Gibson, E. J. (1997). Discovering the affordances of surfaces of support. *Monographs of the Society for Research in Child Development, 62,* 159–162.

Gollwitzer, P. M. (1999). Implementation intentions: Strong effects of simple plans. *American Psychologist, 54,* 493–503.

Grob, A., Little, T. D., & Wanner, B. (1999). Control judgments across the life span. *International Journal of Behavioral Development, 23,* 833–854.

Harlow, R. E., & Cantor, N. (1996). Still participating after all these years: A study of life task participation in later life. *Journal of Personality & Social Psychology, 71,* 1235–1249.

Havighurst, R. J. (1948). *Developmental tasks and education.* New York: David McKay.

Heckhausen, H. (1991). *Motivation and action.* Berlin, Germany: Springer.

Heckhausen, J. (1997). Developmental regulation across adulthood: Primary and secondary control of age-related changes. *Developmental Psychology, 33,* 176–187.

Heckhausen, J. (Ed.). (1999). *Developmental regulation in adulthood: Age-normative and sociostructural constraints as adaptive challenges.* New York: Cambridge University Press.

Heckhausen, J., & Schulz, R. (1995). A life-span theory of control. *Psychological Review, 102,* 284–304.

Higgins, E. T. (1997). Beyond pleasure and pain. *American Psychologist, 52,* 1280–1300.

Higgins, E. T., & Sorrentino, R. M. (Eds). (1990). *Handbook of motivation and cognition: Foundations of social behavior, Vol. 2.* New York: Guilford.

Hobfoll, S. E. (1998). *Stress, culture, and community: The psychology and philosophy of stress.* New York: Plenum.

Hooker, K., & McAdams, D. P. (2003). Personality and adult development: Looking beyond the OCEAN. *Journals of Gerontology Series B-Psychological Sciences & Social Sciences, 58,* P311–P312.

Kelly, G. A. (1955). *The psychology of personal constructs* (Vol. 1). New York: Norton

Klinger, E. (1977). *Meaning and void: Inner experience and the incentives in people's lives.* Minneapolis: University of Minnesota Press.

Labouvie-Vief, G. (1981). Proactive and reactive aspects of constructivism: Growth and aging in life-span perspective. In R. M. Lerner & N. A. Busch-Rossnagel (Eds.), *Individuals as producers of their development* (pp. 197–230). New York: Academic Press.

Labouvie-Vief, G., & Blanchard-Fields, F. (1982). Cognitive Ageing and Psychological Growth. *Aging and Society, 2,* 183–209.

Lang, F. R., & Carstensen, L. L. (2002). Time counts: Future time perspective, goals, and social relationships. *Psychology and Aging, 17,* 125–139.

Lecky, P. (1969). *Self consistency.* Garden City, NY: Doubleday

Lerner, R. M., & Busch-Rossnagel, N. A. (1981). Individuals as producers of their development: Conceptual and empirical bases. In R. M. Lerner & N. A. Busch-Rossnagel (Eds.), *Individuals as producers of their development: A life-span perspective* (pp. 1–36). New York: Academic Press.

Lerner, R. M., Freund, A. M., DeStefanis, I., & Habermas, T. (2001). Understanding developmental regulation in adolescence: The use of the selection, optimization, and compensation model. *Human Development, 44,* 29–50.

Li, K. Z. H., Lindenberger, U., Freund, A. M., & Baltes, P. B. (2001). Walking while memorizing: Age-related differences in compensatory behavior. *Psychological Science, 12,* 230–237.

Little, B. R. (1989). Personal projects analysis: Trivial pursuits, magnificent obsessions and the search for coherence. In D. M. Buss & N. Cantor (Eds.), *Personality psychology: Recent trends and emerging directions* (pp. 15–31). New York: Springer.

Locke, E. A., & Latham, G. P. (2002). Building a practically useful theory of goal setting and task motivation: A 35-year odyssey. *American Psychologist, 57,* 705–717.

Marsiske, M., Lang, F. R., Baltes, P. B., & Baltes, M. M. (1995). Selective optimization with compensation: Life-span perspectives on successful human development. In R. A. Dixon & L. Bäckman (Eds.), *Compensating for psychological deficits and declines: Managing losses and promoting gains* (pp. 35–79). Mahwah, NJ: Lawrence Erlbaum Associates.

Martin, L. L., & Tesser, A. (Eds). (1996). *Striving and feeling: Interactions among goals, affect, and self-regulation.* Mahwah, NJ: Lawrence Erlbaum Associates.

McAdams, D. P. (1996). Personality, modernity, and the storied self: A contemporary framework for studying persons. *Personality Inquiry, 7,* 295–321.

Mischel, W., Cantor, N., & Feldman, S. (1996). Principles of self-regulation: The nature of willpower and self-control. In E. T. Higgins & A. W. Kruglanski (Eds.), *Social psychology. Handbook of basic principles* (pp. 329–360). New York: Guilford.

Nurmi, J. E. (1992). Age differences in adult life goals, concerns, and their temporal extension: A life course approach to future-oriented motivation. *International Journal of Behavioral Development, 15,* 487–508.

Nurmi, J. E. (1994). The development of future-orientation in a life-span context. In Z. Zaleski (Ed.), *Psychology of future orientation* (pp. 63–74). Lublin, Poland: Towarzystwo Naukowe KUL.

Ogilvie, D. M., Rose, K. M., & Heppen, J. B. (2001). A comparison of personal project motives in three age groups. *Basic and Applied Social Psychology, 23,* 207–215.

Palys, T. S., & Little, B. R. (1983). Perceived life satisfaction and the organization of personal project systems. *Journal of Personality and Social Psychology, 44,* 1221–1230.

Riediger, M. (2001). *On the dynamic relations among multiple goals: Intergoal conflict and intergoal facilitation in younger and older adulthood.* Retrieved December 14, 2001, from http://darwin.inf.fu-berlin.de/2001/266/

Riediger, M., & Freund, A. M. (2004). Interference and facilitation among personal goals: Differential association with subjective well-being and persistent goal pursuit. *Personality and Social Psychology Bulletin, 30,* 1511–1523.

Riediger, M., & Freund, A. M. (in press). Focusing and restricting: Aspects of motivational selectivity in adulthood. *Psychology and Aging.*

Riediger, M., Freund, A. M., & Baltes, P. B. (2005). Managing life through personal goals—Intergoal facilitation and intensity of goal pursuit in younger and older adults. *Journal of Gerontology: Psychological Sciences, 60B,* P84–P91.

Sheldon, K. M., & Kasser, T. (1995). Coherence and congruence: Two aspects of personality integration. *Journal of Personality and Social Psychology, 68,* 531–543.

Singer, T., Lindenberger, U., & Baltes, P. B. (2003). Plasticity of memory for new learning in very old age: A story of major loss? *Psychology and Aging, 18,* 306–317.

Staudinger, U. M., Freund, A. M., Linden, M., & Maas, I. (1999). Self, personality, and life regulation: Facets of psychological resilience in old age. In P. B. Baltes & K. U. Mayer (Eds.), *The Berlin Aging Study: Aging from 70 to 100* (pp. 302–328). New York: Cambridge University Press.

Staudinger, U. M., Marsiske, M., & Baltes, P. B. (1995). Resilience and reserve capacity in later adulthood: Potentials and limits of development across the life span. In D. Cicchetti & D. Cohen (Eds.), *Developmental psychopathology* (Vol. 2: Risk, disorder, and adaptation, pp. 801–847). New York: Wiley.

Tversky, A., & Kahneman, D. (1981). The framing of decisions and the psychology of choice. *Science, 211,* 453–458.

Wegner, D. M. (1992). You can't always think what you want: Problems in the suppression of unwanted thoughts. In M. Zanna (Ed.), *Advances in experimental social psychology* (Vol. 25, pp. 193–225). San Diego, CA: Academic.

Werner, H. (1967). The concept of development from a comparative and organismic point of view. In D. B. Harris (Ed.), *The concept of development* (pp. 125–148). Minneapolis: University of Minnesota Press.

Wiese, B. S., & Freund, A. M. (2001). Zum Einfluss persönlicher Prioritätensetzungen auf Maße der Stimuluspräferenz [The influence of setting personal priorities on the magnitude of stimulus preference: Initial empirical findings]. *Zeitschrift für Experimentelle Psychologie, 48,* 57–73.

Wiese, B. S., Freund, A. M., & Baltes, P. B. (2000). Selection, optimization, and compensation: An action-related approach to work and partnership. *Journal of Vocational Behavior, 57,* 273–300.

Wiese, B. S., Freund, A. M., & Baltes, P. B. (2002). Subjective career success and emotional well-being: Longitudinal predictive power of selection, optimization, and compensation. *Journal of Vocational Behavior, 60,* 321–335.

Wrosch, C., & Freund, A. M. (2001). Self-regulation of normative and non-normative developmental challenges. *Human Development, 44,* 264–283.

Wrosch, C., Heckhausen, J., & Lachman, M. E. (2000). Primary and secondary control strategies for managing health and financial stress across adulthood. *Psychology and Aging, 15,* 387–399.

19

Development of Self-Representations in Adulthood

Manfred Diehl
University of Florida

Theory and research about humans' understanding of their own person and the resulting conceptions of the self have been an integral part of scientific psychology for a long time (James, 1890/1981). Building on the early work by James (1890/1981), the last two decades have seen a renewed interest and a plethora of theoretical (Brandtstädter & Greve, 1994; Markus & Wurf, 1987) and empirical contributions to self-concept research in almost all branches of psychology (Baumeister, 1998; Damon & Hart, 1988; Harter, 1999; Leary & Tangney, 2003; Robins, Norem, & Cheek, 1999). Even trait theorists have incorporated the notion of the self-concept into their theoretical models (McCrae & Costa, 1996) and have acknowledged that individuals' cognitive-affective views of themselves are an important part of personality and essential for the understanding of human behavior (McCrae & Costa, 2003).

Although James (1890/1981) already presented a detailed theoretical view of the self, empirical research treated the *self-concept*—the Me-self, the self as object, the self as known—for a long time as a unidimensional and static entity (see Wylie, 1974). The last two decades, however, have seen a return to many of James' original notions and have extended theory and research in important ways (Campbell, Assanand, & DiPaula, 2000; Markus & Wurf, 1987). Thus, current theory and research conceptualize the human self-concept as a multidimensional, contextualized, and dynamic cognitive structure with important self-regulatory functions (Baumeister, 1998; Brandtstädter & Greve, 1994; Higgins, 1996; Markus & Wurf, 1987). This conceptualization implies that individuals' self-concept is seen as a *cognitive schema* that contains knowledge about traits, values, and beliefs, episodic and semantic memories, and is involved when self-relevant information is processed (Campbell et al., 1996). From a life-span developmental perspective, several theorists (Brandtstädter & Greve, 1994; Markus & Herzog, 1991) have pointed out that the self-concept gives individuals a sense of continuity and permanence, allows them to distinguish themselves and their developmental history from others, and gives their experiences meaning within a larger biography or life story (Bluck & Habermas, 2000; McAdams, 2001).

For the purposes of this chapter, the terms *self-concept* and *self-representations* are used interchangeably to refer to those attributes or characteristics that are part of an individual's self-understanding and self-knowledge, the focus of self-reflection, and can be consciously acknowledged by the individual through language or other means of communication (see also Harter, 1999). Other synonyms that are often used in the literature are "self-conceptions," "self-definitions," "self-descriptions," or "self-perceptions." This terminological clarification is necessary to distinguish self-concept from related terms such as "self-esteem," "self-worth," or "self-evaluation." The main distinguishing feature of self-representations compared to self-esteem is that self-representations tend to be descriptive in nature and without explicit evaluative comments. However, this does not mean that self-representations may not implicitly contain evaluations or individuals may not be able to evaluate the characteristics or experiences that constitute their self-representations on a number of dimensions (e.g., valence, importance, centrality, etc.) if asked to do so.

This chapter has three major parts. The first part introduces a conceptual framework in an attempt to organize the diverse body of literature related to research on self-representations across the adult life span. Using this conceptual framework, the second part then reviews the pertinent research with a particular focus on developmental issues, such as age differences in the content and structural organization of self-representations or the continuity/discontinuity of self-representations across the adult life span. Finally, the third part discusses some future directions in research on self-concept development in adulthood.

AN ORGANIZING FRAMEWORK

Because of the multidimensional, contextualized, and dynamic nature of adults' self-concept, it is important to outline a conceptual framework that organizes the different dimensions and perspectives that can be found in this diverse area of research. From a life-span developmental perspective, Filipp and Klauer (1986) proposed the distinction between a *product-oriented* and a *process-oriented* view of self-concept development. The former perspective emphasizes that the self-concept at any point during the life span is the product or outcome, of the processing, encoding, and storing of self-referent information. In contrast, the latter perspective focuses on the cognitive and emotional processes that are at work when individuals generate or make use of their self-referent knowledge. Although the distinction between product and process seems intuitively meaningful, on further examination it appears somewhat arbitrary, because the products of self-concept development can hardly be separated from the processes that have generated them or are involved in their maintenance and elaboration.

Thus, a framework is considered that takes a slightly different approach. Specifically, the proposed framework defines the major dimensions of a matrix within which most issues of self-concept development can be placed. Consistent with a number of theoretical discussions (Harter, 1999; Markus & Wurf, 1987; Staudinger & Greve, 1997), research on the human self-concept and its development can be meaningfully organized by focusing on four different aspects. These four aspects are shown as the columns in Table 19.1 and refer to the contents, structure/organization, functions,

TABLE 19.1

An Organizational Framework for Self-Concept Research in Adulthood: Mapping the Conceptual Space

Perspective	Aspect			
	Contents	*Structure/Organization*	*Functions*	*Outcomes*
Cognitive, Knowledge-related	Role- or domain-specific self-representations	Self-complexity	Self-assessment	Understanding of own biography/life story
		Self-compartmentalization	Self-consistency	
	Self-defining autobiographical memories	Self-concept differentiation	Self-enhancement	Sense of purpose
		Self-concept discrepancies	Self-regulation	Ego integrity/wisdom
	Possible selves		Self-verification	Emotional adjustment
Affective-evaluative	Affective valences associated with:	Sense of coherence or fragmentation	Optimizing positive affect	Understanding of self-referent emotions
	—Role/domain-specific self-representations	Affective evaluation of self-discrepancies	Minimizing negative affect	Self-acceptance
	—Autobiographical memories		Motivating and maintaining behavior	Sense of self-worth
	—Possible selves		Mood management	Well-being

and outcomes of self-concept development. Moreover, these aspects can be examined from two primary perspectives: a cognitive, knowledge-related and an affective-evaluative perspective. These perspectives are shown as the rows in Table 19.1.

As can be seen in Table 19.1, the cognitive, knowledge-related perspective subsumes under the contents aspect the role- or domain-specific self-representations (Diehl, Hastings, & Stanton, 2001; Donahue, Robins, Roberts, & John, 1993; Harter & Monsour, 1992), self-defining autobiographical memories (Pillemer, 1998), or possible selves of individuals (Cross & Markus, 1991; Hooker, 1999; Ryff, 1991). The structural/organizational features that are frequently examined are the complexity (Linville, 1987), compartmentalization (Showers, 1992a), or differentiation (Diehl et al., 2001; Donahue et al., 1993). Examination of functions of self-representations often focuses on aspects of self-assessment, self-enhancement, self-reflection, self-verification, or the overall self-regulation of behavior. Finally, postulated outcomes tend to be conceptualized in terms of self-understanding and self-knowledge (Freund & Smith, 1999a; Labouvie-Vief, Chiodo, Goguen, Diehl, & Orwoll, 1995; Troll & Skaff, 1997), clarity of self-concept definition (Campbell et al., 1996), sense of self-continuity (Brandtstädter & Greve, 1994), and overall person–environment fit.

In contrast, the affective-evaluative perspective focuses on the affective valences of the contents, examines the implications of certain self-concept structures with regard to feelings of coherence or fragmentation, and examines the functions in terms of affect optimization, mood management, and motivation and maintenance of behavior. The postulated outcomes or products of the affective evaluation of self-representations are conceived as improved understanding of self-referent emotions, self-acceptance, feelings of self-esteem, and overall psychological well-being.

To be consistent with the earlier definition and clarification of the term *self-concept*, this chapter exclusively focuses on the top half of this matrix. That is, the discussion is limited to the cognitive, knowledge-related contents, structures, functions, and products of self-concept development across the adult life span.

THE CONTENT OF SELF-REPRESENTATIONS IN ADULTHOOD

Developmental psychologists have shown that during the early life span (i.e., childhood and adolescence), self-representations develop in a predictable order (Damon & Hart, 1988; Harter, 1999, 2003). This developmental order reflects both the different stages of cognitive development as well as the changes in social environments (e.g., family, school, peers), and results in the emergence of role-specific multiple selves in late adolescence and early adulthood (Damon & Hart, 1988; Harter, 1999, 2003; Harter & Monsour, 1992). Specifically, in early adulthood, individuals usually have developed a thorough understanding that different social roles require different behaviors and the differences in behavior do not preclude the existence of a coherent and stable self-concept (Harter & Monsour, 1992; Moneta, Schneider, & Csikszentmihalyi, 2001). Unfortunately, a similar body of research focusing on age-related changes in the content of adults' self-representations does not exist at this time. There are, however, some empirical studies that provide interesting findings on how adults' self-representations may change as they move from early into middle adulthood and old age.

Findings From Cross-Sectional Studies

The commonly held assumptions regarding self-concept development in adulthood are biased in favor of stability and continuity, because self-concept development is perceived as being completed by early adulthood. McCrae and Costa (2003), however, offered a perspective that leaves room for both stability and change with regard to adults' self-representations. Building on the notion that people's self-conceptions draw on multiple dimensions of behavior, McCrae and Costa (2003) proposed that adults' self-representations may remain stable as they relate to their (relatively) stable personality characteristics (i.e., traits). However, self-representations related to roles and relationships may change over time as these roles and relationships change. This more differentiated view is supported by results from several studies.

Age Differences in Role- or Domain-Specific Self-Representations.   Although adults' self-representations are theoretically conceived as being role or domain specific, research that has applied such a perspective is the exception rather than the rule (see Diehl et al., 2001). Mueller, Wonderlich, and Dugan (1986) examined age differences in the self-schemas of young and older adults. In particular, they asked college students and elderly adults to select from a large set of descriptors those attributes that were self-descriptive. They found no age differences in the number of attributes that were judged as self-descriptive, suggesting that older adults' self-representations were as rich as young adults' self-descriptions. However, there were some interesting age differences with regard to other aspects of the self-schemas. For example, although both young and older adults endorsed more positive than negative attributes, this tendency was significantly more pronounced for older adults. In addition, older adults' self-representations were also more varied and included both "elderly" traits (e.g., mature, experienced, tolerant, slow, anxious, cranky) and "young" traits (e.g., active, ambitious, confident, inconsiderate), as judged by independent raters. Mueller et al. (1986) suggested that older adults' self-schemas were reflective of life experiences that permitted them to incorporate both young and elderly attributes.

McCrae and Costa (1988) used the Twenty Statements Test to examine the spontaneous self-representations of adults who ranged from age 32 to age 84. In general, adults in this sample described themselves primarily in terms of their major life roles, personal dispositions, and their day-to-day activities. There were, however, also significant differences between younger and older adults. Younger adults were more likely to describe themselves in terms of family roles, personal relationships, personality traits, and routine tasks, whereas older adults were more likely to mention age, health status, life circumstances, interests, hobbies, and beliefs as part of their spontaneous self-representations. Thus, McCrae and Costa's (1988) study suggests that there are significant age-related differences in adults' spontaneous self-representations, although a similar study by George and Okun (1985) found no significant age differences in the content of the self-definition of three adult age groups.

Diehl, Owen, and Youngblade (2004) employed the method developed by Harter and Monsour (1992) to examine the role-specific self-representations of 158 adults, ranging from age 20 to age 88. Specifically, adults provided, separately for each of five role-specific self-representations (e.g., self with family, self with close friend, self with colleagues, self with significant other, self with a disliked person), up to six attributes that described their own self in the respective role. These self-descriptors were then categorized whether they represented an agency- or communion-related attribute (Bakan, 1966; Guisinger & Blatt, 1994) and age and gender differences were examined. Findings showed that young and middle-aged adults included significantly more agency attributes in their self-representations than older adults, and men included more agency attributes than women. In contrast, older adults included significantly more communion attributes in their self-representations than young adults (see Fig. 19.1), and women listed significantly more communion attributes than men. As hypothesized, the correlation between age and the number of agency words was negative, whereas the correlation between age and the number of communion words was positive.

Using a sample of old and very old adults (age 70–103 years), Freund and Smith (1999a) addressed several questions with regard to the content and function of spontaneous self-definitions in late adulthood. Consistent with McCrae and Costa's (1988) results, Freund and Smith (1999a) found that older adults included a broad spectrum of life domains in their self-definitions, reflecting an activity-oriented lifestyle. In addition, statements about life review and personality traits also played an important role in these older adults' self-representations, indicating they were not exclusively activity oriented, but also engaged in self-reflection about their lives. Moreover, health proved to be an important aspect of participants' self-definition. Overall, there were more similarities than differences between the old (age 70–84) and the very old (age 85–103) with regard to the content of their self-definitions. Of 24 content categories, only 5 revealed statistically significant differences. The multifacetedness of older adults' self-definitions was significantly associated with

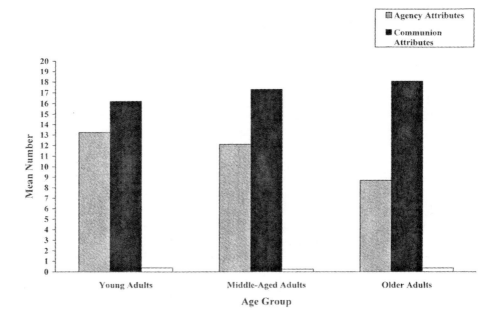

FIG. 19.1.   Mean number of agency- and communion-related attributes across age groups.

emotional well-being. However, multifacetedness did not moderate the negative impact of physical and sensory impairments on well-being.

In summary, a number of studies have documented age differences in adults' spontaneous self-representations. These age differences have been shown with different measurement approaches and different samples of adults. This suggests that these age differences may reflect age-period specific conceptions of the person and may, at least in part, be related to age-associated changes in social roles and relationships (McCrae & Costa, 2003). Further evidence for this notion and for the notion that age differences in self-representations may be reflective of age-specific developmental tasks is provided by research on adults' possible selves.

Age Differences in Possible Selves. Whereas research on age differences in current self-representations is still somewhat tentative, findings on age differences in possible selves in adulthood are more solidly established (Hooker, 1999). In contrast to current self-conceptions, *possible selves* refer to individuals' representations of future selves (Markus & Nurius, 1986). These future selves can include positive representations of the self, or *hoped-for-selves*, or they can include negative representations of one's person, or *feared selves*. Hooker (1999) pointed out that the construct of possible selves has been of particular interest to life-span developmentalists (Baltes, 1987; Cross & Markus, 1991; Hooker, 1999; Ryff, 1991), because they view possible selves as being potentially sensitive to changes in the major developmental contexts of the adult life span (e.g., family, work, leisure, health, etc.). In a similar vein, Markus and Herzog (1991) stated that "aging requires casting away some possible selves and provides opportunities for the creation of new ones" (p. 117)—an assertion that is borne out by most of the empirical research.

Cross and Markus (1991) were among the first to document age differences in possible selves across the adult life span. Specifically, they showed that young and middle-aged adults reported significantly more hoped-for-selves in the family and occupation domain than older adults. In contrast, older adults reported more hoped-for-selves in the physical health and leisure domain. With regard to feared selves, all age groups mentioned possible selves related to physical health most often; although older adults reported significantly more physical health and lifestyle-related feared selves than the younger age groups. In contrast, older adults reported fewer feared selves in the family domain. Cross and Markus (1991) also found that adults who scored low in life satisfaction reported different possible selves than those who scored high in life satisfaction, suggesting that possible selves are not only indicative of individuals' developmental position in adulthood but also indicative of their perceived discrepancies between actual and ideal self-representations.

The findings of Cross and Markus (1991) have been further corroborated by research by Hooker (1999) and Smith and Freund (2002). Hooker and her colleagues showed that across the adult life span, health-related possible selves become increasingly incorporated into adults' self-representations (Hooker & Kaus, 1994). The increasing salience of health-related self-representations is of importance because of how individuals think and plan for the future and the degree to which they may motivate individuals to change their health behaviors so that psychological and physical well-being can be maintained for as long as possible (Hooker, 1999).

Smith and Freund (2002) examined the possible selves in a German sample of old and very old adults (age 70–103). They found that young-olds generated significantly more hoped-for-selves than the old-old age group; there were no age differences in the number of feared selves. Participants' possible selves were predominantly related to personal characteristics, health, and social relationships and were reflective of gain motives. Over a 4-year follow-up period, health became the most frequently mentioned domain for hoped-for-selves.

Ryff (1991) studied the possible selves of young, middle-aged, and older adults in regard to six dimensions of psychological well-being (i.e., self-acceptance, positive relations with others, autonomy, environmental mastery, purpose in life, and personal growth). The findings showed that young and middle-aged adults expected continued improvement in the future for most of these dimensions. In contrast, older adults expected either decline for most aspects of well-being (i.e., environmental mastery, personal growth, purpose in life, positive relations with others) or no change (autonomy, self-acceptance). The future expectations of older adults were consistently lower than the expectations of the two younger age groups. Although this finding may sound discouraging with regard to older adults' possible selves, Ryff (1991) also revealed that age was positively associated with a closer fit between ideal and actual self-representations. This suggests that middle-aged and older adults may adjust their ideal self-representations in response to self-perceived age-related changes in their actual abilities, which may be a very effective accommodative strategy for maintaining high self-esteem and a sense of agency (see Brandtstädter & Greve, 1994).

In summary, research on possible selves in adulthood has documented fairly consistent age differences with regard to the domains of adults' hoped and feared selves. Moreover, findings on possible selves related to psychological well-being have yielded age differences that are consistent with research on normative conceptions of gains and losses across the adult life span (see Heckhausen, Dixon, & Baltes, 1989). Although these patterns of age differences are suggestive of age-related changes, data from longitudinal studies are required to draw conclusions about developmental changes in self-representations across the adult life span.

Findings From Longitudinal Studies

Stability and Change in Self-Representations.   The short-term variability of self-representations, for example, in response to different feedback conditions or in response to different social comparison targets, is well documented in the social psychological literature (for a review, see Kernis & Goldman, 2003) and in the experience sampling literature with adolescents (Savin-Williams & Demo, 1984). However, long-term longitudinal studies that elaborate the developmental antecedents, correlates, and consequences of self-concept variability and/or stability over time are relatively scarce. To date, only a few longitudinal studies exist, providing a relatively tentative description of how adults' self-representations may change or may stay the same over the course of adulthood. Moreover, these studies tend to be limited to particular age periods, such as early or late adulthood, thus making generalizations across the whole adult life span rather difficult, if not impossible.

Mortimer, Finch, and Kumka (1982) analyzed panel data collected from male college students over a 14-year period and assessed four types of stability (i.e., structural invariance, normative, level, and ipsative stability; see Caspi & Roberts, 2001) with regard to the four self-concept dimensions of well-being, sociability, competence, and unconventionality. These dimensions were derived from a semantic differential instrument that was administered during the freshman and senior year in college and 10 years after graduation. Mortimer et al. (1982) found support for the structural invariance of the observed variables (i.e., items) to the latent factors of the multidimensional self-concept. Moreover, the covariances among the latent factors were moderate to high over time, suggesting that the structure of the self-concept remained relatively invariant over the 14-year period. Stability coefficients (i.e., correlation coefficients) were in excess of .60 over the 4 years in college and stayed in the same range over the 10 years after graduation, suggesting a considerable amount of normative or rank-order stability. In terms of level stability, participants' scores on well-being and competence declined significantly over the 4 years in college with subsequent increases over the 10-year period after graduation. In contrast, scores for sociability and unconventionality showed significant declines over the whole 14-year period, suggesting that these young men increasingly committed to their careers and social relationships and settled into their roles as young adults. Thus, whereas the pattern of individual differences (i.e., normative stability) among participants was mostly preserved, the mean levels of scores shifted significantly upward or downward over the 14-year period, suggesting that more attention should be paid to changes in level rather than changes in rank order.

In terms of ipsative stability, Mortimer et al. (1982) examined whether individuals who viewed themselves as higher on some self-concept dimensions than others maintained this intraindividual rank ordering over time. They found that in this sample of young adult men, the intraindividual ordering of the four self-concept dimensions was quite consistent over time. To understand stability and change in self-concept in more detail, Mortimer et al. (1982) also examined the reciprocal relations between self-representations and life events for the dimension of personal competence. They showed that those individuals who maintained a strong sense of personal competence over the decade after graduation differed in a number of ways from those who changed significantly. Participants who maintained a strong sense of personal competence had more positive relationships with their parents, were less likely to experience occupational insecurity (e.g., unemployment or subemployment), were more likely to achieve high income and work autonomy, and were more likely to have good social support and high marital satisfaction. Taken together, these findings suggest that stability in young adults' self-representations of personal competence were to a good extent related to stability in the social circumstances in the family and professional domain.

Filipp and Klauer (1986) reported findings from a similar study in Germany with men from five birth cohorts. These researchers used both a standardized method and unstructured spontaneous self-descriptions to assess the stability of self-representations over a 4-year period. With regard to the standardized assessment, Filipp and Klauer (1986) found support for the structural invariance of the rating scales and for high normative stability of three self-concept dimensions (i.e., efficiency, competence, social integration). Indeed, the correlation coefficients obtained in this study were very similar in size to the stability coefficients obtained by Mortimer et al. (1982). In contrast to Mortimer et al. (1982), however, Filipp and Klauer (1986) failed to find any significant changes in mean level over the 4-year period, which may have been due to the different age range covered in their sample.

With regard to the stability of the unstructured self-descriptions, Filipp and Klauer (1986) found that although the mean number of self-descriptive statements was fairly stable across time, the index of normative stability was rather modest. Moreover, there was considerable change in the content of spontaneous self-descriptions as indicated by increases in the reference to social roles; ideological, religious, or political attitudes; physical appearance and body features; and sociability and social relations. Significant decreases were found in reference to emotionality and autonomy and independence. Overall, this study showed a decrease in the diversification of self-descriptive statements across content domains. In general, the findings from this study suggest that free-response formats may be more sensitive to change in adults' self-representations over time than standardized rating methods, and that the properties of the measurement procedure need to be taken into account in the assessment of the temporal stability of self-representations.

Troll and Skaff (1997) examined the continuity in self-attributes in a sample of very old individuals (age 85 and older) over a 28-month period. Although respondents expressed a great deal of continuity in self-attributes, they also acknowledged that they had changed in some characteristics. The majority of reported changes were in the areas of personality, physical health, and lifestyle adjustments. Interestingly, most of the perceived changes in personality were described as being positive (e.g., "I'm more tolerant," "I'm calmer"), whereas most of the changes in physical health and lifestyle were seen as negative or constraining. Perceptions of continuity were not significantly related to subjective health or affect balance in this sample of very old individuals.

Two studies have examined the temporal stability of adults' self-representations over shorter time frames. Freund and Smith (1999b) examined the temporal stability of spontaneous self-definitions in a sample of German adults (69–92, M age = 78.9) over an 8-week period. They found low intraindividual stability for a free-response format and a card-sorting task and low interindividual stability, suggesting that older adults' spontaneous self-representations exhibited low consistency over a short period of time.

Diehl, Jacobs, and Hastings (in press) investigated the temporal stability of role-specific self-representations (self with family, self with a friend, self with significant other, self with colleagues, real me) in a sample of adults (age 20–88) over a 4-week period. Respondents spontaneously generated a list of up to 20 self-descriptors and rated each descriptor in terms of how characteristic it was of them in each of the five roles. In general, adults' role-specific self-representations exhibited a great deal of temporal stability, with mean stability coefficients ranging from .75 to .80. However, there were significant differences in stability between self-representations. Across age groups, the self with family and with significant other were significantly less stable than the real me representation. In addition, central self-descriptors were significantly more stable than peripheral self-descriptors. Significant age differences in stability were found for several self-representations. For example, middle-aged adults' self with family and self with significant other representations were significantly more stable than young and older adults' self-representations in these roles.

Temporal stability of adults' self-representations was significantly related to authenticity. That is, the more authentic adults reported feeling in a particular role, the more stable their self-representations were in this role.

In summary, findings from longitudinal studies of the stability of adults' self-representations are less than conclusive. On the one hand, there are findings from long-term studies in early adulthood showing high normative and ipsative stability but also significant changes in level stability (Mortimer et al., 1982). Although some of these findings were replicated in a sample of middle-aged and older adults, this study failed to find significant changes in level stability (Filipp & Klauer, 1986). Moreover, the latter study also documented that the obtained results varied by measurement approach, suggesting that findings with standardized rating scales may be biased in favor of stability, whereas free-response measures may be biased in favor of change. This latter conclusion also seems to be supported by findings from short-term longitudinal studies (Diehl et al., in press; Freund & Smith, 1999b).

Stability and Change in Possible Selves.   Only few studies have examined the temporal stability of adults' possible selves. Thus, most theorizing on the development of possible selves in adulthood is guided by the implicit assumption that the age differences that have been documented in cross-sectional, age-comparative studies may be reflective of intraindividual age-related changes. Whether and to what extent this assumption may be justified is currently unknown and warrants systematic empirical investigation.

One of the few studies that have examined longitudinal changes in possible selves is the one by Smith and Freund (2002) with older adults in Berlin, Germany (see earlier). These investigators documented a high degree of intraindividual change over a 4-year observation period. Across all domains, a total of 66% of the participants changed their number of hoped-for-selves and 70% changed the number of feared self-representations. In contrast, analyses at the domain level indicated more stability than change. The largest number of changes occurred in the domains of personal characteristics and health. In the domain of personal characteristics, there was a tendency to delete hopes and fears rather than to add any. In the domain of health, however, more participants added than deleted hoped-for self-representations. These changes did not differ by age/cohort group.

Another interesting finding from this study was related to the motivational orientations of the changes in possible selves. Specifically, Smith and Freund (2002) distinguished three motivational orientations that they referred to as improvement, maintenance, or avoidance of loss. With regard to hoped-for-selves, the majority of participants reported the motivational orientation of improvement over time (i.e., to attain something). Over time, however, an increasing number of older adults mentioned the maintenance orientation as their motivation for hoped-for-selves, and the observed changes differed by age/cohort group. In particular, compared to participants over age 80, more individuals in the age 70 to age 79 range added the maintenance orientation. For feared selves, the motivational orientation of avoidance of loss (e.g., losing independence) was highly stable over time.

In summary, this study provided evidence that older adults' possible selves were highly personalized and covered a range of domains. Older adults' possible selves exhibited a considerable amount of change, suggesting that the participants in this longitudinal study adjusted their possible selves to the changing circumstances of old age. Furthermore, the reported possible selves showed intraindividual changes that were reflective of distinct motivational orientations and of age-related challenges, such as maintaining a sense of identity, agency, and belonging.

Two other studies examined continuity and change in possible selves in specific domains. Frazier, Hooker, Johnson, and Kaus (2000) investigated continuity and change in the possible selves of older adults (M age= 77) in the domains of health, physical functioning, independence/dependence, family, and lifestyle. They showed that continuity was the norm for most domains over a 5-year period. Specifically, continuity was significantly greater than change for hoped-for selves in the independence, physical, and lifestyle domains, and for feared selves in the family domain. These findings suggest that in later life certain domains of self-representations may be best characterized by preservation.

Preservation of self-representations, however, is not the whole story. Frazier et al. (2000) also found some evidence for changes in possible selves. Intraindividual change was generally in the emergent direction (i.e., possible self not present at Time 1 but present at Time 2), with possible selves related to health and physical functioning becoming more important over time. Most participants showed a high degree of balance between their hoped-for and feared selves in the five domains over the 5-year period. Participants who showed a disparity in favor of hoped-for selves in the health domain also reported significantly stronger health-related control beliefs.

Morfei, Hooker, Fiese, and Cordeiro (2001) examined the possible selves of young adults in the parenting domain over a 3-year period. They found that 70% of the mothers and 54% of the fathers reported the same hoped-for selves as parents, showing a good deal of continuity. In contrast, feared parenting selves showed less continuity (54% of the mothers, 29% of the fathers) over the 3-year period. There were significant gender differences in continuity, with fathers reporting significantly less continuity for both hoped-for and feared parenting selves.

Taken together, findings from these two studies showed that there is continuity in adults' possible selves, but the amount of continuity may vary across different stages of the adult life span. In both studies and related to different domains, adults' possible selves also exhibited change and appeared to be responsive to age-related changes in different domains of functioning.

THE STRUCTURAL ORGANIZATION OF SELF-REPRESENTATIONS IN ADULTHOOD

Although the structural organization of individuals' self-representations has been the focus of theorizing for a long time (James, 1890/1981; Lecky, 1945; Rogers, 1959), empirical work examining the organization of self-conceptions from a developmental perspective is rather scarce (cf. Showers & Zeigler-Hill, 2003). The main reason for focusing on the organization of self-knowledge is rooted in the assumption that different self-structures are associated with different ways of processing self-related information, which are in turn associated with either adaptive or maladaptive behavior (Campbell et al., 2000; Showers & Zeigler-Hill, 2003). Thus, a focus on the structural-organizational features of the self-concept goes beyond the content of individuals' self-representations and tries to elucidate how organizational factors, such as coherence, complexity, or differentiation, may moderate the effects of the self-concept content (Campbell et al., 2000; Showers & Zeigler-Hill, 2003). The focus here is on three structural organizations of adults' self-representations (i.e., self-complexity, self-compartmentalization, and self-concept differentiation) and the existing literature on age differences and age-related changes in these structural organizations is reviewed.

Structural Organizations of Self-Representations

The focus on the structural organization of self-representations has been motivated by the desire to elaborate the processes that underlie the dynamic self-concept (Campbell et al., 2000; Markus & Wurf, 1987). Linville (1987) introduced the term *self-complexity* to refer to the number and independence of different self-aspects (e.g., "Me as a parent," or "Me as researcher," etc.). Individuals who organize their self-knowledge in terms of a greater number of self-aspects and maintain greater distinctions among self-aspects show greater self-complexity. The basic assumption is that greater self-complexity moderates the negative effects of stressful events on physical and mental well-being, because when one self-aspect is challenged or thwarted, then the individual with more distinct self-aspects has others to draw on for counterbalance.

The concept of *self-compartmentalization* (Showers, 1992a) builds on Linville's notion of self-complexity, but also includes the valences associated with each self-representation. According to this model, individuals' self-representations can be organized in an *evaluatively compartmentalized* or *evaluatively integrated* way. In an evaluatively compartmentalized organization, positive and negative knowledge about the self is organized into separate self-aspects so that each self-aspect contains primarily positive or primarily negative information. In contrast, in an evaluatively integrated organization, positive as well as negative attributes are represented within self-aspects, suggesting that the individual acknowledges the coexistence of both positive and negative self-knowledge.

The concept of *self-concept differentiation* draws on theorizing in clinical, social, and developmental psychology and refers to the extent to which persons' self-representations are different for different social roles and/or contexts (Block, 1961; Donahue et al., 1993; Harter & Monsour, 1992). Although the emergence of multiple selves in late adolescence is generally seen as the result of increased cognitive flexibility (Harter & Monsour, 1992) and as indication of a higher level of adaptation, it also raises the question of how individuals negotiate potential tensions or conflicts between specific self-representations. That is, how do individuals deal with a differentiated self-concept? Answers to this question have reflected two major positions. On the one hand, there are a number of theorists who have argued that a highly differentiated self-concept reflects a constructive adaptation to the requirements of a highly diverse social world (Gergen, 1991) and, on the other hand, others have argued that high self-concept differentiation may be indicative of an incoherent and fragmented self-concept (Block, 1961; Donahue et al., 1993; Rogers, 1959).

In summary, researchers have started to elaborate different structural organizations of persons' self-representations in an attempt to understand the dynamic nature of the human self-concept. Although a considerable body of empirical research has emerged from these efforts (see Campbell et al., 2000; Rafaeli-Mor & Steinberg, 2002; Showers & Zeigler-Hill, 2003), only a limited number of studies have examined self-structures with regard to development across the adult life span.

Empirical Evidence

Research on the effects of self-complexity and self-compartmentalization has resulted in a fairly consistent pattern of findings. For example, in a number of studies with college students, self-complexity was found to buffer the impact of negative stressful events (Linville, 1987; Rothermund & Meiniger, 2004). Similarly, self-complexity has been shown to be negatively associated with the experience of negative affect after failure and affect variability over time (Linville, 1987; Campbell et al., 1991). Thus, self-complexity clearly seems to moderate the effects of negative events on psychological well-being (see also Rafaeli-Mor & Steinberg, 2002), although the exact processes by which this buffering effect is achieved are not well understood (Rothermund & Meiniger, 2004; Showers & Zeigler-Hill, 2003).

With regard to self-compartmentalization, several studies have shown that positive and negative compartmentalization of self-knowledge is an effective strategy of dealing with short-lived stress (Showers, 1992a, 1992b; Showers & Kling, 1996). From a developmental perspective, two studies are of particular importance because they either adopted a longitudinal design (Showers, Abramson, & Hogan, 1998) or addressed the role of self-compartmentalization in the context of a life transition (Showers & Ryff, 1996). Showers et al. (1998) conducted a prospective study in which they followed a sample of college students over a 2-year period. Findings from this study showed that compartmentalization was associated with less negative mood when stress was short-lived, suggesting that self-compartmentalization was a strategy of first resort. However, participants who were confronted with negative self-beliefs over an extended period of time did not benefit from compartmentalization and showed higher levels of negative mood, as compared to individuals who structured their self-knowledge in an integrated way (Showers et al., 1998). Unfortunately, this study did not report to what extent the self-structure changed in different directions across the 2-year period.

How self-concept structure moderated the stressful effects of a life transition (i.e., residential relocation) was examined by Showers and Ryff (1996) in a sample of older women. They found that high evaluative compartmentalization was associated with lower levels of depressive symptoms and greater well-being when the relocation was associated with improvements in positively evaluated domains of the self. However, if the relocation resulted in a loss in a positive domain, then compartmentalization was associated with higher levels of depression and lower well-being. Thus, this study replicated findings from earlier laboratory studies in a real-life setting and showed that the self-concept structure moderated the stress associated with a life transition in old age (see also Kling, Ryff, & Essex, 1997).

In terms of self-concept differentiation (SCD) only a small number of studies has been conducted with adults. Using a sample of young, middle-aged, and older adults, Diehl et al. (2001) found a U-shaped relation between an index of SCD derived from adults' role-specific self-representations and age (see Fig. 19.2). This means that SCD tended to go down from early adulthood to middle age, reaching its lowest level in middle adulthood. Conversely, SCD tended to increase again from late middle age to old age, showing a positive association with age for this part of the adult life span. Additional analyses showed that age moderated the effect of SCD on measures of emotional adjustment and psychological well-being. That is, greater SCD tended to be associated with poorer emotional adjustment and lower psychological well-being. This relation, however, was significantly more pronounced for older adults as compared to younger adults.

Donahue et al. (1993, Study 2) used data from the Mills Longitudinal Study to examine the precursors of SCD in a sample of middle-aged women. They found that SCD at age 52 showed significant positive correlations with measures of neuroticism and anxiety at ages 21, 27, and 43, and negative correlations with measures of well-being, self-realization, socialization, good impression, and overall emotional adjustment over this time span. Moreover, the bivariate correlations tended to increase over this age range, suggesting that SCD had a lasting effect in the lives of these middle-aged women. Donahue et al. (1993) also examined the relations between SCD and role involvement, role satisfaction, and role changes from age 21 to age 43. Although they found no support for the hypothesis that occupying a larger number of roles resulted in increased SCD, they did find, however, significant negative correlations with role satisfaction and significant positive correlations with the number of experienced role changes. Specifically, individuals who in early adulthood had experienced many role changes, such as marriage, divorce, and job-related changes, tended to have higher levels of SCD in their 50s. Obviously, the correlational nature of Donahue et al's. (1993) data cannot address whether high SCD was a cause or a consequence of the role-related events and the poorer psychological adjustment in

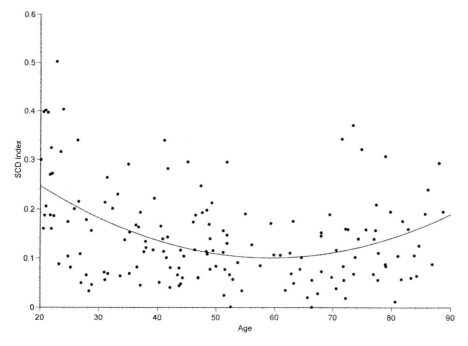

FIG. 19.2.   Relationship between self-concept differentiation (SCD) index and participants' age in Diehl et al. (2001). Reprinted with permission from the American Psychological Association.

these middle-aged women. Nevertheless, these findings suggest that a coherent self-structure is important for psychological adjustment in adulthood and high SCD may be an indication of a fragmented rather than a specialized self.

In summary, there is convincing evidence that different structural organizations of individuals' self-representations are associated with different psychological outcomes (Campbell et al., 2000; Showers & Zeigler-Hill, 2003). Most of these studies have been limited to the age period of young adulthood, although some findings suggest that self-concept structure serves as a moderator at later stages of the adult life span (Diehl et al., 2001; Donahue et al., 1993; Kling et al., 1997; Showers & Ryff, 1996). From a developmental point of view, long-term longitudinal studies are needed to examine intraindividual changes and interindividual differences in intraindividual changes in self-concept structure over longer and different periods of the adult life span.

THE FUNCTIONS AND OUTCOMES
OF SELF-REPRESENTATIONS IN ADULTHOOD

What are self-representations good for? What are the developmental outcomes of certain self-representations in adulthood? These are two fundamental questions that are more frequently asked of researchers who study self-representations across the adult life span. Moreover, these two questions are often asked in combination with the question of whether studying self-representations can help to address fundamental questions of constancy and change in adult personality.

Functions of Self-Representations

The notion that self-representations form a multidimensional and dynamic knowledge structure implies that this structure serves adaptive and self-regulatory functions (Baumeister, 1998; Higgins, 1996; Markus & Wurf, 1987). Life-span developmentalists have emphasized that the self-concept gives individuals a sense of continuity and permanence, allows them to distinguish themselves from others, and gives their experiences meaning within a larger biography (Brandtstädter & Greve, 1994; Markus & Herzog, 1991). Indeed, Markus and Herzog (1991) proposed that adults' self-concept is centrally implicated in all aspects of psychological experience, including goal setting, self-regulation, coping, and well-being.

Social and personality psychologists have also emphasized functions of self-knowledge. For example, Higgins (1996) argued that knowledge about oneself as an object in the world is only relevant to the extent that it is functional in the self-regulation of behavior. Social psychologists, especially, have frequently studied the functions of self-representations in the context of self-esteem maintenance (Crocker & Park, 2003) and have focused on specific functions such as self-enhancement, self-affirmation and self-verification, self-presentation, and social comparisons (Baumeister, 1998; Robins, Norem, & Cheek, 1999). In general, this body of research has shown that individuals can selectively activate positive self-representations in the service of optimizing positive affect. Conversely, people can discount the importance of negative self-related information and withdraw from domains or situations that result in negative affect (Baumeister, 1998; Crocker & Park, 2003;

Kernis & Goldman, 2003). These highly effective strategies related to self-knowledge are often complemented by strategic social comparisons that serve functions of self-enhancement and affect optimization (Rothermund & Brandtstädter, 2003; Wood & Wilson, 2003).

Although strong assertions have been made regarding the functions of self-representations (see Markus & Herzog, 1991), little systematic research exists in support of these assertions. In addition, most work on the functions of self-representations is social psychological in nature and does not address the development of the postulated functions or how their nature and level may change with age. Thus, there is a great need for research investigating the developmental antecedents and long-term consequences of different self-functions, such as self-affirmation or self-enhancement. Specifically, to date almost no research exists about the adaptive value of different self-functions over longer periods of time or at various points of the life span. However, one 4-year longitudinal study with college students found that too much self-enhancement may become maladaptive if it persists over long periods of time, and if it is not supported by a person's objective performance (see Robins & Beer, 2001). Markus and Herzog (1991) suggested that a more systematic analysis of the role of self-functions at various points of the adult life span "may provide a window on the apparent resiliency or invulnerability of the self in adulthood" (p. 121). This suggestion is consistent with the theoretical elaborations of other life span developmentalists who have focused on the flexibility and resiliency of self-representations in the aging process (see Brandtstädter & Greve, 1994; Rothermund & Brandtstädter, 2003).

Besides the need for research investigating the developmental antecedents and long-term consequences of different self-functions, there is also a need for research elaborating to what extent specific self-representations may contribute to stability or change in adult personality. For example, some researchers (McCrae & Costa, 2003) have incidated that role-related self-representations can be expected to change as the nature of the specific roles from which they emanate changes across the life course. Thus, it also seems reasonable to ask whether such changes are, in turn, related to changes in other personality characteristics. To the extent that adults' self-representations are both stable and malleable, more systematic research in this area holds promise for informing the debate on constancy and change of personality across the adult life span.

Outcomes of Self-Representations

Theoretical reasoning suggests that individuals' self-concept is involved in emotion regulation, coping with stressful events, and general self-regulation of behavior (Baumeister, 1998; Markus & Herzog, 1991; Markus & Wurf, 1987; Robins et al., 1999), and should therefore also be related to psychological outcomes over time. However, like research on the functions of self-representations, systematic empirical work on the long-term outcomes of the content and the structural organization of self-conceptions is scarce. The lack of empirical research is particularly obvious when developmental outcomes such as individuals' understanding of their own biography, sense of purpose, ego integrity, or wisdom are considered (see Table 19.1). Currently, most of what is known in terms of outcomes is related to emotional adjustment and psychological well-being.

In terms of the content of self-conceptions, Troll and Skaff (1997) reported for a sample of very old adults that perceived continuity in self-representations was related to positive affect. Similarly, Freund and Smith (1999a) showed that a larger number and more richly elaborated self-definitions tended to be associated with better emotional adjustment. In my own research, I have found that the number of communion-related attributes in adults' role-specific self-representations was positively associated with psychological well-being, whereas the number of agency-related attributes was associated with negative outcomes (i.e., depressive symptoms, negative affect). Consistent with the findings of Troll and Skaff (1997), findings from a short-term longitudinal study with young, middle-aged, and older adults also showed that the temporal stability and authenticity of role-specific self-representations was positively associated with self-esteem and positive affect (Diehl et al., in press). In summary, these findings suggest that the content of adults' self-representations is linked to emotional adjustment and psychological well-being over time. Prospective longitudinal studies, however, are needed to elucidate in more detail the exact pathways by which self-representations exert their effects on well-being (Showers & Zeigler-Hill, 2003).

Findings from several studies suggest that the structural organization of individuals' self-knowledge plays an important role in moderating the effects of stressful events and negative feedback from the environment. For example, the work by Showers et al. (1998), Linville (1987), and Woolfolk, Novalany, Gara, Allen, and Polino (1995) indicates that a positively or negatively compartmentalized self-structure can be a very effective way of dealing with short-term stress. However, a more integrated self-structure seems to be more adaptive when dealing with stress that extends over longer periods of time (Showers et al., 1998). Studies that have examined the role of self-concept structure in the context of real-life transitions have also shown that the ability to highlight self-representations in positively valued domains and to downplay self-representations in negatively valued domains was associated with better adjustment over time (Kling et al., 1997). Finally, both cross-sectional (Diehl et al., 2001) and longitudinal studies (Donahue et al., 1993, Study 2) have provided evidence showing that a highly differentiated self-concept tended to be associated with negative outcomes, such as depressive symptoms or feelings of anxiety.

These findings suggest that the structural organization of individuals' self-representations are intricately involved in the maintenance and optimization of psychological well-being. Research on the role of self-structures is at the interface of affect, cognition, and motivation, because it focuses on the processes by which the self-concept contributes to self-appraisals, emotion regulation, and psychological well-being. Incorporating a developmental perspective into this work holds great promise with regard to gaining a better understanding of the mechanisms that promote constancy or change in personality, and identifying self-concept processes that are at the foundation of the widely observed resiliency of aging individuals (Brandtstädter & Greve, 1994; Rothermund & Brandtstädter, 2003; Staudinger, Marsiske, & Baltes, 1995).

FUTURE DIRECTIONS

To date, most research on personality development in adulthood has focused on the stability and change of personality traits (Caspi & Roberts, 2001; Roberts &

DelVecchio, 2000). Recently, however, theorists have proposed models that address the process aspects of human personality (Hooker & McAdams, 2003; Mischel & Shoda, 1998; Roberts & Wood, chap. 2 in this volume). Among the psychological constructs that are considered to be a dynamic part of human personality, individuals' self-representations are clearly of central importance (Markus & Wurf, 1987; Robins et al., 1999; Showers & Zeigler-Hill, 2003). Even proponents of the Five-Factor model of personality have acknowledged that individuals' cognitive-affective view of themselves plays a distinct role and should be considered separate from enduring dispositions (McCrae & Costa, 1996, 2003). This final section of the chapter, therefore, outlines some future directions that can enrich this domain of personality research in productive ways. In particular, this section focuses on empirical issues related to the role of self-concept in personality continuity or discontinuity, processes involved in the adaptive reorganization of self-knowledge, and developments that have been described as an attempt to "naturalize the self " (Robins et al., 1999).

The Role of Self-Concept in Personality Continuity or Discontinuity

There is an emerging consensus among researchers that personality is both stable and malleable across the adult life span (Caspi & Roberts, 2001; Helson, Jones, & Kwan, 2002; Mroczek & Spiro, 2003). How may adults' self-representations contribute to both stability and change in personality? Several theoretical models propose that self-representations are hierarchically organized and that it is meaningful to distinguish between representations that are more dispositional in nature (i.e., core self-representations) and representations that are highly situation specific. This general idea is expressed in the notion of the working self-concept (Markus & Wurf, 1987).

In order to understand the developmental dynamics of self-representations as part of individuals' personality, future research needs to focus on both core self-representations and situation-specific self-representations and needs to examine them in the context of short- and long-term longitudinal studies (see Demo, 1992). Both traditional research methodologies as well as newly emerging methodologies, such as online experience sampling (see Carstensen, Pasupathi, Mayr, & Nesselroade, 2000; Savin-Williams & Demo, 1984), should be used to assess the constant and changing elements of adults' self-representations. Such an approach and the resulting research designs show promise for detecting individual behavioral signatures as they are reflected in the intraindividual variability patterns of individuals' endorsement of specific self-attributes depending on the situational context. From an adult developmental perspective, such studies may be particularly fruitful when conducted during normative life course transitions (Hooker, 1991) or when individuals are confronted with nonnormative life events. This approach is currently implemented in a study in my own laboratory. Specifically, we follow young, middle-aged, and older adults over 30 consecutive days and examine their self-representations in the context of stressful daily events. One of the objectives of this study is to examine the self-regulatory effects of self-representations by modeling daily variation in affect as a function of self-concept organization and daily stress. In addition, this study will permit the examination of intraindividual variability in self-representations and how such variability covaries with intraindividual variability in affect, and whether there are systematic differences in these patterns across age groups. Showers and Zeigler-Hill (2003) advocated similar approaches and criticized that researchers often neglect the motivational and emotional context in which self-representations are consciously or unconsciously activated.

Adaptive Reorganization of Self-Knowledge

One reason why the self-concept has increasingly been discussed as a psychological resource across the life span has to do with the fact that individuals can flexibly adapt the content and structure of their self-representations to different situations and life circumstances (Markus & Herzog, 1991). Brandtstädter and Greve (1994) proposed a theoretical model in which three main processes are involved in stabilizing individuals' self-representations across the adult life span. These processes involve *assimilative, accommodative,* and *immunizing* strategies. Future empirical work within this theoretical framework can greatly contribute to the understanding of how self-representations are adaptively reorganized.

Greve and Wentura (2003) and Rothermund and Brandtstädter (2003) provided evidence in support of this theoretical model. Greve and Wentura (2003) showed that adults engaged in processes of *self-immunization* by adaptively changing the subjective definition of personal skills and abilities in domains such as cognitive functioning, communicative ability, or physical attractiveness. Specifically, personal skills that individuals believed to be good at in a given domain were conceived of as highly diagnostic and important, whereas skills that individuals believed they were not good at were considered less diagnostic and less important. This selective upgrading and downgrading of skills or traits stabilized individuals' current self-conceptions while at the same time permitting a flexible adjustment of their self-representations to situations where failure or loss was possible. Unfortunately, these researchers did not examine whether or not there were significant age differences in the use of these strategies. If significant age differences were found, then this could be interpreted as evidence that aging individuals use immunizing mechanisms to stabilize their self-representations as they become aware of personal age-related declines or losses.

Rothermund and Brandtstädter (2003) reported another interesting study. Using data from an 8-year longitudinal study, these researchers showed that at the start of the study, participants held more positive views of themselves than of the typical old person (i.e., age stereotype). As the participants aged, their evaluation of the typical old person, however, became increasingly more positive, suggesting that the earlier held age stereotype was gradually assimilated to support the self-view. This assimilative process became increasingly important with advancing age. Furthermore, Rothermund and Brandtstädter (2003) showed that participants who scored high on flexible goal adjustment were more capable of protecting their self-views from negative age stereotypes than individuals who scored low on this variable (see also Wrosch, Scheier, Miller, Schulz, & Carver, 2003). Other studies that have documented the flexible adjustment of self-conceptions over time and in the context of life transitions have been reported by Kling et al. (1997), Kwan, Love, Ryff, and Essex

(2003), and by Showers and Ryff (1996). Although all of these studies describe processes of adaptive reorganization of self-knowledge, further research is still needed to understand these processes and to identify their developmental antecedents and consequences.

In addition to studying fairly specific self-conceptions and how they are reorganized across the adult life span, another promising direction is outlined by researchers who emphasize the construction and reconstruction of personal identities via the use of *autobiographical memories* (Conway & Pleydell-Pearce, 2000; Ross & Conway, 1986). Most of these researchers advocate a functional approach to autobiographical memory and emphasize that a specific subset of autobiographical memories, namely, *self-defining memories*, are crucial elements of any person's self-concept (Cohen, 1998). Although this emerging perspective is theoretically compelling, future research will have to show to what extent this proposition can be supported by actual empirical data.

Naturalizing the Self

Another promising future direction is related to recent developments in cognitive and social neuroscience (Ochsner & Lieberman, 2001; Sarter, Berntson, & Cacioppo, 1996). The approach of "naturalizing the self" represents the attempt to link psychological states such as consciousness, self-awareness, and self-knowledge to the activity and processes of the human brain (Ochsner & Lieberman, 2001; Robins et al., 1999). Recent technological advances in neuroimaging (Raichle, 1994), including methods of functional imaging, such as functional magnetic resonance imaging (fMRI) or positron emission tomography (PET), permit more precise measurement of brain activity when a person is asked to perform certain behavioral, cognitive, or emotional tasks. With regard to self-representations, it has already been documented that semantic and episodic memory rely on different neural structures (Vargha-Khadem, et al., 1997). This is important because semantic memory serves as the foundation for many trait-related self-representations (Klein, Loftus, & Kihlstrom, 1996), whereas episodic memory is mostly the basis for autobiographical memories. For example, Craik et al. (1999) used positron emission tomography to compare patterns of brain activation when participants made judgments about self-relevant trait words or judgments about words that were not self-relevant (i.e., judgments related to a public figure or number of syllables in a trait word). Compared to nonself-judgments, when participants assessed the relevance of self-relevant trait words their brains showed activation of the left frontal lobe as had been documented in earlier work (Kapur et al., 1996). In addition, Craik et al. (1999) found that select areas of the right frontal lobe, which are known to be involved in the retrieval of episodic memories, also showed activation when making self-judgments. These findings suggest that schematic and episodic memory systems may be activated when a person processes self-representations. Based on these findings, it is easy to imagine that future studies on self-representations may draw on neuroimaging techniques and may explore which regions of the brain are activated when the person is asked to produce different kinds of self-representations (e.g., actual self vs. ideal self, ideal self vs. dreaded self, or trait-related self-knowledge vs. autobiographical self-knowledge; see Robins et al., 1999).

CONCLUSIONS

Theoretical discussions on the nature and development of self-representations (Brandtstädter & Greve, 1994; Markus & Wurf, 1987) have provided a solid foundation on which to build empirical work on self-concept development across the adult life span. Although the existing research is not as rich and definitive as research on self-concept development in childhood and adolescence (see Harter, chap. 16 in this volume), promising steps have been made toward describing both the content and the structural organization of adults' self-representations. From a developmental perspective, more longitudinal research is needed to gain a better understanding of the antecedents, correlates, and consequences of adults' self-representations. Furthermore, a more detailed understanding of the processes that guide the structural organization and reorganization of self-knowledge is needed to fully appreciate the dynamic nature of self-representations and their contributions to adjustment and well-being across the adult life span (Showers & Zeigler-Hill, 2003).

ACKNOWLEDGMENT

Work on this chapter was supported by grant R01 AG21147 from the National Institute on Aging.

REFERENCES

Bakan, D. (1966). *The duality of human existence: Isolation and communion in Western man*. Chicago: Rand McNally.

Baltes, P. B. (1987). Theoretical propositions of life-span developmental psychology: On the dynamics between growth and decline. *Developmental Psychology, 23*, 611–626.

Baumeister, R. R. (1998). The self. In D. T. Gilbert, S. T. Fiske, & G. Lindzey (Eds.), *The handbook of social psychology* (4th ed., Vol. 1, pp. 680–740). New York: McGraw-Hill.

Block, J. (1961). Ego-identity, role variability, and adjustment. *Journal of Consulting and Clinical Psychology, 25*, 392–397.

Bluck, S., & Habermas, T. (2000). The life story schema. *Motivation and Emotion, 24*, 121–147.

Brandtstädter, J., & Greve, W. (1994). The aging self: Stabilizing and protective processes. *Developmental Review, 14*, 52–80.

Campbell, J. D., Assanand, S., & DiPaula, A. (2000). Structural features of the self-concept and adjustment. In A. Tesser, R. B. Felson, & J. M. Suls (Eds.), *Psychological perspectives on self and identity* (pp. 67–87). Washington, DC: American Psychological Association.

Campbell, J. D., Trapnell, P. D., Heine, S. J., Katz, I. M., Lavallee, L. F., & Lehman, D. R. (1996). Self-concept clarity: Measurement, personality correlates, and cultural boundaries. *Journal of Personality and Social Psychology, 70*, 141–156.

Carstensen, L. L., Pasupathi, M., Mayr, U., & Nesselroade, J. R. (2000). Emotional experience in everyday life across the adult life span. *Journal of Personality and Social Psychology, 79*, 644–655.

Caspi, A., & Roberts, B. W. (2001). Personality development across the life course: The argument for change and continuity. *Psychological Inquiry, 12*, 49–66.

Cohen, G. (1998). The effects of aging on autobiographical memory. In C. P. Thompson, D. J. Herrmann, D. Bruce, J. D. Read, D. G. Payne, & M. P. Toglia (Eds.), *Autobiographical memory: Theoretical and applied perspectives* (pp. 105–123). Mahwah, NJ: Lawrence Erlbaum Associates.

Conway, M. A., & Pleydell-Pearce, C. W. (2000). The construction of autobiographical memories in the self-memory system. *Psychological Review, 107*, 261–288.

Craik, F. I. M., Moroz, T. M., Moscovitch, M., Stuss, D. T., Winocur, G., Tulving, E., & Kapur, S. (1999). In search of the self: A positron emission tomography study. *Psychological Science, 10,* 26–34.

Crocker, J., & Park, L. E. (2003). Seeking self-esteem: Construction, maintenance, and protection of self-worth. In M. R. Leary & J. P. Tangney (Eds.), *Handbook of self and identity* (pp. 291–313). New York: Guilford.

Cross, S., & Markus, H. (1991). Possible selves across the life span. *Human Development, 34,* 230–255.

Damon, W., & Hart, D. (1988). *Self-understanding in childhood and adolescence.* New York: Cambridge University Press.

Demo, D. H. (1992). The self-concept over time: Research issues and directions. *American Review of Sociology, 18,* 303–326.

Diehl, M., Hastings, C. T., & Stanton, J. M. (2001). Self-concept differentiation across the adult life span. *Psychology and Aging, 16,* 643–654.

Diehl, M., Jacobs, L., & Hastings, C. T. (2003). Temporal stability and authenticity of self-representations in adulthood. *Journal of Adult Development.*

Diehl, M., Owen, S. K., & Youngblade, L. M. (2004). Agency and communion attributes in adults' spontaneous self-representations. *International Journal of Behavioral Development, 28,* 1–15.

Donahue, E.M., Robins, R.W., Roberts, B. W., & John, O.P. (1993). The divided self: Concurrent and longitudinal effects of psychological adjustment and social roles on self-concept differentiation. *Journal of Personality and Social Psychology, 64,* 834–846.

Filipp, S.-H., & Klauer, T. (1986). Conceptions of self over the life span: Reflections on the dialectics of change. In M. M. Baltes & P. B. Baltes (Eds.), *The psychology of control and aging* (pp. 167–205). Hillsdale, NJ: Lawrence Erlbaum Associates.

Frazier, L. D., Hooker, K., Johnson, P. M., & Kaus, C. R. (2000). Continuity and change in possible selves in later life: A 5-year longitudinal study. *Basic and Applied Social Psychology, 22,* 237–243.

Freund, A. M., & Smith, J. (1999a). Content and function of the self-definition in old and very old age. *Journal of Gerontology: Psychological Sciences, 54B,* P55–P67.

Freund, A. M., & Smith, J. (1999b). Temporal stability of older persons' spontaneous self-definition. *Experimental Aging Research, 25,* 95–107.

George, L. K., & Okun, M. A. (1985). Self-concept content. In E. W. Busse, G. L. Maddox, J. B. Nowlin, & I. C. Siegler (Eds.), *Normal aging III: Reports from the Duke Longitudinal Studies 1975–1984* (pp. 267–282). Durham, NC: Duke University Press.

Gergen, K. J. (1991). *The saturated self: Dilemmas of identity in contemporary life.* New York: Basic Books.

Greve, W., & Wentura, D. (2003). Immunizing the self: Self-concept stabilization through reality-adaptive self-definitions. *Personality and Social Psychology Bulletin, 29,* 39–50.

Guisinger, S., & Blatt, S. (1994). Individuality and relatedness. *American Psychologist, 49,* 104–111.

Harter, S. (1999). *The construction of the self: A developmental perspective.* New York: Guilford.

Harter, S. (2003). The development of self-representations during childhood and adolescence. In M. R. Leary & J. P. Tangney (Eds.), *Handbook of self and identity* (pp. 610–642). New York: Guilford.

Harter, S., & Monsour, A. (1992). Developmental analysis of conflict caused by opposing attributes in the adolescent self-portrait. *Developmental Psychology, 28,* 251–260.

Heckhausen, J., Dixon, R. A., & Baltes, P. B. (1989). Gains and losses in development throughout adulthood as perceived by different age groups. *Developmental Psychology, 25,* 109–121.

Helson, R., Jones, C., & Kwan, V. S. (2002). Personality change over 40 years of adulthood: Hierarchical linear modeling analyses of two longitudinal samples. *Journal of Personality and Social Psychology, 83,* 752–766.

Higgins, E. T. (1996). The "self digest": Self-knowledge serving self-regulatory functions. *Journal of Personality and Social Psychology, 71,* 1062–1083.

Hooker, K. (1991). Change and stability in self during the transition to retirement: An intraindividual study using P-technique factor analysis. *International Journal of Behavioral Development, 14,* 209–233.

Hooker, K. (1999). Possible selves in adulthood: Incorporating teleonomic relevance into studies of the self. In T. Hess & F. Blanchard-Fields (Eds.), *Social cognition and aging* (pp. 97–121). San Diego, CA: Academic Press.

Hooker, K., & Kaus, C. R. (1994). Health-related possible selves in young and middle adulthood. *Psychology and Aging, 9,* 126–133.

Hooker, K., & McAdams, D. P. (2003). Personality reconsidered: A new agenda for aging research. *Journal of Gerontology: Psychological Sciences, 58B,* P296–P304.

James, W. (1890/1981). *The principles of psychology* (Vol. 1). Cambridge, MA: Harvard University Press. (Original work published in 1890)

Kapur, S., Tulving, E., Cabeza, R., McIntosh, A. R., Houle, S., & Craik, F. I. M. (1996). The neural correlates of intentional learning of verbal materials: A PET study in humans. *Cognitive Brain Research, 4,* 243–249.

Kernis, M. H., & Goldman, B. M. (2003). Stability and variability in self-concept and self-esteem. In M. R. Leary & J. P. Tangney (Eds.), *Handbook of self and identity* (pp. 106–127). New York: Guilford.

Klein, S. B., Loftus, J., & Kihlstrom, J. F. (1996). Self-knowledge of an amnesic patient: Toward a neuropsychology of personality and social psychology. *Journal of Experimental Psychology: General, 125,* 250–260.

Kling, K. C., Ryff, C. D., & Essex, M. J. (1997). Adaptive changes in the self-concept during a life transition. *Personality and Social Psychology Bulletin, 23,* 981–990.

Kwan, C. M. L., Love, G. D., Ryff, C. D., & Essex, M. J. (2003). The role of self-enhancing evaluations in a successful life transition. *Psychology and Aging, 18,* 3–12.

Labouvie-Vief, G., Chiodo, L.M., Goguen, L.A., Diehl, M., & Orwoll, L. (1995). Representations of self across the life span. *Psychology and Aging, 10,* 404–415.

Leary, M. R., & Tangney, J. P. (2003). The self as an organizing construct in the behavioral and social sciences. In M. R. Leary & J. P. Tangney (Eds.), *Handbook of self and identity* (pp. 3–14). New York: Guilford.

Lecky, P. (1945). *Self-consistency: A theory of personality.* New York: Anchor Books.

Linville, P. W. (1987). Self-complexity as a cognitive buffer against stress-related illness and depression. *Journal of Personality and Social Psychology, 52,* 663–676.

Markus, H. R., & Herzog, R. A. (1991). The role of the self-concept in aging. In K. W. Schaie (Ed.), *Annual review of gerontology and geriatrics* (Vol. 11, pp. 110–143). New York: Springer.

Markus, H. R., & Nurius, P. (1986). Possible selves. *American Psychologist, 41,* 954–969.

Markus, H. R., & Wurf, E. (1987). The dynamic self-concept: A social psychological perspective. *Annual Review of Psychology, 38,* 299–337.

McAdams, D. P. (2001). The psychology of life stories. *Review of General Psychology, 5,* 100–122.

McCrae, R. R., & Costa, P. T., Jr. (1988). Age, personality, and the spontaneous self-concept. *Journal of Gerontology: Social Sciences, 43,* S177–S185.

McCrae, R. R., & Costa, P. T., Jr. (1996). Toward a new generation of personality theories: Theoretical contexts for the five-factor model. In J. S. Wiggins (Ed.), *The Five-Factor model of personality: Theoretical perspectives* (pp. 51–87). New York: Guilford.

McCrae, R. R., & Costa, P. T., Jr. (2003). *Personality in adulthood: A five-factor theory perspective* (2nd ed.). New York: Guilford.

Mischel, W., & Shoda, Y. (1998). Reconciling processing dynamics and personality dispositions. *Annual Review of Psychology, 49,* 229–258.

Moneta, G. B., Schneider, B., & Csikszentmihalyi, M. (2001). A longitudinal study of the self-concept and experiential components of self-worth and affect across adolescence. *Applied Developmental Science, 5,* 125–142.

Morfei, M. Z., Hooker, K., Fiese, B. H., & Cordeiro, A. M. (2001). Continuity and change in parenting possible selves: A longitudinal follow-up. *Basic and Applied Social Psychology, 23,* 217–223.

Mortimer, J. T., Finch, M. D., & Kumka, D. (1982). Persistence and change in development: The multidimensional self-concept. In P. B. Baltes & O. G. Brim, Jr. (Eds.), *Life-span development and behavior* (Vol. 4, pp. 263–313). New York: Academic Press.

Mroczek, D. K., & Spiro, A. III. (2003). Modeling intraindividual change in personality traits: Findings from the Normative Aging Study. *Journal of Gerontology: Psychological Sciences, 58B,* P153–P165.

Mueller, J. H., Wonderlich, S., & Dugan, K. (1986). Self-referent processing of age-specific material. *Psychology and Aging, 1,* 293–299.

Ochsner, K. N., & Lieberman, M. D. (2001). The emergence of social cognitive neuroscience. *American Psychologist, 56,* 717–734.

Pillemer, D. (1998). *Momentous events, vivid memories: How unforgettable moments help us understand the meaning of our lives.* Cambridge, MA: Harvard University Press.

Rafaeli-Mor, E., & Steinberg, J. (2002). Self-complexity and well-being: A review and research synthesis. *Personality and Social Psychology Review, 6,* 31–58.

Raichle, M. E. (1994). Images of the mind: Studies with modern imaging techniques. *Annual Review of Psychology, 45,* 333–356.

Roberts, B. W., & DelVecchio, W. F. (2000). The rank-order consistency of personality traits from childhood to old age: A quantitative review of longitudinal studies. *Psychological Bulletin, 126,* 3–25.

Robins, R. W., & Beer, J. S. (2001). Positive illusions about the self: Short-term benefits and long-term costs. *Journal of Personality and Social Psychology, 80,* 340–352.

Robins, R. W., Norem, J. K., & Cheek, J. M. (1999). Naturalizing the self. In L. A. Pervin & O. P. John (Eds.), *Handbook of personality: Theory and research* (2nd ed., pp. 443–477). New York: Guilford.

Rogers, C. (1959). A theory of therapy, personality, and interpersonal relationships, as developed in the client-centered framework. In S. Koch (Ed.), *Psychology: A study of science: Vol. 3. Formulations of the person and the social context* (pp. 184–256). New York: McGraw-Hill.

Ross, M., & Conway, M. A. (1986). Remembering one's own past: The construction of personal histories. In R. M. Sorrentino & E. T. Higgins (Eds.), *The handbook of motivation and cognition: Foundations of social behavior* (pp. 122–144). New York: Guilford.

Rothermund, K., & Brandtstädter, J. (2003). Age stereotypes and self-views in later life: Evaluating rival assumptions. *International Journal of Behavioral Development, 27,* 549–554.

Rothermund, K., & Meiniger, C. (2004). Stress-buffering effects of self-complexity: Reduced affective spillover or self-regulatory processes? *Self and Identity, 3,* 263–281.

Ryff, C. D. (1991). Possible selves in adulthood and old age: A tale of shifting horizons. *Psychology and Aging, 6,* 286–295.

Sarter, M., Berntson, G. G., & Cacioppo, J. T. (1996). Brain imaging and cognitive neuroscience: Toward strong inference in attributing function to structure. *American Psychologist, 51,* 13–21.

Savin-Williams, R. C., & Demo, D. H. (1984). Developmental change and stability in adolescent self-concept. *Developmental Psychology, 20,* 1100–1110.

Showers, C. J. (1992a). Compartmentalization of positive and negative self-knowledge: Keeping bad apples out of the bunch. *Journal of Personality and Social Psychology, 62,* 1036–1049.

Showers, C. J. (1992b). Evaluatively integrative thinking about characteristics of the self. *Personality and Social Psychology Bulletin, 18,* 719–729.

Showers, C. J., Abramson, L. Y., & Hogan, M. E. (1998). The dynamic self: How the content and structure of the self-concept change with mood. *Journal of Personality and Social Psychology, 75,* 478–493.

Showers, C. J., & Kling, K. C. (1996). Organization of self-knowledge: Implications for recovery from sad mood. *Journal of Personality and Social Psychology, 70,* 578–590.

Showers, C. J., & Ryff, C. D. (1996). Self-differentiation and well-being in a life transition. *Personality and Social Psychology Bulletin, 22,* 448–460.

Showers, C. J., & Zeigler-Hill, V. (2003). Organization of self-knowledge: Features, functions, and flexibility. In M. R. Leary & J. P. Tangney (Eds.), *Handbook of self and identity* (pp. 47–67). New York: Guilford.

Smith, J., & Freund, A. M. (2002). The dynamics of possible selves in old age. *Journal of Gerontology: Psychological Sciences, 57B,* P492–P500.

Staudinger, U. M., & Greve, W. (1997). Das Selbst im Lebenslauf: Brückenschläge und Perspektivenwechsel zwischen entwicklungs- und sozialpsychologischen Zugängen [The self across the life span: Building bridges and exchanging perspectives between developmental and social psychological approaches]. *Zeitschrift für Sozialpsychologie, 28,* 3–18.

Staudinger, U. M., Marsiske, M., & Baltes, P. B. (1995). Resilience and reserve capacity in later adulthood: Potentials and limits of development across the life span. In D. Cicchetti & D. J. Cohen (Eds.), *Developmental psychopathology: Vol. 2. Risk, disorder, and adaptation* (pp. 801–847). New York: Wiley.

Troll, L. E., & Skaff, M. M. (1997). Perceived continuity of self in very old age. *Psychology and Aging, 12,* 162–169.

Vargha-Khadem, F., Gadian, D. G., Watkins, K. E., Connelly, A., Van Paesschen, W., & Miskin, M. (1997). Differential effects of early hippocampal pathology on episodic and semantic memory. *Science, 277,* 376–380.

Wood, J. V., & Wilson, A. E. (2003). How important is social comparison? In M. R. Leary & J. P. Tangney (Eds.), *Handbook of self and identity* (pp. 344–366). New York: Guilford.

Woolfolk, R. L., Novalany, J., Gara, M. A., Allen, L. A., & Polino, M. (1995). Self-complexity, self-evaluation, and depression: An examination of form and content within the self-schema. *Journal of Personality and Social Psychology, 68,* 1108–1120.

Wrosch, C., Scheier, M. F., Miller, G. E., Schulz, R., & Carver, C. S. (2003). Adaptive self-regulation of unattainable goals: Goal disengagement, goal reengagement, and subjective well-being. *Personality and Social Psychology Bulletin, 29,* 1494–1508.

Wylie, R. C. (1974). *The self-concept: A review of methodological considerations and measuring instruments.* Lincoln, NE: University of Nebraska Press.

20

Goal Management Across Adulthood and Old Age: The Adaptive Value of Primary and Secondary Control

Carsten Wrosch
Concordia University

Jutta Heckhausen
University of California, Irvine

Margie E. Lachman
Brandeis University

This chapter addresses the adaptive value of goal-related motivational processes for successful development across the adult life span. Goals play an important role in successful development because they are the building blocks that structure people's lives and imbue life with purpose, both in the short run and on a long-term basis (Carver & Scheier, 1998; Heckhausen, 1999a; Ryff, 1989). Therefore, processes that are functionally associated with achieving personal goals and managing the negative consequences of goal failure can be expected to contribute to pathways of successful development.

On the basis of the life-span theory of control (Heckhausen & Schulz, 1995; Schulz & Heckhausen, 1996), this chapter demonstrates that the adult life span can be characterized by an age-graded structure of opportunities and constraints for attaining personal goals. Whereas young adults usually face plenty and favorable opportunities for attaining personal goals, older adults have to manage increasing constraints on successfully pursuing personal goals. As a consequence, the argument is made that processes aimed at attaining personal goals (e.g., primary control striving) are particularly adaptive in young adulthood. Among older adults, by contrast, adaptive management of personal goals increasingly requires people to disengage from unattainable goals and to protect their selves (e.g., compensatory secondary control striving) in order to safeguard motivational and behavioral resources needed to pursue other important goals (e.g., health-related, highly identity relevant). To provide evidence for the adaptive value of an age-graded management of personal goals, there is a review of recent work that has been conducted to test some of the basic assumptions of the life-span theory of control. In addition, the potential influence of some individual difference variables (e.g., perceived control and general goal management tendencies) on the use of specific control strategies is discussed. The issues discussed in this chapter have the potential to broaden the theoretical scope of a goal-related perspective on adaptive personality functioning and to contribute to a better understanding of successful development across the adult life span.

OPPORTUNITIES FOR GOAL ATTAINMENT ACROSS THE ADULT LIFE SPAN

Many personality theories and empirical studies have pointed to the importance of goal-related processes for successful development. For example, being optimistic, believing in one's own competencies, and using problem-focused coping have been shown to be related to subjective well-being and good health (e.g., Bandura, 1997; Carver et al., 1993; Folkman & Lazarus, 1980). In addition, disengagement and emotion-focused coping have been conceptualized as adaptive processes if people cannot attain their goals (e.g., Baumeister & Scher, 1988; Brockner, 1992; Carver & Scheier, 1990; Nesse, 2000; Vitaliano, DeWolfe, Maiuro, Russso, & Katon, 1990). Although it is clear that contemporary personality approaches to successful living have recognized the role played by personal goals, many of these theories do not address the importance of age as an additional layer of adaptive personality functioning.

This chapter begins with a discussion of the underlying factors that comprise a person's opportunities and constraints involved in the attainment of personal goals. For the past five decades, developmental researchers have become interested in the role played by the time-ordered structure of the life course for individual development (e.g., Erikson, 1968; Havighurst, 1967; Heckhausen, 1999a). At the most general level, these models postulate that successful development depends on effective management of age-graded developmental tasks, developmental goals, or psychosocial crises. Given the relevance of the age-related structure of the adult life span, it is important to discuss the factors that determine opportunities and constraints for goal attainment across the life course and thereby scaffold individual development.

Heckhausen and Schulz (1995) proposed a classification system of factors underlying the structure of the human life course. Their model differentiates biological, societal, and age-normative factors involved in human development. Biological factors are based on maturation and aging and affect the normative development of most individuals to a similar extent. Across the human life span, biological factors produce an inverted U-curve pattern of functional capacity (Heckhausen & Schulz, 1995). During childhood and adolescence, maturation promotes the organism from complete helplessness to a well-functioning individual. In early and middle adulthood, the functional capacities of most human beings plateau on a high level. From middle adulthood on, biological factors negatively affect personal functioning and lead to a progressive decrease of functional capacities. Research on objective markers of biological decline has supported this notion by demonstrating an age-related decrease in cognitive skills and capacities, especially at the limits of individual performance (Baltes, 1987; Kliegl, Smith, & Baltes, 1989). A consequence of the age-related influence of biological factors is that they facilitate the attainment of various developmental tasks during young adulthood and early midlife, but may constrain the attainment of personal goals if people advance in age.

Another factor involved in human development has been described as societal constraints. These constraints are related to the social structure and to social institutions embedded in modern societies in legislative rules associated with an age-specific timing of life course transitions (e.g., school entry, retirement; Heckhausen & Schulz, 1995). Implicit and explicit restrictions based on chronological age provide a structure for entry and transition times of various developmental projects (Hagestad, 1990). For example, school entry, career development, or retirement are often determined by state-regulated and corporate rules about age and sequences of promotion. Such institutionalized age strata for professional development can obstruct the attainment of long-standing career goals, when individuals pass explicit or implicit deadlines for promotion (Heckhausen, 1999a). Societal factors also play an important role in the attainment of other developmental tasks, such as partnership formation. For example, an age-graded marriage market provides better opportunities for partnership formation in young adulthood, as compared to late midlife and old age (cf. Wrosch & Heckhausen, 1999).

More generally speaking, societal factors furnish sequentially organized patterns (Sørensen, 1990) in terms of opportunities and constraints for the attainment of developmental goals. As a consequence, the realization of personal goals in late midlife and old age can be obstructed if a person's age does not fit with institutionalized patterns of age-graded developmental tasks. By contrast, an age-appropriate timing of personal goals (e.g., being "on-time"; Hagestad & Neugarten, 1985) facilitates successful development. Taking advantage of favorable opportunities at the right time in life helps the individual to realize positive outcomes with high efficiency, while trying to attain life-course achievements against external constraints ("swimming against the stream") bears high costs for a person's resources. It must be acknowledged that recent sociostructural changes associated with the idea of disregulation or deinstituionalization of life course patterns (e.g., Held, 1986) have resulted in a broadening of appropriate age ranges for solving specific developmental tasks. An age-related rank order of developmental tasks, however, is still observable and requires the individual to activate adaptive goal management processes to facilitate successful development (e.g., Wrosch & Freund, 2001)

A third factor, influencing the opportunities for goal attainment across the life course has been described as age-normative conceptions about development (Heckhausen & Schulz, 1995). Age norms are socially shared conceptions about normative changes from birth to death (Hagestad & Neugarten, 1985). They can be understood as social constructions of reality and represent assumptions about the predictable life course and age-appropriate behaviors (Berger & Luckmann, 1966; Neugarten, 1969). Empirical evidence from different industrialized cultures has demonstrated a high consensus in age-normative conceptions about the age timing of major developmental tasks (e.g., marriage, starting a career; Neugarten, Moore, & Lowe, 1968; Plath, & Ikeda, 1975; Zepelin, Sills, & Heath, 1986–1987).

Normative conceptions can inform the individual about opportunities and risks concerning intended developmental outcomes, and thereby may function as social reference frames (Festinger, 1954) that provide typical models of possible behavior. An important aspect of age norms relates to the negative consequences for development if an individual violates the norms (Udry, 1982). For example, Settersten and Hagestad (1996a, 1996b) reported that individuals perceive negative developmental consequences of missing personal goals within the age-normative time frame, such as a negative impact on personal abilities, needs, and goals. Moreover, the pursuit of "off-time" developmental tasks is often characterized by a lack of age peers and an associated lack of social support and social models (Brim & Ryff, 1980; Hultsch & Plenoms, 1979; Schulz & Rau, 1985), thereby making the attainment of a goal more difficult and requiring a person to invest much more internal resources for compensating the missing sociostructural support (Heckhausen, 1990; Wrosch & Freund, 2001).

Given that age norms for many of the major developmental tasks are located in young adulthood and early midlife (e.g., starting a career, forming an intimate relationship, having children), normative conceptions of development may help younger individuals to optimize their own development by promoting investments of increased effort in protecting and accelerating intended developmental processes. Moreover, the internalization of age-normative conceptions may enhance the person's commitment to strive for intended goals within the normative time frame (Hagestad & Neugarten, 1985). In addition, normative conceptions are markers for developmental deadlines that indicate when individuals have to disengage from personal goals (Wrosch & Heckhausen, 2005). In the latter case, age norms can obstruct the attainment of a goal, if a person's age does not match the normative time frame. Other things being equal, it may be more difficult for a middle-aged or older person to go back to school and develop a professional career, as compared to a person in young adulthood. However, this latter function of normative conceptions can also be highly adaptive, given that it may prevent individuals from wasting their personal resources in futile developmental projects.

In sum, biological, societal, and age-normative factors produce an age-graded timetable for attaining developmental goals by contributing to age-specific patterns of opportunities and constraints. Whereas biological, societal, and age-normative factors facilitate the attainment of various goals in young and middle adulthood (e.g., having a career, building a family, being in good health), they can obstruct the attainment of many of these goals if people advance in age. An important implication of this argument is that people have to adjust their goal-related processes to the age-specific opportunities for goal attainment. As discussed in more detail later, processes that facilitate the attainment of personal goals are expected to be particularly adaptive in young adulthood, when individuals confront favorable opportunities for goal attainment. Among older adults, by contrast, processes associated with disengagement from unattainable goals and self-protection should become increasingly important to protect and focus remaining behavioral and motivational resources for essential goals of primary control in old age, and thus contribute to pathways of successful development.

AGE-RELATED MANAGEMENT OF PERSONAL GOALS:
THE LIFE-SPAN THEORY OF CONTROL

Individuals take an active part in shaping their own development (Lerner & Busch-Rossnagel, 1981). People select goals, strive for their attainment, and manage the consequences resulting from success and failure. A theoretical model that addresses the importance of goal-related processes from infancy to old age is the life-span theory of control (Heckhausen & Schulz, 1995; Schulz & Heckhausen, 1996). The underlying assumption of this theory is that the ability to produce behavior-event contingencies and thus to effectively change the environment is a fundamental building block of adaptive development in humans (Heckhausen, 2000).

To conceptualize different processes involved in the management of personal goals, the life-span theory of control distinguishes between *primary control* and *secondary control*. Primary control targets the external world and attempts to achieve effects in the immediate environment external to the individual. Secondary control, by contrast, targets the self and attempts to achieve changes directly within the individual (cf. Rothbaum, Weisz, & Snyder, 1982). The life-span theory of control has elaborated and specified the functions of secondary control over the past decade, and arrived at a definition of secondary control as processes involved in optimizing motivational resources, either during goal engagement (i.e., volitional self-commitment) or during goal disengagement (i.e., giving up goal, protecting motivational resources).

The life-span theory of control assumes that human behavior is less predictable, as compared to other species, because of the huge diversity of possible developmental pathways. A consequence of behavioral variability is that it generally enhances the likelihood of failure. This notion of variability in human behavior implies that the individual has to manage two basic requirements throughout the life span: *selectivity* and *failure compensation* (Heckhausen & Schulz, 1995; Schulz & Heckhausen, 1996). First, the variability of goals and behavior requires the individual to be selective. Individuals need to carefully select a certain developmental pathway. In addition, people need to ensure that chosen developmental tracks will be pursued successfully, which also implies that the motivational commitment toward selected goals needs to be high and resilient against conflicting action alternatives (Kuhl, 1983). The second key requirement results from individuals' vulnerability to failure experience. Greater behavioral variability enhances the likelihood of experiencing failure and thereby may result in negative emotional and motivational consequences. Therefore, individuals have to be able to compensate for the negative impact of failure in goal pursuits, and protect their motivational and behavioral resources for future action.

By integrating the distinction between primary and secondary control with the two fundamental requirements of human behavior (selectivity and failure compensation), the life-span theory of control generates a model of Optimization in Primary and Secondary control (OPS model; Heckhausen, 1999a; Heckhausen & Schulz, 1993) that specifies the nature and function of four different types of control strategies involved in successful regulation of development. As illustrated in Table 20.1, four types of control strategies are defined associated with engagement in, and disengagement from, attaining personal goals. First, *selective primary control* striving is de-

TABLE 20.1

**Optimization in Primary and Secondary Control (OPS) Model Specifies
Adaptive Control Processes for Goal Engagement and Disengagement**

Goal Engagement	Goal Disengagement
Selective primary control	Compensatory secondary control
• invests internal resources for goal attainment	• serves two functions:
Compensatory primary control	(1) disengagement from action goal
• recruits external resources for goal attainment	(2) protection of motivational resources after failure/loss
Selective secondary control	
• Focuses volitional resources for chosen goal	

fined as investments of internal resources. These strategies are aimed directly at the realization of chosen developmental goals and involve investments of time and effort, the development of relevant skills, or increased efforts when obstacles emerge. Second, *compensatory primary control* strategies are described as an active search for help and advice, the use of unusual means, and taking a detour for achieving a goal. Compensatory primary control strategies become particularly important in situations in which selective primary control is not sufficient to attain a goal. The active search for external support may secure the attainment of important goals when an individual's internal resources are depleted or the opportunities for goal attainment are expected to become less favorable. Third, *selective secondary control* strategies address individuals' volitional focusing on a chosen goal. This type of strategy comprises enhancement of the goal value, devaluation of competing goals, enhanced perception of control, or the imagination of positive consequences of goal attainment. Selective secondary control striving strengthens the individual commitment to chosen developmental tracks and therefore enhances the likelihood of persistence and goal attainment. Finally, *compensatory secondary control* includes strategies aimed at goal disengagement and the use of self-protective strategies (e.g., external attributions or downward social comparisons). This set of strategies helps individuals to cope with the negative consequences resulting from failure in two different ways. First, external attributions and social comparison processes can directly protect the self after the experience of failure and thereby safeguard a person's resources for future action. Second, disengagement from unattainable goals facilitates the reallocation of time and energy to other goals or life domains that involve more favorable opportunities for goal attainment. Domain-general and domain-specific scales addressing all four sets of control strategies have been developed and can be applied in a wide variety of research contexts (Heckhausen, Schulz, & Wrosch, 1998).

The OPS model assigns both primary control strategies and selective secondary control strategies to the facilitation of goal engagement. In contrast, goal disengagement is fostered by strategies of compensatory secondary control, which help individuals to distance themselves from a previous and now unattainable goal, and to protect themselves against the negative consequences of failure and control loss on motivational resources such as self-esteem, optimism, and hope for success.

It is important to note that the OPS model does not propose that the four types of control strategies are adaptive in and of themselves. The control processes serving goal engagement and goal disengagement are adaptive to the extent that the respective goal pursuit is conducive to optimized development (see detailed discussion of criteria of adaptive development in Heckhausen, 1999a). The criterion for optimized development, according to the life-span theory of control, is whether or not primary control is optimized across the life span (Heckhausen & Schulz, 1995, 1999; Schulz & Heckhausen, 1996). Optimized primary control is not necessarily served by primary control striving with regard to every possible goal. The developing individual needs to be selective and thus engage with appropriate goals and disengage from goals that are exceedingly difficult to obtain or bear consequences that impinge long-term control potential in other domains of life.

Obviously, such assessments about implications for optimal development are not made on the level of the control processes themselves. They are "blind" to such considerations. Instead, the OPS model asserts that optimization, a higher order regulatory process, is used to assess the feasibility of goal pursuits in terms of their fit with developmental opportunities to attain the respective goals. Specifically, assessment and evaluation processes involved in optimization address the opportunity-match of goal pursuits (i.e., the age-appropriateness in developmental contexts), the potential positive and negative implications of goal pursuits for long-term goals and for current goals in other domains (e.g., family-career conflict), and whether the goal pursuit in question is conducive (e.g., learning a skill that can be widely applied) or constraining (e.g., investing in a peak-performance dependent athletic career) to the diversity of developmental goals. Once a decision has been made on the optimization level to pursue a particular goal or to disengage from it, the appropriate primary and secondary control processes are activated. Thus, in any given situation of control opportunities and long-term and cross-domain contingencies, those control processes are adaptive that serve the long-term optimization of primary control. These adaptive control processes may be secondary or primary or they may serve goal disengagement or goal engagement. The critical question regarding adaptiveness of goal engagement, goal disengagement, primary, and secondary control is whether it serves primary control potential on the long run and across domains of functioning (see also Heckhausen, 1999a).

Schulz and Heckhausen (1996) postulated hypothetical life-span trajectories for primary and secondary control. A person's potential for primary control is expected to increase in young adulthood, to plateau in middle adulthood, and to decrease in old age. By contrast, secondary control is expected to start developing in early childhood, become more elaborated during childhood and adolescence, and to increase in use over adulthood and old age. These hypothetical life-span trajectories of primary and secondary control result from the influence of the previously discussed biological, societal, and age-normative factors involved in human development. Biologically based declines of functional capacities, for example, may set limits to an older adult's potential for primary control. As a consequence, older adults should compensate by an increased use of compensatory secondary control. In accordance with the proposed age-related change in the use of control strategies, substantial empirical evidence has demonstrated that the use of processes associated with compensatory secondary control generally increases with age (Brandtstädter & Renner, 1990; Brandtstädter, Wentura, & Greve, 1993; Heckhausen, Wrosch, & Fleeson, 2001; Wrosch & Heckhausen, 1999, 2002; Wrosch, Heckhausen, & Lachman, 2000). With respect to primary control, however, the empirical evidence is inconsistent. Cross-sectional studies have shown an age-graded increase (Wrosch et al., 2000), stability (Heckhausen, 1997), and decrease (Brandtstädter & Renner, 1990) in strategies associated with primary control.

Importantly, research has shown that there is much variance in the use of control strategies within different age groups, above and beyond the normative age-related changes in primary and secondary control. For example, although control striving aimed at attainment of personal goals can be expected to be generally high in young adulthood, not all young adults succeed in investing high levels of primary control in attaining age-normative tasks (e.g., Wrosch & Heckhausen, 1999). In a similar vein, research has demonstrated that some older adults use compensatory secondary control to a greater extent than others (Wrosch & Heckhausen, 1999; Wrosch et al., 2000). Given the age-specific functions of primary and secondary control, an implication of this argument is that individual differences in an age-adjusted use of primary and secondary control should strongly predict successful development. Although control strategies that support the attainment of personal goals can be expected to relate to indicators of successful development across the entire life span, they should be particularly closely associated with successful development among young adults. In contrast, the adaptive value of control strategies associated with goal disengagement and self-protection should increase if people advance in age.

INDIVIDUAL DIFFERENCES AND THE USE OF CONTROL STRATEGIES

To understand the processes of adaptive goal regulation across the life span more completely, it may be useful to discuss how individual variation in various personality characteristics can explain the utilization of control strategies that people choose to manage their goals. For example, other things being equal, people who are more conscientious may use primary control strategies more frequently than people who are not conscientious. In contrast, those who are more neurotic maybe more compelled to use secondary control strategies, but may also use them less effectively. The following sections explore how individual difference variables that are closely associated with the regulation of personal goals may influence the use of specific control strategies. These individual difference variables include people's general sense of control (e.g., perceived mastery and perceived constraints; see Lachman & Weaver, 1998), as well as people's typical reactions toward personal goals (e.g., goal management tendencies; see Wrosch, Scheier, Miller, Schulz, & Carver, 2003).

Control Beliefs

It is useful to clarify the distinction between control beliefs and control strategies. Beliefs about control are general characteristics of the self that influence the way people appraise and respond across situations. Thus, beliefs about control are expected to influence the implementation of control strategies such as primary and secondary control. For example, it is assumed that those people who have a greater sense of control should be more likely to implement strategies (e.g., planning) to take control of a given situation (Lachman & Firth, 2004). Thus, the utilization of the control strategies may vary depending on the particular control beliefs that are held by an individual.

Lachman and colleagues adopted a two-pronged conception of control beliefs, including the general control dimensions of personal mastery and perceived constraints (Lachman & Firth, 2004; Lachman & Weaver, 1998). This multidimensional framework incorporates the control concepts of perceived ability and contingency, as proposed by Bandura (1997) and Skinner (1996). Personal mastery refers to individuals' sense of efficacy or expectancies for competence and effectiveness in carrying out goals. Perceived constraints indicate to what extent people believe there are obstacles or factors beyond their control that interfere with reaching personal goals. High perceived control is best represented by those who have a high sense of mastery and low perceived constraints. These general control beliefs play a role in the implementation of strategies for goal pursuit.

The use of primary and secondary control strategies varies across persons and situations. The situational characteristics (e.g., unexpected obstacles) and contextual factors (e.g., age, timing in the life course) play an important role in the selection of control strategies (Heckhausen & Schulz, 1995). Any given situation provides opportunities and constraints. Such differences in opportunities for goal attainment should be reflected in an individual's perception of control. It is also important to consider generalized perceptions of personal control that are relatively stable and that the person brings to the situation to more fully understand the choice and use of control strategies. Stable personality characteristics and beliefs play a role in the appraisal of the situation and in the selection of strategies for goal attainment.

Little work has been done to investigate the predisposing characteristics of the person that may influence choice of control strategy. However, it is possible to link broader control dispositions with the use of specific control strategies. For example, people who generally have a higher sense of personal mastery should be more likely to implement goal engagement control strategies across situations, because the use of such strategies is consistent with their belief that they generally can be effective. Further, those who are generally confident in their abilities would be expected to show persistent behavior because of their self-conceptions that they possess the skills needed to reach the desired outcomes. Thus, general expectations and situational circumstances can operate interactively to influence the use of control strategies. Of course, an individual's perceptions and evaluations of the situational conditions are not always accurate. Thus, across time a variety of control strategies may be implemented for obtaining a given goal, depending on the feedback regarding the effectiveness of initial control strategies. Nevertheless, general beliefs about the self play an important role in determining behaviors such as persistence and flexibility in using control strategies. Control beliefs reflect general tendencies, which may be manifested in specific behaviors across situations. However, control beliefs may vary across domains of life, and these domain-specific beliefs may be more closely tied to behaviors in a given situation (Lachman & Weaver, 1998).

The expected relation between control beliefs and control strategies is illustrated in Table 20.2. Those who have a high sense of mastery are generally more likely to take goal-directed actions. By contrast, those who perceive high constraints would be less

TABLE 20.2

Predicted Relationship Between Generalized Control Beliefs (Personal Mastery and Perceived Constraints) and the Use of Primary and Secondary Control Strategies

	High Personal Mastery	*Low Personal Mastery*
High perceived constraints	Compensatory primary control strategies	Compensatory secondary control strategies
Low perceived constraints	Selective primary control strategies	Selective secondary control strategies

likely to implement any control strategies to realize an important goal, because they are less likely to see a connection between their efforts and outcomes. Those who have a high sense of mastery and low perceived constraints, the most favorable combination of beliefs, would be most likely to implement selective primary control strategies. This goal-directed behavior would be characterized by persistence and increased effort in the face of obstacles. Those who have high sense of mastery but also a relatively high sense of constraints would be most likely to use compensatory primary control strategies. Although they believe in their own abilities, they are likely to need external supports because of the constraints they foresee. For those with low perceived mastery, secondary control strategies would be the likely approach. Those who have a low sense of mastery and high levels of perceived constraints would be likely to implement compensatory secondary control strategies. They are likely to move to goal disengagement and it would be adaptive to use self-protective strategies, such as blaming external constraints that are not under their control. For those with low mastery and low perceived constraints or with high mastery and high perceived constraints, selective secondary control strategies would be expected. Given their low mastery, they are at risk for not achieving desired goals, but given the favorable low level of constraints they may be able to persist and reach their goals. These predicted associations are based primarily on a conceptual understanding of the links between control beliefs and goal-directed behaviors (Lachman, Ziff, & Spiro, 1994). Empirical work is needed to investigate and test these proposed relations.

The degree of fit between control beliefs and strategies is likely to have an impact on adjustment and adaptation. Those who have higher personal mastery are likely to be more satisfied if they are able to use primary control strategies to reach goals, and would be less content if the social context would constrain their options to compensatory secondary control strategies. The use of secondary control strategies would be compatible with beliefs regarding high-perceived constraints. Generally, those who believe they are in control of their lives have higher levels of well-being. Those who do not believe they have a great deal of control may be able to preserve well-being by using secondary control strategies. Goal management can be adaptive or maladaptive as a function of the fit between a person's general control beliefs and the use of control strategies. For those who have a high sense of mastery, such beliefs would be sustained in response to successful implementation of goal strategies. For those who believe they have high constraints, effective control strategies might serve to boost the sense of mastery or lower the perceived constraints.

Goal Management Tendencies

It has been suggested that people differ more generally in their management of personal goals, irrespective of the nature of the specific goals encountered. For example, some people may generally be more persistent in the pursuit of personal goals than others. Moreover, it may be very difficult for some people to let go of a previously important goal that has become unattainable, whereas other people have an easier time with goal disengagement and finding new pursuits of value. Such individual differences in goal management tendencies are reflected in constructs such as general goal disengagement and goal reengagement tendencies (Wrosch & Scheier, 2003; Wrosch, Scheier, Carver, & Schulz, 2003; Wrosch, Scheier, Miller, Schulz, & Carver, 2003) or tenacious goal pursuit and flexible goal adjustment (Brandtstädter & Renner, 1990).

Individual variation in general goal management tendencies may partly explain the utilization of control strategies that people chose to manage specific personal goals. For example, people who are generally more tenacious should be more likely to invest in primary control and selective secondary control strategies when they do not make enough progress toward a specific desired goal than people who are less tenacious. In addition, people who generally have an easier time with adjusting unattainable goals (e.g., those high in goal disengagement and goal reengagement tendencies) would be particularly likely to reduce their primary control striving when a valuable goal has become unattainable. These individuals should also be more likely to increase the use of compensatory secondary control strategies when they confront a specific unattainable goal. Moreover, people who generally have an easier time with finding and pursuing new goals (e.g., those high on goal reengagement) should be more likely to increase their levels of primary control striving toward new or alternative goals, when they have to stop pursuing an important goal.

More generally speaking, individual differences in general goal management tendencies may influence the choice of specific control strategies and thereby may contribute to pathways of successful development. Interestingly, there has been some research examining the relation between primary and secondary control strategies and Brandtstädter's constructs of tenacious goal pursuit and flexible goal adjustment that support some of the previously mentioned ideas. Peng (1993) found that endorsement of primary control strategies was correlated with tenacious goal pursuit and (compensatory) secondary control was correlated with flexible goal adjustment, as predicted. Moreover, secondary control had a negative correlation with tenacious goal pursuit, suggesting those who are tenacious are less likely to use secondary control. Primary control was also positively related to flexible goal adjustment, suggesting that the adjustment of personal goals may require people to maintain certain levels of primary control (possibly invested toward new or alternative goals). However, more research is needed to examine the relations between general individual differences in goal management tendencies and the use of specific control strategies. In addition, there is a need to better understand how these processes can explain pathways of successful development across the adult life span.

EMPIRICAL EVIDENCE: THE ADAPTIVE VALUE
OF PRIMARY AND SECONDARY CONTROL

As discussed earlier, the life-span theory of control proposes that individuals adjust their goal-related behaviors (in terms of primary and secondary control) to the age-related opportunities and constraints for goal attainment. In addition, the theory predicts that individual differences in an age-adjusted use of control strategies are associated with indicators of successful development. These two propositions of the life-span theory of control have been tested in several studies over the past years (Heckhausen, 2002a; Heckhausen, Wrosch, & Fleeson, 2001; Wrosch & Heckhausen, 1999, 2002; Wrosch et al., 2000; Wrosch, Schulz, & Heckhausen, 2002). These studies cover a wide range of different phenomena and examine groups of people with different opportunities for goal attainment, cultural variation, and fine-grained longitudinal changes in control behavior.

Comparing Groups of People with Different Opportunities for Goal Attainment

Wrosch and Heckhausen (1999) addressed the role played by goal-related process in the adaptation to a partnership separation. They examined the age-related use and predictive value of control strategies in young and late midlife adults who recently had experienced a partnership separation. It is important to note that a person's age plays an important role in realizing intimate relationships: Based on an age-graded partnership market, young adults usually face more favorable opportunities to realize a new partnership than older adults (Braun & Proebsting, 1986). It was predicted that control strategies aimed at attaining partnership goals are particularly adaptive in younger separated individuals. In contrast, compensatory secondary control may preserve older separated people's motivational and emotional resources and facilitate the adjustment of unattainable partnership goals.

The results confirmed that younger, as compared with older, separated adults reported higher levels of selective primary and selective secondary control strategies. In contrast, older separated persons reported higher levels of compensatory secondary control than did younger separated adults. A comparable pattern of result was shown for the nomination of partnership goals (measured with an open-response format questionnaire) and biases in information processing (measured with an incidental memory paradigm). Older, as compared to younger, separated adults reported fewer partnership goals and enhanced recall of negative as compared to positive partnership aspects. In addition, a longitudinal follow-up of the study demonstrated that an age-adjusted use of compensatory secondary control predicted change in positive affect over time (Wrosch & Heckhausen, 1999). Older separated people reported improved positive affect if they used high levels of compensatory secondary control. In contrast, younger separated adults suffered decline in positive affect if they used high levels of compensatory secondary control.

Conceptually similar results have been reported in a study examining the role played by control strategies in managing childbearing goals. Heckhausen, Wrosch, and Fleeson (2001) studied groups of childless women who have and have not passed the biological clock-related deadline for childbearing, based on their chronological age. The main hypothesis of the study was that childless women who have not yet passed the deadline would use control strategies aimed at having their own children. In contrast, women who have passed the biological clock were expected to invest in compensatory secondary control. Moreover, it was expected that an age-adjusted use of control strategies is related to women's subjective well-being.

The results of the study confirmed that women's use of control strategies depend on their age-related status according to having or not having passed the biological clock deadline. Women who had not passed the deadline for having their own children reported higher levels of selective primary, selective secondary, and compensatory primary control than women who had already passed the biological deadline for childbearing. In contrast, women who had passed the deadline reported particularly high levels of compensatory secondary control. In addition, the study showed that, among postdeadline women, those who did not disengage from the goal of having their own children reported more depressive symptoms.

Another study demonstrated the age-related importance of control strategies in a U.S. national probability sample called midlife in the US (MIDUS; see Wrosch et al., 2000). The authors examined the use and predictive value of primary and secondary control strategies for managing health and financial stress. The study assessed generic versions of two prototypical control strategies: persistence in goal striving and positive reappraisals (Peng, 1993). Persistence in goal striving is a core component of selective primary control striving. Positive reappraisals, by contrast, are a compensatory secondary control strategy aimed at protecting a person's motivational and emotional resources after experiencing failure and developmental losses.

The results confirmed age-differential associations between persistence in goal striving and positive reappraisals with subjective well-being. Among young adults, persistence in goal striving showed a significantly stronger effect on subjective well-being than among older adults. In contrast, positive reappraisals as compared with persistence were more strongly associated with subjective well-being in middle-aged and older adults. In addition, the study demonstrated that this pattern of results was more pronounced among participants who confronted problems that involve age-graded opportunities for goal attainment (e.g., chronic health stress in old age, financial problems after retirement; Wrosch et al., 2000).

There will be an opportunity to examine 10-year longitudinal changes in control strategies as adults from the MIDUS sample (Brim, Ryff, & Kessler, 2004) make the transition from midlife into old age and from young adulthood into midlife. Follow-up data collection for the MIDUS II survey was begun in January 2004, and will include a more extensive measure based on Peng's (1993) original items and the OPS scales (Heckhausen et al., 1998). Given the multidisciplinary nature of the MIDUS survey, it will be possible to examine changes in control strategies in relation to changes in life circumstances regarding health, work, social relationships, and psychological well-being.

Wrosch and Heckhausen (2002) also examined the role of control attributions in the management of life regrets across adulthood. Attributions of negative past events can serve different functions, such as protecting the self and supporting goal attainment. For example, research has shown that external attributions may protect the self in uncontrollable situations (Abramson, Seligman, & Teasdale, 1978) and thus may represent a compensatory secondary control strategy. In controllable situations, by contrast, high levels of internal control attributions have been shown to predict successful adjustment (Brown & Siegel, 1988; Janoff-Bulman, 1979, 1982). Given that people can learn from their failure experiences, internal control attributions may promote a person's primary control striving. Considering the differential functions of control attributions, it was expected that low levels of internal control attributions are associated with low regret intensity among older adults, whereas high levels of internal control attributions should predict low levels of regret intensity among young adults.

The results of the study showed that older adults reported significantly lower levels of internal control attributions with respect to their most severe life regret than young adults did, indicating that people generally adjust their control perceptions to the opportunities and constraints involved in undoing their life regrets (Wrosch & Heckhausen, 2002). Moreover, attributions of control predicted the intensity of regret, dependent on a person's age. More specifically, low levels of internal control attributions predicted low levels of regret intensity, but only among older adults. In contrast, high levels of internal control attributions were associated with low levels of regret only among young adults.

Another study examined associations between control strategies and depressive symptomatology among elderly individuals who confronted different types of health problems (Wrosch, Schulz, & Heckhausen, 2002, 2004). This study adds an important aspect to the previously discussed research, because it applies the theoretical principles of the life-span theory of control to people of similar age. Indeed, it can be argued that there is substantial variance with respect to people's opportunities for the attainment of different goals within a certain age group (above and beyond the general life course-related changes in opportunities and constraints for goal attainment). A prototypical example of this phenomenon relates to the management of acute physical health problems (e.g., pain or difficulty breathing) and functional health problems (e.g., restrictions in basic and functional activities of daily living) in the elderly. The adaptive management of both types of health stresses is an important task for elderly individuals, given that acute physical symptoms and functional health problems both may increase an older person's risk of experiencing depressive symptomatology (Williamson, Shaffer, & Parmelee, 2000). With respect to an adaptive management of health problems in the elderly, however, an important implication can be drawn from the distinction between these two types of health stresses. Functional disabilities are often relatively intractable and an older person's active efforts to overcome them may not result in positive outcomes. In contrast, in many cases, the acute physical symptoms associated with chronic disease and disability (e.g., pain) are potentially controllable. Thus, active efforts to counteract acute physical symptoms are likely to alleviate disease symptoms and reduce the negative emotional consequences. Consequently, the use of control strategies that facilitate the attainment of personal goals (primary control and selective secondary control) should be associated with reduced depression, but only among elderly individuals who confront high levels of acute physical symptoms.

To test this hypothesis, Wrosch, Schulz, and Heckhausen (2002) examined the associations between different types of health stresses, depression, and control strategies in a sample of elderly individuals. In support of the hypotheses, the findings demonstrated that control strategies aimed at attaining health goals were associated with low levels of depressive symptoms, but only among older adults who reported high levels of acute physical symptoms. Older adults who experienced acute physical symptoms and did not use control strategies that support the attainment of health goals experienced elevated levels of depression. In addition, a longitudinal follow-up showed that high levels of health engagement control strategies were associated with reduced depression over time, and high levels of depressive symptoms resulted in reduced active attempts to attain important health goals. These results support the theoretical claim that control strategies aimed at attaining health goals can also promote successful development in the elderly, if older individuals face favorable opportunities to overcome a specific health problem. Moreover, the findings indicate that negative emotional consequences of maladaptive control striving can further compromise a person's motivational resources for future action. The psychological distress resulting from maladaptive goal management can result in a reduced motivation to realize important and attainable goals.

Cultural Variation

Control strategies have also been examined in different cultural settings. Peng (1993) examined cultural and age differences in primary and secondary control associated with work and family goals in an age-heterogeneous study of Americans and Chinese Americans. Although Peng (1993) expected that primary control would be lower for older adults than for the young, this was not supported. Primary control remained relatively high for both Americans and Chinese Americans across the age span. This is consistent with more recent work, which shows that across the life span primary control striving is the mode of choice and does not wane in old age (Heckhausen, 1997; Heckhausen & Schulz, 1995). As predicted, secondary control significantly increased with age for both Americans and Chinese Americans. There was an interesting parallel with the age patterns for control beliefs. The use of secondary control strategies showed increases with age, similar to the patterns found for perceived constraints. Personal mastery is usually found to remain stable or decrease slightly with age, as is true for primary control strategies.

It was also expected that Americans would show higher primary control and lower secondary control than Chinese Americans, and this was confirmed (Peng, 1993). Interestingly, the longer the Chinese Americans had lived in the United States, the lower their secondary control strategies, even when age was controlled, suggesting there was some cultural assimilation over time. According to Peng (1993), for Americans, primary control was positively associated with life satisfaction and well-being, as expected. Secondary control was positively related to personal growth and negatively to autonomy. For Chinese Americans, primary control was also positively related to well-being. However, secondary control was not related, contrary to predictions. This may reflect the fact that the measures of well-being were largely based on Western cultural ideals, emphasizing individualism rather than collectivism.

Tracking Control Behavior Across Opportunity Changes in Longitudinal Studies

A final set of studies discussed here has been conducted by a number of research groups that have adopted the life-span theory of control to study ongoing adaptations in primary and secondary control striving across longitudinal spans that include significant shifts in opportunities for primary control. Such longitudinal studies are particularly fruitful because they hold the potential to reveal the system of developmental optimization at work. Longitudinal studies, especially when they involve many and densely spaced assessments of goal endorsement and control strategies, can provide an online, real-time view of the adjustments of control processes to increases or losses of primary control potential in general (e.g., regarding general health and fitness) or in specific goal domains (e.g., regarding certain career goals).

A first example of these longitudinal studies of developmental regulation is the cross-national research program on the transition from school to work (Heckhausen, 1999b, 2002b, 2003b; Heckhausen & Farruggia, 2003; Heckhausen, Haase, & Poulin, 2003; Heckhausen, Nagy, Tomasik, Haase, & Köller, 2002; Heckhausen & Tomasik, 2002). In industrialized societies, the transition from school to work is a period of instability with heightened potential for downward as well as upward mobility, thus bearing significant consequences for adult life. However, different societies, their vocational systems and labor markets, provide more or less institutionalized pathways for this transition. Hamilton (1990) pointed out that Germany and the United States may be at extreme ends on this dimension. The German vocational system channels adolescents through apprenticeships, which provide entry into vocational career tracks for adult employment. In contrast, entry into work life in the United States is much a function of regional and seasonal opportunity and individual choice. Hamilton (1994) coined the terms *transparency* and *permeability* to reflect these fundamental differences in labor markets of different countries. Transparency is high in a more codified vocational system as in Germany and low in a more flexible system as in the United States. At the same time, systems such as the German apprenticeship institution typically come with low permeability once a vocational track has been chosen, whereas the more flexible system in the United States allows for less cumbersome and less costly career changes later on in adulthood.

For adolescents approaching the transition from school to work, these contrasting characteristics of the vocational systems in the two countries make for different challenges to their capacities of developmental regulation. Whereas adolescents in the United States have to navigate a period of "floundering" with all its risk and potential (Hamilton, 1990), German adolescents are confronted with the challenge of choosing and securing an apprenticeship position during a short period of time in 10th grade, which will determine the employment prospects for their entire adult life. Much of the challenge for the German adolescents that approach the end of their school career in 10th grade of the middle tier school (i.e., Realschule) is to shift to an urgent goal engagement during the sensitive period of applying for apprenticeships, that is, during 10th grade and particularly during the second half of 10th grade. The other aspect of challenge in this developmental transition for the German adolescents is to calibrate their choice of a vocational training such as to optimize their developmental resources. Overshooting their potential, especially with regard to school performance, would bear the risk of not securing any apprenticeship position at the time of graduation. On the other hand, underaspiring and thus not using their educational capital (i.e., favorable school grades) would have negative consequences for the long-term career.

An ongoing longitudinal study in Berlin investigated 768 seniors in four middle-tier schools (Realschulen) and is following them for 4 years after graduation (Heckhausen, 1999b). In the German system, the developmental task of entering the workforce is scaffolded by the institution of apprenticeship, which channels youth into vocational career paths and provides them with certificates of vocational qualifications. However, this has become a considerable challenge. Due to globalization and economic strain associated with German reunification, apprenticeship positions have become hard to get, so that about 40% of a given cohort end up with no apprenticeship position when they graduate from school. Thus, in a situation of scarce supply, German adolescents face the challenge of competing for an apprenticeship, which will shape the career and financial prospects for their entire future life. The acuteness of this challenge is heightened by the implicit yet inescapable deadline for starting an apprenticeship. Blossfeld (1990) demonstrated that German adolescents who do not start vocational training within 2 years of graduating from school will not stand a significant chance of ever receiving vocational training, and thus will be doomed to unskilled work for their entire working life. Thus, the pressing task for these adolescents is one of choosing and securing an apprenticeship position during a short period of time in 10th grade, the year before graduating from school. A particularly tricky aspect of this "choosing" and "securing" is to calibrate individuals' aspirations such that their potential for a well-paying vocation is realized, yet overshooting their potential is avoided in order to not risk failure to attain an apprenticeship altogether. Thus, German adolescents have to navigate the Scylla and Charybdis of under- and overaspirations.

Longitudinal follow-ups and analyses in this study are still ongoing. A first set of findings (Heckhausen & Tomasik, 2002) indicates that during the urgent phase adolescents express intense goal engagement for finding an apprenticeship. However, the control strategies involved in goal engagement also showed interindividual variation, which in turn predicted the transition outcome. Adolescents reporting more intense selective primary control striving were more likely to obtain an apprenticeship (Heckhausen, Haase, & Poulin, 2003). Moreover, individual differences in selective secondary control, that is, the strategies aimed at volitional goal commitment (e.g., avoid distractions, enhance optimism about goal attainment), moderated the effect of selective primary control (Haase, 2003).

Regarding the calibration of vocational aspirations, it was found that the adolescents adjusted their "dream job" upwardly and downwardly towards a closer match with the apprenticeships they are considering. This process has been confirmed for three groups of adolescents, those with dream jobs overshooting the social prestige of jobs they expressed a preference to apply for, those with dream jobs similar in prestige than their preference, and those with dream jobs that had less social prestige than their preferred job. These results show that not only those overshooting social prestige in their dream jobs adjusted downwardly, but those who underaspired in their dream jobs upgraded them to more prestigious jobs. This implies that a process of optimization of resource-based vocational striving is underway in this transition from school to work.

In sum, when the challenge of the transition into work life is clear, such as in the case of the German apprenticeship system, adolescents appear to rise to the occasion. They display intense goal engagement with getting an apprenticeship. They also apply for apprenticeships at a level of social prestige that matches their school performance, thus demonstrating adaptive calibration of their vocational aspirations. Moreover, remarkable stability of individual differences in primary control striving was found. Primary control striving for an apprenticeship measured at the beginning of 10th grade, predicts application frequency across grade 10, and also predicts primary control striving in vocational training itself 1 year and 2 years later (Heckhausen, Nagy, Tomasik, Haase, & Köller, 2002). However, those adolescents with dispositionally high selective primary control striving appear to hold an advantage not just for finding an apprenticeship but also for other important outcomes (e.g., investing effort in their vocational training) of the school-to-work transition. In addition, volitional self-regulation (i.e., selective secondary control) played a key role as a moderator of the effectiveness of primary control striving for attaining an apprenticeship.

Primary and secondary control components of goal engagement can be expected to play an even greater role as behavioral and motivational resources of the individual when the societal conditions provide less guidance and support to youth in the transition to work life, as is the case in the United States. A longitudinal study involving more than 1,000 high school graduates from the Los Angeles Unified School District is under way. Processes of goal engagement and goal disengagement with educational and vocational goals will be investigated in all the subgroups of young adults, those who are attending community (junior) colleges, those attending 4-year colleges, and those who work without attending further educational institutions. Trajectories of transition into postsecondary education and work will be identified and related to individual resources in terms of goal aspirations and control striving, as well as social support. Moreover, it will be possible to investigate to what extent adaptive patterns of control striving hold up across ethnic and social differences in this very diverse sample of Los Angeles youth.

Another domain to investigate changes in control behavior across time and across shifting opportunities is the domain of health-related behavior. A number of research teams has adopted the OPS model to study such changes. For example, Horowitz and her colleagues at the Lighthouse Institute in New York are studying control strategies in macular degeneration patients experiencing gradually declining vision. A similar longitudinal study is being conducted by Wahl and his colleagues in Heidelberg, Germany. Pinquart and Silbereisen (2002) addressed the engagement with and disengagement from treatment decisions and related changes in life goals in elderly cancer patients in Jena, Germany. For these health-related goal engagements and disengagements, a general model of sequential retreat and advancement with hierarchically organized health goals is being developed to conceptualize adaptive and maladaptive patterns of engagement and control strategies (Heckhausen, 2003a).

CONCLUSIONS

This chapter addressed the importance of goal-related personality processes for successful development across the life span. It argued that biological, societal, and age-normative factors contribute to an age-graded structure of opportunities for attaining personal goals. Based on the life-span theory of control, it was proposed that successful development requires individuals to adjust their goal-related processes (in terms of primary and secondary control strategies) to their opportunities for goal attainment. In addition, it discussed the relations between some individual difference variables and the use of specific control strategies. Overall, the reviewed literature supports the argument that control strategies aimed at attaining personal goals are particularly adaptive when (younger) adults face favorable opportunities for goal attainment. In contrast, strategies associated with disengagement and self-protection (compensatory secondary control) were shown to support pathways of successful development when (older) adults confront reduced opportunities for attaining personal goals. Together, these findings suggest that age is an important moderating context of adaptive personality functioning. Future research should therefore continue examining the age-specific functions of goal-related personality processes to further illuminate pathways to successful development across the adult life span.

ACKNOWLEDGMENTS

Preparation of this chapter was supported in part by grants from Canadian Institutes of Health Research (CW), NIA AG17920 (MEL) and AG20166 (MEL), Social Sciences and Humanities Research Council of Canada (CW), and "Fonds de la recherche sur la société et la culture, Québec." (CW).

REFERENCES

Abramson, L. Y., Seligman, M. E. P., & Teasdale, J. D. (1978). Learned helplessness in humans: Critique and reformulation. *Journal of Abnormal Psychology, 87,* 49-74.

Baltes, P. B. (1987). Theoretical propositions of life-span developmental psychology: On the dynamics between growth and decline. *Developmental Psychology, 23,* 611–626.

Bandura, A. (1997). *Self-efficacy: The exercise of control.* New York: Freeman.

Baumeister, R. F., & Scher, S. J. (1988). Self-defeating behavior patterns among normal individuals: Review and analysis of common self-destructive strategies. *Psychological Bulletin, 104,* 3–22.

Berger, P. L., & Luckmann, T. (1966). *The social construction of reality.* New York: Doubleday.

Blossfeld, H.-P. (1990). Changes in educational careers in the Federal Republic of Germany. *Sociology of Education, 63,* 165–177.

Brandtstädter, J., & Renner, G. (1990). Tenacious goal pursuit and flexible goal adjustment: Explication and age-related analysis of assimilative and accommodative strategies of coping. *Psychology and Aging, 5,* 58–67.

Brandtstädter, J., Wentura, D., & Greve, W. (1993). Adaptive resources of the aging self: Outlines of an emergent perspective. *International Journal of Behavioral Development, 16,* 323–349.

Braun, W., & Proebsting, H. (1986). Heiratstafeln verwitweter Deutscher 1979/82 und geschiedener Deutscher 1980/83 [Marriage tables of divorced (1980/83) and widowed Germans (1979/82)]. *Wirtschaft und Statistik,* 107–112.

Brim, O. G., & Ryff, C. D. (1980). On the properties of life events. In P. B. Baltes & O. G. Brim, Jr. (Eds.), *Life-span development and behavior* (Vol. 3, pp. 367–388). New York: Academic Press.

Brim, O. G., Ryff, C. D., & Kessler, R. (Eds.). (2004). *How healthy are we? A national study of well-being at midlife.* Chicago: University of Chicago Press.

Brockner, J. (1992). The escalation of commitment to a failing course of action: Toward theoretical progress. *Academy of Management Review, 17,* 39–61.

Brown, J. D., & Siegel, J. M. (1988). Attributions for negative life events and depression: The role of perceived control. *Journal of Personality and Social Psychology, 54,* 316–322.

Carver, C. S., & Scheier, M. F. (1990). Origins and functions of positive and negative affect: A control-process view. *Psychological Review, 97,* 19–35.

418 WROSCH, HECKHAUSEN, LACHMAN

Carver, C. S., & Scheier, M. F. (1998). On the self-regulation of behavior. New York: Cambridge University Press.
Carver, C. S., Pozo, C., Harris, S. D., Noriega, V., Scheier, M. F., Robinson, D. S., Ketchman, A. S., Moffat, F. L., & Clark, K. C. (1993). How coping mediates the effect of optimism on distress: A study of women with early stage breast cancer. Journal of Personality and Social Psychology, 65, 375–390.
Erikson, E. H. (1968). Identity: Youth and crisis. New York: Norton.
Festinger, L. (1954). A theory of social comparison processes. Human Relations, 7, 117–140.
Folkman, S., & Lazarus, R. S. (1980). An analysis of coping in a middle-aged community sample. Journal of Health and Social Behavior, 21, 219–239.
Haase, C. (2003). Urgent goal striving in the transition from school to vocational education. Unpublished master's thesis, University of Jena, Germany.
Hagestad, G. O. (1990). Social perspectives on the life course. In R. Binstock & L. George (Eds.), Handbook of aging and the social sciences (3rd. ed., pp. 151–168). New York: Academic Press.
Hagestad, G. O., & Neugarten, B. L. (1985). Age and the life course. In R. H. Binstock & E. Shanas (Eds.), Handbook of aging and the social sciences (pp. 35–61). New York: Van Nostrand Reinhold.
Hamilton, S. F. (1990). Apprenticeship for adulthood. New York: The Free Press.
Hamilton, S. F. (1994). Employment prospects as motivation for school achievement: Links and gaps between school and work in seven countries. In R. K. Silbereisen & E. Todt (Eds.), Adolescence in context: The interplay of family, school, peers, and work in adjustment (pp. 267–303). New York: Springer.
Havighurst, R. J. (1967). Developmental tasks and education. New York: McKay.
Heckhausen, J. (1990). Erwerb und Funktion normativer Vorstellungen über den Lebenslauf: Ein entwicklungspsychologischer Beitrag zur sozio-psychischen Konstruktion von Biographien [Acquisition and function of normative conceptions about the life course: A developmental psychology approach to the socio-psychological construction of biographies]. Kölner Zeitschrift für Soziologie und Sozialpsychologie, 31, 351–373.
Heckhausen, J. (1997). Developmental regulation across adulthood: Primary and secondary control of age-related challenges. Developmental Psychology, 33, 176–187.
Heckhausen, J. (1999a). Developmental regulation in adulthood. New York: Cambridge University Press.
Heckhausen, J. (1999b). Entwicklungsregulation beim Übergang von der schulischen in die berufliche Ausbildung oder gymnasiale Oberstufe: Anforderungsabhängige Veränderungen im primären und sekundären Kontrollstreben [Developmental regulation in the transition from school-to-work or higher education: Changes in primary and secondary control striving as a function of developmental challenge]. Research proposal funded by the German Research Foundation. Berlin: Max Planck Institute for Human Development.
Heckhausen, J. (2000). Evolutionary perspectives on human motivation. In J. Heckhausen & P. Boyer (Eds.), Evolutionary psychology: Potential and limits of a Darwinian framework for the behavioral sciences [Special Issue]. American Behavioral Scientist, 43, 1015–1029.
Heckhausen, J. (2002a). Developmental regulation of life-course transitions: A control theory approach. In L. Pulkkinen & A. Caspi (Eds.), Paths to successful development: Personality in the life course (pp. 257–280). Cambridge, England: Cambridge University Press.
Heckhausen, J. (2002b). Transition from school-to-work: Societal opportunities and the potential for individual agency. Journal of Vocational Behavior, 60, 173–177.
Heckhausen, J. (2003a, May/June). The life-span theory of control as a paradigm to study illness and disability in old age. Paper presented at the UC/APA Conference on Health Psychology and Aging, Lake Arrowhead, California.
Heckhausen, J. (2003b). School-to-work transition in a multi-ethnic sample. Research proposal, University of California, Irvine.
Heckhausen, J., & Farruggia, S. P. (2003). Developmental regulation across the life span: A control-theory approach and implications for secondary education. In: L. Smith & C. Rogers, & P.

Tomlinson (Eds.), *Development and motivation: Joint perspectives*. British Journal of Educational Psychology, Monograph Series II: Psychological Aspects of Education—Current Trends. Leicester: British Psychological Society.

Heckhausen, J., Haase, C., & Poulin, M. (2003, April). *School-to-work transition in German adolescents: Findings from a longitudinal study*. Colloquium presentation, Department for Psychology and Social Behavior, University of California, Irvine.

Heckhausen, J., Nagy, G., Tomasik, M., Haase, C. M. , & Köller, O. (2002, June). *Motivation and control in the transition from school to work*. Paper presented at the meeting of the American Psychological Society, New Orleans.

Heckhausen, J., & Schulz, R. (1993). Optimization by selection and compensation: Balancing primary and secondary control in life-span development. *International Journal of Behavioral Development, 16*, 287–303.

Heckhausen, J., & Schulz, R. (1995). A life-span theory of control. *Psychological Review, 102*, 284–304.

Heckhausen, J., & Schulz, R. (1999). The primacy of primary control is a human universal: A reply to Gould's critique of the Life-Span Theory of Control. *Psychological Review, 106*(3), 605–609.

Heckhausen, J., Schulz, R., & Wrosch, C. (1998). *Developmental regulation in adulthood: Optimization in primary and secondary control—a multiscale questionnaire*. Technical Report, Max Planck Institute for Human Development and Education, Berlin.

Heckhausen, J., & Tomasik, M. (2002). Get an apprenticeship before school is out: How German adolescents adjust vocational aspirations when getting close to a developmental deadline. *Journal of Vocational Behavior, 60*, 199–219.

Heckhausen, J., Wrosch, C., & Fleeson, W. (2001). Developmental regulation before and after a developmental deadline: The sample case of "biological clock" for childbearing. *Psychology and Aging, 16*, 400–413.

Held, T. (1986). Institutionalization and deinstitutionalization of the life course. *Human Development, 29*, 157–162.

Hultsch, D. F., & Plemons, J. K. (1979). Life events and life-span development. In P. B. Baltes & O. G. Brim, Jr. (Eds.), *Life-span development and behavior* (Vol. 2, pp. 1–37). New York: Academic Press.

Janoff-Bulman, R. (1979). Characterological versus behavioral self-blame: Inquiries into depression and rape. *Journal of Personality and Social Psychology, 37*, 1798–1809.

Janoff-Bulman, R. (1982). Esteem and control bases of blame: "Adaptive" strategies for victims versus observers. *Journal of Personality, 50*, 180–192.

Kliegl, R., Smith, J., & Baltes, P. B. (1989). Testing-the-limits and the study of age differences in cognitive plasticity of a mnemonic skill. *Developmental Psychology, 25*, 247–256.

Kuhl, J. (1983). *Motivation, Konflikt und Handlungskontrolle* [Motivation, conflict, and action control]. Berlin: Springer.

Lachman, M. E., & Firth, K. P. (2004). The adaptive value of feeling in control during midlife. In O. G. Brim, C. D. Ryff, & R. Kessler (Eds.), *How healthy are we?: A national study of well-being at midlife* (pp. 320–349) . Chicago: University of Chicago Press.

Lachman, M. E., & Weaver, S. L. (1998). Sociodemographic variations in the sense of control by domain: Findings from the MacArthur Studies of Midlife. *Psychology and Aging, 13*, 553–562.

Lachman, M. E., Ziff, M. A., & Spiro, A. (1994). Maintaining a sense of control in later life. In R. Abeles, H. Gift, & M. Ory (Eds.), *Aging and quality of life* (pp. 116–132). New York: Sage.

Lerner, R. M., & Busch-Rossnagel, A. (Eds.). (1981). *Individuals as producers of their development: A life-span perspective*. New York: Academic Press.

Nesse, R. M. (2000). Is depression an adaptation? *Archives of General Psychiatry, 57*, 14–20.

Neugarten, B. L. (1969). Time, age, and the life cycle. *American Journal of Psychiatry, 136*, 887–894.

Neugarten, B. L., Moore J. W., & Lowe, J. C. (1968). Age norms, age constraints, and adult socialization. In B. L. Neugarten (Ed.), *Middle age and aging* (pp. 22– 28). Chicago: University of Chicago Press.

Peng, Y. (1993). *Primary and secondary control in American and Chinese American adults: Cross-cultural and life-span developmental perspectives*. Unpublished doctoral dissertation, Brandeis University, Waltham, MA.

Pinquart, M., & Silbereisen, R. K. (2002, November). *Cancer patients' control strategies: Associations with age, course of therapy, and subjective well-being*. Paper presented at the 55th annual meeting of the Gerontological Society of America, Boston.

Plath, D. W., & Ikeda, K. (1975). After coming of age: Adult awareness of age norms. In T. R. Williams (Ed.), *Socialization and communication in primary groups* (pp. 107–123). The Hague: Mouton.

Rothbaum, F., Weisz, J. R., & Snyder, S. S. (1982). Changing the world and changing the self: A two-process model of perceived control. *Journal of Personality and Social Psychology, 42*, 5–37.

Ryff, C. D. (1989). Happiness is everything, or is it? Explorations on the meaning of psychological well-being. *Journal of Personality and Social Psychology, 57*, 1069–1081.

Schulz, R., & Heckhausen J. (1996). A life span model of successful aging. *American Psychologist, 51*, 702–714.

Schulz, R., & Rau, M. T. (1985). Social support through the life course. In S. Cohen & L. Syme (Eds.), *Social support and health* (pp. 129–149). New York: Academic Press.

Settersten, R. A., & Hagestad, G. O. (1996a). What's the latest? Cultural age deadlines for family transitions. *The Gerontologist, 36*, 178–188.

Settersten, R. A., & Hagestad, G. O. (1996b). What's the latest? II. Cultural age deadlines for educational and work transitions. *The Gerontologist, 36*, 602–613.

Skinner, E. A. (1996). A guide to constructs of control. *Journal of Personality and Social Psychology, 71*, 549–570.

Sørensen, A. (1990). Unterschiede im Lebenslauf von Frauen und Männern [Differences in life-course patterns of male and female]. *Kölner Zeitschrift für Soziologie und Sozialpsychologie, Sonderheft 31*, 304–321.

Udry, J. R. (1982). The effect of normative pressure on fertility. *Population and Environment, 5*, 1–18.

Vitaliano, P. P., DeWolfe, D. J., Maiuro, R. D., Russo, J., & Katon, W. (1990). Appraised changeability of a stressor as a modifier on the relationship between coping and depression. A test of the hypothesis of fit. *Journal of Personality and Social Psychology, 59*, 582–592.

Williamson, G. M., Shaffer, D. R., & Parmelee, P. A. (Eds.). (2000). *Physical illness and depression in older adults: A handbook of theory, research, and practice*. New York: Kluwer Academic/Plenum.

Wrosch, C., & Freund, A. M. (2001). Self-regulation of normative and non-normative developmental challenges. *Human Development, 44*, 264–283.

Wrosch, C., & Heckhausen, J. (1999). Control processes before and after passing a developmental deadline: Activation and deactivation of intimate relationship goals. *Journal of Personality and Social Psychology, 77*, 415–427.

Wrosch, C., & Heckhausen, J. (2002). Perceived control of life regrets: Good for young and bad for old adults. *Psychology and Aging, 17*, 340–350.

Wrosch, C., & Heckhausen, J. (2005). Being on-time or off-time: Developmental deadlines for regulating one's own development. In A. N. Perret-Clermont, J. M. Barrelet, A. Flammer, D. Miéville, J. F. Perret, & W. Perrig (Eds.), *Thinking time: A multidisciplinary perspective* (pp. 110–123). Göttingen: Hogrefe & Huber.

Wrosch, C., Heckhausen, J., & Lachman, M. E. (2000). Primary and secondary control strategies for managing health and financial stress across adulthood. *Psychology and Aging, 15*, 387–399.

Wrosch, C., & Scheier, M. F. (2003). Personality and quality of life: The importance of optimism and goal adjustment. *Quality of Life Research, 12*, 59–72.

Wrosch, C., Scheier, M. F., Carver, C. S., & Schulz, R. (2003). The importance of goal disengagement in adaptive self-regulation: When giving up is beneficial. *Self and Identity, 2*, 1–20.

Wrosch, C., Scheier, M. F., Miller, G. E., Schulz, R., & Carver, C. S. (2003). Adaptive self-regulation of unattainable goals: Goal disengagement, goal re-engagement, and subjective well-being. *Personality and Social Psychology Bulletin, 29*, 1494–1508.

Wrosch, C., Schulz, R., & Heckhausen, J. (2002). Health stresses and depressive symptomatology in the elderly: The importance of health engagement control strategies. *Health Psychology, 21,* 340–349.

Wrosch, C., Schulz, R., & Heckhausen, J. (2004). Health stresses and depressive symptomatology in the elderly: A control-process approach. *Current Directions in Psychological Science, 13,* 17–20.

Zepelin, H. R., Sills, A., & Heath, M. W. (1986–87). Is age becoming irrelevant? An exploratory study of perceived age norms. *Journal of Aging and Human Development, 24,* 241–256.

21

Change in Personality Processes and Health Outcomes

Michael R. Levenson
Carolyn M. Aldwin
Oregon State University

Wrath, to which John [Hunter, a cardiologist researching angina] was so prone, exposed him to the direst attacks. A tardy coachman, an inattentive secretary, would throw him into volcanic rages. He realized his danger, yet was powerless to control his temper. "My life," he said, "is at the mercy of any rogue who chooses to provoke me."

—Kligfield (1980, p. 368)

A fairly large literature has documented findings of relations between personality and health (for reviews see Aldwin, Levenson, & Gilmer, 2004; Contrada, Cather, & O'Leary, 1999; Smith & Gallo, 2001). Another has addressed the question of whether and to what extent personality can and does change, especially in adulthood (which is reviewed in chap. 9 of this volume). The obvious next step is to explore relations between personality change and health. Unfortunately, with few exceptions, very little literature addresses whether changing personality results in changes in health status, although logically they would be expected to be related. Thus, this chapter proposes a theoretical framework exploring why change in personality should be related to changes in health status, setting up an agenda for future research. It reviews the evidence for a link between personality and health, focusing on both risk and protective factors. Drawing on a continuity theory of personality and mental health (Claridge & Davis, 2003), the argument is made that mental health symptoms are extreme manifestations of normal personality traits. Thus, interventions to change personality would not endeavor to replace one trait with another (a dubious prospect at best), but rather to return the individual to the normal range of the characteristic. Then there is a review of the small literature on interventions intended to ameliorate the personality process risk factors on which this chapter focuses (hostility, anxiety, and depression).

PERSONALITY PROCESSES AND HEALTH

A relation between personality and health has long been posited, starting in the West with Hippocrates' theory of humors (cf. Friedman, 1991) and in the East with *The Yellow Emperor's Medical Classic* (Veith, 2000), with its emphasis on imbalances of yin and yang. For example, hostility in the Hippocratic system would be characterized as an excess of choler, while in the Chinese system it would be an excess of yang. Conversely, depression would be an excess of bile, or yin, respectively. As physicians learned more about the manifestation of physical disease in organ systems, the importance of blood circulation, and agents of disease such as microbes, the study of the mind and the body became separated. Some physicians are still skeptical of relations between mind and body (Angel, 1985), keeping Cartesian dualism in effect while denying it in principle.

Early theories of psychosomatic illnesses posited relations between psychological processes and specific symptoms and illnesses, for example, heart disease and repressed hostility, or asthma and overprotective mothering (see Weiner, 1977). There were problems with the attempts to test these somewhat simplistic theories. Most of the studies either had no controls or compared healthy controls with people with preexisting illnesses. Thus, causal directionality could not be imputed inasmuch as illnesses can cause psychological and behavioral change, both in the individual and in the family. For example, mothers of asthmatic children might well be "overprotective" *because* their children are very ill, not the other way around. A serious chronic illness can induce frustration and depression. An unfortunate tendency arose to treat so-called psychosomatic illnesses as not "real" illnesses but "in a person's head"—despite the fact that asthma and heart disease can be fatal. This, and the increased understanding of the pathophysiology of disease, led psychosomatic medicine to fall into disfavor.

However, more sophisticated research has reinstated the interest in psychosomatic medicine and, specifically, in possible relations between personality and disease outcomes. Such relations are central to the closely linked fields of health psychology and behavioral medicine.

Even though the results of research being examined use trait measures, our concentration is on personality as process (cf. Allport, 1937) and the view that it is the "active ingredient" in personality that is likely related to disease processes. Therefore, the term *personality processes* is used to emphasize that the psychological factors studied in connection with health include traits, affective states, and psychological symptoms, as well as beliefs and attitudes. For example, sometimes hostility is considered to be a relatively stable personality trait and at other times a short-lived negative affect. Similarly, optimism is sometimes treated as a personality characteristic and at other times as a cognitive style. The term *personality processes* acknowledges the blurring of these traditional distinctions, and permits greater flexibility in the review of this material.

In the past three decades, a robust relation has emerged between personality processes and such diseases as coronary heart disease (CHD) and overall mortality. Three primary negative emotions have been linked to the development of disease and its progression: hostility, depression, and anxiety. Possible protective factors have also been observed, such as control, self-efficacy, optimism, and emotional stability.

Hostility

Cardiologists Friedman and Rosenman (1974) observed that their patients shared other distinctive characteristics, including extreme, easily aroused hostility, high achievement motivation, time urgency, and explosive speech patterns. They dubbed this syndrome "Type A personality," later changed to Type A Behavior Pattern (TABP), in contrast to Type Bs, who were thought to be calmer and more emotionally stable. This initial insight generated a host of studies (see Smith & Gallo, 2001), and the general consensus is that hostility is the key component that relates to heart disease, and contributes significantly even controlling for other risk factors (Niaura et al., 2000).

In a meta-analysis of the relation between hostility and health, T. D. Miller, Smith, Turner, Guijarro, and Hallet (1996) showed conclusively that individuals higher in hostility are more likely to develop CHD, and to show higher overall mortality rates. In the Normative Aging Study, men who were high in anger and hostility had risk ratios of 2.5 for the development of CHD (Kawachi, Sparrow, Spiro, Vokonas, & Weiss, 1996). The state of anger may have immediate CHD effects. In the Determinants of Myocardial Infarction Onset Study, a significant number of individuals with MIs had experienced an episode of anger shortly before the event (Mittleman et al., 1995; Mittleman, Maclure, Nachnani, Sherwood, & Muller, 1997).

T. D. Miller et al. (1996) found that the magnitude of the relation between hostility and CHD was generally greater for the structured interview than for self-report measures, probably due to the expected underreporting of negative traits in the latter measures. Interestingly, studies with a longer follow-up period tended to have weaker effects than those with short-term follow-ups, perhaps because hostility is not a stable personality trait (see McCrae et al., 1999).

Sex and age also play a role in the relation between hostility and CHD. It is stronger for men than for women, and Williams (2000) found TABP was most predictive of coronary artery disease (CAD) among those in their 30s and early 40s. Among those from age 46 to 55, Type A and Type B individuals had about equal rates of CAD. Type Bs over age 56 actually had higher rates. This may have been a survivor effect, with the most vulnerable dying younger, leaving the less vulnerable alive. However, hostility tends to decrease with age (McCrae et al., 1999). Thus, instability of hostility as a trait may account for hostility's greater predictiveness of CHD in shorter term in contrast to longer term follow-up studies. However, in a longitudinal study of men, Aldwin, Spiro, Levenson, and Cupertino (2001) found that hostility was associated with a larger number of physical health symptoms across the adult life span.

There may be multiple pathways linking hostility to CHD. Hostile people tend to have poorer health behavior habits such as smoking, excessive drinking, overeating, and physical inactivity. However, covarying out these behaviors does not necessarily diminish the relation between hostility and CHD (T. D. Miller et al., 1996), suggesting the existence of an independent pathway from hostility to CHD.

A number of laboratory studies have shown that people who are high in hostility show greater cardiovascular reactivity (heart rate and blood pressure increases) to stressors (Krantz & McCeney, 2002), especially interpersonal stressors such as criticism. There is some evidence that hostile people have higher serum lipid levels, such as LDL and triglycerides (Niaura et al., 2000), especially when stressed (Vögele, 1998) or treated unfairly (Richards, Hof, & Alvarenga, 2000). However, these results have not been found consistently (van Doornen, 1997), suggesting that the relation is moderated by other factors, including genetics, sex, ethnicity, diet, and smoking. A possible indirect pathway between hostility and CHD could be that those high in hostility tend to be low in social support, and there is some evidence that individuals low in support are also at higher risk for CHD (T. D. Miller et al., 1996).

Hostility may even be health protective in certain circumstances. Lieberman & Tobin (1983) found that nursing home residents whom the staff perceived to be "ornery" or "cantakerous" actually were more likely to live longer than more passive patients. Their abrasive behavior resulted in their receiving greater attention by the staff, and may have protected them against feelings of helplessness and hopelessness, which may have negative consequences for health, especially in later life (see later).

Thus, for the past quarter-century, hostility has been known to be a risk factor for CHD comparable in magnitude to more traditional risk factors such as high cholesterol, blood pressure, and cigarette smoking (Review Panel on Coronary-Prone Behavior and Coronary Heart Disease, 1978). Therefore, it might be expected that there would be public health campaigns urging people to be less hostile in their everyday lives. Yet, no such campaigns have been mounted. However, there has been a number of interventions designed to modify TABP, which are discussed below in the personality change and health section.

Anxiety

Twenge (2000) conducted meta-analyses showing that successive cohorts of adults and children increased in anxiety by nearly a standard deviation in the second half of the 20th century. Friedman & Booth-Kewley (1987), in their review of personality and health outcomes, found relatively consistent effects of anxiety on heart disease and overall mortality, suggesting that increasing anxiety in a population can constitute a serious public health problem. Anxiety has been studied in several forms, including phobias, self-report anxiety, and worries (see Kubzansky & Kawachi, 2000). In a prospective study with the Normative Aging Study, men who reported worrying were nearly two and a half times more likely to develop CHD (Kubzansky et al., 1997) and those who were high in self-reported anxiety were at four and one half times the risk for sudden cardiac death (Kawachi, Sparrow, Vokonas, & Weiss, 1994). In a national sample, those with phobias had six times the risk for sudden cardiac death (Kawachi et al., 1994). In the Framingham Heart Study, women who were homemakers (but not employed women) and who reported high anxiety had nearly eight times the risk of death from heart attacks and other CHD-related mortality (Eaker, Pinski, & Castelli, 1992). In reviews of the literature, Tennant and McLean (2001) and Smith and Gallo (2001) also concluded that negative affectivity significantly predicted CHD.

Possible mechanisms linking anxiety and CHD have been of special interest. Tennant and McLean (2001) reviewed evidence indicating that emotional distress in general, and anxiety in particular, are associated with heart rate acceleration stimulated by a release of catecholamines. Acute emotional distress and hyperventilation can trigger vasospasm, which cuts off blood flow to the heart muscles, especially in those with underlying ischemic disease. Vasospasm can initiate acute ischemic attacks and changes in blood platelets, which can cause blood clots. Thus, there may be a cascade of events leading from anxiety to CHD.

Gorman and Sloan (2000) offered an alternative insight into the underlying pathophysiology linking anxiety and CHD. Heart rate is under the control of both the sympathetic and the parasympathetic nervous system. In heart disease, there is a loss of normal parasympathetic nervous system control of the heart rate and rhythm. Such a decrease in parasympathetic control results in decreased heart rate variability, and may leave the heart vulnerable to sympathetic nervous system stimulation via catecholamines. Thus, heart rate dysregulation leaves the heart vulnerable to overstimulation. Individuals high in anxiety may have insufficient parasympathetic heart rate regulation leaving them more vulnerable to significant arrhythmias under stress that can lead to arrest and sudden death.

Heart rate variability also decreases with normal aging, but the decrease is especially pronounced among those with diabetic neuropathy and vascular disease. If chronic anxiety is also associated with decreased heart rate variability, it could be speculated that the combination of aging and disease with chronic anxiety may make older individuals at special risk for arrhythmias and sudden death. Anxiety, like hostility, may take its toll in midlife. More research is needed to determine the exact pathway(s) between anxiety and CHD, and if the relation between the two varies significantly by age.

Depression

Perhaps the strongest association between negative affect and health may be with depression. Tennant and McLean (2001) found that 9 of 14 studies they reviewed showed a positive association. The association between depression and mortality is well established in the literature(Zheng et al., 1997), even after taking rates of suicide into account (Tsuang & Woolson, 1978). As in the specific case of bereavement, the impact of depression on mortality may be generally short-lived. Blazer, Hybels, and Pieper (2001) found that depression itself appears to be quite unstable. In a sample of older adults, assessed for 9 years at 3-year intervals, most individuals who were depressed at one point in time were not depressed at the next assessment. This helps to explain why depression significantly predicted mortality only for the next follow-up period. Time 1 depressive symptoms predicted mortality only at Time 2, and Time 2 symptoms predicted mortality only at Time 3.

There is also a link between depression and CHD morbidity (e.g., Anda et al., 1993; Barefoot & Schroll, 1996), especially in men (Ford et al., 1998; Hippisley-Cox, Fielding, & Pringle, 1998; Sesso, Kawachi, Vokonas, & Sparrow, 1998). In general, people with high levels of self-reported depression have risk ratios for CHD one and a half to two times that of their nondepressed peers (Kubzhansky & Kawachi, 2000). Wulsin and Singlan (2003), in their meta-analysis of smoking and CHD, revealed that the relative risk of depression (1.64) was greater than that for passive smoking (1.25) but less than the risk for active smoking (2.5).

The relation between depression and cardiovascular morbidity and mortality appears to be especially strong among those with preexisting CHD, predicting subsequent arrhythmias (Ladwig et al., 1992) and deaths (Carney et al., 1988). Frasure-Smith and his colleagues followed the relation of depression to mortality in CHD patients at 6 (Frasure-Smith, Lespérance, & Talajic, 1993), 12 (Frasure-Smith, Lespérance, Juneau, Talajic, & Bourassa, 1999), and 18 months (Frasure, Lespérance, & Talajic, 1995), and also conducted a long-term (5-year) follow-up (Lespérance, Frasure-Smith, Talajic, & Bourassa, 2002). They indicated that depressed individuals had four times the mortality of the nondepressed and that depression was actually a stronger predictor of mortality than physiological factors such as a previous MI or left ventricular function. This effect was found for women as well as for men, has been shown over 10 years (Welin, Lappas, & Wilhemsen, 2000), and has also been found in chronic congestive heart failure patients (Murburg, Brue, Svebak, Tveteras, & Aarsland, 1999).

The explanation of the association between depression and CHD morbidity and mortality is controversial. Some have argued that it is largely mediated through health behavior habits. Depressed people are more likely to smoke and to have a poor diet, and are less likely to exercise (Hayward, 1995). However, Blazer et al. (2001) argued that effects of depression on mortality are not limited to health behavior habits, but also include functional health and cognitive impairment. Pulska, Pahkala, Laippala, and Kivelä (2000) found that the primary differences between depressed older adults who had died and those who survived after 6 years were anorexia and weight loss.

There is also evidence for a direct effect of depression on physiological processes. Depression is also linked to physiological processes such as atherogenesis (Appels, F. W. Bar, J. Bar, Bruggeman, & de Baets, 2000) and arrhythmias (Ladwig, Kieser, Konigh, Breithardt, & Borggrefe, 1992), perhaps because of a decrease in heart rate variability (Nemeroff, Musselman, & Evans, 1998). As we saw with anxiety, decreased heart rate variability with depression can leave the heart vulnerable to overstimulation by stress reactions of the sympathetic nervous system. Decreased heart rate variability has also been associated with such pathophysiological processes as atherogenesis and ischemia, as well as with arrhythmias, MIs, and sudden death (Tennant & McLean, 2001).

The relation of depression to other illnesses, such as cancer, has not, so far, proved to be as strong. Nevertheless, depression and other psychosocial factors are widely believed to be associated with cancer (K. I. Baghurst, P. A. Baghurst, & Record, 1992). One possible mechanism is through depressed immune function, although this relation has not yet been found prospectively (Stein, A. H. Miller, & Trestman, 1991). Retrospective studies have shown a link, but such studies may suffer from recall bias—that is, post hoc, individuals with any disease may attribute the disease to some stressor or feeling state that preceded it.

In their meta-analysis of six prospective studies on depression and cancer, McGee, Williams, and Elwood (1994) found that the relation between depression and cancer was weak, with an excess cancer rate of only 1–2%. The strongest relations were found in studies with older participants and with larger numbers of smokers. This is consistent with the finding that depression is associated with a greater likelihood of smoking (Covey, Glassman, & Dalack, 1991) and being overweight (DiPietro, Anda, Williamson, & Stunkard, 1992), both of which are associated with increased risk of cancer.

Temoshok and her colleagues (1985) hypothesized that women with rather passive personalities who suppressed emotional expression were more likely to develop cancer, coining the "Type C" personality. Similarly, helplessness appeared to result in poorer prognoses in cervical cancer (Goodkin, Antoni, & Bloom, 1986). However, Cooper and Fagher (1992) found that older women were both more likely to exhibit this personality and to develop breast cancer. Controlling for age eliminated the significance of the relation.

In summary, there is abundant evidence for relations of anxiety, hostility, and depression to coronary heart disease, but the relation to cancer is less clear. Less attention has been paid to protective factors, such as an emotional stability, an internal locus of control and optimism.

Optimism

Optimism has been conceptualized both as an explanatory style (Abramson, Seligman, & Teasdale, 1978; Peterson & Seligman, 1984) and as a personality disposition (Scheier & Carver, 1985). Optimism as explanatory style is assessed by the Attributional Style Questionnaire (ASQ; Peterson et al., 1982), and dispositional optimism by the Life Orientation Test (LOT; Scheier & Carver, 1985). The ASQ seeks explanations for past events, whereas the LOT assesses expectations for the future. The two measures tend to be only modestly correlated; however, optimism, assessed either way, is associated with better health. The effects of optimism on health outcomes may be mediated through better health behavior habits (Scheier & Carver, 1992), although not entirely (Tomakowsky, Lumley, Markowitz, & Frank, 2001).

People with optimistic explanatory styles report fewer illnesses (Peterson, 1988) and fewer contacts with physicians (Lin & Peterson, 1990). Explanatory optimists report fewer illnesses over the life span (Peterson, Seligman, & Vaillant, 1988), and are at lower risk for premature mortality (Peterson & Seligman, 1987). Optimistic older adults have better cell-mediated immunity (Kamen-Siegel, Rodin, Seligman, & Dwyer, 1991).

Dispositional optimists also report better health in general (Scheier & Carver, 1985) and fewer influenza symptoms (Hamid, 1990). Scheier and his colleagues conducted research showing that optimistic individuals have better short- and long-term recovery from coronary artery bypass surgery, as indicated by fewer hospitalizations (Scheier & Carver, 1992; Scheier et al., 1989; Scheier et al., 1999). Helgeson and Fritz (1999) also found optimists suffered fewer coronary events following angioplasty.

However, optimism is not always protective, especially with chronic stress. Under these circumstances, optimists have been shown to be more depressed (Frese, 1992; Isaacowitz & Seligman, 2002). The same may be true for immune functioning (Cohen et al., 1999), with optimists showing lower NK cell activity during uncontrollable stressors (Sieber et al., 1992). Optimistic HIV patients' CD4+ counts worsened more rapidly over a 2-year follow-up, whereas pessimists' CD4+ counts actually increased slightly (Tomakowsky et al., 2001).

Control

The effects of control on health have been studied for some time (for reviews, see Devine, 1992; Gatchel & Baum, 1983). However, many of these were intervention studies, and thus are reviewed under that section.

Many of the more naturalistic studies of control and health outcomes have been conducted in occupational settings. Karasek & Theorell (1990) proposed that there is an interaction effect between control and responsibility in occupational settings. Workers with a great deal of responsibility but also a fair amount of control, like executives, had lower levels of work-related stress, whereas those with responsibility but little control, like secretaries, reported the greatest amount of stress. In controls, individuals who have little control but relatively few responsibilities, like janitors, also reported low amounts of stress. Indeed, subsequent work has shown that individuals with high responsibility but little control are more likely to develop to cardiovascular disease.

Having a sense of control may be especially important for more disadvantaged groups. Lachman and Weaver (1998) showed that a sense of control moderates the effects of social class on health. Using national data from the MacArthur Studies of Midlife, they found that lower SES individuals with a strong sense of control had self-rated health that was as high as more prosperous SES groups, but those with a low sense of control reported much worse health. Controlling for perceived control reduced the relation between social class and mortality by about 50% (Bosma, Schrijvers, & Mackenbach, 1999).

However, control can be a double-edged sword. Most control is rather illusory, and when that sense of control is shattered, people may "give up," sometimes with quite devastating consequences. For example, Seligman (1975) related a relevant anecdote of a prisoner of war (POW) in Vietnam. He was a strong young man and in relatively good physical and mental shape, despite the horrors of the conditions under which the POWs were kept. He firmly believed that if he did everything his captors requested, he would be given an early release. Gradually, however, he realized that this promise was, in fact, a lie. He became profoundly depressed and refused to eat or drink. He curled up in a fetal position, lying in his own waste. He died shortly thereafter.

Further, there are many different types of control measures. Some assess control in specific domains, such as work or health, whereas others assess more global feelings. Thus, it is not surprising that the literature on control and mortality is inconsistent. For example, low work control is associated with cardiovascular mortality (Johnson, Steward, Hall, Fredlund, & Theorell, 1996). An external locus of control has been associated with increased overall mortality (Dalgard & Lund Haheim, 1998), but health locus of control was not significantly related to all-cause mortality after an MI (Welin et al., 2000). Krause and Shaw (2000) suggested that part of the inconsistency in the literature is due to a failure to look at control with regard to an individual's most important role. In a nationwide survey of older adults, they found that global measures of control were unrelated to mortality, but feelings of control over the most important role reduced the odds of dying during the study period.

Feelings of control change in some interesting ways with age. Lachman (1986) reviewed the rather mixed literature on aging and locus of control, and concluded that control is a multidimensional construct. Although some aspects appear to change with age, others do not. Older adults begin to realize that they do not have the sort of control over the external environment they thought they had when they were younger, but they do maintain other types of control. Aldwin (1991) investigated this hypothesis and found that older individuals were less likely to say they felt responsibility for either the occurrence or the management of problems they faced. Nonetheless, they did just as much problem-focused coping as younger individuals. In some ways, acknowledging lack of control is protective, as long as individuals do what they can to mitigate problems. Acknowledging that circumstances are often beyond control allows them to avoid self-blame, but this is very different from a sense of helplessness. Schulz and Heckhausen (1998) made the shift from primary to secondary control a key element of their life-span theory of change in control, with primary referring to control over the environment and secondary referring to control over their reactions to it.

Recent studies have provided a more refined examination of control and its influences. For example, Bandura (1997) differentiated between control beliefs and self-efficacy. The classic definition of locus of control focused on generalized expectancies about outcomes. An individual with an internal locus of control would expect to be able to affect the outcome of a given situation (Rotter, 1954). However, Bandura reasoned that there is a subtle difference between thinking a situation can be under individuals' control and the belief that they can actually perform the behaviors required to affect the outcome. Thus, a person could believe that the responsibility to quit smoking lies with an individual, but not think that they personally are capable of stopping (B. M. DeVillis & R. F. DeVillis, 2001).

Emotional Stability

Clearly, part of the negative effect of anxiety, hostility, and depression is related to emotional lability. Thus, it would make sense that emotional stability would be protective. However, only a handful of studies has examined this possibility. Spiro, Aldwin, Ward, and Mroczek (1995) examined the relation between personality and the development of hypertension (HT) in the NAS men. They hypothesized that hostility would be positively associated with the incidence of HT, but found only marginal results. Instead, the strongest personality predictor was emotional stability, and it was inversely associated with the development of HT.

A second study examined personality and the self-reported symptom trajectories across 25 years. Aldwin, Spiro, Levenson, and Cupertino (2001) identified different patterns of symptom trajectories. Two patterns had very low levels of symptoms that increased only slightly from midlife to late life. The men in these trajectory groups reported the highest level of emotional stability and also had among the highest survival rates of any of the groups. This study raises the interesting possibility that emotional stability is protective of health in mid- and later life.

Summary

The past several decades have witnessed a dramatic increase in the understanding of how personality processes affect health. Sometimes there appear to be direct physiological effects, as in the relation between hostility and increased cholesterol levels under stress, while at other times the effect is mediated through health behavior habits such as smoking, diet, or alcohol consumption.

PERSONALITY CHANGE AND HEALTH

Issues concerning personality stability and change are addressed elsewhere in this book; therefore, this discussion does not dwell on the question of whether or not personality changes in adulthood (see chap. 9). There appears to be a growing consensus that change in personality traits or processes is often observed (McCrae et al., 1999; Mroczek & Spiro, 2003; Roberts & DelVecchio, 2000). As noted earlier, hostility and neuroticism tend to decrease with age, but other characteristics such as mastery increase (Parker & Aldwin, 1997; Srivastava, John, Gosling, & Potter, 2003).

However, very few studies examine naturalistic change and its relation to health outcomes. As mentioned earlier, most longitudinal studies find that the longer the follow-up time, the weaker the predictive power of personality for health outcomes. A possible interpretation for this finding is that personality does change. So, for example, hostility assessed in adolescence may not predict CHD in midlife, because hostility decreases during early adulthood. Therefore, hostility in midlife is a stronger predictor. This is supported by the finding, mentioned earlier, that the effects of depression on mortality in an older sample were short-lived (Blazer et al., 2001).

Another argument for this line of reasoning lies in the continuity theory of the origins of mental health symptoms, which argues that all psychopathologies arise as an exaggerated form of a normal personality dimension (Claridge & Davis, 2003). In the cases of anxiety and depression, evidence is consistent with this theory. Krueger (1999) found that high negative emotionality at age 18, assessed by the Multidimensional Personality Questionnaire (Tellegen, 1982), associated prospectively with anxiety, affective, antisocial, and substance dependence disorders diagnosed by DSM–III–R criteria at age 21, controlling for such disorders at age 18. As with physical disease (Kaplan, 2003), there may be a deep reservoir of subclinical mental health symptoms that contribute to the development of physical disease. Interventions to reduce anxiety may be expected also to lower the risk of CHD.

From the perspective of continuity theory, interventions intended to ameliorate mental heath symptoms work at the level of underlying personality to reduce a person's level on a dimension to a normal, nondistressing level. With respect to the personality processes addressed in the present chapter—hostility, anxiety, and depression—interventions have been devised that do seem to induce long-term reductions, such as TABP interventions (Bracke & Thoresen, 1996), Cognitive Behavior Therapy for depression (Beck, 1967), and mindfulness meditation for anxiety disorders (Kabat-Zinn et al., 1992; J. J. Miller, Fletcher, & Kabat-Zinn, 1995), which are reviewed here.

Type A Interventions

A number of studies has examined interventions for Type A Behavior Pattern, and the outcomes are variable. However, sufficient evidence exists in the literature to suggest that Type A interventions, if well designed, can be effective in reducing risk factors and the recurrence of disease in cardiac patients (Bennett, 1994; Smith & Gallo, 1994; Thoresen & Powell, 1992). For example, Friedman et al. (1986) evaluated a Type A Behavior Pattern Intervention among cardiac patients; an astounding 95% of these patients could be classified as Type As. They initiated a longitudinal study in which 270 patients received cardiac counseling, which consisted of information about nutrition, exercise, drug treatments, and surgical options. The second group consisted of 592 participants who received both cardiac counseling and Type A behavioral counseling, which included instruction in progressive muscle relaxation, strategies to change behavior, alterations in belief systems, restructuring of the environment, and cognitive-emotional education. The control group consisted of 151 individuals who received neither type of intervention.

Over the course of 4½ years, Type A behavior was significantly decreased in the second group more than the other two groups. Further, they had a substantially reduced rate of recurrence of cardiovascular events, about half that of the other two groups, as did patients who had bypass surgery. Interestingly, cardiac counseling alone seemed to have little effect. Further, cholesterol levels were comparable across the two intervention groups, and these levels did not differentiate between patients with or without recurrences. Unfortunately, this study did not clearly examine the pathways through which the Type A intervention had its effect. However, other studies have shown that these interventions do decrease systolic and diastolic blood pressure reactivity (Bennett, Wallace, Carrol, & Smith, 1991).

Kasl (1983) argued that the causal directionality between Type A and cardiovascular reactivity was questionable, and argued that the reactivity may be the source of the behavior. Interestingly, other types of cardiac interventions may decrease Type A Behavior. An aerobic exercise training program decreased heart rate and blood pressure, and also decreased Type A behaviors. Change in diet may also affect these behavior patterns. Weidner (1994) showed that dietary interventions improved plasma lipid levels and was also associated with reductions in depression and aggressive hostility.

Issues in causal directionality may appear critical in these types of interventions. However, as has been argued elsewhere (Aldwin, Levenson, & Gilmer, 2004), emotional reactivity may be a key factor in cardiovascular risk. The Type A interventions, exercise, and diet may have much of their effect through mood. Anxiety and hostility can both affect heart rate variability and responsivity, leading both to MIs and sudden cardiac death. Clearly, more studies are needed that trace the specific pathways through which these various interventions have their impact on morbidity and mortality (Krantz & McCeney, 2002).

Depression Interventions

A number of studies have examined depression interventions and physical health outcomes. The most common (and effective) depression intervention is cognitive behavioral therapy (CBT), especially in older adults (Pinquart & Soerensen, 2001). CBT has been shown to be effective in reducing insomnia (Espie, Inglis, Tessier, & Harvey, 2001), chronic pain (Dahl & Nilsson, 2001), irritable bowel syndrome (Tkachuk, Graff, Martin, & Bernstein, 2003), and chronic fatigue syndrome (Raine et al., 2002). Although depression has been shown to predict mortality after an MI, surprisingly little work has been done examining psychosocial intervention for depression in cardiac patients (Burg & Berkman, 2002).

The Enhancing Recovery in Coronary Heart Disease Patients (ENRICHD) study (Berkman et al., 2003) was designed to remedy that gap, and illustrates some of the difficulty in conducting psychosocial interventions in medically frail populations. This study enrolled 2,481 MI patients, of whom 39% were depressed. Half of these patients were randomly assigned to 6 months of CBT, and the other half to usual care. For those who had low perceived social support, the therapy was supplemented with social learning theory-based interventions that addressed relevant cognition, behaviors, and affect. In addition, the experimental group was offered an additional 12 weeks of group therapy, if desired. Note that not all patients completed the 6 months of therapy, if they met strict criteria for optimal treatment outcome. In both groups, depressed patients who did not respond to the psychosocial intervention after 5 weeks received antidepressants.

The psychosocial intervention was successful in reducing depressive symptoms, although the effect faded by 30 months, mainly due to the improvement in the control group. However, there were no significant differences in both subsequent MIs and mortality between the two groups, although there was a gender by treatment interaction that disappeared once adjusted for age and a number of preexisting medical conditions. Interestingly, receiving antidepressants was related to lower rates of subsequent MIs and mortality.

Ethically, depression had to be treated in the usual care group, but, following standard epidemiological protocols, no attempt was made adjust for antidepressant use in the analyses examining the effect of the psychosocial intervention. Also, no analyses were done directly relating amount of decrease in depressive symptoms with subsequent risk of morbidity and mortality. Unfortunately, therefore, the results are inconclusive and further explication of subgroups would be helpful.

Others have demonstrated that it is important to consider individual differences among MI patients in interpreting the results of psychosocial interventions. For example, Frasure-Smith, Lesperance, and their colleagues conducted a series of studies called the Montreal Heart Attack Readjustment Trial (M-HART). The initial publication (Frasure-Smith et al., 1997) examined the impact of individualized interventions directed at problem solving and providing emotional and technical support by nurses on 1,376 post-MI patients. Overall, there was little effect of this intervention; indeed, women in the treatment group were marginally more likely to show higher cardiac and all-cause mortality.

A follow-up analysis of just those in the treatment group who manifested high levels of emotional distress ($N = 433$) showed that those who decreased in depression and anxiety were less likely to die of cardiac causes, less likely to be readmitted to the hospital, and had marginally lower all-cause mortality rates (Cossette, Frasure-Smith, & Lesperance, 2001). A further analysis divided the patients into three groups, low anxious, repressors, and high anxious, and followed them for 5 years (Frasure-Smith et al., 2002). The initial results were confirmed; there was no effect of treatment in men, and worse outcomes for the women. However, there were subgroup differences. Highly anxious men showed significant positive long-term effects from the intervention, but repressors in both sexes showed significantly worse survival. Thus, it is possible that intervention increased emotional distress among repressors, who likely preferred more avoidant coping styles.

Anxiety Interventions

Despite the relation between anxiety and health, psychosocial intervention programs targeting anxiety in medical settings have been surprisingly ineffective. Dusseldorp, van Elderen, Maes, Meulman, and Kraaij (1999) conducted a meta-analysis of psychoeducational programs for CHD patients. Although such programs, on average, decreased recurrence of MIs as well as cardiac mortality by an average of 29% and 34%, respectively, this effect was not due to a decrease in either depression or anxiety. Rather, the effects were probably mediated through health behavior habits, which were significantly changed by the interventions.

Studies that utilize self-reported outcomes tend to show greater effects. For example, Cheung, Molassiotis, and Chang (2003) found that a progressive muscle relaxation intervention significantly decreased state anxiety, but not trait anxiety, and improved perceived quality of life in colorectal cancer patients after surgery. However, cognitive behavioral therapy in panic disorder patients reduced anxiety and physical health symptoms, but the effect of CBT on physical symptoms was apparently not mediated through anxiety (Schmidt et al., 2003).

Meditation appears to have the most consistent effects on anxiety in health contexts. Pioneering research conducted by Kabat-Zinn and his colleagues (1992) showed that a short-term course of mindfulness meditation resulted in significant decreases in anxiety and depression symptoms in anxiety disorder patients. These effects persisted after 3 years (J. J. Miller et al., 1995). Subsequent work in health contexts also shows promise. Alexander et al.'s (1994) meta-analysis showed that transcendental meditation (TM) was more effective than other forms of relaxation therapy on psychophysiological arousal and trait anxiety. Randomized clinical trials found that TM was associated with reduction of hypertension mortality in older people.

Continuing the work of Kabat-Zinn and his colleagues, Reibel, Greeson, Brainard, and Rosenzweig (2001) found that a mindfulness-based stress reduction intervention in a heterogeneous patient population resulted in a 38% decrease in the Global Severity Index of the SCL–90R, and a 44% decrease in the anxiety subscale. The intervention also led to an improvement on all subscales of the SF–36, including pain and role limitations due to physical health. In addition, 28% fewer medical symptoms were reported on the Medical Symptom Checklist.

Cantor (2003) cautioned that the evidence for the therapeutic effects of meditation, although abundant, has a number of methodological problems. The most frequently-researched meditation technique is transcendental meditation, and unfortunately most of the research is conducted by individuals officially affiliated with this movement. Cantor criticized them for frequently omitting control groups and with using self-selected TM practitioners rather than randomly assigning individuals to meditative versus control conditions. In response to these types of criticisms, Fields et al. (2002) conducted a randomized study comparing vedic medicine, which includes meditation, with a standard care group and a "modern medicine" group (which included exercise and nutrition) on coronary artery thickness. Patients in the vedic medicine group showed better improvement in coronary artery thickness, especially those in the high risk category. Unfortunately, the vedic medicine group also received herbal supplements, diet, and exercise interventions, and it was not possible to establish independent effects of meditation.

However, recent research has begun to examine the physiological mechanisms through which meditation can affect health outcomes. Davidson and his colleagues (2003) found both EKG and immune effects of a mindfulness meditation intervention. Meditation resulted in left-sided anterior activation, associated with positive affect, and increased antibody titers to an influenza vaccination. Further, the two effects were correlated, suggesting that positive affect mediated the relation between meditation and increased immune responsivity. Further, Carlson, Speca, Patel, and Goodey (2003) found that meditation in patients with breast cancer and prostate cancer decreased negative affect and shifted the immune profile toward more normal functioning. Whether these intermediate changes are associated with improved physical health, however, remains to be seen.

Control

Laboratory studies dating back to the 1970s showed that control over aversive stimuli lessened physiological arousal (Glass & Singer, 1972). Johnson and Leventhal (1974) enhanced patients' sense of control by giving them information about medical procedures and means of coping. They found that such patients experienced less distress. A number of studies by Frankenhauser (1978) showed lower neuroendocrine stress responses among workers who had control over the speed of assembly lines.

During this decade, Seligman also demonstrated the existence of learned helplessness and its damaging physiological consequences. In light of these findings, Langer and Rodin (1976) reasoned that increasing control should have beneficial effects. Nursing homes of that era tended to promote learned helplessness with residents given very few choices even about what to wear or when to eat and sleep. Langer and Rodin's intervention simply gave one group of residents options (e.g., about movie choices and meal selection). These residents were also each given a plant and told that they were responsible for its care. The other group of residents remained without any choices and, although they were also given a plant, they were informed that the staff would care for it. Residents who had been given some control and responsibility had better self-rated health (Langer & Rodin, 1976), as well as lower mortality after 18 months (Rodin & Langer, 1977).

The most consistent results of control interventions are seen with pain. Devine (1992) conducted a meta-analysis of 191 studies. He found modest but statistically reliable effects for a variety of types of pain, including post-operative pain. Nearly 80% of those studies found that individuals who received pain management interventions had shorter stays in the hospital. Thus, it appears to be easier to modify personality processes such as control appraisals to affect health than personality traits such as hostility.

CONCLUSIONS

Despite the fact that there is a clear link between personality and health, there is a surprising paucity of research on the relation between change in personality and health, despite the growing evidence that personality can and does change with age. We found few naturalistic studies examining this phenomenon, and thus turned to intervention research. Here the results were promising, if not as strong as one would have hoped. Clearly, well-designed Type A and depression psychosocial interventions can affect health. However, there is little evidence to suggest that these can prevent the occurrence of illness, but rather may mitigate its impact once it occurs. The evidence for anxiety interventions is weaker. Although meditation appears to decrease psychological distress in clinical populations, better designed studies with solid health indicators are needed.

The control literature is surprisingly dated, perhaps because the evidence that it does work has been widely accepted—at least in the pain literature. There is a huge gap in the literature, however, on control interventions and other types of physical health outcomes, especially illnesses. We were unable to locate any studies on learned optimism and physical health outcomes, suggesting an important are for future research in positive psychology.

Given the relatively large number of longitudinal studies with personality data, it is very surprising that few have examined the issue of change in personality and its relation to health. Researchers are urged to pursue this extremely interesting question.

ACKNOWLEDGMENTS

Preparation of this chapter was supported by an NIA grant R01AG13006. We would like to thank Linda Kelly, Ray Shiraishi, and Dr. Loriena Yancura for their helpful comments on an earlier draft.

REFERENCES

Abramson, L. Y, Seligman, M. E. P., & Teasdale, J. D. (1978). Learned helplessness in humans: Critique and reformulation. *Journal of Abnormal Psychology, 87*, 49–74.

Aldwin, C. M. (1991). Does age affect the stress and coping process? The implications of age differences in perceived locus of control. *Journal of Gerontology: Psychological Sciences, 46*, P174–180.

Aldwin, C. M., & Levenson, M. R. (2001). Stress, coping, and health at mid-life: A developmental perspective. In M. E. Lachman (Ed.), *The handbook of midlife development* (pp. 188–214). New York: Wiley.

Aldwin, C. M., Levenson, M. R., & Gilmer, D. F. (2004). The interface between physical and mental health. In C. M. Aldwin & D. F. Gilmer, *Health, illness and optimal aging: Biological and psychosocial perspectives* (pp. 229–253). Thousand Oaks, CA: Sage.

Aldwin, C. M., Spiro, A., III, Levenson, M. R., & Cupertino, A. P. (2001). Longitudinal findings from the Normative Aging Study: III. Personality, individual health trajectories, and mortality. *Psychology and Aging, 16*, 450–465.

Alexander, C. N., Robinson, P., Orme-Johnson, D. W., Schneider, R. H., & Walton, K. G. (1994). The effects of transcendental meditation compared to other methods of relaxation and meditation in reducing risk factors, morbidity, and mortality. *Homeostasis in Health and Disease, 35*, 243–263.

Allport, G. W. (1937). *Personality: A psychological interpretation*. New York: Henry Holt.

Anda, R., Williamson, D., Jones, D., Macea, C., Eaker, E., Glassman, A., & Marks, J. (1993). Depressed affect, hopelessness, and the risk of ischemic heart disease in a cohort of U.S. adults. *Epidemiology, 4*, 285–294.

Angel, M. (1985). Disease as a reflection of the psyche. *New England Journal of Medicine, 312*, 1570–1572.

Appels, A., Bar, F. W., Bar, J., Bruggeman, C., & de Baets, M. (2000). Inflammation, depressive symptomatology, and coronary artery disease. *Psychosomatic Medicine, 62*, 601–605.

Baghurst, K. I., Baghurst, P. A., & Record. S. J. (1992). Public perceptions in the role of dietary and other environmental factors in cancer causation or prevention. *Journal of Epidemiology and Community Health, 46,* 120–126.

Bandura, A. (1997). *Self-efficacy: The exercise of control.* New York: Freeman.

Barefoot, J. C., & Schroll, M. (1996). Symptoms of depression, acute myocardial infarction, and total mortality in a community sample, *Circulation, 93,* 1976–1980.

Beck, A. T. (1967). *Depression: Clinical, experimental and theoretical aspects.* New York: Harper & Row.

Bennett, P. (1994). Should we intervene to modify Type A behaviours in patients with manifest heart disease? *Behavioural and Cognitive Psychotherapy, 22,* 125–145.

Bennett, P., Wallace, L., Carroll, D., & Smith, N. (1991). Treating Type A behaviours and mild hypertension in middle-aged men. *Journal of Psychosomatic Research, 35,* 209–223.

Berkman, L. F., and the Writing Committee for the ENRICHD investigators. (2003). Effects of treating depression and low perceived social support on clinical events after myocardial infarction: The Enhancing Recovery in Coronary Heart Disease Patients (ENRICHD) randomized trial. *Journal of the American Medical Association, 289,* 3106–3116.

Blazer, D. G., Hybels, C. F., & Pieper, C. F. (2001). The association of depression and mortality in elderly persons: A case for multiple, independent pathways. *Journal of Gerontology: Medical Sciences, 65A,* M505–M509.

Bosma, H., Schrijvers, C., & Mackenbach, J. P. (1999). Socioeconomic inequalities in mortality and importance of perceived control: Cohort study. *British Medical Journal, 319,* 1469–70.

Bracke, P. E., & Thoreson, C. E. (1996). Reducing Type A behavior patterns: A structured-group approach. In R. Allan & S. S. Scheidt (Eds.), *Heart and mind: The practice of cardiac psychology* (pp. 255–290). Washington, DC: American Psychological Association.

Burg, M., & Berkman, L. (2002). Psychosocial intervention in coronary heart disease. In S. A. Stansfeld & M. G. Marmot (Eds.), *Stress and the heart: Psychosocial pathways to coronary heart disease* (pp. 278–293). Williston, VT: BMJ Books.

Cantor, P. H. (2003). The therapeutic effects of meditation. *British Medical Journal, 326,* 1049–1050.

Carlson, L. E., Speca, M., Patel, K. D., & Goodey, E. (2003). Mindfulness-based stress reduction in relation to quality of life, mood, symptoms of stress, and immune parameters in breast and prostate cancer outpatients. *Psychosomatic Medicine, 65,* 571–581.

Carney, R., Rich, M., Freedland, K., Saini, J., Tel Velder, A., & Simeone, I. (1988). Major depressive disorder predicts cardiac events in patients with coronary artery disease. *Psychosomatic Medicine, 59,* 627–633.

Cheung, Y. L., Molassiotis, A., & Chang, A. M. (2003). The effect of progressive muscle relaxation training on anxiety and quality of life after stoma surgery in colorectal cancer patients. *Psycho-oncology, 12,* 254–266.

Claridge, G., & Davis, C. (2003). *Personality and psychological disorders.* London: Arnold.

Cohen, F., Kearney, K. A., Zegans, L. S., Kemeny, M. E., Neuhaus, J, M., & Stites, D. P. (1999). Differential immune system changes with acute and persistent stress for optimists vs. pessimists. *Brain, Behavior, and Immunity, 13,* 155–174.

Contrada, R. J., Cather, C., & O'Leary, A. (1999). Personality and health: Dispositions and processes in disease susceptibility and adaptation to illness. In L. A. Pervin & O. P. John (Eds.), *Handbook of personality: Theory and research* (2nd ed., pp. 576–604). New York: Guilford.

Cooper, C., & Fagher, E. (1992). Coping strategies and breast disorders/cancer. *Psychological Medicine, 22,* 447–455.

Cossette, S., Frasure-Smith, N., & Lesperance, F. (2001). Clinical implications of a reduction in psychological distress on cardiac prognosis in patients participating in a psychosocial intervention program. *Psychosomatic Medicine, 63,* 257–266.

Covey, L. A., Glassman, A., & Dalack, G. W. (1991). Re: Depressed mood and the development of cancer. *American Journal of Epidemiology, 134,* 324–326.

Dahl, J. C., & Nilsson, A. (2001). Evaluation of randomized preventive behavioural medicine work site intervention for public health workers at risk for developing chronic pain. *European Journal of Pain, 5,* 421–432.

Dalgard, O. S., & Lund Haheim, L. (1998). Psychosocial risk factors and mortality: A prospective study with special focus on social support, social participation, and locus of control in Norway. *Journal of Epidemiology and Community Health, 52,* 476–481.

Davidson, R. J., Kabat-Zinn, J., Schumacher, J., Rosenkranz, M., Muller, D., Santorelli, S. F., Urbanowski, F., Harrington, A., Bonus, K., & Sheridan, J. F. (2003). Alternations in brain and immune function produced by mindfulness meditation. *Psychosomatic Medicine, 65,* 654–570.

DeVellis, B. M., & DeVellis, R. F. (2001). Self-efficacy and health. In A. Baum, T. A. Revenson, & J. E. Singer (Eds.), *Handbook of health psychology* (pp. 235–248). Mahwah, NJ: Lawrence Erlbaum Associates.

Devine, E. C. (1992). Effects of psychoeducational care for adult surgical patients: A meta-analysis of 191 studies. *Patient Education and Counseling, 19,* 129–142.

DiPietro, L., Anda, R. F., Williamson, D. F., & Stunkard, A. J. (1992). Depressive symptoms and weight change in a national cohort of adults. *Internal Journal of Obesity, 16,* 745–753.

Dusseldorp, E., Van Elderen, T., Maes, S., Meulman, J., & Kraaij, V. (1999). A meta-analysis of psycho-educational programs for coronary heart disease patients. *Health Psychology, 18,* 506–529.

Eaker, E. D., Pinsky, J., & Castelli, W. P. (1992). Myocardial infarction and coronary death among women: Psychosocial predictors from a 20-year follow-up of women in the Framingham Study. *American Journal of Epidemiology, 135,* 854–864.

Espie, C. A., Inglis, S. J., Tessier, S., & Harvey, L. (2001). The clinical effectiveness of cognitive behaviour therapy for chronic insomnia: Implementation and evaluation of a sleep clinic in general medical practices. *Behaviour Research and Therapy, 39,* 45–60.

Fields, J. Z., Walton, K. G., Schneider, R. H., Nidich, S., Pomerantz, R., Suchdev, P., Castillo-Richmond, A., Payne, K., Clark, E. T., & Rainforth, M. (2002). Effect of a multimodality natural medicine program on carotid atherosclerosis in older subjects: A pilot trial of Maharishi vedic medicine. *American Journal of Cardiology, 89,* 952–958.

Ford, D. E., Mead, L. A., Chang, P. P., Cooper-Patrick, L., Wang, N.-Y., & Klag, M. J. (1998). Depression is a risk factor for coronary artery disease in men. *Archives of Internal Medicine, 158,* 1422–1426.

Frankenhaeuser, M. (1978). *Coping with job stress: A psychobiological approach.* Sweden: University of Stockholm.

Frasure-Smith, N., Lespérance, F., Prince, R. H., Verrier, P., Garber, R. A., Juneau, M., Wolfson, C., & Bourassa, M. G. (1997). Randomized trial of home-based psychosocial nursing intervention for patients recovering from myocardial infarction. *Lancet, 350,* 473–479.

Frasure-Smith, N., Lesperance, F., Gravel, G., Masson, A., Juneau, M., & Bourassa, M. G. (2002). Long-term survival differences among low-anxious, high-anxious, and repressive copers enrolled in the Montreal Heart Attack Readjustment Trial. *Psychosomatic Medicine, 64,* 571–579.

Frasure-Smith, N., Lespérance, F., Juneau, M., Talajic, M., & Bourassa, M. G. (1999). Gender, depression, and one-year prognosis after myocardial infarction. *Psychosomatic Medicine, 61,* 26–37.

Frasure-Smith, N., Lespérance, F., & Talajic, M. (1993). Depression following myocardial infarction. *Journal of the American Medical Association, 270,* 1819–1825.

Frasure-Smith, N., Lespérance, F., & Talajic, M. (1995). Depression and 18-month prognosis after myocardial infarction. *Circulation, 91,* 999–1005.

Frese, M. (1992). A plea for realistic pessimism: On objective reality, coping with stress, and psychological dysfunction. In L. Montada, S. H. Filipp, & M. J. Lerner (Eds.), *Life crises and experiences of loss in adulthood* (pp. 81–94). Hillsdale, NJ: Lawrence Erlbaum Associates.

Friedman, H. S. (1991). *The self-healing personality: Why some people achieve health and others succumb to illness.* New York: Holt.

Friedman, H. S., & Booth-Kewley, S. (1987). The "disease-prone personality." A meta-analytic view of the construct. *American Psychologist, 42,* 539–555.

Friedman, M., & Rosenman, R. H. (1974). *Type A behavior and your heart.* New York: Knopf.

Friedman, M., Thoresen, C. E., Gill, J. J., Ulmer, D., Powell, L. H., Price, V. A., Brown, B., Thompson, L., Rabin, D. D., Breall, W. S., Bourg, E., Levy, R., & Dickson, T. (1986). Alteration of Type A behavior and its effect on cardiac recurrences in post-myocardial infarction patients: Summary results of the Recurrent Coronary Prevention Project. *American Heart Journal, 112*, 653–665.

Gatchel, R. J., & Baum, A. (1983). *An introduction to health psychology*. Reading, MA: Addison-Wesley.

Goodkin, K., Antoni, M., & Bloom, P. (1986). Stress and hopelessness in the promotion of cervical intraepithelial neoplasm to invasive squamous cell carcinoma of the cervix. *Journal of Psychosomatic Research, 30*, 67–76.

Gorman, J. M., & Sloan, R. P. (2000). Heart rate variability in depression and anxiety disorders. *American Heart Journal, 140*(Suppl. 4), 77–83.

Glass, D. C., & Singer, J. E. (1972). *Urban stress: Experiments on noise and social stressors*. New York: Academic Press.

Hamid, P. N. (1990). Optimism and the reporting of flu episodes. *Social Behavior and Personality, 18*, 224–234.

Hayward, C. (1995). Psychiatric illness and cardiovascular disease risk. *Epidemiological Review, 17*, 129–138.

Helgeson, V. S., & Fritz, H. L. (1999). Cognitive adaptation as a predictor of new coronary events after percutaneous transluminal coronary angioplasty. *Psychosomatic Medicine, 61*, 488–495.

Hippisley-Cox, J., Fielding, K., & Pringle, M. (1998). Depression as a risk factor for ischaemic heart disease in men: Population based case-control study. *British Medical Journal, 316*, 1714–1719.

Isaacowitz, D. M., & Seligman, M. E. P. (2002). Is pessimism a risk factor for depressive mood among community dwelling older adults? *Behavioral Research and Therapy, 39*, 255–272.

Johnson, J. E., & Leventhal, H. (1974). Effects of accurate expectations and behavioral instructions on reactions during a noxious medical examination. *Journal of Personality and Social Psychology, 29*, 710–718.

Johnson, J. V., Stewart, W., Hall, E. M., Fredlund, P., & Theorell, T. (1996). Long-term psychosocial work environment and cardiovascular mortality among Swedish men. *American Journal of Public Health, 86*, 324–331.

Kabat-Zinn, J., Massion, A. O., Kristeller, J., Peterson, L. G., Fletcher, K. E., Pbert, L., Linderking, W. R., & Santorelli, S. F. (1992). Effectiveness of a meditation-based stress reduction program in the treatment of anxiety disorders. *American Journal of Psychiatry, 149*, 936–943.

Kamen-Siegel, L., Rodin, J., Seligman, M. E., & Dwyer, J. (1991). Explanatory style and cell-mediated immunity in elderly men and women. *Health Psychology, 10*, 229–235.

Kaplan, R. (2003, May). *Changing diagnostic thresholds and the definition of disease*. Paper presented at the UC/APA Health Psychology and Aging Conference, Lake Arrowhead, CA.

Karasek, R., & Theorell, T. (1990). *Healthy work: Stress, productivity, and the reconstruction of working life*. New York: Basic Books.

Kasl, S. (1983). Pursuing the link between stressful life experiences and disease: A time for reappraisal. In C. I. Cooper (Ed.), *Stress research* (pp. 79–102). New York: Mentor Books.

Kawachi, I., Colditz, G. A., Ascherio, A., Rimm, E. B., Giovannucci, E., Stampfer, M. J., & Willett, W. C. (1994). Prospective study of phobic anxiety and risk of coronary heart disease in men. *Circulation, 89*, 1992–1997.

Kawachi, I., Sparrow, D., Spiro, A., Vokonas, P., & Weiss, S. T. (1996). A prospective study of anger and coronary heart disease. The Normative Aging Study. *Circulation, 94*, 2090–2095.

Kawachi, I., Sparrow, D., Vokonas, P. S., & Weiss, S. T. (1994). Symptoms of anxiety and risk of coronary heart disease. The Normative Aging Study. *Circulation, 90*, 2225–2229.

Kligfield, P. (1980). John Hunter, angina pectoris and medical education. *American Journal of Cardiology, 45*, 36–369.

Krantz, D. S., & McCeney, M. K. (2002). Effects of psychological and social factors on organic disease: A critical assessment of research on coronary heart disease. *Annual Review of Psychology, 53*, 341–369.

Krause, N., & Shaw, B. A. (2000). Role-specific feelings of control and mortality. *Psychology of Aging, 15*, 617–626.

Krueger, R. F. (1999). Personality traits in late adolescence predict mental disorders in early adulthood: A prospective-epidemiological study. *Journal of Personality, 67*, 39–65.

Kubzansky, L. D., Kawachi, I., Spiro, A., III, Weiss, S. T., Vokonas, P. S., & Sparrow, D. (1997). Is worrying bad for your heart? A prospective study of worry and coronary heart disease in the Normative Aging Study. *Circulation, 95*, 818–824.

Kubzansky, L. D., & Kawachi, I. (2000). Going to the heart of the matter: Do negative emotions cause coronary heart disease? *Journal of Psychosomatic Research, 48*, 323–337.

Lachman, M. E. (1986). Locus of control in aging research: A case for multidimensional and domain-specific assessment. *Psychology and Aging, 1*, 34–40.

Lachman, M. E., & Weaver, S. L. (1998). The sense of control as a moderator of social class differences in health and well-being. *Journal of Personality and Social Psychology, 74*, 763–773.

Ladwig, K. H., Kieser, M., Konigh, J., Breithardt, G., & Borggrefe, M. (1991). Affective diseases and survival after acute myocardial infarction. *European Heart Journal, 12*, 959–964.

Ladwig, K. H., Lehmacher, W., Rorth, R., Breithardt, G., Budde, T. H., & Borggrefe, M. (1992). Factors which provoke post infarction depression: Results from the Post Infarction Late Potential Study (PILP). *Journal of Psychosomatic Research, 36*, 723–729.

Langer, E. J., & Rodin, J. (1976). The effects of choice and enhanced personality responsibility for the aged: A field experiment in an institutional setting. *Journal of Personality and Social Psychology, 34*, 191–198.

Lesperance, F., Frasure-Smith, N., Talajic, M., & Bourassa, M. G. (2002). Five-year risk of cardiac mortality in relation to initial severity and one-year changes in depression symptoms after myocardial infarction. *Circulation, 105*, 1049–1053.

Lieberman, M. A., & Tobin, S. (1983). *The experience of old age: Stress, coping, and survival*. New York: Basic Books.

Lin, E. H., & Peterson, C. (1990). Pessimistic explanatory style and response to illness. *Behavior Research and Therapy, 28*, 243–248.

McCrae, R. R., Costa, P. T., Jr., Pedroso de Lima, M., Simoes, A., Ostendorf, F., Angleitner, A., Marusic, I., Bratko, D., Caprara, G. V., Barbaranelli, C., Chae, J. H., & Piedmont, R. L. (1999). Age differences in personality across the adult life span: Parallels in five cultures. *Developmental Psychology, 35*, 466–77.

McGee, R., Williams, S., & Elwood, M. (1994). Depression and the development of cancer: A meta-analysis. *Social Science and Medicine, 38*, 187–192.

Miller, J. J., Fletcher, K., & Kabat-Zinn, J. (1995). Three-year follow-up and clinical implications of a mindfulness meditation-based stress-reduction intervention in the treatment of anxiety disorders. *General Hospital Psychiatry, 17*, 192–200.

Miller, T. D., Smith, T. W., Turner, C. W., Guijarro, M. L., & Hallet, A. J. (1996). A meta-analytic review of research on hostility and physical health. *Psychological Bulletin, 119*, 322–348.

Mittleman, M. A., Maclure, M., Nachnani, M., Sherwood, J. B., & Muller, J. E. (1997). Educational attainment, anger, and the risk of triggering myocardial infarction onset. The Determinants of Myocardial Infarction Onset Study Investigators. *Archives of Internal Medicine, 157*, 769–75.

Mittleman, M. A., Maclure, M., Sherwood, J. B., Mulry, R. P., Tofler, G. H., Jacobs, S. C., Friedman, R., Benson, H., & Muller, J. E. (1995). Triggering of acute myocardial infarction onset by episodes of anger. Determinants of Myocardial Infarction Onset Study. *Circulation, 92*, 1720–1725.

Mroczek, D., & Spiro, A., III. (2003). Modeling intraindividual change in personality traits: Findings from the Normative Aging Study. *Journals of Gerontology: Psychological Sciences, 58B*, P153–P165.

Murberg, T. A., Bru, E., Svebak, S., Tveteras, R., & Aarsland, T. (1999). Depressed mood and subjective health symptoms as predictors of mortality in patients with congestive heart failure: A two-year follow-up study. *International Journal of Psychiatry and Medicine, 29*, 311–326.

Nemeroff, C. B., Musselman, D. L., & Evans, D. L. (1998). Depression and cardiac disease. *Depression and Anxiety, 8* (Suppl. 1), 71–79.

Niaura, R., Banks, S. M., Ward, K. D., Stoney, C. M., Spiro, A. III, Aldwin, C. M., Landsberg, M.D., & Weiss, S. T. (2000). Hostility and the metabolic syndrome in older males: The Normative Aging Study. *Psychosomatic Medicine, 62*, 7–16.

Parker, R., & Aldwin, C. M. (1997). Do aspects of gender identity change from early to middle adulthood? Disentangling age, cohort, and period effects. In M. Lachman & J. James (Eds.), *Multiple paths of mid-life development* (pp. 67–107). Chicago: University of Chicago Press.

Peterson, C. (1988). Explanatory style as a risk factor for illness. *Cognitive Therapy and Research, 12,* 117–130.

Peterson, C., & Seligman, M. E. P. (1984). Causal explanations as a risk factor for depression: Theory and evidence. *Psychological Review, 91,* 347–74.

Peterson, C., & Seligman, M. E. P. (1987). Explanatory style and illness. *Journal of Personality, 55,* 237–265

Peterson, C., Seligman, M. E. P., & Vaillant, G. E. (1988). Pessimistic explanatory style is a risk factor for physical illness: A thirty-five year longitudinal study. *Journal of Personality and Social Psychology, 55,* 23–27.

Peterson, C., Semmel, A., von Baeyer, C., Abramson, L. Y., Metalsky, G. I., & Seligman, M. E. P. (1982) The Attributional Style Questionnaire. *Cognitive Therapy Research, 6,* 287–299.

Pinquart, M., & Soerensen, S. (2001). How effective are psychotherapeutic and other psychosocial interventions with older adults? A meta-analysis. *Journal of Mental Health and Aging, 7,* 207–243.

Pulska, T., Pahkala, K., Laippala, P., & Kivelä, S.-L. (2000). Depressive symptoms predicting six-year mortality in depressed elderly Finns. *International Journal of Geriatric Psychiatry, 15,* 940–1046.

Review Panel on Coronary-Prone Behavior and Coronary Heart Disease (1978). Coronary-prone behavior and coronary heart disease: A critical review. *Circulation, 65,* 1199–1215.

Raine, R., Haines, A., Sensky, T., Hutchings, A., Larkin, K., & Black, N. (2002). Systematic review of mental health interventions for patients with common somatic symptoms: Can research evidence from secondary care be extrapolated to primary care? *British Medical Journal, 325,* 1082–1085.

Reibel, D. K., Greeson, J. M., Brainard, G. C., & Rosenzweig, S. (2001). Mindfulness-based stress reduction and health-related quality of life in a heterogeneous patient population. *General Hospital Psychiatry, 23,* 183–192.

Richards, J. C., Hof, A., & Alvarenga, M. (2000). Serum lipids and their relationships with hostility and angry affect and behaviors in men. *Health Psychology, 19,* 393–398.

Roberts, B. W., & DelVecchio, W. F. (2000). The rank-order consistency of personality traits from childhood to old age: A quantitative review of longitudinal studies *Psychological Bulletin, 126*(1), 3–25.

Rodin, J., & Langer, E. J. (1977). Long-term effects of a control-relevant intervention with institutionalized aged. *Journal of Personality and Social Psychology, 35,* 897–902.

Rotter, J. B. (1954). *Social learning theory and clinical psychology.* Englewood Cliffs, NJ: Prentice-Hall.

Scheier, M. F., & Carver, C. S. (1985). Optimism, coping, and health: Assessment and implications of generalized outcome expectancies. *Health Psychology, 4,* 219–247.

Scheier, M. F., & Carver, C. S. (1992). Effects of optimism on psychological and physical well-being: Theoretical overview and empirical update. *Cognitive Therapy Research, 16,* 201–228.

Scheier, M. F, Matthews, K., Owens, J. F., Magovern, G. J., Lefebvre, R. C., Abbott, R. A., & Carver, C. S. (1989). Dispositional optimism and recover from coronary artery bypass surgery: The beneficial effects on physical and psychological well-being. *Journal of Personality and Social Psychology, 57,* 1024–1040.

Scheier, M. F., Matthews, K., Owens, J. F., Schulz, R., Bridges, M. W., Magovern, G. J., & Carver, C. S. (1999). Optimism and rehospitalization after coronary artery bypass graft surgery. *Archives of Internal Medicine, 159,* 829–835.

Schmidt, N. B., McCreary, B. T., Trakowski, J. J., Santiago, H. T., Woolaway-Bickel, K., & Ialongo, N. (2003). Effects of cognitive behavioral treatment on physical health status in patients with panic disorder. *Behavior Therapy, 34,* 49–63.

Schulz, R., & Heckhausen, J. (1998). Emotion and control: A life-span perspective. In K. W. Schaie & M. P. Lawton (Eds.), *Annual review of gerontology and geriatrics: Vol. 17. Focus on emotion and adult development* (pp. 185–205). New York: Springer.

Seligman, M. E. P. (1975). *Helplessness: On depression, development, and death.* San Francisco: Freeman.

Sesso, H. D., Kawachi, I., Vokonas, P. S., & Sparrow, D. (1998). Depression and the risk of coronary heart disease in the Normative Aging Study. *American Journal of Cardiology, 82,* 851–856.

Sieber, W. J., Rodin, J., Larson, L., Ortega, N., Cummings, N., Levy, S., Whiteside, T., & Herberman, R. (1992). Modulation of human natural killer cell activity by exposure to uncontrollable stress. *Brain, Behavior, and Immunity, 6,* 141–156.

Smith, T. W., & Gallo, L. C. (1994). Psychosocial influences on coronary heart disease [Special issue]. *Irish Journal of Psychology, 15,* 8–26.

Smith, T. W., & Gallo, L. C. (2001). Personality traits as risk factors for physical illness. In A. Baum, T. A. Revenson, & J. E. Singer (Eds.), *Handbook of health psychology* (pp. 139–173). Mahwah, NJ: Lawrence Erlbaum Associates.

Spiro, A. III, Aldwin, C. M., Ward, K. D., & Mroczek, D. K. (1995). Personality and the incidence of hypertension among older men: Longitudinal findings from the Normative Aging Study. *Health Psychology, 14,* 563–569.

Srivastava, S., John, O. P., Gosling, S. D., & Potter, J. (2003). Development of personality in early and mid-life: Set in plaster or consistent change? *Journal of Personality and Social Psychology, 84,* 1041–1053.

Stein, M., Miller, A. H., & Trestman, R. L. (1991). Depression: The immune system, and health and illness. *Archives of General Psychiatry, 48,* 171–177.

Tellegen, A. P. (1982). *Manual for the Multidimensional Personality Questionnaire.* Department of Psychiatry, University of Minnesota.

Temoshok, L., Heller, B., Sagebiel, R., Blois, M., Sweet, D., Diclemete, R., & Gold, M. (1985). The relationship of psychosocial factors to prognostic indicators in cutaneous melanoma. *Journal of Psychosomatic Research, 29,* 137–155.

Tennant, C., & McLean, L. (2001). The impact of emotions on coronary heart disease risk. *Journal of Cardiovascular Risk, 8,* 175–183.

Thoresen, C. E., & Powell, L. H. (1992). Type A Behavior Pattern: New perspectives on theory, assessment, and intervention. *Journal of Consulting and Clinical Psychology, 60,* 595–604.

Tkachuk, G. A., Graff, L. A., Martin, G. L., & Bernstein, C. N. (2003). Randomized control trial of cognitive-behavioral group therapy for irritable bowel syndrome in a medical setting. *Journal of Clinical Psychology in Medicine Settings, 10,* 57–69.

Tomakowsky, J., Lumley, M. A., Markowitz, N., & Frank, C. (2001). Optimistic explanatory style and dispositional optimism in HIV-infected men. *Journal of Psychosomatic Research, 51,* 577–587.

Tsuang, M., & Woolson, R. (1978). Excess mortality in schizophrenia and affective disorders: Do suicides and accidental deaths solely account for this excess? *Archives General Psychiatry, 35,* 1181–1185.

Twenge, J. M. (2000). The age of anxiety? The birth cohort change in anxiety and neuroticism, 1952–1993. *Journal of Personality and Social Psychology, 79,* 1007–1021.

van Doornan, L. J. P. (1997). Lipids and the coronary-prone personality. In M. Hillbrand & R. T. Spitz (Eds.), *Lipids, health, and behavior* (pp. 81–98). Washington, DC: American Psychological Association.

Veith, I. (2000). *The Yellow Emperor's Classic of Internal Medicine.* Berkeley: University of California.

Vögele, C. (1998). Serum lipid concentrations, hostility, and cardiovascular reactions to mental stress. *International Journal of Psychophysiology, 28,* 167–179.

Weidner, G. (1994). Correlates of health behavior change: The Family Heart Study. *Homeostasis in Health and Disease, 35,* 235–242.

Weiner, H. (1977). *Psychobiology and human disease.* New York: Elsevier.

Welin, C., Lappas, G., & Wilhelmsen, L. (2000). Independent importance of psychosocial factors for prognosis after myocardial infarction. *Journal of Internal Medicine, 247,* 629–639.

Williams, R. B. (2000). Psychological factors, health, and disease: The impact of aging and the life cycle. In S. B. Manuck, R. Jennings, B. S. Rabin, & A. Baum (Eds.), *Behavior, health, and aging* (pp. 135–151). Mahwah, NJ: Lawrence Erlbaum Associates.

Wulsin, L. R., & Singal, B. M. (2003). Do depressive symptoms increase the risk for the onset of coronary disease? A systematic quantitative review. *Psychosomatic Medicine, 65,* 201–210.

Zheng, D., Macera, C., Croft, J., Giles, W., Davis, D., & Scott, W. (1997). Major depression and all-cause mortality among white adults in the United States. *Annuals of Epidemiology, 7,* 213–218.

22

Social Relationships, Transitions, and Personality Development Across the Life Span

Frieder R. Lang and Franziska S. Reschke
Martin-Luther-Universität Halle-Wittenburg, Germany

Franz J. Neyer
Humboldt-Universität zu Berlin, Germany

Changes of social relationships are part and parcel of personality development over the life course. The continuity and coherence of personality is manifested in the enduring ways in which individuals shape and manage their social relationships. The social world reflects the individual's concerns and behaviors, which in turn reflect affordances of the social environment. Over the past two decades, the theoretical and empirical understanding of change and continuity of personality over the life course has seen enormous growth (Caspi, 1998; Roberts & Caspi, 2003; Roberts & DelVecchio, 2000). However, the dynamic role and functions of social relationships in the lifelong stabilization and continuity of personality is still not well understood. For example, there is no quantitative review of the stability or change of social environments over the life course (see Neyer, 2004; Roberts & Caspi, 2003). One possible explanation for this apparent gap of knowledge lies in the dynamic and interwoven nature of social contexts at various phases of the life course. Moreover, social relationships typically are multidimensional, malleable, and characterized by mutuality and interdependence. Any change in mood, trait characteristics, attitudes, or affect of one partner in a relationship affects the other person and, thus, requires the other to adjust. For example, since the birth of his first child, Peter has become less irritable and more reliable over the years. Mary, his wife (as well as everyone else), expresses greater joy in being with Peter than ever before. But in what ways do such changes of social relationships contribute to the continuity and stabilization of personality over the life course? In this context, personality is defined as a set of relatively stable behaviors, feelings, or cognitions that characterize an individual's behavior consistently across different contexts. Personality characteristics can be classified with respect to their plasticity, stability, and malleability over the life course in two broad classes (Asendorpf & van Aken, 2003): Core personality characteristics such as the Big Five personality are relatively stable, whereas surface personality characteristics are less stable and more closely intertwined with relationship influences.

This chapter focuses on how individuals make use of motivational resources in order to regulate their social relationships and social experience and thus create developmental adaptive environments that enhance or protect their action potentials. It is argued that the shaping and managing of social relationships involves goal-related processes that are likely to contribute to the continuity, coherence, and stabilization of core personality traits over the life course. The central argument is that the adaptation and stabilization of personality characteristics, as a result of regulatory processes in social relationships, prototypically occur in the context of expected and normative transitions. This is not to say that other more unexpected and more undesirable life transitions (e.g., divorce, death of a child) do not also involve relationship regulation. However, for reasons of clarity and space, the discussion here focuses exclusively on the mastery of *normative* life tasks and events. Normative life course transitions are defined here as highly predictable events that are expected to occur to most people in a society and are well structured with respect to the involved demands and challenges for the individual's motivational and self-regulatory resources and capacities (Brandtstaedter & Rothermund, 2003; Cantor, Norem, Niedenthal, Langston, & Brower, 1987; Caspi & Moffitt, 1993; Heckhausen, 1999). The term *norm* here pertains to a social expectation rather than to a statistical norm. Prototypical examples of normative events are the birth of a sibling, school entry, entering the first job, marriage, first parenthood, and retirement. Normative transitions require adaptive efforts in personality-relationship transactions that are prototypical for the understanding of the lifelong dynamic interplay of personality, motivation, and social relationships. Typically, normative events involve necessary and inevitable changes in the individuals' social world, which are related to the activation (initiation, selection) or protection (reorganization, transformation, dissolution) of their social relationships. In this context, the term *life transitions* is used interchangeably with *normative life events*.

This chapter is organized in three sections: First, theoretical models on the stability and change of social relationships and personality over the life course as it is structured around normative life transitions are presented. The second section provides empirical illustrations of the ways in which the regulation of relationships in the course of normative life transitions contributes to the stabilization of personality over the life course. The mastery of normative life course transitions is typically accompanied by both change and continuity in personality characteristics. The third section focuses on specific mechanisms of normative and regulatory relationship change across the life course. Prospective research on personality development, motivation, and social resources is discussed and a roadmap for future research is provided.

STABILIZATION OF PERSONALITY AND SOCIAL RELATIONSHIPS OVER THE LIFE COURSE

From birth to death, individuals are confronted with educational, vocational, and family transitions that typically arise from the age-graded social structure in modern societies and that organize and sequence the individual's life course (Hagestad, 1990; Riley, 1985; Settersten, 1999). Theories of life-span management and developmental regulation address the ways in which individuals master the challenges and constraints associated with developmental tasks over the life course (Baltes, Staudinger, & Lindenberger, 1999; Brandtstädter & Rothermund, 2003; Carstensen, Isaacowitz, & Charles, 1999; Wrosch, Heckhausen, & Lachman, chap. 20 in this volume). The idea that individuals create and shape their social environments in accordance with their motives, goals, and basic traits has a rather long tradition in psychology (Allport, 1937; Caspi, Bem, & Elder, 1989; Snyder & Ickes, 1985). Furthermore, the ways in which processes of shaping environments lead to the stabilization and continuity of personality has been discussed from developmental (e.g., Lang & Heckhausen, 2005), social (e.g., Ickes, Snyder, & Garcia, 1997), and evolutionary (e.g., Buss, 1999) perspectives. The common ground of these perspectives is related to the idea that when facing environmental affordances or constraints individuals make use of motivational and regulatory strategies, which enhance their action potentials (i.e., adaptivity).

How Do Social Relationships Contribute to the Continuity of Personality?

Some scholars suggest that personality provides a scaffold of social relationships (Vangelisti, Reis, & Fitzpatrick, 2002), whereas others argue that social contexts constitute vehicles for the individual's personality over the life course (Antonucci & Jackson, 1990; Lang, 2004). Both perspectives are complementary rather than contradictory: The first perspective is corroborated by empirical evidence according to which core personality characteristics influence social relationships rather than vice versa (e.g., Asendorpf & van Aken, 2003; Asendorpf & Wilpers, 1998; Neyer & Asendorpf, 2001). In this view, core personality characteristics are associated with social choices and preferences that cumulate over time and thus create enduring person–environment fit (Caspi, 1998; Caspi et al., 1989; Roberts & Caspi, 2003). Such person–environment fit is stable, but not necessarily contributing to the individual's action potential. The second perspective, in contrast, emphasizes the individual's regulation of social relationships, which serves to create adaptive contexts that enhance developmental resources and thus contribute to increasing continuity of personality characteristics over the life course (Antonucci & Jackson, 1990; Lang, Featherman, & Nesselroade 1997). In this tradition, the activation and protection of adaptive social resources is seen as fostering the mastery of developmental transitions or normative life tasks.

Normative Transitions Entail Strong Situations. There has been some debate about how and in what ways normative life transitions and the involved changes of social relationships may differently contribute to the continuity of personality over the life course as compared to unexpected life events and relationship changes (e.g., Cantor & Kihlstrom, 1987; Caspi & Moffitt, 1993; Wrosch & Freund, 2001). Caspi and Moffitt (1993) suggested that predictable, normative life transitions are associated with an increased likelihood of personality change, because individuals are "knifed off" from preexisting environments while at the same time being confronted with structured scripts of how to behave after the transition. According to this, situations differ with respect to the kind of environmental pressures they exert on the individual. This is consistent with the idea that personality effects on social behavior differ in weak and in strong situations (Snyder & Ickes, 1985). Normative life events (e.g., first parenthood) often result in strong situations that require individuals to give up existing preferences and behavioral styles and to adapt to the new environmental pressures. Consequently, personality differences may have less impact on changes in social relationships. Narrowly structured environments allow only for specific behaviors and thus wipe out individual preferences and behavioral styles. One result is that personality may change. In strong situations, individuals have a low degree of freedom to change the environment according to their personality. In contrast, unexpected life events are often related to weak situations that are less regulated by social rules or norms and, thus, allow the individual to invest in existing preferences and behavioral styles. These personality differences may have relatively strong impact on changes in social relationships. One result is that social relationship changes contribute to stabilization rather than to change of personality (Neyer, 2004). This is not to say that the distinction between weak or unexpected and strong or expected life transitions is empirically clear. Rather, this is conceived of as a continuum from relatively weak to relatively strong situations. However, the analytic distinction is of heuristic value and contributes to an improved understanding of the underlying regulatory mechanisms. Weak and strong situations imply two kinds of relationship change, which are conceptualized as regulatory and normative relationship change.

Regulatory and Normative Relationship Change: A Distinction.   Age-graded life transitions are associated with relatively explicit scripts and societal expectations about the ways in which such normative transitions ought to be mastered. If, in contrast, individuals are confronted with ambiguity of solutions and have free choice, they will select a personality-congruent way of adapting to a transition. In the first case, personality change is likely to occur, whereas in the latter case, there will be much continuity and stabilization of the individual's personality. There are two broad classes of relationship changes that emerge in the context of normative life transitions.

The first type of relationship changes defines specific tasks as constituents of the normative life course transition. For example, the transition to the first job necessarily implies gaining new colleagues. Marriage involves that partners show enhanced commitments in the partnership. Changes in an individual's social roles and social identity are necessary features of most transitions that occur over the life course (Erikson, 1959; Lewis, 1999). The involved changes are normative, because they define the salient tasks of the specific life course transition (e.g., retirement). Such normative changes entail several challenges. They limit the continuity in the quality of people's social relationships (e.g., change in professional friendships after retirement), they threaten their social resources (e.g., status change after retirement), and they imply ambiguity or insecurity about the future of their social relationships. These challenges require adaptive efforts of individuals to protect their motivational and self-regulatory resources.

The second type of relationship change is related to the individuals' purposeful effort to shape and manage their social relationships in order to master the transitional tasks (e.g., finding a supportive colleague on the new job, activating kinship relationships after retirement). These changes of relationships result from the individual's active and reactive efforts of shaping and molding the social environment. Such relationship changes are regulatory, because they represent the individual's striving for control and enhanced action potentials over the life course.

In the following discussion, the first type is referred to as *normative relationship change* and the second is called *regulatory relationship change*. Normative relationship changes follow culture-specific scripts that are highly predictable because they are accompanied by new social roles, which are clearly defined by new tasks and social norms (e.g., being a reliable husband, a caring parent, or a responsible coworker). The course and direction of such normative relationship changes can only be influenced or altered within limited margins (e.g., marriage implies living in the same household). One implication is that adapting to such normative change requires activation of self-regulatory resources, which may subsequently lead to change (increase or decrease) of enduring personality characteristics (e.g., becoming more reliable). Regulatory relationship changes, in contrast, reflect the individual's social preferences and behavioral styles, through which individuals protect their control over their social environmental resources. Regulatory relationship changes imply that individuals shape their social world so that it fits best with their personality. Consequently, such regulatory changes contribute to the stabilization and continuity of the personality over the life course (e.g., remaining a reliable person). Using the terms of Sanderson and Cantor (1999), it is suggested that normative relationship change across the life course "generally acts as a *push* toward personality change" (p. 373), whereas regulatory relationship change acts as a "pull" toward enhanced stabilization of personality. For example, when individuals transition into a first job, this involves a push to develop new social behaviors and social roles (normative changes). During the transition, social relationships with friends and family are also challenged and managed (pulled) to fit with one's own goals and tasks in this phase of life (regulatory changes). This may also serve to illustrate that both types of relationship changes typically co-occur simultaneously. Similarly, most life course transitions involve change in some personality dimensions but also much continuity in other personality dimensions (Mroczek & Spiro, 2003; Small, Hertzog, Hultsch, & Dixon, 2003). For example, becoming a parent involves prescribed new and normative tasks related to taking care of one's family. Mastering this task may involve social behaviors that promote qualitative increases in traits related to conscientiousness and agreeableness (Srivastava, John, Gosling, & Potter, 2003). Regulatory changes of relationships refer to individual styles of selecting, shaping, and organizing the specific type or quality of relationship (e.g., spouse, child or other persons of the social network) in the course of the transition.

Life Course Transitions Involve Regulatory Relationship Change. Social relationships are malleable and dynamic. They never involve scripts for individual action that allow just for one type of individual behavior. Although there are general pressures on individual behaviors in social relationships such as the norm of reciprocity (Gouldner, 1960) or kinship orientations (Neyer & Lang, 2003), the course and the quality of a specific social relationship are always unique for at least two individuals. There is no personal relationship that is identical to another one either within the individual's network or between individuals' social networks.

Social relationships are often classified according to role-specific scripts such as friendship or kinship (Hartup & Stevens, 1997; Neyer & Lang, 2003). However, the heterogeneity within each of such relationship roles may be at times greater than the heterogeneity between the roles. In other words, it is not possible to replace one friend with another friend or to replace a child with a friend. This is not to say that relationship loss cannot be compensated or substituted (e.g., Rook & Schuster, 1996), rather, compensation processes imply regulatory relationship change. At times, individuals may loosen one tie while intensifying another tie. Often this is done for reasons that lie in the self (i.e., the individual's goals) or in the particular characteristics of the relationship. Many transitions confront individuals with new social partners that they have not, and perhaps never would have, deliberately chosen as social partners. For example, in professional transitions and career advancements it is fairly usual to enter a new team, to have a new boss, a new colleague, or a new client, whom individuals did not select themselves. However, there are few legal situations, in which individuals have very limited choice of their prospective social partners. Even in extreme prisonlike situations, individuals may still have (rather limited) options to choose among social partners. In such situations, individuals may apply their individual, personality-based scripts of shaping and regulating their social world. It is plausible to expect that such regulatory changes of social relationships in the course of normative life course transitions contribute to the stabilization of personality over time.

Regulatory Relationship Changes Stabilize Personality. By definition, normative transitions are age-graded and reflective of social-structural and societal environments that are typically not self-selected. Consequently, the occurrence of normative life transitions does not depend on personality characteristics (with a few exceptions), whereas unexpected life events are often associated with stable personality differences. For example, there is evidence for personality and genetic influences on the occurrence of favorable or adverse life events (e.g., Billig, Hershberger, Iacono, & McGue, 1996; Headey & Wearing, 1989; Saudino, Pedersen, Lichtenstein, McClearn, & Plomin, 1997).

Changes of social relationship that occur in the context of normative transitions are typically not under the individual's deliberate control. For example, in most societies, marrying implies that individuals behave according to predefined social scripts that require being loyal, faithful, and trustful toward their partner. Consequently, the transition to marriage may trigger qualitative changes toward more positive social-behavioral traits and behaviors (Neyer & Asendorpf, 2001). However, such normative relationship changes occur within a structure of other social relationships. This means that all normative transitions also provide many opportunities for individual preferences and social-behavioral styles, which might counterbalance the effects of the normative environmental press. For example, the extent to which spouses share relationships with their relatives predicts the stability of their marital relationship (Orbuch, Veroff, Hassan, & Horrocks, 2002).

Individuals use motivational and self-regulatory strategies to protect or enhance their action potentials (Heckhausen, 1999; Heckhausen & Schulz, 1995). This involves strategies that may either aim at the other partner's or the individual's own internal states or behaviors. For example, individuals may adapt their expectations and internal goals during a transition in order to change or stabilize the quality of their existing relationship(s).

Strategies and Motivational Processes of Developmental Regulation

Developmental research literature indicates that prototypical strategies of life management can be subdivided in two general groups of strategies. The first group aims at changing or stabilizing the external world. The second group of strategies aims at changing or protecting the internal states of the individual's mind (Brandtstaedter & Rothermund, 2003; Heckhausen, 1999, Rothbaum, Weisz, & Snyder, 1982). The functionality of such strategies was described with respect to the involved adaptation processes, which either pertain to investing or activating resources, to protect resources or to compensate for loss (e.g., Baltes et al., 1999; Wrosch, Heckhausen, & Lachman, chap. 20 in this volume). According to Heckhausen and Schulz (1995), all individuals are evolutionarily optimized to strive for the maximization to exert control over their external world. Primary control striving involves strategies that are directed toward the environment (e.g., taking influence on others) in the course of a transition. Secondary control striving pertains to the readjustment of internal standards and to the reduction of cognitive discrepancies in a given situation. Primary and secondary control strategies operate hand-in-hand during the mastery of normative life transitions. Both, primary and secondary control striving involve mobilization of behavioral, social, and motivational resources either in the self or in the social environment.

Life Course Theories of Relationship Change. The motivational processes underlying developmental changes of social relationships were addressed in socioemotional selectivity theory (e.g., Carstensen et al., 1999). The theory posits that individuals adapt their social motives over the life course in response to perceptions of the remaining time in their future life. When time is perceived as expansive, individuals prioritize goals and motives that optimize the future in the long run. Typically, this implies that they seek to enhance their social and self-related knowledge, which may be useful in the future. In contrast, when time is perceived as limited, emotionally meaningful goals are more salient and more adaptive. One reason is that emotional gratification does not require much effort. Whereas long-term rewards often require investment and the pursuit of information, short-term goals may allow for more immediate albeit meaningful benefits. There is robust empirical support for the basic assumptions of socioemotional selectivity theory (overview: Carstensen et al., 1999), as well as many demonstrations of its validity and usefulness in the domains of memory (Mather & Carstensen, 2003), the processing of commercial messages (Fung & Carstensen, 2003), and the shaping of social networks over the life course (Lang & Carstensen, 2002). For example, when individuals approach endings or experience that their remaining time in life is limited, they tend to dissolve less meaningful and distant social relationships while preferably pursuing goals related to belongingness needs such as generativity (Lang & Carstensen, 2002).

Patterns of structural changes of social relationships over the life course were also described with the metaphor of a "social convoy over the life course" (Kahn & Antonucci, 1980). According to the *social-convoy model,* individuals move through their lives surrounded by social partners, to whom they maintain diverse, multifaceted, and ever-changing relationships as in a convoy of vehicles. In this metaphor, personality may be seen as the engine that steers the individual through the convoy of lifelong relationships (and thus, transports the individual across the life course). Continuity of personality, in this perspective, may be seen as a catalyst as well as a product of social experience, which leads to improvements of the social convoy driver's driving capacities. With increasing life management expertise, individuals may become better at selecting those individuals in their environment that better fit with their personality, thus producing increased continuity and coherence over time.

CONTINUITY AND CHANGE OF SOCIAL RELATIONSHIPS AND PERSONALITY IN THE COURSE OF LIFE TRANSITIONS

Environments are not rigid and enduring cocoons that either do or do not fit the individual. Rather, environments are hierarchical, dynamic, and malleable systems that surround the individual (Lerner & Kauffman 1985; Lewis, 1999). Environments evoke, shape and select individual behavior, and are also selected, shaped, and interpreted by the individual (Caspi, 1998; Sanderson & Cantor, 1999). It may even be argued that developmental ecologies like social relationships reflect "extensions" of an individual's personality. As Lewontin (1982, p. 160) put it: "Environment is nature organized by organisms."

The stability and change of social relationships entail great challenges to theoretical and empirical work on personality development over the life course (Lang & Fingerman, 2004; Vangelisti et al., 2002). There is some evidence for moderate stability in specific relationship contexts. For example, in an 8-year longitudinal study, McNally, Eisenberg, and Harris (1991) found substantial stabilities of parental orientation and behavioral styles toward their 7- to 18-year-old children. There is also evidence for moderate continuity of structural indicators of the social environment such as professional status in the job context (Roberts & Caspi, 2003). In the studies of Asendorpf and Wilpers (1998; Neyer & Asendorpf, 2001), Big Five Personality traits were generally more stable than indicators of the quality of social relationship.

Is There Continuity of Social Environments Over the Life Course?

In general, assumptions of social-environmental continuity over the life course are challenged by at least three considerations: First, social relationships are most vulnerable to change. Each relationship consists of two individuals with different personalities. Most individuals have more than one relationship (i.e., a personal network), and some of these social relationships (e.g., within the family) are often interdependent (Cook, 1993). By nature, the stability of a given relationship context cannot be larger than the stability of the social behavior of all involved individuals. If the personality of one relationship partner is unstable, this inevitably also changes the relationship context of other partners as well. Second, human societies are characterized by continuous social-structural change, related to technological innovations or to socioeconomic change. Elder (1974) demonstrated that economic crises have a strong impact on personality stability and development in adolescence and adulthood. Third, in modern societies, individual life courses are organized around educational, vocational, and family transitions, which confront the individual with age-graded tasks and challenges (Hagestad, 1990; Havighurst, 1948/1981; Sanderson & Cantor, 1999; West & Graziano, 1989).

One implication of these considerations is that at all phases of the life course individuals are equally likely to experience discontinuity and change in their social environments. Consequently, evidence for increases in consistency of personality over the life course (e.g., Roberts & DelVecchio, 2000) may not simply be attributed to increased stability in the individual's social environment. On the contrary, when considering that in most modern societies an overwhelming majority of children grows up in one household together with both their (married) biological parents (e.g., Amato & Fowler, 2002; Nauck, 1991), social-environmental changes are more likely to occur across adulthood than in childhood and adolescence. What then accounts for continuity of personality over the life course? It is argued that when individuals experience environmental change in the course of life transitions, they invest in social-regulatory strategies that aim at creating (and reconstructing) social environments that match best with their enduring behavioral and social preferences.

The distinction of normative and regulatory changes of social relationships in the course of normative life course transitions has several implications for the development of personality. First, normative relationship change may affect personality development in different ways than regulatory relationship change. Whereas normative relationship changes (e.g., the transition to partnership) may contribute to personality change, the individual's regulatory efforts to activate or protect social relationships, in response to a transition, may contribute to continuity and stability of the personality. Second, regulatory relationship changes may counterbalance the effects of normative relationship change on personality development. Selection and transformation of social relationships are likely to contribute to the continuity of an individual's personality. This may also improve the understanding of apparent contradictory effects of normative life transitions on continuity or change of personality over the life course. For example, whereas some empirical findings suggest that normative life transitions are associated with change of personality (e.g., Neyer & Asendorpf, 2001), other findings suggest that there is much continuity of personality in the course of life transitions (Asendorpf & Wilpers, 1998; Hope, Rodgers, & Power, 1999). Third, individuals may develop specific relationship-regulatory strategies and competences that lead to improved mastery of normative relationships over the life course. According to theories on social-developmental regulation over the life course (Carstensen et al., 1999; Heckhausen & Schulz, 1995), it is expected that as individuals begin to experience limitations of resources (e.g., time remaining in life), they seek to protect the quality of their social relationships in order to protect their sense of life purpose and action potentials. For example, normative relationship changes that occur during early life course transitions (e.g., school entry) may generalize more strongly to other domains of social functioning than relationship changes that occur in late-life transitions (e.g. retirement). As individuals grow older, they acquire social-regulatory strategies, which help them protect their motivational resources as well as their meaningful social relationships in the course of a transition. This may, in part, account for the increasing continuity and stabilization of personality over the life course.

The following discussion focuses on normative life course transitions that arise in the context of family development and in the context of educational and vocational development. Table 22.1 gives an overview of empirical evidence on exemplar normative transitions across the life course and the specific challenges and constraints, as well as the regulatory tasks, associated with these transitions. Another relevant class of normative life transitions is associated with spiritual and religious development. Initiation rites of group membership or spiritual "rites des passage" (Caspi & Moffitt, 1993) also produce changes of social opportunity structures that may contribute to the stabilization of personality. Not much is known, however, about the ways in which social relationships are affected through spiritual passages in the life course.

The Family Context

Birth of a Sibling. Becoming a (older) sibling often is the first normative life course transition in an individual's life course. Firstborn children, who experience the birth of a sibling, are confronted with the task of having to share the previously undivided love and care of the parents. Firstborn children typically begin to develop behavioral changes during the mother's pregnancy and before the sibling's birth (Kramer & Ramsburg, 2002). Two- and 3-year-old children even engage in anticipatory efforts to master the event (Stewart, 1990). In a longitudinal study, Baydar and Brooks-Gunn (1997) explored effects of the birth of a sibling over 6 years. Findings illustrate changes of family interactions such as reduced positive interactions with the mother and increased interaction with the father. The firstborn child's mastery of the siblinghood transition depends on the quality of the family's relationships, such as the mother's attachment (e.g., Teti, Sakin, Kucera, & Corns, 1996). Also, birth of a younger sibling often is associated with a temporary phase of regressive problems and at the same time provides opportunities for enhanced intellectual and socioemotional capacities (Baydar, Hyle, & Brooks-Gunn, 1997). Siblings who are around 2 years old at the time of the birth of their sibling often experience greater regressive problems. One reason may be that, at this age, children still lack some of the self- and social-regulatory skills that are required to master the siblinghood transition.

The transition to siblinghood appears to enhance and support the development of social-regulatory skills in the child. There are findings (although not fully consistent) suggesting that being a sibling affects the child's relationships to peers (Dunn, 1992). In general, the transition to siblinghood contributes to the child's improved understanding of family and rules and to improved learning of social skills such as taking care of a family member.

Marriage. When couples marry (or move in together), new challenges and tasks arise in the partnership, which typically involve the sharing of household responsibilities, family relationships, other relatives, and friendship relationships (Sprecher, Felmlee, Orbuch, & Willetts, 2002; Veroff, Douvan, Orbuch, & Acitelli, 1998). A critical issue in early marriage phases is to what extent the spouses do or do not develop overlapping or close-knit social networks. For example, having shared friendships and networks is associated with greater marital relationship quality (e.g., Stein,

TABLE 22.1

Personality Development, Relationship Change and Transitions: Exemplary Illustrations of Challenges, Constraints, and Strategies

		Challenges and Constraints		Regulatory Relationship Strategies (Activation/Protection)
Transition	Personality Change or Continuity	Normative Relationship Change		
		Family transitions		
First siblinghood	—Regressive problems	—Change of family interactions		• Taking responsibility for sibling
				• Sharing parental love
First Marriage	—Increase of positive personality	—Adjustment to partner		• Readjustment of other relationships
		—New relatives		• Dyadic network regulation
First parenthood	—Increase of agreeableness	—Changing family structure		• Activating supportive networks
		—Reduced marital satisfaction		• Role negotiation in family
		Educational and vocational transitions		
School entry	—Increase of competence and academic achievement	—New peers and teachers		• Cooperative/prosocial behaviors
				• Adjust to peer group norms
School-to-school, School-to-work	—Increase of job-congruent personality characteristics	—Multiple new roles		• Activate professional support
				• Balance family with work demands
Retirement	(—Continuity)	—Loss of professional roles		• Readjustment of social network
				• Changing family involvement

455

Bush, Ross, & Ward, 1992), and is known to predict more traditional role segregation in the marriage (Milardo & Allan, 1996). Marital satisfaction in the early years of marriage is greater when husbands and wives manage to mobilize support from their respective relatives. However, this also entails risks, when the involvement of relatives from both partners is not balanced or when relatives are too demanding or intrusive (e.g., Timmer, Veroff, & Hatchett, 1996). Managing the transition to early marital phases involves that couples develop a dyadic network regulation, which requires specific communicative competence, interdependence, and the delegating and dividing of shared responsibilities.

Whereas some challenges that emerge in the transition to marriage or to romantic partnership appear to contribute to the continuity of personality, first partnership also entails great potentials for positive and qualitative change in personality. Moving from the status of being single to (first) partnership in early adulthood was found to be associated with a change toward more positive personality traits such as emotional stability and conscientiousness (Neyer & Asendorpf, 2001). Moreover, such growth of positive personality appears to even persist after the partnership ends. It is an open question as to what extent the transition to a first partnership differs from the marriage transition (which typically occurs later than the beginning of partnership). In a longitudinal study based on an entire cohort of children born in England, Scotland, and Wales in the first week of March 1958, Hope et al. (1999) explored associations between marital status and levels of distress among respondents at age 23 ($N = 12\ 357$) and at age 33 ($N = 11\ 405$). In this study, the transition to marriage was not associated with much change in symptoms of psychological distress (anxiety, depression, somatic complaints). The findings suggest that activation and sharing of supportive friends and relatives in the social network stabilize the marriage and thus also contribute to the continuity of personality. There needs to be empirical testing of the ways the couples' dyadic shaping and regulating of relationship changes in the transition to partnership or marriage is associated with more stable personalities over time. Overall, it is an established finding that, in the long run, being married (as compared to singlehood) has beneficial effects on psychological well-being and physical health (e.g., Brown, 2000; Horwitz & White, 1998; Stack & Eshleman, 1998). Additionally, marital transitions often involve regulatory change in other social relationships (friends, relatives) that may counteract the effects of marriage transition on personality change.

First Parenthood.   In an overview of research on the transition to parenting, Heinicke (2002) concluded that there is much continuity of personality and marital quality after birth of the first child. However, there is also evidence for change in the quality of family relationships. In general, the transition to parenthood involves tasks and demands that challenge the family system. It is a robust finding that the quality of the marital relationship decreases in the months following the birth of a first child (e.g., Gloger-Tippelt & Huerkamp, 1998; Helms-Erikson, 2001), whereas the risk of divorce or separation of parents increases (Orbuch et al., 2002). The specific motivational and regulatory mechanisms underlying changes in family interactions are not yet fully understood. There is some indication that parenthood typically leads to increased activation of supportive and network resources that may also contribute to improved adaptation (Bost, Cox, Burchinal, & Payne, 2002).

It still is an open question as to what extent such changes are associated with continuity or discontinuity of personality. Fathers who were more involved with a newborn child showed decreases in self-esteem over the first 15 months following the child's birth (Hawkins & Belsky, 1989). In this case, the level of involvement may reflect efforts that enhance personality continuity among fathers over time. When investing more into the new role, fathers will experience less self-esteem enhancing success with goals and plans in other domains of life. Srivastava and collaborators (2003) suggested that normative changes in agreeableness occur in the beginning of the fourth decade of life (age 30) where people in Western societies typically undergo the transition to parenthood. However, the empirical evidence for this is still relatively scarce.

Educational and Vocational Contexts

School Entry and School-to-School. Early educational transitions involve adaptations to new learning environments and to complex new social situations. Moreover, school settings are typically associated with the pressure to acquire socially adaptive academic behaviors and to find adequate roles within the peer group. Consequently, school entry for the child typically involves challenges related to normative tasks such as learning appropriate social behaviors in the classroom toward peers and teachers (Ladd, 1999; Perry & Weinstein, 1998). There is good evidence that the quality of peer relationships in the school context influences the child's academic as well as socioemotional performance (Buhs, & Ladd, 2001; Dunn, Cutting, & Fisher, 2002). The relationship quality with parents and with teachers is relevant for the children's mastery of normative relationship changes in school entry as well as in school-to-school transitions. For example, Grolnick, Kurowski, Dunlab, and Hevey (2000) interviewed mothers and their children at the transition to junior high school. Involvement of mothers predicted mean-level stability of perceived competence and learning performance. Obviously, school entry involves great vulnerability to the quality of the child's other relationships.

In a study investigating the transition to on-campus residence of female and male college freshman, Perl and Trickett (1988) observed that the formation of new social networks was associated with adaptations of social preferences and exploration behaviors among students. Similarly, Zirkel (1992) explored the task-specific influences on the transition to college in two groups of first-year college students: A first group of students entered an academically challenging (high) college, and a second group of students entered a sorority. The two groups differed with respect to their salient concerns during the transition. The first group experienced fear of academic failure, whereas students in the second group were concerned about their family and their social acceptance in the peer group. Regulatory relationship changes in early adulthood appear to reflect responses to challenges of situation-specific tasks during a transition rather than to the transitional task in general.

School-to-Work and Career Transitions. The transition from school to work is complex because it often involves a myriad of normative relationship changes such as moving to a new city, a change of social status, balancing work and leisure demands, formal relationships with colleagues in hierarchical structures, and mastery of new professional demands while having relatively few job experience (e.g., Bynner, 1998). Whereas there is some evidence for influences of macro-contextual and so-cial-structural influences on the course and timing of school-to-work transition (e.g., Reitzle, Vondracek, & Silbereisen, 1998; Weidman, 1987), not much is known about the regulatory changes that accompany such transitions. For example, in a longitudional study with adolescents approaching the end of school, Heckhausen and Tomasik (2002) observed adjustments of aspirations and job preferences in the course of seeking and applying for apprenticeships. These findings suggest that indi-viduals adapt their internal standards in anticipation of the transition. However, not all regulatory changes of social relationships that accompany the transitions to the first job are yet well understood. For example, regulatory relationship changes in the school-to-work transition also involve tasks such as seeking job-relevant informa-tion, mobilizing support from colleagues, and differentiating formal roles in the job context, as well as choosing partners for adaptive upward and downward social com-parisons (e.g., Bynner, 1998; Heckhausen & Krueger, 1993).

Based on data from the longitudinal Dunedin study, Roberts, Caspi, and Moffitt (2003) investigated the association between personality and work experience during early adulthood (from age 18 to 26). Findings suggest that specific work experiences (e.g., achieving power, work autonomy) predicted personality change at age 26. When work experience (e.g., achieving power or status) was congruent with the young adult's personality (e.g., social agency or potency), personality change was more pronounced than when there was less congruence (i.e., *lack of corresponsiveness* in the terms of Roberts et al., 2003). Career transitions and work experiences seem to be related both to the continuity and stabilization (or deepening) of positive (or job congruent) personality characteristics as well as to changes of personality. One ex-planation is that regulatory relationship changes may bolster and train the individ-ual's congruent personality characteristics. Therefore, job tasks that are congruent with personality traits reinforce respective social behaviors, whereas job tasks that are incongruent may result in greater efforts to protect one's social- and self-regulatory resources.

Retirement. Over the past decades, the timing and process of retirement as well as the life quality of the postretirement phase of life, has changed enormously (Hay-ward, Friedman & Chen, 1998; Settersten, 1998). Most professionals expect an ex-tended period of relatively healthy living when they retire from the job (Kim & Moen, 2001). However, the transition also bears many challenges, which typically emerge in the social context. Kim and Moen (2001) argued that the course and qual-ity of the retirement process depends on the broader social-ecological context, in-cluding the marital relationship. Mastering the transition to retirement also involves challenges that arise from an enormous discontinuity in the individual's professional relationships. In a longitudinal study of social network change before and after re-tirement, Van Tilburg (1992) observed substantive changes in the structure and functions of supportive networks. One year after retirement, most relationships with former colleagues had disappeared from the network, but the overall size of social networks did not change much. However, individuals were very likely to maintain most of their nonprofessional relationships and begin new relationships with net-work partners to which they experienced reciprocity in social exchanges. These findings may underscore that even if dramatic changes occur during a transition, older adults appear to be able to protect meaningful and instrumental relationships from the effects of normative relationship changes. Considering the great continuity and coherence of personality in later adulthood (Roberts & DelVecchio, 2000; Small et al., 2003), together with findings that suggest great interindividual differences in stability and change of personality (Mroczek & Spiro, 2003; Small et al., 2003), regulatory adaptations in the social networks would be expected to greatly contribute to general stabilization of personality in the postretirement phase. Further research needs to address the possible effects of relationship regulation on change or continuity of personality in the retirement process.

To sum up, empirical evidence shows that family, educational, and vocational transitions over the life course often involve changes in the social environment. These changes are a result of the individual's proactive mastery of the transition rather than a result of the normative changes of the transition per se. Distinguishing between normative relationship changes that emerge in the course of a transition, on the one hand, and the individuals' adaptive efforts to shape and organize the environment in accordance with their needs and preferences while mastering the transition, on the other hand, may also contribute to improved understanding of stabilization processes in personality development over the life course. From early childhood, individuals develop strategies to shape and organize their social environments when being confronted with age-graded and normative changes in their social world (i.e., siblinghood, partnership, school and job entry, parenthood, retirement). Such transitions entail prototypical environmental challenges for the individual. Mastering the tasks of these transitions involves that individuals activate and transform their social relationships in ways that protect or enhance their action potentials. This also appears to be critical for the stabilization and continuity of personality across adulthood. Empirical illustrations also suggest that with increasing age there is a general shift from an activation to a protection modus in the shaping and organizing of social relationships during a life course transition.

STABILIZATION OF PERSONALITY AND REGULATION OF SOCIAL RELATIONSHIPS OVER THE LIFE COURSE

From early childhood until late in life, the human life course is structured around normative life transitions and tasks, which entail inevitable and normative changes in the individual's social relationships. Such transitional challenges are typically accompanied by the individual's efforts to activate or protect social resources in the network, which contribute to mastery or control potentials. Such *regulatory* adjustments in the social environment may thus minimize or counterbalance the instability of environments associated with most life course transitions. Regulatory relationship changes may contribute to improved understanding of increasing stabilization and positive changes of personality over the life course (Lang, Lüdtke, & Asendorpf, 2001; McCrae et al, 1999; Neyer & Asendorpf, 2001; Roberts & DelVecchio, 2000; Small et al., 2003; Srivastava et al., 2003). Dealing with the tasks of balancing and mastering the changing demands of social relationships within a complex social network during transitional changes may lead to increased expertise in the regulation of social relationships. The stabilization of positive personality characteristics over the life course may be attributed to a growing expertise in organizing the social environment in ways that fit best with individuals.

Building on assumptions of theories on developmental regulation over the life course, such as socioemotional selectivity theory (Carstensen et al., 1999) and the life course theory of control (Heckhausen & Schulz, 1995), individuals shape and organize their relationships not only through processes of activation (vs. nonactivation), but also through protection (vs. breaking-off). Both processes involve strategies that may either aim at the self (secondary control) or at the social partner in a relationship (primary control). Self-focused strategies of relationship regulation refer to the activation and protection of individuals' own motivational resources for maintaining and transforming the quality of a relationship in the course of a life transition, such as choosing standards for social comparisons (Heckhausen & Krueger, 1993), emotion regulation (Carstensen et al., 1999), or accommodative behaviors (Yovetich & Rusbult, 1994). Other-focused regulation of relationships refers to the choice of social partners (Fredrickson & Carstensen, 1990), interpersonal sense of control (Cook, 1993), dissolution of social relationships (Lang, 2004) or acts of generativity or social responsibility (McAdams & de St. Aubin, 1992).

After reviewing selected empirical illustrations, it appears that individuals shift from activation to protection modes and from other-focus to self-focus in organizing their social relationships over the life course. For example, older adults appear to adapt their goals and needs as they experience limitations of resources or remaining time in life (Carstensen et al., 1999; Lang, 2003). In a study with a representative sample of adults, who were between age 20 and age 90, Lang and Carstensen (2002) found that individuals benefited from committing to emotion-regulatory goals in organizing their social networks, when perceiving their future time as limited. In another study with married couples in middle and later adulthood, Levenson, Carstensen, and Gottman (1993; Carstensen, Gottman, & Levenson, 1995) discovered that older couples were better at expressing mutual affection and better at avoiding conflictual issues in interactions with their spouse. These findings are consistent with the contention that older adults are better at differentiating normative and regulatory tasks of relationship changes across adulthood.

In earlier phases of life, children, adolescents, and young adults appear to generalize across relationships and social roles. For example, externalizing problems and acts of aggression toward other people often culminate in late adolescence (Curtner-Smith, 2000). Empirical findings on family–work spillover (Rogers & May, 2003) suggest that, particularly in early adulthood, individuals often generalize from the quality of family relationships to work relationships and vice versa. Shaping and organizing one's social environment accompanies the individual's efforts to master life course transitions. Doing so is critical for the understanding of personality development and stabilization over the life course. The review on associations between social relationships, transitions, and the stabilization of personality also points to a couple of pertinent research issues that need to be addressed in the future.

Future Outlook and Pertinent Research Issues

More research on the dynamics of the social environments of individuals is needed. Understanding the dynamic transactions between personality and social relationships requires reliable measures of social environment. There are two implications: First, there is a need to theoretically link models of personality development with models of change or stability in social relationships. It is still not well understood in which ways personality-dependent differences in social relationships relate to adaptive processes of shaping social relationships. For example, changes of relationship status (e.g., siblinghood) may characterize groups of individuals, in which personality effects on changes in the quality of the individual's social network relationships differ. Moreover, when relying on more frequent measurement occasions in longitudinal designs, it is possible to identify some of the processes that underlie the stabilization of personality characteristics during changes of the relationship quality. Second, research on environmental stability or continuity often relies on self-report data. Obviously, quality and exchanges of social relationships are difficult to observe from the outside (cf. Neyer, in press). One possible solution is that other informants are included in research that can either validate or inform about the quality of an individual's social relationships. Additionally, research is needed that also addresses possible age differences across adulthood in the associations between personality and social relationships.

Another critical issue in research on personality change and coherence pertains to the interplay of personality, motivation, and regulatory processes that organizes the individual's adaptation over the life course. There are few domains of life management in which this is as obvious as in the social domain. Evocative, responsive, and manipulative transactions between the individual and the social environment depend on the individual's goals and life tasks. Not much is known about the ways in which individuals shape their social relationships in congruence with specific goals and personality resources. Future research needs to more explicitly address the intersection of interpersonal regulation and personality development. This chapter has argued that social relationships should be seen as part and parcel of any developmental transition. Understanding stabilization and change of personality requires a focus on the specific relationship processes in which individuals select, adjust their standards, or exert control in their social ties with others. Future research needs to address intra- as well as interindividual variation of change and continuity in personality as it relates to constraints and challenges of relationship changes that occur in the context of life course transitions.

ACKNOWLEDGMENTS

Work on this chapter was supported by a grant of the Alice-Aeppli Foundation Zürich, Switzerland, to the first author. We would like to express our gratitude to Michael R. Levenson and to Judith Lehnart for their valuable comments on an earlier version.

REFERENCES

Allport, G. W. (1937). *Personality: A psychological interpretation*. New York: Holt, Rinehart & Wilson.

Amato, P. R. & Fowler, F. (2002). Parenting practices, child adjustment and family diversity. *Journal of Marriage and Family, 64*, 703–716.

Antonucci, T. C., & Jackson, J. S. (1990). The role of reciprocity in social support. In B. R. Sarason, I. G. Sarason & G. R. Pierce (Eds.), *Social support: An interactional view* (pp. 173–198). New York: Wiley.

Asendorpf, J. B., & van Aken, M. (2003). Personality-relationship transaction in adolescence: Core versus surface personality characteristics. *Journal of Personality, 71,* 629–666.

Asendorpf, J. B., & Wilpers, S. (1998). Personality effects on social relationships. *Journal of Personality and Social Psychology, 74,* 1531–1544.

Baltes, P. B., Staudinger, U. M., & Lindenberger, U. (1999). Lifespan psychology: Theory and application to intellectual functioning. *Annual Review of Psychology, 50,* 471–507.

Baydar, N., & Brooks-Gunn, J. (1997). A longitudinal study of the effects of the birth of a sibling during the first 6 years of life. *Journal of Marriage and the Family, 59,* 939–956.

Baydar, N., Hyle, P., & Brooks-Gunn, J. (1997). A longitudinal study of the effects of the birth during preschool and early grade school years. *Journal of Marriage and the Family, 59,* 957–965.

Billig, J. P., Hershberger, S. L., Iacono, W. G., & McGue, M. (1996). Life events and personality in late adolescence: Genetic and environmental relations. *Behavior Genetics, 26,* 543–554.

Bost, K. K., Cox, M. J., Burchinal, M. R., & Payne, C. (2002). Structural and supportive changes in couples' family and friendship networks across the transition to parenthood. *Journal of Marriage and the Family, 64,* 517–531.

Brandtstädter, J., & Rothermund, K. (2003). Intentionality and time in human development and aging. In U. M. Staudinger & U. Lindenberger (Eds.), *Understanding human development* (pp. 105–124). Boston: Kluwer Academic.

Brown, S. L. (2000). The effect of union type on psychological well-being: Depression among cohabitators versus marrieds. *Journal of Health and Social Behavior, 41*(3), 241–255.

Buhs, E. S., & Ladd, G. W. (2001). Peer rejection as an antecedent of young children's school adjustment: An examination of mediating processes. *Developmental Psychology, 37,* 550–560.

Buss, D. M. (1999). Human nature and individual differences: The evolution of human personality. In L. A. Pervin & O. P. John (Eds.), *Handbook of personality* (2nd ed., pp. 31–56). New York: Guilford.

Bynner, J. (1998). Education and family components of identity in the transition from school to work. *International Journal of Behavioral Development, 22,* 29–53.

Cantor, N., & Kihlstrom, J. F. (1987). *Personality and social intelligence.* Englewood Cliffs, NJ: Prentice-Hall.

Cantor, N., Norem, J. K., Niedenthal, P. M., Langston, C. A., & Brower, A. M. (1987). Life tasks, self-concept ideals, and cognitive strategies in a life transition. *Journal of Personality and Social Psychology, 53,* 1178–1191.

Carstensen, L. L., Gottman, J. M., & Levenson, R. W. (1995). Emotional behavior in long-term marriage. *Psychology and Aging, 10,* 140–149.

Carstensen, L. L., Isaacowitz, D. M., & Charles, S. T. (1999). Taking time seriously: A theory of socioemotional selectivity. *American Psychologist, 54,* 165–181.

Caspi, A. (1998). Personality development across the life course. In N. Eisenberg (Ed.), *Handbook of child psychology: Vol. 3. Social, emotional, and personality development* (5th ed., pp. 311–388). New York: Wiley.

Caspi, A., Bem, D. J., & Elder, G. H., Jr. (1989). Continuities and consequences of interactional styles across the life course. *Journal of Personality, 57,* 375–406.

Caspi, A., & Moffitt, T. E. (1993). When do individual differences matter? A paradoxical theory of personality coherence. *Psychological Inquiry, 4,* 247–271.

Cook, W. J. (1993). Interdependence and the interpersonal sense of control: An analysis of family relationships. *Journal of Personality and Social Psychology, 64,* 587–601.

Curtner-Smith, M. E. (2000). Mechanisms by which family processes contribute to school-age boy's bullying. *Child Study Journal, 30*(3), 169–186.

Dunn, J. (1992). Siblings and development. *Current Directions, 1,* 6–9.

Dunn, J., Cutting, A., & Fisher, N. (2002). Old friends, new friends: Predictors of children's perspective on their friends at school. *Child Development, 73,* 621–635

Elder, G. H. (1974). *Children of the great depression.* Chicago: University of Chicago Press.

Erikson, E. H. (1959). *Identity and the life cycle.* New York: Norton.

Fredrickson, B. L., & Carstensen, L. L. (1990). Choosing social partners: How old age and anticipated endings make people more selective. *Psychology and Aging, 5,* 335–347.

Fung, H. H., & Carstensen, L. L. (2003). Sending memorable messages to the old: Age differences in
preferences and memory for advertisements. *Journal of Personality and Social Psychology, 85,* 163–178.

Gouldner, A. W. (1960). The norm of reciprocity: A preliminary statement. *American Sociological
Review, 25,* 161–178.

Gloger-Tippelt, G., & Huerkamp, M. (1998). Relationship change at the transition to parenthood
and security of infant-mother attachment. *International Journal of Behavioral Development, 22,*
633–655.

Grolnick, W. S., Kurowski, C. O., Dunlap, K. G., & Hevey, C. (2000). Parental resources and the
transition to junior high. *Journal of Research on Adolescence, 10,* 465–488.

Hagestad, G. O. (1990). Social perspectives on the life course. In R. Binstock & L. George (Eds.),
Handbook of aging and the social sciences (3rd ed., pp. 151–168). New York: Academic Press.

Hartup, W. W., & Stevens, N. (1997). Friendships and adaptation in the life course. *Psychological
Bulletin, 121,* 355–370.

Havighurst, R. (1981). *Developmental tasks and education.* New York: Longman. (Original work
published 1948)

Hawkins, A. J., & Belsky, J. (1989). The role of father involvement in personality change in men
across the transition to parenthood. *Family Relations, 38,* 378–384.

Hayward, M. D., Friedman, S., & Chen, H. (1998). Career trajectories and older men's retirement.
Journals of Gerontology: Social Sciences, 53B, S91–S103

Headey, B., & Wearing, A. (1989). Personality, life events, and subjective well-being: Toward a dynamic equilibrium model. *Journal of Personality and Social Psychology, 57,* 731–739.

Heckhausen, J. (1999). *Developmental regulation in adulthood.* New York: Cambridge University
Press.

Heckhausen, J., & Krueger, J. (1993). Developmental expectations for the self and most other
people: Age grading in three functions of social comparison. *Developmental Psychology, 29,*
539–548.

Heckhausen, J., & Schulz, R. (1995). A life span theory of control. *Psychological Review, 102,*
284–302.

Heckhausen, J., & Tomasik, M. J. (2002). Get an apprenticeship before school is out: How German adolescents adjust vocational aspirations when getting close to a developmental deadline.
Journal of Vocational Behavior, 60, 199–219.

Heinicke, C. M. (2002). The transition to parenting. In M. H. Bornstein (Ed.), *Handbook of
parenting: Vol. 3. Being and becoming a parent* (2nd ed., pp. 363–388). Mahwah, NJ: Lawrence
Erlbaum Associates.

Helms-Erikson, H. (2001). Marital quality ten years after the transition to parenthood: Implications of the timing of parenthood and the division of housework. *Journal of Marriage and the
Family, 63,* 1099–1110.

Hope, S., Rodgers, B., & Power, C. (1999). Marital status transitions and psychological distress:
Longitudinal evidence from a national population sample. *Psychological Medicine, 29,* 381–389.

Horwitz, A. V., & White, H. R. (1998). The relationship of cohabitation and mental health: A
study of a young adult cohort. *Journal of Marriage and the Family, 60,* 505–514.

Ickes, W., Snyder, M., & Garcia, S. (1997). Personality influences on the choice of situations. In R.
Hogan, J. Johnson, & S. Briggs (Eds.), *Handbook of personality psychology* (pp. 166–195). San
Diego: Academic Press.

Kahn, R. L., & Antonucci, T. C. (1980). Convoys over the life course. Attachment, roles and social support. In P. B. Baltes & O. G. Brim (Eds.), *Life-span development and behavior* (pp.
254–283). New York: Academic Press.

Kim, J. E., & Moen, P. (2001). Is retirement good or bad for subjective well-being? *Current Directions in Psychological Science, 10,* 83–86.

Kramer, L., & Ramsburg, D. (2002). Advice given to parents on welcoming a second child: A critical review. *Family Relations, 51,* 2–14.

Ladd. G. W. (1999). Peer relationships and social competence during early and middle childhood. *Annual Review of Psychology, 50,* 333–359.

Lang, F. R. (2004). Social motivation across the life span. In F. R. Lang & K. L. Fingerman (Eds.), *Growing together: Personal relationships across the lifespan* (pp. 341–367). New York: Cambridge University Press.

Lang, F. R., & Carstensen, L. L. (2002). Time counts: Future time perspective, goals, and social relationships. *Psychology and Aging, 17,* 125–139.

Lang, F. R., Featherman, D. L., & Nesselroade, J. R. (1997). Social self efficacy and short-term variability in social relationships: The MacArthur successful aging studies. *Psychology and Aging, 12,* 657–666.

Lang, F. R., & Fingerman, K. L. (Eds.). (2004). *Growing together: Personal relationships across the life span.* New York: Cambridge University Press.

Lang, F. R., & Heckhausen, J. (2005). Stabilisierung und Kontinuität der Persönlichkeit im Lebenslauf [Stabilization and continuity of personality over the life course]. In J. B. Asendorpf (Ed.), *Enzyklopaedie der Psychologie. Band C/V/3. Soziale, emotionale und Persoenlichkeitsentwicklung* (pp. 525–562). Göttingen, Germany: Hogrefe.

Lang, F. R., Lüdtke, O., & Asendorpf, J. B. (2001). Validity and psychometric equivalence of the German version of the Big Five Inventory in young, middle-aged and old adults. *Diagnostica, 47,* 111–121.

Lerner, R. M., & Kauffman, M. B. (1985). The concept of development in contextualism. *Development Review, 5,* 309–333.

Levenson, R. W., Carstensen, L. L., & Gottman, J. M. (1993). Long-term marriage: Age, gender, and satisfaction. *Psychology and Aging, 8,* 301–313.

Lewis, M. (1999). On the development of personality. In L. A. Pervin & O. P. John (Eds.), *Handbook of personality* (2nd ed., pp. 327–346). New York: Guilford.

Lewontin, R. C. (1982). Organism and environment. In H. C. Plotkin (Ed.), *Learning, development and culture* (pp. 151–170). Chichester, England: Wiley.

Mather, M., & Carstensen, L. L. (2003). Aging and attentional biases for emotional faces. *Psychological Science, 14,* 409–415.

McAdams, D. P., & de St. Aubin, E. (1992). A theory of generativity and its assessment through self-report, behavioral acts and narrative themes in autobiography. *Journal of Personality and Social Psychology, 62,* 1003–1015.

McCrae, R. R., Costa, P. T., Lima, M. P., Simöes, A., Ostendorf, F., Angleitner, A., Marusic, I., Bratko, D., Caprara, G. V., Barbaranelli, C., Chae, J.-H. & Piedmont, R. L. (1999). Age differences in personality across the adult life span: Parallels in five cultures. *Developmental Psychology, 35,* 466–477.

McNally, S., Eisenberg, N., & Harris, J. D. (1991). Consistency and change in maternal childrearing practices and values: A longitudinal study. *Child Development, 62,* 190–198.

Milardo, R. M., & Allan, G. (1996). Social networks and marital relationships. In S. Duck, K. Dindia, W. Ickes, R. Milardo, R. Mills, & B. Saranson (Eds.), *Handbook of personal relationships* (pp. 505–522). London: Wiley.

Mroczek, D. K., & Spiro, A., III. (2003). Modeling intraindividual change in personality traits: Findings from the Normative Aging Study. *Journal of Gerontology: Psychological Sciences, 58,* P153–P165.

Nauck, B. (1991). Familien- und Betreuugssituationen im Lebenslauf von Kindern [Family- and caregiving situations over the life course]. In H. Bertram (Ed.), *Die Familie in Westdeutschland. Stabilität und Wandel familaler Lebensformen* (pp. 389–428). Opladen, Germany: Leske & Budrich.

Neyer, F. J. (in press). Informant assessment. In M. Eid & E. Diener (Eds.), *Handbook of psychological measurement: a multimethod perspective.* Washington, DC: American Psychological Association.

Neyer, F. J. (2004). Dyadic fits and transactions in personality and relationships. In F. R. Lang & K. L. Fingerman (Eds.), *Growing together: Personal relationships across the lifespan* (pp. 290–316). New York: Cambridge University Press.

Neyer, F. J., & Asendorpf, J. B. (2001). Personality-relationship transaction in young adulthood. *Journal of Personality and Social Psychology, 81,* 1190–1204.

Neyer, F. J., & Lang, F. R. (2003). Blood is thicker than water: Kinship orientation across adulthood. *Journal of Personality and Social Psychology, 84,* 310–321.

Orbuch, T. L., Veroff, J., Hassan, H., & Horrocks, J. (2002). Who will divorce: A 14-year longitudinal study of Black couples and White couples. *Journal of Social and Personal Relationships, 19,* 179–202.

Perl, H. I., & Trickett, E. J. (1988). Social network formation of college freshmen: Personal and environmental determinants. *American Journal of Community Psychology, 16,* 207–224.

Perry, K. E., & Weinstein, R. S. (1998). The social context of early schooling and children's school adjustment. *Educational Psychologist, 33,* 177–194

Reitzle, M., Vondracek, F. W., & Silbereisen, R. K. (1998). Timing of school-to-work transitions: A developmental-contextual perspective. *International Journal of Behavioral Development, 22,* 7–28

Riley, M. W. (1985). Age strata in social systems. In R. Binstock & E. Shanas (Eds.), *Handbook of aging and the social sciences* (2nd ed., pp. 369–411). New York: Van Nostrand Reinhold.

Roberts, B. W., & Caspi, A. (2003). The cumulative continuity model of personality development: Striking a balance between continuity and change in personality traits across the life course. In U. M. Staudinger & U. Lindenberger (Eds.), *Understanding human development* (pp. 183–214). Boston: Kluwer Academic.

Roberts, B. W., Caspi, A., & Moffitt, T. E. (2003). Work experiences and personality development in young adulthood. *Journal of Personality and Social Psychology, 84,* 582–593.

Roberts, B. W., & DelVecchio, W. F. (2000). The rank-order consistency of personality from childhood to old age: A quantitative review of longitudinal studies. *Psychological Bulletin, 126,* 3–25.

Rogers, S. J., & May, D. C. (2003). Spillover between marital quality and job satisfaction: Long-term patterns and gender differences. *Journal of Marriage and the Family, 65,* 482–495.

Rook, K. S., & Schuster, T. L. (1996). Compensatory processes in the social networks of older adults. In G. R. Pierce, B. R. Sarason, & I. G. Sarason (Eds.), *Handbook of social support and the family* (pp. 219–248). New York: Plenum.

Rothbaum, F., Weisz, J. R., & Snyder, S. S. (1982). Changing the world and changing the self: A two-process model of perceived control. *Journal of Personality and Social Psychology, 42,* 5–37.

Sanderson, C. A., & Cantor, N. (1999). A life task perspective on personality coherence. Stability versus change in tasks, goals, strategies, and outcomes. In D. Cervone & Y. Shoda (Eds.), *The coherence of personality* (pp. 372–392). New York: Guilford.

Saudino, K. J., Pedersen, N. L., Lichtenstein, P., McClearn, G. E., & Plomin, R. (1997). Can personality explain genetic influences on life events. *Journal of Personality and Social Psychology, 72,* 196–206.

Settersten, R. A., Jr. (1998). Time, age, and the transition to retirement: New evidence on life-course flexibility? *International Journal of Aging and Human Development, 47,* 177–203.

Settersten, R. A., Jr. (1999). *Lives in time and place: The problems and promises of developmental science.* Amityville, NY: Baywood.

Small, B. J., Hertzog, C., Hultsch, D. F., & Dixon, R. A. (2003). Stability and change in adult personality over 6 years: Findings from the Victoria Longitudinal Study. *Journal of Gerontology: Psychological Sciences, 58,* P166–P176.

Snyder, M., & Ickes, W. (1985). Personality and social behavior. In G. Lindzey & E. Aronson (Eds.), *The handbook of social psychology* (Vol. 2, pp. 883–947). New York: Random House.

Sprecher, S., Felmlee, D., Orbuch, T. L., & Willetts, M. C. (2002). Social networks and change in personal relationships. In A. L. Vangelisti., H. T. Reis & M. A. Fitzpatrick (Eds.), *Stability and change in relationships* (pp. 257–284). New York: Cambridge University Press.

Srivastava, S., John, O. P., Gosling, S. D., & Potter, J. (2003). Development of personality in early and middle adulthood: Set like plaster or persistent change. *Journal of Personality and Social Psychology, 84,* 1041–1053.

Stack, S., & Eshleman, J. R. (1998). Marital status and happiness: A 17 nation study. *Journal of Marriage and the Family, 60,* 527–536.

Stein, C. H., Bush, E. G., Ross, R. R., & Ward, M. (1992). Mine, yours and ours: A configural analysis of the networks of married couples in relation to marital satisfaction and individual well-being. *Journal of Social and Personal Relationships, 9,* 365–383.

Stewart, R. B. (1990). *The second child: Family transition and adjustment.* Newbury Park, CA: Sage.

Teti, D. M., Sakin, J. W., Kucera, E., & Corns, K. M. (1996). And baby makes four: Predictors of attachment security among preschool-age firstborns during the transition to siblinghood. *Child development, 67,* 579–596.

Timmer, S. G., Veroff, J., & Hatchett, S. (1996). Family ties and marital happiness: The different marital experiences of black and white newlywed couples. *Journal of Social and Personal Relationships, 13,* 335–359.

Vangelisti, A. L., Reis, H. T., & Fitzpatrick, M. A. (Eds.). (2002). *Stability and change in relationships.* New York: Cambridge University Press.

Van Tilburg, T. (1992). Support networks before and after retirement. *Journal of Social and Personal Relationships, 9,* 433–445.

Veroff, J., Douvan, E., Orbuch, T. L., & Acitelli, L. K. (1998). Happiness in stable marriages: The early years. In T. N. Bradbury (Ed.), *The developmental course of marital dysfunction* (pp. 152–179). New York: Cambridge University Press.

Weidman, J. C. (1987). Problems in the transition from school to work for adolescents in West Germany and the United States. *Journal of Adolescent Research, 2,* 175–182

West, S. G., & Graziano, W. G. (1989). Long-term stability and change in personality: An introduction. *Journal of Personality, 57,* 175–193.

Wrosch, C., & Freund, A. M. (2001). Self-regulation of normative and non-normative developmental challenges. *Human Development, 44,* 264–283.

Yovetich, N. A., & Rusbult, C. E. (1994). Accommodative behavior in close relationships: Exploring transformation of motivation. *Journal of Experimental Social Psychology, 30,* 138–164.

Zirkel, S. (1992). Developing independence in a life transition: Investing the self in the concerns of the day. *Journal of Personality and Social Psychology, 62,* 506–521.

V

Capstone

23

How Does Personality Develop?

Dan P. McAdams
Jonathan M. Adler
Northwestern University

Our university library lists no entries for "handbooks" on "personality develop-ment." Either our collection is inadequate or, more likely, nobody before Dan Mroczek and Todd Little has ever succeeded in putting together a volume like this one. The editors of the current handbook may be crazy or visionary, or else things may be different today than they have been for the past 100 years, because there are good reasons to be skeptical about any efforts to bring together two fields of inquiry that have historically had little to do with each other—that is, personality psychol-ogy and the study of human development. Personality psychologists are, by training and maybe even temperament, suspicious of the idea of development, for to them it means *change* (i.e., instability, inconsistency), and personality is nothing if it is not at least somewhat enduring. Developmentalists, on the other hand, specialize in a cer-tain kind of change—meaningful and orderly change over time. For them, lives are dynamic and evolving, resistant to the neat categorizations of traits and types. To make matters worse for any handbook editor, a vocal contingent of social scientists (e.g., Mischel, 1968; Shweder, 1975) has long questioned the utility of the very con-cept of "personality." Does personality even exist? What is it anyway? If scientists don't know what it is and they even doubt its very existence, then how can they say that personality develops?

WHAT IS PERSONALITY? HOW MIGHT IT DEVELOP?

Near the top of any list of fruitless intellectual pursuits is the search for a common defi-nition of personality. Going back even before Allport's (1937) classic textbook in the field, authors have defined the term *personality* in at least 100 ways. (Allport himself spelled out 50 definitions.) Personality has been defined as a set of traits that assure in-dividual continuity, as the motivational core of human behavior, as a self-regulating system designed to maximize adaptation to life's challenges, and on and on. Some defi-

469

nitions are better than others. If you look beyond the sexist language, one of the best is the definition that Allport (1937) finally settled on: Personality is "the dynamic organization within the individual of those psychophysical systems that determine his [the individual's] unique adjustments to his environment" (p. 48). But what makes even Allport's effort insufficient is the assumption that personality itself is a single, tangible thing with a single, well-designed function. In Allport's case, the thing is a "psychophysical system" designed to promote "adjustments." But why does personality need to be any*thing* at all? Almost 50 years ago, the authors of the most famous textbook on personality theories wondered the same thing. C. Hall and Lindzey (1957) concluded that even Allport's well-regarded conception was somewhat arbitrary. Every theorist defines personality differently, C. Hall and Lindzey (1957) observed. As a result, "it is our conviction that no substantive definition of personality can be applied with any generality" (p. 9). Instead, they argued, personality may be variously defined in terms of the major themes highlighted in different theories and by the particular constructs that personality psychologists invoke in their research. In other words, personality is such a broad, diffuse category that for pragmatic reasons it may be best defined by focusing on what personality psychologists try to do.

But what do they try to do? From the time of Allport to the present day, what personality psychologists have mainly aimed to do is to account for human individuality (McAdams, 1997, 2006a). What this means is that personality psychologists have endeavored to formulate theories and test hypotheses regarding how individual people are, in general, similar to and different from each other. (In contrast, other types of psychologists, such as cognitive and social psychologists, are more focused on human universals.) To paraphrase one of the canonical quotes in the history of personality psychology, "Every individual person is like *all* other persons, like *some* other persons, and like *no* other person" (from Kluckhohn & Murray, 1953, p. 53). The research emphasis in personality psychology has traditionally been on the latter two of Kluckhohn and Murray's three-part characterization. With their focus on individual differences, personality psychologists have traditionally sought to spell out how individuals are similar to and different from some other individuals and how they are also unique. If anything, this emphasis is what has unified personality psychology as a field. What are those features of individuals that differentiate them from others? Although many features might be identified, personality psychologists have tended to focus on those differences that make a difference—those aspects or features of human individuality that help account for socially consequential behaviors and outcomes. After all, people differ from each other in countless ways. But only certain differences count in the minds of personality psychologists—those differences that appear to be centrally implicated in social life and human adaptation.

How do researchers decide what differences are centrally implicated in social life? The answer to this question depends on an awareness of the nature of social life, which derives ultimately from the exigencies of the societies and cultural frameworks within which personality psychologists live and work. It is no accident that American and European psychologists decided that authoritarianism was an important personality construct shortly after Hitler's rise to power and the transformation of Germany and Italy into authoritarian states (Adorno, Frenkel-Brunswik, Levinson, & Sanford, 1950). It should be no surprise that whereas concepts like achievement motivation (McClelland, 1961) and Machiavellianism (Christie &

Geis, 1970; Hawley, chap. 8 in this volume) enjoyed considerable currency among American personality psychologists in the 1960s and 1970s, it took a Japanese psychologist writing around the same time to articulate the concept of *amae*, which means depending on or presuming another's benevolence (Doi, 1962).

Not only do personality theories and constructs reflect the particularities of social life as it exists in time and culture, but personality itself—as a scientific accounting of psychological individuality—is a social and cultural construction. The fact that personality constructs like extraversion and neuroticism are highly heritable and can be linked to psychophysiological functioning does not undermine this claim, because unless one adopts a Cartesian split between body and mind/soul, all human behavior and experience is 100% biological, even as it plays out in culture (Buss, 1995). As a social and cultural construction, personality is still in the brain (where else could it be?). The fact that the first author of this chapter tends to take large steps when he walks and the fact that he chose a green shirt to wear this morning (instead of a blue one), whereas the second author takes shorter strides and chose a white shirt this morning, reflect brain processes of one kind or another, which themselves may or may not be strongly influenced by social forces. But although these individual differences between the authors are observed, they are aspects that are socially and culturally trivial, and personality psychologists, therefore, are not likely to study them. Those aspects of human individuality that are deemed socially consequential—things like extraversion and neuroticism, amae in Japan, liberal and conservative belief systems in modern democratic societies, soothability in infants, the tendency for certain midlife American adults to see their lives as narratives of redemption—come to comprise the social construction of personality. This is what personality psychologists study. Ipso facto, this is what personality—here and now—is.

In looking at the broad field of contemporary research, there are three levels that help organize this construct of personality. Personality is viewed as a culturally shaped and evolving patterning of dispositional traits (Level 1), characteristic adaptations (Level 2), and integrative life narratives (Level 3) (Hooker & McAdams, 2003; McAdams, 1994, 1995, 2006a; Sheldon, 2004). Dispositional traits provide a broad sketch of human individuality, characteristic adaptations (which include motives and goals) fill in many of the motivational and strategic details, and integrative life narratives spell out what a person's life means in the overall. The patterning is multifaceted, complex, and sometimes contradictory, reflecting the complex realities of contemporary social life. But, the three different levels or domains for personality do not necessarily add up to a single, integrated thing. They do not function together to accomplish a cohesive overarching aim. They do not work as a structure, a blueprint, or any other kind of organized and integrated entity. Taken together, they comprise instead those broad and socially consequential aspects of psychological individuality that contemporary personality psychologists, reflecting the cultural discourses within which they live and work, tend to invoke to describe and explain how one person is like another and different from others. The three-level system is therefore a conceptual framework for organizing the accumulated knowledge about personality.

How do these different features of human individuality develop? The short answer is differently. Dispositional traits, characteristic adaptations, and integrative life narratives tend to develop in diverse ways. As the sum total of the many fine chapters in this volume show, there is no single, all-encompassing course of development for personality. There is no universal stage sequence that adequately encompasses our current understanding of meaningful and orderly change in personality over time. How development happens depends on what feature of personality is considered. The chapters in this handbook spell out the current scientific understanding of how different features of psychological individuality appear to develop over time, from infancy to old age. This chapter organizes the many insights of the previous chapters within the conception of personality as a culturally shaped and evolving patterning of dispositional traits, characteristic adaptations, and integrative life stories. It then focuses on four developmental milestones in the life course: the move from attachment to self in the second year, the transition from late childhood to adolescence, the protracted period of emerging adulthood, and midlife tipping points. (The last also raises questions regarding how personality and developmental psychologist might consider old age.) So, what makes each of these four milestones especially interesting is the way in which features related to traits, adaptations, and life stories appear at these times either to change dramatically or to interact with each other in important ways as they come to the developmental fore.

DISPOSITIONAL TRAITS: FROM TEMPERAMENT TO THE BIG FIVE

Dispositional traits are broad, internal, and comparative features of psychological individuality that account for consistencies perceived or expected in behavior and experience from one situation to the next, and over time. Typically assessed via self-report questionnaires or observer ratings, dispositional traits position an individual on a series of bipolar, linear continua that describe the most basic and general dimensions on which persons are typically perceived to differ. Although it is possible to invoke hundreds of trait labels to account for broad individual differences in behavior, thought, and feeling, recent years have witnessed a near-consensus in personality psychology that the many possible trait terms may be reduced to a small number of factors—between three and seven, but most often five (i.e., Big Five; see Saucier & Simonds, chap. 6 in this volume, regarding the ongoing debate on the precise number of factors). Basic traits therefore provide a dispositional signature for psychological individuality. They sketch an outline of those broad and more-or-less decontextualized differences between people that are readily detected as general, cross-situational trends on which people may be compared. Mary is friendlier than Jessica. Fernando is highly conscientious. Alicia is very low on openness to experience, but not as low as Doug.

The most important scientific advance in personality psychology over the past 25 years has been the reestablishment and validation of the trait concept. In the 1960s and 1970s, neo-behaviorist critics and social psychologists argued forcefully that variability in human behavior is largely driven by situational constraints and affordances rather than internal personality factors. They asserted that individual differences in traits were, at best, weak predictors of behavior (Mischel, 1968). Trait attributions were little better than stereotyping labels, misleading fictions in the minds of observers, and/or trivial artifacts of the structure of language (Mischel, 1973; Nisbett & Ross, 1980; Shweder, 1975). Eventually, however, these arguments proved to be more clever than true. In the 1980s and 1990s, personality psychologists amassed empirical evidence to show that individual differences in dispositional traits predict important cross-situational consistencies in behavior, especially when behavior is aggregated across different environmental contexts; are powerfully implicated in important life outcomes like physical and mental health, leadership, creativity, morality and altruism, job success, the quality of relationships, and even longevity; and demonstrate considerable interindividual consistency over time, especially in the adult years (see Matthews, Deary, & Whiteman, 2003, for a comprehensive review of trait research; see Levenson & Aldwin, chap. 21 in this volume, on relations between traits and health). In the first decade of the 21st century, those few empirically minded psychologists who still dismiss the trait concept out of hand appear to be driven by a shocking misreading, or nonreading, of the past 25 years of personality research and/or a quasi-Lockean ideology that imagines individuals to be repeatedly erased blank slates as they move cluelessly from one situation in life to the next.

Along with McCrae and Costa (chap. 7 in this volume), we view dispositional traits to be basic tendencies in personality, comprising what is described as Level 1 of psychological individuality (McAdams, 1995). Dispositional traits are basic in at least two ways. First, they describe those most general, most fundamental, and least contingent differences between persons that are most readily detected as researchers observe different people's behavior across different situations and over time. Second, they speak to broad differences and consistencies that appear even at the very beginning of the human life span.

Although it is probably not right to suggest that newborn infants posses full-fledged personality traits, the broad differences in temperament that are observed in the first few months of life seem to signal the eventual emergence, development, and consolidation of basic, cross-situational tendencies in human behavior, thought, and feeling. Indeed, Saucier and Simonds (chap. 6 in this volume) describe temperament as the "early-in-life framework" from which personality traits develop. Developmentally speaking, how do we get from temperament to the Big Five? Genetics appear to play a strong role. Twin studies tend to show heritabilities of around 50% for most personality traits, with some especially well-designed assessment strategies suggesting even higher figures (e.g., Loehlin, Niederhiser, & Reiss, 2003; Riemann, Angleitner, & Strelau, 1997). Krueger, Johnson, and Kling (chap. 5 in this volume) review research on behavior genetics to conclude that the primary source for stability in temperament across time is genetic, with unique environmental influences (nonshared environments) accounting for change. It is hardly a stretch to suspect that some, if not many, of the genes involved in shaping early temperament differences are the same genes implicated in the development of later personality traits. The developmental move from temperament to the Big Five may be the protracted, lifelong unfolding of a genetic blueprint. According to this conception, traits emerge naturally out of early, genetically determined temperament dimensions. McCrae and Costa (chap. 7 in this volume) appear to be this volume's strongest adherents to a genetic-determinist point of view. Not only do genetic differences drive the emergence and consolidation of individual differences in dispositional traits, they argue, but to the extent traits show change over time, those changes are also driven by biological factors (e.g., biological maturation).

Sometimes it is useful to take an extreme view in science in order to provoke a dialogue and help to move the field forward. Indeed, McCrae and Costa have certainly stirred an excellent tradition of research investigating the deterministic view of traits. Let us, then, take this most charitable view of McCrae and Costa's claims regarding the biology of traits, because the evidence and the arguments against their position are considerable. For example, Saarni (chap. 13 in this volume) shows that temperament dimensions related to emotional regulation are sometimes surprisingly inconsistent from one situation to the next and rather less stable over time than many might suspect. Her contextualist perspective on temperament raises doubts about an easy mapping of broad and consistent personality traits onto equally broad and consistent temperament dimensions. Shiner (chap. 11 in this volume) and Krueger, Johnson, and Kling (chap. 5 in this volume) review research showing that parental behaviors interact with biologically contoured temperament dispositions to shape the development of personality. For example, when children are high on irritability, several parenting variables (e.g., unskilled discipline tactics, negativity toward the child, lack of restrictive control) predict higher levels of acting out and aggression, whereas skillful and warm parenting appears to protect these negative and hard-to-manage children from developing high levels of externalizing behaviors (e.g., Belsky, Hsieth, & Crnic, 1998).

Genetics and environment appear to work together as well. Donnellan, Trsesniewski, and Robins (chap. 15 in this volume), in keeping with Caspi (1998) and Scarr and McCartney (1983), outline three mechanisms whereby environmental factors conspire with genotype to solidify the continuity of dispositional traits. First, genotypically driven tendencies may elicit responses from the environment that feed back to reinforce those same tendencies: Smiley and approachable infants evoke friendly responses from others, reinforcing their sociability and (perhaps) helping to set them on the path for high extraversion. Second, genotypically driven tendencies may shape how individuals construe the world: Children prone to hostility may interpret neutral situations in a threatening manner, serving to reinforce their hostile tendencies and make for a kind of self-fulfilling prophecy in the development of dispositional traits. Third, genotypically driven tendencies may influence the choice of situations and the manipulation of environments: Young adults high in openness to experience may seek out dynamic and complex environments that are simpatico with their high levels of openness, again reinforcing the tendencies that they have been developing all along.

Therefore, through mechanisms and pathways that are just beginning to be understood, temperament dimensions of infancy and early childhood may eventually morph into those full-fledged personality dimensions that are recognizable in the Big Five and related taxonomies. This process of *developmental elaboration* (Caspi, 1998) surely involves complex and unpredictable interactions between unfolding behavioral patterns linked to genotypes and a wide range of environmental forces and factors. Once dispositional traits resembling the Big Five emerge, they show reasonable interindividual stability in adolescence, higher levels of interindividual stability in young adulthood, and even higher levels of interindividual stability in the middle adult years (Roberts & DelVecchio, 2000). The comparative ordering of individuals along trait dimensions becomes increasingly stable as people move through the young and middle adult years. Nonetheless, some shifting around in the distribution still happens. Donnellan, Trzesniewski, and Robins (chap. 15 in this volume) point to responses to contingencies, self-reflection, observation of significant others, and reflected appraisals from others as four mechanisms that may promote change in personality traits during the adolescent years. Roberts and Wood (chap. 2 in this volume) suggest that changes in traits during the adult years may correspond to the assumption of age-graded social roles.

Issues related to interindividual stability and change (e.g., where different people rank relative to each other on any given bipolar continuum) are independent of issues related to continuity and change on mean levels for any given trait, as Little, Bovaird, and Slegers (chap. 10 in this volume) make clear. Even as adults show relatively high levels of interindividual stability on personality traits, mean levels appear to vary as a function of age. As Roberts and Wood (chap. 2 in this volume) and McCrae and Costa (chap. 7 in this volume) show, levels of agreeableness and conscientiousness appear to rise gradually from the adolescent years through middle age, whereas traits associated with neuroticism or negative affectivity generally decline somewhat. Certain features of extraversion (e.g., excitement seeking) may also decline. Openness may increase during adolescence and the early adult years, but decline somewhat thereafter. These mean-level changes are small but important, and they appear to show up in a number of different societies (McCrae et al., 1999).

As people move into and through their early-to-middle-adult years, therefore, they appear in general to become somewhat more comfortable with themselves as adults, less inclined to moodiness and negative emotion, more responsible and caring, more focused on long-term life tasks and plans, and less susceptible to extreme risk taking and the expression of unbridled internal impulses. This general process of maturation and adult socialization is probably driven by both biological changes (McCrae & Costa, chap. 7 in this volume) and the development and articulation of social roles (Roberts & Wood, chap. 2 in this volume). At the same time, not everybody follows the same developmental path, as Mroczek, Almeida, Spiro, and Pafford (chap. 9 in this volume) show. New research methods have exposed important individual differences in intraindividual change during the adult years. For example, married men tend to show declines in neuroticism that are less steep over time than those shown by unmarried men (Mroczek & Spiro, 2003). Furthermore, important life events may exert short-term, and sometimes long-term, influence on adult traits. The death of one's spouse appears to produce strong spikes in neuroticism in the short term, to be followed by a more gradual decline that eventually approaches the levels shown before the loss. Dispositional traits, although likely the most stable of the three levels of personality, are never completely set in stone, or even plaster. Up until one's own death, the prospects of dispositional change in any given life never completely vanish.

CHARACTERISTIC ADAPTATIONS: PERSONAL GOALS AND THE AGENTIC SELF

There is more to personality than traits. The broad and relatively stable dimensions of psychological individuality that eventually come to comprise a person's dispositional signature sketch the general outline of personality. But many of the particulars are located at a second conceptual level. In the first decade of the 21st century, what aspects of psychological individuality do (mainly Western) personality psychologists deem to be within the conceptual orbit of personality? The term *characteristic adaptations* is used to refer to a wide range of variables in psychological individuality that speak to specific motivational, strategic, cognitive-social, and developmental concerns (McAdams, 1995). What do people want in life? How do they seek what they want and avoid what they fear? How do people develop plans, goals, and programs for their lives? How do people think about and cope with the challenges of social life? What psychological and social tasks await people at particular stages or times in their lives? To answer these kinds of questions (and many others), it is necessary to move beyond the realm of broad, stylistic dispositions and consider the manifestations and development of motives, values, interests, goals, projects, coping strategies, defense mechanisms, self-schemas, possible selves, relational schemas, and other variables of human individuality contextualized, as they are, in time, situations, and social roles. (Note that Roberts and Wood, chap. 2, split this level into two, distinguishing values and motives from abilities. Our conceptualization deemphasizes the ability domain because many behavioral scientists associate abilities and skills with cognitive psychology, intelligence testing, and related fields, as opposed to the study of personality.) If dispositional traits sketch an outline for personality, then characteristic adaptations begin to fill in many of the details.

Characteristic adaptations are better suited than are dispositional traits to address the issues of time, contingency, and agency in human personality. The problem of time is central in the chapter by Fleeson and Jolley (chap. 3 in this volume), who focus attention on the relation between day-to-day, even moment-to-moment, fluctuations in personality and more long-term dispositional trends. For Fleeson and Jolley, dispositional traits themselves are but density distributions of momentary states. Over time, people high in extraversion tend to find themselves more often in an extraverted state, compared to a dispositional introvert. More interestingly, the personality psychologist may be able to compare and contrast individuals with respect to the properties of their state distributions—how it is, for example, that some extraverts express their characteristic state at certain times and situations while certain other kinds of extraverts express their characteristic state at other times and situations. In this regard, Fleeson and Jolley's approach recalls Mischel and Shoda's (1995) model of person × situation contingencies. From this standpoint, the most important features of human individuality are not cross-situationally consistent dispositions, but instead those particular contingent patterns wherein Person A shows Characteristic B in Situations C, D, and E, and Person F shows Characteristic B in Situations G, H, and I.

Like Mischel and Shoda (1995), Fleeson and Jolley are trying to model temporal and situational contingencies into their formal conceptualizations of persons. But their conceptualizations still rely mainly on the discourse of traits. In both models, traitlike states (described in terms like this: extraversion, dominance, warmth, etc.) are distributed across different situational contexts, inviting the psychologist to examine the pattern of the distribution. Other personality psychologists have found it easier to let go of the trait language altogether and adopt in its place the Level 2 discourse of motivation. Motivational constructs like goals, strivings, plans, and projects are explicitly temporal and contingent. They spell out how people pursue ends over time and with respect to particular situational roles and affordances. Moreover, motivational constructs place human agency at the center of personality inquiry. As agentic and self-determining actors, people make choices; they plan their lives; they will their very identity into being. Dispositional traits may help in describing and understanding the general ways in which people do this. But motives and goals tell us more precisely what, in fact, they aim to do.

Many of the chapters herein focus on the development of motives and goals. Little, Snyder, and Wehemeyer (chap. 4 in this volume) set forth the credo of this overall approach. Drawing from the humanistic tradition in personality psychology and its contemporary heir in self-determination theory (Deci & Ryan, 1991), these authors proclaim that human beings are self-determining and self-regulating agents who organize their lives around goal pursuit. Life is about choice, goals, and hope—the hope that individuals can achieve their most desired goals. Walls and Kollat (chap. 12 in this volume) define agency as selecting and acting on goals, and they trace its development in the early childhood years. Moving forward in the life course, Freund and Riediger (chap. 18 in this volume) characterize goals as the "building blocks" of adult personality. Goals speak to "personality-in-context." They contribute to the "specialization of general potentials," spelling out how general dispositional trends play themselves out in particular lives. Although goals sometimes connect thematically to dispositional traits, often they do not, as Roberts and Wood (chap. 2 in this volume) maintain. People's goals, furthermore, may even contradict their traits. An introverted 40-something man may decide that his new, number one goal in life is to find a mate. To launch the project, he may need to engage in many behaviors and move through many states and situations that do not seem especially "introverted." He resolves to do it. The developmental project trumps his dispositional traits. When he achieves the goal (there is always hope), he may settle back into his day-to-day dispositional routine.

What are the main goals in life? Roberts and Wood (chap. 2 in this volume) draw from evolutionary theory and Hogan's (1982) socioanalytic approach to suggest that personal goals often serve the deeper needs that were critical to survival and reproductive success in the environment of evolutionary adaptedness (see also Hawley, chap. 8 in this volume). For Hogan (1982), these are the needs for social acceptance and social status—getting along and getting ahead in social groups. Yet, as Roberts and Wood (chap. 2 in this volume) argue, the ways in which these meta-goals are pursued and managed are intricately contoured by culture and by the emergence of different social roles across the life course. Little, Snyder, and Wehemeyer (chap. 4 in this volume) argue that self-determined behavior often fulfills the deeper needs for autonomy, relatedness, and competence. Relatedness and competence appear to map roughly on to Hogan's getting along and getting ahead, respectively; autonomy appears to represent the very need to act as a goal-directed, agentic being—the motivational core of what these authors call the *agentic self*.

A number of other authors suggest that different life stages set forth different goals to achieve. Freund and Riediger (chap. 18 in this volume) review research to show that education, partnership, friends, and careers are salient goal areas for young adults; middle-aged adults focus their goals on the future of their children, securing what they have already established, and property-related concerns; older adults show more goals regarding health, retirement, leisure, and understanding current events in the world. Helson, Soto, and Cate (chap. 17 in this volume) suggest that goals in early adulthood often focus on expanding the self and gaining new information, whereas goals in later adulthood may be more calibrated to the emotional quality of relationships. Wrosch, Heckhausen, and Lachman (chap. 20 in this volume) show how people approach and manage their goals in different ways over the course of life. In young adulthood, they may rely on primary control strategies whereby they act on the world to attain the goals they desire. As people move through midlife and approach their later years, however, they may rely more on secondary control processes, whereby they act on the self to adjust their thoughts, feelings, and expectations in order to maximize satisfaction in those goal areas that remain viable and minimize the disappointment that might follow the pursuit of no-longer realistic goals.

Developmental theories that focus on dispositional traits (Level 1) tend to begin with infant temperament and trace the gradual elaboration of basic emotional and self-regulatory differences into the full-fledged, cognitively elaborated dispositional dimensions that are readily observed among adults. Broad, stylistic differences emerge early in the life span, determined largely by varieties in genotypes, and they continue to spread out and become more articulated over time through the cumulative interplay between genes and environment. By contrast, developmental theories that focus on motives and goals, as representatives of characteristic adaptations (Level 2), tend to begin with the first evidence of human intentionality (around age 1) and the early emergence of the agentic "I" (in the second year of life) (see Walls & Kollat, chap. 12 in this volume). From the Level 2 perspective, personality is fundamentally about the self-determining, goal-directed projects that individuals take on in life. Certain basic needs, such as those related to getting along (relatedness, communion) and getting ahead (competence, agency), may underlie goal striving. However, individual human beings pursue many different goals over the course of life, determined by a wide range of factors that include, but are not limited to, genetic differences in basic preferences and approaches to goals, parental influences, neighborhood and school environments, changing social roles, and on-time and off-time life events. Against a backdrop of increasing dispositional stability (Level 1), personal goals and motives—and the many (Level 2) features of human individuality linked to goal striving—continue to change in response to changing environmental and developmental demands. Even if she is no more or less extraverted than she was at age 30, a 50-year-old woman likely "has a different personality" than she had at age 30 because she is seeking and managing different goals today, involved in different life projects, defending against different losses and failures, and enjoying different developmental gains today than she did 20 years ago.

LIFE STORIES:
THE CONSTRUCTION OF NARRATIVE IDENTITY

At different points in the human life course, different kinds of constructs are required to capture the full gamut of psychological individuality. At birth, parents and psychologists may begin to see some of the rudiments of individual differences in dispositional traits, manifest as basic dimensions of temperament. Yet, it makes little sense at this early point in the life course to differentiate one newborn from the next in terms of the different motives and goals they are pursuing in life. Goal-oriented, Level 2 constructs begin to become salient features of psychological individuality later in childhood. An 8-year-old girl is a more personologically complex organism than a newborn in the sense that a full accounting of the young girl's psychological individuality seems to require a greater variety of constructs than what is needed for infants. The 8-year-old may be especially sociable and moderately conscientious in the overall (Level 1), but it is also important to note that she fears her father and adores her teachers, struggles to be accepted by the pretty girls in her class, believes in the loving and merciful God described by her Sunday School teacher and in heaven (but not in hell), hates bossy boys (because they are like her father), and strives hardest to attain the goals of getting good grades in school, landing her axel as an ice skater, and teaching her dog how to fetch (Level 2). Her characteristic adaptations are layered on top of her dispositional traits.

As this 8-year-old grows up, another set of constructs is needed to convey the most socially consequential features of her psychological individuality. Especially in modern, democratic societies, emerging adults are expected to explore the various ideological, occupational, and interpersonal options available to them and eventually commit themselves to a configuration of self-in-the-world that is right for them and right for the societal niches they will come to occupy (Arnett, 2000; Erikson, 1963). Dispositional traits and characteristic adaptations continue to assume importance, but the new psychological challenge of emerging adulthood transcends these constructs, to some extent, as it comes to involve what Erikson (1963) described as the exploration and development of *identity*. Among other things, the identity configuration that begins to come together in the emerging adulthood years provides the individual's life with some degree of unity and purpose, specifying who he or she is, was, and will be in the future. Many contemporary theorists describe this configuration as an integrative and evolving *life story* (Giddens, 1991; McAdams, 1985; Singer, 2004). In their late teens and twenties, young people living in modern societies begin to see their own lives as self-defining stories (Habermas & Bluck, 2000). These stories, or narrative identities, reconstruct the past and imagine the future in such a way as to spell out what a person's life means, both for the person who is living it and for the social world wherein the person lives. Level 3 of personality, then, is the level of narrative identity. What kind of story is the individual person working on? How does that story function to provide the person with unity, purpose, and meaning?

Like dispositional traits, people's life stories speak to broad thematic lines in human lives. But as traits sketch a dispositional outline for determining what kind of person a person is, narrative identity tells the story of who the person is. In the terms described by Diehl (chap. 19 in this volume), dispositional traits (Level 1) are *semantic* self-representations, providing the most important abstract categories and adjectival descriptors of the person, whereas narrative identities (Level 3) are the *episodic* self-representations, the most important reconstructed scenes from the past, combined with the imagined future, wherein the "me" serves as protagonist, even as the "I" narrates the story. As Diehl points out, semantic (trait-based) and episodic (narrative-based) memory may rely on different neural structures and functions, suggesting that different levels of personality may correspond to different self-relevant processes in the brain (Klein, Loftus, & Kihlstrom, 1996). Furthermore, certain narrative styles have been shown to relate to mental health variables including depression and life satisfaction above and beyond the contribution of lower levels of personality such as traits (Adler, Kissel, & McAdams, 2006).

Like characteristic adaptations (Level 2), people's life stories also address issues of time, contingency, and agency in personality. Stories make sense of a full life in time—from the reconstructed past, to the perceived present, to the broad contours of the imagined future (Bruner, 1990; Ricouer, 1984). As Helson, Soto, and Cate (chap. 17 in this volume) write, life narratives provide a person with the sense that one part of life leads coherently and meaningfully to another. Stories spell out in clear detail the particular contingencies through which people believe their life has come to be, and where it may be going in the future. As agentic authors, people construct their own life stories. But they do so with the material, ideological, political, and cultural resources they have at hand. As such, life stories say as much about the society and culture wherein a person makes a life as they do about the person making it (Bruner, 1990; McAdams, 2006b; Rosenwald & Ochberg, 1992). It is mainly through life narrative, rather than through traits and adaptations, that individuals and their culture come to terms with each other. For example, McAdams (2006b) showed how especially generative midlife American adults often construct narrative identities that draw on quintessentially American discourses of redemption—ways of narrating caring and productive lives that move from sin to salvation, rags to riches, slavery to freedom, addiction to recovery, and immaturity to the full actualization of the good Emersonian self. These redemptive story forms can be traced back to 17th-century Puritan spiritual testimonials, to Benjamin Franklin's autobiography, and to de Tocqueville's 19th-century observations of American cultural life, and they can be followed forward to the 20th-century American self-help industry, Hollywood, and Oprah (see also Cushman, 1995).

Narrative theories of personality (e.g., Gregg, 1991; Hermans & Kempen, 1993; Josselson & Lieblich, 1993; McAdams, 1985, 1999; Singer, 2005; Tomkins, 1987) view life stories as qualitatively different from and not reducible to dispositional traits and characteristic adaptations, and they argue that life stories follow a developmental course that also differs from what may be observed for other features of psychological individuality. Although children can tell autobiographical stories about the self from about age 3 onward, it is not until late adolescence that individuals have the cognitive wherewithal to conceive of and construct their own lives as full-fledged life stories (Habermas & Bluck, 2000). Emerging adulthood is prime time for the narrative construction of self. As they explore different identity options and begin to make commitments to adult roles and niches, emerging adults reconstruct their own lives into coherent narratives that explain how and why they came to be and where they may be going in life. These narratives may also serve to integrate disparate roles and goals in life, explaining how the many different selves that an individual person knows and lives exist and develop within the same self-defining life narrative. As people living in modern societies move into and through their middle adult years, furthermore, they continue to work on their life stories, incorporating new experiences, framing new aims and outlooks, and continually editing the past in light of the changing present and future (Helson, Soto, & Cate, chap. 17 in this volume). In old age, they may move from author to critic of their own narrative, looking back now on the story that has been and pondering over the extent to which they now see it has having been good and worthwhile (McAdams, 1996). A move from life story construction to life story acceptance may be at the heart of what Erikson (1963) described as *ego integrity versus despair*—the last stage of psychosocial development.

FOUR DEVELOPMENTAL MILESTONES

When it comes to personality development, researchers and theorists tend to privilege certain periods of the life span over others. Because we believe that beginnings offer hints at lifelong patterns to come, infancy has traditionally garnered more than its fair share of attention. Accordingly, current theory and research in early personality development tend to highlight the emergence of temperament and the development of caregiver–infant attachment in the first year of life. Going back to G. Stanley Hall (1904), adolescence has also been a favorite, if controversial, period for developmental inquiry. Some theorists have viewed adolescence as a time of storm and stress; others have suggested that adolescence ushers in a period of identity search; still others maintain that claims for the uniqueness of adolescence are overblown. Until the 1970s, by contrast, few researchers and theorists paid much attention to the adult years. Before the advent of life-span psychological approaches and ideas like the *midlife crisis* (Jacques, 1965) and Levinson's (1978) *seasons* of adult life, most authorities assumed that very little by way of personality development could occur after adolescence.

A reading of the chapters in this volume highlights the theoretical importance of four particular periods in the human life course. The four milestones are the movement from the establishment of caregiver–infant attachment at the end of the first year of life to the emergence of a basic sense of self at the end of the second year; the difficult transition between late childhood and early adolescence; the protracted period of emerging adulthood (late teens through mid-20s), especially as it is currently played out in modern industrial societies; and developmental shifts that mark important tipping points in the midlife years. Each of these four milestones may be viewed from the standpoints of dispositional traits, characteristic adaptations, and integrative life stories.

From Attachment to the Emergence of an Agentic, Autobiographical Self

Ever since Bowlby (1969) formulated his monumental theory of attachment, psychologists have carefully examined how the caregiver–infant bond develops in the first year of life. Bowlby viewed attachment as a goal-corrected behavioral system designed to assure mother–infant proximity so as to protect infants from predators and other dangers in the environment of evolutionary adaptedness. By the end of the first year, nearly all infants have consolidated an affective bond with one or a handful of primary caregivers in their environment. Nonetheless, not all attachment bonds are created equal. Although some 1-year-olds use the caregiver as a safe haven during periods of stress and a secure base from which to explore the world, other infants show patterns of insecure and even disorganized attachment (Ainsworth, Blehar, Waters, & Wall, 1978). Many theorists and researchers believe that these individual differences in the quality of caregiver–infant attachment hold significant ramifications for subsequent personality development (Fraley, 2002; Main, 1991). Furthermore, many view the attachment relationship to be the primary interpersonal matrix out of which emerges a coherent sense of self in the second year of life (Kohut, 1977; Sroufe & Waters, 1977). In terms that are quite reminiscent of Erikson's (1963) characterization of the first two stages of the human life span, infants ideally enjoy a relatively secure and trusting bond in the first year of life (*trust vs. mistrust*), which paves the way for the consolidation of an autonomous self in the second (*autonomy vs. shame and doubt*).

In a most basic sense, the movement from attachment at age 1 to more-or-less autonomous selfhood at age 2 establishes an internalized working model or schema of how self and other—"I" and "you"—can and do relate to each other (Baldwin, 1992; Bowlby, 1980). Theoretical descriptions of the development of attachment and the subsequent emergence of an agentic, goal-directed self tend to be couched in the personality language of Level 2. Attachment itself is the first, broad psychosocial *goal* in development. It marks the organization of an evolutionarily adaptive and culturally sensitive system designed to assure the proximal goal of caregiver–infant proximity. Infants (and caregivers) learn how to achieve and regulate this goal through vocalizing, following, smiling, and other attachment behaviors. These sequences of goal-directed, intentional behavior begin to become organized around the time (age 8–12 months) that infants are beginning to show a rudimentary understanding of human *intentionality*. Walls and Kollat (chap. 12 in this volume) chart how the 1-year-old's implicit apperception of intentionality in the behavior of others develops into something more sophisticated and deeper in the second year of life, culminating in the consolidation of an agentic self (see also Little, Snyder, & Wehemeyer, chap. 4 in this volume).

At the same time that the attachment-to-self dynamic marks the first clear expression of goal-related adaptations in personality, so too does this developmental move showcase the early manifestations of personality features from Levels 1 and 3. Shiner (chap. 11 in this volume) suggests that more cognitively elaborated personality traits (Level 1) may have their developmental origins in basic, emotionally anchored temperament dimensions such as positive emotionality, irritability/frustration, inhibition/fear, discomfort, attention/persistence, and activity level. Some of the most exciting research in personality development today is focused on documenting longitudinal connections between temperament dimensions in very early life and the development of personality traits in children, adolescents, and adults. Current work seems to be most supportive of three potential long-term linkages: A surgency factor in temperament (positive approach, positive affectivity) may herald the development of traits like extraversion and positive emotionality; a negative affectivity factor in temperament may foreshadow the development of neuroticism; and a temperament factor of constraint (impulse control, persistence) may lay the groundwork for the later emergence of traits such as agreeableness and conscientiousness. With respect to the third proposition, the regulation of self and emotion appears to be a central theme in conceptions of both early temperament and later personality (see also Tobin & Graziano, chap. 14 in this volume). The well-socialized adult who is warm and caring to others (agreeableness) and diligent, hard working, and focused in life (conscientiousness) is adept at controlling short-term emotional exigencies and channeling energy into longer term patterns of committed love and work. Furthermore, as Saarni (chap. 13 in this volume) suggests, temperament dimensions may have a profound impact on the quality of caregiver–infant attachment. Irritable babies (and their caregivers) may have an especially difficult time establishing the smooth, goal-corrected partnership that is so characteristic of securely attached infants and toddlers. Secure attachment may be easier to achieve with temperamentally easy babies. In addition, in that both temperament dimensions and attachment are viewed to be instrumental in emotional regulation in the first few years of life (Tobin & Graziano, chap. 14

in this volume), it should not be surprising if features from Levels 1 and 2 of personality (i.e., traits and goals) sometimes mix together and influence each other in complicated ways during this time.

As far as personality at Level 3 is concerned, 2-year-olds have a long way to go before they are composing life stories. But some theorists have suggested that the quality of early attachment may lay down a set of implicit expectations regarding the likelihood that protagonists' strivings over time may result in satisfying endings, providing emotional material for what McAdams (1999) described as the narrative tone of life stories. Furthermore, the same developments that mark the emergence of a sense of human intentionality and the consolidation of an agentic self in the second year of life may be reframed to describe the origins of autobiographical memory and the beginnings of self-narration. According to Howe and Courage (1997), the authorial "I" begins to remember, own, and tell autobiographical memories at around age 2, "my" little stories about things that happened to "me," and about things "I" intended (wanted, desired) to do. The autonomous 2-year-old self starts to become the intentional, goal-directed striver and the autobiographical narrator, which are the beginnings of both agency (Level 2) and authorship (Level 3) in personality.

The Transition to Adolescence

Whether viewed as a period of storm and stress or an uncertain limbo betwixt and between two well-defined developmental epochs, adolescence has traditionally been conceived of as a transitional phase, identified roughly as the teenaged years. Textbooks tell us what our memories recall: Teenagers are no longer children, but they are not yet adults either. But when does adolescence really begin? And how does it end? On the one hand, hormonal and psychological shifts heralding a transition to come seem to occur years before the advent of puberty's most obvious signs—as early as age 8 or 9. On the other, surveys of Americans and Europeans show that an increasing number of individuals in their mid-20s still do not consider themselves adults and have not as yet assumed those roles traditionally associated with adulthood—stable jobs, marriage, parenthood (Arnett, 2000). Furthermore, the psychological and psychosocial issues facing individuals in their early teens (i.e., peer pressure, delinquency) appear to be dramatically different from those facing college freshmen and sophomores (i.e., vocation, intimacy) (see Steinberg & Morris, 2001). In that it seems to begin earlier and end later than once expected and in that its beginning looks nothing like its ending, adolescence is not what it used to be, if it ever was. Rather than view adolescence itself, then, as an especially critical phase of personality development, this discussion distinguishes between two very different periods in the life span: the transition from childhood to adolescence (roughly age 8–13) and what Arnett (2000) described as emerging adulthood (roughly the late teens through the mid-20s).

A number of chapters in this volume describe this first period as an especially difficult one. Most strikingly, Harter (chap. 16 in this volume) documents two very interesting changes in self-esteem associated with the late childhood and early teenage years. Before about age 7 or 8, Harter contends, children's self-esteem seems to be uniformly high. But thereafter it begins to drop and show more-or-less consistent individual differences. Put differently, most first- and second-graders feel pretty good about themselves. By the time they hit fourth or fifth grade, however, some feel much better about themselves than do others, and the mean level of self-esteem for the whole group has, correspondingly, gone down as well. Harter shows that these changes result in part from increasing expectations for performance coming from parents and teachers and cognitive developmental changes that enable older children to compare their own performance in various domains—from sports to academics to moral behavior—to the performance of others. The transition from a small and nurturing grade school to larger and more impersonal junior high settings may also contribute to the difficulties experienced by many children/adolescents during this time (Eccles & Midgely, 1989). Donnellan, Trzesniewski, and Robins (chap. 15 in this volume) also describe drops in self-esteem beginning around age 9 and continuing through the junior high years, cross-culturally and for both genders. They report that this developmental period also manifests the first signs of depression (especially in girls) and increases in antisocial behavior (especially among boys). Scores on openness to experience also begin to rise around age 10 (see also McCrae & Costa, chap. 7 in this volume).

From the standpoint of Level 1 in personality, it is as if a new dispositional trait emerges in the late childhood years—the individual's overall evaluation of self. Although Harter resists labeling self-esteem as a "trait" (she argues that it is traitlike for some children/adolescents and statelike for others), it is clear that the emergence of self-esteem as a new individual-difference dimension during the late childhood years has implications for the development of dispositional traits during this time. In adolescence and adulthood, low self-esteem may be associated with high neuroticism and low extraversion.

These changes may also have implications for the development of characteristic adaptations and life stories. Older children and young adolescents are now able to evaluate the worth and progress of their own goal pursuits and projects. They begin to see what they need to do to promote those projects on which their self-esteem depends, be they in the realm of athletics, friendship, schoolwork, or values. They may also begin to utilize strategies for what Wrosch, Heckhausen, and Lachman (chap. 20 in this volume) call *failure compensation* in goal management. At the same time, older children and young adolescents may hold grandiose fantasies about achievement and fame in the future. What Elkind (1981) described as the *personal fable* begins to emerge around this time—a fantastical first draft of narrative identity. The same cognitive skills and social developments that enable older children and young adolescents to evaluate themselves (positively or negatively) vis-à-vis their peers may also help to launch their first full autobiographical narratives, as evidenced in early adolescent diaries, fantasies, and conversations (Elkind, 1981; McAdams, 1999). It is during the transition to adolescence, revealed Habermas and Bluck (2000), that individuals begin to see in full what makes up an entire life, from birth through childhood, career, marriage, parenting, and so on, to death. Their first efforts at imaging their own life stories may be unrealistic, grandiose, and somewhat incoherent. But one has to begin somewhere.

Emerging Adulthood

Arnett (2000, 2004) argued that the period running from about age 17 or so up through the mid-20s constitutes an integral developmental epoch in and of itself, which he called *emerging adulthood*. This demarcation makes increasingly good sense in modern industrial and postindustrial societies wherein schooling and the preparation for adult work often extend well into the 20s and even beyond. The betwixt and between nature of what was once called adolescence appears to be extending for almost a decade beyond the teenage years for many young men and women today, who are putting off marriage, "settling down," and raising children until their late 20s and 30s. The movement through this developmental period is strongly shaped by class and education. Less-educated, working-class men and women may find it especially difficult to sustain steady and gainful employment during this period. Some get married and/or begin families anyway, but others may drift for many years without the economic security required to become a stakeholder in society. Those more privileged men and women headed for middle-class professions may require many years of schooling and/or training and a great deal of role experimentation before they feel they are able to settle down and assume the full responsibilities of adulthood. Many social and cultural factors in modern societies have come together to make emerging adulthood the prime time in the life course for the exploration and development of what Erikson (1963) described as ego identity.

At Level 1 in personality, emerging adulthood marks a relative stabilization in dispositional traits, a recovery in self-esteem, and the beginning of an upward swing for agreeableness and conscientiousness (Roberts & Wood, chap. 2 in this volume; McCrae & Costa, chap. 7 in this volume; Donnellan, Trzesniewski, & Robins, chap. 15 in this volume). As emerging adults eventually come to take on the roles of spouse, parent, citizen, and stakeholder, their traits may shift upward in the direction of greater warmth and care for others, higher levels of social responsibility, and greater dedication to being productive, hard working, and reliable (Roberts & Wood, chap. 2 in this volume). At the same time, levels of openness to experience may begin to decline (McCrae & Costa, chap. 7 in this volume), indicating that individuals in their late 20s are now less interested in exploring new experiences in life and more focused on consolidating the commitments they have begun to make.

At Levels 2 and 3 in personality, emerging adulthood marks the exploration of and eventual commitment to new life goals and new narrative understandings of the adult self. Diehl (chap. 19 in this volume) describes the emergence of role-specific multiple selves in late adolescence and young adulthood. Emerging adults begin to see life as a complex and multifaceted challenge in role performance and role display (see also Hawley, chap. 8 in this volume). At the same time, they seek to integrate the many different selves they display and the many different role performances they enact into an organized self pattern that provides their increasingly complex lives with some semblance of unity, purpose, and meaning. Narrative theories of identity describe this effort as a process of bringing different voices together into a common self-dialogue (Hermans, Kempen, & van Loon, 1992) or integrating different *imagoes* (internalized personifications of the self) as dynamic main characters within a single self-defining life story (McAdams, 1985). In any case, the main psychosocial act of emerging adulthood is the development of narrative identity. By the time young people have finally "emerged" from emerging adulthood, they have articulated and internalized a more-or-less coherent story of who they were, are, and will be. The story affirms their former and ongoing explorations and their newly established commitments, and it sets them up, psychologically speaking, for the daunting challenges of generative adulthood in the modern world.

Midlife Tipping Points: From Expansion to Contraction

When psychologists began to consider the possibility that personality continues to develop in the adult years, one of the concepts around which they initially rallied was the *midlife crisis* (Gutmann, 1980; Jacques, 1965; Levinson, 1978). Strange things happen to men (and maybe some women) around age 40, some theorists maintained. Suddenly cognizant that they are at least half way on their way to mortality, midlife adults come to question anew who they are and what their lives mean. As a result, they come to reject many of the vestiges of their old selves (including old spouses and jobs). They redesign their life structures and transform their consciousness to focus on those long-suppressed aspects of self—playfulness, mysticism, the hidden woman in men, the hidden man in women. In Jung's (1939) terms, midlife adults are now ready to embark on an adventure of *individuation,* or a search for greater wholeness and fullness in life.

Early conceptions of the midlife crisis were almost absurdly romantic and mainly centered on the discontents (and longings) of wealthy professional men, all Americans of course, who were hitting their 40s in the 1960s and 1970s (Dannefer, 1984). If the midlife crisis were truly a tumultuous transition in adult life, then sudden increases in neuroticism or openness to experience, or perhaps sudden decreases in conscientiousness, around age 40 to 45 would be expected. Yet, cross-sectional and longitudinal studies of adult dispositional traits (Level 1) have never documented any dramatic shifts like this (McCrae & Costa, chap. 7 in this volume). Still, modest shifts in certain features of personality have been observed during the midlife years. For example, generativity strivings appear to peak in the 40s and 50s and decline somewhat thereafter (Rossi, 2001). Diehl (chap. 19 in this volume) reports decreases in spontaneous self-attributions regarding agency and increases in communion in the midlife years, as well as changes in hoped-for possible selves. Stewart and Ostrove (1998) reported longitudinal data suggesting less of a midlife crisis and more of what they called *midcourse corrections* in the lives of American women. Stewart and Ostrove suggested that, for many women, the 40s may be a time when they make subtle shifts in their lives in order to maximize the fulfillment of those goals that are most important to them.

Against the backdrop of increasingly stable dispositional traits, midlife adults express substantial change in the realm of goals and goal management (Freund & Riediger, chap. 18 in this volume). For example, younger adults appear to tolerate substantial conflict among their different goals, but midlife and older adults seek to manage goals in ways that minimize conflict and produce mutual regulation. As adults begin to experience the physical and informational-processing declines that begin even in early midlife, they select goals and strategies for accomplishing goals that optimize their best skills and compensate for areas of weakness. Carstensen's (1993) *socioemotional selectivity theory* suggests that young adults expend considerable energy in pursuing goals that maximize experiential diversity and informational intake, but older adults shift their focus toward goals that enhance and regulate emotional experiences with close friends and family. According to Carstensen, time is the major factor in accounting for this shift. When individuals feel that they have relatively little time left in life, they focus on emotional goals. Relatedly, Wrosch, Heckhausen, and Lachman (chap. 20 in this volume) argue that primary control (changing the environment to fit one's needs and goals) may predominate in young adulthood, but secondary control (changing the self to fit the environment) gains in importance as people move into and through the midlife years. Lang, Reschke, and Neyer (chap. 22 in this volume) describe a similar shift from activation to protection modes over the adult life course.

This volume's chapters devoted to adult personality development converge on the general idea of a midlife tipping point. At some point in the middle-aged years, the authors seem to be suggesting, adults shift their perspectives on life from one emphasizing expansion, activation, primary control, and information seeking to one emphasizing contraction, protection, secondary control, and the quality of emotional life. The shift is not likely to be sudden, may occur in some domains before others, and is sure to play itself out differently for different people. But however and whenever it happens, the shift marks a tipping from a life narrative of ascent to one of maintenance and eventual decline.

Helson, Soto, and Cate (chap. 17 in this volume) suggest that this kind of tipping point may be reached in late middle age, after the person has traversed through "ascendant" and "executive" phases of the midlife years and moved into a period of "acceptance." Diehl (chap. 19 in this volume) suggests that young and midlife adults expect continued improvement in life, but in late middle age people begin to adjust their expectations for something rather less. As they move into their later adulthood years, individuals are likely to experience increasingly negative ratios of gains to losses (Freund & Riediger, chap. 18 in this volume). Even as their traits remain relatively stable, then, midlife and older adults continue to adjust their goals and strategies (Level 2) to accommodate a wide range of on-time and off-time developmental demands. In addition, they may rewrite their narrative identities (Level 3), simplifying plots to accentuate harmony and balance in life, focusing more attention on the story's most important characters (usually close colleagues, close friends, and family), and specifying in more detail and with more poignancy how they hope to leave a generative legacy for the future (McAdams, 1985, 1996; Singer, 2005).

The idea of midlife tipping points signals the beginnings of old age. Yet the study of personality development has, with few exceptions, had little to say about what happens to personality traits, goals, and stories in the last decade or two of life. There are fewer age-normative changes that distinguish old age from the later stages of midlife. Indeed, compared to periods like infancy and adolescence, old age has received far less attention in the field of personality research as a whole. Lang, Reschke and Neyer (chap. 22 in this volume) indicate that they do not know of a study on the effects of retirement, one of the hallmark milestones of this transition, on change or continuity of personality. Still, Erikson (1963) emphasized that development does not cease at midlife and several of the chapters included in this volume do speak to some of those changes.

What happens to traits in the last years of life? Roberts and DelVecchio (2000) showed that interindividual stability in traits increases with age, but most of the studies they reviewed do not push the inquiry into the last years. It is possible that old age may represent the most stable period for traits across the life span. A counterpossibility is a decomposition, as it were, of traits in the last years, as has been shown with certain physical and cognitive skills associated with what gerontologists sometimes call the *terminal drop*.

To the extent that personality researchers have examined old age, they have tended to focus on Level 2, specifically goals. As individuals increasingly conceive of their lives in terms of time left to live, as opposed to time alive, both the type of goals people have and their strategies for pursuing them shift. Freund and Riediger (chap. 18 in this volume) indicated that a recalibration of future-oriented aspirations is a key factor in successful adaptation to old age. They add that, as the ratio of gains to losses in one's life becomes increasingly negative (due to the attenuation of available resources and the decreased efficiency of existing resources; see Wrosch, Hechhausen, & Lachman, chap. 20 in this volume), individuals shift their investment of resources toward the maintenance of functioning and counteracting loss as opposed to focusing on growth. In addition, old age involves increasingly more secondary control strategies such as goal disengagement, as opposed to primary control strategies of goal attainment (Wrosch, Hechhausen, & Lachman, chap. 20 in this volume). Furthermore, the salience of limited time in life tends to lead elderly individuals to dissolve less meaningful and distant relationships, thus restricting their social networks (Lang, Reschke, & Neyer, chap. 22 in this volume).

As far as life narratives (Level 3) are concerned, there has been little work represented in these chapters. As suggested earlier, in old age life stories may show a shift in perspective from a position of narrator to that of critic, evaluating the story that has been told in an effort to come to some degree of acceptance of the life that has been lived (McAdams, 1996). People in their last years may no longer be actively engaged in constructing narrative identity. They may return instead to those most basic issues involved with living day to day, conserving energy to focus on the moments left in life, surviving and holding on as well as possible, before death closes the door.

CONCLUSION

We conceive of personality as comprising those features of psychological individuality that a given society or culture deems to be the most socially consequential and important for overall human adaptation. In this place and at this point in history, personality is well-represented as a three-level framework consisting of an evolving constellation or patterning of dispositional traits, characteristic adaptations, and integrative life narratives. Dispositional traits provide a broad sketch of psychological individuality, characteristic adaptations fill in many of the motivational and strategic details, and integrative life narratives spell out what a person's life means in the overall. In recent years, personality and developmental psychologists have made considerable scientific progress in accounting for psychological individuality from the perspectives of traits, adaptations, and life narratives. This concluding chapter has provided a broad-brush overview of some of the main themes running through the preceding chapters, from the standpoint of how dispositional traits, characteristic adaptations, and integrative life stories develop over the human life course. It has also zeroed in on four developmental milestones: the move from attachment to the emergence of self in the second year of life, the often difficult transition from late childhood to adolescence, the increasingly protracted period now called emerging adulthood, and what we call midlife tipping points. During each of these periods, important trends and developments may be observed for dispositional traits like those subsumed within the Big Five framework, characteristic adaptations like personal goals and coping strategies, and the integrative life stories that comprise narrative identity.

This handbook does a very fine job of conveying the current excitement and progress in the scientific study of personality development. Of course, the chapters, including this final chapter, are not without their biases. The volume neglects certain areas that have traditionally enjoyed strong representation in the field of personality development, such as attachment, moral development, and the development of wisdom in adulthood. Furthermore, no chapter focuses exclusively on the development of abnormal personality (e.g., personality disorders) or on efforts to change personality through structured interventions (e.g., therapy). At the same time, certain concepts (e.g., agency, self-regulation, and self-esteem) may receive more emphasis than some readers might want. Despite a few limitations, nonetheless, this volume covers most of the important terrain in the study of personality development. The editors have done an excellent job of assembling some of the strongest and most articulate spokespersons for the major developments in the field today.

In personality development, timing is critical. We agree with the editors that the time seems very right to bring together for the first time the major advances that scientists have made in recent years in understanding the development of human personality. The chapters contained in this first handbook of personality development tell us what we have learned already and suggest many of the most important questions we need to pursue in the years to come.

ACKNOWLEDGMENT

The production of this chapter was supported by a grant to the first author from the Foley Family Foundation.

REFERENCES

Adler, J. M., McAdams, D. P., & Kissel, E. (2006). Emerging from the CAVE: Attributional style and the narrative study of identity in midlife adults. *Cognitive Therapy and Research, 30.*

Adorno, T. W., Frenkel-Brunswik, E., Levinson, D. J., & Sanford, N. (1950). *The authoritarian personality.* New York: Harper & Brothers.

Ainsworth, M. D. S., Blehar, M. C., Waters, E., & Wall, T. (1978). *Patterns of attachment.* Hillsdale, NJ: Lawrence Erlbaum Associates.

Allport, G. W. (1937). *Personality: A psychological interpretation.* New York: Holt, Rinehart & Winston.

Arnett, J. J. (2000). Emerging adulthood: A theory of development from the late teens through the twenties. *American Psychologist, 55,* 469–480.

Arnett, J. J. (2004). *Emerging adulthood.* New York: Oxford University Press.

Baldwin, M. W. (1992). Relational schemas and the processing of social information. *Psychological Bulletin, 112,* 461–484.

Belsky, J., Hsieh, K., & Crnic, K. (1998). Mothering, fathering, and infant negativity as antecedents of boys' externalizing problems and inhibition at age 3: Differential susceptibility to rearing influence? *Development and Psychopathology, 10,* 301–319.

Bowlby, J. (1969). *Attachment.* New York: Basic Books.

Bowlby, J. (1980). *Loss.* New York: Basic Books.

Bruner, J. (1990). *Acts of mind.* Cambridge, MA: Harvard University Press.

Buss, D. M. (1995). Evolutionary psychology: A new paradigm for psychological science. *Psychological Inquiry, 6,* 1–30.

Carstensen, L. L. (1993). Motivation for social contact across the life span: A theory of socioemotional selectivity. In J. E. Jacobs (Ed.), *Nebraska symposium on motivation, 1992: Developmental perspectives on motivation* (Vol. 40, pp. 209–254). Lincoln, NE: University of Nebraska Press.

Caspi, A. (1998). Personality development across the life course. In W. Damon (Ed.), *Handbook of child psychology: Vol. 3: Social, emotional, and personality development* (5th ed., pp. 311–388). New York: Wiley.

Christie, R., & Geis, F. (1970). *Studies in Machiavellianism*. New York: Academic Press.

Cushman, P. (1995). *Constructing the self, constructing America*. Reading, MA: Addison-Wesley.

Dannefer, D. (1984). Adult development and social theory: A paradigmatic reappraisal. *American Sociological Review, 49,* 100–116.

Deci, E., & Ryan, R. M. (1991). A motivational approach to self: Integration in personality. In R. Dienstbier & R. M. Ryan (Eds.), *Nebraska symposium on motivation: 1990* (pp. 237–288). Lincoln, NE: University of Nebraska Press.

Doi, L. T. (1962). Amae: A key concept for understanding Japanese personality structure. In R. J. Smith & R. K. Beardsley (Eds.), *Japanese culture: Its development and characteristics* (pp. 132–139). Chicago: Aldine.

Eccles, J. S., & Midgley, C. (1989). Stage/environment fit: Developmentally appropriate classrooms for early adolescents. In R. E. Ames & C. Ames (Eds.), *Research on motivation in education* (Vol. 3, pp. 139–186). San Diego: Academic Press.

Elkind, D. (1981). *Children and adolescents* (3rd ed.). New York: Oxford University Press.

Erikson, E. H. (1963). *Childhood and society* (2nd ed.). New York: Norton.

Fraley, R. C. (2002). Attachment stability from infancy to adulthood: Meta-analysis and dynamic modeling of developmental mechanisms. *Personality and Social Psychology Review, 6,* 123–151.

Giddens, A. (1991). *Modernity and self-identity: Self and society in the late modern age*. Stanford, CA: Stanford University Press.

Gregg, G. (1991). *Self-representation: Life-narrative studies in identity and ideology*. New York: Greenwood Press.

Gutmann, D. (1980). The post-parental years: Clinical problems and developmental possibilities. In W. H. Norman & T. J. Scaramella (Eds.), *Midlife: developmental and clinical issues* (pp. 38–52). New York: Bruner/Mazel.

Habermas, T., & Bluck, S. (2000). Getting a life: The emergence of the life story in adolescence. *Psychological Bulletin, 126,* 748–769.

Hall, C., & Lindzey, G. (1957). *Theories of personality*. New York: Wiley.

Hall, G. S. (1904). *Adolescence: Its psychology and its relation to physiology, anthropology, sociology, sex, crime, religion, and education*. New York: Appleton.

Hermans, H. J. M., & Kempen, H. J. G. (1993). *The dialogical self: Meaning as movement*. New York: Academic Press.

Hermans, H. J. M., Kempen, H. J. G., & van Loon, R. J. P. (1992). The dialogical self: Beyond individualism and rationalism. *American Psychologist, 47,* 23–33.

Hogan, R. (1982). A socioanalytic theory of personality. In M. Page (Ed.), *Nebraska symposium on motivation: 1981* (pp. 55–89). Lincoln, NE: University of Nebraska Press.

Hooker, K., & McAdams, D. P. (2003). Personality reconsidered: A new agenda for aging research. *Journal of Gerontology: Psychological Sciences, 58B,* 296–304.

Howe, M.L., & Courage, M.L. (1997). The emergence and early development of autobiographical memory. *Psychological Review, 104,* 499–523.

Jacques, E. (1965). Death and the midlife crisis. *International Journal of Psychoanalysis, 46,* 502–514.

Josselson, R., & Lieblich, A. (Eds.). (1993). *The narrative study of lives*. Thousand Oaks, CA: Sage.

Jung, C. G. (1939). *The integration of personality*. New York: Farrar & Rinehart.

Klein, S. B., Loftus, G., & Kihlstrom, J. K. (1996). Self-knowledge of an amnesiac patient: Toward a neuropsychology of personality and social psychology. *Journal of Experimental Psychology: General, 125,* 250–260.

Kluckhohn, C., & Murray, H. A. (1953). Personality formation: The determinants. In C. Kluckhohn, H. A. Murray, & D. M. Schneider (Eds.), *Personality in nature, society, and culture* (pp. 53–67). New York: Knopf.

Kohut, H. (1977). *The restoration of the self*. New York: International Universities Press.

Levinson, D. J. (1978). *The seasons of a man's life*. New York: Knopf.

Loehlin, J. C., Neiderhiser, J. M., & Reiss, D. (2003). The behavior genetics of personality and the NEAD study. *Journal of Research in Personality, 37*, 373–387.

Main, M. (1991). Metacognitive knowledge, metacognitive monitoring, and singular (coherent) vs. multiple (incoherent) model of attachment. In C. M. Parkes, J. Stevenson-Hinde, & P. Marris (Eds.), *Attachment across the life cycle* (pp. 127–159). London: Tavistock/Routledge.

Matthews, G., Deary, I., & Whiteman, W. (2003). *Personality traits* (2nd ed.). Cambridge, England: Cambridge University Press.

McAdams, D. P. (1985). *Power, intimacy, and the life story: Personological inquiries into identity*. New York: Guilford.

McAdams, D. P. (1994). Can personality change? Levels of stability and growth in personality across the life span. In T. F. Heatherton & J. L. Weinberger (Eds.), *Can personality change?* (pp. 299–314). Washington, DC: APA Books.

McAdams, D. P. (1995). What do we know when we know a person? *Journal of Personality, 63*, 365–396.

McAdams, D. P. (1996). Narrating the self in adulthood. In J. Birren, G. Kenyon, J. E. Ruth, J. J. F. Shroots, & J. Svendson (Eds.), *Aging and biography: Explorations in adult development* (pp. 131–148). New York: Springer.

McAdams, D. P. (1997). A conceptual history of personality psychology. In R. Hogan, J. Johnson, & S. Briggs (Eds.), *Handbook of personality psychology* (pp. 3–39). San Diego, CA: Academic Press.

McAdams, D. P. (1999). Personal narratives and the life story. In L. Pervin & O. P. John (Eds.), *Handbook of personality: Theory and research* (2nd ed., pp. 478–500). New York: Guilford.

McAdams, D. P. (2006a). *The person: A new introduction to personality psychology* (4th ed.). New York: Wiley.

McAdams, D. P. (2006b). *The redemptive self: Stories Americans live by*. New York: Oxford University Press.

McClelland, D. C. (1961). *The achieving society*. New York: D. Van Nostrand.

McCrae, R. R., Costa, P. T., Jr., de Lima, M. P., Simoes, A., Ostendorf, F., Angleitner, A., Marusic, I., Bratko, D., Caprara, G. V., Barbaranelli, C., Chae, J.-H., & Piedmont, R. L. (1999). Age differences in personality across the adult life span: Parallels in five cultures. *Developmental Psychology, 35*, 466–477.

Mischel, W. (1968). *Personality and assessment*. New York: Wiley.

Mischel, W. (1973). Toward a cognitive social learning reconceptualization of personality. *Psychological Review, 80*, 252–283.

Mischel, W., & Shoda, Y. (1995). A cognitive-affective system theory of personality: Reconceptualizing situations, dispositions, dynamics, and invariance in personality structure. *Psychological Review, 102*, 246–268.

Mroczek, D. K., & Spiro, A, III. (2003). Modeling intraindividual change in personality traits: Findings from the Normative Aging Study. *Journal of Gerontology: Psychological Sciences, 58B*, 153–165.

Nisbett, R. E., & Ross, L. D. (1980). *Human inference: Strategies and shortcomings of social judgment*. Englewood Cliffs, NJ: Prentice-Hall.

Ricoeur, P. (1984). *Time and narrative*. Chicago: University of Chicago Press.

Riemann, R., Angleitner, A., & Strelau, J. (1997). Genetic and environmental influences on personality: A study of twins reared together using the self- and peer report NEO–FFI scales. *Journal of Personality, 65*, 449–475.

Roberts, B., & DelVecchio, W. (2000). The rank-order consistency of personality from childhood to old age: A quantitative review of longitudinal studies. *Psychological Bulletin, 126*, 3–25.

Rosenwald, G. C., & Ochberg, R. L. (Eds.). (1992). *Storied lives: The cultural politics of self-understanding*. New Haven, CT: Yale University Press.

Rossi, A. (Ed.). (2001). *Caring and doing for others*. Chicago: University of Chicago Press.

Scarr, S., & McCartney, K. (1983). How people make their environments: A theory of genotype → environment effects. *Child Development, 54*, 424–435.

Sheldon, K. (2004). *Optimal human being: An integrated, multilevel perspective.* Mahwah, NJ: Lawrence Erlbaum Associates.

Shweder, R. (1975). How relevant is an individual difference theory of personality? *Journal of Personality, 43,* 455–484.

Singer, J. A. (2004). Narrative identity and meaning making across the adult life span: An introduction. *Journal of Personality, 72,* 437–459.

Singer, J. A. (2005). *Personality and psychotherapy: Treating the whole person.* New York: Guilford.

Sroufe, L. A., & Waters, E. E. (1977). Attachment as an organizational construct. *Child Development, 48,* 1184–1199.

Steinberg, L., & Morris, A. S. (2001). Adolescent development. In S. T. Fiske, D. L. Schacter, & C. Zahn-Waxler (Eds.), *Annual review of psychology* (Vol. 52, pp. 83–110). Palo Alto, CA: Annual Reviews, Inc.

Stewart, A. J., & Ostrove, J. M. (1998). Women's personality in middle age: Gender, history, and midcourse corrections. *American Psychologist, 53,* 1185–1194.

Tomkins, S. S. (1987). Script theory. In J. Aronoff, A. I. Rabin, & R. A. Zucker (Eds.), *The emergence of personality* (pp. 147–216). New York: Springer.

Author Index

Note: *f* indicates figure.

Y

Z

Subject Index

Note: *f* indicates figure; *t* indicates table.

A

Abilities, 15
Ability, 71, 233–238
    to bounce back, 216
    cognitive, 13, 23
    to cope, 250
    domains, 31–32
    to focus, 217
    to model, 25
Accommodation, 18, 31
Accommodative strategies, 29
Accumulation, 42–43
Achievement, 24
    motivation, 217
Actions, 61–62
Action-control
    beliefs, 70–72
    sequence, 69–70
Activity level, 119
Adaptability, 119, 170, 216, 218
Adjustment, 23–24, 29, 70, 219, 221, 248, 268, 294, 330
Adolescence
    behavior during, 325
    mechanisms that promote change during, 298–299
    methodological concerns in the study of, 299–301
    personality development in, 6, 286–289
    role of peers during, 295
    romantic relationships during, 295–296

school and extracurricular activities during, 296
    transition in, 289–294
    transition to, 483–484
Adoptive siblings, 32, 82, 97
Adult development
    of intraindividual variability in trait behavior, 51–55
    traditional theories of, 11–12
Adult Temperament Questionnaire, 120
Adulthood (see also Young adulthood)
    content of goals in, 355–359
    development of personality traits in, 20–23
    emerging, 484–485
    goal-focus in, 364–365
    personality change in, 338–339
    in Western culture, 337–338
Affect and self-regulation, 69
Affiliation, 15, 24, 120, 156, 258, 290
Affordances, 355, 445, 447, 472, 476
Age (see also Old age)
    change in personality traits with, 25, 129–132
        cross-cultural comparisons of, 134–142
        interpreting, 132–133
    consistency of personality traits with, 23
    and decline in functioning, 12
    differences
        in possible selves, 379–380
        in role- or domain-specific self-representations, 377–379
    and the increase of personality traits,

F

Facial expression
  coding, 5
  neutral, 251
Failure compensation, 403, 484
Family
  change in context of, 454–457
  establishing, 18
  of origin, 25
  processes, 224–225
  quality, 24
Fearfulness, 220
Feedback
  emotional, 73
  mechanisms, 25–26
  persistent, 27
  self-evaluative, 63
Feelings, 14, 17–18, 22, 69, 430, 478
  concealing, 272
  of discomfort, 216
  negative, 73
  positive, 24, 315
  verbalizing, 252
Feelings About Life, 342–343
Flexibility, 48
Fit, 33
Five Factor model, 12
Fixed effects, 166–167
Force of will, 64
Freud, Sigmund, 3, 5
Friendliness, 48

G

Gemeinschaft, 293
Gender, 347
  bias, 71
  differences in genetic influences on personality, 89–90, 96, 131, 291, 356, 378
  in rates of change in personality, 131
Genetic
  influences, 12, 20, 23, 50, 53, 87–88
    and gender differences, 89–90
    for personality change in late adulthood, 97–100
    understanding, 6
  polymorphism, 86
  processes of change, 222–225
  structure underlying observed personality, 90–92
Genetically informative studies, 301
  of temperament in infants and children, 84–85
Genetics
  molecular, 86, 95

role of, 32
Gesellschaft, 293
Global self-esteem
  determinants of, 314–316
Global self-worth (see also Global self-esteem), 323–324
  historical perspectives on the causes of, 313–314
Goal
  attainment, 410
    across the adult life span, 400–402
    cultural variation in, 413
  difficulty, 72
  discrepancy
    analysis, 70
    problem, 70
  generation process, 69–70
  management, 409
Goal-focus in adulthood, 364–365
Goal-relevant behavior, 359–360
Goals, 14, 45
  as anchor of hope, 72
  content of (across adulthood), 355–359
  Kurt Lewin's theory of, 64–65
  personal, 353, 365–367, 475–478
    age related management of, 403–406
  as personality-in-context, 354–355
  pursuit of, 29, 67–68
    action-control beliefs during, 70–72
    in adulthood, 359–360
Gregariousness, 116
Growth curves in multilevel modeling framework, 166
  fixed effects, 166–167
  linear and quadratic growth models in personality, 168–169
  random effects, 166–168
Guilt, 220

H

Harlow, Harry, 3
Health, 342, 345, 356, 377–384 (see also Mental health)
  behaviors, 18
  changes in, 170
  deterioration of, 170
  disorders, 48
  and personality
    change, 431–437
    processes, 424–436
  risks, 21–22
  stress in old-age, 411–413
  variability of, 52
Heider, Fritz, 63–64
Helson, Ravenna, 3